Food: In Context

Food: In Context

Brenda Wilmoth Lerner & K. Lee Lerner, Editors

VOLUME 1

ADVERTISING FOOD TO INTERNATIONAL FUND FOR AGRICULTURAL DEVELOPMENT

GALE
CENGAGE Learning

Detroit • New York • San Francisco • New Haven, Conn • Waterville, Maine • London

GALE
CENGAGE Learning™

Food: In Context

Brenda Wilmoth Lerner and K. Lee Lerner, Editors

Project Editor: Elizabeth Manar

Editorial: Kathleen Edgar

Rights Acquisition and Management: Margaret Chamberlain-Gaston, Leitha Etheridge-Sims, Robyn Young

Composition: Evi Abou-El-Seoud, Mary Beth Trimper

Manufacturing: Wendy Blurton, Dorothy Maki

Imaging: John Watkins

Product Design: Kristine Julien, Jennifer Wahi

Indexing: Dow Jones & Company, Factiva, Inc.

For product information and technology assistance, contact us at **Gale Customer Support, 1-800-877-4253.**
For permission to use material from this text or product, submit all requests online at **www.cengage.com/permissions**.
Further permissions questions can be emailed to **permissionrequest@cengage.com**

Cover photographs: Image of earthquake survivors reaching for boxes of food reproduced by permission of AP Images. All others used under license from Shutterstock.com: Image copyright Dmitriy Karelin, 2010 (cow); Image copyright Tan Wei Ming, 2010 (dairy plant in Switzerland); Image copyright Vishal Shah, 2010 (Indian woman cleaning grain); Image copyright Certe, 2010 (olives); Image copyright Sandra Caldwell, 2010 (corn cob); Image copyright apdesign, 2010 (wheat); Image copyright @amp;erics, 2010 (grapes); Image copyright Sveta San, 2010 (poultry farm); Image copyright Anna Jurkovska, 2010 (fishermen); Image copyright Laurent Renault, 2010 (rows of lettuce).

While every effort has been made to ensure the reliability of the information presented in this publication, Gale, a part of Cengage Learning, does not guarantee the accuracy of the data contained herein. Gale accepts no payment for listing; and inclusion in the publication of any organization, agency, institution, publication, service, or individual does not imply endorsement of the editors or publisher. Errors brought to the attention of the publisher and verified to the satisfaction of the publisher will be corrected in future editions.

LIBRARY OF CONGRESS CATALOGING-IN-PUBLICATION DATA

Food: In Context/Brenda Wilmoth Lerner & K. Lee Lerner, editors.
  p. cm.
  Includes bibliographical references and index.
  ISBN-13: 978-1-4144-8652-9 (set) ISBN-10: 1-4144-8652-9 (set) ISBN-13: 978-1-4144-8653-6 (v. 1) ISBN-13: 978-1-4144-8654-3 (v. 2) [etc.]
  1. Food. 2. Nutrition. 3. Food supply. I. Lerner, Brenda Wilmoth. II. Lerner, K. Lee.
TX354.F6657 2011
641.3--dc22   2010054584

Gale
27500 Drake Rd.
Farmington Hills, MI, 48331-3535

ISBN-13: 978-1-4144-8652-9 (set)   ISBN-10: 1-4144-8652-9 (set)
ISBN-13: 978-1-4144-8653-6 (vol. 1)   ISBN-10: 1-4144-8653-7 (vol. 1)
ISBN-13: 978-1-4144-8654-3 (vol. 2)   ISBN-10: 1-4144-8654-5 (vol. 2)

This title is also available as an e-book.
ISBN-13: 978-1-4144-8655-0 (set)   ISBN-10: 1-4144-8655-3 (set)
Contact your Gale, a part of Cengage Learning, sales representative for ordering information.

Printed in China
1 2 3 4 5 6 7 15 14 13 12 11

Contents

Contents

Advisors and Contributors

While compiling this volume, the editors relied upon the expertise and contributions of the following chefs, scientists, scholars, and researchers, who served as advisors and/or contributors for *Food: In Context*.

Andrea Abel, MPAff
*Independent Scholar and Food
Writer*
Austin, Texas

Susan Aldridge, Ph.D.
*Independent Scholar
and Writer*
London, England

Steven J. Archambault
Department of Economics
University of New Mexico
Albuquerque, New Mexico

Stephen A. Berger, M.D.
Director, Geographic Medicine
Tel Aviv Medical Center
Tel Aviv, Israel

Melissa Carson, Ph.D.
Sustainability Expert
London, England

Bryan Davies, J.D.
*Independent Scholar and
Science Writer*
Whitby, Ontario, Canada

Sandra Dunavan, M.S.
Journalist
Saline, Michigan

Emily Walden Harris
Writer, Cook
Portland, Oregon

Brian D. Hoyle, Ph.D.
Microbiologist
Nova Scotia, Canada

Tiffany Imes, M.S.P.H.
*Congressional Hunger Center
International Fellow*
Arlington, Virginia

Phillip McIntosh
*Science Journalist
and Writer*
Colorado Springs,
Colorado

Pamela S. Michaels, M.S.
*Independent Scholar
and Writer*
Santa Fe, New Mexico

Matthew Munsey
Independent Scholar and Writer
Tucson, Arizona

Caryn Neumann, Ph.D.
*Visiting Assistant Professor,
History*
Miami University
Middletown, Ohio

Anna Marie Roos, Ph.D.
*Research Fellow in Modern
History*
University of Oxford
Oxford, England

Blake J. Stabler, M.A.
*Policy Analyst, Agriculture
and Food Security*
Washington, D.C.

David Brennan Tilove
Independent Writer and Chef
Hollywood, California

Melanie Barton Zoltán, M.S.
Independent Scholar
Amherst, Massachusetts

Acknowledgments

The editors are grateful to the global group of scholars, researchers, and writers who contributed to *Food: In Context* as academic advisors: Andre Able, Steve Berger, Melissa Carson, Brian Hoyle, Anna Marie Roos, Blake Stabler, and David Tilove.

The editors also wish to thank John Krol, whose keen eyes and sound judgment greatly enhanced the quality and readability of the text.

The editors gratefully acknowledge and extend thanks to Julia Furtaw, Janet Witalec, and Debra Kirby at Cengage Gale for their faith in the project and for their sound content, advice, and guidance. Without the able guidance and efforts of talented teams in IT, rights and acquisition management, and imaging at Cengage Gale this book would not have been possible.

Deep and sincere thanks and appreciation are also due to Project Manager Elizabeth Manar who, despite encountering the usual myriad of publishing hurdles and woes, managed miracles with wit, skill, grace, and humor.

Introduction

As memorialized in the opening chapter of his book *A Moveable Feast*, the American writer Ernest Hemingway sets out on one of most renowned walks in literary history, a walk that takes him from his humble apartment in Paris to eventually write in a "good café on the Place St. Michel."

Nearly ninety years later, one can still, as Hemingway recalled, walk past the Lycée Henri-IV and the ancient church Saint-Étienne-du-Mont, into the Place du Panthéon. The wind is still bitter on cold, rainy days, and shelter can still be sought by cutting right and slipping behind a remnant of the Université de Paris to reach the Boulevard St. Michel. Turning right and walking down the slight grade toward the river Seine, the Musée de Cluny and Boulevard St. Germain still mark the journey.

Just shy of the Place St. Michel itself, the boulevard flattens, as do the hopes of finding a café similar to those that existed in Hemingway's day. Such cafés exist in many other parts of Paris, but in this heavily touristed area, the only café open early one morning was a Starbucks coffee shop—albeit one culturally assimilated enough to have Parisian-style café tables outside.

In the Place St. Michel proper, there are now only high-traffic cafés that have signs and menus in multiple languages. Looking left and downstream along the river in the direction of the Louvre museum, a blue awning advertising "Pizza" and "Pasta" shades the opposing corner café. Wheeling back to look across the river to the Île de la Cité and then over a bit to view the westward façade of the Cathedral Notre Dame de Paris, the view of a flying buttress of the famed Gothic cathedral is partially obscured by signs perched on top of the closest corner: a café advertising Ben and Jerry's ice cream, along with an Italian brand of coffee that brews beans grown and harvested from farms around the world.

In the most important and profound ways, Hemingway's words remain true. Paris is a movable feast for the soul, but globalization has, for better and worse, also moved the feast of the world to Paris.

Food: In Context is not, however, a book about gastronomy or the impacts of globalization on cuisine *per se*. It is, rather, a book dedicated to offering a first course in food-related science, politics, and issues. While food is art—its history and expression both mirroring and articulating subtle cultural differences—its provision in some areas devolves to more sharply drawn struggles with outcomes measured in health or sickness, life or death.

The editors are humbled and fortunate that a lifetime of work covering science and disease-related issues has taken us, quite literally, around the world. We must more humbly, however, also confess to hubris, hunger, and family-driven folly regarding food choices. We know parental pangs of paying far too much for unremarkable sandwiches at tourist-trap cafés in Venice's Piazza San Marco and the profound shame of indulging in a celebratory seafood feast in Chennai, India, when only meters away, people scavenged for food. We know the joys of seeking out wonderfully intimate back-alley restaurants run by families in Bonnieux, France, Girona, Spain, Cairo, Egypt, and in the Moslem quarter of Xi'an, China. In addition to experiencing the cultural diversity of food, these intimate encounters invariably led to long discussions about food set in the context of the local geography and politics held by the owners, chefs, servers, and local patrons. Perhaps more influential in shaping *Food: In Context*, however, we have too often and too closely seen the devastating impacts of malnutrition and the folly of government policies that provide food to a fortunate few while others are left to undernourishment. We have seen food, separated from hungry people only by bad policies and inept distribution, allowed to rot instead of benefiting a population. Nothing expresses the frailty of the human condition more than a malnourished mother determined to feed a starving infant with what little milk her body will yield.

In the West, we are normally privileged to fight food wars with less dramatic outcomes. Regardless, matters of nutrition, food integrity, labeling, equitable treatment of workers, lunches for school children, etc. are also vibrantly debated and vital to creating healthy and sustainable societies. Although headlines are often consumed with the potentially deadly impacts of higher food prices or famine globally, it would be imprudent to simply ignore what are often local issues in order to focus only on more fully global issues. The motivation to tackle global issues can often come from awareness and involvement at the local level. Moreover, many of the lifestyle and sustainability issues have vital overlaps with energy and ecology issues critically important in an increasingly environmentally challenged world. Lastly, many of the health related issues are profound. While not as immediately deadly as famine, diabetes and obesity are akin to modern plagues in the West and growing in importance globally.

We also know the passions aroused when local cultures deeply entwined with local foods are imperiled. We raised children along the Gulf Coast of the United States and have long sailed the waters between New Orleans, Louisiana, and Pensacola, Florida. We lived and worked on the Gulf Coast through the worst parts of the 2010 *Deepwater Horizon* oil spill, experiencing first-hand the mounting anxiety of people fearful of losing their unique resources, cuisine, and culture.

Similarities and differences in context and perspective are an essential component of *Food: In Context* entries. Talking with farmers or workers in a market in Cambodia translates surprisingly well to similar uncertainties about keeping and maintaining family lands voiced at struggling roadside family markets in Alabama. Struggles to carve out and preserve a local niche in markets dominated by large food companies are, given minor differences in context, similar for both a family dairy in Georgia and a family farm in Ireland.

Concerns over food safety can dominate discussions with public health officials in Berlin or Kuala Lumpur.

These personal insights are important because food is not a dispassionate topic. No topic we have ever tackled has so deeply stirred passions among writers, editors, and advisors as have the issues explored in *Food: In Context*. Provided that opinions were supported by well-established science or policy, our disposition as editors was to best serve students by allowing the widest divergence of expert opinion. There were however, tough editorial calls to be made.

For example, the treatment and depiction of agribusiness is often quick to inflame passionate debate. After weeks of internal debate over which material to cover in a ballooning entry on agribusiness, we decided to retain older material related to the Nestle baby formula scandal even though more modern issues rage in the press. While the current issues were well covered in other topics (e.g., seed monopolies, GMO issues, treatment of migrant workers, child labor, etc.) we made difficult space-related choices about including the "textbook" Nestle scandal. In the end, we felt it was vital to developing a base for critical thought that we include the classic material. Such material may be classic to more advanced readers, but it is often foundational to younger students.

Accordingly, if a reader were only to read the one entry of agribusiness, we would expect to brace ourselves for a charge that we failed to more fully explore the market power of agribusinesses. As before, there are treatments of related issues throughout *Food: In Context*. We also specifically retained the Nestle baby formula example, because as one advisor advocated, he could not think of "anything worse to accuse agribusinesses of as being responsible for infant deaths." At times, providing the "textbook" example is vital.

On the other hand, we also tried to acknowledge that there is a wide diversity of opinion, especially outside the West, on the value of agribusiness. As scientists attempting to provide introductory material for students, we made a deliberate attempt to heavily rely on vetted material and avoid the inclusion of material that, although abundantly supported, did not rest on established science, or was subject to extreme, highly speculative, or conspiratorial interpretations. As editors, we considered it prudent to initially provide a diverse, but solid base of issues that will allow students to build toward their own conclusions as their studies progress.

The editors acknowledge and take responsibility for the fact that our personal experiences and perspectives from around the world have shaped *Food: In Context* to a far greater extent than our other science-related and "In Context" work. Although we attempt scholarly balance within each topic, the selection of topics—limited by space—was more subjectively driven than, for example, the topics one might cover in a book on infectious disease or climate change. Regardless, as editors, we attempted to select those topics that provide a solid foundation for beginners and a reference for more advanced students. To the extent that there are omissions, or where topics seem too briefly covered, the editors accept full responsibly. Much good material went to the editing bin.

We respectfully submit that while *Food: In Context* is more subjective editorially, it is most decidedly not self-indulgent. There are many assertions made by expert authors with which we as editors disagree or might modify if the article was in our voice alone. If the authors could, however, substantiate their positions with peer-reviewed supporting evidence, we welcomed and included divergent viewpoints and assertions.

Accessibility is a key concept for the book. Rather than detached scholarly discourse, our personal experiences drove us to seek experts with "hands on" experience grappling with an array of food issues, especially in developing nations. While we attempted to make *Food: In Context* readable for a wide audience, we also attempted to allow experts to challenge a range of student abilities, and did not shy away from promoting awareness of those causes that likely will stir a reader's own intellect and passions.

As different styles and interpretations of art, music, and literature are manifestations of the need to communicate and connect, so the many viewpoints regarding food and food issues reflect and reveal communal beliefs, deep differences, and the manifest complexities of civilization. We will consider *Food: In Context* a success if it leaves readers hungry to learn more about the vital issues covered in these pages.

To a man with an empty stomach, food is God.
—Mohandas Karamchand Gandhi (Mahatma Gandhi)

K. Lee Lerner & Brenda Wilmoth Lerner, Senior Editors

PARIS, FRANCE, DECEMBER 2010

Although grateful for the assistance of colleagues working around the world, *Food: In Context* was also a dedicated family effort within a family-run company. The senior editors wish to extend profound thanks to our senior assistant editors on this project, Joseph Patterson Hyder, J.D., and Adrienne Wilmoth Lerner, J.D., who tirelessly tackled the enormous challenges of reconciling internationally disparate food related policies. Our editorial intern and assistant editor, Adeline Wilmoth Lerner, a student at Auburn University (now also studying at *Le Cordon Bleu* in Paris), provided a solid selection of photos and helped ensure that the text remained accessible to our target audience.

The Lerner & Lerner/LernerMedia portfolio includes award-winning books, media, and film that bring global perspectives to science related issues. Since 1996, they have contributed to more than 60 academic books and served as editors-in-chief for more than 30 books related to science and society. Their book *Infectious Diseases: In Context* was designated an ALA Outstanding Academic title, and their book, *Climate Change: In Context,* both published by Cengage Gale, was named a ALA RUSA Outstanding Reference Source for 2009.

About the *In Context* Series

Written by a global array of experts yet aimed primarily at high school students and an interested general readership, the *In Context* series serves as an authoritative reference guide to essential concepts of science, the impacts of recent changes in scientific consensus, and the impacts of science on social, political, and legal issues.

Cross curricular in nature, *In Context* books align with and support national science standards and high school science curriculums across subjects in science and the humanities and facilitate science understanding important to higher achievement in science testing. The inclusion of original essays written by leading experts and primary source documents serve the requirements of an increasing number of high school and international baccalaureate programs and are designed to provide additional insights on leading social issues, as well as spur critical thinking about the profound cultural connections of science.

In Context books also give special coverage to the impact of science on daily life, commerce, travel, and the future of industrialized and impoverished nations.

Each book in the series features entries with extensively developed words-to-know sections designed to facilitate understanding and increase both reading retention and the ability of students to advance reading in context without being overwhelmed by scientific terminology.

Entries are further designed to include standardized subheads that are specifically designed to present information related to the main focus of the book. Entries also include a listing of further resources (books, periodicals, Web sites, audio and visual media) and references to related entries.

Each *In Context* title has approximately 300 topic related images that visually enrich the content. Each *In Context* title will also contain topic-specific timelines (a chronology of major events), a topic-specific glossary, a bibliography, and an index especially prepared to coordinate with the volume topic.

About This Book

Food: In Context is a collection of entries on topics designed to provide an introduction to the global diversity of viewpoints on a broad array of food related issues. In addition to life-and-death decisions reflecting the fundamental importance of food, policies related to food issues both reflect and shape societies, social justice, and social change. While the entries contained in *Food: In Context* include treatments of traditional food related issues grounded in peer-reviewed science, they also provide insight into the development and implementation of polices shaped by history and contemporary geopolitical realities.

General Structure

Food: In Context is a collection of entries on diverse topics selected to provide insight into increasingly important and urgent topics associated with the study of food science and issues.

Intended for a wide and diverse audience, every effort has been made to set forth *Food: In Context* entries in everyday language and to provide accurate and generous explanations of the most important scientific terms. Entries are designed to instruct, challenge, and excite less experienced students, while providing a solid foundation for reference for more advanced students. *Food: In Context* provides students and readers with essential information and insights that foster critical thinking about food science and policy issues.

In an attempt to enrich the reader's understanding of the mutually influential relationships of history, science, and culture, as space allows, the editors have included primary sources that enhance the content of *In Context* entries. In keeping with the philosophy that much of the benefit from using primary sources derives from the reader's own process of inquiry, the contextual material introducing each primary source provides an unobtrusive introduction and springboard to critical thought.

- Entries are arranged alphabetically, rather than by chronology or scientific subfield.

- The **chronology** (timeline) includes many of the most significant events in the history of food. Where appropriate, related scientific advances are included to offer additional context.

- An extensive **glossary** section provides readers with a ready reference for content-related terminology. In addition to defining terms within entries, specific Words-to-Know sidebars are placed within each entry.

- A **bibliography** (citations of books, periodicals, and Web sites) offers additional resources to those resources cited within each entry.

- A comprehensive **general index** guides the reader to topics and persons mentioned in the book.

Entry Structure

In Context entries are designed so that readers may navigate entries with ease. Toward that goal, entries are divided into easy-to-access sections:

- **Introduction:** A opening section designed to clearly identify the topic.

- A **Words to Know** sidebar contains essential terms that enhance readability and critical understanding of entry content.

- A **Historical Background and Scientific Foundations** section provides the historical context of the topic.

- An **Impacts and Issues** section relates key scientific, political, or social considerations related to the topic.

- More than 200 sidebars added by the editors enhance expert contributions by focusing on key areas, providing material for divergent studies, or providing evidence from key scientific or official agency reports.

- If an entry contains a related primary source, it is appended to end of the author's text. Authors are not responsible for the selection or insertion of primary sources.

- A **Bibliography** section contains citations of books, periodicals, Web sites, and audio and visual material used in preparation of the entry or that provide a stepping stone to further study.

- **"See also"** references clearly identify additional content-related entries.

Food: In Context special style notes

Please note the following with regard to topics and entries included in *Food: In Context*:

- Primary source selection and the composition of sidebars are not attributed to authors of signed entries to which the sidebars may be associated. Sources for sidebars containing external content (e.g., a quote from an Intergovernmental Panel on Climate Change (IPCC) report related to the entry) are clearly indicated.

- Equations are, of course, often the most accurate and preferred language of science. To better serve the intended audience of *Food: In Context*, however, the editors attempted to minimize the inclusion of equations in favor of describing the elegance of thought or essential results such equations yield.

- A detailed understanding of nutrition, physiology, or chemistry is neither assumed nor required for *Food: In Context*. Accordingly, students and other readers should not be intimidated or deterred by the sometimes-complex names of chemical molecules or biological classification. Where necessary, sufficient information regarding chemical structure or species classification is provided. If desired, more information can easily be obtained from any basic reference.

Bibliography citation formats

In Context titles adopt the following citation format:

Books

De, Dipak; Basavaprabhu Jirli; and K. Kiran. *Empowerment of Women in Agriculture.* Varanasi, India: Ganga Kaveri, 2010.

Hovorka, Alice, Henk de Zeeuw, and Mary Njenga. *Women Feeding Cities: Mainstreaming Gender in Urban Agriculture and Food Security.* Warwickshire, UK: Practical Action, 2009.

Jacobs, Susie M. *Gender and Agrarian Reforms.* New York: Routledge, 2010.

Kristof, Nicholas D., and Sheryl WuDunn. *Half the Sky: Turning Oppression into Opportunity for Women Worldwide.* New York: Knopf, 2009.

Periodicals

de Brauw, Alan, Qiang Li, Chengfang Liu, Scott Rozelle, and Linxiu Zhang. "Feminization of Agriculture in China? Myths Surrounding Women's Participation in Farming." *China Quarterly London* (2008): 327–348.

Giarracca, Norma, and Miguel Teubal. "Women in Agriculture." *Latin American Perspectives* 35, no. 6 (2008): 5–10.

Gill, Jatinderjit Kaur, M. K. Dhillon, and Muninder K. Sidhu. "Women in Agriculture." *International Journal of Rural Studies* 14, no. 1 (2007): 2–6.

Motzafi-Haller, Pnina, and Paul J. Kaldjian. "Geographical Reviews—Women in Agriculture in the Middle East." *Geographical Review* 96, no. 4 (2006): 721–722.

Ngowi, Aiwerasia Vera Festo. "Women's Work in Agriculture." *African Newsletter on Occupational Health and Safety* 18, no. 3 (2008): 48–49.

Web Sites

"Agriculture and Achieving the Millennium Development Goals." *International Food Policy Research Institute.* http://www.ifpri.org/publication/agriculture-and-achieving-millennium-development-goals (accessed September 18, 2010).

"Asia's Women in Agriculture, Environment, and Rural Production." *Food and Agriculture Organization of the United Nations (FAO).* http://www.fao.org/sd/wpdirect/WPre0108.htm (accessed September 18, 2010).

Using Primary Sources

The definition of what constitutes a primary source is often the subject of scholarly debate and interpretation. Although primary sources come from a wide spectrum of resources, they are united by the fact that they individually provide insight into the historical *milieu* (context and environment) during which they were produced. Primary sources include materials such as newspaper articles, press dispatches, autobiographies, essays, letters, diaries, speeches, song lyrics, posters, works of art—and in the twenty-first century, web logs—that offer direct, first-hand insight or witness to events of their day.

Categories of primary sources include:

- Documents containing firsthand accounts of historic events by witnesses and participants. This category includes diary or journal entries, letters, email, newspaper articles, interviews, memoirs, and testimony in legal proceedings.

- Documents or works representing the official views of both government leaders and leaders of other organizations. These include primary sources such as policy statements, speeches, interviews, press releases, government reports, and legislation.

- Works of art, including (but certainly not limited to) photographs, poems, and songs, including advertisements and reviews of those works that help establish an understanding of the cultural milieu (the cultural environment with regard to attitudes and perceptions of events).

- Secondary sources. In some cases, secondary sources or tertiary sources may be treated as primary sources. For example, if an entry written many years after an event, or to summarize an event, includes quotes, recollections, or retrospectives (accounts of the past) written by participants in the earlier event, the source can be considered a primary source.

Analysis of primary sources

The primary material collected in this volume is not intended to provide a comprehensive or balanced overview of a topic or event. Rather, the primary sources are intended to generate interest and lay a foundation for further inquiry and study.

In order to properly analyze a primary source, readers should remain skeptical and develop probing questions about the source. Using historical documents requires that readers analyze them carefully and extract specific information. However, readers must also read "beyond the text" to garner larger clues about the social impact of the primary source.

In addition to providing information about their topics, primary sources may also supply a wealth of insight into their creator's viewpoint. For example, when reading a news article about the effects of biofuel production on the 2008 world food crisis, consider whether the reporter's words also indicate something about his or her origin, bias (an irrational disposition in favor of someone or something), prejudices (an irrational disposition against someone or something), or intended audience.

Students should remember that primary sources often contain information later proven to be false, or contain viewpoints and terms unacceptable to future generations. It is important to view the primary source within the historical and social context existing at its creation. If for example, a newspaper article is written within hours or days of an event, later developments may reveal some assertions in the original article as false or misleading.

Test new conclusions and ideas

Whatever opinion or working hypothesis the reader forms, it is critical that they then test that hypothesis against other facts and sources related to the incident. For example, it might be wrong to conclude that factual mistakes are deliberate unless evidence can be produced of a pattern and practice of such mistakes with an intent to promote a false idea.

The difference between sound reasoning and preposterous conspiracy theories (or the birth of urban legends) lies in the willingness to test new ideas against other sources, rather than rest on one piece of evidence such as a single primary source that may contain errors. Sound reasoning requires that arguments and assertions guard against argument fallacies that utilize the following:

- false dilemmas (only two choices are given when in fact there are three or more options);
- arguments from ignorance (*argumentum ad ignorantiam*; because something is not known to be true, it is assumed to be false);
- possibilist fallacies (a favorite among conspiracy theorists who attempt to demonstrate that a factual statement is true or false by establishing the possibility of its truth or falsity. An argument where "it could be" is usually followed by an unearned "therefore, it is.");
- slippery slope arguments or fallacies (a series of increasingly dramatic consequences is drawn from an initial fact or idea);
- begging the question (the truth of the conclusion is assumed by the premises);
- straw man arguments (the arguer mischaracterizes an argument or theory and then attacks the merits of their own false representations);
- appeals to pity or force (the argument attempts to persuade people to agree by sympathy or force);
- prejudicial language (values or moral goodness, good and bad, are attached to certain arguments or facts);
- personal attacks (*ad hominem*; an attack on a person's character or circumstances);
- anecdotal or testimonial evidence (stories that are unsupported by impartial observation or data that is not reproducible);
- *post hoc* (after the fact) fallacies (because one thing follows another, it is held to cause the other);
- the fallacy of the appeal to authority (the argument rests upon the credentials of a person, not the evidence).

Despite the fact that some primary sources can contain false information or lead readers to false conclusions based on the "facts" presented, they remain an invaluable resource regarding past events. Primary sources allow readers and researchers to come as close as possible to understanding the perceptions and context of events and thus to more fully appreciate how and why misconceptions occur.

Glossary

A

ACT: A statute, rule, or formal lawmaking document enacted by a legislative body or issued by a government.

ADAPTATION: Adaptation to global climate change refers to projects and initiatives designed to reduce the vulnerability of agriculture, infrastructure, and other human and natural systems to the effects of global climate change.

ADDITIONALITY: The extent to which food aid reaches those who would not otherwise have access to food and to which additional food is not available in the targeted area and must come from the outside. Additionality refers both to the food deficit of a region or country and to the food deficit within a household.

ADOLESCENT: A person who has started puberty and continues to mature by experiencing a period of physical and psychological development. Also known as a transitional period of development between youth and maturity, this period usually starts at age 12 or 13 and lasts until 18 or 19 years of age. This time period is informally referred to as the teenage years.

ADULT-ONSET DIABETES: Also known as non-insulin-dependent or Type-2 diabetes, a form of diabetes that is often associated with obesity and often can be controlled by diet, exercise, and oral medication rather than daily injections of insulin.

AEROPONICS: A hydroponic method of growing plants in which a well-aerated root environment is maintained by enclosing the root zone in a container and pumping a steady mist of nutrient solution directly onto the roots.

AFICIONADO: An ardent follower, supporter, or enthusiast.

AGE OF DISCOVERY: A period from the late fifteenth through early seventeenth centuries, during which European maritime powers explored, mapped, and claimed previously unexplored parts of the world.

AGRARIAN: Rural, agricultural, or relating to the land. Also, a person who follows agrarianism.

AGRARIANISM: A philosophy that advocates rural living, agriculture, and equitable distribution of land.

AGRIBUSINESS: Any business involved at any point in the value chain in agriculture, livestock production, or the food industry. The term is also narrowly used as a synonym for corporate farming or industrial farming by opponents of large, corporate-run farms.

AGRICULTURAL COMMODITIES: Variable quantities of grain, livestock, poultry, fruit, timber, or other items produced from agricultural activities. Agricultural commodities are frequently traded on commodities exchanges.

AGRICULTURAL SUBSIDY: Financial assistance paid to farmers or agribusinesses by the government to supplement income or to affect the price of agricultural commodities.

AGRICULTURE: The production and management of crops and livestock, primarily for the production of food.

AGROECOLOGY: The study of how agricultural systems react with and integrate into the natural environment.

AGRONOMIST: A researcher who applies various agricultural sciences to improve soil management practices and improve crop production.

AGRONOMY: The science of cultivation of land, soil management, and crop production.

AGROTERRORISM: A subset of bioterrorism that involves the use of pathogens or pests to infect or destroy livestock or crops.

AID: Aid (also known as international aid, overseas aid, or foreign aid, especially in the United States) is a voluntary transfer of resources from one country to another, given with the objective of benefiting the recipient country.

ALEURONE: The thin layer just beneath the outside of a grain that is rich in proteins, oils, vitamins, minerals, and fiber. The aleurone layer is the outer layer of the endosperm.

ALGACULTURE: The branch of aquaculture that concerns the cultivation and harvesting of algae, the aquatic plant species. All forms of algae are produced through photosynthesis. Micro-algaculture involves the production of various types of plankton, the tiny organisms that are the foundation for virtually all aquatic organism food chains. Macro-algaculture products are more complex plant forms such as seaweed and kelp. Algae have a number of important commercial uses.

ALLERGEN: Any substance that causes an allergic reaction. Typically, various proteins are the most common food allergens.

ALLERGY: An abnormal immune reaction to an allergen introduced into the body by ingestion, inhalation, or contact with skin. The reaction produced, which can take many forms, is commonly known as an allergic reaction.

ALMS: Money or food given to the poor, typically by religious groups or by individuals for religious reasons.

AMYLOPHAGY: The consumption of uncooked starches, such as cornstarch, flour, or rice grains.

ANAPHYLAXIS: A severe, multi-system hypersensitivity reaction requiring immediate treatment to avert life-threatening symptoms such as vascular collapse, respiratory distress, and shock.

ANIMAL RIGHTS MOVEMENT: Individuals and groups concerned with protecting animals from perceived abuse or misuse. Supporters are specifically concerned with the use of animals for medical and cosmetics testing, the killing of animals for furs, hunting for pleasure, and the raising of livestock in restrictive or inhumane quarters.

ANOREXIA NERVOSA: An eating disorder in which the patient intentionally restricts eating to the point of near starvation with the purpose of weight loss and control over weight.

ANTHROPOGENIC: Being caused by, or coming from, human activities.

ANTHROPOPHAGY: Cannibalism; eating humans.

ANTIBODIES: Antibodies, or Y-shaped immunoglobulins, are proteins found in the blood that help to fight against foreign substances called antigens.

ANTIGENS: Antigens, which are usually proteins or polysaccharides, stimulate the immune system to produce antibodies. Antigens can be the source of infections from pathogenic bacteria and viruses. Organic molecules detrimental to the body from internal or environmental sources (such as allergens) also act as antigens.

ANTIOXIDANT: A substance that inhibits oxidization or slows the progress of oxidization. Biochemical reactions involving oxygen within the cells of the body produce substances called free radicals that can damage both genes and proteins. Over time, this free radical damage increases the likelihood of chronic diseases such as cancer and heart disease. Antioxidants are compounds that are thought to block free radical damage.

ANTISENSE TECHNOLOGY: The use of DNA to generate RNA molecules that bind to a target RNA and prevent it from being translated into protein.

AQUACULTURE: The process of raising fish, crustaceans, mollusks, and other aquatic plants and animals in confinement.

AQUAPONICS: A method for producing both fish and plant crops using the same water supply.

AQUIFER: An underground bed or layer of permeable rock, gravel, sand, silt, or clay that contains groundwater.

ARCHAEOBOTANY: Also known as paleoethnobotany, this is the identification and interpretation of plant remains from archaeological sites. Zooarchaeology is the related specialization that focuses on animal remains.

AROMATIC OIL: Plants used as herbs and spices synthesize oils with compounds that have distinctive aromas and flavors and result in aromatic oils. The aromatic oils are used not only in cuisine but also for medicinal purposes. Several natural essential oils may be combined to make aromatic oil, or plant material can be combined with oil to make an aromatic oil.

ARRONDISSEMENT: In France, an administrative division or compartment. The city of Paris is currently subdivided into 20 municipal arrondissements. There are also national departmental arrondissements, dividing France into 100 departments.

ARTISAN: One who is skilled in a particular trade that typically involves making products by hand using traditional methods.

ARTISANAL: Any product made by hand by an artisan or skilled craftsperson.

ARTISANAL FOOD: Handcrafted, often gourmet, food that is usually made from high-quality ingredients by traditional methods.

ASCETICISM: A way of life characterized by self-restraint, abstinence, and the rigorous self-denial of earthly pleasures, such as certain foods.

ASEPTIC: Free of agents that could cause disease.

ASSIMILATION: The process by which one ethnic group is absorbed by another, losing or altering unique cultural traits, customs, and attitudes, including those about food. Less pervasive changes associated with colonialism and migration are more accurately described as acculturation, with cultural groups remaining distinct but altering each other's cultures.

AUROCHS: Aurochs, or urus (*Bos primigenius*) is a species of wild cattle that existed across Eurasia and North Africa, from which modern cattle breeds were derived. Humans hunted wild aurochs into extinction, with a hunter killing the last known aurochs in Poland in 1627.

AUSTRALOPITHECINE: A member of the genus *Australopithecus*, australopithecines are the extinct ancestors and side branches of humans that lived 4 million to 1.4 million years ago in Africa, preceding the genus *Homo*.

AUTOTROPHS: Organisms that make their own food.

B

BAN: To prohibit something.

BARREL (OF OIL): The traditional unit of measure by which crude oil is bought and sold on the world market. One barrel of oil is equivalent to 42 U.S. gallons (159 liters).

BATTERY CAGES: An industrial, agricultural confinement system used primarily for egg-laying hens. The battery cage has generated conflict between industrial egg producers and advocates for animal welfare and animal rights due to the restrictions on movement these high-density cages impose on the hens.

BIG PHARMA: This refers to the largest multinational pharmaceutical companies, often reported in the media as having the financial ability to exert considerable influence on governments and other decision-making bodies.

BILE: A bitter, greenish fluid secreted by the liver and stored in the gall bladder that aids in the digestion of fats and oils in the body.

BINGE EATING: An eating disorder that is commonly described as continuously snacking or eating large amounts of food in a short period of time. To be considered binge eating disorder, a person must binge eat two times per week for at least six months.

BIOACCUMULATION: A progressive increase in the amount of a substance in an organism due to the inability of the organism to clear the substance from the body faster than it is accumulated.

BIOAVAILABILITY: The degree to which an ingested substance, including a vitamin or mineral, can be absorbed and used by the body. For instance, iron in meat is more bioavailable than iron in spinach, although both foods are rich in the mineral.

BIODIESEL: A biofuel produced from vegetable or other plant oils that is used to power diesel engines.

BIODIVERSITY: The number, variety, and variability of living organisms, including diversity within a species, between species, and among ecosystems. Agricultural biodiversity is particularly important for food security.

BIOFUEL: A fuel derived from biomass, which may be any living organism.

BIOMASS: Plant material, agricultural debris, or animal waste that is used as a fuel or energy source, most commonly by burning.

BIOPIRACY: Claiming patents for existing plant and animal species in order to restrict their use.

BIOTECHNOLOGY: The manipulation or use of organisms for industrial or agricultural purposes.

BIOTERRORISM: A form of terrorism that uses bacteria, viruses, or other organisms to attack people or disrupt societies.

BIOTOXIN: A toxin that is a component of, or is produced by, a living organism.

BIPEDALISM: The ability to walk upright on two feet.

BLACK CARBON: A pollutant emitted during the burning of biomass, coal, diesel, and other fossil fuels; a component of soot.

BLIGHT: A plant disease inflicted by a pathogen that causes the plant to brown, wither, and die.

BLOG: A weblog, or journal, maintained on an Internet website.

BLOOD ALCOHOL LEVEL (BAL) OR BLOOD ALCOHOL CONCENTRATION (BAC): The amount of alcohol present in the bloodstream, determined by the number of ounces of alcohol consumed per hour, the period of time in which drinking occurred, and gender and weight of the individual.

BLOOD PRESSURE: The pressure exerted by circulating blood upon the walls of the blood vessels. Blood pressure is measured in millimeters of mercury (mm Hg), and a reading is composed of two figures. The lower figure is the diastolic blood pressure, which corresponds to blood pressure in the resting phase of a heartbeat. The higher figure, the systolic blood pressure, is the blood pressure when the heart is actually contracting.

BLUE WATER: A term used to refer to all bodies of groundwater and surface waters together: rivers, lakes, and aquifers.

BODY MASS INDEX (BMI): A measurement of body fat based on a person's height and weight.

BOTULISM: A deadly form of food poisoning, botulism is caused by the bacterium *Clostridium botulinum*, which produces a potent nerve toxin. Spores of the bacterium can survive cooking. Although botulism has become rare, its most common cause in Europe is cured pork; in Japan it is salted fish; and in North America it is home-canned vegetables.

BOVINE SPONGIFORM ENCEPHALOPATHY (BSE): Also called mad cow disease. A fatal, slow-developing, prion disease affecting the nervous system of cattle. It is thought to cause a variant form of Creutzfeldt-Jakob disease (vCJD) in humans.

BRAN: The hard outer layers of a cereal grain, bran is high in fiber and also contains micronutrients.

BREMSTRAHLUNG: Electromagnetic energy given off by an electron that passes near a positively charged nucleus.

BRIGADE SYSTEM: A system of kitchen organization in which each person in the kitchen is assigned a specific station and task.

BROILER CHICKEN: A chicken intended for slaughter for food, the broiler chicken has been bred to have bigger thighs and breasts, as these are the most popular parts for consumption.

BROWNING: The color change that occurs when some foods are heated, progressing from yellow to brown, then black. The chemical reactions responsible for this color change produce new flavors. The dehydration of sugars in food, known as caramelization, and the reaction between proteins and sugars, called Maillard reactions, are the two main browning processes.

BROWNING AGENT: A chemical that causes food to turn brown to give it the appearance of having been cooked.

BUCKWHEAT: A grain prominent in the macrobiotic diet that is unusual in being a complete protein source, supplying all essential amino acids. Buckwheat also contains a compound called D-chito-inositol, which plays a role in insulin signaling and is deficient in some people with type 2 diabetes.

BULIMIA NERVOSA: An eating disorder in which the patient eats large volumes of food (binge eating) and later purges the food via forced vomiting, the use of diuretics and/or laxatives, and/or excessive exercise.

C

CALORIE: The energy value of different foods is measured in kilocalories (kcal) or calories. One kilocalorie is 1,000 calories, and one calorie is the amount of energy required to raise the temperature of one gram of water by one degree Celsius. When talking about diet and nutrition, the word calorie actually refers to a kilocalorie.

CANNING: A method of food preservation in which food is heat processed and sealed in a vessel.

CAPITALISM: An economic system in which private owners control the means of production and operate trade and industry for a profit.

CARBOHYDRATES: Molecules composed of carbon, hydrogen, and oxygen. For many animals carbohydrates are a primary source of energy, mainly in the form of starches and sugars. This term can also be used to refer to foods that are high in carbohydrates such as bread and grains.

CARBON FOOTPRINT: A measure of the amount of carbon dioxide released into the atmosphere by a single endeavor or by a company, household, or individual through day-to-day activities over a given period.

CARCINOGEN: A compound that increases the risk of cancer. Carcinogens found in food include nitrosamines, heterocyclic amines, and polycyclic aromatic hydrocarbons and acrylamide that occur in red meat or from cooking meat and other foods at high temperatures that produce charring.

CARRYING CAPACITY: The ability of an ecosystem to sustain a certain population of a species. The carrying capacity defines the maximum load of population the ecosystem can support without disrupting other species' populations.

CATALYST: A substance added to a chemical process that remains unchanged throughout, but which speeds up the rate of the reaction.

CELIAC DISEASE: Celiac (or coeliac) disease, also known as gluten-sensitive enteropathy or gluten intolerance, involves an autoimmune reaction to the gluten found in wheat and some other grains. It causes an acute inflammation of the lining of the small intestine that leaves the intestinal villi unable to absorb nutrients from food that passes through the digestive tract. Symptoms of celiac disease include chronic diarrhea, fatigue, and in infants, failure to thrive.

CELLULOID: A tough, highly flammable substance consisting essentially of cellulose nitrate and camphor, used in the manufacture of motion-picture and x ray film and other products.

CERTIFIED ORGANIC: In the United States, the states manage and regulate the use of the label "certified organic" and associated claims by supervising programs designed to give consumers confidence that products claimed to be organic meet certain standards.

CETACEAN: Any member of the marine mammal order Cetacea, including whales, dolphins, and porpoises.

CHEMOSYNTHETIC AUTOTROPH: An organism that uses carbon dioxide as a carbon source but obtains energy by oxidizing inorganic substances.

CHEMOTROPHS: Animals that make energy and produce food by breaking down inorganic molecules.

CHOLESTEROL: A waxy lipid found in animal foods and also produced in the body by the liver. Cholesterol is needed for essential bodily functions such as synthesis of cell membranes and hormones. Excess cholesterol may clog the arteries and lead to coronary heart disease and stroke.

CHROMOSOME: In higher plants and animals, discrete structural bodies composed of DNA, supporting histones, and proteins that exist in the cell nucleus and divide genetic material into entities and regions bearing specific genes.

CHUTNEY: A type of sauce originating from India with many different styles of preparation. Traditionally, a chutney is made by blending fruits, vegetables, spices, and oil.

CINEMA: The art or business of making films.

CISGENIC ORGANISM: A genetically modified organism that contains genetic sequences from the same, or closely related, species that have been spliced together in a different order.

CLOACA: The cavity into which the intestinal, genital, and urinary tracts open in vertebrates such as fish, reptiles, birds, and some primitive mammals.

CODEX ALIMENTARIUS: A collection of standards, guidelines, and codes of practices related to food production, hygiene, and food safety produced by the Food and Agriculture Organization (FAO) of the United Nations.

CODEX ALIMENTARIUS COMMISSION: Formed as a joint effort between the Food and Agriculture Organization (FAO) of the United Nations and the World Health Organization (WHO) in 1963, the Codex Alimentarius Commission works to supervise international cooperation for safe food practices across borders.

COEVOLUTION: The joint evolution of two different species, interacting with and changing each other in turn. Human societies and domesticated plants and animals evolved together, with human actions altering the other species, and the domesticated species in turn altering human cultures. Coevolution is generally seen as the unintentional consequence of long-term interactions.

COLLECTIVE AGRICULTURE: The organization of agricultural production wherein farmers jointly work on a large farm. Collective agriculture typically involves state ownership of the means of production, including the land

COLLECTIVIZATION: The organization of the economy, or some sector thereof, on the basis of ownership by the people as represented by the state.

COLUMBIAN EXCHANGE: The products and ideas that were traded between the Americas and Europe as the result of Christopher Columbus' voyage to the Americas.

COMMENSALISM: A relationship involving two organisms, in which one organism benefits, and the other is not affected.

COMMENSALITY: The act of eating with other people.

COMMODITY: A uniform good about which it is difficult to make distinctions based on quality in the market. In agriculture, grains and oilseeds are often referred to as commodities, as are some meat and dairy products.

COMMON AGRICULTURAL POLICY (CAP): The European Economic Community (EEC) and then the European Union (EU) systems of agricultural subsidies, tariffs, and controls designed to create a single agricultural market without giving advantage to particular countries within the customs union are examples of common agricultural policies.

COMMON POOL RESOURCE (CPR): A resource that is open to use by many individuals. Pastures, fisheries, and irrigation systems can all be organized as common pool resources. Unlike a pure public good, additional users do have a cost. These users can negatively affect the resource, but unlike a public good, they can be excluded from using the resource.

COMPARATIVE ADVANTAGE: Efficiency in production of one good over another that makes trade possible even if one country lacks absolute efficiency in either good. Even if one country is more efficient at producing every product, it can gain from specializing in the products it is comparatively more efficient at producing. Then the country can move out of producing products in which it lacks comparative advantage and trade with other countries for those products.

COMPLETE PROTEINS: Protein sources that contain all eight amino acids in adequate amounts. Animal foods are complete proteins but many plant foods are not.

CONCENTRATED ANIMAL FEEDING OPERATION (CAFO): Agricultural facilities (or "factory farms") where a single facility confines a large number of animals. The animals, waste, and production are highly concentrated in a small area of land. Legally, in the United States, the Environmental Protection Agency (EPA) defines a CAFO as a farm that has at least 1,000 beef cattle, 700 dairy cows, 2,500 hogs, or 125,000 broiler chickens.

CONNECTIVE TISSUE: The tissue between muscle fibers in meat and between muscle tissues and other tissues, such as bone. Connective tissue is made up of three proteins—collagen, elastin, and reticulin—and contributes to the texture of cooked meat.

CONQUISTADOR: A conqueror, especially one of the sixteenth-century Spanish soldiers who defeated the indigenous civilizations of Mexico, Central America, or Peru.

CONSUMER ADVOCACY GROUP: An organization dedicated to protecting consumers from corporate abuses, including unsafe products and false advertising.

CONSUMER PRICE INDEX: A measure of price changes, or inflation, through the monitoring of the average price of a set basket of goods.

CONTAMINATION: The unwanted presence of a microorganism or compound in a particular environment. That environment can be in the laboratory setting, for example, in a medium being used for the growth of a species of bacteria during an experiment. Another environment can be the human body, where contamination by bacteria can produce an infection.

CONVENTION ON INTERNATIONAL TRADE IN ENDANGERED SPECIES (CITES): The Convention on International Trade in Endangered Species of Wild Fauna and Flora, often known as the CITES agreement, is a voluntary international agreement to restrict trade in animal or plant products from endangered or threatened species.

COOKING: The transfer of heat to a food by conduction, convention, or radiation. The heat brings about chemical reactions between food molecules that transform the food's texture and flavor.

COOKING SHOW: A type of food-related television programming dedicated to providing instruction to home cooks on food preparation.

COPING STRATEGY: A way in which a household seeks to avoid the negative consequences of a reduction in income, agricultural production, or livestock production.

CORN SYRUP: An aqueous solution composed of glucose chains of different lengths derived from the acidic or enzymatic breakdown of corn starch, a glucose polymer.

CORONARY HEART DISEASE: In atherosclerosis, which is the main cause of coronary heart disease, fatty material, including cholesterol, forms a deposit called plaque on the inner walls of the arteries. This causes them to narrow—slowing or even stopping the flow of blood to the heart.

COSMETICS: Products that by direct application to the skin, nails, lips, or hair of a person are intended to promote attractiveness by cleansing, enhancing, or otherwise altering one's appearance.

COTYLEDON: The seed leaves that form part of a seed, storing its food supplies. Most nuts and seeds consist of two swollen cotyledons packed with oil, protein, and other nutrients.

COUNTRY OF ORIGIN LABELING (COOL): Labeling on a food item that shows the country in which the product was farmed, grown, or raised.

CREOLE: Refers to both the people and the culture of French settlements in the Caribbean and Louisiana beginning in the fifteenth century.

CROP ROTATION: An agricultural practice that involves growing different crops in sequential seasons or letting fields lie fallow for a season in order to preserve soil fertility.

CROSS-CONTAMINATION: The movement of a pathogen or potentially dangerous or uncooked material from one surface to another. For example, if a cook uses the same knife to cut raw chicken and a tomato, the tomato may become cross-contaminated with a pathogen from the raw chicken.

CULTIVAR: A variety of a plant that has been created or selected intentionally and maintained through cultivation.

CURING: A method of food preservation involving salt, smoking, and dehydrating that works by drawing water out of the food so that bacteria are less likely to grow on it.

CURRY: A technique for making a stewed food dish common in India and South Asia that can be made with meat or vegetables with curry spices.

D

DEBEAKING: Also called beak trimming, this is the partial removal of the beak of poultry, especially chickens and turkeys. Most commonly, the beak is shortened permanently, although regrowth can occur. The term debeaking implies that the entire beak is removed during the trimming process, though in reality only half or less of the beak is generally removed. Debeaking is done in order to reduce instances of cannibalistic pecking among birds in dense populations, where such behavior is more common.

DECOLLECTIVIZATION: The process of moving from collective agriculture to private land ownership or removing state control over agriculture.

DECOLONIZATION: The process of transforming from a colony to an independent nation.

DECOMPOSITION: Breakdown of cells and tissues.

DEFICIENCY DISEASE: A disease caused by a lack of a specific nutrient, whether that nutrient is missing from the diet or is unable to be absorbed or metabolized by the body.

DEFORESTATION: The clearing of forest cover through human activity.

DENTAL CARIES: The condition when the enamel or outermost surface of a tooth is eroded or damaged to the point at which food particles and bacteria can pass through the protective enamel covering and into the living tissue of the tooth where blood vessels are stored. Signs that a person may have caries include sensitivity or pain to foods that are cold, hot, sour, or sweet.

DESERTIFICATION: The degradation of fertile, habitable land, typically semi-arid dryland, into arid desert, usually due to climate change or misuse of the land. Desertification is identified as a main barrier to food security and sustainable livelihoods.

DETRITUS: Dead organic matter.

DIABETES: Diabetes mellitus is a disease of glucose metabolism that is defined by blood glucose levels. There are three types of diabetes: insulin dependent diabetes mellitus, IDDM (type 1), non-insulin dependent diabetes mellitus, NIDDM (type 2), and gestational diabetes (onset occurs in women during pregnancy).

DIET: The word *diet* really has two meanings. It can mean simply what a person happens to eat, and diets are influenced by many factors, such as access to food, culture, personal preferences, and beliefs. Diet can also mean eating with a certain goal in mind, such as a reducing food intake to lose weight.

DIETARY GUIDELINES FOR AMERICANS: The *Dietary Guidelines for Americans* contains science-based, nutritional advice for Americans and outlines the U.S. government's nutrition policy and education initiatives. The U.S. Department of Agriculture (USDA) and U.S. Department of Health and Human Services (HHS) jointly publish the *Dietary Guidelines for Americans* every five years.

DIETARY REFERENCE INTAKES (DRIS): Developed by the Institute of Medicine of the National Academy of Sciences, Dietary Reference Intakes (DRIs) are intended to plan and assess nutrient intake for healthy people. DRIs include the recommended daily allowance (RDA) and also the tolerable upper intake level (UL), which is the maximum daily intake unlikely to result in adverse health effects. DRIs are intended to plan and assess nutrient intake for healthy people.

DIETARY SUPPLEMENT: A product, such as a vitamin, mineral, or herb, that is intended to be consumed in addition to the regular diet in the expectation that it will improve health.

DIETARY TABOO: A prohibition of a food or a type of food preparation.

DIGESTION: The physical and chemical processes that transform the food a person eats into nutrients that the body can use.

DIOXINS: A group of highly toxic, carcinogenic compounds produced during the manufacturing process of various substances, such as herbicides.

DIRECT FOOD AID: The provision of food or rations of food to individuals. Direct food aid can also include providing the infrastructure for delivering and distributing food aid.

DISASTER RECOVERY: Distinct from disaster management, disaster recovery encompasses the processes, policies, and procedures related to preparing for recovery or continuation of technology infrastructure critical to an organization after a natural or human-induced disaster.

DISEASE SURVEILLANCE: Routine monitoring of important diseases conducted by state health departments. Salmonellosis and *E. coli* 0157:H7 bacteria are foodborne illnesses subject to surveillance.

DISPARAGEMENT: A communication that belittles, undermines, or damages the reputation of someone or something.

DOCUMENTARY: A factual film or television program about an event, person, etc., presenting the facts with little or no fiction.

DOMESTICATION: The process by which humans selectively alter plant and animal species, resulting in new varieties or new species with different behaviors and physical characteristics. This may done consciously, through controlled breeding, or through repeated interactions with unintended consequences in a coevolutionary fashion. Domesticates rely on humans to reproduce themselves; without human aid they will go extinct or revert back to wild forms.

DRY NURSING: The term for the practice common in the 1800s and 1900s of feeding of infants, via spoon, finger, or bottle, any mixture of animal milk and other foods as a substitute for breast milk.

DRYLAND: Arid desert or semi-arid xeric shrubland biomes.

DUMPING: Food aid that consists of free, subsidized, or below market price food, which undercuts local farmers and can lead to the destruction of local farming and economies and to an ongoing cycle of poverty and hunger.

DYSPHAGIA: Dysphagia refers to experiencing difficulty swallowing.

E

E. COLI: *Escherichia coli* is a form of bacteria found in the lower intestine of humans and many warm-blooded animals. Many *E. coli* forms are harmless; the *E. coli* strain O157:H7 is associated with food poisoning, and its presence has precipitated numerous food product recalls in North America and Europe.

EATING DISORDERS: Eating disorders include anorexia nervosa, bulimia nervosa, and binge eating. Individuals suffering from bulimia and anorexia exhibit excessive control over their body weight by controlling their food intake. Anorexia nervosa and bulimia nervosa are disorders that are more prevalent among young women in industrialized countries where food exists in abundance yet there is pressure to diet and to achieve a perceived ideal, thin body.

EATING HABITS: Describes what foods people eat, why and how people eat, and with whom they eat. Individual, social, cultural, religious, economic, and environmental factors can influence people's eating habits. Acceptable and learned eating behaviors can vary by cultural group and are reflected in a person's meal and snack patterns, portion sizes, and food combinations.

ECONOMIC STATECRAFT: The use of economic power by one country to influence how other countries behave.

ECONOMY OF SCALE: A reduction in the cost of the production of a product attained by producing more. Economies of scale also refer to cost reductions accrued by geographic concentration of an industry.

EDIBLE: The ability to be eaten or used as a source of nutrients.

ELECTROLYTES: Compounds that ionize in a solution; electrolytes dissolved in the blood play an important role in maintaining the proper functioning of the body.

ELECTROMAGNETIC RADIATION: A phenomenon consisting of oscillating magnetic and electric waves existing at right angles to each other. Waves with shorter wavelengths (higher frequencies) have higher energies.

ELECTRON BEAM: A focused stream of electrons emitted from the hot filament of an electron gun.

EMERGENCY RELIEF: The aspect of humanitarian assistance that seeks to directly preserve life, health, and safety and directly protect livelihoods and dignity during a crisis.

EMULSIFIER: A chemical used to suspend oils in water.

ENCEPHALOPATHY: A disorder or disease of the brain.

ENDOCANNIBALISM: Eating people from within one's own group, usually as part of a religious rite involving dead ancestors. In contrast, exocannibalism is defined by eating outsiders, usually the enemies of the one's group.

ENDOCRINE SYSTEM: A system comprising glands that secrete specific hormones into the bloodstream to regulate body functions.

ENDOSPERM: The central and largest portion of a grain, filled with starch granules embedded in a protein matrix.

ENGEL'S LAW: As a household's income increases, it will spend a lower percentage of income on food though its actual food expenditures may increase. The increase in spending is due to a shift in the diet away from grains to more expensive foods such as meats, dairy products, fruits, and vegetables. Engel's Law is named after Ernst Engel (1821–1896), the German economist and statistician who first noted the tendency.

ENTERAL NUTRITION: Feeding through a tube that goes in through the nose and down to the stomach. Long-term enteral nutrition may involve a gastrostomy tube being inserted into the stomach through an incision in the abdomen.

ENTERIC: Involving the intestinal tract or relating to the intestines.

ENTEROTOXIN: Enterotoxin and exotoxin are two classes of toxin that are produced by bacteria.

ENTITLEMENT PROGRAM: A program that uses government resources to provide assistance to needy families.

ENTITLEMENTS APPROACH: An approach to understanding famine, hunger, malnutrition, and poverty based on understanding how a population acquires food and on what resources a population has available to acquire food. Pioneered by Amartya Sen, the approach looks at the right to food and other goods and to changes in exchange conditions to explain sudden deprivation events such as a famine.

ENVIRONMENTAL LITERACY: Basic knowledge of environmental connections, ecology, and the environmental issues that are important in the early twenty-first century.

ENZYME: Proteins found in living cells that act as catalysts for chemical reactions, including digestion. Some raw food advocates argue that cooking kills the enzymes found in freshly harvested foods that are beneficial to human health.

EPHEDRA: An herbal supplement, derived from the plant *Ephedra sinica*, which is a stimulant that may increase blood pressure and heart rate. Ephedra-containing supplements were banned in the United States in 2004.

EPOXY RESINS: Short chain polymers or monomers formed by the reaction of bisphenol A (or other compounds) and epichlorohydrin. When mixed with a hardener, the resin forms a very tough epoxy copolymer.

ESSENTIAL AMINO ACIDS: All the proteins in the body are made from 20 different amino acid building blocks. Humans can synthesize 12 of these but eight need to be obtained from the diet. These eight are known as essential amino acids.

ESSENTIAL OIL: A concentrated liquid containing volatile aromatic compounds extracted from plants.

ESTROGENIC: Having an effect similar to that of the female sex hormone estrogen.

ETHANOL: A term often used to refer to bioethanol, a type of ethanol (ethyl alcohol) derived from plants and used as a fuel.

ETHNOBIOLOGY: The study of the interrelations between people and the plants and animals in their environment, including cultural classifications and perceptions of other species, as well as traditional ecological knowledge and the utilization of plants and animals. Researchers may specialize in ethnobotany or ethnozoology.

ETHNOECOLOGY: The study of how people, agriculture, economics, and the environment interact with an emphasis on culture.

EUTROPHICATION: The depletion in water of oxygen available for fish and other animals resulting from the rapid growth of algae and other organisms in the presence of excess nutrients in the water system.

EVAPO-TRANSPIRATION: Loss of water through both evaporation from the surface and the transpiration of moisture from the aboveground parts of plants.

EVIDENCE-BASED: Using scientific method and research studies to determine the best practice in a specific discipline.

EXISTENTIALIST: A philosopher who argues existential philosophical principles, typically (but with many variations) emphasizing the uniqueness of the individual and the isolation of the individual imposed by mortal existence in an indifferent natural world. The philosophy stresses freedom of individual choice and responsibility for personal actions.

EXOCANNIBALISM: Exocannibalism is defined by eating outsiders, usually the enemies of the one's group.

EXPERIENTIAL LEARNING: A form of education that emphasizes learning by doing, or through direct experience.

EXTERNALITY: Something external to a production process for which the producer does not pay or get paid. An externality can be negative, such as pollution for which a producer incurs no cost. It can also be positive, such as bees from one farm pollinating other farms' crops in an area for free. Externalities are external to the accounting and decision making process of the producer.

EXTINCTION: The state or process of a species or larger taxonomic group ceasing to exist.

EXTRA VIRGIN OLIVE OIL: Olive oil derived from the first press of the olives and not chemically processed.

F

FAD DIET: A specific food regimen, typically restricted to no more than five foods or to one food group, designed to create extreme, short-term weight loss.

FAIR TRADE: A process that incorporates equitable distribution of profit, environmental and ecological consequences, human rights, and cultural issues into capitalist markets. In the late twentieth century, advocacy groups pushed for fair trade in the coffee industry.

FALAFEL: Ground chickpeas formed into a ball or patty and fried, sometimes served in a pita sandwich.

FAMILY FARM: Defined by the U.S. Department of Agriculture (USDA) as any farm organized as a sole proprietorship, partnership, or family corporation. The definition excludes co-operatives and farms with hired managers.

FAMINE: A generalized and extreme scarcity of food, prolonged extreme hunger, undernourishment, or lack of food.

FARM BILL: A comprehensive omnibus bill adopted by the United States Congress that sets the agricultural and food policy of the United States.

FARMER'S MARKET: A local, decentralized produce market in which farmers sell directly to the public, without the middleman of produce brokers or grocery stores.

FARM-TO-SCHOOL PROGRAMS: Local partnerships that public school districts, or individual schools, can form with area farmers to deliver agricultural and nutritional curricula to students while serving local produce and crops. These programs often include field trips to farms, cooking classes that incorporate local crops, and unit studies on nutritional composition and growing conditions for local foods.

FAST FOOD: Food that can be prepared and served rapidly, usually involving precooked or preheated ingredients. Fast food is usually taken away, rather than eaten where it is prepared.

FAT: A type of lipid or chemical compound used as a source of energy, to provide insulation, and to protect organs in an animal body.

FATTY ACIDS: A group of organic chemicals consisting of a carbon backbone linked to a carboxylic acid group. The length of the carbon backbone varies. The simplest fatty acid is acetic acid, the main ingredient in vinegar, which has a backbone consisting of just one carbon atom, bonded to three hydrogen atoms. Naturally occurring fatty acids have carbon backbones containing up to 35 carbon atoms.

FEAST: A large and usually elaborate banquet, often prepared for many people, and often in recognition of a celebratory event or religious occasion.

FECAL-ORAL ROUTE: The transmission of minute particles of fecal material from one organism (human or animal) to the mouth of another organism.

FERMENTATION: Biological process performed by many microorganisms in which sugars are converted to carbon dioxide and alcohol.

FERTILIZERS: Fertilizers are soil amendments applied to promote plant growth and are usually directly applied to soil and also sprayed on leaves.

FIBER: Fiber is not always defined as a nutrient because it is not digested. Yet it plays a useful role in maintaining good bowel function. Diets high in fiber may also protect against diabetes and certain types of cancer.

FIXED MENU: A style of restaurant service in which instead of having a list of dishes from which the diner can choose, there is only one list of courses that every diner receives.

FLORA: In microbiology, flora refers to the collective microorganisms that normally inhabit an organism or system. Human intestines, for example, contain bacteria that aid in digestion and are considered normal flora.

FOIE GRAS: A traditional French product, the name of which in English means "fat liver." It is the liver of overfed ducks or geese and contains about 65 percent fat. Foie gras production is banned in some countries because the method of overfeeding the animals is considered inhumane.

FOOD ADDITIVE: A substance, not normally consumed by itself, that is added to a food product to increase shelf life, appearance, or taste.

FOOD AID: Emergency food aid is distributed to victims of natural or human-made disasters. It is freely distributed to targeted beneficiary groups and usually provided on a grant basis. Food aid is channeled multilaterally, through nongovernmental organizations (NGOs), or sometimes bilaterally, given by one country directly to another.

FOOD ALLERGY: An allergy is an adverse reaction to a substance called an allergen that is usually harmless. In food allergy, the allergen is contained in one or more foodstuffs. Allergic reactions always involve the allergen triggering a response from the immune system.

FOOD ALLIANCE CERTIFICATION: A comprehensive certification program for sustainably-produced food in North America.

FOOD ASSISTANCE: Any intervention to address hunger and undernutrition (e.g., food stamps, WIC, food subsidies, food price stabilization, etc.). It is distinct from food aid in that it is not related to international sourcing of resources tied to the provision of food, whether by a donor or to a recipient.

FOOD BANK: An organization that stores and distributes food to the hungry.

FOOD CO-OP: A member-owned and run grocery store.

FOOD CRITIC: A person who writes reviews of dining experiences at restaurants for publication in newspapers, magazines, or on the Internet.

FOOD EMULSIFIERS: Emulsifiers are chemicals that facilitate the complete mixture of substances that naturally separate when they are added one to another, such as oil and water.

FOOD GUIDE: A book or website that contains information on restaurants, often including restaurant ratings.

FOOD INSECURITY: A situation that exists when people lack secure access to sufficient amounts of safe and nutritious food for normal growth and development and an active and healthy life. It may be caused by the unavailability of food, insufficient purchasing power, inappropriate distribution, or inadequate use of food at the household level.

FOOD INTOLERANCE: An adverse reaction to food that does not involve the immune system.

FOOD JUSTICE: The concept that society should arrange its relationships so everyone can have sufficient food.

FOOD MILES: The distance that food products or the raw ingredients used in food travel between the farm gate and the final producer. Food miles are used as a comparative measure of the environmental impact of transportation in the food industry.

FOOD PRESERVATION: Techniques of food handling, processing, or packaging that slow down the decomposition of the food.

FOOD QUALITY PROTECTION ACT OF 1996: Also known as the FQPA, this act changed the way the Environmental Protection Agency (EPA) regulates pesticides and set stricter standards for acceptable exposure levels for infants and children.

FOOD RECALLS: In a recall, the Food Safety and Inspection Service (FSIS), a Food and Drug Administration (FDA) agency, asks the public to return products from a specific batch produced by a manufacturer or farm, for reasons such as contamination by foodborne illness. Most FSIS-originated recalls involve voluntary recalls, in which the manufacturer works proactively with government agencies to remove a product from shelves and to educate consumers to return or destroy defective products.

FOOD SAFETY MODERNIZATION ACT (FSMA): Passed by the U.S. House of Representatives in 2009, FSMA authorizes the Food and Drug Administration (FDA) to order the recall of any contaminated foods commercially available in the United States.

FOOD SECURITY: Access to sufficient, safe, and nutritious food to meet dietary needs and food preferences for an active and healthy life.

FOOD SOVEREIGNTY: The right of peoples and sovereign states to determine democratically their own agricultural and food policies.

FOOD STAMPS: A form of government assistance to low-income citizens that enables the recipient to acquire food from grocery stores, markets, or other locations.

FOOD WASTE: Food that is not consumed, from domestic and commercial food scraps not eaten at the table to harvested foods rotting before they are delivered and everything in between.

FOODBORNE ILLNESS: An illness caused by the consumption of contaminated food that has usually been improperly stored, handled, or prepared.

FOODIE: A person who follows food fads and trends for interest or entertainment.

FOODS FOR SPECIFIED HEALTH USE (FOSHU): A legal term in Japan used to regulate the health claims made by functional foods. FOSHU producers can receive a seal and verification of their health claims from the Japanese government.

FOODSHED: A foodshed is defined by the area within which one's food is produced, as a watershed defines where water drains. Modern foodsheds may be global in scale, but locavores' foodsheds are much smaller and regionally restricted.

FOODWAYS: Customs and traditions that accompany the production, selection, preparation, consumption, and culture of food.

FOUR BASIC FOOD GROUPS: The four basic food groups were part of nutrition education in the United States from the 1950s until the development of the Improved American Food Guide Pyramid. These groups were meats (including poultry, eggs, nuts, and legumes), dairy, fruits and vegetables, and grains.

FOWL: Often used to describe birds in general, but more accurately applies to the orders Galliformes, which includes chickens, turkeys, pheasants, partridges and quail, and Anseriformes, which includes waterfowl such as ducks and geese.

FRANCHISE: Many restaurants and other outlets serving fast food are franchises, or branches, of a chain in which the food is delivered from a central location and is standardized.

FREE AND REDUCED PRICE LUNCH: Students from families with incomes below 130 percent of the federal poverty line generally qualify for free school lunches through the National School Lunch Program (NSLP), with the fee for lunch reduced for children from families earning between 131 percent and 185 percent of the federal poverty line, per United States Department of Agriculture Guidelines.

FREE RANGE: A food-source animal that is permitted to pasture graze for food rather than being confined to a feed house or feed lot.

FUNCTIONAL FOODS: Also known as nutraceuticals, functional foods are foods, beverages, or nutritional supplements that contain additives with purported medicinal or health benefits.

FUNGIBLE: The condition of one unit of a commodity being absolutely identical to another unit of a commodity and thus being a perfect substitute.

FUSION CUISINE: Food that contains combinations of traditions, techniques, and ingredients of varying cultures.

G

GAMMA RAYS: Electromagnetic radiation of wavelengths from about 0.003 to 0.03 nanometers.

GASTROENTERITIS: Gastroenteritis is an inflammation of the stomach and the intestines. More commonly, gastroenteritis is called the stomach flu.

GENDER MAINSTREAMING: The incorporation into organizations, development programs, and research of concern and understanding about how women and men work, live, and earn money differently.

GENE: A loosely defined term describing a DNA sequence that contains a discrete coding unit for a single protein or RNA molecule.

GENETIC ENGINEERING: General term for using a wide variety of techniques to introduce specific changes in an organism's DNA.

GENETICALLY MODIFIED (GM) FOODS: Foods derived from genetically modified organisms that have had changes introduced into their DNA by techniques in genetic engineering to introduce a new trait that does not occur naturally in the species.

GENETICALLY MODIFIED ORGANISM (GMO): Any living organism, including plants, animals, and bacteria, in which the genetic material has been altered so the organism expresses desired traits.

GENOCIDE: According to the United Nations (UN) Convention on Genocide of 1948, "any of the following acts committed with intent to destroy, in whole or in part, a national, ethnical, racial or religious group, as such: killing members of the group, causing serious bodily or mental harm to members of the group, deliberately inflicting on the group conditions of life calculated to bring about its physical destruction in whole or in part, imposing measures intended to prevent births within the group; forcibly transferring children of the group to another group."

GENOME: The total genetic material contained in a single cell of an organism.

GENRE: A class or category of artistic endeavor having a particular form, content, technique, or the like: the genre of epic poetry; the genre of symphonic music.

GEOPHAGY: Also known as geophagia or geophagism, this is the consumption of substances taken from the earth, such as dirt, clay, and ground stone. Certain types of smooth clay, such as kaolin or "white dirt," are often preferred. In some parts of the world, clay that has been processed for eating is sold at markets and convenience stores.

GERMPLASM: Genetic material, especially in a form that that can be used to reproduce an organism. Seeds, tubers, cuttings, breeding colonies of living animals, and frozen sperm and embryos are all types of germplasm.

GESTATION CRATE: A metal pen typically two feet wide and seven feet long in which a pregnant sow is kept during its four-month gestation period. The use of these enclosures is controversial because they often do not include any kind of bedding material, and the cramped conditions within the pen do not allow the animal to turn around or even to lie down comfortably. Most sows in factory farms are kept in a lifelong state of impregnation and birth and will therefore spend most of their lives in these crates.

GINGIVITIS: A mild form of periodontal or gum disease that causes inflammation or swelling of the gums. If a person's gums bleed when being brushed, gingivitis is a likely cause. Daily brushing and flossing of the teeth can help to prevent this disease.

GLOBALIZATION: The integration of national and local systems into a global economy through increased trade, manufacturing, communications, and migration.

GLUCOSE: A type of sugar that serves as the body's fuel. Other sugars include sucrose (or table sugar), lactose, and fructose.

GLUTEN: Elastic protein molecules specific to certain cereal grains. It is found in high concentrations in wheat and in smaller concentrations in barley and rye.

GOITER: A swelling of the thyroid gland, located in the neck, that is caused primarily by iodine deficiency.

GOLDEN RICE: A variety of rice that has been genetically modified to contain beta carotene using genes from corn.

GOURMET: A connoisseur of fine food and drink.

GRAIN: The edible part of a cereal grass plant. A grain is a whole fruit, containing a seed and a thin, dry layer of ovary tissue.

GRAM CALORIE: The small calorie; the amount of heat energy necessary to raise the temperature of one gram of water by one degree Celsius.

GREEN COFFEE: The dried berries from the coffee bush. Green coffee has a long shelf life, and beans are sold in large volume as green coffee. Leaving the beans in their green state prolongs the life of the berries. Coffee cannot be brewed until the green coffee beans are roasted and ground.

GREEN CONSUMER: A consumer who puts the environment at the top of his or her shopping list by buying products made from natural ingredients that cause minimal or no environmental damage. The term was made popular by a book called *The Green Consumer Guide* written by sustainability pioneers Julia Hailes (1961–) and John Elkington (1949–) in 1987.

GREEN WATER: A term used to refer to rainwater.

GREENHOUSE EFFECT: A process by which atmospheric greenhouse gases absorb radiation from the Earth's surface and reemit the radiation—some of which returns to the surface—instead of allowing the radiation to escape into space. The greenhouse effect results in an increase of the Earth's surface temperature.

GREENHOUSE GAS: A greenhouse gas (GHG) is any gas that contributes to the greenhouse effect by absorbing and emitting radiation within the thermal infrared range. Carbon dioxide, methane, ozone, nitrous oxide, and water vapor are the most common greenhouse gases.

GROUNDWATER: Water that exists underground in aquifers, streams, soil, or rock.

GUSTATORY: Relating to the sense of taste.

H

HABILINE: An early human ancestor in the genus *Homo*, particularly *Homo habilis* but also including such fossil species as *Homo rudolfensis*, *Homo georgicus*, and some transitional forms of australopithecines. Habilines evolved into *Homo ergaster* and *Homo erectus* and several other species during the Pleistocene, including Neanderthals.

HALAL: Foods that adhere to Islamic dietary laws.

HALVAH: A Middle Eastern and Mediterranean confection made by grinding almonds into a sweet paste and combining them with other ingredients and flavorings.

HARMONIZATION OF FOOD STANDARDS: Harmonization occurs when all member nations adopt the same standards to the same degree.

HAZARD ANALYSIS AND CRITICAL CONTROL POINT (HACCP): According to the Food and Drug Administration (FDA), HACCP is a "management system in which food safety is addressed through the analysis and control of biological, chemical, and physical hazards from raw material production, procurement and handling, to manufacturing, distribution and consumption of the finished product."

HEAT: A form of energy that makes molecules travel faster. When heat is transferred to a food, it causes physical and chemical changes that transform the food into a palatable dish.

HEIFER: A young female cow that has not yet given birth to its first calf.

HEIRLOOM: A variety of plant or breed of animal that has not been subjected to industrialized modification. Heirloom chickens, for example, include mostly free-range breeds that are slow-growing, as opposed to the fast-growing chickens that are used in conventional poultry operations.

HEIRLOOM VARIETY: A particular cultivar of plant that was previously grown in agriculture, but experienced decreased cultivation with the rise of industrialized agriculture.

HERB: A plant with aromatic leaves, seeds, or flowers that are used, fresh or dried, to flavor food, scent perfume, or as an ingredient in medicine.

HERITAGE BREED: Traditional, genetically distinct livestock and poultry breeds that were raised by farmers in the past before the reduction of breed variety caused by industrial agriculture.

HETEROCYCLIC AMINES (HCAs): Potentially cancer-causing compounds that are formed on meat when it is charred or cooked at high temperatures.

HETEROTROPHS: Organisms that do not make their own food.

HIERARCHICAL SOCIETIES: Social groups characterized by an inherited political hierarchy (ruled by few, with many agricultural producers below), and different levels of social inequality. In anthropology, complex chiefdoms, states, and empires are classified as hierarchical societies. More egalitarian societies may be organized into tribes or bands.

HIGH-FRUCTOSE CORN SYRUP (HFCs): High-fructose corn syrup is a sweetener and preservative that is commonly used in baked goods, soda, dairy treats, and many other processed foods. It is made by converting the glucose in corn starch to fructose, and then adding more glucose.

HILUM: The small pore in the center of the curved edge of a bean that allows water in during soaking to make a dried bean edible

HOLISTIC DEVELOPMENT: Sometimes used interchangeably with sustainable development, holistic approaches involve agroecology and development that does not compromise future generations or cause environmental damage.

HOLOCENE: The current geological epoch, which began approximately 12,000 years ago.

HOMININ: A taxonomic term used to describe humans, their ancestors, and closely related species, including all members of the genera *Homo* and *Australopithecus*. Hominid, which anthropologists previously used to describe humans and their ancestors, now includes chimpanzees and gorillas as part of the family Hominidae.

HOMOGENIZATION: Milk is an emulsion of fat in water, and if left standing will separate into two layers. Homogenization involves passing the milk through a fine nozzle, which breaks up its fat globules into smaller particles that form a uniform liquid with the watery component of milk.

HORIZONTAL INTEGRATION: Controlling a single step or stage of a value chain.

HOST: Organism that serves as the habitat for a parasite, or possibly for a symbiont. A host may provide nutrition to the parasite or symbiont or simply a place in which to live.

HUMAN TRAFFICKING: To move a person, often from one country to another, for the purpose of exploiting that person.

HUNGER: No internationally recognized legal definition of hunger exists. However, it is widely accepted that it goes beyond a minimum calorie intake sufficient to prevent death by starvation. The term "starvation" refers to the most extreme form of hunger; death by starvation is the end result of a chronic, long-lasting, and severe period of hunger.

HUNTER-GATHERERS: People whose subsistence depends on hunting and gathering or foraging for their food. In the Paleolithic period, all humans were hunter-gatherers, but in the early twenty-first century most of the world's population eats an agriculturally based diet.

HYDROCARBON: A chemical containing only carbon and hydrogen.

HYDROGENATED FAT: The fatty acids in fats and oils may contain carbon-carbon double bonds that are capable of reacting with hydrogen. The hydrogenation of a fat, as in the manufacture of margarine, increases the degree of saturation of a fat.

HYDROLOGIC CYCLE: The hydrologic cycle, or water cycle, is the cycle in which water circulates between the earth's oceans, atmosphere, and land. During the hydrologic cycle water falls to the surface as precipitation, flows as runoff into streams and rivers, and returns to the atmosphere via evaporation and transpiration.

HYGIENE: Actions that help maximize health, particularly by controlling the growth of bacteria on surfaces.

HYPERTENSION: Long-term elevation of blood pressure defined by two readings, systolic and diastolic blood pressure, that are above the normal of 140 and 90 mm Hg, respectively. Hypertension risks damage to the blood vessels and complications including stroke, heart attack, and kidney failure.

I

ICSR NUMBER: The Reportable Food Registry issues Individual Case Safety Report (ICSR) numbers when a responsible party inputs a reportable food to the registry. Responsible parties and the Food and Drug Administration (FDA) then use this number to track developments in the case.

IDEOLOGY: A system of knowledge, myths, and beliefs guiding the behavior of a group.

IMMUNOGLOBULIN: Globulins are a type of protein found in blood. The immunoglobulins (also called immune globulins) are Y-shaped globulins that act as antibodies, attaching themselves to invasive cells or materials in the body so that they can be identified and attacked by the immune system. There are five immunoglobulins, designated IgM, IgG, IgA, IgD, and IgE.

IMPROVED AMERICAN FOOD GUIDE PYRAMID: The formal name for the food pyramid, the Improved American Food Guide Pyramid, was introduced by the U.S. Department of Agriculture (USDA) in 1992.

INACTIVATED VIRUS: Inactivated virus is incapable of causing disease but still stimulates the immune system to respond by forming antibodies.

INDEPENDENT CONTRACTOR: A person who contracts do a specified project or type of work for another person using his or her own resources and processes to accomplish the work; an independent worker rather than an employee.

INDIGENOUS: Native. The definition of indigenous peoples varies across the world, but usually refers to those whose ancestors were born in a particular area and who retain traditional knowledge of their environment and culture (including food). Indigenous peoples may be also be described as ethnic groups, and aboriginal, tribal, or First Peoples.

IN-KIND DONATIONS: Donations that are made in goods and services rather than money (or cash).

INSTITUTE OF MEDICINE: Founded in 1970, the Institute of Medicine is non-governmental organization established under the U.S. National Academy of Sciences that advises the government and policymakers on issues related to medicine and health.

INSULIN: A hormone produced by the pancreas after eating that carries glucose in the blood to muscle, liver, and fat cells after a meal. Too much insulin makes blood glucose levels too low, whereas insufficient insulin results in high blood sugar that is stored as excess glucose. The right amount of insulin is needed to keep blood glucose levels under control.

INTEGRATED PEST MANAGEMENT (IPM): A pest-management technique that involves balancing the need to increase crop yield and protect crops from damage with the desire to protect the environment and cause the least damage. Rather than never using pesticides, or always spraying regardless of need, IPM seeks a middle ground to reduce the pesticide load as much as possible.

INTELLECTUAL PROPERTY RIGHTS (IPR): Rights to produce or reproduce intangible property such as music, written words, ideas, or processes that are protected through patents, copyrights, and other means. In agriculture, recent disputes in IPR include controversies surrounding patenting genes or seeds in biotechnology and the effort to grant IPR to indigenous or traditional knowledge.

INTENSIVE PLANTING: Planting seeds more densely than traditional methods to increase yields.

INTERGENERATIONAL EQUITY: The principle that the actions of one generation must take into account their impact on subsequent generations, and that some resources must be preserved for use by future generations.

INTERNATIONAL COFFEE ORGANIZATION (ICO): Founded in 1963, the ICO works to coordinate coffee trade worldwide and to set industry standards for farmers, middlemen, and large manufacturers. The ICO has a loose association with the United Nations (UN).

INTERNATIONAL MONETARY FUND (IMF): An international non-governmental organization that supervises the global financial system with the objectives of stabilizing exchange rates and facilitating economic development through liberal economic policies.

INTESTINAL MOTILITY: Intestinal motility refers to the movement of smooth muscles in the small and large intestines that aids in mixing, digestion, absorption, and movement of foodstuffs.

INTOXICATION: The point at which the amount of alcohol consumed causes impaired judgment, behavior, and decision-making.

IODINE: A chemical element required by the thyroid gland in the body to produce thyroid hormone. Iodine is commonly added to table salt to help prevent goiter development.

IRRIGATION: The agricultural practice of artificially supplying land with water, usually for the purpose of growing crops.

I-TAL: The Rastafarian food code, which specifies that foods should be eaten unprocessed, whole (uncooked and unchanged), or minimally cooked.

J

JAUNDICE: Jaundice is a condition in which a person's skin and the sclera (whites of the eyes) are discolored a shade of yellow due to an increased level of bile pigments in the blood resulting from liver disease. Jaundice is sometimes called *icterus*, from a Greek word for the condition.

K

KASHRUT (KOSHER): Jewish dietary laws.

KILOGRAM CALORIE: The heat energy necessary to increase the temperature of one kilogram of water by one degree Celsius.

KNEADING: The process of rolling dough made from wheat flour to develop and align the gluten molecules

KOSHER: Foods that adhere to Jewish dietary laws.

KURU: An incurable, degenerative type of transmissable spongiform encephalopathy (TSE), a fatal brain disease transmitted by infection with prions (abnormal protein particles). Kuru is found in New Guinea and was mainly contracted by the Fore people during endocannibalistic funeral rituals. A gene protecting its carriers from kuru (and possibly other TSE diseases) has been discovered among the Fore.

L

LA LECHE LEAGUE INTERNATIONAL: Founded in 1956 in Franklin Park, Illinois, at a time when breast-feeding rates were close to 20 percent in the United States, La Leche League International supports on-demand breastfeeding for mother and child pairs, with monthly meetings for women seeking breast-feeding support in 68 countries.

LABOR UNION: An organization of workers formed to negotiate terms of employment with employers.

LACTASE: An enzyme that hydrolyzes lactose. It is found in the intestines of most young mammals.

LACTOSE: The sugar in milk, lactose, is not found in any other food. It is a disaccharide made up of glucose and galactose and requires the enzyme lactase to break it down into molecules that the body can utilize as fuel.

LAND TENURE: A system under which land is acquired, used, and possibly bought and sold. A variety of land tenure systems exist, including legal land titles, land use rights without land ownership, untitled family farms, and shifting cultivation.

LANDRACE: A traditional crop variety.

LEAKAGE: In international food aid, the use of food by someone other than the targeted recipient. Leakage can occur through sale, barter, or use of food as a gift by a recipient to another party.

LEAVENING: The volume expansion of baking dough caused by the formation and inclusion of gas bubbles.

LIBEL: The negligent or intentional publication of a defamatory statement.

LIBERALIZATION: In trade, the reduction or removal of tariffs and other barriers to trade. In agricultural policy, liberalization refers to reduction or elimination of domestic subsidies, price and production controls, export subsidies, and other agricultural support programs.

LIPIDS: Molecules that include fats such as oils from plants, animal fats such as butter and lard, and fat-soluble vitamins.

LIPOPOLYSACCHARIDE (LPS): Lipopolysaccharide (LPS) is a molecule that is a constituent of the outer membrane of Gram-negative bacteria. The molecule can also be referred to as endotoxin. LPS can help protect the bacterium from host defenses and can contribute to illness in the host.

LISTERIA: A genus of bacteria that includes the pathogenic species *Listeria monocytogenes.*

LISTERIOSIS: An infectious disease caused by ingestion of food contaminated with *Listeria monocytogenes* bacteria.

LIVELIHOOD PORTFOLIO: A collection of strategies a household uses to earn income or otherwise obtain goods and services.

LIVING MODIFIED ORGANISM (LMO): Any living organism that has been genetically modified through the use of biotechnology.

LOCAL AND REGIONAL PROCUREMENT (LRP): The purchase of commodities for food aid either within the recipient country or in a nearby country as opposed to the shipment of food aid from the donor country.

LOCAVORE: Someone who attempts to eat a high proportion of foods that are grown or raised locally. Local food can be defined as that produced within a certain radius (e.g. 50 or 100 or 250 miles), a geographic region or a foodshed, or even a state or a country. The term localvore may also be used.

LONGLINE FISHING: Longline fishing is a technique used extensively in the commercial swordfish and tuna fisheries. Monofilament lines equipped with hundreds of baited hooks and flotation devices are extended for up to 100 miles (160 km) over open ocean waters. Longline fishing is controversial because of its indiscriminate bycatch of other fish species.

M

MALNUTRITION: A condition in which a person is not consuming or absorbing adequate and balanced nutrients in order to sustain a healthy, active life. Diets with caloric deficits, deficits of protein or fat, or deficits of key vitamins and minerals cause malnutrition. Obesity is also sometimes considered a form of malnutrition if it contributes to a state of decreased health or disease.

MARBLING: The internal fat in meat, which can often be seen as white veining within the red muscle matrix. Marbling differs from the adipose fat on the outside of a cut of meat, which can be trimmed off. It contributes to the flavor of meat but is saturated fat and may raise cholesterol levels.

MARICULTURE: Mariculture is the aquaculture variant in which seawater is used to cultivate desired aquatic life forms for harvest. Mariculture is practiced in open ocean environments through the use of specialized protective nets and enclosures or in natural or artificial sea water ponds.

MARKET ACCESS: The ability to get goods to market and sell them to willing buyers of the seller's choice.

MARKET ECONOMY: An economy that permits the open exchange of goods and services and relies on market forces to determine price, production, investment, and savings without government intervention.

MARKET POWER: The ability to influence price through increasing or decreasing production in the market or choosing customers.

MARZIPAN: A type of confection made from almond paste. It is often made into fruit or animal shapes as a stand-alone treat. It can also be used as a topping for cakes and pastries.

MAXIMUM SUSTAINABLE YIELD: The maximum extraction of a species from an ecosystem by humans that can occur without reducing the long-term average population of the species.

MEALTIME: The period of time at which a meal is habitually or customarily eaten. All meals, whether at home or in a restaurant, are usually structured events. Current standard meals include breakfast, lunch, and dinner. The components of a meal vary across cultures, but generally include the consumption of two or more foods.

MEAT: The edible parts of an animal, usually excluding the skin and bone. The term meat often excludes poultry and fish, and refers to beef, lamb, pork, and veal. However, these meats are sometimes known as red meat, whereas poultry may be referred to as white meat.

MEATPACKING: The process of slaughtering animals and preparing meat for sale to consumers.

MELAMINE: Melamine ($C_3H_6N_6$) is a synthetic chemical that is primarily used to produce commercial resins, laminates, and glues. Prohibited for use as a food additive, melamine attained world-wide notoriety in 2008 when a number of Chinese milk products were found to contain the chemical. When added to food products, melamine will tend to disguise low levels of protein and other nutrients in milk adulterated by adding water.

MERCANTILISM: An economic theory that advocates increasing capital through beneficial, government-controlled balance of trade with other nations, often through the imposition of import restrictions.

MESOAMERICA: A region extending south and east from central Mexico to include parts of Guatemala, Belize, Honduras, and Nicaragua.

METABOLIC SYNDROME: A group of risk factors including elevated blood pressure, insulin resistance, increased abdominal fat, elevated lipids in the blood, and overweight or obesity, that together are linked to future development of heart disease and/or diabetes in an individual.

METABOLISM: The total of all the chemical reactions that keep the body alive. Metabolic reactions include the breakdown of proteins and carbohydrates to their constituent parts and their use in various bodily functions. Metabolism depends upon action of enzymes to achieve reactions at a rate compatible with life.

MICRO-COMMUNITIES: Groups of people who communicate on the Internet and via social media that come together based upon a shared interest, regardless of the physical distance between them; for example, people in different countries who are car enthusiasts or fans of an artist that communicate on a public message board.

MICROCREDIT: Loan programs that give people, many times women, access to small sums of money by developed-nation standards (often less than $100), enabling people who are unable otherwise to access capital to buy equipment necessary for creating surpluses to sell in a small business or at market.

MICROLOAN: A small sum of money loaned to persons living in poverty in order to promote entrepreneurship and alleviate hardship.

MICRONUTRIENT: A vitamin or mineral necessary for growth, metabolic functions, and other biological processes in humans, other animals, and plants.

MICRONUTRIENT MALNUTRITION: Different from general malnutrition, micronutrient malnutrition occurs largely in women and children in developing countries with low food security and with low food variety, evidenced by conditions such as anemia and vitamin A deficiency.

MIDDLE-INCOME COUNTRY (MIC): A country that when compared to other countries in the world is neither very poor nor very rich. According to the World Bank, a middle-income country has a per capita gross national income (GNI) between 996 and 12,195 U.S. dollars. In 2010 middle income countries included Botswana, Brazil, Chile, China, Fiji, India, Indonesia, Jordan, Kazakhstan, Mexico,

Nigeria, Russia, Senegal, South Africa, Thailand, and Turkey among others.

MIGRANT WORKER: A person who moves from one region to another to find or follow employment. Migrant workers are used extensively in agriculture, moving frequently during the course of the year to follow the harvest seasons.

MISO: A traditional Japanese seasoning paste made from fermented soybeans, which can be used for sauces, soups, pickling vegetables, and many other dishes.

MONOCULTURE: The agricultural practice of cultivating only a specific crop within a given area.

MONOMER: A small molecule used as a chemical building block. Monomers can be linked together to form much larger molecules called polymers.

MONOSODIUM GLUTAMATE (MSG): Monosodium glutamate (MSG) is one of the best known food additives, used widely as a flavor enhancing agent since the early twentieth century. In addition to the general health concerns associated with excess sodium consumption in modern human diets, such as high blood pressure and increased risk of stroke, MSG symptom complex is a condition experienced by persons who have MSG intolerance.

MONOUNSATURATED OIL: Oil with a fatty acid carbon chain containing one double or triple bond per molecule. Peanut oil, canola oil, and olive oil are examples of monounsaturated oils, which are thought to help lower LDL cholesterol levels in the blood.

MOUTHFEEL: The textural properties of a food when it is perceived in the mouth. Mouthfeel includes qualities such as crunchiness and creaminess and is an important concept in food technology.

MUCKRAKERS: Late nineteenth-century and early-twentieth century journalists, authors, and photographers who sought social change by featuring injustices in such a way as to create maximum interest and action in the public.

MULTI-CROPPING: The practice of growing two or more crops on the same plot of land during one growing season.

MYOGLOBIN: An iron-containing, oxygen-transporting protein in red blood cells that gives meat its red appearance.

N

NaCl: The chemical formula for sodium chloride, or table salt.

NARCOTERRORISM: The use of terrorist techniques to promote, protect, or fund the trade of illicit drugs.

NATIONAL SCHOOL LUNCH PROGRAM (NSLP): The National School Lunch Program is a U.S. government-assisted program that provides low-cost or free lunches to American schoolchildren in public schools, non-profit private schools, and residential child care institutions.

NEOLITHIC: The archaeological period during which agriculture first appeared, no earlier than 12,000 years ago in the Middle East. The Paleolithic (or "Stone Age") and the Mesolithic (or "Middle Stone Age") preceded the Neolithic, and in Europe, the Neolithic is followed by the Bronze Age. The Neolithic Revolution refers to the changes in human societies correlated with agricultural economies.

NEUROTOXIN: A poison that interferes with nerve function, usually by affecting the flow of ions through the cell membrane.

NITRITES: A group of salts, including sodium nitrite, which are derived from nitrates by either chemical or bacterial action. They play a role in curing meats through stopping the growth of bacteria, preventing oxidation of fat, preserving color, and adding flavor.

NO ACCESS–NO FOOD: The principle that humanitarian food aid will be distributed only under regimes in which the distribution and storage can be monitored by humanitarian relief workers, usually by foreign humanitarian relief workers. Food refers to food aid, and access refers to the ability to travel to the locations where food aid is stored and distributed.

NOMADIC: Individuals or groups who do not have a static place of residence; a lifestyle or culture characterized by periodic relocation without a permanent dwelling. Herding cultures are frequently nomadic.

NONGOVERNMENTAL ORGANIZATION (NGO): This generally refers to organizations that are created and directed outside of any governmental affiliation. Often, NGOs are involved with human rights and health-related issues. They are typically dedicated to development and service.

NON-TARIFF BARRIER: Any barrier to trade other than tariffs. Usually refers to quotas and restrictions on trade or to rules and regulations that affect trade but may be set for other reasons.

NOUVELLE CUISINE: A culinary trend beginning in the late 1970s that pulled away from classic French cooking to find new, lighter techniques and more artistic presentations.

NUT: The strict botanical definition of a nut is a one-seeded fruit in which the fruit tissue is dry and tough rather than juicy. A broader definition is any large seed of certain long-lived trees.

NUTRACEUTICAL: A food that may treat illness or prevent disease due to its nutritional qualities.

NUTRIENT: A component of food that has some useful role in the body's functioning. Macronutrients are required in larger quantities and consist of carbohydrates, protein, and fat, whereas the micronutrients, the vitamins and minerals, are required in much smaller quantities.

NUTRIENT FILM TECHNIQUE (NFT): Hydroponic technique in which a thin layer of nutrient solution is continuously passed over the plant roots, which are enclosed in a tray or pipe.

NUTRIENT FORTIFICATION: The process of adding concentrated micronutrients to processed foods.

NUTRITION: The process of providing or obtaining the nourishment necessary for health and growth.

NUTRITION LABEL: A listing of all ingredients and nutritional information, including calories, fat, sodium, protein, and carbohydrates, contained in the product.

NUTRITION TRANSITION: Process of change that is occurring more in low and middle-income countries, whereby people are transitioning to a more sedentary lifestyle with decreased activity patterns and access to more high-fat, high-sugar, and low-nutrient based foods. The combination of these lifestyle changes results in an increase in conditions such as heart or cardiovascular disease, diabetes, and high-blood pressure.

O

O157: A recently emergent strain of *E. coli* that causes mild to severe diarrhea and, in advanced cases, brain and kidney damage that may be fatal.

OBESITY: Excess amount of body fat; usually defined by a body mass index (BMI) measurement of 30 or more, based on age and gender. Obesity is a risk factor for developing heart disease, high blood pressure, high cholesterol, type 2 diabetes, and other chronic diseases.

OFFAL: The internal organs of animals prepared for consumption.

OIL: A fat that is liquid at room temperature. Oils generally come from vegetable sources, and a wide range of oils are available for cooking.

OMNIVORE: An animal that derives food from both plant and animal sources.

ORAL DISEASE: May be any of a number of diseases and disorders that affect more than just the teeth.

This group of diseases refers to an infection or ailment affecting the mouth, throat, tongue, lips, the salivary glands, the chewing muscles, and the upper and lower jaws.

ORGANIC AGRICULTURE: Agriculture and livestock production that uses no chemical, mineral, or otherwise artificial inputs. Organic agriculture is thought to be more natural and to have less impact on the environment than the conventional methods associated with the input-dependent technologies of the twentieth century. Certain human-made fertilizers, soil amendments, herbicides, and pesticides are prohibited by organic standards that define organic agriculture.

ORGANIC CHEMICAL: Any compound containing carbon is technically referred to as an organic compound, which includes most chemical pesticides. This use of the term organic should not be confused with its use with respect to farming methods.

ORGANICALLY GROWN: This term means that no synthetic fertilizers or pesticides are used in the growing of a particular food. Biological pesticides are permitted for food labeled "organically grown" according to U.S. Department of Agriculture (USDA) standards.

ORGANISATION FOR ECONOMIC CO-OPERATION AND DEVELOPMENT (OECD): An economic forum of 33 countries focused on promoting democracy and market economies.

ORTHOREXIA: An unhealthy obsession with healthy eating, modeled by an analogy with anorexia nervosa. Orthorexia is not a medically recognized diagnosis, but may be useful in describing individuals who are fixated on eating only certain types of food.

OSTEOPOROSIS: A loss in bone density that may be the result of a chronic calcium deficiency, early menopause, certain endocrine diseases, certain medications, advanced age, or other risk factors.

OUTBREAK: Occurrence of disease. Most cases of foodborne disease are individual or sporadic, but sometimes a group of people will eat the same contaminated food, and several or many will become ill. Such incidents are defined as outbreaks and may need further investigation to stop them from spreading.

OVARY: The part of a plant that produces a seed and nourishes it until it is ready to grow into another plant.

OVERWEIGHT: Defined as having a body mass index (BMI) of 25.0–29.9, based on age and gender.

OWNER-MEMBER: A member and employee of a food co-op.

P

PADDY: Rice in its unprocessed, raw form without the hull removed, which is also called paddy rice or rough rice. Can also mean the flooded field used in rice growing.

PAGOPHAGY: The excessive consumption of ice, especially common during pregnancy, which is highly correlated with iron deficiency anemia.

PALEOLITHIC: Also known as the Stone Age, this archaeological period of time began when human ancestors and their relatives began making stone tools and ended with the transition to agriculture, from about 2.6 million to 12,000 years ago.

PANDEMIC: Pandemic, which means "all the people" describes an epidemic that occurs in more than one country or population simultaneously.

PAPILLAE: Small projections on the upper surface of the tongue that give it a rough appearance. Each papilla houses 25 to 250 taste buds. Papillae are also located in the throat, sides of the mouth, and soft palate.

PARENTERAL NUTRITION: Parenteral nutrition is nutritionally complete feeding delivered directly to the stomach, by means of a tube. For short-term nutritional replacement, the tube is generally inserted through the nose. In patients with severe gagging issues, the tube may be surgically placed into the abdomen, connecting directly to the stomach.

PASTEURIZATION: A process by which food is heated to a high-enough temperature for a specific period of time to kill bacteria. Pasteurization is named after French bacteriologist Louis Pasteur (1822–1895), who developed the process in 1864. By the early 1950s, most milk in the United States was pasteurized, leading to a significant decline in milk-related food-borne illnesses.

PATENT MEDICINES: Tonics, remedies, compounds, and drugs of untested effectiveness that were popularly sold in the nineteenth and early twentieth centuries. Ingredients were most often kept secret from consumers, and manufacturers advertised "patented formulas." Many of the so-called patent medicines were in fact trademarked instead of patented because the application for patents required revealing ingredients and quantities.

PATHOGEN: A disease-causing organism.

PECTIN: A glue-like compound located between plant cell walls. Pectin forms a matrix that traps water into a smooth and viscous gel. It is an essential component in making jams and jellies to preserve fruit.

PERIODONTAL DISEASE: Diseases of the gums that can result in tooth loss. When a bacterial infection starts in the mouth, the gums become inflamed. The tissue that supports and holds the teeth in the mouth breaks down, and the teeth are loosened. One of the main causes of this disease is a buildup of bacterial plaque on the surfaces of the teeth.

PERMACULTURE: A method and philosophy of local land management stressing integration of people and the land in harmony with natural biological patterns and cycles.

PHENOLS: A broad group of alcohol-like compounds.

PHENYLETHYLAMINE: Informally known as "the love drug," phenylethylamine raises blood pressure and blood sugar slightly, causing a state of alertness.

PHOBIA: A phobia is a fear of an object or situation that is sufficient in intensity to cause an individual considerable distress and result in avoidance not only of the feared object but of situations associated with it.

PHOTOSYNTHESIS: The process by which plants use chlorophyll, their green pigment, to capture sunlight and carbon dioxide in the atmosphere to make glucose. Photosynthesis is the primary source of energy for both plants and the animals that eat them.

PHOTOSYNTHESIZING AUTOTROPHS: Animals that produce their own food by using sunlight to convert other substances to food.

PHYTOCHEMICALS: Trace chemicals found in plants that often perform some biological function, such as protecting the plant from predators. Some phytochemicals, such as the purple anthocyanins, have antioxidant properties in humans that may help protect against disease.

PHYTOESTROGEN: Phytochemicals that mimic the action of human estrogen and so may block its role in activating cells, potentially preventing the development of some cancers.

PLAINTIFF: A person, group of people, or legal entity that brings suit against another party in court.

PLEISTOCENE: The geological period of time from 2.58 million years ago to 12,000 years ago. By the end of the Pleistocene epoch, which was also the end of the archaeological period known as the Paleolithic, or "Stone Age," human hunters and gatherers had spread across the world. The Pleistocene was preceded by the Pliocene and is followed by the current period, the Holocene.

POACHING: Illegal hunting and killing of animals, often to sell their meat, skins, tusks, or other parts.

PODCASTS: Spoken word shows, similar to talk radio shows, that are recorded and posted on the Internet for download. The word is derived from the name of Apple's "iPod" mp3 player. Whereas many podcasts are homemade, some traditional radio stations record their shows and post them as podcasts on the Internet for fans to download.

POLYCARBONATE PLASTIC: A versatile, transparent, malleable polymer with many commercial applications, synthesized by combining bisphenol A and phosgene.

POLYETHYLENE TEREPHTHALATE (PET): Also known as PET, polyethylene terephthalate is a lightweight, rigid polymer resin that is widely used for food and beverage containers.

POLYMER: A molecule of relatively high molecular weight, consisting of repeated chemical subunits that are linked together by chemical bonds.

POLYUNSATURATED: Substances such as oils composed of molecules containing more than one carbon-carbon double bond are said to be polyunsaturated.

POLYUNSATURATED OIL: Oil with a fatty acid carbon chain that contains multiple double or triple bonds in each molecule. Corn oil, safflower oil, soybean oil, and sesame oil are examples of polyunsaturated oils. Polyunsaturated oils are thought to help reduce LDL cholesterol levels in the blood.

POPULATION: A group with similar demographic characteristics such as geographic location, species, gender, age, habits, nationality, ethnicity, productive requirements, or needs.

POTABLE: Potable water (or drinking water) is water fit for human consumption. Water that is not potable may be made potable by filtration, distillation, or by a range of other methods.

POULTRY: General term describing all birds raised for their meat, feathers, or eggs, including chickens, quail, turkeys, ducks, geese, doves, and pheasants.

POVERTY TRAP: A level of poverty below which a household no longer has the means to increase income over time, especially a decreased level of productive assets such as livestock, land, or tools. Once a household is in a poverty trap, the household lacks the tools to escape poverty or to improve its condition in any way.

PRECAUTIONARY PRINCIPLE: A principle that any product, action, or process that might pose a threat to public or environmental health should not be introduced in the absence of scientific consensus regarding its safety.

PREHYPERTENSION: A term that reflects increased risk through mildly raised blood pressure. Prehypertension is defined as having systolic blood pressure greater than or equal to 120 and/or diastolic blood pressure greater than or equal to 80.

PRESERVATIVES: A type of food additive that preserves the life of a food. The use of preservatives increases the range of foods available to the consumer by extending their shelf lives and improving food safety.

PRION: A proteinaceous infectious particle, or prion, is a deformed protein that converts other proteins into the same form, resulting in a buildup of abnormal proteins causing one of several types of transmissible spongiform encephalopathy (TSE), a type of fatal brain disease, such as BSE (bovine spongiform encephalopathy, or "mad cow disease"), scrapie in sheep and goats, and Creutzfeldt-Jakob Disease (CJD) in humans. Variant CJD (vCJD) is usually contracted by human consumption of BSE-infected beef.

PRIX FIXE: A menu style in which there is one price for a meal consisting of many small courses.

PROCESSED FOOD: A food that has been modified during production to transform raw ingredients into different forms of food.

PRODUCER SUPPORT ESTIMATE (PSE): A commonly used measure of the impact of agricultural subsidies and other agricultural policy measures. The PSE combines estimates of government spending in agriculture along with the higher prices consumers in a country may pay due to agricultural trade policies and the price effects of subsidies.

PROGRESSIVE ERA: A period of social and political reform in the United States from the 1890s to the 1920s. Progressive Era reforms included labor, education, food safety, and anti-corruption laws.

PROOFING: Allowing dough that has risen once to rise again.

PROSPECTIVE STUDY: A research study that starts with healthy people and gathers information about factors such as diet or medication intake and then follows up their medical history for a number of years to deduce the influences of these factors upon health. A prospective study generally has high scientific validity if well designed and carried out.

PROTECTIONISM: The theory or practice of protecting a nation's domestic industry or agriculture from foreign competition through the imposition of trade barriers or regulations that discriminate against imports.

PSYCHROPHILES: Organisms that live and grow more efficiently in moderate temperatures between 14–68°F (–10–20°C).

PULSES: Legumes dry well, and the dried versions are known as pulses. They consist mainly of starch and protein, and their water-resistant, hard coat makes them easy to store.

PUNCHING DOWN: Pressing on risen dough to expel excess carbon dioxide.

PURE FOOD AND DRUG ACT OF 1906: This Act created the agency that is now known as the Food and Drug Administration (FDA); the Center for Food Safety and Applied Nutrition (CFSAN) operates under the authority of the FDA.

Q

QUOTA: A trade restriction that limits the number of goods that may be imported into a nation within a certain period.

R

RAMADAN: The ninth month of the Islamic calendar year and a period of fasting, prayer, charity, and family celebration.

RATION: Ration, when used within a military context, refers to a daily food allowance designed to meet the dietary and nutritional needs of service members.

RAWIST: A person who consumes a diet of mostly plant-based foods in an uncooked state.

READY-TO-EAT FOOD: Prepared food that can be consumed as soon as it is purchased.

REALITY-BASED COMPETITION: Television shows in which contestants compete against each other in mock, real-life situations.

RECALL: In a recall in the United States, the Center for Food Safety and Applied Nutrition (CFSAN) asks the public to return products from a specific batch produced by a manufacturer, for reasons such as contamination or foodborne illness. Most CFSAN-originated recalls involve voluntary recalls, in which the manufacturer works proactively with CFSAN to remove a product from the shelves and to educate consumers to return or destroy defective products.

RECOMBINANT BOVINE GROWTH HORMONE (rBGH): A genetically engineered hormone given to cattle to increase milk production.

RECOMBINANT DNA: A form of artificial DNA that contains two or more genetic sequences that normally do not occur together, which are spliced together.

RECOMMENDED DIETARY ALLOWANCE (RDA): Sometimes known as the recommended daily allowance, RDA is the level of intake of a vitamin or mineral required to prevent deficiency disease. In real life, people will tend to consume more of a vitamin or mineral on one day than another, so it is probably best to think in terms of average, rather than daily, intakes.

RECOVERY: The aspect of humanitarian assistance that seeks to prevent further deterioration of an affected area and to restore basic living conditions, services, livelihoods, security and rule of law, and national capacities.

REDUCTION: Thickening or intensifying the flavor of a liquid by evaporation.

REGULATION: Controlling behaviors, business practices, or industrial practices through rules, restrictions, or laws to encourage preferred outcomes or prevent undesired outcomes that may otherwise occur.

REPORTABLE FOOD: Any food item that, if consumed by humans or animals, may be believed to cause serious health problems or death.

RESPONSIBLE PARTY: Any registered food facility or manufacturer, processor, or packager that manages food for human or animal consumption.

RHEOLOGY: The science of deformation and flow when a force is applied to a material, including a food. Materials vary widely in their rheological behavior.

RHIZOBIA: Species of soil bacteria that form a symbiotic relationship with legume plants, living inside nodules in their roots.

RIPENING: A series of chemical processes occurring in a fruit that make it more attractive to animals. Ripening includes increasing sweetness and decreasing starch and acid content, as well as characteristic color changes from green to red or yellow and the development of texture and aroma.

RURAL DEVELOPMENT: Rural development refers to actions, programs, or projects designed to increase the living standards of people living in rural areas, typically through agricultural improvement or poverty reduction.

S

SALMONELLA: The genus *Salmonella* includes more than 2,500 types of bacteria. Salmonellosis, a common form of food poisoning, is the illness that results when food contaminated by this bacterial strain is consumed. *Salmonella* causes a variety of illnesses in humans, animals, and birds; poultry are especially vulnerable to *Salmonella* outbreaks.

SALTATION: The process by which sand or soil particles move across an uneven surface when carried by the wind.

SANITARY AND PHYTOSANITARY (SPS) MEASURES: Laws, rules, and regulations intended to help protect human and animal health (sanitary) or plant health (phytosanitary). Regulations regarding food safety, animal diseases, plant diseases, and pests are referred to as SPS restrictions.

SAPROPHYTE: Saprophytes are organisms that obtain nutrients from dead and/or decaying matter in the environment. They are important decomposers of organic material.

SATAY: Marinated, grilled meat on a kabob skewer often served with a dipping sauce, a dish that originated in Indonesia and Thailand.

SATURATED FAT: Fat in which the fatty acid chain contains only single bonds between carbon atoms in each molecule. Saturated fats are usually obtained from animal products, including lard and butter, but are also derived from plants, such as coconut oil and palm oil. Saturated fats are thought to increase LDL cholesterol levels in the blood.

SAXITOXIN: A neurotoxin that is the basis of paralytic shellfish poisoning.

SCIENTIFIC RELIABILITY AND VALIDITY: Reliability refers to the consistency or replicability of a measurement across repetition. A reliable instrument is one that gives the same results for the same object measured at different times. Validity is concerned with the accuracy of a measure and the determination of whether a result accurately reflects what was being measured.

SEA LICE: A naturally occurring aquatic parasite. These small creatures prey on the blood, skin, and mucous membranes of juvenile or adult fish hosts, causing damage to the flesh and immune systems of its targets. Salmon farms have been identified as key sites where sea lice proliferate. From the farms the lice migrate to nearby wild salmon populations, causing widespread destruction. Pacific salmon and sea trout are fish species that are especially vulnerable to sea lice infestations.

SEED: A compact package containing a plant's embryo and the food stores it needs to develop into a new plant.

SELF ESTEEM: A state of being that is grounded in self acceptance and self respect. In the context of body image and food, a person with high self esteem feels good about his or her body and has a positive self perception about their size and shape. Individuals with low self esteem will most likely be unsatisfied with their body image and size. Unfortunately this could result in a repetitive pattern of self deprivation, followed by bingeing, weight gain, and worsening self image.

SEMOLINA: A rougher, uncooked durum wheat product made as a precursor to the final grinding of flour or for use in pastas, breads, or cereals.

SEROTYPES: Serotypes or serovars are classes of microorganisms based on the types of molecules (antigens) that they present on their surfaces. Even a single species may have thousands of serotypes, which may have medically quite distinct behaviors.

SEVEN Ms: Money, muscle, motivation, milk, materials, manure, and meat.

SHARK FIN SOUP: Shark fin soup, *yu chi* (translated Mandarin for shark wing) has been regarded as a delicacy in Chinese food culture for centuries. This soup was a dish traditionally available only to the very wealthy due to the scarcity of shark fins needed for its preparation. The emergence of a consumer middle class in late twentieth century China broadened the soup's appeal as a status symbol. Chinese consumer demand for shark fins helped spur a dramatic decrease in world shark populations.

SHELF LIFE: The amount of time a food product can be stored without noticeable changes to its quality or significantly increased risks of foodborne illness.

SILT: Fine particles of clay, sand, or other matter that are carried by running water and deposited as sediment.

SLASH-AND-BURN: A deforestation technique in which trees and other vegetation are cut and burned to clear land for planting crops or grazing livestock.

SLOW FOOD: A movement promoting traditional and regional cuisines, deliberately (and often slowly) prepared, eaten at leisure with friends and family, and opposed to corporate-produced fast food consumption.

SLOW FOOD MOVEMENT: Founded by the Italian writer Carlo Petrini (1949–) in 1989, the international Slow Food Movement acts as an antidote to fast food, with its campaigning for the pleasure of food, preservation of traditional dishes, and respect for community and environment.

SMALLHOLDER: A farming or livestock-raising rural household with small amounts of land or otherwise limited access to land. Smallholders typically have less than two hectares of arable land, and many have access to far smaller plots.

SMOKE POINT: The temperature at which a cooking fat breaks down into visible gaseous products.

SOCIAL SAFETY NET: A public program designed to prevent households from falling into extreme poverty or reducing their consumption of necessary nutrients, medical services, and education.

SOIL EROSION: The process by which soil is carried away by wind or water.

SOOT: A particulate air pollutant, primarily composed of carbon, produced by the incomplete combustion of biomass and fossil fuels.

SOVEREIGNTY: Supreme and independent power or authority in government as possessed or claimed by a state or community; rightful status, independence, or prerogative; a sovereign state, community, or political unit.

SPECIES: A taxonomic group of living organisms capable of exchanging genes or interbreeding.

SPICE: The fragrant roots, barks, fruits, seeds, or nuts of a plant. Often found in tropical regions, spices can be dried and transported. They develop their characteristic flavors and aromas on drying, but can be used both dried and fresh.

SPORE: A dormant form assumed by some bacteria, such as anthrax and *Clostridium botulinum*, that enables the bacteria to survive high temperatures, dryness, and lack of nourishment for long periods of time. Under proper conditions, the spore may revert to the actively multiplying form of the bacteria.

SPRING ROLLS: A traditional appetizer in several Asian countries. Often they consist of vegetables or seafood rolled in rice paper, but the finishing varies from country to country. Some countries, such as China, fry their spring rolls, whereas in Vietnam the rice paper of the spring rolls is dipped in water, and the spring rolls are served cold.

SPRING WATER: Spring water refers to groundwater that emanates from a spring.

STANDARD AMERICAN DIET (SAD): The standard American diet includes large amounts of red meat, eggs, and refined grain products that are generally high-fat, high-sugar, and heavily-processed foods.

STARVATION: The most extreme form of undernutrition, in which there is a partial or total lack of nutrients for a long time. Total starvation, in which no food is consumed, is usually fatal within 8 to 12 weeks.

STERILIZATION: Refers to any procedure that kills all of the microorganisms in or on a product. May be done with high temperature and pressure, by use of chemicals, or by irradiation.

STRAIN: A subclass of a particular tribe and genus.

SUBSIDY: A form of financial assistance granted by the government to assist a particular business or industry, usually so that the price of a commodity remains competitive.

SUBSISTENCE: Methods of obtaining food. Subsistence was based on hunting and gathering until relatively recently in human prehistory.

SUBSISTENCE FARMER: A farmer who grows food primarily to feed his or her family, with little or no surplus remaining for selling at market.

SUBSTITUTE: In economics, any good that can be used instead of another good with little or limited reduction in consumer satisfaction.

SUBSTRATE: In hydroponics, the root supporting medium used to grow plants. Substrate may consist of any inert material that does not directly supply nutrients to the plants.

SUGAR: The common name for the smaller molecules of the carbohydrate family, known as the monosaccharides and disaccharides, composed of one sugar unit and two sugar units respectively. Glucose is the monosaccharide that is used as the body's fuel. Sugar is also the common name for sucrose, a disaccharide composed of glucose and fructose, which is also known as fruit sugar.

SUPPLY CHAIN: All of the steps between a raw material and the final consumer.

SURPLUS FOOD: Food that is near or past its expiration date but remains edible, as well as an oversupply of food.

SUSTAINABILITY: Often defined as being able to meet the needs of the present without compromising the needs of future generations. Sustainability is an important concept in environmental protection.

SUSTAINABLE AGRICULTURE: Methods of producing food that can be sustained without depleting resources for future generations.

SUSTAINABLE DEVELOPMENT: Sustainable development involves economic development and the fulfillment of human requirements in an environmentally responsible manner.

SUSTAINABLE FOOD: Food that is grown in a manner that is profitable for the farmer, nutritious for the consumer, and preserves the environment.

SWADESHI: The Swadeshi movement was a facet of the Indian independence movement that advocated boycotting British goods in favor of strengthening domestic production.

SWEETNESS: One of the five basic tastes, long associated with pleasure. There are taste buds that detect sweet-tasting molecules on the tongue, and these relay messages to the brain, creating the sensation of sweetness. There are many sweet-tasting compounds, both natural and synthetic.

SYNTHETIC FERTILIZER: A commercially-prepared chemical mixture containing plant nutrients, such as nitrates, phosphates, and potassium.

SYNTHETIC PESTICIDE: A commercially-prepared chemical mixture designed to kill or repel insects.

T

TANNINS: Astringent chemical compounds found in the skins, stems, and seeds of wine grapes that produce a sense of bitterness and tactile drying sensation in wine. As a wine ages, tannins form long polymerized chains resulting in the wine "mellowing" its taste and mouthfeel.

TAP WATER: Tap water refers to water produced by a municipal water system and transported to consumers through home plumbing systems.

TARIFF: A duty or tax imposed on imports or exports.

TASTE BUD: A group of cells that are responsive to taste molecules. Taste buds consist of a barrel shaped arrangement of alternating taste receptor cells and supporting cells, the latter acting as a source of new taste receptor cells.

TEIKEI: The Japanese word for "cooperation," a connection between consumer and farmer to form an economic relationship similar to that of community supported agriculture (CSA). *Teikei* was part of the foundation of the international CSA movement.

TEMPERATE CLIMATE FRUITS: Fruits that grow on trees, bushes, and vines and need a period of cold before they flower.

TERMS OF TRADE (TOT): The relative prices of goods or of goods traded between countries.

TERROIR: The special characteristics of soil, weather, and techniques of farming that contribute to the unique qualities of wine.

TEXTURE: The qualities of a food, or other material, that can be felt with the fingers, tongue, palate, or teeth. Foods have many different textures, which contribute to their imparted sensation of taste.

THEOBROMINE: A vasodilator and a diuretic, theobrimine is found in the cacao bean.

THIRD-PARTY CERTIFICATION: A system in which an organization independent of all the companies in a supply chain certifies that a good reaches particular standards or has particular attributes. Most international organic standards, fair trade standards, humane animal treatment standards, claims of being not genetically modified, and a variety of environmental claims are substantiated by third-party certification.

TOFU: Curdled soy milk, made by heating soy milk and adding salts to solidify its protein content. Tofu is often used as a meat substitute in macrobiotic and vegetarian diets.

TOXIN: A poison that is produced by a living organism.

TRACE ELEMENTS: Elements such as copper, molybdenum, boron, selenium, chromium, iron, and manganese, the trace elements are the minerals that the body requires in much smaller amounts than calcium, for instance, or phosphorus. There are only a few grams of each trace element in the body.

TRACEABILITY: The ability to follow a product through each step in a supply chain.

TRADE AGREEMENT: An accord or contract among participating nations or trade groups that establishes rules for trade, including taxes, import fees, tariffs, duties, levies, subsidies, or restrictions on the exchange of goods and money.

TRADE BARRIER: Anything that impedes or distorts the movement of goods between countries. Examples of trade barriers include tariffs, export taxes, export subsidies, quotas, country of origin rules, safety regulations, licensing requirements, and product standards.

TRADITIONAL FOODS: The Traditional Foods Movement is a byproduct of the Weston A. Price Foundation and the book *Nourishing Traditions* by Sally Fallon Morell, the co-founder of A Campaign for Real Milk. Using principles from Price's research, Fallon advocates a diet of raw milk, grassfed meats, raw liver, coconut oil, and sprouted grains.

TRADITIONAL KNOWLEDGE: Sometimes called indigenous knowledge, traditional knowledge is information related to practices that are often preserved and passed on by methods other than through academic study or formal writings. Although components of beliefs and practices may not be fully tested by scientific experimentation, many experts argue that traditional knowledge and practices contain useful insights about the environment, medicine, and agriculture.

TRANS FATS: Hydrogenated, unsaturated fats often present in processed foods that lower the HDL (good) cholesterol and raise the LDL (bad) cholesterol in the blood and are, therefore, associated with an increased risk for developing heart disease.

TRANSGENIC ORGANISM: A genetically modified organism that contains genetic sequences from multiple species.

TRANSMISSABLE SPONGIFORM ENCEPHALOPATHY (TSE): Transmissable spongiform encephalopathies, or prion diseases, are incurable brain diseases transmitted by infection with prions, protein-based infectious agents.

TRANSMISSION: Microorganisms that cause disease in humans and other species are known as pathogens. The transmission of pathogens to a human or other host can occur in a number of ways, depending upon the microorganism.

TRIGLYCERIDES: The chemical name for the form in which most fats exist both in the body and in foods. Higher levels of triglycerides in the blood, resulting from a high fat diet, are a known risk factor for coronary heart disease.

TROPHIC LEVEL: The division of species in an ecosystem by their main source of nutrition.

TROPICAL PRODUCT: An agricultural product that can be cultivated only in a relatively warm climate. Tropical products include tea, coffee, cocoa, cotton, pineapples, bananas, and a wide variety of other tropical fruits.

tTG TEST: tTG is the standard diagnostic blood test performed when gluten intolerance is suspected. Short for anti-tissue transglutaminase antibody, the tTG test measures the presence of antibodies to gluten in the blood. Higher results indicate a likely gluten intolerance disorder.

TURBIDITY: A condition in which water (or another liquid) becomes opaque due to suspended particles of clay or other matter.

U

ULTRA HIGH TEMPERATURE (UHT) PROCESSING: A food processing procedure in which the product is heated for a very short time to a temperature higher than the setting used for pasteurization, which accomplishes a result close to sterilization.

ULTRAVIOLET: Electromagnetic radiation of wavelengths from about 100 to 400 nanometers.

UMAMI: Sometimes known as the fifth basic taste, umami is a savory taste triggered by the presence of amino acids in meat or aged cheese.

UMBRELLA ORGANIZATION: A federation or other grouping of organizations for a single purpose. An umbrella organization unites many organizations, often from various countries, to represent a cause or movement on a broader level or internationally.

UNDERNUTRITION: Undernutrition describes the status of people whose food intake does not include enough calories (energy) to meet minimum physiological needs. The term is a measure of a country's ability to gain access to food and is normally derived from Food Balance Sheets prepared by the United Nations Food and Agriculture Organization (FAO).

UNDOCUMENTED (WORKER): A person of unverified immigration status; someone who entered a country without advance permission, entered without required paperwork, or who cannot prove that he or she legally entered a country under its immigration laws.

UNITED NATIONS FOOD AND AGRICULTURE ORGANIZATION (FAO): Organization that leads international efforts to defeat hunger. Serving both developed and developing countries, the FAO acts as a neutral forum where all nations meet as equals to negotiate agreements and debate policy. The FAO is also a source of knowledge and information and assists developing countries and countries in transition to modernize and improve agriculture, forestry, and fisheries practices and ensure good nutrition for all.

UNITED STATES DEPARTMENT OF AGRICULTURE (USDA): A department of the United States government, the role of which is to provide leadership on food, agriculture, natural resources, and related issues based on sound public policy, the best available science, and efficient management.

UNITED STATES FOOD AND DRUG ADMINISTRATION (FDA): The Food and Drug Administration (FDA) is an agency of the U.S. Department of Health and Human Services (HHS) that is responsible for regulating and ensuring the safety and effectiveness of foods, drugs, cosmetics, tobacco, and other products.

URINARY INCONTINENCE: Inability to retain urine in the bladder until the person chooses to empty it.

USDA NATURAL LABELED FOOD: Food that is minimally processed with no artificial ingredients or coloring according to USDA standards. This does not include genetically altered food.

USDA ORGANIC LABELED FOOD: A food that is at least 95 percent organically grown or produced product according to USDA standards.

V

VALUE CHAIN: A series of steps between a raw material and a finished good that reaches a final consumer.

VARIANT CREUTZFELDT-JAKOB DISEASE (vCJD): A fatal neurological disorder that is transmitted by prions, or protein-based infectious agents, contained in the brains or spinal cords of cattle infected with bovine spongiform encephalopathy (BSE).

VEGAN: A person who does not eat any animal products, including eggs, milk, cheese, and honey (as opposed to a vegetarian, who does not eat meat).

VEGETABLE: A culinary term, which excludes fruits, describing the edible part of a plant. In a botanical sense, both fruits and vegetables are edible parts of plants.

VIGNERON: A person who cultivates grapes for winemaking.

VINICULTURE: The science, art, and social customs that surround the practices of growing grapes and making wine.

VINTNER: A person who makes wine.

VISA: A certificate or other evidence of permission to enter a country legally for work, residential, or visiting purposes.

VOLATILE: Easily vaporized at moderate temperatures and pressures.

VOLATILE ORGANIC COMPOUND (VOC): Any organic liquid that changes easily (volatilizes) to a gas.

W

WAGE SLAVERY: The practice of being dependent on a wage from hiring out of a person's labor. For some critics of capitalism, all workers who receive wages and live by hiring out their labor are wage slaves. For others not opposed to wage employment *per se*, wage slavery usually denotes forms of indebtedness or other forced systems in which a worker is unable to leave a poor work environment for fear of the consequences.

WATERSHED: The surface waters or streams, rivers, deltas, wetlands, and lakes that share sources of water from both above and below the ground.

WEIGHT CONTROL BEHAVIORS: Behaviors exhibited when someone is trying to control his or her body weight. Some of these behaviors include skipping meals, using diet pills, self-induced vomiting, excessive exercise, and dietary restrictions.

WET NURSING: A term for a woman, not an infant's biological mother, who breastfeeds an infant due to the biological mother's inability to breastfeed. Wet nurses were typically women who had recently had an infant, whose infant had died, or women who maintained lactation easily and charged a fee for wet nursing services to provide economic support for their families.

WIC: The Special Supplemental Nutrition Program for Women, Infants, and Children (WIC) provides nutrition assistance to more than 45 percent of all infants in the United States. WIC supplies specific foods via a voucher system to pregnant women, postpartum women, breastfeeding mothers, infants, and children through age five for families with incomes below 185 percent of the federal poverty line.

WORKSHARE: A type of community supported agriculture (CSA) share in which the shareholder pays a reduced price to the CSA farmer in return for spending an agreed-upon number of hours working on the farm.

WORLD BANK: The World Bank is part of a group of international financial institutions that provides loans and other financial assistance to developing nations to promote economic growth and reduce poverty.

WORLD FOOD PROGRAMME (WFP): The front-line food agency of the United Nations (UN), the World Food Programme (WFP) is the largest food aid organization in the world dedicated to hunger issues, delivering aid to more than 90 million persons in more than 70 countries per year.

WORLD TRADE ORGANIZATION (WTO): An international non-governmental organization that implements and supervises international trade agreements.

X

X RAYS: Electromagnetic radiation of wavelengths from about 0.03 to 3 nanometers.

Y

YEAST: A naturally occurring single-celled fungus that ferments sugar to produce carbon dioxide bubbles to leaven dough and to produce alcoholic beverages such as beer and wine.

YIELD: The amount of a crop produced per planting or per growing season.

Z

ZOONOSIS: A zoonosis is a disease of microbiological origin that can be transmitted from animals to people. The disease may be caused by bacteria, viruses, parasites, or fungi.

ZOONOTIC DISEASE: A disease transmitted from animals to humans.

Chronology

A chronology of events related to the history of food and agriculture.

BC

c.18000 BC
Nile valley sees rise of agricultural techniques; cereal grains are specifically cultivated.

c.10000 BC
Neolithic Revolution: transition from a hunting and gathering mode of food production to farming and animal husbandry, the domestication of plants and animals.

c.9000 BC
Sheep and goats domesticated in Mesopotamia, other livestock in Persia.

c.8750 BC
Pumpkins and other members of the squash family are known to have been cultivated in what is now Persia and Central Asia.

c.8000 BC
Settled agriculture occurs in the Near East and other centers of human habitation.

c.8000 BC
The first forms of fired clay are used by Neolithic people to keep track of agricultural products. They are unmarked and have geometric shapes.

c.8000 BC
With the beginning of settled agriculture come the first simple digging and harvesting tools.

c.8000 BC
Beer is brewed in Mesopotamia.

c.8000 BC
Potatoes are cultivated in the Andes of Peru.

c.7000 BC
The water buffalo is domesticated in eastern Asia and China.

c.7000 BC
Durum wheat is cultivated in Anatolia (Turkey). This important variety is used to make alimentary paste-like foods and much later becomes a staple for pastas.

c.7000 BC
Wheat, barley, and millet are cultivated in the east Mediterranean basin.

c.7000 BC
Pigs and cattle are domesticated in what is today Turkey.

c.6500 BC
A primitive plough called the ard is used in the Near East.

c.6400 BC
Beer is known to be brewed in the Andes at this time.

c.6000 BC
Millet is cultivated in Africa. These various types of grasses produce small edible seeds that are used as forage crops and as food cereals. High in carbohydrates, millet becomes an important food staple.

c.6000 BC

Peaches are known to be grown in central China, and citrus fruits are cultivated in Indonesia.

c.6000 BC

Bread-making wheat called *Triticum vulgare* is cultivated in southwestern Asia. This is the most important variety of wheat, because it is used for bread making; it becomes a major source of energy in the human diet.

c.6000 BC

Wine-making begins in northern Mesopotamia and in the Levant (along the eastern Mediterranean shore).

c.5600 BC

The saddle quern is used for grinding grain. A type of mortar and pestle, it consists of a flat stone bed and a rounded stone that is operated manually against it.

c.5000 BC

Date palms are grown in India, and rice is cultivated in the Yangtze Delta in China.

c.5000 BC

Iraq develops formal irrigation methods and tools.

c.4500 BC

Fired clay tokens are used for agricultural record-keeping.

c.4000 BC

Maize or corn is cultivated in what is now the Tehuacan Valley of Mexico.

c.4000 BC

Grapes are grown around the Caspian Sea and the coastal regions of the Black Sea.

c.4000 BC

With the appearance of the plow in Mesopotamia, planting can be done in rows or furrows instead of in holes, allowing more crops to be planted in less time and more food to be produced.

c.4000 BC

The Sumerians make cheese in Mesopotamia.

c.4000 BC

The yoke is used possibly for the first time in the Near East. It is a wooden bar or frame that rests on the shoulders or withers of draft animals and is tied to the neck or horns to assure that they pull together.

c.3500 BC

The edible olive is grown on the island of Crete. It is eventually used primarily for its oil.

c.3500 BC

Sumerians describe methods of managing the date harvest.

c.3400 BC

Opium is first cultivated in lower Mesopotamia. The Sumerians called the poppy Hul Gil or the "joy plant." The art of poppy cultivation subsequently spreads from the Sumerians to the Assyrians, and from the Assyrians to the Babylonians and Egyptians.

c.3100 BC

Peanuts and sweet potatoes are domesticated and grown on the west coast of South America in what is now Peru.

c.3000 BC

Making sugar from sugarcane in India is known to be practiced at this time.

c.2700 BC

Certain cereal and forage grasses, now classed as millet, form one of the chief sources of food in China. The Chinese claim that wheat used as food during this period is a direct gift from Heaven.

c.2700 BC

Tea drinking begins in China.

c.2500 BC

Apiculture or beekeeping begins in Egypt around this time. One of the oldest forms of animal husbandry, it involves the care and manipulation of colonies of honeybees (of the "Apis" species) so that they will produce and store a quantity of honey above their own requirements.

c.2400 BC

Food is known to have been stored by primitive man below ground in pits during winter months in what is now Eastern Europe. This is an early form of cold storage and food preservation.

c.2000 BC

The shduf or shadoof, a hand-operated device for lifting water, appears in Egypt and Mesopotamia. It consists of a long, tapering pole mounted like a seesaw with a skin or bucket hung from one end and a counter weight at the other end. It is still used in India and Egypt today.

c.1500 BC

A primitive seed drill for planting seeds is introduced in Sumer.

c.1500 BC

The beam press is used in Greece to squeeze olives and grapes mechanically. It is a considerable improvement over the old manual "bag press."

c.1400 BC

Fatty matter (animal and vegetable oils and fats) are used to lubricate the axles of chariot wheels.

c.1350 BC

The Rollins papyrus, containing elaborate bread accounts, is dated to this time. It indicates how large numbers are used in everyday, practical ways.

c.1100 BC

The rotary or true quern for grinding grain appears in the Mediterranean area. It uses a handle that rotates one stone atop a stationary stone. It is the precursor of the heavy querns used later by the Greeks and Romans that are operated by slaves or donkeys.

c.1000 BC

Oats are cultivated in central Europe. This important cereal plant is used primarily for livestock feed but also is processed for human consumption. It is not used for breads.

c.1000 BC

The Chinese preserve their foods by salting, drying, smoking, and fermenting them in wine vinegar.

c.1000 BC

Flax is known to have been harvested by people living in what is now Switzerland. It is not known if it is used solely for food.

AD

35

Marcus Gavius Apicius, Roman epicure, writes what many consider to be the oldest cookbook. Titled *De Re Coquinaria* (On the Subject of Cooking), it contains glimpses of Roman cooking and eating habits as well as recipes.

75

Pliny (23–79) recommends eating animal testicles to improve the sexual function of men.

1000

In Naples, a food called "pieca" is eaten and is regarded by some as the forerunner of modern pizza.

1100

In western North America, the Hopi tribe of Native Americans uses coal for both heating and cooking purposes.

1200

Buckwheat is introduced into Europe from Asia. It becomes a staple grain crop for poultry and livestock and is also cooked and served much like rice. It is not considered suitable for bread-making.

1202

King John of England (1167–1216) proclaims England's first food law. The Assize of Bread prohibits adding undisclosed ingredients such as ground peas or beans to bread.

1560

Jean Nicot de Villemain (1530–1600), French ambassador to Portugal, sends tobacco seeds from the New World to Paris and introduces tobacco into France and the rest of Europe. Tobacco is already being smoked in Portugal and Spain.

1600

French agronomist Olivier de Serres (1539–1619) publishes *Theatre d'Agriculture et Mesnage de Champs*, a textbook on French agricultural practices. He is also the first to practice systematic crop rotation.

1609

The first yield of corn that is produced by American colonists is harvested by the Jamestown colony in Virginia. The Jamestown settlers learned how to grow corn from the Native Americans two years earlier.

1623

Flax is first introduced in America and is cultivated solely for its fiber, from which linen and yarn are made. The seeds of the plant are called linseed from which linseed oil is made.

1650

Glass bottles replace stoneware for conserving wine and beer. They are made by the mouth-blowing technique and are surprisingly standardized.

1670

The first cookbook written by a woman is published. Written by Hannah Woolley (1622–c.1675) of England, *The Queen like Closet; or, Rich Cabinet* sees several editions.

1679

French physicist Denis Papin (1647–1712) develops a steam digester that is the forerunner of the pressure cooker. Work on this device leads him to later experiment with steam pushing a piston.

1701 English agriculturalist and inventor Jethro Tull (1674–1741) invents a seed drill that sows seed in neat rows, saving seed and making it easier to keep weeds down. His horse-drawn hoes destroy weeds and keep the soil between the rows in a friable condition.

1716 The first unambiguous account of plant hybridization is given by the American writer Cotton Mather (1663–1728). He describes a case involving red and blue kernels of *Zea mays* (corn).

1727 English botanist and chemist Stephen Hales (1677–1761) studies plant nutrition and measures water taken up by plant roots and released by leaves. He states that something in the air (CO_2) is converted into food, and that light was necessary for this purpose. His work *Vegetable Staticks*, published in this year, lays the foundation for plant physiology.

1728 Italian physician Jacopo Bartolomeo Beccaria (1682–1766) discovers gluten in wheat flour. This is the first protein substance of plant origin to be found.

1731 English agriculturalist and inventor Jethro Tull (1674–1741) publishes *Horse-Hoeing Husbandry*; its advanced ideas help form the basis of the modern system of British agriculture.

1742 The first cookbook published in the American colonies is *The Compleat Housewife; or, Accomplished Gentlewoman's Companion*, published at Williamsburg, Virginia. It was first written by a cook and published in London in 1727. Following this first edition, this popular work went through a total of 18 editions.

1747 Agricultural seeds are first sold commercially in the American colonies.

1747 One of the most popular cookbooks of the eighteenth century, *The Art of Cookery Made Plain and Easy* is published. It is reprinted in the first year and goes through 20 editions, continuing to be in publication until 1843. Its author is Hannah Glasse (1708–1770), though it was published anonymously.

1752 French physicist and physiologist René-Antoine Ferchault de Réaumur (1683–1757) studies the physiology of digestion and obtains gastric juice.

1753 Scottish physician James Lind (1716–1794) first publishes his *Treatise of the Scurvy*. This vitamin-deficiency disease, which killed more sailors on long voyages than did battle with the enemy, was finally eliminated in the British Navy some years after Lind's book. The Navy's practice of giving lime juice to their crews resulted in British sailors being called "limeys."

1768 Italian biologist Lazzaro Spallanzani (1729–1799) concludes that boiling a sealed container prevents microorganisms from entering and spoiling its contents. (See 1795.)

1770 Swedish chemist Karl Wilhelm Scheele (1742–1786) discovers tartaric acid. One of the most widely distributed of the plant acids, it eventually assumes a wide variety of food and industrial uses.

1780 Swedish chemist Karl Wilhelm Scheele (1742–1786) discovers lactic acid. Found in the soil, in the blood and muscles of animals, and in fermented milk products, it eventually is used in food processing and for tanning leather and dyeing wool.

1783 Chinch bug is first noted as a pest of wheat in the United States in North Carolina.

1784 David Landreth opens the first seed business in the United States in Philadelphia, Pennsylvania.

1785 The first organization of American agricultural societies convenes in Philadelphia, Pennsylvania.

1795 French inventor and chef Nicolas François Appert (1752–1841) discovers how to hermetically seal food and creates what becomes known as canning. He devises a method of putting food in corked glass bottles and immersing them in boiling water. This destroys microorganisms in the food (although bacteriology has not yet discovered this). Appert sets up a bottling plant at Massy, south of Paris, in 1804. (See 1810.)

1801 American legendary figure John Chapman (1774–1845), called "Johnny Appleseed," begins planting apple seeds throughout

Indiana and the adjacent territory. He uses the broadcast or scatter method of seeding, and he lives to see 100,000 acres with apple trees in them.

1802   The sugar beet is first introduced as a field crop into Germany where it becomes a commercial success.

1804   The soybean is first cultivated in the United States. It becomes a major crop after World War II (1939–1945).

1804   The first agricultural fair in America is held in Washington, DC.

1805   French agriculturalist Antoine-Augustin Parmentier (1737–1813) produces the first powdered milk.

1810   French inventor Nicolas François Appert (1752–1841) publishes *L'Art de Conserver les Substances Animals et Vegetables* (The Art of Preserving Animal and Vegetable Substances), which founds the commercial canning industry. He describes how to preserve food over long periods of time by putting it in corked and sealed bottles and submerging them in boiling water. He applies heat to kill anything that might cause spoilage and then excludes air. Appert also develops the bouillon cube.

1810   Peter Durand of England patents an improved version of food preservation by using tin-plate canisters instead of glass. He does not offer an easy method of opening the cans, however. (See 1811.)

1810   Scottish physicist and mathematician John Leslie (1766–1832) is the first to create artificial ice when he freezes water using an air pump.

1810   The first farm magazine in the United States, *The Agricultural Museum*, begins publication.

1811   Bryan Donkin (1768–1855) and John Hall of England buy Peter Durand's patent for canning food and establish the first cannery in England in 1812. They supply canned goods to the Royal Navy and to various Arctic expeditions.

1811   French industrialist Bernard Courtois (1777–1838) discovers iodine in the ashes of seaweed. The ingestion of burnt seaweed was recommended as a treatment for goiter by Spanish alchemist Arnold of

Villanova (c.1235–1311) around 1300 and is known to have been used by the Chinese around 1600 BC.

1811   A horse-drawn version of a circular-blade reaper is patented by an Englishman named Smith. Reapers are used to harvest mature grain crops.

1815   The secrets of the new canning methods are introduced into the United States by the Englishman Ezra Daggett, who begins a business hermetically sealing food in containers.

1819   The first distinctively agricultural journal in America, *American Farmer*, is published in Baltimore, Maryland.

1819   The canning industry in the United States begins in Massachusetts and New York. In Boston, Thomas Underwood packs fruits, pickles, and condiments in bottles, while in New York Thomas Kensett and Ezra Daggett pack seafood in bottles.

1820   The "wheat belt" in the U.S. Midwest begins its successful spread. Seventy-two percent of the U.S. population who are gainfully employed are engaged in agriculture.

1822   A wheat and barley reaper that uses a serrated horizontal bar moving side-to-side is developed by two Englishmen named Ogle and Brown.

1823   French chemist Michel-Eugène Chevreul (1786–1889) publishes his classic work *Recherches sur les corps gras d'origine animale* (Research on Animal Fats), which deals with oils, fats, and vegetable colors. He shows that fat is a compound of glycerol with an organic acid. This is one of the first works addressing the issue of the fundamental structure of a large class of compounds, and it has a revolutionary effect on the soap and candle industries.

1824   First preservation of meat in cans is made.

1827   French inventor and chef Nicolas François Appert (1752–1841) first condenses milk to make it keep better. Seven years later he invents the method of evaporating milk.

1827   The first slaughterhouse in Chicago is a log structure built by Archibald Clybourne. This marks the beginning of Chicago's meat packing industry.

1827   English chemist and physiologist William Prout (1785–1850) first classifies the components of food into carbohydrates, fats, and proteins. He uses the words saccharinous, oleaginous, and albuminous for the three respective groups.

1832   German chemist Heinrich Wilhelm Ferdinand Wackenroder (1798–1854) discovers carotene (carotin) in carrots. This organic compound is usually found as a pigment in plants, giving them a yellow, red, or orange color, and is converted in the liver of animals into vitamin A.

1835   German physiologist Theodor Schwann (1810–1882) discovers pepsin, the active digesting principle in the stomach.

1837   American inventor John Deere (1804–1886) develops a steel plow that he fashions from a circular saw blade. It is able to cut through the difficult prairie soils. He also realizes that a successful self-scouring steel moldboard depends upon its shape. His steel plow plays a large role in opening the western states to agriculture. His company becomes a leading maker of farm equipment.

1840   German chemist Justus von Liebig (1803–1873) publishes *Die Organische Chemie in ihrer Anwendung auf Agrikultur und Physiologie* (Organic Chemistry in Its Application to Agriculture and Physiology), in which he shows that plants synthesize organic compounds from carbon dioxide in the air, but take their nitrogenous compounds from the soil. He also says that ammonia (nitrogen) is needed for plant growth and introduces the use of mineral fertilizers.

1842   English agriculturalist John Benne Lawes (1814–1900) patents a process for treating phosphate rock with sulfuric acid to produce superphosphate. He also opens the first fertilizer factory this year, thus beginning the artificial fertilizer industry.

1845   The Irish potato famine begins and lasts for 15 years. Called "late blight," this fungus disease of potato and tomato plants destroys plants in two weeks' time and results in more than 30 percent of the population of Ireland either dying or being forced to emigrate.

1846   Robert Reid of the United States develops a new variety of corn known as "Reid's Yellow Dent" that eventually comes to dominate the Corn Belt.

1856   American surveyor and inventor Gail Borden (1801–1874) cans his sweetened, condensed milk using a heat and vacuum method. In 1858 he establishes the New York Condensed Milk Company.

1859   The Great Atlantic and Pacific Tea Company (A&P) is founded and eventually becomes one of the largest food chains in the United States.

1862   President Abraham Lincoln (1809–1865) signs legislation that creates the U.S. Department of Agriculture (USDA).

1864   French chemist and microbiologist Louis Pasteur (1822–1895) invents the process of slow heating that kills bacteria and other microorganisms. Called pasteurization, it is used first as a way of keeping wine and beer from turning sour.

1864   F. S. Davenport of the United States invents the sulky plow, which offers the farmer a seat to ride on behind his team.

1869   French chemist Hippolyte Mege-Mouries (1817–1880) patents his "oleomargarine" and wins a government prize given to the inventor of the best "cheap butter." His product consists of liquid beef tallow, milk, water, and chopped cow's udder churned into a solid form. It is first produced commercially in 1873 as "butterine."

1870   Superphosphates begin to be used as fertilizers. This soluble mixture is made from mineral phosphates treated with sulfuric acid, and its use as a rapid-acting fertilizer boosts agricultural production.

1874   German physician Adolf Kussmaul (1822–1902) explains diabetic coma as due to acetonaemia and describes the labored breathing or air hunger that accompanies that condition. It becomes known as "Kussmaul's respiration."

1877   Swedish inventor Carl Gustaf Patrik de Laval (1848–1913) invents the first cream separator. Operated by a steam engine, his device centrifugally spins milk and separates out the heavier cream from it.

1877   Frozen meat is packed in ice and successfully shipped from Argentina to France.

1878   Joseph Lister (1827–1912) publishes a paper describing the role of a bacterium he names *Bacterium lactis* in the souring of milk.

1879   A bread slicing machine is manufactured in England.

1883   A machine for making a self-opening, pleated, flat-bottomed grocery bag is patented by Charles Stilwell of the United States.

1886   Franz von Soxhlet (1848–1926) first suggests that milk given to infants be sterilized.

1888   Meat is shipped in railroad cars cooled by mechanical refrigeration for the first time in the United States.

1890   American agricultural chemist Stephen Moulton Babcock (1843–1931) perfects a test for determining the buttermilk content of milk and offers a standard method of grading milk.

1892   Scottish chemist and physicist James Dewar (1842–1923) improves the Violle vacuum insulator by constructing a double-walled flask with a vacuum between the walls. He then coats all sides with silver so heat will be reflected and not absorbed. His Dewar flask keeps hot liquids hot and cold liquids cold. This flask eventually becomes the first Thermos bottle.

1893   The first ready-to-eat breakfast cereal, "Shredded Wheat," is introduced by Henry D. Perky (1843–1906) of the United States.

1894   Max Rubner (1854–1932), a German physiologist, makes accurate caloric measurements of food and discovers that the energy produced by food being consumed by the body is the same amount as if that quantity had been consumed in a fire.

1895   Refrigeration is introduced for commercial and home food preservation.

1896   English engineer William Joseph Dibdin (1850–1925) and his colleague Schweder improve the sewage disposal systems in England with the introduction of a bacterial system of water purification. These improvements greatly reduce the number of waterborne diseases like typhoid fever.

1898   American agricultural chemist George Washington Carver (1860–1943) publishes his first agricultural paper. During his long and productive career, he develops hundreds of products from sweet potatoes, peanuts, and soybeans that prove valuable alternatives to cotton and tobacco as staple crops. He also emphasizes crop rotation and diversification.

1901   Prince Edward Island, Canada, becomes the first province to enact prohibition legislation banning alcohol.

1902   The Horn & Hardart Baking Company of Philadelphia, Pennsylvania, creates an early automat that offers food for a "nickel in a slot."

1904   Russian physiologist Ivan Petrovich Pavlov (1849–1936) is awarded the Nobel Prize for physiology or medicine for his work establishing that the nervous system plays a part in controlling digestion and by helping to found gastroenterology.

1906   English biochemist Frederick Gowland Hopkins (1861–1947) first argues that certain "accessory factors" in food are necessary to sustain life. This theory of trace substances becomes the starting point of further work on vitamin requirements.

1906   Freeze-drying is invented by Jacques Arsène d'Arsonval (1851–1940) of France and his colleague, George Bordas. This food preservation process works on the principle of removing water from food. It is not perfected until after World War II (1939–1945). (See 1946.)

1906   Japan begins the production of monosodium glutamate (MSG) as a flavor-enhancer for foods. By 1926, production reaches industrial proportions.

1906   The Pure Food and Drug Act of 1906 and its companion bill the Federal Meat Inspection Act are passed in the United States. The two pieces of legislation sought to remedy the adulteration of food, addition of intoxicating ingredients, and unsanitary conditions in the food processing industry that had been exposed by Progressive Era reformers.

1908   George H. Shull (1874–1954) proposes using self-fertilized lines in the production of commercial seed corn. This results in highly successful hybrid corn programs.

1912   American biochemist Casimir Funk (1884–1967) coins the word "vitamine." Since the dietary substances he discovers are in the amine group, he calls all of them "life-amines" or "vitamines."

1913 Swedish inventor Carl Gustaf Patrik de Laval (1849–1913) perfects a vacuum milking machine. Despite its efficiency, it is painful to the cows.

1913 American biochemist Elmer Verner McCollum (1879–1967) discovers that a factor essential to life is present in water-soluble fats; it is soon named vitamin A.

1914 Pasteurization of milk begins in many large cities.

1917 American inventor Clarence Birdseye (1886–1956) begins to develop a process for freezing foods in small packages suitable for retailing. His process is highly efficient, and he founds the General Seafoods Company in 1924.

1917 German organic chemist Adolf Windaus (1876–1959) extracts cholestrin (later known as vitamin D) from cod liver oil and formulates it.

1917 Canada enacts legislation restricting the import, sale, and manufacture of alcohol. Several provinces have total bans on alcohol by this time, but the union government permits the importation of beverages with 2.5 percent alcohol or less into Canada for sale in those provinces without bans.

1920 The Prohibition Era begins in the United States as the nationwide alcohol ban enacted the previous year takes effect.

1922 The first canned baby food is manufactured in the United States by Harold H. Clapp of New York.

1922 American biochemist Ernest Verner McCollum (1879–1967) discovers and names vitamin D as a substance found in cod liver oil that prevents the deficiency disease rickets.

1922 Herbert McLean Evans (1882–1971), an American anatomist, embryologist, and physician, and his colleagues discover vitamin E.

1926 American pathologist Joseph Goldberger (1874–1929) and his colleagues discover the cause and cure of the disease pellagra. This disease leads to a severe skin condition, diarrhea, and eventually coma and death. He discovers that it is caused by a diet totally deficient in niacin (vitamin B3) and protein.

1926 Dutch biochemists Barend C. P. Jansen and Willem F. Donath first isolate vitamin B1.

1927 Hungarian-American physicist Albert Szent-Gyorgyi (1893–1986) discovers ascorbic acid or vitamin C while studying oxidation in plants.

1927 The first stainless steel cookware is made in the United States by the Polar Ware Company.

1928 Hungarian-American biochemist Albert Szent-Gyorgyi (1893–1986) first isolates and describes ascorbic acid. In 1931, he shows this to be identical to vitamin C.

1929 Dutch physician Christiaan Eijkman (1858–1930) is awarded the Nobel Prize for physiology or medicine for his discovery that the disease beriberi is the result of a nutritional deficiency. He is also the first to experimentally establish a deficiency disease. English biochemist Frederick Gowland Hopkins (1861–1947) is also awarded the Nobel Prize for physiology or medicine for his discovery of growth-stimulating vitamins.

1930 The first sliced and packaged bread, "Wonder Bread," is introduced in the United States.

1930 The first stationary electric food mixer, the Mixmaster, is introduced in the United States by the Sunbeam Company.

1930 The first modern supermarket is the chain of King Kullen food stores operated in New York by Michael Cullen of the United States.

1931 Erma Rombauer's *The Joy of Cooking*, a modern comprehensive cookbook intended for homemakers, is first published. The book becomes the bestselling cookbook of the twentieth century.

1932 American biochemist John Howard Northrop crystallizes trypsin, a protein-splitting digestive enzyme of pancreatic secretions.

1933 Prohibition of alcohol ends in the United States, reintroducing the legal manufacture, importation, and sale of liquor, beer, and wine.

1934 German biochemist Philipp Ellinger (1888–1952) and Walter Koschara discover vitamin B2 (riboflavin) and establish its chemical formula.

1934 Danish biochemist Carl Peter Henrik Dam (1895–1976) discovers vitamin K and finds it to be a factor in blood clotting.

1937   Shopping carts are made available to food customers at Humpty Dumpty Stores in Oklahoma. They are a basket attached to a folding chair on wheels.

1937   English chemist Walter Norman Haworth (1883–1950) is awarded the Nobel Prize for chemistry for his investigations on carbohydrates and vitamin C. Swiss chemist Paul Karrer (1889–1971) is also awarded the Nobel Prize for chemistry for his investigations on carotenoids, flavins, and vitamins A and B2. Hungarian-American physicist Albert Szent-Gyorgyi (1893–1986) receives the Nobel Prize in physiology and medicine for his work on vitamin C.

1938   Austrian-German chemist Richard Kuhn (1900–1967) first isolates vitamin B6 (pyridoxine) from skim milk.

1939   Food stamps program is introduced in the United States.

1940   American biochemist Vincent Du Vigneaud (1901–1978) identifies a compound called biotin as being what previously had been known as vitamin H.

1940   The first MacDonald's and Dairy Queen restaurants open in the United States, sparking the spread of fast-food culture worldwide.

1941   *Gourmet* magazine publishes its first issue.

1942   American food manufacturer Wrigley Company develops packed rations military personnel serving overseas during World War II (1939–1945). Typical ration packets contained items like graham biscuits, canned meat, cigarettes, sugar, pickles, flavoring sauces, and chewing gum.

1943   Danish biochemist Henrik Carl Peter Dam (1895–1976) is awarded the Nobel Prize for physiology or medicine for his discovery of vitamin K. American biochemist Edward Adelbert Doisy (1893–1986) is awarded the Nobel Prize for physiology or medicine for his discovery of the chemical nature of vitamin K.

1944   The worldwide introduction of mechanized agricultural practices and bioengineered crops in developing nations struggling with food insecurity begins, sparking what becomes known as the Green Revolution.

1945   Earl Tupper (1907–1983) invents Tupperware plastic food storage containers.

1945   The Food and Agriculture Organization (FAO) is formally organized as part of the United Nations (UN). It is the oldest permanent specialized agency in the UN, and its objective is eliminating hunger and improving nutrition.

1946   American bacteriologist Earl W. Flosdorff (1904–1958) demonstrates that the process of freeze-drying can be used to preserve coffee, orange juice, and even meat. When food is flash frozen in a vacuum, the water in it sublimates or changes directly from a liquid into a vapor. Because the water sublimates rather than melts, the food's tissues do not collapse.

1946   The Culinary Institute of America, dedicated to educating professional chefs and restaurant owners, opens.

1947   The microwave oven is introduced. The first commercial model is known as the Radarange.

1948   American biochemist Edward Lawrence Rickes, with N. G. Brink, F. R. Koniusky, T. R. Wood, and K. Folkers, first crystallizes vitamin B12.

1948   Prince Edward Island is the last Canadian province to repeal its prohibition laws.

1963   The United Nations Food and Agricultural Organization (FAO) and the United Nations General Assembly establish the World Food Programme (WFP) on a trial basis. The WFP provides food aid and agricultural development assistance to developing regions.

1964   Automated irrigation systems are field-tested for agricultural use in the United States.

1965   Dwarf, high-yield rice is introduced in India and other Asian nations. It requires higher-than-usual amounts of fertilizer and insecticides. It also contributes to what becomes known as the Green Revolution.

1965   After a successful trial period, The World Food Programme (WFP) is made a permanent agency.

1967   The U.S. Wholesome Meat Act of 1967 requires the inspection of meat that stays within state lines. Meat must be certified as truthfully labeled, sanitary, unadulterated, and free of disease.

1968   The Poultry Products Inspection Act passes, requiring the inspection of most poultry sold in the United States. The law also creates a unified inspection division for all meats subject to federal inspection.

1970 American agronomist Norman Borlaug (1914–2009), dubbed the "Father of the Green Revolution," is awarded the Nobel Peace Prize for promoting food security by increasing the global food supply.

1970 The U.S. Food and Drug Administration (FDA) orders the recall of canned tuna fish after mercury levels above 0.5 parts per million are discovered in it.

1971 American chemist Robert Burns Woodward (1917–1979) first synthesizes vitamin B12.

1981 The artificial sweetener aspartame is approved for general use by the U.S. Food and Drug Administration (FDA). Discovered in 1965, it does not have saccharin's bitter aftertaste.

1986 The U.S. Department of Agriculture (USDA) approves the release of the first genetically altered virus as well as the first outdoor test of genetically altered plants. The virus is to be used to combat swine herpes, and the plants are high-yield tobacco plants.

1986 Italian advocate Carlo Petrini founds the International Slow Food movement.

1992 Nutrition fact labels indicating nutrition information such as calories per serving appear on all manufactured or processed foods sold in the United States, as directed by the Nutrition Labeling and Education Act of 1990.

1994 The first genetically-altered food for human consumption, the Flavr Savr tomato, gains approval by the Food and Drug Administration (FDA) and is sold in U.S. food stores.

1993 The Food and Drug Administration (FDA) approves bovine somatropin (BST), a genetically-engineered synthetic hormone that increases the amount of milk given by dairy cows.

1994 The Dietary Supplement Health and Education Act declares supplements a food ingredient, thereby permitting regulation. The law establishes specific labeling requirements, manufacturing practices, and evaluation of claims or use of a disclaimer that the product is evaluated for effectiveness.

1996 Olestra, a calorie-free fat substitute, is approved by the Food and Drug Administration (FDA) for use in processed foods, despite reports that its ingestion can cause gastrointestinal side effects.

1997 A record El Niño develops in the Pacific Ocean, altering the typical hurricane pattern and causing severe drought in Australia, Northern Africa, and Southeast Asia.

1997 The Food and Drug Administration (FDA) revises its recommendations for vitamin intake, replacing the recommended dietary allowances (RDAs), with dietary reference intakes (DRIs), intended to support optimum health.

1997 The Food and Drug Administration (FDA) permits manufacturers of low-fat, oat-rich cereals that are found to lower cholesterol in the blood to advertise the claim.

1997 A study argues that women who eat whole-grain foods and other rich sources of phytoestrogens are found less likely to develop breast cancer.

1998 The Food and Drug Administration (FDA) approves a bacterial spray for newly hatched chicks laden with beneficial bacteria which prevent their picking up *Salmonella* and other bacteria that cause food poisoning.

1999 The United States leads the world in corn production, a crop grown on every continent except Antarctica, due to scientists' development of diverse hybrid varieties that suit growing conditions and locations worldwide.

1999 A U.S. federal study reveals that dioxins in breast milk can permanently weaken children's molars, and repeated occupational exposure to dioxins can increase a person's risk of developing fatal cancers.

1999 Scientists develop plants that infuse crop soils with biodegradable pesticides.

2000 The Cartagena Protocol on Biosafety is adopted in Montreal, Canada. The protocol, negotiated under the United Nations Convention on Biological Diversity, is one of the first legally binding international agreements to govern the trade or sale of genetically modified organisms of agricultural importance.

2000   Food irradiation is endorsed by the United States Food Protection Agency, the American Medical Association, and the World Health Association, and over 40 countries sterilize food by irradiation.

2000   The Institute of Medicine of the U.S. National Academy of Sciences increases the recommended daily consumption of dietary antioxidants, such as vitamins C and E.

2001   European countries, including France and Germany, push for tough European Union rules regulating the sale of genetically modified foods. The U.S. State Department brands the new rules without scientific merit.

2001   New food labels will identify choline-rich foods. Choline is a nutrient essential for learning and brain health.

2002   The United Nations holds an Earth Summit in Johannesburg, South Africa, to focus on international regulations that address environmental problems: water and air quality, accessibility of food and water, sanitation, agricultural productivity, and land management, that often accompany the human population's most pressing social issues: poverty, famine, disease, and war.

2002   Drought conditions again threaten eastern Africa, with an estimated 15 million people in Ethiopia, 3 million in Kenya, 1.5 million in Eritrea, and 3 million in Sudan facing the risk of starvation as a result.

2002   Reports surface that scaremongering concerning genetically modified foods causes several African countries fighting starvation to reject genetically modified food supplements that may have reduced starvation and death rates.

2002   The agricultural chemical atrazine, used in weed control, is thought to be partially responsible for the dramatic global decline in amphibians, as it is found to disturb male frog sex hormones, altering their gonads.

2002   Biochemists discover that starchy foods become contaminated by the animal carcinogen acrylamide when fried, and scientists

attempt to find the threshold for human exposure and risk.

2003   An obesity working group is established by the U.S. Commissioner of Food and Drugs to study ways that food and advertising regulation could help address the U.S. obesity epidemic.

2004   The Food Allergy Labeling and Consumer Protection Act requires food labels to disclose whether a food contains any protein derived from peanuts, soybeans, cow milk, eggs, fish, crustacean shellfish, tree nuts, or wheat—the eight most common sources of food allergies.

2004   The Food and Drug Administration (FDA) bans dietary supplements containing ephedrine.

2004   A joint advisory by the Food and Drug Administration (FDA) and Environmental Protection Agency (EPA) suggests limiting consumption of tuna and certain other fish by children and women of childbearing age after findings show low levels of mercury contamination. Coal-fired power plants are suspected to release into lakes and streams up to half of the mercury that eventually makes its way into oceans and contaminates fish.

2004   Amid the worst drought in over 100 years, Australian scientists warn that the continent faces an environmental crisis unless scarce water resources in the world's most arid inhabited continent are carefully managed.

2006   Norway announces plans to build a "doomsday vault" in a mountain close to the North Pole that will house a two-million-crop seed bank in the event of catastrophic climate change, nuclear war, or rising sea levels.

2006   The Oakland, California, city council passes a measure to ban Styrofoam packaging for restaurant takeout food.

2006   Researchers report that carbon dioxide from industrial emissions is raising the acidity of the world's oceans, threatening plankton and other organisms that form the base of the entire marine food web.

2007   The World Wildlife Fund (WWF; also known as the World Wide Fund for Nature) conservation group states that climate change, pollution, over extraction of water, and encroaching development are killing some of the world's major rivers, including China's Yangtze, India's Ganges, and Africa's Nile.

2008   Oil and food prices rise sharply on a global scale, increasing widespread dangers of famine and poverty. Critics contend increased prices for petroleum lead to the diversion of food crops to biofuel production.

2008   Global agricultural experts issue a warning that UG99, a plant rust fungus that kills up to 80% of current wheat strains, threatens crops (most immediately those in developing countries). The spread of UG99 raises the specter of widespread wheat crop destruction on a global scale. Such destruction would, of course, result in massive poverty for farmers, widespread economic damage, increased global wheat prices (at a time when wheat prices have already experienced sharp increases), and possible famine.

2008   Despite initial studies suggesting that vitamin C and vitamin E supplements might offer some protection against prostate cancer, two major separate studies published in the *Journal of the American Medical Association* argue that taking vitamin C and vitamin E supplements fails to reduce risk of any cancers. Public health researchers also argue that improper use of vitamins can lessen the importance of following a healthy diet known to reduce cancer risk.

2009   The last issue of *Gourmet* magazine is published in November. Publishers cite decreased readership and the global economic crisis as reasons for ceasing publication.

2009   Falling prices and reduced U.S. demand for dairy products prompt dairy farmers to sell hundreds of thousands of dairy cows, up to 15 percent of the U.S. herd, for meat slaughter.

2010   The Food Network, the most popular cable channel devoted to food and cooking themes, reaches almost 100 million homes.

2010   A trans fat ban takes effect in California, the first state to ban trans fats in restaurants and retail food establishments. Several U.S. cities, including New York, had previously enacted similar bans.

Advertising Food

■ Introduction

Manufacturers use food advertisements to inform the public about new products or increase sales of existing products. Food advertising began in the mid-seventeenth century to promote new products imported from Asia and the Americas. In the mid-twentieth century, food advertising took advantage of the rising popularity of television (and continues to exploit television's home saturation) to promote convenience foods to time-crunched, modern families. Processed foods and fast food restaurants remain the most advertised food products. Food advertising has become a multi-billion dollar industry and is the second-largest advertising sector.

Food advertisements influence the food choices made by both children and adults. Consumer and health advocacy groups have criticized food advertisements, which overwhelmingly promote high-fat, high-calorie foods. Critics assert that food advertisements contribute to increasing obesity, diabetes, and heart disease rates by persuading consumers to consume more of the unhealthy foods featured in advertisements for fast food restaurants and junk food.

■ Historical Background and Scientific Foundations

Food advertisements date back to at least the mid-seventeenth century. Before this period, virtually all food products were prepared and consumed locally. Increased trade with Asia and the Americas, however, made many exotic food products more readily available for Europe's growing middle class, which primarily consisted of merchants and professionals. The earliest advertisements usually informed consumers about the arrival of new shipments of goods from faraway lands. In 1652 advertisements for coffee appeared in English weekly newspapers. Advertisements for chocolate and tea appeared in 1657 and 1658, respectively.

Food advertisements became more frequent and more prominent in the mid- to late nineteenth century.

The development of canning and other preservation methods enabled manufacturers to produce and transport a variety of food products across great distances, which expanded the markets for food manufacturers' products. Rising literacy rates also meant that food producers' advertisements could reach a wider audience. During this period, food advertisements placed an emphasis on wholesome and healthy food to take advantage of recently publicized studies linking health and nutrition. Many of these advertisements, however, made outlandish claims about a product's single-handed ability to prolong life, improve physical appearance, or improve mood.

In the late nineteenth and early twentieth centuries, many food advertisements adopted characters to represent and advertise food, a good number of which remain in use in the twenty-first century. The Quaker Oats Man, America's oldest food advertising icon, appeared in 1877. In 1916 Planters Nuts adopted Mr. Peanut, a cartoon peanut with a top hat, cane, and monocle. The use of advertising icons enabled consumers to identify a company's products quickly.

The rise of television in the mid-twentieth century introduced a new medium with which companies and advertisers could reach consumers. Some companies merely transformed their existing branding for use on television. Green Giant's Jolly Green Giant, which first appeared in print advertisements in 1928, was animated for use in television commercials. The elves named Snap, Crackle, and Pop were introduced in radio commercials for Rice Krispies in 1933 and first appeared on television in the 1960s, when they became prominent fixtures during *Howdy Doody* and other children's shows. Other companies developed characters for use on television or used actors to promote their products.

■ Impacts and Issues

The World Health Organization (WHO) cites obesity and being overweight as a major contributor to the rise of diet-related chronic diseases, including diabetes,

WORDS TO KNOW

DIABETES: Refers to group of metabolic diseases that result in high blood sugar, resulting in frequent urination, increased hunger, and increased thirst.

HYPERTENSION: A chronic medical condition in which an individual's blood pressure is elevated.

OBESITY: Excess amount of body fat; usually defined by a body mass index (BMI) measurement of 30 or more, based on age and gender.

heart disease, hypertension and stroke, and some forms of cancer. WHO cites an increased consumption of high-fat, high-calorie foods as one of the major contributing factors to increasing rates of obese and overweight adults and children. (A reduction in physical activity is cited by WHO as the other major contributing factor.) Children's health advocates note the causal relationship between food advertisements and childhood obesity. Since 1980 the number of overweight children or those at risk of becoming overweight has more than tripled in the United States to 37 percent. The number of overweight and at-risk adolescents in the United States also more than tripled during the same period to 34 percent.

According to a 2007 report by the U.S. Federal Trade Commission, the average American child views 15 television food commercials per day—or almost 5,500 commercials per year. Approximately 98 percent of these advertisements feature foods that are high in fat, calories, or sodium. The majority of the commercials also promote unhealthy eating habits, including snacking (58 percent of commercials), or encourage eating unhealthy foods in order to have fun, be cool, or be happy. A 2009 study by researchers from Yale University in Health Psychology revealed that children exposed to food advertisements during an experiment

A child enjoys a McDonald's Happy Meal, a fast-food boxed meal marketed especially to children. Eleven food and drink companies adopted new rules to limit advertising to children under the age of 12, a move that restricts ads for products such as McDonald's Happy Meals and the use of popular cartoon characters. *AP Images.*

consumed 45 percent more food than children exposed to non-food advertisements. The study found that food advertisements also lead adults to consume more unhealthy foods than adults that were not exposed to food advertisements.

Critics of food advertisements also note that some advertisements perpetuate gender- and race-based stereotypes. Food advertisements often feature a woman preparing meals for her family. Gender stereotypes provide audiences with a cultural frame of reference—although not necessarily an accurate one—through which to view advertisements. Some food advertisements also promote racial stereotypes, usually featuring Native Americans or African-Americans. Native American characters are used in advertisements to promote food products as wholesome, pure, or "of the earth." Land O'Lakes butter and Calumet baking powder continue to represent Native Americans on packaging and advertisements. Aunt Jemima syrup, Uncle Ben's rice, and Cream of Wheat products featured stereotypical African-American characters on their packaging. Following a public criticism, however, advertisers removed Aunt Jemima's stereotypical "mammy" kerchief, and updated the character to a more modern version in the 1960s, and again in 1989.

■ Primary Source Connection

As the following article—published in a U.S. Department of Agriculture (USDA) magazine—discusses, the influx of new technologies and shopping experiences available to the American public creates new opportunities and challenges for food manufacturers, merchants, and advertising agencies. Advertising experts argue that marketing focus is forced to adapt at a remarkable pace. Large food stores and niche market stores must all compete to lure customers. Marketing that relies on communication technologies, such as cell phones and social networking sites, is becoming increasingly common. This type of marketing focuses on ways to attract shoppers with individualized marketing solicitations. In many cases, however, traditional grocers have struggled to compete.

Twenty Years of Competition Reshape the U.S. Food Marketing System

The share of food and beverage (excluding alcohol) manufacturers' media budgets spent on TV advertising fell from 81 percent in 1990 to 64 percent in 2006, illustrating a fragmenting of food advertising media over recent decades. The decline may reflect TV commercial-skipping technologies, such as TiVo, difficulty in measuring ads' effectiveness, and the growing variety of advertising options, including Internet sites and video games.

The Internet accounts for only 2 percent of food manufacturers' advertising expenditures, but it is becoming increasingly important in targeting children, with games and contests built around the brands. Other Internet options include search-related advertising and social networking sites, such as MySpace and Facebook, which allow advertisers to reach a specific demographic segment.

Some companies are turning to video games, cell phones, in-store advertising, and product placement in entertainment programs to tout their brands. To attract teenagers, Coca-Cola is creating a cell-phone networking site for its Sprite brand, similar to online social networking sites. Kroger announced plans to offer in-store television broadcasts that, besides delivering information on new products and promotions, will allow food manufacturers to air commercials. Each store will have programs specific to its location. Food company brands are also featured in movies and at sports events, such as the National Association of Stock Car Racing's (NASCAR) Nextel Cup. PepsiCo Inc.'s Mountain Dew recently financed a documentary on snowboarding, and the brand could be seen occasionally in the movie.

Another factor contributing to more customized marketing and product offerings is changing consumer preferences. The convergence of labor-force participation rates between men and women has increased the value of households' time and convenience foods. New information about the relationship between diet and health has led to increased demand for more healthful foods. As wealthier consumers seek new experiences and ways to broaden their tastes, new niche products allow consumers to express their individuality and social position through food purchases.

Product proliferation, in part, serves the needs and desires of different consumer segments. Each year, thousands of new food and beverage products are introduced. From 1988 to 2007, the number of new product introductions rose by 181 percent. Based on new product claims tracked by Datamonitor, a leading international supplier of information on new packaged products, health and convenience-related attributes accounted for 7 of the top 10 subject categories for claims on packages in 2007. Five of these categories have ranked in the top 10 since 2001, including "natural," "organic," "single serving," "quick," and "fresh." From 2003 to 2007, "upscale" ranked as the leading new product claim category, including "unique" and "premium" products.

Steve Martinez
Phil Kaufman

MARTINEZ, STEVE, AND PHIL KAUFMAN. "TWENTY YEARS OF COMPETITION RESHAPE THE U.S. FOOD MARKETING SYSTEM." *AMBER WAVES*. APRIL (2008): 33–34.

SEE ALSO *Fast Food; Food and the Internet; Food Fads; Food Styling; Gender Equality and Agriculture; Gourmet Hobbyists and Foodies; Junk Food; Movies,*

Documentaries, and Food; Truth in Labeling; Women's Role in Global Food Preparation.

BIBLIOGRAPHY

Books

Cartere, Jason Y. *TV, Food Marketing and Childhood Obesity.* New York: Nova Science, 2009.

Gantz, Walter. *Food for Thought: Television Food Advertising to Children in the United States.* Menlo Park, CA: Henry J. Kaiser Family Foundation, 2007.

Parkin, Katherine J. *Food Is Love: Food Advertising and Gender Roles in Modern America.* Philadelphia: University of Pennsylvania, 2006.

Periodicals

Kelly, Bridget, et al. "Television Food Advertising to Children: A Global Perspective." *American Journal of Public Health* 100, no. 9 (2010): 1730–1736.

Web Sites

"Ban on Fast Food TV Advertising Would Reverse Childhood Obesity Trends, Study Shows." *Science Daily,* November 29, 2008. http://www.sciencedaily.com/releases/2008/11/081119120149.htm (accessed October 31, 2010).

Harris, Jennifer L., John A. Bargh, and Kelly D. Brownell. "Priming Effects of Television Food Advertising on Eating Behavior." *Health Psychology* 28, no. 4, 2009. http://www.yale.edu/acmelab/articles/Harris_Bargh_Brownell_Health_Psych.pdf (accessed October 31, 2010).

Joseph P. Hyder

African Famine Relief

■ Introduction

A famine is a rapid reduction in the availability or supply of food that may be linked to a crop failure or to changing economic conditions. Every reduction in food supply or rapid change in food prices does not necessarily lead to famine. Famine occurs when food supply has been reduced to the point that some residents of an area are unable to feed themselves sufficient amounts of food, and these people suffer from hunger, malnutrition, disease, and even starvation. Following independence, the countries of Sub-Saharan Africa (SSA) experienced a series of famines in the 1970s and 1980s. Famines most often appear in the Sahel, the area just south of the Sahara desert, and in the Horn of Africa. Political unrest and civil war are often correlated with famine, so Somalia, lacking a government since the early 1990s, has been decimated by famine since that time. Repeated famine and other disasters exhaust the ability of smallholder households to cope. Specially formulated fortified foods have helped international food aid programs combat malnutrition during emergencies. Also, a better understanding of how households cope with famine has led to improved programs to prevent households from adopting negative coping strategies such as reducing their food consumption.

■ Historical Background and Scientific Foundations

The countries of Sub-Saharan Africa (SSA) became independent starting in the 1950s and 1960s. Formerly colonies of Western European countries, the region experienced moderate, positive economic growth rates in the 1950s and early 1960s. However, starting in the late 1960s and early 1970s, the Sahel, the region of savanna and dry grasslands just south of the Sahara desert, began to experience a series of droughts. Famines resulted from some of these droughts. Some observers blamed the phenomenon of desertification, in which the Sahara desert was argued to be slowly expanding into the savanna regions as they became increasingly dry and the land unusable for agriculture. Many blamed the practices of smallholder farmers as the source of desertification. While much of the Sahel experienced drought and famine, famine was also triggered in 1973 and 1974 in the Wollo province of Ethiopia, a country in the Horn of Africa, which had not been a European colony. International organizations and relief agencies began to try to combat both desertification and famine through a wide variety of relief and development programs including the distribution of international food aid.

Again, in the early 1980s, several parts of Africa experienced a series of droughts and associated falls in grain production. The countries of southern Africa, such as Botswana and Zimbabwe, did not experience famines during this period however, due at least in part to successful interventions by governments and international organizations to prevent famine. However, in 1984 Ethiopia once again experienced a severe famine that may have resulted in one million deaths, according to United Nations (UN) reports, bringing in the attention of the world press. This famine occurred during a period of civil war and insurgency, including the civil war that eventually led to Eritrea, a province of Ethiopia from 1952 until 1991 along the Red Sea coast, becoming an independent country in 1993. Political turmoil in the Horn of Africa appears to lead to famine often, as famines have recurred since the 1970s in several regions of Ethiopia, in southern Sudan (which fought a war for independence from 1983 to 2004), and in the Darfur region of Sudan, in the first decade of the twenty-first century. Probably the best example of civil war correlating with famine is Somalia.

In Somalia there has been no stable central government since the early 1990s. For years the country was ruled by numerous warlords and fighting clans. Armed patrols prevented passage of supplies to farmers

WORDS TO KNOW

COPING STRATEGY: A way in which a household seeks to avoid the negative consequences of a reduction in income, agricultural production, or livestock production.

POVERTY TRAP: A level of poverty, especially a level of productive assets such as livestock, land, or tools, below which a household no longer has the means to increase income over time. Once a household is in a poverty trap, the household lacks the tools to escape poverty or to improve its condition in any way.

SMALLHOLDER: A farming or livestock-raising rural household with small amounts of land or otherwise limited access to land. Smallholders typically have less than two hectares of arable land, and many have access to far smaller plots.

SOCIAL SAFETY NET (SSN): A public program designed to prevent households from falling into extreme poverty or reducing their consumption of necessary nutrients, medical services, and education.

An aid worker serves *phala*, a maize porridge, to hungry children as part of the Joseph Project feeding program in the village of Kendekeza, Malawi, Africa. *© Joseph Project – Malawi / Alamy.*

and movement of harvested crops and often barred imported staple food and food assistance of international organizations from entering into areas that needed them desperately. The obstacles have led to widespread starvation even in times of successful crop production. In 1992, under the auspices of the United Nations (UN), the United States and other countries sent ground forces into Somalia in an effort to restore the safe movement of goods. For about two years, their mission was successfully accomplished and hunger decreased. But conflict escalated in 1995, and the UN-sponsored forces withdrew after coming under attack. In 2000, under international peace processes, Somalia formed the Transitional National Government (TNG). The TNG was weak and was overthrown for a period of about six months in 2006 by the Council of Islamic Courts (CIC). Although the TNG regained power, as of October 2010 order had not been restored, and Somalia's fighting and civil unrest have involved neighboring countries, such as Ethiopia, Eritrea, Djibouti, and others. The result is that in 2009 the World Food Program reached 3.3 million Somali people in the hope of reducing the world's highest rate of child malnutrition—affecting one of every six children. The conflicts continue to make delivery of assistance difficult and dangerous, and aid deliveries to some areas were suspended in early 2010.

■ Impacts and Issues

Continued climactic stresses, along with the rapid rise in food prices from 2004 until 2008, placed additional stresses on poor smallholder households in Sub-Saharan Africa. These recent stresses may have triggered a famine in Niger, a country in the Sahel in Western Africa, in 2008. When people are consistently exposed to severe stress and trauma, such as that encountered by people living in extreme poverty in the rural areas of Africa, with limited resources, under climatic conditions that repeatedly lead to failed crops, they lose the ability to be resilient. At the initial onset of disaster, a smallholder household may be able to employ coping strategies such as seeking additional day labor opportunities, sending away a household member as a migrant, or drawing down stored food. However in the face of repeated droughts and disasters, reserves on every level become diminished, and smallholder households lose the ability to strive to make their lives better. To lose the ability to slowly increase the level of income over time and to be below the level at which any improvement is possible is known by development economists as falling into a poverty trap.

Success stories in the effort to combat famine and starvation in Africa come both from technological innovations in food fortification and from better understanding of the economics of poverty traps. Widespread

Aid workers and locals in southern Sudan unload bags of unimix, a nutrient-dense grain mixture, delivered to the area by plane. © *Jenny Matthews / Alamy.*

distribution of ready-to-use foods (RTUFs) in emergency situations have saved many lives. RTUFs require no mixing or refrigeration and include high energy biscuits (HEB) for adults and a variety of special foods for malnourished children and infants. Some foods are formulated to be easily digested by children in advanced states of malnutrition. These foods have become less expensive, with the World Food Programme (WFP) estimating that in 2010 it costs 12 U.S. cents to provide 100 grams of HEB or 33 U.S. cents to provide a dose of supplementary peanut paste for malnourished children.

Improved understanding of poverty traps has led to a variety of innovations including new forms of insurance for the poor and improved use and targeting of cash transfers from remittances or government programs. Also, better designed government-sponsored or international organization-sponsored food-for-work and cash-for-work programs take advantage of vulnerable populations' excess labor capacity following disasters and droughts. Most of these relief and development programs seek to provide a social safety net to vulnerable populations so they do not adopt coping strategies that could harm their nutritional status or allow them to fall into a poverty trap.

■ Primary Source Connection

Indian-born Amartya Sen is a professor of economics and philosophy at Harvard University and is best known for his work on the causes of famine. Sen was awarded the 1998 Nobel Prize in economics for his contributions to welfare (development) economics and social choice theory. Sen's work led to practical solutions in preventing or lessening famines, and also considers gender inequalities, ageism, poverty, and illiteracy as it relates to food shortages.

In Sen's 1983 book *Poverty and Famines: An Essay on Entitlement and Deprivation*, he discusses what he sees as the main factors that contributed to the 1972–1974 Ethiopian famine, which killed between 50,000 and 200,000 people. Although this famine was precipitated by a drought and subsequent crop failures in the early 1970s, Sen argues that the decline of food availability is not a sufficient explanation of how and why this disaster occurred. In the following passage from his book, Sen argues the Ethiopian famine was caused primarily by a series of entitlement failures within the country and a hostile market mechanism that prevented people from getting the food they needed.

Poverty and Famines

The famine of 1972–74 in Ethiopia had two rather distinct parts: one affecting the north-east—especially the Wollo province—in 1972–73, and the other happening in the more southern provinces—especially Harerghe—in 1973–74. Total famine mortality seems to have been much higher in the north-eastern famine, for which relief came much too late. While in the north-eastern famine the relative incidence of starvation was probably greatest for the pastoral people, a majority of the famine victims in absolute numbers seem to have come from the agricultural community. In the southern famine—especially in Hareghe—the pastoral population has been the main group to suffer from the famine.

The Ethiopian famine took place with no abnormal reduction in food output, and consumption of food per head of the height of the famine in 1973 was fairly normal for Ethiopia as a whole. While the food output in Wollo was substantially reduced in 1973, the inability of Wollo to command food from outside was the result of the low purchasing power in that province. A remarkable feature of the Wollo famine is that food prices in general rose very little, and people were dying of starvation even when food was selling at prices not very different from predrought levels. The phenomenon can be understood in terms of extensive entitlement failures of various sections of the Wollo population.

The pastoral population—severely affected in both the north-eastern and southern parts of the famine—belonged to nomadic and semi-nomadic groups. They were affected not merely by the drought but also by growth of commercial agriculture, displacing some of these communities from their dry-weather grazing land, thereby vastly heightening the impact of the drought. The effect of the loss of animal stock was also compounded by a severe worsening of terms of trade of animals for grain, disrupting the pastoralist's normal method of meeting his food requirements. The characteristics of exchange relations of the herdsmen by making price movement reinforce—rather than counteract—the decline on the livestock quality, the pastoralist, hit by drought, was decimated by the market mechanism.

Amartya Sen

SEN, AMARTYA. "POVERTY AND FAMINES: AN ESSAY ON ENTITLEMENT AND DEPRIVATION." OXFORD: OXFORD UNIVERSITY PRESS, 1983.

SEE ALSO *Ethical Issues in Food Aid; Famine; Famine: Political Considerations; Food Security; Hunger; International Food Aid; International Fund for Agricultural Development; Malnutrition; Rome Declaration on World Food Security (1996); UN Millennium Development Goals; U.S. Agency for International Development (USAID); World Food Programme.*

BIBLIOGRAPHY

Books

Cliggett, Lisa. *Grains from Grass: Aging, Gender, and Famine in Rural Africa.* Ithaca, NY: Cornell University Press, 2005.

De Waal, Alex. *Famine Crimes: Politics & the Disaster Relief Industry in Africa.* London: African Rights, 2006.

Soyinka, Wole. *Changing Attitudes and Behaviors: The Role of Africa's Cultural Leaders.* Washington, DC: International Food Policy Research Institute, 2007.

Periodicals

"The Horn of Africa—Famine Looms Again." *The Economist* 389, no. 8604 (2008): 44.

"Out of Africa: Famine-Ridden Ethiopia Is Home to New Commercial Farms Growing Fresh Tomatoes and Lettuce—for Export." *Maclean's* 123, no. 32 (2010): 46–47.

Web Sites

"Countries: Sudan." *World Food Programme.* http://www.wfp.org/countries/sudan (accessed October 18, 2010).

"The Current State of World Hunger." *East Africa Famine,* March 19, 2010. http://www.eastafricafamine.com/ (accessed October 18, 2010).

Agenda 21

■ Introduction

Agenda 21 was adopted at the United Nations Conference on Environment and Development (UNCED), which was held in Rio de Janeiro, Brazil, in 1992. Agenda 21 was meant to be a plan of action for sustainable development, including sustainable agriculture and sustainable rural development. The UN Commission on Sustainable Development (CSD) gathers information, encourages programs, and reports on progress toward adoption of Agenda 21 by signatory countries. Proponents of Agenda 21 state that sustainable development, including sustainable agricultural and rural development, will use environmentally friendly technologies to meet the challenge of increased need for food production. Critics of Agenda 21 point to its deterministic view of population and carrying capacity and worry that it is unsuited to meet the natural resource challenges of the twenty-first century.

■ Historical Background and Scientific Foundations

Building upon a long history of other United Nations (UN) environmental conferences, starting with the UN Conference on the Human Environment in Stockholm, Sweden, in 1972, environmental activists pleaded for international bodies and national government to consider the environmental aspects of development throughout the 1970s and 1980s. As this view that the environment must be considered as countries industrialized and increased their populations became more common, the UN system organized a response through the UN Conference on Environment and Development (UNCED) which was held in Rio de Janeiro, Brazil, from June 3–14, 1992. This conference is also known as the Rio Earth Summit. Among the documents

adopted at the UNCED was Agenda 21, a plan of action for sustainable development. Following the Brundtland Report, which was published by the United Nations-sponsored World Commission on the Environment and Development in 1987 under the title *Our Common Future*, sustainable development was defined as "the ability to meet the needs of the present without compromising the ability of future generations to meet their needs." This concept of environmental protection and conservation for sustainable development rests on the idea of intergenerational equity: Resources should be evenly available between generations, so they must be conserved for the future. Because agriculture and food production are major users of land and environmental resources, agriculture was one topic of the UNCED and of Agenda 21.

The UN Commission for Sustainable Development (CSD) was established in 1992 as an adjunct to Agenda 21. Its charge is to ensure that decisions made at UNCED, including Agenda 21, are carried out at national, regional, and international levels, and to further international cooperation and decision-making on these issues. The full Commission meets once per year. Ad hoc working groups meet periodically to address specific issues, including trade and environmental development, consumption patterns, financial resources, and technology transfer. Open-ended working groups address such issues as integrated management of land resources, forests, combating desertification, sustainable mountain development, sustainable agriculture, rural development, and biological diversity.

In 2002 the role of the CSD was evaluated at the World Summit on Sustainable Development (WSSD) in Johannesburg, South Africa, as part of a 10-year review of the 1992 Earth Summit. The WSSD reaffirmed the mandate and functions of the CSD. The WSSD review also expanded the role of the CSD to accommodate the sustainable development goals that emerged from the Johannesburg summit.

WORDS TO KNOW

CARRYING CAPACITY: The ability of an ecosystem to sustain a certain population of a species. The carrying capacity defines the maximum load of population the ecosystem can support without disrupting other species' populations.

INTERGENERATIONAL EQUITY: The principle that the actions of one generation must take into account their impact on subsequent generations, and that some resources must be preserved for use by future generations.

SUSTAINABLE DEVELOPMENT: According to the Brundtland Report published by the United Nations-sponsored World Commission on the Environment and Development in 1987 under the title *Our Common Future,* "the ability to meet the needs of the present without compromising the ability of future generations to meet their needs."

■ Impacts and Issues

Proponents of Agenda 21 and of sustainable agriculture and sustainable development point to the problem of an increasing population needing an increasing amount of food. In the words of Agenda 21, "Agriculture has to meet this challenge, mainly by increasing production on land already in use and by avoiding further encroachment on land that is only marginally suitable for cultivation." To meet this challenge and protect the environment, ensuring intergenerational equity, lower impact agricultural methods will need to be found. Reducing the use of inputs produced from natural gas, such as nitrogen fertilizer, and a variety of other chemicals used in agricultural production is seen as one way to protect the environment. However, many of the increases in yields per hectare in the second half of the twentieth century came from heavy use of inputs such as nitrogen fertilizers. New technologies, revival of traditional technologies, and better policy, education, and management are hoped to increase yields over time without degrading the land or the environment.

Most proponents of and the writers of Agenda 21 have what their critics refer to as a neo-Malthusian view of the relationship between population and land. According to the writings of British economist Thomas Robert Malthus (1766–1834), an increasing population only serves to impoverish that population through falling wages. A larger population simply cannot be maintained on a certain amount of land in this view. So Agenda 21 proposes that, at least in lower yielding agricultural regions, "conserving

The BedZed eco development in the London neighborhood of Beddington aims to be energy-efficient and carbon neutral. Agenda 21 encourages the development of sustainable human housing and the transfer of technology from developed to less-developed nations to facilitate sustainable growth everywhere. © *Global Warming Images / Alamy.*

and rehabilitating the natural resources on lower potential lands in order to maintain sustainable man/land ratios is also necessary" or in other words, population growth must be limited to the carrying capacity of the land.

Critics of neo-Malthusian views come from several angles. In non-equilibrium ecology, a field emerging primarily from work in grasslands and drylands known as the new range ecology, carrying capacity can be based only on a static view of the environment, an environment at equilibrium. Because non-equilibrium ecology studies systems in which the environment is constantly changing and adapting, no carrying capacity can be calculated. In this view, population density or a person/land ratio is difficult or impossible to calculate in a dynamic natural environment. These ecologists doubt the ability of current scientific management practices to preserve natural resources for future generations, as proposed throughout Agenda 21. Other critics point to the ability of technology to overcome limitations to population. Other critics argue that inequalities within countries and between countries within a single generation are a much bigger problem than intergenerational equity. These critics worry that a focus on sustainability serves to limit the options of developing countries and to keep these countries in poverty by restraining their development.

SEE ALSO *Agroecology; Food Security; Population and Food; Sustainable Agriculture.*

BIBLIOGRAPHY

Books

Culture 21: Agenda 21 for Culture. Barcelona, Spain: Institut de Cultura de Barcelona, 2007.

Implementing Agenda 21. Geneva, Switzerland: United Nations Economic and Social Council, 2002.

Overview of Progress towards Sustainable Development: A Review of the Implementation of Agenda 21, the Programme for the Further Implementation of Agenda 21 and the Johannesburg Plan of Implementation: Report of the Secretary-General. New York: United Nations, 2010.

Robinson, Nicholas A. *Strategies toward Sustainable Development: Implementing Agenda 21.* Dobbs Ferry, NY: Oceana Publications, 2004.

Web Sites

"Agenda 21." *Division for Sustainable Development, UN Department of Economic and Social Affairs.* http://www.un.org/esa/dsd/agenda21/ (accessed October 18, 2010).

Agribusiness

■ Introduction

An agribusiness can be any business involved in any aspect of agriculture. Agribusinesses include firms all along the value chain. A value chain refers to the chain of processes and trades between the farmer and the final consumer. Agribusinesses include firms such as input suppliers that produce and sell seeds, fertilizers, pesticides, herbicides, and animal feed. Food processors are the agribusinesses that buy raw goods from farmers and transform them into processed foods, beverages, fiber products, forest products, and tobacco products. Other firms are directly involved in agriculture, such as agricultural equipment manufacturers, banks or credit unions that provide agricultural loans, veterinary services firms, manufacturers of veterinary medicines, and insurance agencies that specialize in crop or weather insurance for farms. Additionally, some definitions of agribusiness include firms further down the value chain such as restaurants, food retail businesses, or traders in wet markets or green markets. Some critics of agribusiness use the term to mean larger, typically multinational firms that they accuse of unfairly extracting profits from the value chain and participating in a variety of supposed abuses in their business practices.

■ Historical Background and Scientific Foundations

Although the term agribusiness probably did not start being commonly used in the English language until the 1950s, by the 1970s university departments of agribusiness and master's degree programs in agribusiness were common. The roots of agribusiness go back much further into history. Some of the first joint stock companies would be called agribusinesses in the early twenty-first century. For example, the British East India Company, founded in 1600, primarily traded cotton, silk, and indigo from India. However, the start of many modern agribusinesses can be traced to the increasing use of fertilizers from bone meal and guano in the early part of the nineteenth century in Europe and the Americas. By the end of the nineteenth century, technological changes had produced a wide variety of active agribusinesses in Europe and the Americas, which were involved in many lines of business that continue to this day such as: the manufacturing of tractors, hybrid corn seed production, slaughter-houses and meatpacking, the production of branded canned foods, and refrigerated transport by rail and ship.

Agribusiness has grown in terms of the roles it plays in agriculture and in terms of its geographic scope in the twentieth and twenty-first centuries. One way in which agribusiness has expanded is through contracts. Contracts with individual farmers and producers enable agribusinesses to receive raw materials from farmers or products supplied by manufacturers that meet certain specifications and give agribusinesses the means to protect their intellectual property. Contracts have vastly increased the scope of agribusiness and cover almost every imaginable matter from specifying how a farmer will use seeds that have just been purchased to guaranteeing forward prices for delivery of a product on a particular date.

At the start of the twentieth century, agricultural commodities would primarily be traded through spot markets instead of contracts. Spot markets are places where buyers and sellers who do not necessarily know each other may meet, such as at crop or livestock auctions, physical commodity markets, grain elevators, wholesale markets, farmers' markets, or green markets. Transactions at these markets are, in economics, called arms length transactions, since presumably the buyer and seller interact. As use of contracts increases, they have virtually eliminated the use of spot markets for some crops and livestock products. The lower volume of products in spot markets may increase price volatility in those spot markets as they will presumably have price reactions more quickly due to decreased supply and demand. Reduced volume or closed spot market opportunities may reduce choices for farmers regarding where and when they sell their production.

Large agribusinesses tend not to actually operate farms to provide their raw materials or to use their inputs. According to the data from the 2005 agricultural census conducted by the U.S. Department of Agriculture's (USDA) National Agricultural Statistics Service (NASS), corporations not owned by a single family only made up to 0.4 percent of total number of U.S. farms and up to 7 percent of total U.S. farm sales for the preceding five years. Though average farm size has increased in most of the developed world and in developing parts of Latin America, large corporations still tend not to be in the business of owning or operating farms. Instead, larger agribusinesses use contracts with farmers and landowners to receive raw materials or otherwise limit the ways in which their product is used.

Another way agribusinesses have expanded has been through horizontal integration. Agribusinesses tend to expand across a single step in the value chain, and many agribusinesses use this strategy to expand into additional countries. Horizontal integration, by spreading geographically and repeating the same process in multiple locations, differs from vertical integration. In vertical integration, for example, a single company or a parent company might produce various parts of a product, such as a car, in factories it owns or controls and then assembles these parts, with all trade occurring within a single company or parent company. The car company may control the manufacturing process for all the parts and even have special dealerships to sell the finished car to the final customer. In horizontal integration, on the other hand, a seed company based in the Netherlands may seek to sell seeds in many other countries. It is unlikely that a seed company would also move into wholesaling or retailing of the tomatoes grown from those seeds or produce tomato paste from tomatoes grown from the seeds. A food processor or soft drink producer may produce the same product but set up processing facilities in every country in which it operates.

Several explanations have been offered for why agribusiness and the food industry operate based on horizontal integration internationally instead of the vertical integration more typical of manufactured goods. First, agribusinesses may do this as a means to protect their technology. Second, agricultural trade continues to face high tariffs and a variety of non-tariff barriers to international trade unique to food, agricultural products, and plant and animal genetic materials. Third, some food products have a limited shelf life or a high weight relative to their value, such as soda or beer, which increases the advantage of being located near local markets. For these reasons and others, international agribusinesses tend to expand horizontally.

WORDS TO KNOW

AGRIBUSINESS: Any business involved at any point in the value chain in agriculture, livestock production, or the food industry. For some critics of agribusiness, the term refers to large, typically multinational firms that these critics accuse of having unfair market power.

HORIZONTAL INTEGRATION: Controlling a single step or stage of a value chain.

VALUE CHAIN: A series of steps between a raw material and a finished good that reaches a final consumer.

■ Impacts and Issues

Larger agribusinesses and international agribusinesses have been accused of many wrongdoings, related to environmental practices, food safety, labor practices, and intellectual property. One of the most controversial accusations was against the Swiss agribusiness Nestle in 1977. Nestle was accused of improperly marketing infant formula, also called breast milk substitute, in several developing countries to mothers of children who may not have been able to read the directions or may not have had clean water with which to reconstitute the formula. Some activists accused Nestle of promoting formula at the expense of breastfeeding. In 1984 Nestle changed its infant formula marketing practices partially in response to this boycott. In this case, the critics of agribusiness brought evidence of wrongdoing forward and promoted change in industry practices.

More contemporary critics of larger agribusinesses point to a variety of potential abuses. The use of migrant labor by agribusinesses for picking horticultural crops such as tomatoes and lettuce, in seed breeding operations, and in food processing may lead to abuse of labor rights. Especially in the United States, agribusinesses large and small have been accused of withholding wages from migrant and minority workers, using known illegal immigrants, and contributing to the problem of human trafficking. Legislation proposed in 2001 to guard against child trafficking and slavery among Africa's chocolate producers was opposed by the industry, which pledged to eliminate the problem. The resulting Harkin-Engle Protocol pledged to develop certification standards for slave labor-free chocolate and to eliminate child slave labor in chocolate production by 2005. Neither objective was met.

Intellectual property protections, specifically of some of the genetically modified seed patents in the United States held by Monsanto, have caused accusations that Monsanto is disrupting normal seed use patterns by farmers and is abusive toward small farmers in enforcement of its

Workers process freshly harvested bananas at a plantation in northeastern Costa Rica owned by U.S.-based agribusiness Dole. The bananas are soaked in water to remove pests and a sticky resin that is exuded by the plant. © *Martin Shields / Alamy.*

seed purchase contracts. Monsanto does not allow its genetically modified seeds to be saved and reused, which is common practice with other seeds. Monsanto takes these actions to protect its market and to protect the research investments the company has made in developing these seeds. Purchasers are aware of these restrictions, but some critics question the right of a company to own rights to a seed variety in this manner and to enforce these rights by actively searching for misuse of its seed.

Also, agribusinesses receive blame from some critics for producing and promoting high calorie, ready-to-eat foods. These snack foods are certainly an attractive market for larger agribusinesses as they are often low cost to produce and are sometimes shelf stable, not requiring a cold chain, a series of refrigerated or frozen transport and storage facilities, to distribute fresh meat, cheese, or ice cream. These products proliferated starting in the nineteenth century in the developed countries and have spread to most developing countries. However, the supply side is only part of the rise of these low nutrient, calorie dense foods, as consumers continue to purchase these foods in a variety of retail markets.

■ Primary Source Connection

The U.S. Department of Agriculture (USDA) publishes a journal called *Amber Waves* dedicated to the "Economics of Food, Farming, Natural Resources, and Rural America." It is published four times a year. The following article on the benefits and perils of agricultural or agribusiness contracts was a Best of *Amber Waves* 2004 award winner.

Contract Use Continues to Expand

The desire for specific attributes in agricultural products is making contracts the method of choice for moving products through the production and marketing system. These attributes cover everything from oil content in corn, which affects feed digestion, to the weight of market hogs, because uniform weights can reduce processing costs. Other examples include milk produced according to organic standards, or attributes tied to a product's delivery, such as a certain volume of peas provided during a specified time window, that can reduce processing costs and better meet consumer demands.

Buyers—processors, elevators, and retailers—use production contracts to control input choices and production methods. They also use marketing contracts that offer farmers price premiums for desired attributes. Farmers can benefit from contracting as well, in that contracts can reduce income risks, ease credit requirements, and provide higher prices for providing specific product attributes.

But there are downsides to contracting. Specific features of contracts, like requiring use of a specific feed ration, can limit farmers' decision making freedom. Contracts can reduce volumes traded on spot markets (where individual buyers and sellers agree to a price at the time the product changes hands), thereby increasing price volatility and risks of trading in spot markets. They can also be structured to limit competition among buyers.

An observed expansion in contract use is closely tied to consolidation in agriculture. Among farms with at least $500,000 in annual sales, 61 percent used contracts for at least some of their production in 2001, compared with only 8 percent of farms with sales under $250,000. Because most farms are small, only 11 percent of all farms used contracts in 2001, up from 6 percent in 1969. But because large farms account for most agricultural production, contracts cover a large and growing share of production—36 percent in 2001, up from 12 percent in 1969 and 28 percent in 1991.

The use of contracts can spread rapidly through an industry. Virtually nonexistent in tobacco marketing in 1999, contracts covered half of 2001 production and almost 100 percent of 2002 production. In just 5 years, from 1996 to 2001, contract coverage grew from one-third to two-thirds of hog production, as spot markets commensurately diminished. By 2001, contracts covered 54 percent of cotton and 39 percent of rice production, compared with 30 percent and 20 percent, respectively, in 1991.

Growing demand for specific product attributes should lead to continuing expansion of contracting. In turn, spot markets will come under continuing pressure to adapt to the challenge posed by the contracting alternative, by providing better means of defining, measuring, and communicating product attributes.

James MacDonald
Janet Perry

MACDONALD, JAMES, AND JANET PERRY. "CONTRACT USE CONTINUES TO EXPAND." *AMBER WAVES.* NOVEMBER (2004): 5–6.

SEE ALSO *Advertising Food; Agricultural Land Reform; Agriculture and International Trade; Banana Trade Wars; Biofuels and World Hunger; Breastfeeding; Commission on Genetic Resources for Food and Agriculture; Decollectivization; Ethical Issues in Agriculture; Fair Trade; Family Farms; Food Sovereignty; Free Trade and Agriculture; Genetically Modified Organisms (GMO); Import Restrictions; Infant Formula and Baby Food; International Federation of Organic Agriculture Movements; International Fund for Agricultural Development; Political Food Boycotts; Sustainable Agriculture; U.S. Department of Agriculture (USDA); World Trade Organization (WTO).*

BIBLIOGRAPHY

Books

Hamilton, Lisa M. *Deeply Rooted: Unconventional Farmers in the Age of Agribusiness.* Berkeley, CA: Counterpoint, 2009.

Jansen, Kees, and Sietze Vellema. *Agribusiness and Society: Corporate Responses to Environmentalism, Market Opportunities and Public Regulation.* London: Zed Books, 2004.

Larsen, Kurt, Ronald Kim, and Florian Theus. *Agribusiness and Innovation Systems in Africa.* Washington, DC: World Bank, 2009.

Ricketts, Cliff, and Kristina Ricketts. *Agribusiness: Fundamentals and Applications.* Clifton Park, NY: Delmar Cengage Learning, 2009.

Periodicals

"Agribusiness Is Booming." *Business Week New York* (October 20, 2008): 50–51.

Tillotson, James. "Agribusiness—The Backbone of Our Diet for Better—or for Worse, Part 1." *Nutrition Today* 41, no. 5 (2006): 233–238.

Web Sites

"Agribusiness." *North Dakota State University, College of Agriculture, Food Systems, and Natural Resources.* http://www.ndsu.edu/ndsu/academic/factsheets/ag/agbus.shtml (accessed September 9, 2010).

"Large Agribusiness Hurting Small Landholders, Says UN Rights Expert." *UN News Centre,* March 5, 2010. http://www.un.org/apps/news/story.asp?NewsID=33984&Cr=agriculture&Cr1= (accessed September 9, 2010).

Blake Jackson Stabler

Agricultural Deforestation

■ Introduction

Deforestation refers to the process by which humans clear forested land, generally for use in agriculture or for raw materials. For millennia, humans have cut forests for agricultural purposes, such as growing crops or raising livestock. Humans have also exploited forests to obtain wood for fuel, for material for building structures and ships, or for producing paper or other wood products.

Deforestation causes a host of environmental, social, and economic problems, particularly in the absence of proper forest management. Slash-and-burn is one of the primary deforestation techniques. Slash-and-burn involves cutting trees for timber or other purposes, and then burning the remaining trees, stumps, and brush. Although this method quickly clears the land for growing crops or raising livestock, it contributes to global climate change, habitat loss, desertification, and other environmental problems. Slash-and-burn also produces poor soil, which, after a few growing seasons, often requires farmers to move on to another part of the forest.

■ Historical Background and Scientific Foundations

Archaeological evidence indicates that deforestation began occurring during the Mesolithic period. Pollen records indicate a dramatic decline in oak, ash, and elm populations in Europe between 8600 and 7000 BC. Archaeologists hold that Mesolithic peoples cleared land to allow for easier hunting of game. With the rise of agriculture, the demand for open land for farming increased. The people of the Late Mesolithic and Early Neolithic periods used axes and fire to clear large swaths of forests.

Deforestation became the norm for most preindustrial civilizations around the world. In addition to the need for cleared land for crops and livestock grazing, wood became a vital source of energy and served as one of the predominant building and shipbuilding materials.

The tremendous demand for agricultural land and wood led to significant deforestation around settlements and towns, which were relocated frequently once inhabitants consumed the forest's raw materials or the agricultural land became unproductive—a common problem in deforested areas.

■ Impacts and Issues

Whether for agricultural or other purposes, deforestation is destructive to the environment and the economic and social lives of indigenous peoples. In addition to potentially devastating effects on local ecosystems, deforestation may affect regional and even the global environment by polluting the atmosphere, altering weather patterns, silting rivers, and destroying biodiversity, in addition to other adverse consequences.

According to a 2007 report by the United Nations Framework Convention on Climate Change, "Investment and Financial Flows to Address Climate Change," approximately 13 million hectares (32,123,700 acres), or 130,000 square kilometers (50,193 square miles) of forests were cleared each year between 2000 and 2005. The rate of deforestation varies greatly by region. According to the Food and Agriculture Organization (FAO) of the United Nations, between 2000 and 2005 Central America, South Asia, and Southeast Asia experienced the greatest deforestation rate with an annual loss of 1.2 percent of remaining forests. Tropical Asia followed with a 1 percent annual deforestation rate. Eastern, Southern, and Northern Africa lost forests at an annual rate of 0.7 percent. Reforestation efforts produced an increase in forested areas in East Asia, Europe, and the Caribbean.

Among individual countries, Brazil and Indonesia accounted for more than 50 percent of global deforestation between 2000 and 2005. The demand for cleared land for cattle grazing and soybean production in Brazil and for coffee and palm oil production in Indonesia were the primary reasons for deforestation in these countries.

During the same period, China accounted for approximately 80 percent of reforestation efforts. China's forests grew by more than 4,000,000 hectares (9,884,215 acres) per year from 2000 to 2005.

Subsistence agriculture is the greatest driver of deforestation. Subsistence agriculture accounts for approximately 42 percent of all deforestation each year. The use of wood for fuel and other household uses accounts for 6 percent of annual deforestation. Commercial agriculture is behind 32 percent of annual deforestation, with commercial crop production resulting in 20 percent of deforestation and livestock ranching responsible for 12 percent. Commercial wood extraction for building materials, commercial fuel wood and charcoal, and other commercial uses account for the remaining 20 percent of global deforestation annually.

Deforestation produces extensive environmental damage, regardless of the method used or reason for deforestation. Trees capture and store carbon dioxide (CO_2), a major greenhouse gas and one of the primary contributors to global climate change. The United Nations Environment Programme (UNEP) estimates that the world's forests store 283 gigatonnes (metric), or 312 gigatons (short tons), of carbon. When forests are burned, they release CO_2 into the atmosphere, which

contributes to global climate change. UNEP estimates that deforestation released 1.1 gigatonnes (metric) or 1.2 gigatons (short tons) of carbon into the atmosphere annually between 1990 and 2005. Deforestation,

Farmers burn rain forests to clear farmland for raising cattle and soybeans in the Amazon, west of Juara city in the upper Mato Grosso state, Brazil, on September 18, 2008. As demand for meat increases across the globe, high prices for livestock food grains are encouraging farmers to increase soybean and corn production, removing massive tracks of pristine forest in their wake. *AP Images.*

therefore, produces more greenhouse gas emissions each year than the transportation sector.

Deforestation may also result in numerous environmental and agricultural issues related to the soil, including erosion, nutrient loss, siltation of rivers and streams, and desertification. The roots of trees and other plants hold soil in place. The cycle of growth and decay also maintains the balance of nutrients that plants need to grow. Once an area is cleared of its forests, soil erosion typically occurs at a much higher rate. Much of this soil washes away into streams and rivers. Siltation of rivers contributes to turbidity in water, which may increase the prevalence of some waterborne diseases and reduce the presence of aquatic plants. A reduction in aquatic plants typically results in decreased fish populations.

Deforestation also reduces biodiversity by destroying the habitats on which many species of flora and fauna rely. According to a United Nations report, "Global Biodiversity Outlook 3," forests cover 31 percent of the Earth's land surface but contain more than 50 percent of the world's terrestrial flora and fauna species. The majority of these forest-dependent, terrestrial plant and animal species are found in tropical forests.

In many regions, deforestation has produced tension between commercial agricultural interests and indigenous peoples. The United Nations' "Global Biodiversity Outlook 3" report states that the traditions and tribal laws of indigenous peoples are responsible for preserving large tracts of forest. Between four million and eight million square kilometers (1,544,408 to 3,088,817 square miles) of forests are governed by indigenous peoples as community conserved areas (CCAs). Commercial agriculture interests that clear these areas for grazing or cultivation deprive these indigenous peoples of the forests on which their livelihoods have relied for centuries.

The United Nations, World Bank, and other international organizations increasingly have focused on reducing deforestation. Their efforts have included reforestation, forest management, and providing an economic incentive not to cut forests. Between 2000 and 2005, reforestation efforts resulted in the planting of approximately 8,000,000 hectares (19,768,431 acres) of new forests each year. Proper forest management results in a more productive use of forest resources, thereby negating the need to clear additional forest.

Because deforestation contributes to global climate change by both releasing carbon and preventing the capture of additional carbon, global climate change initiatives have been concerned with deforestation. Reducing Emissions from Deforestation and Forest Degradation (REDD) is a policy that provides economic incentives to curtail deforestation in order to reduce greenhouse gas emissions. International negotiations over a comprehensive global climate change and greenhouse gas reduction treaty indicate that REDD will be a primary component of such an agreement.

■ Primary Source Connection

David Kaimowitz, one of the authors of the following article, "Soybean Technology and the Loss of Natural Vegetation in Brazil and Bolivia," holds a Ph.D. in agricultural economics. He directs the Natural Assets and Sustainability Department of the Ford Foundation. In addition, he has served as a principal economist with the Center for International Forestry Research (CIFOR). Joyotee Smith is an economist with CIFOR.

CABI (Commonwealth Agricultural Bureaux International) is a not-for-profit science-based organization that is involved in publishing and projects that help solve agricultural and environmental problems of global concern.

Soybean Technology and the Loss of Natural Vegetation in Brazil and Bolivia

Thirty-five years ago, South American farmers grew virtually no soybeans. Now, Brazilian farmers plant almost 13 million ha of soybeans and Brazil ranks as the world's second largest exporter (Waino, 1998). Bolivian farmers cultivate an additional 470,000 ha (Pacheco, 1998).

Soybean expansion in southern Brazil contributed to deforestation by stimulating migration to agricultural frontier regions in the Amazon and the Cerrado. Since producing soybeans requires much less labour than producing coffee or food crops, when soybeans replaced those crops many small farmers and rural labourers lost their jobs and moved to the frontier. Elsewhere, in the Brazilian Cerrado and in Bolivia, farmers cleared large areas of Cerrado vegetation (natural savannah and open woodlands) and semi-deciduous forest to plant soybeans.

Technology was the key in all this. In a sense, soybeans themselves were a new technology, since, up to the 1970s, Brazilian and Bolivian farmers knew little about how to produce them. The development of new varieties adapted to the tropics and the use of soil amendments permitted farmers to grow soybeans in the low latitudes and poor acid soils of the Brazilian Cerrado. More generally, new varieties, inoculants, pest control agents, postharvest technologies and cultural practices made growing soybeans more profitable in both Bolivia and Brazil and stimulated their expansion.

Favourable policies and market conditions reinforced the new technologies' effect. Together, they helped soybean production attain a level that justified establishing the associated services and infrastructure competitive soybean production requires. High international prices and government subsidies encouraged the spread of soybeans in Brazil. Export promotion policies, favourable exchange rates and preferential access to the Andean market stimulated Bolivia's production. In both countries, road construction, government land grants and rising domestic demand for soybeans accelerated the crop's advance. This in turn increased the political power of the soybean lobby and enabled farmers and processors to obtain further government support.

David Kaimowitz
Joyotee Smith

KAIMOWITZ, DAVID, AND JOYOTEE SMITH. "SOYBEAN TECHNOLOGY AND THE LOSS OF NATURAL VEGETATION IN BRAZIL AND BOLIVIA." *AGRICULTURAL TECHNOLOGIES AND TROPICAL DEFORESTATION.* EDITED BY ALRID ANGELSEN AND DAVID KAIMOWITZ. NEW YORK: CABI PUBLISHING, 2001: 195–196.

SEE ALSO *Agroecology; Biodiversity and Food Supply; Climate Change and Agriculture; Desertification and Agriculture; Ecological Impacts of Various World Diets; Free Trade and Agriculture; Land Availability and Degradation; Subsistence Farming; Sustainable Agriculture.*

BIBLIOGRAPHY

Books

Cairns, Malcolm. *Voices from the Forest: Integrating Indigenous Knowledge into Sustainable Upland Farming.* Washington, DC: Resources for the Future, 2007.

Chomitz, Kenneth M., and Piet Buys. *At Loggerheads?: Overview: Agricultural Expansion, Poverty Reduction, and Environment in the Tropical Forests.* Washington, DC: World Bank, 2007.

Gradwohl, Judith, and Russell Greenberg. *Saving the Tropical Forests.* London: Earthscan, 2009 (originally published 1988).

Greenpeace International. *Eating up the Amazon.* Amsterdam: Greenpeace, 2006.

Millington, A. C., and Wendy Jepson. *Land-Change Science in the Tropics: Changing Agricultural Landscapes.* New York: Springer, 2008.

Palm, C. A. *Slash-and-Burn Agriculture: The Search for Alternatives.* New York: Columbia University Press, 2005.

Periodicals

Benhin, James K. A. "Agriculture and Deforestation in the Tropics: A Critical Theoretical and Empirical Review." *Ambio* 351 (2006): 9.

Carr, David. "Population and Deforestation: Why Rural Migration Matters." *Progress in Human Geography* 33, no. 3 (2009): 355–378.

Pacheco, Pablo. "Smallholder Livelihoods, Wealth and Deforestation in the Eastern Amazon." *Human Ecology* 37, no 1 (2009): 27–41.

Web Sites

"Slashing Slash-and-Burn Agriculture." *USAID.* http://www.usaid.gov/stories/madagascar/ss_mdg_slash.html (accessed August 3, 2010).

Joseph P. Hyder

Agricultural Demand for Water

■ Introduction

The rise of agriculture—the practice of farming to raise crops and livestock—is one of the key developments in the rise of human civilization. Agriculture enabled nomadic hunter-and-gatherer societies to settle in more densely populated communities. Early farmers, however, discovered that relying solely on the weather to supply crops and animals with water could have disastrous consequences in times of drought or other severe weather. Human civilizations developed methods of supplying crops and animals with a consistent supply of water from rivers, lakes, and aquifers through a process known as irrigation.

The amount of water required for agriculture varies greatly depending on the crop grown or livestock raised, the applied technology, and the production level. Modern agriculture accounts for approximately 70 percent of the world's water usage. Inefficient irrigation methods result in the loss of between 15 and 35 percent of all irrigation water, primarily through evaporation or runoff. Animal husbandry places an even greater burden on water resources, because livestock requires greater water input than crops to produce an equal weight of product.

■ Historical Background and Scientific Foundations

Archaeological evidence indicates that humans in Egypt and Mesopotamia employed irrigation as early as the sixth millennium BC. The Egyptians and Mesopotamian civilizations would divert water from the Nile and Tigris-Euphrates river systems, respectively, into nearby fields. After several weeks of inundation, depending on the growth cycle of each crop, the water would be diverted back to the river system. The Egyptian pharaoh Menes undertook the world's first large scale irrigation project around 3100 BC. Menes and his successors constructed a series of dams and canals, one of which was 12 miles

(20 kilometers) long, to divert flood waters from the Nile to a lake that served as a reservoir.

As civilizations became more dependent on agriculture, irrigation became prevalent around the world. Archaeological evidence shows that civilizations in the Andes Mountains of modern day Peru constructed irrigation canals in the fourth millennium BC, and the Indus River civilization of modern day India and Pakistan created large-scale canal and reservoir systems around 2600 BC. Over the centuries, irrigation systems became more complex. In China around 600 BC, Sunshu Ao, a court minister and engineer, constructed a dam that created a large reservoir that reportedly irrigated 2,428,000 hectares (6,000,000 acres) of land. In 256 BC Chinese engineers constructed a levee and cut a 66 feet (20 meters) wide channel through a mountain to divert water from the Min River to a reservoir. This irrigation system, the Dujiangyan irrigation system, continues to provide water for the irrigation of 530,000 hectares (1,300,000 acres) of land.

The demand for irrigation prompted numerous innovations to transport water across distances, uphill, or without the use of floodwaters. Around 2000 BC the Mesopotamians developed the shadoof (or shaduf) to transport water from rivers, canals, and reservoirs to fields or different canals. A shadoof consists of a bucket tied to the end of a counterbalanced pole that is mounted on a crossbeam. With minimal effort water may be raised and then swung to and emptied into a field or canal. The shadoof permits irrigation when rivers are not at flood stage and enables the irrigation of higher ground.

As early as 1000 BC the Persians developed the qanat, a system of underground channels that delivers a constant supply of groundwater to lower elevations. Approximately 20,000 qanats are still in use around the world. In late centuries, numerous civilizations, including China, Egypt, Greece, Persia, and Rome, used waterwheels to move water. Waterwheels consist of a large wheel with buckets around its perimeter. As the wheel turns, the buckets dip into and fill with water, which is then lifted and dumped into a channel. Waterwheels may be powered by humans or animals or the flow of a river.

■ Impacts and Issues

Irrigation fueled the rise of industrial agriculture beginning in the nineteenth century. Industrial agriculture has enabled food production to keep pace with the world's rapidly growing human population. In 1800, fewer than 8,000,000 hectares (19,760,000 acres) of land was irrigated, whereas in the early twenty-first century, approximately 250,000,000 hectares (618,000,000 acres) of land is irrigated for crop production. The increased demand for water for irrigation has resulted in numerous problems, including the exhaustion of water supplies and conflict over water sources.

Technological innovations have decreased the amount of water required for irrigation. However, the irrigation systems that conserve water are often prohibitively expensive in many parts of the world.

Inundation is the oldest form of large-scale crop irrigation. This method involves flooding a field and then draining the water away or allowing it to evaporate. Inundation irrigation is water-intensive because much of the water is lost to evaporation. It continues used in many parts of the world, particularly for growing rice.

Sprinkler irrigation is one of the most common forms of large-scale irrigation utilized on modern farms. Sprinkler irrigation uses high-pressure sprinklers or

A sprinkler irrigates crops on a farm near Wiggins, Colorado, an area prone to water use restrictions because of scarcity. *AP Images.*

This aerial view of circular pivot farming in the American southwest illustrates the dry desert that surrounds the irrigated areas. Though pivot irrigation wastes less water than some other methods, it is frequently used in extremely dry climates and usually pulls fossil water deposits from underground aquifers, an unsustainable method of irrigation. *Image copyright Glenn Young, 2010. Used under license from Shutterstock.com.*

guns to spray water over a large area of crops. It is more water-efficient than inundation irrigation, but some water is still lost to evaporation and runoff. Drip irrigation, like sprinkler irrigation, uses pipes to deliver water to crops. Drip irrigation, however, slowly applies water near the roots of the plants. Drip irrigation is water-efficient and minimizes evaporation and runoff. Drip irrigation systems, however, are typically more expensive than sprinkler systems.

Raising livestock requires a more intensive agricultural use of water than crop irrigation. The spread of the Western diet, which is high in meat consumption, is one of the greatest threats to the world's future supply of fresh water. People who once relied primarily on vegetables and grains in their diets have increased meat consumption in recent decades as incomes have risen in many parts of the world. Raising cattle and other livestock requires a far greater input of water per weight output than growing crops.

A 2004 study by the International Water Management Institute (IWMI) concludes that increased meat consumption will stress water systems around the world.

According to IWMI, 2.2 pounds (1 kg) of beef requires approximately 2,557 gallons (9,680 liters) of water input. However, 2.2 pounds (1 kg) of wheat only requires 473 gallons (1,790 liters) of water to grow. On average, people who consume a large amount of meat in their diets require approximately 1,321 gallons (5,000 liters) of water input to produce the food they consume each day. People in developing countries with vegetarian diets require only 264 to 528 gallons (1,000 to 2,000 liters) of water to produce their daily food supply.

With a burgeoning world population, global food production remains at historically unprecedented levels. Approximately 250 million hectares (approximately 618 million acres) of land around the world is equipped with irrigation equipment. More than two-thirds of the world's irrigated land is located in population-dense Asia. The widespread deployment of electrical and diesel powered water pumps fueled the rapid expansion of irrigated land around the world in the twentieth century. These pumps typically produce a seemingly endless supply of groundwater from aquifers. Although this technological development allowed for the needed growth of food production, the widespread use of electrical and diesel pumps is capable of draining aquifers faster than they can recharge. The heavy reliance on groundwater for agriculture threatens the continued food production in North China, the American Plains, Punjab, and other areas.

■ Primary Source Connection

According to the Food and Agriculture Organization of the United Nations (FAO): "Food security exists when all people, at all times, have physical, social and economic access to sufficient, safe and nutritious food which meets their dietary needs and food preferences for an active and healthy life. Food insecurity exists when people do not have adequate physical, social or economic access to food." As the following primary source, from the report *Coping with Water Scarcity: Challenge of the Twenty-First Century*, which was written in conjunction with the World Water Day, March 22, 2007, demonstrates, in recent years the FAO has increasingly recognized and included the importance of access to clean water as fundamental to attempts to address food and poverty issues.

The Vicious Cycle of Water & Poverty—An Issue of Life & Livelihood

First and foremost, water scarcity is an issue of poverty. Unclean water and lack of sanitation are the destiny of poor people across the world. Lack of hygiene affects poor children and families first, while the rest of the world's population benefits from direct access to the water they need for domestic use. One in five people in the developing world lacks access to sufficient clean water (a suggested minimum of 20 litres/day), while average water use in Europe and the United States of America ranges between 200 and 600 litres/day. In addition, the poor pay more. A recent report by the United Nations Development Programme shows that people in the slums of developing countries typically pay 5–10 times more per unit of water than do people with access to piped water (UNDP, 2006).

For poor people, water scarcity is not only about droughts or rivers running dry. Above all, it is about guaranteeing the fair and safe access they need to sustain their lives and secure their livelihoods. For the poor, scarcity is about how institutions function and how transparency and equity are guaranteed in decisions affecting their lives. It is about choices on infrastructure development and the way they are managed. In many places throughout the world, organizations struggle to distribute resources equitably.

Water for life, water for livelihood. While access to safe water and sanitation have been recognized as priority targets through the Millennium Development

IN CONTEXT: AGRICULTURAL IRRIGATION PERILS

In 2010 a study published in the science journal *Nature* predicted that 30 percent of the world's population is vulnerable to freshwater supply shortages. Threats to freshwater supplies for more than 3.4 billion people range through a myriad of problems related to scarcity, pollution, improper management (including badly placed reservoirs and dams), and political instability. The study concluded that safeguarding watersheds, wetlands, and flood plains is essential to preserving freshwater resources. Whereas the industrialized world increasingly relies on expensive aqueducts, canals, dams, pipelines, and pumping systems to address localized freshwater shortages, such "concrete and steel" solutions often remain beyond the reach of a large percentage of the developing world's population. Moreover, even well-intentioned attempts to safeguard or enhance drinking water supplies require analysis that weighs both costs and benefits from proposed solutions. For example, a proposal to drain wetlands along the Barotse Floodplain in Zambia to serve a needed agricultural irrigation scheme ultimately proved to be a net economic loss to the region when factoring in losses anticipated in current fishing and farming yields. International Union for Conservation of Nature (IUCN) representatives who participated in the study also noted that although use of "concrete and steel" watershed management often temporarily solved human use and consumption needs, many solutions created unintentional stress on fish and other wildlife populations.

Goals (MDGs) and the Johannesburg plan of action of the World Summit on Sustainable Development (WSSD), there is increasing recognition that this is not enough. Millions of people rely in one way or another on water for their daily income or food production. Farmers, small rural enterprises, herders and fishing people—all need water to secure their livelihood. However, as the resources become scarce, an increasing number of them see their sources of income disappear. Silently, progressively, the number of water losers increases—at the tail end of the irrigation canal, downstream of a new dam, or as a result of excessive groundwater drawdown.

It is probably in rural areas that water scarcity affects people most. In large parts of the developing world, irrigation remains the backbone of rural economies. However, small-holder farmers make up the majority of the world's rural poor, and they often occupy marginal land and depend mainly on rainfall for production. They are highly sensitive to many changes—droughts, floods, but also shifts in market prices. However, rainwater is rarely integrated into water management strategies, which usually focus exclusively on surface water and groundwater. Countries need to integrate rainwater fully into their strategies to cope with water scarcity.

"THE VICIOUS CYCLE OF WATER & POVERTY—AN ISSUE OF LIFE & LIVELIHOOD," FROM *COPING WITH WATER SCARCITY: CHALLENGE OF THE TWENTY-FIRST CENTURY.* ROME: FOOD AND AGRICULTURE ORGANIZATION OF THE UNITED NATIONS, 2007: 4, 8.

SEE ALSO *Agroecology; Climate Change and Agriculture; Desertification and Agriculture; Food and Agriculture Organization (FAO); Food Security; Sustainable Agriculture; UN Millennium Development Goals; Water; Water Scarcity.*

BIBLIOGRAPHY

Books

Aswathanarayana, U. *Food and Water Security.* London: Taylor & Francis, 2008.

Merkaz Peres Leshalom (corporate author). *Peacebuilding through Regional Agriculture, Water, Agrotechnology and Food Security Programs.* Tel-Aviv: Peres Center for Peace, 2007.

Opportunity Untapped: Water for Food, Agriculture and Rural Livelihood. Rome: Food and Agriculture Organization of the United Nations, 2006.

Pascual, Unai, and Amita Shah. *Water, Agriculture, and Sustainable Well-Being.* New Delhi: Oxford University Press, 2009.

Periodicals

Rosegrant, Mark W., Claudia Ringler, and Tingiu Zhu. "Water for Agriculture: Maintaining Food Security under Growing Scarcity." *Annual Review of Environment and Resources* 34 (2009): 205–222.

Tarver, Toni. "'Just Add Water': Regulating and Protecting the Most Common Ingredient." *Journal of Food Science* 73, no. 1 (2008): R1–R13.

Web Sites

"FAO Urges Action to Cope with Increasing Water Scarcity." *FAO Newsroom, Food and Agriculture Organization of the United Nations (FAO),* March 22, 2007. http://www.fao.org/newsroom/en/news/2007/1000520/index.html (accessed August 22, 2010).

Joseph P. Hyder

Agricultural Land Reform

■ Introduction

Agricultural land reform involves the redistribution of agricultural land, typically through government action. Agricultural land reform may be referred to as agrarian reform; however, agricultural land reform is technically a subset of agrarian reform. In addition to land reform, agrarian reforms may include credit and finance manipulation, training, and price and market controls.

Agricultural land reform usually involves redistributing arable land from large-scale, wealthy landowners to landless persons. The government may compensate the landowners for their land—often below market value—or the government may simply seize the land without the owner's consent. Agricultural land reform may espouse one or more of the following goals: increased agricultural productivity, decreased poverty, promotion of rural development, resettlement to rural areas, equitable redistribution of land, or a return of the land to its original owners.

In practice, however, governments often promote agricultural land reform for more political reasons. Governments may utilize agricultural land reform to transform the agricultural sector or as part of a more ambitious overhaul of the economy and society. Agricultural land reform may become a key component in the shift from the prevailing economic, social, and political landscape, such as feudalism, mercantilism, capitalism, or communism.

Agricultural land reform may also arise out of populist movements. Populist land reforms typically involve taking land from the wealthy in order to redistribute the land to the poor. Populist land reforms merely signal a shift in government policy. Governments often conduct populist land reforms as a means of rewarding political allies or quelling social unrest.

■ Historical Background and Scientific Foundations

Controversies and social upheaval surrounding agricultural land reform stretch back over thousands of years. The land reforms implemented by Tiberius Gracchus (c.165–133 BC), known as Lex Sempronia Agraria, limited the size of estates and seized land from wealthy landowners for redistribution. The political upheaval created by the Graccian land reforms led to the assassination of Tiberius Gracchus and indirectly contributed to the fall of the Roman Republic. In the early sixteenth century, calls for land reform led to the Peasants' War (1524–1525) in central Europe, in which an estimated 100,000 people died in armed revolts. The Peasants' War was the most widespread popular revolt in Europe until the French Revolution.

The twentieth century saw two major developments in the history of land reforms: the collectivization of land in Communist nations and the land reforms that emerged in post-colonial Africa, Asia, and other parts of the world. Collectivization refers to the organization of ownership by the people, typically represented through the state. Collectivized agriculture is the consolidation of land and labor into communal, or collective, farms. In 1917, following the Russian Revolution, Vladimir Lenin (1870–1924) abolished the private ownership of land and announced a redistribution of land to the peasants. Although the government theoretically owned all land in the Soviet Union, peasants continued to farm individual plots of land. Following severe grain shortfalls in 1928, Josef Stalin (1878–1953) accelerated plans to reorganize land into large collective farms.

The idea of agricultural collectivization spread to other Communist nations in Eastern Europe and Asia.

The forced relocation of workers and state-directed agricultural policies proved problematic in the implementation of collective agriculture in most countries. The collectivization of agriculture in China, which culminated with the Great Leap Forward Program, was a disastrous agricultural collectivization policy. China began collectivizing land in 1949, but the process accelerated with the Great Leap Forward Program of Chairman Mao Zedong (1893–1976) during the late 1950s and early 1960s. The disruption in agricultural production caused by the Great Leap Forward resulted in widespread famine. Although the Chinese government officially estimates that 14 million people starved to death because of the Great Leap Forward, scholars place the number of dead between 20 and 48 million.

During the twentieth century, European colonies in Africa, Asia, and Latin America gained independence. Decolonization, however, resulted in the need for agricultural land reform. Non-native landowners owned the vast majority of arable land in most colonies. The transition from large-scale, colonial landowners to small-scale, native landowners has experienced mixed success. For example, India inherited a semi-feudal agrarian system after the country gained independence from the United Kingdom in 1947. A small number of landowners owned the majority of land, and intermediaries of the landlords extracted rent from those who worked the soil. In the years since decolonization, the gradual land reforms of the Communist Party of India (Marxist) in the states of Kerala and West Bengal have been successful in redistributing land equitably and with little decrease in agricultural production. Land reforms in other areas have resulted in violence and the continued inequitable distribution of land.

■ Impacts and Issues

Agricultural land reforms historically have had a mixed record of equitable distribution of land and increased agricultural output. Agricultural land reform may fail for numerous reasons. First, land reform typically replaces skilled farmers with unskilled workers who have little or no technical knowledge. Unskilled, or even absentee,

landowners become an issue particularly when land is redistributed to political allies rather than to landless farmers. Second, large commercial farms rely on economies of scale, or the savings realized through mass production, to produce more goods for a lower cost per good. Smaller farms must pay more to produce the same level of agricultural output, thereby increasing the cost of food. Finally, commercial farms have greater access to capital to invest in machinery, fertilizers, pesticides, and infrastructure improvement. Smaller farms with little or no access to capital cannot make necessary investments to increase production.

Post-colonial sub-Saharan Africa has a particularly poor agricultural land reform record. Many African nations established "willing seller, willing buyer" programs that required colonial landowners to sell to the government or permitted the government a right of first refusal on agricultural land sells. These programs have caused several problems. First, governments must buy the land with tax dollars, which often come from high taxes on large farms. The taxes decrease the profitability and, often, the production on these farms. Second, the requirement to sell to the government or allow the government a right of first refusal drives down the value of the land, because the land is not sold in a competitive market—the government is the only purchaser. Finally, the "willing seller, willing buyer" programs force many landowners to hold onto their land rather than sell the land at depressed prices. This has resulted in a slow transfer of arable land to native farmers.

To accelerate the process of land transfer, some countries have forced large-scale landowners to sell or have seized the land for redistribution. The failed land reforms of President Robert Mugabe (1924–) in Zimbabwe are the most notable and disastrous seizures of land in sub-Saharan Africa. In 2000 paramilitary groups began seizing large farms of white landowners for redistribution to landless black Zimbabweans. In the first decade of the land reforms, the government seized more than 4,000 white-owned commercial farms. Agricultural output in Zimbabwe—once known as the breadbasket of Africa—plummeted. Unskilled, subsistence farmers replaced the commercial farm system, which relied on technical knowledge, economies of scale, and access to capital for machinery and fertilizers. The United Nations estimates that approximately 1.7 million Zimbabweans required international food assistance in 2010.

Decollectivization, or the privatization of publicly-owned land, became a major issue in agricultural land reform in the late twentieth century, following the collapse of Communist governments in the Soviet Union and Eastern Europe. In Russia, the privatization of land exists in theory, but in practice most farmers remain on state-controlled farms. Only about 300,000 farms have been converted to privately owned family farms since the mid–1990s. Most Russian farmers continue to work on state-controlled cooperative farms, because most farmers

A farmer works on the outskirts of Havana, Cuba, in 2008. The nation has begun accepting applications from private farmers, both with and without experience, who want to till idle government land. President Raul Castro hopes the private farmers will raise more food than underperforming state cooperatives. *AP Images.*

find it impossible to work the large farms without access to credit for machinery. Other countries that were part of the former Soviet Union have also struggled with land reform. Like Russia, many of the farmers in these countries continue to work on collective farms. Armenia, Azerbaijan, Georgia, and Moldova, however, have made a relatively smooth transition to private farm ownership. Land reform in the former Communist states of Eastern Europe has also gone well. In some areas of Eastern Europe, however, state-owned collective farms have morphed into corporate-run farms.

China began its decollectivization efforts in the 1970s, following the failure of the Great Leap Forward. The conversion of large collective farms into small, family-run farms initially increased productivity. Later, however, stagnation set in because the system encouraged productivity over proper land management. Land degradation resulted in decreased productivity in many areas. The loss of economies of scale in agricultural production also contributed to agricultural stagnation in China. In the early twenty-first century, China is faced with a new generation of 70 million landless peasants, many of whom work as migratory factory workers. The degree to which these peasants are integrated into the

Chinese economy may have an impact on China's continued economic growth and political stability.

Land reform in Latin America suffers from a lack of rural workforce: Only about 20 percent of the workforce remains in the agricultural sector. Most workers have fled to industrial and service jobs in the cities. Many countries in Latin America suffer from an extremely inequitable distribution of land. In Brazil, for example, the top 3.5 percent of landowners own approximately 56 percent of all arable land. The poorest 40 percent of Brazil's population own approximately 1 percent of the arable land. Over decades of land reform, Brazil has extended land ownership opportunities to millions of families, although much of the progress has come about through deforestation of the Amazon rainforest.

■ Primary Source Connection

Comprehensive land reform can be a complicated and controversial endeavor, especially when the process involves the transfer of land from those parties who have the power and the resources needed to acquire and administer agricultural land to those who have neither money to acquire land, nor the necessary experience to successfully manage it. The following excerpt from Mike Lyne and Michael Roth's *Innovating Institutions to Help Land Reform Beneficiaries*, published under the auspices of the U.S. Agency for International Development (USAID), illustrates some of the major challenges and issues involved in undertaking this type of large-scale land reform.

In 1961, the Foreign Assistance Act was passed and USAID was created by executive order. USAID is an independent federal agency whose purpose is to extend aid to countries recovering from disaster. It supports U.S. foreign policy in Africa, Asia, Latin America, Europe and the Middle East.

Author Mike Lyne teaches Agricultural Economics at the University of Natal-Pietermaritzburg in South Africa. He has been an active member of the Agricultural Economics Association of South Africa (AEASA) and the International Association of Agricultural Economists (IAAE). Michael Roth is a faculty member at the University of Wisconsin-Madison.

Innovating Institutions to Help Land Reform Beneficiaries

Group Ownership of Land Resources

Central Asia and Southern Africa are undergoing political and economic transition, the former from state and collective farm ownership to private groups and individuals, and the latter to redress the apartheid and colonial heritage of racially biased and unequal landownership. Despite different histories and policy contexts, countries in these regions share a core problem: poor people in rural areas are unable to make productive use of their land resources.

The problem is most acute where it has not been feasible to privatize land, water, infrastructure, or movable assets to individual owners. Many beneficiaries of land reform in these regions find themselves co-owning resources, often in diverse groups that lack the constitutional rules and operational arrangements needed for effective management. Historically, these cooperative ownership models have led to low productivity, free ridership, and an inability to encourage investment by the co-owners or external financiers.

Yet, as demonstrated by some successful arrangements in South Africa as well as globally, group ownership need not be unproductive or unprofitable. By helping to identify and resolve the social, institutional, and organizational problems associated with group ownership in the Kyrgyz Republic and South Africa, BASIS endeavors to develop institutional models that increase enterprise profitability and improve the livelihoods and asset holdings of the rural poor.

Problems with Land Reform and Farm Restructuring

In South Africa, progress with land reform has fallen far short of the goals set by the government. In 1994, the post-apartheid government projected land redistribution at the rate of six million hectares per year. Between 1994 and 2000, just one million hectares was redistributed. In the province of KwaZulu-Natal, where BASIS has monitored farm transactions since 1997, less than 0.5% of the farmland owned by whites has transferred to historically disadvantaged people each year despite the presence of an active land market and the availability of public grants to purchase land on a willing buyer–willing seller basis. Two obstacles have contributed to the slow pace of land reform. It is expensive to subdivide commercial farms and to survey, register, and transfer smaller units to aspiring farmers. Prospective farmers also lack capital and are unable to finance land with conventional mortgage loans from commercial banks due to cash flow problems caused by high nominal interest rates.

Most of the disadvantaged people who have acquired farmland have done so by pooling resources and purchasing farms collectively, a trend that is likely to continue even if the inflation rate falls and the statutory costs associated with subdivision, registration, and transfer of farmland decline. From 1997–2001, more than half the farmland purchased by historically disadvantaged people in KwaZulu-Natal transferred to groups, not individuals. This poses a major challenge to policymakers, since farms acquired by groups of land reform beneficiaries already show symptoms of becoming open access resources.

In the Kyrgyz Republic, the agricultural transition is unfolding rapidly, with swift and far-reaching structural change. Between independence in 1991 and January 2000, 47% of the arable land formerly held by state and collective farms had been transferred to 69,000 small- and medium-sized farms (usually operated by groups of families). The other 53% is managed by 600 corporate-collective farm enterprises that have many of the same features as their predecessors but operate under a variety of new legal forms.

The economic conditions facing these enterprises are severe. The collapse of the Soviet system of production and distribution has left Kyrgyz agriculture starved for operating capital and long-term investment. Farm enterprises that managed to stay afloat with depreciating capital stock and self-financing during the 1990s presently are challenged in attracting new sources of capital and moving beyond subsistence into profitable commercial activities.

Sustainable growth in both countries will be difficult to achieve without improving the efficiency of these emerging enterprises and increasing public and private investment. To a large extent, these improvements will depend on the ability of the newly created, member-owned enterprises to innovate and expand under adverse economic conditions.

Mike Lyne
Michael Roth

LYNE, MIKE, AND MICHAEL ROTH. *INNOVATING INSTITUTIONS TO HELP LAND REFORM BENEFICIARIES.* BASIS BRIEF NUMBER 8. MADISON, WI: UNIVERSITY OF WISCONSIN, 2002. THIS PUBLICATION WAS MADE POSSIBLE BY SUPPORT PROVIDED IN PART BY THE US AGENCY FOR INTERNATIONAL DEVELOPMENT (USAID) AGREEMENT NO. LAG-A-C0-96-90016-00 AWARDED TO THE BASIS COLLABORATIVE RESEARCH SUPPORT PROGRAM (BASIS CRSP). ALL VIEWS, INTERPRETATIONS, RECOMMENDATIONS, AND CONCLUSIONS EXPRESSED IN THIS PAPER ARE THOSE OF THE AUTHOR(S) AND NOT NECESSARILY THOSE OF THE SUPPORTING OR COLLABORATING INSTITUTIONS.

SEE ALSO *Decollectivization; Ethical Issues in Agriculture; Food and Agriculture Organization (FAO); Food Sovereignty; Rome Declaration on World Food Security (1996); Subsistence Farming; UN Millennium Development Goals; War, Conquest, Colonialism, and Cuisine.*

BIBLIOGRAPHY

Books

Chamabati, Walter, and Sam Moyo. *Land Reform and the Political Economy of Agricultural Labour in Zimbabwe.* Harare, Zimbabwe: African Institute for Agrarian Studies, 2007.

General Agricultural and Plantation Workers of Zimbabwe (GAPWUZ). *If Something Is Wrong: The Invisible Suffering of Commercial Farm Workers and Their Families Due to "Land Reform."* Harare, Zimbabwe: Weaver Press, 2010.

Lerman, Zvi. *Russia's Agriculture in Transition: Factor Markets and Constraints on Growth.* Lanham, MD: Lexington Books, 2008.

Nzioki, Akinyi. *Land Policies in Sub-Saharan Africa.* Nairobi, Kenya: Center for Land, Economy and Rights of Women, 2006.

Ondetti, Gabriel A. *Land, Protest, and Politics: The Landless Movement and the Struggle for Agrarian Reform in Brazil.* University Park: Pennsylvania State University Press, 2008.

Wietersheim, Erika. *This Land Is My Land!: Motions and Emotions around Land in Namibia.* Windhoek, Namibia: Friedrich Ebert-Stiftung, 2008.

Periodicals

Binswanger-Mkhize, Hans, Alex McCalla, and Praful Patel. "Structural Transformation and African Agriculture." *Global Journal of Emerging Market Economies* 2, no. 2 (2010): 113–152.

Eastwood, Robert, Johann Kirsten, and Michael Lipton. "Premature Deagriculturalisation? Land Inequality and Rural Dependency in Limpopo Province, South Africa." *The Journal of Development Studies* 42, no. 8 (2006): 1325–1349.

Ghatak, Maitreesh, and Sanchari Roy. "Land Reform and Agricultural Productivity in India: A Review of the Evidence." *Oxford Review of Economic Policy* 23, no. 2 (2007): 251–269.

Lerman, Zvi. "Land Reform, Farm Structure, and Agricultural Performance in CIS Countries." *China Economic Review* 20, no. 2 (2009): 316.

Web Sites

"Land Tenure." *Food and Agriculture Organization of the United Nations (FAO).* http://www.fao.org/nr/tenure/lt-home/en/ (accessed August 23, 2010).

Joseph P. Hyder

Agriculture and International Trade

■ Introduction

Trade of goods produced through agriculture is almost as old as agriculture itself. According to economists, international trade occurs for the reasons of absolute advantage, comparative advantage, and economies of scale. However, trade is restricted through trade barriers. Some trade barriers attempt to restrict trade using quotas to limit quantities or imposition of tariffs (taxes on trade to raise the price of imported goods and increase government revenue). Among non-tariff barriers, sanitary (animal health) and phytosanitary (plant health) measures (SPS measures) are designed to protect the safety, productivity, and health of a country's population

and agricultural sector. Many countries have attempted to lower trade barriers since forming the General Agreement on Tariffs and Trade (GATT) in 1946, but agricultural trade was not included until the creation of the World Trade Organization in 1995 as a result of the Uruguay round trade negotiations (1986–1993). Further reductions of trade barriers for agricultural goods have reached a standstill due to disagreements between developed and developing countries.

■ Historical Background and Scientific Foundations

Farmers have traditionally played an important role in the economies of many countries, and there has always been international trade in agricultural goods. According to economists, countries trade for three reasons. First, they may trade for reasons of absolute advantage. Given that a nation may need products that it cannot or does not grow, trade can substitute for production. Imports of tropical products such as coffee, tea, cocoa, and bananas to temperate countries is one example of trade based on absolute advantage. The second reason countries trade is comparative advantage. Countries can gain from trade even if both countries could produce the same goods. They can gain purchasing power through lower prices for certain imported goods, or they can gain efficiency by concentrating on products for which they are relatively, but not absolutely efficient. Because two countries produce goods at different levels of efficiency, countries' different opportunity costs lead to opportunities for trade. By concentrating on goods for which it has comparative advantage, a country can specialize in some products and trade with other countries for those products that it no longer produces. The resulting trade benefits both trading partners due to specialization allowing the countries to use their resources more efficiently. The third reason countries trade is economies of scale. Large markets and large scale production have a tendency to

---

WORDS TO KNOW

COMPARATIVE ADVANTAGE: Efficiency in production of one good over another that makes trade possible even if one country lacks absolute efficiency in either good. Even if one country is more efficient at producing every product, it can gain from specializing in the products it is comparatively more efficient at producing. Then the country can move out of producing products in which it lacks comparative advantage and trade with other countries for those products. The resulting trade benefits both trading partners due to specialization allowing countries to use their resources more efficiently.

NON-TARIFF BARRIER: Any barrier to trade other than tariffs. Usually refers to quotas and restrictions on trade or to rules and regulations that affect trade but may be set for other reasons.

SANITARY AND PHYTOSANITARY (SPS) MEASURES: Laws, rules, and regulations intended to help protect human and animal health (sanitary) or plant health (phytosanitary). Regulations regarding food safety, animal diseases, plant disease, and pests are referred to as SPS restrictions.

---

reduce costs both for producers and consumers, and this phenomenon is known as an economy of scale.

Trade barriers, which are government policies or regulations regarding imports, can be used to adjust this situation. Quotas, restrictions on how much can be imported, and tariffs, taxes paid on imported goods, can raise the cost of the imported goods so that local farmers can compete despite their higher production cost for a product. In this case, consumers subsidize farmers through higher cost goods. Trade barriers may also increase government revenues, helping fund necessary government services or government investments in the economy. Unlike trade in other goods, though, agricultural trade faces a special set of barriers called sanitary and phytosanitary (SPS) measures. Because imported food products can bring with them diseases or health risks to humans, animals, and plants, countries have barriers designed to prevent the spread of human, animal, and plant diseases or the introduction of exotic pests that could harm crops.

Discussions about how to control international trade through trade barriers and other mechanisms began in 1946 and led to the General Agreement on Tariffs and Trades (GATT). However, the six subsequent rounds of GATT negotiations excluded discussions of agricultural trade. During this time, developed and developing countries erected many trade barriers in agriculture to protect their domestic industries, to deal with the trade implications of their domestic agricultural support programs, and to prevent the spread of human, plant, and animal diseases through SPS measures. Despite these limits on trade, between 1961 and 1995 agricultural trade increased more than thirteen-fold. With the Uruguay round of negotiations (1986–1993), which led to the formation of the World Trade Organization (WTO) in 1995, agricultural trade began to become a part of international trade rules.

One of the main aims of the WTO is to try to reform international agricultural trade and improve both predictability and security of food and other agricultural products for both importing and exporting countries. Member states have agreed to a variety of rules for trade, including rules for agricultural trade. Under the Agreement on Agriculture (1995), member countries agreed to phase out subsidies for agricultural exports and set maximum, bound rates for tariffs on agricultural goods. More controversially, the Agreement on Agriculture sets some limits on the amount a country spends on agricultural subsidies. Non-tariff barriers are also subject to some discipline and rules under the WTO. Under the Agreement on Sanitary and Phytosanitary (SPS) Measures, known as the SPS Agreement (1995), countries must use scientific risk assessment and internationally accepted standards as the basis for their rules that protect human, plant, and animal health. From 1995 until 2005, the first decade of the WTO's existence, agricultural trade increased more than 100 percent.

IN CONTEXT: BACTERIAL BLIGHTS

Bacterial blights, outbreaks of bacterial growth, can severely impact agricultural production and result in substantial economic loss. The impacts can range from crop loss to blights that diminish crop quality or economic value. For example, during the 2009 and 2010 growing seasons, onion crops in Argentina suffered a blight that resulted in onions with excess water retention. This condition accelerated spoilage during storage and transport, causing substantially reduced exports to traditional European markets.

Bacterial blights can spread internationally and subside and erupt in outbreaks over several years. Blights are most common in tropical and subtropical areas. Heavy rains may provide the environmental trigger for an outbreak.

Blights can be caused by subtle changes in bacteria that create bacterial pathovars. A pathovar is a pathological (disease causing) variation of normally nonpathological bacteria. It may refer to one specific bacterial strain or a set of closely related strains with similar characteristics. Pathovars can spread in seed or be carried by wind and water. In addition to genus and species names, pathovars are often designated and differentiated by a suffix. For example, the pathovar responsible for an onion blight in Japan in 2000 was designated *Xanthomonas axonopodis pv. allii.*

Pathovars may also infect specific crops. For example, there are variations of *Xanthomonas axonopodis* that infect different crops. *Xanthomonas axonopodis pv. s citri* causes citrus crop blights whereas *Xanthomonas axonopodis pv. vesicatoria* causes a bacterial blight in tomato crops.

Growers generally respond by trying to develop varieties of plants resistant to specific pathovars.

■ Impacts and Issues

The Doha Round of multilateral trade negotiations began on November 14, 2001, in Doha, Qatar. They were intended to be the development round, and developing countries and developed countries thought many agricultural trade issues would be settled by this round. However, the talks collapsed in 2008 due to disagreements between countries. Current WTO rules cover market access, domestic support of local farmers, and the issue of export subsidies. Developing countries make up about three-quarters of WTO membership. They are given more time to fulfill their commitments to the WTO, and there are supposed to be special provisions for those who rely on imports to feed their populations. But critics of the WTO contend that the organization marginalizes poorer countries' aspirations, as some rich countries held up the Doha round negotiations. These critics contend that WTO rules fail to balance market conditions.

A group of Peruvian protesters pretend to grasp at food and medicine, commenting on the possible effects of a free trade agreement between the United States and Peru. Opponents of free trade agreements fear subsidized U.S. products will make it impossible for Peru to compete in agriculture and will raise other consumer prices. *AP Images.*

One of the reasons for this failure is that some developed, or industrialized, nations heavily subsidize their farmers. Thus, farmers in wealthier nations can sell their products at lower prices than can the farmers of developing nations. For example, subsidies for cotton production in the United States may lower the world price of cotton and reduce the prices received by smallholder cotton farmers in developing countries in West Africa, South America, and Central and South Asia. Representatives of developing nations argue that differences in trade barriers do not balance out inequities caused by agricultural subsidies. Developing countries want the developed nations to stop subsidizing farmers and to simplify the SPS measures necessary to export to those countries. The developed nations, however, want developing nations to

open up their markets to foreign agricultural goods by reducing both tariffs and non-tariff barriers to trade.

SEE ALSO *Agribusiness; Aid and Subsidies to Promote Agriculture and Reduce Illicit Drug Production; Banana Trade Wars; Biofuels and World Hunger; Embargoes; Ethical Issues in Agriculture; Fair Trade; Food and Agriculture Organization (FAO); Food Security; Free Trade and Agriculture; Import Restrictions; International Fund for Agricultural Development (IFAD); Subsidies; World Trade Organization (WTO).*

BIBLIOGRAPHY

Books

Achterbosch, Thom.*Consumer Health Hazards in International Food Trade.* The Hague, The Netherlands: LEI, 2007.

Australian Farm Institute.*China—Emerging Opportunity or Emerging Threat?* Surry Hills, NSW: Australian Farm Institute, 2007.

Gibbon, Peter, Evelene Lazaro, and Stefano Ponte. *Global Agro-Food Trade and Standards: Challenges for Africa.* Houndmills, Basinstoke, Hampshire, UK: Palgrave Macmillan, 2010.

Kastner, Justin, and Jason Ackleson. "Global Trade and Food Security: Perspectives for the Twenty-First Century." In *Homeland Security: Protecting America's Targets, Vol. 1: Borders and Points of Entry.* Westport, CT: Praeger Security International (2006): 98–116.

Millstone, Erik, and Tim Lang. *The Atlas of Food: Who Eats What, Where, and Why.* Berkeley: University of California Press, 2008.

Morgan, Kevin, Terry Marsden, and Jonathan Murdoch. *Worlds of Food: Place, Power, and Provenance in the Food Chain.* Oxford, UK: Oxford University Press, 2006.

Murray, Sarah. *Moveable Feasts: From Ancient Rome to the 21st Century, the Incredible Journeys of the Food We Eat.* New York: St. Martin's Press, 2007.

Nütsenadel, Alexander, and Frank Trentmann. *Food and Globalization: Consumption, Markets and Politics in the Modern World.* Oxford, UK: Berg, 2008.

Patel, Raj. *Stuffed and Starved: The Hidden Battle for the World Food System.* Brooklyn, NY: Melville House Pub, 2008.

Thomas, Harmon C. *Trade Reforms and Food Security: Country Case Studies and Synthesis.* Rome: Food and Agriculture Organization of the United Nations, 2006.

Weis, Anthony J. *The Global Food Economy: The Battle for the Future of Farming.* London: Zed Books, 2007.

Wright, Simon, and Diane McCrea. *The Handbook of Organic and Fair Trade Food Marketing.* Oxford, UK: Blackwell Pub., 2007.

World Trade Organization Agreement: Significance to Food Trade. Geneva, Switzerland: AFIST, 2005.

Periodicals

Sawhney, Aparna. "Quality Measures in Food Trade: The Indian Experience." *The World Economy* 28, no. 3 (2005): 329–348.

Web Sites

"Agriculture." *World Trade Organization (WTO).* http://www.wto.org/english/tratop_e/agric_e/agric_e.htm (accessed October 18, 2010).

"Trade and Agriculture." *Food and Agriculture Organization of the United Nations (FAO),* September 2003. http://www.fao.org/english/newsroom/focus/2003/wto.htm (accessed October 4, 2010).

Agriculture Brings Hierarchical Societies

■ Introduction

Anthropologists and historians have long recognized that the origins of agriculture are inextricably linked to the origins of civilization. All ancient state-level civilizations were characterized by certain features, including high population densities, complex social systems with a political hierarchy, centralized authority, and social inequality (characterized by a small set of rulers, a middle class, and a larger populace of farmers), as well as sedentary villages and urban centers with monumental architecture and armies. Literacy and well-established artistic traditions were not uncommon in these societies. All of this was supported by the large-scale agriculture of storable, starchy staples, sometimes augmented with animal husbandry.

The question of how these civilizations evolved independently in South America, Mexico, India, China, Africa, and the Middle East during the last five or six thousand years has been an enduring one. Similarly, the role that the rise of agricultural economies played in this sociocultural evolution has been a topic of much recent archaeological research. Although it is clear that the cultivation of domesticated crops and the presence of livestock did not automatically ensure the development of hierarchical societies, crops were a definite prerequisite for state-building, and various kinds of food and drink were used by high-status people in some very intriguing social and economic ways. Agricultural resources and access to food also played an important role in the historic growth and collapse of states, nations, and empires, and continue to do so in the early twenty-first century.

■ Historical Background and Scientific Foundations

In the late 1800s, American anthropologist Lewis Henry Morgan (1818–1881), who was inspired by classical ideas about the stages of humankind and Charles Darwin's (1809–1882) concept of natural evolution, proposed that all human cultures evolved through three distinct states: savagery, barbarism, and civilization. This sociocultural evolution was unilinear and progressive, and different levels of social organization and modes of production characterized each stage. Bands of hunter-gatherers were followed by tribes of settled agriculturalists, which in turn evolved into chiefdoms, culminating in the primitive states, which were the basis of modern civilization. It was widely assumed that the invention of agriculture during the tribal stage enabled farmers to produce a surplus that allowed civilizations to flourish.

Archaeologist V. Gordon Childe (1892–1957) coined the terms "Neolithic Revolution" and "Urban Revolution" in the 1920s and 1930s to describe the transformation from foraging (or hunting and gathering) societies to agricultural ones, and the subsequent change from settled villages to urban centers. The flaws inherent in unilinear theories of sociocultural evolution were also demonstrated during these years, and many different multilinear models explaining these cultural transformations were put forth by anthropologists, sociologists, and economists during the rest of the twentieth century. As more evidence for the domestication of plants and animals accumulated, it became obvious that not all societies with crops and livestock were characterized by social inequality and political hierarchy. Agriculture alone—at least on a small scale—did not always seem to promote the growth of complex chiefdoms, let alone states.

Karl Wittfogel (1896–1988), a professor of Chinese history, put forth his "hydraulic theory" in 1957, which suggested that the construction of irrigation systems necessary to produce crops in dry areas required centralized political power and hierarchy. In 1965 Danish economist Ester Boserup (1910–1999) argued that population pressure—an imbalance between the quantity of people and available land—caused agricultural intensification (such as irrigation), echoing some of the British scholar Thomas Malthus's (1766–1834) ideas about population growth and food supply in the nineteenth

A pictography shows agricultural laborers as the base of ancient Mayan society. The tier above depicts bakers, millers, and other food stuff workers.   © *The Art Archive / Alamy.*

century. Agronomists, cultural anthropologists, and archaeologists continued to examine the ecology of agricultural strategies and methods of intensification, such as terracing, fertilization, multi-cropping, and crop rotation in subsequent years, pondering the roles that these technological advances played in the emergence of early states. They also noted the constraints that the natural environment and particular crops and livestock (or the lack of animals suitable for domestication) placed on the evolution of cultural and political systems, especially in Australia and some parts of the New World.

Most archaeologists have come to acknowledge that more complex political systems do not contribute much to the maintenance or productivity of an agricultural system, but point out that individuals and lineages with high status certainly co-opt agricultural resources for social reasons. In the most recent social models, hierarchical political systems, which may emerge in response to the military or defensive needs of agrarian villages, or for other economic, social, and ritual reasons, result in agricultural intensification.

Archaeologists have come to view feasting as an especially important aspect of the control of food by the elites in emergent chiefdoms and in a variety of early states and empires. Feasts were useful for defining and maintaining political hierarchies. The consumption of

WORDS TO KNOW

AGRICULTURE: The production of food using domesticated plants and animals. Anthropologists often draw a distinction between horticulture or cultivation in gardens, which may be economically important and may or may not be based on domesticated plants, and large-scale field agriculture, which is economically fundamental, may be quite labor intensive, and produces a storable surplus important to more than its producers.

DOMESTICATION: The process by which humans selectively alter plant and animal species, resulting in varieties or new species with different behaviors and physical characteristics. This may done consciously, through controlled breeding, or through repeated interactions with unintended consequences in a coevolutionary fashion. Domesticates rely on humans to reproduce themselves; without human aid they will go extinct or revert back to wild forms.

HIERARCHICAL SOCIETIES: Social groups characterized by an inherited political hierarchy (ruled by few, with many agricultural producers below), and different levels of social inequality. In anthropology, complex chiefdoms, states, and empires are classified as hierarchical societies. More egalitarian societies may be organized into tribes or bands.

food at large social gatherings was qualitatively different from that served at everyday meals (which continues to be the case) and highlighted differential access to food by different social groups, the negotiation of social power and identity, and traditional gender roles. The consumption of alcohol was also particularly important in this context.

■ Impacts and Issues

Since the early 1990s, an understanding of the origins of agriculture has become more clear through detailed investigations of particular prehistoric (and sometimes historic) developments. The origins of political and social hierarchies, and the roles that agriculture, agricultural resources, and food in general play in this transformation, have also been successfully examined on a case by case basis. Population growth, circumscribed agricultural lands, feasts, and agricultural intensification–especially of easily stored, starchy crops–are all factors that appear to have been critical in the different trajectories that led to early states in widely varied parts of the world.

The social inequality that characterized complex prehistoric societies had some significant implications in terms of political and economic power and individual health. Malnutrition left permanent marks on the bones and teeth of prehistoric people with relatively low social standing in both the Old World and the New World. Vitamin and protein deficiencies and periods of famine were much more common and widespread than they were in pre-agricultural times. A lifetime of agricultural labor or food processing activities such as maize grinding also left indelible marks on the human skeleton. Because people in these societies were so dependent on a few major crops, and generally had a much less diverse diet than hunter-gatherers or less sedentary horticulturists enjoyed, natural disasters and the resulting crop losses were much more problematic. Sedentary, populous communities were also more vulnerable to contagious diseases, including zoonotic illnesses transmitted from animals to people, and parasites.

The social control of food in these societies ensured that only ruling elites had access to certain exotic foodstuffs, the best foods (especially the most meat, and the choicest cuts), and to the greatest quantities of food. State granaries were used to fund the construction of public works by lower classes and to feed conquering armies. Agricultural innovations, technological advances in food preservation, and the destruction of agricultural resources became important military strategies for states and empires and continue to be so in the second decade of the twenty-first century. Many of the economic and agricultural problems that plagued early states, in fact, continue to be issues of importance to modern nations.

SEE ALSO *Agricultural Deforestation; Agricultural Demand for Water; Agricultural Land Reform; Agriculture and International Trade; Agroecology; Desertification and Agriculture; Ethical Issues in Agriculture; Gender Equality and Agriculture; History of Food and Man: From Hunter-Gatherer to Agriculture; Indigenous Peoples and Their Diets; Nutrition's Role in Human Evolution; Paleolithic Diet.*

BIBLIOGRAPHY

Books

Bray, Tamara L., ed. *The Archaeology and Politics of Food and Feasting in Early States and Empires.* New York: Kluwer Academic/Plenum, 2003.

Cohen, Mark N., and Gillian M. M. Crane-Kramer, eds. *Ancient Health: Skeletal Indicators of Agricultural and Economic Intensification.* Gainesville: University of Florida Press, 2007.

Diamond, Jared M. *Collapse: How Societies Choose to Fail or Succeed.* New York: Viking, 2005.

Manning, Richard. *Against the Grain: How Agriculture Has Hijacked Civilization.* New York: North Point Press, 2005.

Marcus, Joyce, and Charles Stanish, eds. *Agricultural Strategies.* Los Angeles: Cotsen Institute of Archaeology, 2005.

Standage, Tom. *An Edible History of Humanity.* New York: Walker, 2009.

Periodicals

Dietler, Michael. "Alcohol: Anthropological/Archaeological Perspectives." *Annual Review of Anthropology* 35, no. (2006): 229–249.

Web Sites

"Early Agriculture and Development." *Oregon State University.* http://oregonstate.edu/instruct/css/330/one/index.htm#EarlyAgriculture (accessed October 22, 2010).

"Go West, Early Man: Modeling the Origin and Spread of Early Agriculture." *PLoS Biology* 3, no. 12, 2005. http://www.ncbi.nlm.nih.gov/pmc/articles/PMC1287510/ (accessed October 22, 2010).

Sandra L. Dunavan

Agroecology

■ Introduction

Agroecology is the study of agricultural systems in their ecological context. Agroecologists use theories and techniques from agronomy to study how agriculture reacts and adapts to changes in the environment. Agroecologists also study the influence of agriculture on component ecosystems, utilizing research techniques commonly employed in ecology and other environmental science areas to articulate how agricultural lands interact with surrounding ecosystems.

Agricultural interaction with human societies and economics are also component areas of study, especially when attempting to define and measure specific interrelationships between agriculture and ecology. Researchers may apply theories and methodology common to sociology, economics, political science, and anthropology. There are, however, agroecologists who restrict their studies to the physical interactions of agriculture and ecosystems (e.g., chemical, biological, microbiological interactions) and who do not study the cultural or social contexts of agriculture. In contrast, the field of ethno-ecology is more focused on human and cultural factors involved both in agriculture and in environmental impacts of agriculture.

In some developing countries, agroecology is associated with political movements with goals of increasing agricultural sustainability and preserving traditional knowledge and practices related to agriculture and the environment. Less politicized practitioners of agroecology may also focus on integrating sustainable agricultural techniques into local farming systems based on agroecological research.

■ Historical Background and Scientific Foundations

The term agroecology first appears in the work of scientists in both Germany and the United States during the 1930s. However, the field began to develop more fully in the 1950s as the science of ecology developed the terminology and concepts related to the modern definition and understanding of ecosystems. Interest in studying agricultural ecosystems or agro-ecosystems grew again in reaction to developments in population ecology in the 1960s. Population ecology brought concerns about human overpopulation to a wide variety of scientific fields and to the social sciences. Garrett Hardin's (1915–2003) seminal article on the "Tragedy of the Commons" in the journal *Science* and P. R. Ehrlich's (1932–) best-seller *The Population Bomb* (1968) raised concerns about human overpopulation and modern civilization's negative impacts on the environment. These works focused scientists, along with many non-specialists, on human-caused environmental problems and on negative human impacts on the environment. More specifically, agroecology emerged as a field of research and study to address the

---

WORDS TO KNOW

AGROECOLOGY: The study of agricultural systems in their ecological context.

AGRONOMY: The scientific study of soil and plants as applied to land management and crop production.

ETHNO-ECOLOGY: The study of how people, agriculture, economics, and the environment interact with an emphasis on culture.

TRADITIONAL KNOWLEDGE: Sometimes called indigenous knowledge, traditional knowledge is information related to practices that are often preserved and passed on by methods other than through academic study or formal writings. Although components of beliefs and practices may not be fully tested by scientific experimentation, many experts argue that traditional knowledge and practices contain useful insights about the environment, medicine, and agriculture.

need to feed more people in an environmentally sustainable manner.

The growth of the environmental movement in the 1970s brought broad attention to ecology including the developing discipline of agroecology. Some scholars cite the primary influence on the growth of agroecology in the 1970s as the school of process ecology. Process ecologists study cycles and processes in both organisms and in organisms' interactions with soil, water, air, and other components of the environment. For process ecologists interested in the role of crops or livestock in component ecosystems, the agro-ecosystem solidified as a unit of study. The agro-ecosystem includes agricultural lands and organisms on that land, as well as water and other environmental factors.

Also during the 1970s, agronomy as a field began to change. Agronomy had achieved large increases in crop productivity known as the Green Revolution during the 1960s. As the Green Revolution spread, increased use of expensive chemical inputs such as fertilizer led some agronomists to study the environmental and economic impacts of the Green Revolution's recommended cropping patterns. The focus of agronomy slowly moved from research that had the single goal of increasing production to research that examined both the costs and the benefits of production agriculture. Studies integrated, compared, and articulated the monetary and the environmental costs of inputs such as fertilizers with the results or benefits in terms of profit, productivity, and long-term impact on physical resources (e.g. soil fertility conditions). Studies also examined impacts on human capital, or knowledge, of farmers involved in the agricultural system.

Some agroecologists became activists promoting agricultural sustainability, or more specifically argued for agricultural practices that reduced negative environmental impacts. Other scientists began to draw more on the social sciences, arguing that the problems associated with the environment and agriculture could not be solved by purely technical, scientific means that did not account for human factors. Activists in developing countries who sought to preserve traditional knowledge or modify existing agricultural practices to protect environmental resources were attracted to agroecology. Starting in the 1980s, several

A booth of local, food-producing plants at a cooperative greenmarket in Neptune Beach, Florida. Selecting native, same-climate, or developed-for-the-region plants that need fewer resources to achieve high yield adheres to basic agroecology principles of sustainable productivity. *Brenda Lerner / Lerner & Lerner / LernerMedia Global Photos.*

universities added agroecology departments. As of 2010 the discipline is still in development, with continuing arguments and discussion about the scope of agroecology and applicable research methodology.

■ Impacts and Issues

As with other emerging fields of study, agroecology depends on integrating techniques and findings from a variety of research fields. Differences in interpretation create tensions between fields and also lead to internal debates among agroecologists. One key debate in agroecology concerns the scale at which agriculture and the environment should be studied. Agronomists have traditionally studied individual plots of land, not entire farms. However, ecology demands examination of agroecosystems, which can include many types of agricultural production interacting with the environment, often over large areas of land. Social scientists, including rural sociologists and agricultural economists, often study agricultural systems at a still larger scale, looking at how large, national markets operate or how certain practices exist over wide areas of land with varying geographic features. Deciding at what level agricultural systems and their ecological context can be studied remains an ongoing debate in agroecology.

Agroecology issues can also derive from differences in outlook, practices, and application of data between natural scientists and social scientists. For example, the idea of research as an activity that has no impact on the place or the people who are studied has evolved into the understanding that those conducting research can affect the people and places under study. Aside from research bias, a study itself can distort results. This evolution of thinking is actually an extension of long-held physical science theory (on the smallest scale, for example, the Heisenberg Uncertainty Principle) that study of a system alters and disrupts the system itself. For practical reasons, however, many agronomists, soil scientists, veterinarians, and other natural scientists continue to view their work as purely objective because it employs the scientific method and uses controlled experiments.

Critics contend that it is too often the practice of many scientists concentrating on the physical aspects of agricultural science to discount or disregard the impacts of the study itself. Critics also contend that without attention to the scale of a study, the validity of the study is often compromised. As a result, in agricultural sciences there is an emerging emphasis on applied field research on actual, working farms. This research acknowledges the integrated role of the farmer and of the researcher in the research. For example, agricultural researchers who work in agricultural extension services often spend large amounts of time on farms and in personal interaction with farmers. As a result, others must factor in the possibility that they may employ a more subjective approach to studies that accommodates views held by farmers and local cultural influences.

This debate on objectivity of research is not limited to agroecology and is similar to debates in a wide range of academic disciplines.

SEE ALSO *Agribusiness; Population and Food; Sustainable Agriculture.*

BIBLIOGRAPHY

Books

Babe, Robert E. *Culture of Ecology: Reconciling Economics and Environment.* Toronto, Ontario, Canada: University of Toronto Press, 2006.

Begon, Michael, Colin R. Townsend, and John L. Harper. *Ecology: From Individuals to Ecosystems*, 4th ed. Malden, MA: Blackwell, 2006.

Clements, David, and Anil Shrestha, eds. *New Dimensions in Agroecology.* Binghamton, NY: Food Products Press, 2004.

Diaz, Laia, and Marta Perez. *Ecology Research Trends.* New York: Nova Science Publishers, 2008.

Gliessmann, Stephen, Eric Engles, and Robin Kreiter. *Agroecology: Ecological Processes in Sustainable Agriculture.* Chelsea, MI: Ann Arbor Press, 1998.

Hatfield, Jerry L., ed. *The Farmer's Decision: Balancing Economic Agriculture Production with Environmental Quality.* Ankeny, IA: Soil and Water Conservation Society, 2005.

Lyson, Thomas A. *Civic Agriculture: Reconnecting Farm, Food, and Community.* Medford, MA: Tufts University Press, 2004.

Warner, Keith. *Agroecology in Action: Extending Alternative Agriculture through Social Networks.* Cambridge, MA: MIT, 2007.

Web Sites

"Ecosystems: Agroecosystems: Agriculture." *United States Environmental Protection Agency (EPA).* http://www.epa.gov/ebtpages/ecosagroecosystemsagriculture.html (accessed August 4, 2010).

"USAID-Agriculture." *United States Agency for International Development (USAID).* http://www.usaid.gov/our_work/agriculture (accessed August 4, 2010).

Blake Jackson Stabler

Aid for Agriculture to Replace Illicit Drug Production

■ Introduction

The United Nations Office on Drugs and Crime (UNODC) estimates that between 155 and 250 million people, 3.5–5.7 percent of the world's population between the ages of 15 and 64, used illicit drugs in 2008. The majority of these individuals used drugs derived from plants, including cannabis, cocaine, and opiates. Whereas most cannabis is produced and consumed locally or regionally, opiates and cocaine are trafficked internationally from points of production in Central Asia and South America, respectively.

Many foreign and domestic governments have attempted to provide financial and technical assistance to farmers that grow crops used in the production of illicit drugs. These aid programs may be designed to achieve one or more of the following: a reduction in international drug trafficking; elimination or reduction of funding to extremist or terrorist groups that benefit from the drug trade; and the promotion of sustainable licit agriculture as part of nation-building efforts.

Nations may also fund agricultural programs within their own countries to aid farmers in the transition from the production of illicit crops to legal crops such as coffee or cocoa beans. These domestic subsidy programs attempt to make licit crop cultivation more profitable in order to lure farmers away from lucrative illicit crop cultivation or to decrease funding to domestic separatist or narco-terrorist groups.

■ Historical Background and Scientific Foundations

Historically, attempts to reduce the flow of illicit drugs have focused on drug interdiction and eradication. Police, military, and border control forces work together to prevent the production and distribution of illicit drugs. Domestic police and military forces may implement drug interdiction and eradication campaigns individually or in concert with foreign forces. Since the 1980s, drug enforcement forces in nations with heavy drug production and trafficking have received substantial foreign aid to combat drug trade. The vast majority of this aid is used to fund police and military personnel and equipment.

Since the turn of the twenty-first century, however, nations have earmarked some of this foreign aid to promote the transformation of the recipient nation's agricultural sector from the production of illicit drugs to legal crops. A few nations have also created domestic agricultural subsidy programs to assist their farmers in making this transition. Foreign aid and domestic subsidy programs that seek to move farmers from the cultivation of coca, cannabis, or poppies to legal crop production are designed to reduce the economic burden of shifting agricultural production. Many farmers cultivate crops used in drug production as a means to escape the poverty that exists in rural areas of developing nations.

In 2000 the United States began providing assistance to Colombia under Plan Colombia, a multi-year strategic plan to strengthen Colombia's military and police forces and combat drug production and trafficking. Plan Colombia contains provisions for financial assistance for social and economic development aid, some of which goes to assist farmers in the transition to legal agricultural production. The United States Agency for International Development (USAID), a U.S. federal government agency that oversees civilian foreign aid, administers Plan Colombia's social and economic programs. One of USAID's Colombian assistance programs, Areas for Municipal Level Alternative Development (ADAM), works with Colombian farmers, communities, and the private sector to develop licit agricultural production, including cacao and coffee. In the first eight years of Plan Colombia, the United States contributed more than $1 billion to promote social and economic programs. The government of Colombia has also contributed money for these purposes under Plan Colombia.

Opium poppy production in Afghanistan soared following the U.S.-led invasion of Afghanistan in 2001.

Opiates, including opium, morphine, and codeine, are produced from opium poppy. Heroin, a semi-synthetic opioid, is synthetically derived from morphine. USAID has spent more than $500 million on agricultural programs in Afghanistan since 2002, including more than $100 million in agricultural assistance to Afghan farmers to transition to licit crops. USAID also funds programs that provide agricultural services and technical assistance and education. Following the invasion of Afghanistan, opium poppy cultivation in Afghanistan rose from 7,606 hectares (18,795 acres) to a high of 193,000 hectares (476,913 acres) in 2007. USAID programs—which administer microloans for the purchase of farm equipment or seeds, provide technical training and assistance, and improve infrastructure—may explain part of the reduction in opium poppy cultivation in Afghanistan from 2007 to 2010 noted by the UNODC in February 2010.

■ Impacts and Issues

Agricultural aid and subsidy programs designed to reduce the flow of illicit drugs must effectively reduce production, while providing farmers with other financially viable agricultural opportunities. Eradication of crops used in illicit

drug production through herbicidal spraying is an effective way of reducing drug production; however, it often only produces short-term benefits. Eradication efforts harm farmers by destroying their livelihood, and most farmers in developing countries have little or no access to credit to fund the replanting of their land with licit crops. The farmers targeted by eradication schemes often have to return to narcotics producers to assist with replanting efforts. Eradication schemes, therefore, may reduce drug

Three saleswomen trade coca leaves in the Coca Market in downtown in La Paz, Bolivia. Soaring food prices may achieve what the United States has spent millions of dollars trying to do: persuade Bolivian farmers to sow their fields with less potent crops than cocaine's raw ingredient. Bolivia's government is now asking coca farmers to supplement their crops with rice and corn as a way of holding down coca production. *AP Images.*

IN CONTEXT: AGRICULTURAL VERSUS MILITARY AID

According to a report released by the United Nations Food and Agriculture Organization (FAO) in November 2009, direct foreign investment in agriculture increased from $1 billion in 2000 to $3 billion in 2007 (the latest year for which complete data is available). However, analysts contend that even with this increase, aid for non-agriculture programs (military and security interests, industrial development, etc.) accounts for approximately 99 percent of all foreign aid and investment and falls significantly short of the level of investment FAO estimates is needed to mitigate global poverty and famine.

production temporarily, but such programs rarely result in transitioning the agricultural sector to licit crops.

Nations may contribute agricultural aid to farmers as direct financial contributions, loans, services, or technical assistance and education. Short-term direct financial contributions may be used to assist farmers in the transition to the cultivation of licit crops. Long-term direct aid may also subsidize discrepancies in income following the transition from higher-priced illicit crops to lower-priced licit crops. Corruption involving narcotics producers becomes an issue with direct financial contributions, particularly long-term subsidies. In the mid-1990s, Mexico began an agricultural subsidy program to assist small-scale farmers who had to compete with corporate farms in the United States under a free trade agreement. In 2010 the *Los Angeles Times* reported that family members and associates of known drug lords received money under the subsidy program, ostensibly for the production of licit crops.

United States assistance to farmers in Afghanistan has relied more heavily on loans, services, and technical assistance and education. In fiscal year 2009, for example, USAID provided more than 52,000 agricultural loans to Afghan farmers. Most of these USAID loans are microloans, or small-scale loans that farmers may use to purchase seed and fertilizer, and have the capital to cultivate and harvest licit crops. The loans also make the farmers stakeholders in the future success of licit crops in Afghanistan, which encourages continued participation in the production of licit crops. Yet, according to the U.S. State Department, replacing illicit poppies with licit crops is difficult due to the value of such crops. USAID reviewed several alternative crop suggestions including soy, cotton, and sunflower, but high value horticultural crops that grow well in Afghanistan, such as grapes, almonds, pistachios, pomegranates, apricots, and melons, might provide food and allow farmers to invest in agricultural crops for which prices would be competitive with poppy production.

The technical assistance, infrastructure improvements, and education programs funded by USAID, the British government, and other groups have provided Afghan farmers with the tools and education needed to transition to the production of licit crops. USAID has trained more than 200,000 Afghan farmers in methods to increase crop yields and store harvested crops, and in business and finance management. Foreign investments have also improved irrigation infrastructure in Afghanistan, which increases arable land and crop yields. Foreign investment in Afghan agriculture played a part in the steady decline in opium poppy cultivation from 2007 to 2010.

SEE ALSO *Ethical Issues in Agriculture; Food Security; Subsistence Farming; Sustainable Agriculture; U.S. Agency for International Development (USAID).*

BIBLIOGRAPHY

Periodicals

Contreras, Joseph. "Failed Plan: After Five Years and Billions of U.S. Aid in the Drug War, Cocaine Production Still Thrives." *Newsweek International,* (August 29, 2005): 40.

Web Sites

"Afghanistan: Drug Industry and Counter-Narcotics Policy." *World Bank.* http://www.worldbank.org/ZTCWYL49P0 (accessed September 9, 2010).

"Afghanistan Opium Survey 2007: Executive Summary (August 2007)." *United Nations Office on Drugs and Crime.* http://www.unodc.org/documents/crop-monitoring/AFG07_ExSum_web.pdf (accessed September 9, 2010).

"Alternative Development: Myanmar." *United Nations Office on Drugs and Crime.* http://www.unodc.org/unodc/en/alternative-development/Myanmarprogramme.html (accessed September 6, 2010).

"Fact Sheet: Plan Columbia." *U.S. Bureau of Western Hemisphere Affairs, U.S. Department of State,* March 28, 2000. http://www.state.gov/www/regions/wha/colombia/fs_000328_plancolombia.html (accessed September 6, 2010).

"Myths & Facts about Fighting the Opium Trade in Afghanistan." *International Narcotics and Law Enforcement Affairs, U.S. Department of State.* http://www.state.gov/documents/organization/142643.pdf (accessed September 9, 2010).

"Opium Production in Afghanistan May Fall in 2010, UN Reports." *United Nations Office on Drugs and Crime.* http://www.un.org/apps/news/story.asp?NewsID=33727&Cr=afghan&Cr1= (accessed December 27, 2010).

Joseph P. Hyder

Alice Waters: California and New American Cuisine

■ Introduction

Alice Waters is an American chef and restaurateur who was among those credited with pioneering California cuisine, also called New American cuisine. Born in 1944, Waters opened the restaurant Chez Panisse in Berkley, California, in 1971. The restaurant focused on using fresh, organic ingredients and had a fixed menu that changed based upon what was available at its peak freshness. The focus on freshness and organic produce, as well as developing relationships with farmers and purveyors, laid the groundwork for the New American cuisine. Waters is also a notable member of the Slow Food movement, which is an organization that seeks to protect and educate about regional cuisine, as well as enhance the relationship between the food service industry and farmers and local specialty purveyors, such as cheese makers, bakers, or wine makers.

■ Historical Background and Scientific Foundations

Alice Waters learned to cook while she was studying abroad in France, earning a degree in French Cultural Studies from the University of California at Berkley in the late 1960s. She opened Chez Panisse after finishing college. Initially, it operated as a collaborative effort with the intention of having a place where Waters could cook for her friends. When purchasing supplies for Chez Panisse, Waters found that most of what was available was not of the same quality as the meat and produce she was able to get at farmers' markets while she was in France. In search of satisfactory supplies, she began contacting farmers and specialty food producers directly, building direct relationships with them. Eventually, Waters was able to obtain all organic ingredients at their peak of freshness, all from local farms and purveyors.

Chez Panisse became popular due to Waters' unique cooking style, which is referred to as a "fusion" style because it combines influences from many different cuisines. Additionally, her cooking style focuses on the flavor of every ingredient used, which is why she attempts to procure the best, freshest ingredients possible. By avoiding any ingredients that do not meet this criteria, the finished dishes are all intensely flavorful, as well as prepared in an innovative style. However, the extreme selectiveness with which she chooses her ingredients restricts what she can offer on a given night, which is why she serves a fixed menu. Not allowing the diners to choose their own meals was an unusual method when introduced, but was an inextricable element of a meal at Chez Panisse because the menu relied so heavily on locally sourced food.

As well as using techniques from varied cuisines, Waters' cooking focuses on lighter dishes. Instead of the cream- and *roux*-based sauces of classic French and Haute Cuisine, Waters favors lighter sauces such as vinaigrettes. It is this move toward lighter, fresher fare that has become the hallmark of California, or New American, cuisine. Rather than *roux*, sauces are thickened with pure starches such as cornstarch or via reduction, which means to cook a sauce slowly so the water evaporates out, and the sauce becomes thicker. Brighter, sharper flavors are also favored, so vinegars and citrus are popular ingredients.

■ Impacts and Issues

New American cuisine spread out from California to the rest of the country with remarkable efficacy. In a matter of years, one could see the techniques and flavor concepts of Alice Waters and other chefs in California becoming common in restaurants all across the United States.

Chez Panisse has been a famous restaurant for many years. Waters received the prestigious James Beard Foundation award for Best Chef in America in 1992, and Chez Panisse has received numerous accolades, including being named the best restaurant in America

WORDS TO KNOW

FIXED MENU: A style of restaurant service in which instead of having a list of dishes from which the diner can choose, there is only one list of courses that every diner receives.

FUSION CUISINE: Food that contains combinations of traditions, techniques, and ingredients of varying cultures.

ORGANIC: Organic refers to food that is produced using only natural techniques. Organic food cannot be produced or grown with pesticides, hormones, industrial fertilizers, antibiotics, or any other chemicals. Instead, organic farmers use techniques such as natural fertilizers and crop rotation.

REDUCTION: Thickening or intensifying the flavor of a liquid by evaporation.

ROUX: A cooked mixture of flour and butter, used as the base for many sauces in classic French cuisine.

SLOW FOOD MOVEMENT: A food culture that values traditional, seasonal, and local ingredients and preparation methods.

by *Gourmet* magazine. Many cooks who worked under Waters went on to become notable chefs in their own right, some continuing to contribute to the creation of California cuisine. One example is Californian chef Deborah Madison, who after working for Waters went on to open The Greens restaurant, which is a renowned vegan and vegetarian restaurant in San Francisco, California.

In addition to her work with the Slow Food movement, Waters has been an outspoken figure in the drive to improve the quality of food served in public schools. To that end, she started the Edible Schoolyard program, in which schoolchildren grow, harvest, and prepare organic ingredients for their lunches; as well as the School Lunch Initiative, which sought to bring healthier food to the Berkley school district in which Chez Panisse is located.

While Waters pursued organic food and continues to be an outspoken proponent for its attributes, there remains a controversy in the food service industry as to organic food's benefits. Although there is evidence that organic techniques are better for the environment and, in the case of certain growth hormones and pesticides also creates healthier products, organic food does

Alice Waters, the executive chef and owner of Chez Panisse in Berkeley, California, looks over the produce at a farmer's market in Washington, 2009. Waters has been advocating the use of seasonal, local food since the 1960s. *AP Images.*

not necessarily result in better tasting or more nutritious food. Also, in comparison to traditionally grown produce, organic fruits and vegetables are markedly more expensive due to the fact that organic techniques generally produce less yield per acre than traditional techniques. There is sometimes public pressure on restaurants to use more organic ingredients, but in certain situations it is not a feasible alternative for restaurants when fresh, in-season, and well-grown produce from a farm or purveyor may be a better option both in price and in the interest of the final dish.

Organic food has also come into controversy concerning the legitimacy of foods claiming to be organic. In the United States, the term was not regulated until 2002, when the United States Department of Agriculture passed legislation that the term could not be used to describe food that did not meet certain organic requirements. Throughout the world, enforcement of the term often comes into question, with some critics asking if foods that claim to be organic are actually grown or raised that way. Though there are pros and cons to organic methods, the term itself is a relatively recent addition to the restaurant and food marketing lexicon and as such will continue to spark controversy as more legislation is passed in various countries.

SEE ALSO *Community Supported Agriculture (CSAs); Edible Schoolyard Movement; Ethical Issues in Agriculture; Family Farms; Farm-to-Table Movement; Fusion; Improving Nutrition for America's Children Act of 2010; Locavore; Michael Pollan: Linking Food and Environmental Journalism; Organic Foods Production Act of 1990; Organics; School Lunch Reform; Slow Food Movement; Standard American Diet and Changing American Diet; Sustainable Table; Urban Farming/Gardening.*

BIBLIOGRAPHY

Books

McNamee, Thomas. *Alice Waters & Chez Panisse: The Romantic, Impractical, Often Eccentric, Ultimately Brilliant Making of a Food Revolution*. New York: Penguin Press, 2007.

Waters, Alice. *In the Green Kitchen: Techniques to Learn by Heart*. New York: Clarkson Potter, 2010.

Waters, Alice, Daniel Duane, and David Liittschwager. *Edible Schoolyard: A Universal Idea*. San Francisco: Chronicle Books, 2008.

Waters, Alice, Patricia Curtan, Kelsie Kerr, and Fritz Streiff. *The Art of Simple Food: Notes, Lessons, and Recipes from a Delicious Revolution*. New York: Clarkson Potter, 2007.

Periodicals

"My Kitchen: Locavore Pioneer Alice Waters." *Vanity Fair* (October 2010): 148.

Waters, Alice. "Slow Food Nation." *The Nation* 283, no. 7 (2006): 13ff.

Web Sites

Slow Food International. http://www.slowfood.com/ (accessed October 4, 2010).

The Edible Schoolyard. http://www.edibleschoolyard.org/ (accessed October 4, 2010).

David Brennan Tilove

America's Second Harvest/ Feeding America

■ Introduction

Feeding America, known until 2008 as America's Second Harvest, provides food to hungry Americans by partnering with major corporations. It is the leading hunger-relief charity in the United States and serves more than 37 million low-income people annually, including 14 million children and 3 million seniors. Feeding America seeks to eliminate hunger by matching people with surplus food. The organization operates through about 200 local food banks that serve all 50 states, the District of Columbia, and Puerto Rico. These banks obtain and distribute more than 2.5 billion pounds of food and grocery products to approximately 61,000 local charitable agencies and 70,000 programs that directly serve individuals and families in need.

The national organization manages logistics necessary to funnel food donations to the food banks that need them most. Feeding America secures food from the U.S. government and large corporate manufacturers, including Barilla, Coca-Cola, Dannon, Del Monte, General Mills, Hershey, Kellogg, Nestlé, Pepsi, Quaker-Tropicana-Gatorade, Sara Lee, Seashare, J.M. Smucker, SYSCO, and Tyson. It also works with trade associations such as the United Egg Producers and the American Farm Bureau Federation. Grocery stores that back Feeding America include Albertson's, Food Lion, Kroger, Publix, Safeway, and Walmart.

■ Historical Background and Scientific Foundations

The United States is rarely viewed as a nation in which hunger exists. With the end of the Great Depression (1929–1941), most Americans thought that poverty had virtually disappeared from the land, and with it went concern over the nutrition of the poor. Unlike its 1920s and 1930s editions, the 1954 version of Lydia Roberts's (1879–1965) standard text on child nutrition, *Nutrition Work with Children*, did not even mention poverty as a cause of malnutrition. In 1962 Michael Harrington (1928–1989) opened the eyes of many people about poverty with his book, *The Other America: Poverty in the United States*. Harrington inspired President Lyndon B. Johnson (1908–1973) to start the Great Society, which included a food stamp program that expanded the choice of free foods for the poor. There was also revived interest in school lunch programs, as well as federal aid to subsidize them.

When the late 1970s and early 1980s brought a renewal of complacency regarding malnutrition, as well as a turn against government programs for the poor, hunger and malnutrition rose. Various advocates for the poor reported that low-income individuals did not receive enough fresh vegetables, fruit, milk, beef, or chicken, resulting in deficiencies in vitamins A and C, iron, calcium, and protein. Malnutrition caused stunted growth, learning disabilities, and significantly higher infant mortality rates. While the government continued to fund nutrition programs, albeit at reduced numbers, private groups stepped into the breach.

Feeding America was established in 1979 and is headquartered in Chicago. However, its roots are in Arizona. American activist John van Hengel (1923–2005), a retired businessman, volunteered at a soup kitchen in Phoenix in the early 1960s. When he solicited food donations, he typically wound up with more food than the soup kitchen could use. At the same time, a client advised van Hengel that she found food for her family by searching through dumpsters behind grocery stores. The discarded food had acceptable quality. Van Hengel subsequently founded the nation's first food bank, St. Mary's Food Bank. As food banks developed around the country, they consolidated into America's Second Harvest, then Feeding America.

■ Impacts and Issues

According to the U.S. Department of Agriculture (USDA), one in six Americans does not get enough food to eat. At the end of 2009, the USDA Economic Research Service reported that food insecurity had increased dramatically. It estimated that more than 49 million Americans struggled with hunger on a daily basis, including nearly 17 million children. The rate of hunger jumped 36 percent over the previous year, likely as a result of the economic downturn. Nearly 15 percent of American households lacked access to an adequate supply of nutritious food. In its survey, *Hunger in America 2010*, Feeding America reported that more than one in three of the households that it served experienced low food security or hunger, which is a 54 percent increase in the number of households compared with four years earlier.

As the problem of hunger is immense, it will take considerable effort to solve it. The USDA measures 1.28 pounds of food as equivalent to one meal, meaning that millions of pounds of food are needed on a daily basis for hungry Americans. Feeding America is successfully bringing together government, nonprofit organizations, and the private sector as well as charitable individuals to

reduce food insecurity. In 2010 it received a $2 billion cash and in-kind commitment from Walmart. The donation is expected to expand the capacity of food banks, help the banks become more efficient in their operations, and provide healthy meals for children. At the time of this contribution, Walmart already contributed 45 percent of donations from its retailers to Feeding America. If the rate of hunger continues to rise, Feeding America will need to continue to expand its operations.

SEE ALSO *Food Price Crisis; Food Security; Government Food Assistance for Citizens; Waste and Spoilage.*

The Second Harvest food bank of Greater New Orleans has food ready to distribute early Saturday, November 17, 2007, in New Orleans, Louisiana. *AP Images.*

BIBLIOGRAPHY

Books

America's Second Harvest—the Nation's Food Bank Network: Ending Hunger. Chicago: America's Second Harvest, 2007.

Cohen, Rhoda, Myoung Kim, and James C. Ohls. *Hunger in America 2006: A Project of America's Second Harvest—the Nation's Food Bank Network: Full Report, March 2006.* Chicago: America's Second Harvest, 2006.

Periodicals

Daponte, Beth, and Shannon Bade. "How the Private Food Assistance Network Evolved: Interactions between Public and Private Responses to Hunger." *Nonprofit and Voluntary Sector Quarterly* 35, no. 4 (2006): 668–690.

"Features—News & Trends—America's Second Harvest." *Dairy Foods* 101, no. 12 (2000): 19.

"Hurricane Katrina Response—Food Processors, America's Second Harvest Help." *Food Processing* 66, no. 10 (2005): 11.

"Warehousing & Distribution—Do Something—America's Second Harvest Is Working to See That No One in America Goes Hungry." *Material Handling Management* 59, no. 7 (2004): 46.

Web Sites

AmpleHarvest.org. http://www.ampleharvest.org/LP/Pantry.php?gclid=CKy6_sXC1qQCFc5i2godzkNnJQ (accessed October 18, 2010).

Feeding America. http://feedingamerica.org/ (accessed October 18, 2010).

Caryn E. Neumann

Aquaculture and Fishery Resources

■ Introduction

The plant and animal life found in oceans, lakes, and rivers is an important food source for much of the world's population. Throughout human history, the apparent abundance of aquatic life created the impression that the supply of fish and other animals for human purposes was inexhaustible. In the twentieth century, two main anthropogenic forces contributed to the significant depletion of many aquatic species populations that humans use for food: harvesting methods that led to overfishing, with the resulting inability of threatened species to sustain themselves, and environmental degradation of aquatic habitats—the physical destruction of natural ecosystem habitats through ill-considered shoreline and marshland development.

Aquaculture is the cultivation and harvesting of animal or plant life in a controlled aquatic environment. It can be carried out in freshwater and saltwater environments depending upon nature of the cultivated species. Aquaculture has achieved global prominence as a means to increase human food supplies and to counter the observed effects of overfishing in many jurisdictions. The popular expressions "fish farming" and "shrimp farming" describe two well-known facets of aquaculture.

Fishery resources are the elements of a natural aquatic resource that include its species, populations, and stocks. A fishery is an industry devoted to harvesting, processing, and/or the ultimate sale of specific aquatic species taken in their natural habitat. The North Atlantic cod fishery and the Pacific salmon fishery are examples.

■ Historical Background and Scientific Foundations

China, one of the earliest aquaculture societies, first established inland freshwater aquaculture systems more than 2,000 years ago. Carp was the most prominent fish species cultivated by the Chinese, in specialized ponds constructed and maintained to provide optimal growing conditions. These early aquaculturalists determined that several different aquatic species could be raised in a single controlled habitat. Polyculture is based on the principle that because different species have distinct feeding habits, the mixed aquatic population will fully utilize the natural foods available. In modern times, rice paddies have been used to cultivate simultaneously this important aquatic plant food source and various fish species.

Successful aquaculture is directed by the basic principle that an aquatic species can be nurtured to optimal size and quality in a protected and controlled environment. Fish farming is the most common form of aquaculture. A typical fish farm is a fully integrated system where fish are cultivated from egg to larvae, through fingerling and yearling stages, to maturity, at which point they are harvested and processed. To achieve these results, aquaculture depends on a number of specific scientific disciplines that include genetics and selective breeding, parasite reduction processes, and strict control exercised over contact between the farmed fish and wild species.

Aquaculture is practiced in two distinct ways; the degree of human control exercised over the cultivation process is the distinguishing factor. The first method is *extensive aquaculture*, in which the cultivated aquatic life is grown using available natural food sources. This form of aquaculture is generally practiced in bodies of water where the temperature is not controlled and the intended aquatic product is shielded from natural predators. *Intensive aquaculture* involves the creation and maintenance of aquatic environments in which the intended product is nourished with high protein food formulations that increase growth rates and the ultimate product size. Intensive systems often require specialized filtration and waste product removal to protect the aquatic life from accumulating toxins.

WORDS TO KNOW

ALGACULTURE: The branch of aquaculture that concerns the cultivation and harvesting of algae, the aquatic plant species. All forms of algae are produced through photosynthesis. Micro-algaculture involves the production of various types of plankton, the tiny organisms that are the foundation for virtually all aquatic organism food chains. Macro-algaculture products are more complex plant forms such as seaweed and kelp. Algae have a number of important commercial uses, including their emerging role in biofuel production, as fertilizer ingredients, and as a component in bacteria elimination systems used for pollution control.

MARICULTURE: Mariculture is the aquaculture variant in which seawater is used to cultivate desired aquatic life forms for harvest. Mariculture is practiced in open ocean environments through the use of specialized protective nets and enclosures or in natural or artificial sea water ponds.

SEA LICE: A naturally occurring aquatic parasite. These small creatures prey on the blood, skin, and mucous membranes of a juvenile or adult fish host, causing damage to the flesh and immune system of its target. Salmon farms have been identified as key sites where sea lice proliferate. From the farms the lice migrate to nearby wild salmon populations, causing widespread destruction. Pacific salmon and sea trout are fish species that are especially vulnerable to sea lice infestations.

■ Impacts and Issues

In theory, aquaculture should be a safe and effective means to ensure that the all humans have access to a guaranteed supply of cost-effective and nutrient-rich foods. Aquaculture is compatible with the sustainable harvest practices universally advocated for all global aquatic species populations. Aquaculture should be a mechanism that contributes to the preservation of global fishery resources. It is estimated that approximately 50 percent of the world's current food demands will be supplied through aquaculture production by 2015. As the global population nears 7 billion people, the need to increase world food production in sustainable and environmentally sound ways should encourage additional aquaculture development. Further, the cost to produce food from aquaculture is less than the cost of many forms of terrestrial food production, such as cattle and pork farms.

The overall environmental impact of aquaculture on natural aquatic life and associated habitats is a source of continuing international controversy. Fish farming is a particular source of concern. If farmed fish species escape from their enclosures, there is a heightened risk that sea lice and other parasites that flourish in fish farm environments will contaminate wild fish populations. These circumstances contribute to widespread fears that fish caught in natural habitats may not be safe for human consumption. In addition, the antibiotics used on fish farms to control pathogens and parasites also can be

Extensive farming techniques are used to farm mussels growing in underwater socks in Rustico, Prince Edward Island, Canada.
© *Philip Scalia / Alamy.*

introduced by escaped fish into natural fish populations. The long-term genetic impact of farmed fish interbred with natural populations is not fully understood.

Genetic modification (GM) of aquatic species is a further aquaculture issue that raises environmental concerns. In September 2010, the U.S. Food and Drug Administration (FDA) gave preliminary approval for the human consumption of a new transgenic salmon species created from DNA extracted from Pacific salmon and the faster-growing eelspout fish. The resulting species, called "Frankenfood" by critics, has all of the physical and biological characteristics of salmon, but it grows to its commercial harvest weight on 25 percent less food in approximately one half of the normal maturation period for wild salmon. Critics assert that breeding between GM species that escape from salmon farms into natural habitats could destroy wild salmon populations.

Aquaculture presents another specific environmental risk: Intensive aquaculture practices tend to remove large amounts of nutrients from aquatic habitats from relatively small areas in short periods. The large volume of fish waste generated by these operations also tends to upset the optimal ecological balance in the locale.

The harvest of natural ocean fish stocks is subject to a variety of international agreements. The enforcement of the specific fishing quotas established as measures to protect fishery resources has limited effect given the natural mobility of fish populations and their movements beyond specific territorial waters.

■ Primary Source Connection

According to the Fisheries and Aquaculture Department of the Food and Agriculture Organization (FAO) of the United Nations, aquaculture is "set to contribute half of the fish consumed by the human population worldwide." As the following primary source articulates, however, increasing energy and food costs offer substantial challenges to aquaculture-based industries. Complex issues such as climate change and energy costs can make dramatic impacts on fish supply and the sustainability of aquaculture ventures.

The State of World Fisheries and Aquaculture—2008

Will land and water suffice for agriculture to feed a growing human population? The question about humankind's ability to feed itself is old and recurring. However, only fairly recently has fish been included in this concern. As late as the first half of the twentieth century, the sea was considered a virtually inexhaustible reservoir of fish for people to exploit. It was only in mid-century that marine biologists started to gain an audience when they affirmed that wild fish stocks were finite and could be fished too heavily. These concerns became serious early in the second half of the century, when the capacity to overfish wild stocks became apparent. However, aquaculture started to grow at about that time and,

A fish farm off Frioul Island near Marseille, France.   *Image copyright Ekaterina Pokrovsky, 2010. Used under license from Shutterstock.com.*

for many, this was reassuring. It sustained the hope that there would be enough fish to eat also in the future.

In the last three decades, aquaculture has grown rapidly. In the 1970s, it accounted for about 6 percent of fish available for human consumption; in 2006, the figure was 47 percent.

However, overall the rate of growth in aquaculture (measured in production volume) has started to slow. For the world as a whole, while the average yearly growth rate had been 11.8 percent in the period 1985–94, it was 7.1 percent in the following decade.

This slowdown is also reflected in the quantities of fish and fish products made available for human consumption. Per capita availability, which grew, albeit slowly, in the 1990s and early years of the following decade, seems to be leveling off. The question is whether per capita supplies of fish for human consumption will remain steady or peak in the near future and then start to fall.

The world's supply of fish available for human consumption is determined by capture fisheries production (marine and freshwater) and aquaculture production, less the share of this total withdrawn from human consumption and used for other purposes. Given the strong likelihood that fish landings will remain stagnant in capture fisheries, aquaculture remains the only apparent means to expand world supplies. So, what does the future look like for aquaculture?

In the late twentieth century, when capture fishery production levelled off and aquaculture production increased rapidly, most observers tended to conclude that any supply shortfall would be filled by aquaculture production. This opinion is still widely held.

More serious attempts to predict future fish supplies have tended to predict capture fisheries production independently (by considering the state of stocks and fishing effort in capture fisheries) and then deduct projected landings from demand (arrived at by considering population growth and income elasticities of demand for fish) in order to arrive at the quantity that aquaculture would have to produce. There have been few attempts to predict future aquaculture production by examining the prospects for culture of various species, culture systems and economic conditions.

However, the popular assumption—that aquaculture production will grow as long as demand does, and do so in volumes that will virtually match demand growth—is unfortunate as it sends a surreptitious message that there is a considerable degree of automatism in the expected aquaculture response and, thus, little need for enabling public policies. Such a view of the seafood sector is misleading for those who formulate public policies towards aquaculture and capture fisheries. Aquaculture-enabling policies are essential for the steady and sustainable growth of the sector. . . .

Worldwide, the rate of growth in aquaculture production is slowing. Surveys of fish farmers and other aquaculturists show that, generally, the reasons for this are that those who want to expand production face various constraints and obstacles. They would probably be better equipped to overcome them, and increase production, if the price levels for fish rose. However, it would seem unwise to rely only on an increase in price, which, if it happens, is likely to be in nominal rather than real terms. . . .

FOOD AND AGRICULTURE ORGANIZATION (FAO) OF THE UNITED NATIONS: FISHERIES AND AQUACULTURE DEPARTMENT. "THE STATE OF WORLD FISHERIES AND AQUACULTURE–2008 (SOFIA)." HTTP://WWW.FAO.ORG/DOCREP/011/I0250E/I0250E00.HTM (ACCESSED NOVEMBER 2, 2010).

SEE ALSO *Agriculture Demand for Water; Agroecology; Climate Change and Agriculture; Factory Farming; Free Trade and Agriculture; Genetically Modified Organisms (GMO); Gulf Oil Spill Food Impacts; Paralytic Shellfish Poisoning; Population and Food; Seafood; Water; Water Scarcity.*

BIBLIOGRAPHY

Books

Leung, PingSun, Cheng-Sheng Lee, and P. J. O'Bryen. *Species and System Selection for Sustainable Aquaculture.* Ames, IA: Blackwell, 2007.

Molyneaux, Paul. *Swimming in Circles: Aquaculture and the End of Wild Oceans.* New York: Thunder's Mouth, 2007.

World Bank. *Changing the Face of the Waters: The Promise and Challenge of Sustainable Aquaculture.* Washington, DC: World Bank, 2007.

Periodicals

Cressey, Daniel. "Aquaculture: Future Fish." *Nature* 458, no. 7237 (2009): 398–400.

Rosenberg, Andrew A. "Aquaculture: The Price of Lice." *Nature* 451, no. 7174 (2008): 23–24.

Sachs, Jeffrey D. "The Promise of the Blue Revolution. Aquaculture Can Maintain Living Standards While Averting the Ruin of the Oceans." *Scientific American* 297, no. 1 (2007): 37–38.

Web Sites

"Aquaculture." *Fisheries and Aquaculture Department, Food and Agriculture Organization of the United Nations.* http://www.fao.org/fishery/aquaculture/en (accessed October 8, 2010).

"Aquaculture." *U.S. Department of Heath & Human Services.* http://www.fda.gov/AnimalVeterinary/DevelopmentApprovalProcess/Aquaculture/default.htm (accessed October 8, 2010).

Bryan Thomas Davies

Asian Diet

Introduction

The Asian diet tends to be based on rice as the staple food, and also includes many vegetables. Compared to other world diets, the Asian diet features more fish and seafood, but with lower consumption overall of other sources of animal protein. Japan has avoided many of the diet-related health problems associated with other high-income countries. Many credit this to the Asian diet, and some have outlined an Asian food pyramid as a guide to the Asian diet. Despite having high incomes in some countries, such as Japan, food insecurity remains common in many parts of Asia, and the majority of the underweight children under five in the world live in South Asia. Vitamin A deficiency is also common in Asia, although scientists have engineered a type of genetically modified rice that contains beta-carotene in an effort to prevent the deficiency. Diets in middle-income countries in Asia are rapidly changing and becoming more like diets in Europe and the Americas, with reliance on supermarkets and fast food. The relatively high levels of fish and seafood in the Asian diet present some challenges to maintaining fish populations at sea as both incomes and populations continue to increase in the region.

Historical Background and Scientific Foundations

According to the World Health Organization's (WHO) 2009 data, Japan had the highest life expectancy of any country in the world in 2007: 86 years for women and 79 years for men. Due to high income, high-quality health care, and a healthy diet, the Japanese appear to experience fewer diet-related health conditions such as diabetes, obesity, heart disease, and certain cancers compared to other industrialized countries. According to Engel's law, as incomes rise, a smaller percentage of income will be spent on food, though more real income

will be spent. This means that as their incomes rise, people all over the world tend to purchase more expensive calories, often in the form of fruits, vegetables, meat, and dairy products rather than grain. However, instead of suffering from too many calories and associated high levels of fat, which is often a hallmark of high-income countries, Japan consumes only 2,900 calories per capita per day, compared to the average of high-income nations of 3,364 calories per capita per day, according to a study conducted by the U.S. Department of Agriculture's Economic Research Service (USDA/ERS). Part of the story is that Japan has high food costs, with rice, fruits, and meat priced higher than in other high-income countries, at least partly due to protective agricultural trade policies and high domestic agricultural prices maintained by agricultural policy and subsidies. However, cultural preferences also appear to play a role.

Because the Japanese diet is 80 percent vegetable products and uses fish and seafood for animal protein, these low-fat products help maintain the health of the Japanese population and may explain the difference in this diet with others in high income countries. Other East Asian and South Asian diets have many health benefits similar to the Japanese diet. Based on studies conducted by scientists from Cornell University and the Harvard University School of Public Health, an Asian diet pyramid was developed in 1995. Somewhat similar to the U.S. Department of Agriculture's (USDA) 1992 food pyramid, the Asian diet pyramid highlights the role of whole grains and vegetables, along with rare consumption of red meat, sweets, poultry, and eggs. Nutritionists who worked on this project stressed that the Asian diet was lower in fat content than most other diets.

Despite a diet with many potential health benefits, East and South Asia also have areas with large populations experiencing food insecurity. More than half of the world's underweight children under the age of five live in South Asia, with 42 percent of those in India and

WORDS TO KNOW

AQUACULTURE: The process of raising fish, crustaceans, mollusks, and other aquatic plants and animals in confinement.

ENGEL'S LAW: As a household's income increases, it will spend a lower percentage of income on food, though its actual food expenditures may increase. The increased spending is due to a shift in the diet away from grains to more expensive foods such as meat, dairy, fruits, and vegetables. Engel's law is named after Ernst Engel (1821–1896), the German economist and statistician who first wrote about it.

MIDDLE-INCOME COUNTRY (MIC): A country that when compared to other countries in the world is neither very poor nor very rich. According to the World Bank, a middle-income country has a per capita gross national income (GNI) between 996 and 12,195 U.S. dollars. In 2010 middle income countries included Botswana, Brazil, Chile, China, Fiji, India, Indonesia, Jordan, Kazakhstan, Mexico, Nigeria, Russia, Senegal, South Africa, Thailand, and Turkey among others.

5 percent each in Bangladesh and Pakistan, according to the International Food Policy Research Institute's (IFPRI) 2010 "Global Hunger Index" report. However, between 1990 and 2000 North Korea was the only Asian country to experience deterioration in its Global Hunger Index score, an indexed measure of food insecurity based on several other measurements. Bangladesh, Cambodia, India, Nepal, and Timor-Leste had the highest scores in Asia, reflecting high levels of hunger and malnutrition in those countries.

■ Impacts and Issues

Despite having traditional diets that include a large number of vegetables, Asian diets and persistent poverty have failed to eradicate vitamin A deficiency. According to the International Rice Research Institute (IRRI), an international research center based in the Philippines, half of the world's population depends on rice as a staple food. Rice lacks vitamin A, and vitamin A deficiency can lead to blindness or night blindness in children. Vitamin A deficiency also increases the risk of death from infections as an infant and of contracting a variety of communicable diseases. In Southeast Asia alone, more than

A woman prepares fresh fish at a market in Vietnam. The diet of many Asian nations, especially those with substantial coastlines, heavily relies on fish. *Image copyright Simone van den Berg, 2010. Used under license from Shutterstock.com.*

90 million children may have vitamin A deficiency according to IRRI.

For this reason, two scientists, Ingo Potrykus (1933–), a German plant biologist, and Peter Beyer (1952–), a German biologist and biochemist, created "golden rice" by combining traditional breeding methods and genetic modification. Using genes from corn and a variety of other genes, golden rice contains beta-carotene, which the human body converts into vitamin A. The scientists have donated the intellectual property rights for golden rice, so that it can be freely used by public agricultural research institutions to develop rice varieties suitable for local growing conditions. Although golden rice was developed by 2001, it has yet to enter markets, because fear of genetically modified organisms (GMOs) and slow regulatory processes have not made it commercially available to farmers in Asia. While grown in research settings in several countries, golden rice has yet to clear regulatory barriers. The Philippines may be the first country to approve non-research growing of golden rice by 2012 at the earliest.

IN CONTEXT: ASIAN OBESITY RATES ALSO ON THE RISE

Asia is not immune to the rising obesity rates found in America and Europe. World Health Organization (WHO) officials cite rising obesity and diabetes rates across Asia. In a 2005 study, about 30 percent of the population of Asia was estimated to be clinically overweight. WHO officials predict that obesity levels in Asia could grow to levels rivaling those in the United States and Europe by 2015. A study released in 2009 concluded that approximately 23 percent of the population of China could be considered overweight. In some areas of India—especially major urban centers and areas of rising income due to technology-related jobs—approximately one quarter of the population could be considered clinically obese. In India, there are more than 40 million reported cases of diabetes, and some experts predict that the number of persons with diabetes could double by 2025.

A local merchant serves a variety of foods at a traditional floating market in Bangkok, Thailand. Vegetables, fish, and rice- or noodle-based dishes are common in many Asian countries. *Image copyright gh19, 2010. Image used under license from Shutterstock.com.*

Diets in Asian countries are rapidly changing due to shifting preferences and wider availability of processed and imported foods. Supermarkets have entered Asian middle-income countries such as China, Thailand, and Indonesia, replacing or competing with ubiquitous street markets and street food vendors. Whereas supermarkets provide convenient access to a wide variety of foods, possibly increasing dietary diversity and improving access to some foods, they also carry a wide array of highly processed, high-calorie foods that may have low nutritional content. Between 1999 and 2005, supermarket sales in China increased 600 percent. Also, Asian countries are experiencing a remarkable expansion of fast food outlets from developed countries: Sales of fast food in Indonesia and China doubled between 1999 and 2005. In these rapidly developing countries, health systems have been strained by obesity and other associated health problems.

Asian countries have also responded to these trends with novel policy responses. Singapore has altered school lunches, improved access to drinking water at schools, and encouraged more physical activity at school to change the habits of its youth. In 1992 only 60 percent of students could pass the national physical fitness test, but by 2002 80 percent passed according to USDA/ERS.

As incomes increase in Asia, a high relative consumption of fish and seafood may have positive health outcomes as was the case in Japan. Instead of shifting to high fat foods, it appears income growth in Asia may lead to increased consumption of fish and seafood. However, the environmental impact of increasing demand for seafood troubles many ecologists and environmental activists. In Malaysia, for example, the World Wide Fund for Nature (WWF; formerly the World Wildlife Fund) warns that fish stocks in the seas off the Malaysian coast may be exhausted by 2050. Other East Asian and Southeast Asian countries face similar problems of increasing demand for seafood but decreasing stocks at sea.

While being a large consumer of fish and seafood from the oceans, Asia also leads the world in aquaculture, the process of farming fish, crustaceans, and other aquatic plants and animals. In 2007, according to the Food and Agriculture Organization (FAO) of the United Nations, Asia provided 92 percent of production and 80 percent of the value of world aquaculture. While not without its own environmental concerns, growth of Asian aquaculture has been rapid and offers one possible response to shrinking fish populations at sea. Production of fish, crustaceans, and mollusks increased 20 percent by weight between 2002 and 2005 in Asia according to FAO data. Balancing environmental concerns with increasing demand for seafood and fish will remain a challenge for the Asian diet in the twenty-first century.

SEE ALSO *Aquaculture and Fishery Resources; Diet and Cancer; Diet and Diabetes; Diet and Heart Disease; Diet and Hypertension; Dietary Changes in Rapidly Developing Countries; Food Security; Fusion; Genetically Modified Organisms (GMO); Immigration and Cuisine; Malnutrition; Rice; Shark Harvesting; Street Food; Tea; Vegetables; Whaling.*

BIBLIOGRAPHY

Books

Asia Society. *Never an Empty Bowl: Sustaining Food Security in Asia.* New York: Asia Society, 2010.

Huang, Bochao. *Diet, Nutrition and Optimal Health: From Food Supply to Nutrigenomics, the 10th Asian Congress of Nutrition, September 2007.* Middle Park, Victoria, Australia: HEC Press, 2008.

Mack, Glenn R., and Asele Surina. *Food Culture in Russia and Central Asia.* Westport, CT: Greenwood Press, 2005.

Periodicals

Akamatsu, Rie. "A Content Analysis of the Japanese Interpretation of 'Eating a Balanced Diet'." *Psychological Reports* 100, no. 3 (2007): 727–730.

"Fresh Market to Supermarket: Nutrition Transition Insights from Chiang Mai, Thailand." *Public Health Nutrition* 13, no. 6 (2010): 893–897.

Lukacs, Gabriella. "Iron Chef around the World." *International Journal of Cultural Studies* 13, no. 4 (2010): 409–426.

Paik, HeeYoung. "The Issues in Assessment and Evaluation of Diet in Asia." *Asia Pacific Journal of Clinical Nutrition* 17, suppl. 1 (2008): 294–295.

Palmer, Amanda, and Keith West. "A Quarter of a Century of Progress to Prevent Vitamin A Deficiency through Supplementation." *Food Reviews International* 26, no. 3 (2010): 270–301.

Wu, Anna H., Mimi C. Yu, Chiu-Chen Tseng, Frank Z. Stanczyk, and Malcolm C. Pike. "Dietary Patterns and Breast Cancer Risk in Asian American Women." *The American Journal of Clinical Nutrition* 89, no. 4 (2009): 1145–1154.

Web Sites

"Asian Cuisine & Foods." *Asian Nation.* http://www.asian-nation.org/asian-food.shtml (accessed October 21, 2010).

"What Is the Asian Diet Pyramid?" *Oldways.* http://www.oldwayspt.org/asian-diet-pyramid (accessed October 21, 2010).

Blake Jackson Stabler

Avian Influenza

■ Introduction

Few phenomena in the field of infectious diseases have so captured world attention as avian (bird) influenza. By September 2010, 62 countries had reported cases of highly pathogenic avian influenza H5N1 in poultry and wild birds. As of August 30, 2010, a total of 504 cases of H5N1 influenza were officially reported to World Health Organization (WHO) officials, with 299 of the reported cases resulting in death (a lethality rate near 60 percent).

While a cautious fear of a highly pathogenic H5N1 pandemic remains, there are immediate and serious consequences for food producers and on public confidence in the safety of avian (especially poultry) products. Outbreaks in flocks of birds have resulted in culls, or organized killings, of selected birds; as of September 2010, the number of birds killed for this reason was in excess of 300 million birds. In some cases, outbreaks of H5N1 have killed 100 percent of the birds in infected flocks.

■ Historical Background and Scientific Foundations

The term "avian influenza" is a misnomer: Virtually all strains (types) of the influenza virus pass through ducks or other birds before emerging into the human population. The first recorded outbreak of influenza occurred in 1580, and an additional 32 pandemics (global epidemics) had been documented as of 2010. The Spanish flu H1N1 pandemic of 1918–1919 resulted in an estimated 21 to 40 million deaths. The Asian flu (H2N2, 1957) and Hong Kong flu (H3N2, 1968) pandemics each resulted in one to four million deaths. Excess deaths attributable to influenza in the United States numbered 603,600 during the epidemics of 1918–1919, 1957–1958, and 1968–1969; and an additional 600,000 were estimated to have died in non-pandemic years during 1957 to 1990.

Whereas most human infection is caused by virus types H1, H2 and H3, types H5 and H7 are known to be more virulent. In fact, before the current outbreak of H5N1 virus, small clusters of human infection by H7N7, H7N3, and even H5N1 had been reported in persons having close exposure to poultry in several countries. Infections were generally mild, often limited to a mild cough and conjunctivitis (inflammation of the membranes of the eye). Nevertheless, prior outbreaks of H5N1 virus in Hong Kong in 1997 and 1998 resulted

A woman in Medan, Indonesia, in 2006, kisses her chicken to show her belief that it is safe. Dozens of people from the Karo regency of north Sumatra province, where seven family members died of avian influenza, held a protest in front of the governor's office, slaughtering their chickens, drinking the chickens' blood, cooking them, and consuming them to protest the government's plan to kill all poultry. *AP Images.*

in six deaths. Antibody (a protein produced by the immune system in response to the presence of the specific H5N1 antigen) was demonstrated in 17.2 percent of poultry workers during the outbreak. Approximately 1.5 million chickens and other birds were slaughtered in an attempt to control the virus.

H5N1 mutates rapidly and has a propensity to acquire genes from other animal species. Birds may excrete the virus from the mouth and cloaca (the excretory vent of a bird) for up to ten days. H5N1 virus was found to survive in bird feces for at least 35 days at low temperature (39.2°F, 4°C). At a much higher temperature (98.6°F, 37°C), H5N1 viruses have been shown to survive in fecal samples for 6 days.

Scope and Distribution

Despite the H5N1 cases and deaths in 1997, epidemiologists define the current outbreak as starting in 2003, when one fatal case of human H5N1 was reported in China and three fatal cases in Vietnam. The H5N1 virus responsible for the outbreak in 1997 was transitory and a different strain of H5N1 than the one causing outbreaks

and circulating since 2003. In 2004, 17 cases (12 fatal) were reported in Thailand, and 29 (20 fatal) in Vietnam. Several asymptomatic (without symptoms) infections were subsequently reported in South Korea. In 2005, 20 cases (13 fatal) were reported in Indonesia, 5 (2 fatal) in Thailand, and 61 (19 fatal) in Vietnam. By the end of 2006, cases were being reported in Azerbaijan, Cambodia, China, Indonesia, Iraq, Turkey, and Africa (Djibouti and Egypt). In 2007 the list of infected countries expanded to include Laos and Nigeria.

In 2009 WHO recorded 72 cases of human H5N1 influenza infection in 17 countries spanning Europe, Africa, the Middle East, and Asia. Lethality rates are high, but vary according to region. For example, as of July 2010 a total of 166 cases of H5N1 influenza in humans, resulting in 137 deaths, were confirmed in Indonesia. The H5N1-related fatality rate in Indonesia of 82.5 percent is significantly higher than the global H5N1 fatality rate.

In addition to human cases, as of September 2010 numerous outbreaks limited to wild and domestic birds have been reported in 62 countries. Thus far, spread of highly pathogenic H5N1 is primarily through wild birds, and still has a very low transmissibility to and among humans.

H5N1 infection has, however, already appeared in a number of non-avian hosts, including pigs, tigers, leopards, dogs, civet cats, domestic cats, Cynomolgus macaques, ferrets, New Zealand white rabbits, leopards, rats, mink, and stone marten. Indeed, infected blow flies (*Calliphora nigribarbis*) have been identified in the vicinity of poultry infected with H5N1 influenza virus in Japan.

Avian influenza is characterized by fever greater than 100.4°F (38°C), shortness of breath, and cough. The incubation period is two to four days. Some persons have reported sore throat, conjunctivitis, muscle pain, rash, and runny nose. Watery diarrhea or loose stools is noted in approximately 50 percent of the cases, a symptom that is uncommon in the more familiar forms of influenza. All patients reported to date have presented with significant lymphopenia (diminished concentration of lymphocytes, white blood cells, in the blood) and marked chest x-ray abnormalities consisting of diffuse, multifocal or patchy infiltrates (areas of inflammatory cells, foreign organisms, and cellular debris, often indicating pneumonia). Physical examination reveals the patient to be short of breath, with signs of lung inflammation. Myocardial (heart muscle) and hepatic (liver) dysfunction are also reported. Approximately 60 percent of patients have died, on an average of ten days after the onset of symptoms.

Treatment and Prevention

Diagnosis depends on demonstration of the virus or serum antibody toward the virus in specialized laboratories. Because of intense media reporting (and misinformation) a given patient may be reported repeatedly; or a case of unrelated respiratory infection may be reported as "avian influenza." Thus, only reports issued by qualified centralized laboratories should be considered valid. As of 2007, only four anti-viral agents have been used for the treatment of influenza: Amantadine, Rimantadine, Oseltamivir, and Zanamivir. Although some success has been claimed in the use of Oseltamivir for the treatment of H5N1, a large controlled clinical trial is not feasible. Vaccines against this strain are under development.

■ Impacts and Issues

Influenza is one of the most contagious of human diseases, and though most strains of the virus are rarely fatal, influenza creates a large economic medical care burden. The new avian influenza strain, however, causes a very severe disease. The chance of dying of the better-known common strains is lower than one tenth of one percent; the case-fatality rate for avian influenza is much

---

IN CONTEXT: INFLUENZA VIRUS NAMES

An influenza A virus, including the pandemic H1N1 virus (inappropriately named the "swine flu" virus) and the H5N1 avian flu virus are often designated by the presence of two specific proteins on the virus surface that are important in determining how the specific virus infects humans. These proteins, known as antigens, bear the names hemagglutinin (HA) and neuraminidase (NA). The HA and NA proteins are complex and vary subtly in their chemical structure over time. This process, termed antigenic drift, results in virus particle proteins with different binding and recognition abilities. As of 2010, fifteen different HA subtypes were known to exist; there were nine different NA subtypes. These subtypes receive different number designations, and the various influenza strains are named by the specific HA and NA proteins on the virus. For example, the H5N1 virus contains HA protein 5 and NA protein 1.

Other traits of viruses also help them evade the immune system or to create an influenza virus for which humans have no immunity at all. A form of the influenza virus exists in nearly all animals, including domesticated birds and pigs, and the animal viruses bear a close genetic relationship to human influenza viruses. This occasionally enables new virus strains to develop in animals and then leap to humans. A novel virus produced this way, to which humans have no immunity, can be an ideal candidate to create an epidemic or pandemic if the virus is also highly transmissible.

---

higher. Thus, the fear of all those who deal with this outbreak is that the virus will one day revert to a contagious form, while retaining its high virulence ability to cause disease. At that point, public health officials fear millions of cases . . of a highly lethal disease.

In 2009 and 2010 the majority of new H5N1 cases were reported in Egypt. As of September 2010, Egyptian officials reported 112 confirmed cases of H5N1 avian influenza, with death resulting in approximately one-third of all cases. In Egypt, avian influenza in humans occurs mostly among young children, and poultry is one of the mainstays of the diet. Chickens are often kept on the rooftops of homes, and children are frequently responsible for their care. Many Egyptian people are reluctant to report ill or dying chickens to local authorities for fear that their chickens and possibly those of their neighbors will be removed. Unlike many other countries, Egypt does not compensate citizens for culled or seized poultry.

Other countries reporting cases of H5N1 avian influenza between January 2010 and September 2010 include Cambodia (1 case), China (1 case), Egypt (22 cases), Indonesia (6 cases), and Vietnam (7 cases).

SEE ALSO *Poultry.*

BIBLIOGRAPHY

Books

Alcabes, Philip. *Dread: How Fear and Fantasy Have Fueled Epidemics from the Black Death to Avian Flu.* New York: PublicAffairs, 2009.

Bethe, Marilyn R. *Global Spread of the Avian Flu: Issues and Actions.* Hauppauge, NY: Nova Science, 2006.

Nandi, Sukdeb. *Avian Influenza or Bird Flu.* Delhi, India: Daya Pub. House, 2009.

U.S. Department of Health and Human Services. *2006 Guide to Surviving Bird Flu: Common Sense Strategies and Preparedness Plans—Avian Flu and H5N1 Threat.* Mount Laurel, NJ: Progressive Management, 2006.

Periodicals

Gorman, Christine. "The Avian Flu: How Scared Should We Be?" *Time* (October 17, 2005): 30–34.

Kaiser, Jocelyn. "Resurrected Influenza Virus Yields Secrets of Deadly 1918 Pandemic." *Science* 310 (2005): 28–29.

The Writing Committee of the World Health Organization Consultation on Human Influenza A/H5. "Avian Influenza A (H5N1) Infection in Humans." *New England Journal of Medicine* 353 (September 29, 2005): 1374–1385.

Web Sites

"Avian Influenza." *Centers for Disease Control and Prevention (CDC).* http://www.cdc.gov/flu/avian (accessed September 23, 2010).

"Avian Influenza." *World Health Organization (WHO) Global Alert and Response (GAR).* http://www.who.int/csr/disease/avian_influenza/en/index.html (accessed September 23, 2010).

"Avian Influenza (Bird Flu)." *World Health Organization (WHO) Medical Centre.* http://www.who.int/entity/mediacentre/factsheets/avian_influenza/en/index.html (accessed September 23, 2010).

"Avian Influenza: Current H5N1 Situation." *Centers for Disease Control and Prevention (CDC).* http://www.cdc.gov/flu/avian/outbreaks/current.htm (accessed September 23, 2010).

"Bird Flu (Avian Influenza)." *Mayo Clinic.* http://www.mayoclinic.com/health/bird-flu/DS00566 (accessed September 23, 2010).

"Influenza." *Centers for Disease Control and Prevention (CDC).* http://www.cdc.gov/flu (accessed September 23, 2010).

Stephen A. Berger

Baking Bread

■ Introduction

Breads, more specifically the most familiar leavened breads, are part of a rich tradition dating back thousands of years. However, the process by which dough leavens has only been understood relatively recently. With current understanding and technology, bakers have much more control over the process and the final product. Leavened bread utilizes the process of fermentation, the metabolic process in which yeast consumes carbohydrates and produces two primary byproducts: carbon dioxide and alcohol. Yeast is a naturally occurring microorganism, of which there are thousands of different species. Much as the first beer brewers discovered that a mash of grains would ferment and become beer if left in the open, leavened bread first occurred when raw wheat gruel was left in the open and airborne yeast caused the mixture to ferment.

■ Historical Background and Scientific Foundations

The earliest archeological evidence of leavened bread dates back to Egypt around 4000 BC. The technological turning point for creating leavened bread was the cultivation of a strain of wheat that could be easily husked without being cooked. As with most grains, wheat was cultivated so it could be ground into wheat flour, which would then be mixed with water to make dough and cooked into flatbreads. Wild wheat, however, is tough and difficult to grind, so oftentimes it was cooked beforehand to aid the milling process. Wheat that is cooked before it is ground cannot become leavened bread, because the heat of cooking affects the protein structure inside the grain and prevents the development of gluten, a key aspect of leavened bread. Gluten is a long, elastic protein molecule that is specific to grains in the grass family, including wheat, rye, and barley. Of these grains, wheat has the highest gluten content, which provides a greater elasticity that is good for leavened bread. Gluten is created when grains are milled into flour while raw.

Ancient farmers developed wheat that could be ground raw simply so they could produce more flour faster. However, when this new flour was mixed with water and left in the open, some batches would be exposed to airborne yeast. The yeast would start to ferment in the dough, consuming carbohydrates and producing carbon dioxide. The released carbon dioxide is caught by the gluten, which stretches and expands as it fills up, causing the dough to rise and become leavened. Because yeast could not be cultivated at the time, the batches that leavened would be saved and fed more flour, and then broken off in to pieces to make more batches, similar to how modern sourdough starter is used. Because gluten is specific to certain grains, cultures in areas where these grains are not common (such as Asia, where the primary grain is rice) have fewer leavened breads in their cuisine.

Now that yeast can be cultivated and stored, the process of baking bread is much easier and more versatile. For a modern baker, the options are almost endless: There are different types of flour that can be chosen, each with a different starch to protein ratio that affects the final texture of the bread. There are many different types of yeast readily available on the market, such as brewer's yeast and active dry yeast. There are also recipes that call for fat to be added in the form of eggs, butter, or oil for a richer bread. Breads without added fat, such as baguettes, traditional white bread, and rye are called lean breads. Breads with added butter or oil, such as brioche and challah, are enriched breads.

Whatever recipe the baker is using, the modern process is much the same. First, the yeast is combined with warm water and sometimes a small amount of sugar. This activates the yeast and begins the fermentation process, and as the yeast feeds on the sugar the mixture will become frothy. Next the flour and any additional

WORDS TO KNOW

FERMENTATION: The metabolic process by which yeast consumes carbohydrates and produces carbon dioxide and alcohol.

GLUTEN: Elastic protein molecules specific to certain cereal grains. It is found in high concentrations in wheat and in smaller concentrations in barley and rye.

KNEADING: The process of rolling dough made from wheat flour to develop and align the gluten molecules.

LEAVENING: The process of causing dough to rise and puff up with carbon dioxide prior to cooking.

OVEN SPRING: The sudden rapid rising of dough shortly after it is put in to the oven.

PROOFING: Allowing dough that has risen once to rise again.

PUNCHING DOWN: Pressing on risen dough to expel excess carbon dioxide.

YEAST: A naturally occurring single-celled fungus.

ingredients in the recipe are mixed in with the yeast to form dough. Then the dough is kneaded, or mixed consistently for several minutes. Kneading develops the gluten in the dough and also causes the gluten's long molecules to align. Different doughs, depending on the amount of protein in the flour, need to be kneaded for different amounts of time, so kneading itself can be an art because it has an enormous impact on the final texture of the bread. Once kneaded, the dough is allowed to rise for the first time, often expanding to more than twice its original size. This stretches the gluten for the first time, helping to produce a finer texture in the finished bread.

Next, the dough is punched down—pressed and folded—to expel the excess carbon dioxide. The punched down dough is separated and shaped into loaves. The loaves are allowed to rise a second time in a step called proofing. This time, the dough is allowed to rise to slightly less than the final expected size of the bread, after which it is baked. While the dough cooks, the yeast works faster as the environment gets hotter until the dough reaches about 140°F (60°C), at which point the yeast dies. This final burst of carbon dioxide causes

An Afghan war widow takes flat nan bread from an earthen oven at one of the World Food Programme (WFP) bakeries west of Kabul, Afghanistan, 2002. WFP provides a daily ration of bread to approximately 250,000 highly vulnerable people living in Afghanistan's major cities. Of the 116 bakeries in operation, 56 are run and managed by women. *AP Images.*

became more commercialized, meat and processed foods increased in abundance and occupied a larger share of calories, and most baking was taken on by professional bakers and bread companies. However, the art has not been lost. In Europe many small bakeries have persisted despite the commercialization of bread. Also, in many parts of the world there are a growing number of modern artisanal bread companies and small bakeries that specialize in bread, either to meet dietary restrictions or to create inventive new recipes. In developing countries, breads (especially unleavened breads) are often still made daily by hand.

Many grains essential to bread making are also essential commodities, subject to the influences of climate, market, and politics, which can ultimately affect the supply and price of bread. In the summer of 2010, for example, Russia experienced a record-setting heat wave and a series of crop fires that eventually resulted in a diminished wheat harvest. In order to conserve supplies and avert a food crisis in Russia, wheat exports were prohibited. Countries such as Egypt that depend on imported Russian grains faced soaring bread prices. The United Nations estimates that 20 percent of the Egyptian population relies on government subsidies to make bread affordable, and that for these people, bread constitutes 45 percent of their total caloric intake.

SEE ALSO *Building Better Ovens; Dietary Reference Intakes; Extreme Weather and Food Supply; Foodways; Free Trade and Agriculture; Genetically Modified Organisms (GMO); Gluten Intolerance; Gourmet Hobbyists and Foodies; Grains; Nutrient Fortification of Foods; Religion and Food; Women's Role in Global Food Preparation; Yeast and Leavening Agents.*

BIBLIOGRAPHY

Books

Kaplan, Steven L. *Good Bread Is Back: A Contemporary History of French Bread, the Way It Is Made, and the People Who Make It.* Durham, NC: Duke University, 2006.

Marchant, John, Bryan G. Reuben, and Joan P. Alcock. *Bread: A Slice of History.* Stroud, UK: History, 2008.

Whitley, Andrew. *Bread Matters: Why and How to Make Your Own.* new ed. London: Fourth Estate, 2009.

Periodicals

Bobrow-Strain, Aaron. "White Bread Bio-Politics: Purity, Health, and the Triumph of Industrial Baking." *Cultural Geographies* 15, no. 1 (2008): 19–40.

"Egypt: Not by Bread Alone." *Economist* 387, no. 8575 (2008): 47

Two Romanian women bake bread the traditional way in an outdoor oven in their village. They then beat the fresh loaves to remove the burnt crust. © *Paul Glendell / Alamy.*

the bread to puff up quickly, which is referred to as oven spring. When oven spring has taken place, the bread has risen for the final time.

■ Impacts and Issues

In every culture dependent upon wheat, bread has played an important social role. In some cases bread can even be an indicator of world history. For example, the years of French occupation of Vietnam imparted many French cooking techniques into the local cuisine, which is why the Vietnamese *bon mai* sandwich is served on freshly baked baguette.

Although still considered a staple in most cultures, bread's importance in the diets of many people in industrialized countries has declined since the 1800s. Before meat was readily available, bread served as the primary source of calories in most people's diets and was often made in the home. As the food industry grew and

"Me & My Factory: MD David Rixon Talks about the Art of Baking and Getting a Slice of the Artisan Bread Market." *Food Manufacture* 84, no. 9 (2009): 24–25.

Reuben, Bryan, and Tom Coultate. "On the Rise— The Ancient Tradition of Bread Baking Depends on a Cascade of Chemical Reactions." *Chemistry World* 6, no. 10 (2009): 54–57.

Web Sites

Bread Bakers Guild of America. http://www.bbga.org/ (accessed September 14, 2010).

Turecamo, David. "The Art of Baking Bread." *CBS News,* March 28, 2010. http://www.cbsnews.com/video/ watch/?id=6341065n (accessed September 14, 2010).

David Brennan Tilove

Banana Trade Wars

■ Introduction

The banana trade wars were a long-running trade dispute over preferential treatment granted by Europe to certain banana exporting nations. A trade war involves two or more nations imposing trade restrictions on exports from each other or closely allied trading partners. Trade restrictions may include tariffs, import quotas, or other trade barriers. A tariff is a tax or duty levied on a class of import or export goods. An import quota restricts the quantity of a good or certain class of goods allowed into a country.

The longest multilateral trade dispute since World War II (1939–1945), the banana trade wars began in 1993 and concluded in 2009. The dispute embroiled the United States, Europe, Latin American banana-producing nations, and African, Caribbean, and Pacific (ACP) banana-producing nations in a series of arbitrations and negotiations within the framework of international trade agreements. The banana trade wars highlighted the vulnerability of developing nations when seeking redress under multilateral trade agreements.

■ Historical Background and Scientific Foundations

Since the late nineteenth century, American corporations have engaged in large-scale banana trade with Central and South America. By the early twentieth century, the United Fruit Company and the Standard Fruit Company, two American corporations, forged strong political ties and established near monopolies over fruit trading in certain areas of Latin America. These companies exerted such political influence in Latin American nations that those nations became known as "banana republics." United Fruit Company and Standard Fruit Company ultimately transformed into Chiquita Brands International and Dole Food Company, respectively.

These two companies, along with Fresh Del Monte Produce, another U.S.-based fresh fruit producer and distributor, played a central role in the banana trade wars. In 1993 the European Commission (EC), the predecessor to the European Union (EU), established a tariff-free trading zone among its member nations. The EC also extended the benefits of its tariff-free trading zone to 12 former colonies, which are often referred to as the African, Caribbean, and Pacific (ACP) countries. Under the EC's European Banana Regime, the EC initially imposed a quota on non-ACP bananas and a tariff of 100 euros per metric ton.

In 1993 five non-ACP banana exporting nations requested that countries that were a part of the General Agreement on Tariffs and Trade (GATT), the predecessor to the World Trade Organization (WTO), investigated the EC's trade policy. A GATT panel agreed that the EC's banana trade policy violated trade agreements, but the EC led a productive campaign to have the full GATT membership overturn this decision. In 1996 Chiquita Brands International persuaded the United States to support the Latin American nations in the banana trade case. The United States filed a complaint with the newly formed WTO on behalf of Chiquita Brands International and other U.S. fruit producers and distributors. In September 1997 the WTO ruled that the EU's banana import restrictions violated WTO rules.

The EU implemented a new banana trade policy in January 1999. Ecuador argued that the EU's new trade policy continued to impose trade restrictions in violation of WTO rules and petitioned the WTO to examine the new trade policy. The United States, however, feared that a new WTO ruling would take years. With Chiquita Brands International facing financial difficulties, the United States, acting unilaterally, stated that it would impose $500 million in trade sanctions against European goods if the EU did not change its banana trade policy. The EU responded by claiming that it would place trade restrictions on a variety of American goods.

Latin American countries protested that they had been absent from negotiations. Years of negotiations over the amount of the EU tariff followed with little progress.

In 2009 representatives from the United States, the EU, Latin America, and ACP nations met on more than 100 occasions to negotiate a settlement to the banana trade issue. In December 2009 the four sides announced an agreement. The EU agreed to lower its tariffs on bananas from 176 euros to 114 euros per metric ton. ACP nations will continue to receive tariff-free access to the European market along with a one-time 200 million euro payment from the EU.

The WTO's decision came quickly, however, and averted an all-out trade war between the United States and Europe. The WTO ruled in favor of the United States and Latin America. It authorized the United States to impose $191.4 million in trade sanctions on European exports, including French handbags, British linens, and Danish hams. In 2001 Ecuador, the United States, and the EU reached an agreement on the banana trade issue. The new agreement eliminated quotas but permitted the EU to impose tariffs on non-ACP bananas.

■ Impacts and Issues

The major players of the 16-year banana trade wars—the United States, Europe, Latin America, and ACP nations—will experience repercussions for years to come. The banana trade wars provided a significant test for the nascent WTO and demonstrated the influence that the United States and Europe wield in global trade. A 1999 report by Oxfam International, "Loaded against the Poor: The World Trade Organization," stated that the banana trade wars highlighted how major world

Workers unload bananas from a truck in La Terminal market, Guatemala City. 2010. The European Union, Costa Rica, El Salvador, Guatemala, Honduras, Nicaragua, and Panama completed discussions on an agreement that will open up trade in beef, bananas, rice, and cars during the EU and Latin America summit in Madrid, Spain. *AP Images.*

FOOD: IN CONTEXT

trading powers such as the United States and Europe could override and coerce developing nations on trade issues. Indeed, in 1999 the WTO authorized Ecuador to impose $201.6 million in sanctions against European goods, but Ecuador did not do so out of fear of retaliation against Ecuadorian goods.

The banana trade wars demonstrated that developing nations that rely heavily on the export of only a few products or that rely heavily on the import of essential goods are at a distinct disadvantage in negotiating unilateral trade agreements. The existing WTO arbitration process, which dragged on for more than 10 years on Ecuador's 1999 petition, also places these nations at a disadvantage within the dispute resolution framework established under international trade agreements. Developing nations do not have the financial resources or the economic diversity to sustain a prolonged trade war with a trading power.

The trade agreement will have a significant impact on ACP banana producing nations. Although ACP nations will continue to receive preferential treatment in the European market through tariff-free trading, ACP nations will lose market share to cheaper non-ACP bananas. The International Centre for Sustainable Trade and Development, a non-profit organization, estimates European banana imports from ACP nations will fall 14 percent, resulting in a loss of $40 million per year. Furthermore, banana prices in Europe will decline 12 percent. The one-time 200 million euro payment to ACP nations will ease the initial economic impact to ACP banana producers. ACP producers and distributors will have to devise a long-term solution to the diminished market share and decreased revenue without participating in a race to the bottom.

■ Primary Source Connection

The Food and Agriculture Organization of the United Nations (FAO) has its headquarters in Rome, Italy. Founded in 1945, the FAO's purpose is to reduce and eliminate world hunger. The FAO provides scientific and technical knowledge to developing countries on ways to modernize agriculture, forestry, and fisheries practices. The FAO also promotes good nutrition.

In this 2004 article the FAO explains a long-standing trade dispute over bananas up to that time.

Will the Banana Trade War Ever End?

Numerous complaints to the World Trade Organisation (WTO) have necessitated successive reforms of the EU banana trade regime since the establishment of the Common Market Organisation for Bananas (CMOB) in 1993.

Before that date, European countries pursued their own trade regimes. The Single European Market of 1992 provided the impetus to eliminate internal EU border restrictions since it would be no longer possible to enforce Article 115 of the Treaty of Rome to prevent intra-community trade. From 1993 to 1998, the trade regime consisted of two tariff-rate quotas. The ACP quota allowed the twelve traditional ACP producer countries to enter the EU market duty free up to a maximum cumulated volume of 857,700 tonnes per year. During this first period, there were country-specific allocations of the ACP quota. The annual quota for dollar and non-traditional ACP countries was initially set at 2 million tonnes with an in-quota duty of 100 euros per tonne. It was progressively raised up to 2,553 million tonnes from 1995 (following EU enlargement) with a reduced in-quota duty of 75 euros per tonne. Following the so-called Framework Agreement of 1994, there were also country-specific allocations of the dollar quota to four LA countries (23.4 % for Costa Rica, 21.0 % for Colombia, 3 % for Nicaragua and 2 % for Venezuela).

The 1998 reform of the CMOB that came into force on 1 January 1999 considerably simplified the import and export licensing system, allocated nearly 90 % of the dollar quota to the four main LA exporters (Ecuador, Costa Rica, Colombia and Panama) and suppressed the country-specific allocations of the ACP quota. Each traditional ACP country could export as much as it wanted up to a cumulated annual volume of 857,700 tonnes for the twelve traditional ACP suppliers. Despite these changes, the regime remained under heavy scrutiny. A new WTO panel initiated in January 1999 concluded that the modified EU policy was still not fully compatible with WTO rules. After two unsuccessful proposals, on 10 November 1999 and 4 October 2000, the EU finally adopted a regulation on 2 May 2001 to implement a new banana import regime in line with understandings arrived with both the United States and Ecuador. The mutually agreed solution is a two-step process toward a tariff-only regime that should enter into force no later than 1 January 2006. During the transitional period 2001–2005, bananas continue to be imported into the EU under a two tariff-rate quota system through import licences distributed on the basis of past trade. The transitional regime also includes a transfer, from 1 January 2002, of 100,000 tonnes from the quota reserved to ACP suppliers to the non-reserved quota.

Impacts of the Various Forms of the CMOB on Banana Exports to the EU

Since the establishment of the first CMOB in 1993, EU producing regions have benefited from income support under the form of coupled direct aids. This income support policy has resulted in a positive growth rate of exports from EU territories, 2.38 % over the period 1993–2003. EU territory supply represented 18.24 %

of EU consumption in 1990–1992. It now represents 18.85 % of this consumption (average 2002–2003). EU imports from ACP countries represented 16.13 % of EU consumption in 1990–1992. This share increased to 18.81 % during the period 1993–1998 where there were country-specific allocations of the ACP quota. It decreased to 18.03 % in 1999–2001 where there were no longer country-specific allocations of the ACP quota. It now represents 18.46 % of EU consumption (average 2002–2003). After an important decrease during the first years of application of the CMOB, EU imports from dollar zone countries stabilised and then have increased. Over the whole period 1993–2003, the growth rate of dollar zone exports to the EU is slightly positive (0.34 %). Their share in EU consumption however has continuously decreased with a much more pronounced decline during the first version of the CMOB (from 65.63 % in 1990–1992 to 63.34 % in 1993–1998, 62.95 % in 1999–2001 and 62.69 % in 2002–2003).

Over the period 1993–2001, EU imports from traditional ACP countries always remained below the ACP quota limit of 857,700 tonnes. But while exports from Caribbean countries have decreased, exports from West African countries (Cameroon and Ivory Coast) have increased. . . .

More specifically, the decline of Caribbean country exports appears much more pronounced after the cancellation of country-specific allocations of the ACP quota in 1999. Inversely, exports from West African countries have mainly increased after that date. While Caribbean country exports represented 58.54 % of total ACP exports to the EU in 1990–1992 and still 44.85 % in 1993–1998, they now only represent 24.18 %. By contrast, the share of exports from Cameroon and Ivory Coast to the EU has continuously increased, from 34.68 % in 1990–1992 to 61.68 % in 2002–2003. One non-traditional ACP country, the Dominican Republic, has substantially increased its exports to the EU. While this country represented 2.64 % of ACP exports to the EU in 1990–1992,

its share is now equal to 13.66 %. For a large part, these volumes correspond to organic and/or fair trade bananas mainly exported to the United Kingdom.

Hervé Guyomard
Chantal Le Mouël
Fabrice Levert
F. Jahir Lombana

GUYOMARD, HERVÉ, CHANTAL LE MOUËL, FABRICE LEVERT, AND F. JAHIR LOMBANA. "WILL THE BANANA TRADE WAR EVER END?" NOVEMBER 2004. FOOD AND AGRICULTURE ORGANIZATION OF THE UNITED NATIONS (FAO) CORPORATE DOCUMENT REPOSITORY. HTTP://WWW.FAO.ORG/DOCREP/008/AE593E/AE593E00.HTM (ACCESSED NOVEMBER 4, 2010).

SEE ALSO *Agribusiness; Ethical Issues in Agriculture; Fair Trade; World Trade Organization (WTO).*

BIBLIOGRAPHY

Books

Soluri, John. *Banana Cultures: Agriculture, Consumption, and Environmental Change in Honduras and the United States.* Austin: University of Texas Press, 2005.

Wiley, James. *The Banana: Empires, Trade Wars, and Globalization.* Lincoln: University of Nebraska Press, 2008.

Periodicals

Hamer, Ed. "Bananas." *The Ecologist* (September 2007): 24.

Web Sites

"Trade and Markets: Bananas." *Food and Agriculture Organization of the United Nations (FAO).* http://www.fao.org/es/esc/en/15/190/index.html (accessed September 6, 2010).

Joseph P. Hyder

Biodiversity and Food Supply

■ Introduction

Increasing environmental awareness led to more widespread public appreciation for natural biodiversity in the 1970s, but except for some scientists and farmers, the recognition of the importance of agricultural biodiversity did not arrive until a decade or two later. The realization that the loss of traditional varieties of crops and animals was a serious threat to world food supplies, security, and national economies came just as the rate of extinction of these varieties accelerated with worldwide agricultural intensification and industrialization.

The world's population depends on an alarmingly small number of plants and animals for food. About 15 species of plants and 8 animal species produce 90 percent of the global food supply. Three single grains—rice, corn, and wheat—account for half of the worldwide human diet. This makes the loss of the genetic variation found in traditional cultivars and heirloom breeds particularly troubling. The ability to selectively alter plants and animals is essential to agricultural production and an important buffer against famines caused by plant and animal diseases, insect pests, natural disasters, and even climate change. Germplasm is an irreplaceable resource, and one that future generations will need to survive.

■ Historical Background and Scientific Foundations

Russian agronomist Nikolai Vavilov (1887–1943) was one of the first scientists to investigate the diversity of both cultivated and wild varieties of crops. He began collecting seeds and other types of germplasm in 1916, and he made more than 100 expeditions to 64 countries for an agricultural research center in St. Petersburg (now called the Vavilov Research Institute of Plant Industry) before he was arrested, imprisoned, and finally starved to death by Soviet government forces in 1943. Vavilov's scientific work on "centers of diversity," areas harboring the greatest biodiversity of crop species, had a profound effect on plant science and crop breeding around the world, though few outside academia or agriculture understood its importance at the time. In short, Vavilov demonstrated how the germplasm from a wide variety of different cultivars of a single plant species was indispensable to improving food production. He also understood that traditional crop varieties were often isolated amongst different ethnic groups and found that an understanding of local languages and farming techniques was important in building his seminal collection.

As American journalist Kenny Ausubel pointed out in 1994 in *Seeds of Change*, the gene pool of human crops is a living treasure created by "billions of years of evolution and at least twelve thousand years of human selection for agriculture . . . the legacy of countless generations of seed savers and collectors, farmers, gardeners, and world cultures." In the 1980s, as more researchers realized that this genetic legacy was rapidly disappearing, they surveyed the world's agricultural resources and began attempting to conserve them. According to the Food and Agriculture Organization (FAO) of the United Nations, at least 75 percent of the world's genetic crop diversity has been lost since 1900. In the United States, almost 96 percent of the vegetable varieties that could be purchased in 1900 are now extinct. The dangers of monoculture (the cultivation of a single crop), especially when a particular crop is descended from a few plants (i.e., with low genetic variability) was highlighted in the United States in 1970, when a disease called the Southern corn leaf blight nearly wiped out a year's entire corn crop. Fortunately, agronomists were able to use genes from a corn variety that had been grown in China since the 1500s to produce a new hybrid corn variety that was resistant to the fungus, averting a disaster that was potentially as wide-ranging as the Irish Potato Famine of the 1840s.

In many nations, the creation and expansion of seed banks where germplasm is stored for future use, such as Russia's historic Vavilov Research Institute, began in

WORDS TO KNOW

BIODIVERSITY: Also known as biological diversity, biodiversity is the sum total of life in an area. It includes the number of species, the richness of the ecological niches, and the amount of genetic diversity in the plants and animals. Agricultural biodiversity is particularly important for food security.

CULTIVAR: A term for a cultivated variety of plant, this is a subspecies of a cultivated plant that may also be called a landrace, a traditional or peasant variety, or an heirloom. These varieties, along with wild relatives of cultivated plants, are important sources of germplasm for both agronomists and traditional farmers.

GERMPLASM: Genetic material, especially in a form that can be used to reproduce an organism. Seeds, tubers, cuttings, breeding colonies of living animals, and frozen sperm and embryos are all types of germplasm.

earnest in the 1980s and 1990s. This *ex situ* ("off site") conservation preserves seeds and other kinds of germplasm exactly as they were when harvested, as a kind of snapshot of crop evolution. The Svalbard Global Seed Vault, popularly known as the "Doomsday Vault," is probably the most famous of these collections, but most nations and many non-profit groups also save seeds. The Svalbard Vault began operations in 2008 on a remote Norwegian island far above the Arctic circle, serving as both the ultimate safety net for food supplies and a source to resupply other seed banks that meet with disaster. It is clear that this kind of backup is necessary–in 2003, the Iraqi seed bank of ancient Middle Eastern crops (such as wheat and barley) located in Abu Ghraib was looted; in 2006 the Philippine repository for rice germplasm was destroyed by a typhoon.

An equally important, though less well publicized aspect of preserving agricultural biodiversity is *in situ* ("on site") conservation. *In situ* programs encourage farmers to continue growing traditional varieties, which keeps crops evolving along with the indigenous knowledge of how to grow them and use them. In the hands of traditional farmers, seed crops (and even traditional animal breeds) change dynamically in response to local conditions, such as climate change, disease, and pests, in a manner that crops grown in the more controlled fields of corporate and academic plant breeders can only attempt to substitute. Publications such as *The Future is an Ancient Lake* (2004) document ongoing conservation

The Svalbard Global Seed Bank, located inside a mountain on the Artic island Svalbard, warehouses millions of seeds in freezing temperatures. The seed bank preserves biodiversity for future generations by storing seeds of thousands of species of plants for centuries. © *deadlyphoto.com / Alamy.*

projects including the FAO's *in situ* project in the area around Lake Chad in the African nations of Niger, Nigeria, Cameroon, and Chad, where the co-evolution of human cultures, ecosystems, and a diverse suite of plant and animal species occurred. In addition to promoting sustainable agriculture and indigenous cultures, this kind of program can also enhance natural biodiversity and the traditional use of wild plants in a way that industrial agriculture cannot.

■ Impacts and Issues

The greatest threat to agricultural biodiversity continues to be industrial and corporate agriculture. Although the Green Revolution of the 1960s and 1970s produced many hybrid varieties of crops with dramatically higher yields that were resistant to the pests and diseases that plagued traditional farmers, these seeds came with a price. Most of these hybrid varieties do not reproduce "true"—the seed to grow a particular crop is created by crossing two different varieties, and though the resulting offspring show hybrid vigor with higher yields, when the seeds from this hybrid are planted, the next generation does not germinate properly or may revert back to different varieties. Thus, farmers need to continue to buy their seeds from the companies from which they were originally obtained, and they often stop experimenting with their own crops and selecting the best varieties for local conditions. Plant breeding is taken out of the hands of a multitude of farmers and turned over to a few scientists. In addition, hybrid seeds are often patented or protected by intellectual property right laws and other proprietary laws.

Native farmers and traditional gardeners are sometimes angered by what has been termed biopiracy, which includes the corporate hijacking of traditional germplasm to make hybrids that are controlled and owned in a manner that is not possible with the open-pollinated heirloom varieties of plants that breed true. Although the Green Revolution's hybrid varieties may be more productive, these crops typically require more fertilizer and more intensive farming methods than do the traditional cultivars. The most alarming consequence of the adoption of hybrid crops, however, is that some farmers abandon older varieties. In some cases, traditional varieties are merely seen as less productive than modern hybrids, but sometimes, financial aid or other forms of assistance are tied to "progress" as defined by the adoption of new crops, hybrid varieties, or new methods of agriculture. Thousands of varieties of rice, wheat, and corn alone have been irrevocably lost in this manner.

Unfortunately, crops are more vulnerable to plant pests, diseases, and weather when biodiversity is reduced, either in the number of crops grown—with

IN CONTEXT: SPECIES PROTECTION

Many nations have laws that protect threatened and endangered species. The International Union for Conservation of Nature (IUCN), the world's oldest international conservation organization, works with nations and organizations worldwide to protect the world's natural resources. The *IUCN Red List of Threatened Species* presents scientifically based information on the status of threatened species around the world. Important international conventions, ratified by most of the world's nations, are intended to offer protections against human activities that threaten species. These conventions include: (1) the 1971 Convention on Wetlands of International Importance; (2) the 1972 Convention Concerning the Protection of the World Cultural and Natural Heritage, which designates high-profile World Heritage Sites for protection of their natural and cultural values; (3) the 1973 Convention on International Trade in Endangered Species of Wild Fauna and Flora (CITES); (4) the 1992 Convention on Biological Diversity (CBD), which was presented by the United Nations Environment Program (UNEP) at the United Nations Conference on Environment and Development (UNCED) in 1992; and (5) the 1979 Convention on the Conservation of Migratory Species of Wild Animals (CMS or Bonn Convention), also enacted under the aegis of the UNEP.

Within the framework of the Bonn Convention, member states are encouraged to enter into specific agreements. These agreements—which are legally binding international treaties—aim to conserve a wide range of threatened animals, including species prized as traditional foods. For example, the CMS Agreement on the Conservation of Gorillas and their Habitats—signed by Central African Republic, Republic of Congo, Democratic Republic of Congo, Equatorial Guinea, Nigeria, and Uganda (six of the 10 African countries where gorillas are usually found)—provides a legal framework to reinforce and integrate conservation efforts to reduce threats to gorilla populations from hunting for the bushmeat trade and other perils.

In March 2010, CITES officials, scientists, and wildlife preservation specialists meeting in Doha, Qatar, asserted that organized crime continues to drive the illegal trade in animal species used as exotic foods. World Bank leader Robert Zoellick (1953–) claimed that a multi-billion dollar global black market exists in wildlife products. That same month, Interpol and local law enforcement agencies announced a coordinated global emphasis on preventing trade in medicines and foods that use illegally obtained animal parts.

Although scientists estimate that extinctions caused by humans are taking place at 100 to 1,000 times nature's normal rate, there are not reliable estimates as to what percentage of species are threatened or endangered due to their value as human food sources.

intensive monoculture being the most susceptible—and within a particular crop, when only one or a few varieties of crops are available. Once traditional farmers lose native varieties, they may also lose the skills and knowledge necessary to select and breed these plants effectively, especially if enough time has passed so that new generations of sons and daughters are working the land. Even if saved germplasm can be re-introduced to an area, it may take many years for farmers to regain the intimate knowledge of the crops, animals, and ecosystems that is necessary for productive and sustainable agriculture and plant breeding.

After much debate, several international laws and treaties have been passed in support of global biodiversity, with specific statements addressing agricultural biodiversity, including the Convention on Biological Diversity (CBD) and the International Treaty of Plant Genetic Resources for Food and Agriculture (ITPGRFA). Unfortunately, much of this legislation is unenforceable and lacks penalties for violation. And despite all the recent publicity accompanying the opening of the Svalbard Vault and an award-winning documentary on agricultural biodiversity (*Diverseeds*; 2009), most people and many governments still do not fully understand the importance of preserving these resources. In the fall of 2010, the Russian government was planning to sell the Pavlosk Experimental Station, the division of the Vavilov Research Institute that houses Europe's greatest collection of fruit trees and berries, to a developer planning to level the land. More than 600 types of apple trees and 1,000 different kinds of strawberries (including some collected by Vavilov himself) are grown at Pavlosk, and 90 percent of these varieties are found nowhere else in the world. Unlike the cryogenically preserved seeds at some seed banks, most of these plants cannot be easily transported. The destruction of the Pavlosk station is still being debated in the courts.

■ Primary Source Connection

The Food and Agriculture Organization (FAO) of the United Nations, an agency dedicated to reducing hunger, is headquartered in Rome, Italy. The FAO works in four main areas: to provide information; to share policy expertise; to provide meeting places for nations; and to provide knowledge to the projects around the world aimed at reducing hunger.

This article discusses the establishment of a multilateral system to share genetic resources among nations.

Global Interdependency for Local Sustainability

Studies by FAO show that most countries depend on crops that originated outside their own regions for more than 90% of their food. The future development of agriculture in all parts of the world—for example to cope with challenges of climate change and newly evolved pests and diseases—will require secure access to the genetic qualities inherent in existing diversity. The use of these genetic resources can be encouraged in two ways; through bilateral agreements between donors and recipients, or through a multilateral system with an agreed set of rules accepted by all countries and codified in a treaty. The CGIAR supports the concept of a multilateral system for a variety of reasons, including the fact that it is efficient and simpler to operate.

For example, if a county wishes to gain access to existing diversity for rice, it would have to make separate bilateral agreements with each of the more than 100 countries that hold samples. A multilateral system gives access to all the thousands of varieties held in trust by the International Rice Research Institute (IRRI) under a single agreement.

SGRP has worked with data supplied by CGIAR genebanks to chart the flows of germplasm around the world. While many conclusions have been drawn from these studies, one example highlights the global interdependence of local agriculture. The International Maize and Wheat Improvement Center (CIMMYT) distributes more than 11 tonnes of cereal seed samples a year, three-quarters of it to developing countries. From 1966 to 1997, 6 of every 7 new spring varieties released in developing countries had CIMMYT varieties in their ancestry. It is important to note that this does not represent a narrowing of the genetic base for spring wheat. CIMMYT varieties recombine vast amounts of diverse materials from around the world. A recent study indicates that the genetic diversity of parents in the pedigrees and the overall diversity of genes in CIMMYT varieties have both increased considerably over the past 30 years. What is true of wheat is true of many other crops managed by the CGIAR genebanks under the FAO in-trust agreements.

FOOD AND AGRICULTURE ORGANIZATION OF THE UNITED NATIONS (FAO). "GLOBAL INTERDEPENDENCY FOR LOCAL SUSTAINABILITY." *FACT SHEETS ON THE FIFTH ANNIVERSARY OF THE WORLD FOOD SUMMIT: UNDERPINNING THE FOUNDATIONS OF FOOD PRODUCTION: THE SGRP AND CONSERVATIVE GENETIC RESOURCES, 2007.*

SEE ALSO *Agribusiness; Agroecology; Commission on Genetic Resources for Food and Agriculture; Convention on Biological Diversity (1992); Ecological Impacts of Various World Diets; Ethical Issues in Agriculture; Food and Agriculture Organization (FAO); Organics; Sustainable Agriculture.*

BIBLIOGRAPHY

Books

Batello, Caterina, Marzio Marzot, and Adamou Harouna Touree. *The Future Is an Ancient Lake: Traditional Knowledge, Biodiversity, and Genetic Resources for Food and Agriculture in Lake Chad Basin Ecosystems.*

Rome: Food and Agriculture Organization of the United Nations, 2004.

Nabhan, Gary Paul. *Where Our Food Comes From: Retracing Nikolay Vavilov's Quest to End Famine.* Washington, DC: Island Press, 2009.

Tansey, Geoff, and Tasmin Rajotte. *The Future Control of Food: A Guide to International Negotiations and Rules on Intellectual Property, Biodiversity and Food Security.* London: Earthscan, 2008.

Periodicals

Pimentel, David. "Ethical Issues of Global Corporatization: Agriculture and Beyond." *Poultry Science* 83, no. 3 (2004): 321–329.

Pimentel, David, Harold Brookfield, Helen Parsons, and Muriel Brookfield. "Producing Food, Protecting Biodiversity." *Bioscience* 55, no. 5 (2005): 452–453.

Web Sites

Diverseeds: Plant Genetic Resources for Food and Agriculture. http://www.diverseeds.eu/DVD/Home. html (accessed October 18, 2010).

Global Crop Diversity Trust. http://www.croptrust.org/ main/ (accessed October 18, 2010).

Pearce, Fred. "The Battle to Save Russia's Pavlovsk Seed Bank." *The Guardian,* September 20, 2010. http://www.guardian.co.uk/environment/2010/ sep/20/campaign-russia-pavlovsk-seed-bank (accessed October 18, 2010).

Revkin, Andrew C. "Buried Seed Vault Opens in Arctic." *The New York Times,* February 26, 2008. http://dotearth. blogs.nytimes.com/2008/02/26/buried-seed-vault-opens-in-arctic/ (accessed October 18, 2010).

Sandra L. Dunavan

Biofuels and World Hunger

■ Introduction

Biofuels, which include bioethanol and biodiesels, are fuels produced from living organisms such as plants. Many environmentalists argue that biofuels, many of which have lower greenhouse gas emissions than fossil fuels, should become an important aspect of the world's energy production. Biofuels may also contribute to energy self-sufficiency for the United States, Europe, and other parts of the world that currently rely heavily on oil imports from the Middle East or other regions.

A substantial number of humanitarian organizations and agricultural policy analysts, however, warn that biofuel production, which relies on many of the same crops used for food, may contribute to increases in global hunger. Biofuels can potentially divert needed grains or other food crops to biofuel production. In addition, biofuel production stimulates demand for these crops, thereby leading to rising global food prices. In the United States alone, 107 million metric tons (118 short tons) of grain—primarily corn—was used for the production of bioethanol in 2009. The amount of U.S.-produced corn used for bioethanol production in 2009 accounted for one-fourth of the U.S. grain production. This amount of grain could provide enough food for 330 million people for one year.

■ Historical Background and Scientific Foundations

Biofuel played a major role in the early development of the automobile. In the late 1890s Rudolf Diesel (1858–1913), inventor of the diesel engine, developed an engine that ran on fuel derived from peanut oil. Fuels derived from biomass, primarily peanuts and vegetables, remained the primary source of fuel for diesel engines until the petroleum industry developed and promoted petroleum-derived diesel fuel in the 1920s.

American automaker Henry Ford (1863–1947) also designed the Ford Model T, one of the first successful mass-produced automobiles, to run on ethanol derived from corn and hemp. The expansion of the petroleum industry due to the expansion of petroleum production in California, Texas, and Pennsylvania lowered the price of petroleum-derived fuel. The lower-priced petroleum fuels, combined with a massive marketing campaign, replaced biofuels as the dominant source of automobile fuel by the 1940s.

The discovery of large oil deposits in the Middle East drove down the cost of petroleum-derived fuels even further in the mid-twentieth century. By the 1970s, however, political instability in the Middle East and concerns over a growing American and European reliance on Middle Eastern oil rekindled interest in biofuels. Tougher clean air and automobile emissions standards in the United States and Europe in the 1970s through 1990s also made cleaner-burning biofuels more attractive.

By the early years of the twenty-first century, massive government subsidies and government-mandated biofuel production levels dramatically increased biofuel production and consumption. In the United States, the Energy Security and Independence Act of 2007 mandated the use of 36 billion gallons (136 billion liters) of ethanol in the United States by 2022. In 2010 the United States produced approximately 12.5 billion gallons (47.3 billion liters) of ethanol—up from 1.63 billion gallons (6.17 billion liters) in 2000.

Most of the ethanol produced in the United States is blended with gasoline up to the federal limit of 10 percent ethanol, which is known as E10. With 138 billion gallons of oil consumed in the United States each year, the U.S. ethanol market is approaching domestic saturation. Brazil, the world's second leading producer of ethanol, requires that all gasoline contain 25 percent ethanol, or E25. China has mandated the usage of E10 in several provinces.

Europe relies more heavily on biodiesel than bio-ethanol. Under the European Union's (EU's) biofuels directive, all EU member nations should achieve 5.75 percent biofuel usage by 2010 and 10 percent usage by 2020. India's National Biofuel Policy of 2008 calls on meeting 20 percent of India's diesel demand with biodiesel. India has a growing biodiesel industry that produces fuel from oil extracted from the seeds of the jatropha plant.

Many of the current biofuels are similar to those used in the early twentieth century by Diesel and Ford. All biofuels are liquid fuels derived from biomass, or organic matter derived from plants or animals. Two main types of biofuels exist: bioethanol and biodiesel. Fermenting the carbohydrates that exist within the sugars found in plants produces bioethanol, often referred to as simply "ethanol." The fermented product is then distilled and dried to produce bioethanol. Because bioethanol relies on the fermentation of carbohydrates, plants that are high in sugars or starches, including corn, sugar cane, wheat, and sugar beets, are used most often for bioethanol production.

Biodiesel production involves transforming vegetable or other plant oils into fuel through a process called transesterification. Vegetable or plant oil is mixed with an alcohol, typically methanol, and a catalyst. The resulting chemical reaction produces biodiesel and waste glycerol.

WORDS TO KNOW

BIODIESEL: A biofuel produced from vegetable or other plant oils that is used to power diesel engines.

BIOFUEL: A fuel derived from biomass, which may be any living organism.

ETHANOL: A term often used to refer to bioethanol, a type of ethanol (ethyl alcohol) derived from plants and used as a fuel.

■ Impacts and Issues

Despite the benefits of biofuels, including increased energy security and decreased greenhouse gas emissions, many human rights groups and non-governmental organizations argue that growth of the biofuel energy sector could exacerbate world hunger. Increased demand for corn, soybeans, or other crops for biofuel production leads to higher prices for these commodities, which, in turn, raises the price of food. For the billions of people that live on less than $2 per day, a sharp rise in the cost of essential foods, such as grains, could lead to increased hunger.

World food prices rose dramatically in 2007 and 2008, creating a crisis that produced social unrest in

A man evaluates plants on an experimental farm with jatropha oil plants for the production of biodiesel. Jatropha is resistant to drought and pests and produces seeds containing up to 40% oil. © *Joerg Boethling / Alamy.*

IN CONTEXT: JATROPHA

A number of food aid and environmental groups have consistently warned that too rapid a shift to the production of biofuels without time for adequate study, or as a result of intense economic pressures, has unintentionally increased poverty and food shortages in areas of the developing world. For example, in some regions farmers were encouraged to grow the plant jatropha, which was thought to be an "ethical" biofuel alternative crop because the plant could grow on land otherwise unsuitable for food production. The plant was also naturally very resistant to drought and pests. To increase yields, and in anticipation of a stronger market for the plant that has thus far failed to develop, some farmers started using richer land once used for food production to grow jatropha. However, in several countries—especially India and Tanzania—yields proved to be low, and lack of industry investment in facilities to process the plants in biofuels resulted in wasted crops or low prices.

A woman protests against biofuels at the offices of the UK Department for Transport in London, England, on March 15, 2008.
© *David Hoffman Photo Library / Alamy.*

numerous countries. Between 2006 and 2008, the price of corn increased by 125 percent, soybeans by 107 percent, and rice by 217 percent.

Many factors contributed to the sudden surge in food prices, including higher oil and fertilizer prices, poor grain harvests in some parts of the world, commodities speculation, and more demand for resource intensive food. Many analysts, however, attribute some or most of the price increases to the burgeoning biofuels sector. In February 2008 Josette Sheeran (1954–), executive director of the United Nations World Food Programme (WFP), stated that increased biofuel production, particularly production that relied on grains, was driving up the cost of food and increasing hunger. Increased food costs even hampered the ability of the WFP, the world's largest humanitarian organization dedicated to hunger issues, to deliver food aid. By 2008, the amount of food that the WFP could purchase and distribute as food aid had decreased by 40 percent compared to 2003 levels.

In July 2008 *The Guardian*, a British daily newspaper, uncovered an internal World Bank report from the previous April, "A Note on Rising Food Prices," which states that biofuel production was responsible for a 75 percent increase in global food prices. The report asserts that "large increases in biofuels production in the United States and Europe are the main reason behind the steep rise in global food prices." The report claims that biofuels contributed to rising food costs in three ways. First, biofuel production shifts crops from food to fuel production. Second, farmers dedicate arable land for biofuel production. Finally, increasing biofuel production spurs financial speculation in grain commodities.

In late 2008 the price of corn commodities fell by 50 percent. Other food commodities also declined sharply despite continued growth in the ethanol industry. These price declines indicate that commodities speculation may have fueled much of the food price increases in 2007 and 2008. Analysts, however, estimate that ethanol production is responsible for a 20 to 33 percent increase in corn prices.

Proponents of biofuel argue that biofuel production does not contribute, or only contributes negligibly, to world hunger. Biofuel advocates dismiss the food versus fuel dilemma as a false dichotomy. They argue that if prices for corn, for example, increase greatly because of biofuel production, then the free market will lead farmers to put more land into corn production. As a worst-case scenario, corn prices would spike briefly before the market catches up with demand. Many biofuel advocates also support growing crops that will not adversely affect world food supplies. The World Bank report found that Brazil's ethanol industry, which relies on sugarcane, did not push food prices appreciably higher.

■ Primary Source Connection

The U.S. Department of Agriculture (USDA) publishes *Amber Waves*, a journal dedicated to the "Economics of Food, Farming, Natural Resources, and Rural America." It is published four to six times per year. The article below is a feature article from the February 2008 issue that addresses the impact of rising global food prices on food security.

Rising Food Prices Intensify Food Insecurity in Developing Countries

Recent hikes in oil prices have raised serious concerns in low-income countries, both because of the financial burden of the higher energy import bill and potential constraints on imports of necessities like food and raw materials. Higher oil prices also have sparked energy security concerns worldwide, increasing the demand for biofuel production. The use of feed crops for biofuels, coupled with greater food demand spurred by high income growth in populous countries, such as China and India, has reversed the long-term path of declining price trends for several commodities.

Worldwide agricultural commodity price increases were significant during 2004–06: corn prices rose 54 percent; wheat, 34 percent; soybean oil, 71 percent; and sugar, 75 percent. But this trend accelerated in 2007, due to continued demand for biofuels and drought in major producing countries. Wheat prices have risen more than 35 percent since the 2006 harvest, while corn prices have increased nearly 28 percent. The price of soybean oil has been particularly volatile, due to high demand growth in China, the U.S., and the European Union (EU), as well as lower global stocks.

The Food and Agriculture Organization of the United Nations (FAO) estimated that the high food prices of 2006 increased the food import bill of developing countries by 10 percent over 2005 levels. For 2007, the food import bill for these countries increased at a much higher rate, an estimated 25 percent.

Stacey Rosen
Shahla Shapouri

ROSEN, STACEY, AND SHAHLA SHAPOURI. "RISING FOOD PRICES INTENSIFY FOOD INSECURITY IN DEVELOPING COUNTRIES." *AMBER WAVES* 6, NO. 1 (FEBRUARY 2008): 16–21.

SEE ALSO *Agribusiness; Agriculture and International Trade; Agroecology; Biodiversity and Food Supply; Climate Change and Agriculture; Food and Agriculture Organization (FAO); Food Security; Gulf Oil Spill Food Impacts; World Trade Organization (WTO).*

BIBLIOGRAPHY

Books

Joshi, Satish V. *Agriculture as a Source of Fuel: Prospects and Impacts, 2007 to 2017.* Washington, DC: U.S. Department of Agriculture, Office of Energy Policy and New Uses, 2007.

Rogers, Heather. *Green Gone Wrong: How Our Economy Is Undermining the Environmental Revolution.* New York: Scribner, 2010.

Rosillo, Callé F., and Francis X. Johnson. *Food versus Fuel: An Informed Introduction to Biofuels.* London: Zed, 2010.

Soetaert, Wim, and Erick J. Vandamme. *Biofuels.* Chichester, UK: Wiley, 2009.

Periodicals

"Biofuels: Food, Fuel and Climate Change." *Opec Bulletin* 40, no. 5 (2009): 72–75.

Molony, Thomas, and James Smith. "Biofuels, Food Security, and Africa." *African Affairs* 109, no. 436 (2010): 489–498.

Schmid, Heinrich O. E. "Biofuels, Food and Population." *World Watch* 21, no. 1 (2008): 2–3.

Tenenbaum, David. "Food vs. Fuel: Diversion of Crops Could Cause More Hunger." *Environmental Health Perspectives* 116 no. 6 (2008): A254–A257.

Web Sites

Rosegrant, Mark W., Siwa Msangi, Timothy Sulser, and Rowena Valmont-Santos. "Biofuels and the Global Food Balance." *International Food Policy Research Institute.* http://www.globalbioenergy.org/uploads/media/0612_IFPRI_-_Biofuels_and_the_Global_Food_Balance_01.pdf (accessed September 9, 2010).

Woods Institute for the Environment. "The Impacts of Large Scale Use of Biofuels on Food, Agriculture, and Trade." *Stanford University.* http://woods.stanford.edu/docs/biofuels/Biofuels3a.pdf (accessed September 9, 2010).

Joseph P. Hyder

Bioterrorism:
Food as a Weapon

■ Introduction

The U.S. Centers for Disease Control (CDC) defines bioterrorism as "the deliberate release of viruses, bacteria, or other germs (agents) used to cause illness or death in people, animals, or plants." Most of the pathogens, or microorganisms, used in bioterrorism occur in nature. Some pathogens may be modified, however, to increase resistance to pharmaceuticals or to increase their ability to spread among humans, animals, or plants.

The anthrax attacks of 2001 that killed five people in the United States renewed interest in bioterrorism. Whereas the anthrax attacks focused on directly infecting humans with a pathogen, counterterrorism officials also began to focus on the possibility of a bioterror attack on agriculture or the food supply, often referred to agroterrorism. A bioterror attack on the food supply could subsequently infect humans, causing illness or death. An agroterrorism attack also could focus solely on the agricultural sector. Infecting livestock or crops with pathogens could disrupt agricultural production, weaken the economy, cause panic, and erode faith in the government's ability to protect the food supply.

■ Historical Background and Scientific Foundations

The use of bioterrorism against military and civilian targets stretches back more than 2,000 years. Military leaders, who often lost more troops to disease than battle, understood the important role that disease could play in siege or battle. In the sixth century BC, the Assyrians poisoned enemy wells with rye ergot, a fungi. Consumption of ergot can cause severe gastrointestinal complications, seizures, hallucinations, paresthesia, and gangrene. Around 400 BC, Sycthian archers were reported to dip the tips of arrows in blood, manure, or decomposing bodies in order to make the arrows more lethal or spread disease.

In the Middle Ages, well before scientists articulated the germ theory of disease, many people assumed that

disease was spread by malaria, or the foul smell of decomposing bodies of people who died of disease. Items that had come into contact with the diseased were also thought to be a possible source of disease. Despite a lack of scientific understanding of germ theory, the crude tactics of military leaders were frequently successful.

During the Tartar siege of Kaffa in 1346 and 1347, the Tartars catapulted the plague-ridden bodies of dead comrades over the city walls. A plague outbreak in Kaffa forced the residents to surrender. The fleeing Genoese residents of Kaffa, and the rats that traveled with them on ships, may have started the Black Death that swept through Europe, killing from 25 million to 50 million people between 1348 and 1350. In the New World, European explorers and military leaders exploited the lack of immunity to smallpox and other diseases among the indigenous peoples. In one of the few historical accounts of true bioterrorism involving food or agriculture, in 1495 the Spanish presented French troops with wine that had been contaminated with the blood of lepers. Given the pathology of leprosy, however, this tactic was likely unsuccessful.

By the twentieth century, scientists had articulated the germ theory of disease, which made biological warfare and bioterrorism more effective. The greatest obstacle to biological warfare and bioterrorism in the twentieth-century became weaponizing the pathogens to maximize their effectiveness. Government-funded biological research programs achieved great success in weaponizing biological agents. Potential terrorists, however, have been less successful in acquiring and weaponizing biological agents, leading many of these groups to rely on cruder methods of transmission.

Few documented cases of modern bioterrorism that targeted the food supply or agriculture exist. In 1952 a Kenyan insurgent group poisoned 33 cattle. In 1978 the Arab Revolutionary Council injected Israeli oranges with mercury, poisoning twelve people; the incident resulted in a 40 percent decline in Israeli orange exports. In 1982 a religious cult in Oregon contaminated restaurant salad bars with *Salmonella typhimurium* in order to derail local elections. More than 750 people became ill, but no deaths occurred.

■ Impacts and Issues

Despite the relatively few incidents of biological attacks on agriculture or food supplies, such bioterror attacks remain a grave concern for counterterrorism organizations. Bioterror attacks on the food supply continue to pose the potential for injury or death. Furthermore, mass panic and loss of public faith in food safety would create severe economic consequences for the agricultural sector.

Weakness in agricultural production and distribution makes the food supply a relatively vulnerable target. Farms typically do not employ widespread surveillance, which would be difficult to conduct over an entire industry that spreads across millions of hectares or acres. Most food processing facilities, particularly small- and medium-sized operations, also do not have uniform security practices or surveillance. In December 2004, U.S. Secretary of Health and Human Services (HHS) Tommy Thompson (1941–) cited poisoning of the U.S. food supply as one of his greatest concerns during an exit press conference. Thompson stated, "I, for the life of me, cannot understand why the terrorists have not, you know, attacked our food supply because it is so easy to do." During Thompson's tenure as HHS Secretary, inspection of imported foods by U.S. officials increased dramatically.

The crowded breeding and rearing conditions among intensive livestock operations increase the likelihood that

livestock diseases could spread quickly. Current livestock disease monitoring and reporting systems in the United States and other countries focus on a statistical diagnosis and monitoring of disease rather than on individual animals. This system decreases the likelihood of detecting emerging diseases early. Livestock, grains, and processed foods are often commingled during processing and distribution. Commingling these products potentially increases contamination by biological agents and makes determining the source of contamination more difficult.

The threat posed to humans by a bioterror attack on the food supply remains relatively low. Potential pathogens that terrorists could release into the food supply

Two workers light a funeral pyre of cattle and sheep suspected to have foot and mouth disease. A report by the U.S. General Accounting Office indicated that terrorists could intentionally introduce foot and mouth disease to U.S. livestock. An outbreak of food and mouth disease could cause tens of billions of dollars of damage to the U.S. cattle industry and erode public confidence in the food supply. *© Agripicture Images / Alamy.*

FOOD: IN CONTEXT

include anthrax, *Clostridium botulinum*, *Salmonella*, *Escherichia coli*, and cholera. While some of these pathogens are highly toxic to humans, the manner in which they would pass through the food supply decreases the likelihood of deaths occurring. *C. botulinum*, which causes botulism, a serious and often deadly condition, grows best in a low-oxygen environment. Botulism, therefore, is mainly a concern with canned foods. Sanitation and processing requirements in most Western countries, however, pose little chance for deliberate contamination. Other pathogens, including *Salmonella* and *E. coli*, could be passed through the food supply more easily, but pose a significantly lower threat of lethality.

A bioterror attack on the food supply, however, would not have to produce widespread human death or injury in order to be effective. A bioterror attack that has little or even no effect on humans could disrupt the agriculture sector and all associate industries, including transportation, distribution, and the restaurant industries. Demand for products targeted by an attack, for example, beef, poultry, pork, dairy, grains, fruits, or vegetables, would likely drop. Demand for other food products would increase as consumers sought substitutes, leading to food price increases. The presence or even rumors of infected livestock or commodities could lead to international restrictions on exports, thus further decimating the affected agricultural sector.

A 2004 report by the Congressional Research Service, "Agroterrorism: Threats and Preparedness," notes that agriculture has not been an attractive target for terrorists because such attacks lack the shock value of bombings or other high profile attacks. Nevertheless, the report concludes that a bioterror attack on the food supply would be relatively easy to achieve and produce serious economic and psychological impacts. Also in 2004, the U.S. Department of Homeland Security launched the National Center for Food Protection and Defense (NCFPD), which is charged with identifying and addressing vulnerabilities in the nation's food system to intentional biological or chemical attack. NCFPD has aided other countries that have experienced attacks to their food supply. In August 2010, for example, seven million fruit and vegetable seedlings at a nursery in northern Australia were destroyed after herbicides were mixed into the irrigation system. Another 20,000 mature produce plants were simultaneously destroyed at nearby farms. Damage to the local economy is estimated at more than 30 million U.S. dollars, and although the motivation for the attacks is unknown and no injuries to the health of the population occurred, the NCFPD is working with Australian authorities to share information that could prevent further similar attacks.

SEE ALSO *Botulism; Center for Food Safety and Applied Nutrition; Consumer Food Safety Recommendations; Disasters and Food Supply; Food Inspection and Standards; Food Safety and Inspection Service; Food Security; Import Restrictions; Produce Traceability; Salmonella.*

BIBLIOGRAPHY

Books

Gullino, Maria Lodovica. *Crop Biosecurity: Assuring Our Global Food Supply.* Dordrecht: Springer, 2008.

Pampel, Fred C. *Threats to Food Safety.* New York: Facts on File, 2006.

Satin, Morton. *Food Alert!: The Ultimate Sourcebook for Food Safety,* 2nd ed. New York: Facts on File, 2008.

Sherrow, Victoria. *Food Safety.* New York: Chelsea House, 2008.

Spellman, Frank R. *Food Supply Protection and Homeland Security.* Lanham, MD: Government Institutes, 2008.

Periodicals

Just, David R., Brian Wansink, and Calum G. Turvey. "Biosecurity, Terrorism, and Food Consumption Behavior: Using Experimental Psychology to Analyze Choices Involving Fear." *Journal of Agricultural and Resource Economics* 34, no. 1 (2009): 91–108.

Liu, Yifan, and Lawrence M. Wein. "Mathematically Assessing the Consequences of Food Terrorism Scenarios." *Journal of Food Science* 73, no. 7 (2008): M346–M353.

Mohtadi, Hamid, and Antu P. Murshid. "Risk Analysis of Chemical, Biological, or Radionuclear Threats: Implications for Food Security." *Risk Analysis* 29, no. 9 (2009): 1317–1335.

Setola, Roberto, and Maria Carla De Maggio. "Security of the Food Supply Chain." *Proceedings: Annual International Conference of the IEEE Engineering in Medicine and Biology Society* (2009): 7061–7064.

Web Sites

"Food Defense & Emergency Response." *Food Safety and Inspection Service, U.S. Department of Agriculture (USDA).* http://www.fsis.usda.gov/Food_Defense_&_Emergency_Response/FSIS_Security_Guidelines_for_Food_Processors/index.asp (accessed September 11, 2010).

FoodSHIELD. http://www.foodshield.org/ (accessed September 11, 2010).

"Guidance for Industry: Food Producers, Processors, and Transporters: Food Security Preventive Measures Guidance." *Office of Food Defense, Communication and Emergency Response, U.S. Food and Drug Administration (FDA).* http://www.fda.gov/Food/GuidanceComplianceRegulatoryInformation/GuidanceDocuments/FoodDefenseandEmergencyResponse/ucm083075.htm (accessed September 11, 2010).

National Center for Food Protection and Defense (NCFPD). http://www.ncfpd.umn.edu/Ncfpd/ (accessed September 6, 2010).

Joseph P. Hyder

Bisphenol A

■ Introduction

Bisphenol A (BPA) is used as a starting material in the synthesis of polycarbonate plastics and epoxy resins. Polycarbonate is used in the manufacture of beverage containers, CDs and DVDs, lenses, medical devices, auto parts, toys, equipment housings, and a host of other products. A wide range of uses may be found for polycarbonate due to its light weight, transparency, thermostability, electrical insulating properties, and impact resistance. BPA-based epoxy resins are mechanically tough and highly resistant to chemical degradation, making them ideal as protective coatings and adhesives, and for fabricating laminates and composites. Cured epoxy is used to line the inside of food cans to prevent the cans from rusting.

Bisphenol A is an organic compound consisting of two phenol groups linked together by a propane (3-carbon) backbone. The International Union of Pure and Applied Chemistry (IUPAC) name of BPA is *4,4′-dihydroxy-2,2-diphenylpropane.*

BPA is a monomer, meaning it is a building block used in the synthesis of larger molecules called polymers. Polymers consist of long chains of monomers that have been linked by chemical reactions. All the plastics that most people are familiar with are manufactured by polymerization of monomers.

Because of its prevalence in so many products that are in everyday use, BPA finds it way into the environment as a contaminant. Small amounts of BPA escape from manufacturing plants to enter air and water supplies. Although the polymerized form of BPA found in epoxies and polycarbonates is relatively stable, not all of the BPA is polymerized during synthesis, and over time the monomeric form can be released from products to enter the environment. Small amounts of BPA are also leached from food containers, especially when heated, and then consumed by humans.

■ Historical Background and Scientific Foundations

The first report of BPA in the chemical literature appeared in 1891, and a method for the synthesis of BPA was published in 1905. Use in the synthesis of epoxy resins was initiated in the 1930s, by which time BPA was recognized as an endocrine disruptor capable of estrogenic effects.

In the early 1950s, German and American scientists independently developed commercially viable production methods that used BPA as a starting material for

WORDS TO KNOW

ENDOCRINE SYSTEM: A system comprising glands that secrete specific hormones into the bloodstream to regulate body functions.

EPOXY RESINS: Short chain polymers or monomers formed by the reaction of bisphenol A (or other compounds) and epichlorohydrin. When mixed with a hardener, the resin forms a very tough epoxy copolymer.

ESTROGENIC: Having an effect similar to that of the female sex hormone estrogen.

MONOMER: A small molecule used as a chemical building block. Monomers can be linked together to form much larger molecules called polymers.

POLYCARBONATE PLASTIC: A versatile, transparent, malleable polymer with many commercial applications, synthesized by combining bisphenol A and phosgene.

POLYMER: A molecule of relatively high molecular weight, consisting of repeated chemical subunits that are linked together by chemical bonds.

Canadian Environment Minister John Baird, left, and Health Minister Tony Clement hand out baby bottles that are free of the chemical bisphenol A, or BPA, following a news conference in Ottawa, Canada, in 2008. Canada has announced its intention to ban the use of the chemical in baby bottles, U.S. lawmakers have introduced legislation to ban it in children's products, and Wal-Mart and Toys "R" Us say they will stop selling baby bottles made with the chemical.   *AP Images.*

synthesizing polycarbonate plastic. More and more uses for polycarbonate plastic were found, which eventually led to the use of BPA in manufacturing polycarbonates on an industrial scale in the late 1950s. A similar expansion in the demand for epoxy resins further increased the popularity of BPA as a feedstock in chemical plants. In the early twenty-first century, millions of metric tons of BPA are used annually by the chemical manufacturing industry.

■ Impacts and Issues

From 2003 to 2004 scientists at the U.S. Centers for Disease Control and Prevention (CDC) measured the concentrations of BPA in urine samples collected from more than 2,000 people of all ages, from six years old and up. Nearly every sample tested positive for BPA. Although this study showed that the American population was widely exposed to BPA, it did not address how much of a health risk this exposure might be.

Industry-standard toxicity tests indicate BPA is non-toxic. Studies of BPA in aquatic ecosystems indicate that it is readily biodegradable and does not persist in the environment or bioaccumulate in tissues. Bisphenol concentrations of less than 100 micrograms per liter in water are unlikely to cause adverse effects in aquatic life. The concentration of BPA found in natural waters is generally significantly less than this. However, experiments designed to detect small effects on neurological and reproductive function in animals suggest that BPA may be harmful to humans, especially young children. Some researchers also report data indicating that BPA may be a contributing factor in contracting breast and prostate cancers, early onset of female puberty, diabetes, obesity, and attention deficit disorders.

Some studies on the health risks of BPA are under increased scientific scrutiny due to an appearance of bias. Research funded by industry groups tends to report no risk or minimal risk from exposure to BPA, whereas those sponsored by non-profit or government organizations have found some evidence of health hazards. This makes it difficult for consumers to decide whether the convenience offered by many BPA-containing products outweighs any potential risk.

In the United States, the National Toxicology Program (NTP) and the Food and Drug Administration (FDA) are proceeding with plans to further and more definitively answer questions about the safety of continuing widespread use of BPA in food containers. In January 2010 the FDA stated that "both the National Toxicology Program at the National Institutes of Health and FDA have some concern about the potential effects of BPA on the brain, behavior, and prostate gland in fetuses, infants, and young children" and announced it was taking steps to reduce human exposure to BPA in the food supply, including the elimination of BPA polymers from baby bottles and food can linings. The FDA is also considering tougher regulation and oversight of BPA.

Many container companies, such as Rubbermaid, Tupperware, Nalgene, Kleen Kanteen, Eco, and Thermos have voluntarily introduced BPA-free food storage containers, water or sports beverage bottles, lunch boxes, and food wrappers into the market. At least one dozen manufacturers also offer BPA-free baby bottles, pacifiers, teethers, and sippy cups. Consumers often pay a small premium for BPA-free products.

SEE ALSO *Food Packaging; Food Safety and Inspection Service; U.S. Food and Drug Administration (FDA).*

BIBLIOGRAPHY

Books

Seeking Safer Packaging: Ranking Packaged Food Companies on BPA. Boston: Green Century Capital Management, 2009.

U.S. Food and Drug Administration. *Draft Assessment of Bisphenol A for Use in Food Contact Applications.* Bethesda, MD: U.S. Food and Drug Administration, 2008.

Periodicals

Cao, Xu-Liang, Jeannette Corriveau, and Svetlana Popovic. "Migration of Bisphenol A from Can Coatings to Liquid Infant Formula during Storage at Room Temperature." *Journal of Food Protection* 72, no. 1212 (2009): 2571–2574.

"European Food Safety Authority Dismisses Safety Concerns over Bisphenol A." *Pesticide and Toxic Chemical News* 35, no. 15 (2007): 1.

"European Food Safety Authority Plans to Review Bisphenol A." *Pesticide and Toxic Chemical News* 36, no. 27 (2008): 11–12.

Kotz, Deborah. "Anxieties in a Bottle (or a Can)." *U.S. News & World Report* 145, no. 7 (September 29, 2008): 84.

Mitka, Mike. "BPA Ban Proposed." *JAMA: The Journal of the American Medical Association* 301, no. 18 (2009): 1868.

Roseler, Deanna. "Industry and Consumers Are Still Hearing Mixed Messages about the Use of Bisphenol-A in Food Packaging." *Food in Canada* 69, no. 2 (2009): 25–25.

"Study Links Bisphenol A to Heart Disease in Adults." *Food Chemical News* 51, no. 46 (2010): 12.

Tanne, Janice Hopkins. "FDA Says That Bisphenol A in Food Is Safe, Despite Controversy." *BMJ* 337 (2008): a1429.

Web Sites

"Bisphenol A (BPA)." *U.S. Food and Drug Administration (FDA).* http://www.fda.gov/newsevents/publichealthfocus/ucm064437.htm (accessed September 20, 2010).

"Since You Asked: Bisphenol A (BPA)." *National Institute of Environmental Health Sciences.* http://www.niehs.nih.gov/news/media/questions/sya-bpa.cfm (accessed September 20, 2010).

Philip McIntosh

Bottled Water

■ Introduction

Bottled water refers to any drinking water that is packaged in containers for consumption at a later date. Bottled water has served an important role in providing people with clean drinking water in situations where the local water supply is unavailable or unsafe to drink. It continues to fill this role during emergency relief, on the battlefield, or during outbreaks of waterborne diseases.

Over the last several decades, however, bottled water has become one of the most popular beverage choices around the world, even in areas with high-quality municipal water supplies. Consumers often choose bottled water as an alternative to carbonated soft drinks, coffee, tea, beer, or other beverages. Increased bottled water consumption has raised a number of environmental issues, including energy required for production and waste generated by water bottles.

■ Historical Background and Scientific Foundations

Bottled water may come from natural springs or municipal water systems. A survey of more than 1,000 bottles of water conducted by the Natural Resources Defense Council (NRDC) in 1999 revealed that at least 25 percent of the bottled water tested was repackaged municipal tap water. Some manufacturers further treat tap water before bottling, but others do not. Labels may indicate whether bottled water comes from municipal water systems, but the NRDC survey revealed that some bottled water claiming to be either "glacier water" or "spring water" was actually tap water.

Bottled water is not necessarily safer than tap water in areas with high-quality municipal water systems. The NRDC's survey of bottled water revealed that 22 percent of the bottled water tested contained chemical contaminants above the health limit allowed in one or more U.S. states. At least some samples from 18 out of the 103 brands tested also contained microbiological contaminants above allowable limits for tap water. Furthermore, the U.S. Environmental Protection Agency (EPA) and similar agencies in other countries regulate contaminant levels in municipal water systems. Most countries do not similarly regulate contaminant levels in bottled water. In the United States, for example, the Food and Drug Administration (FDA), not the EPA, regulates bottled water using lower testing standards than used for municipal water systems.

Since the 1990s, bottled water has emerged as one of the largest segments of the beverage industry. Global bottled consumption increased by an average of 6.3 percent per year between 2003 and 2008, with China leading the way with 15.6 percent annual growth. According to the Beverage Marketing Corporation, in 2008 consumers purchased approximately 52.7 billion gallons (199.4 billion liters) of bottled water. In the United States, the largest bottled water market by volume, consumers drank 8.7 billion gallons (32.9 billion liters) of bottled water in 2008. Mexico and China are the second and third largest bottled water markets with consumption of 6.5 and 5.2 billion gallons (24.6 billion and 19.7 billion liters), respectively, in 2008.

The bottled water market remains regional with great disparities in consumption among countries. In

---

WORDS TO KNOW

POLYETHYLENE TEREPHTHALATE (PET): Polyethylene terephthalate, also known as PET, is a lightweight, rigid polymer resin that is widely used for food and beverage containers.

SPRING WATER: Spring water refers to groundwater that emanates from a spring.

TAP WATER: Tap water refers to water produced by a municipal water system and transported to consumers through home plumbing systems.

2008 the average per capita global consumption of bottled water was 7.9 gallons (29.9 liters). Mexico was the global leader in per capita bottled water consumption in 2008 with 59.1 gallons (223.7 liters), followed by Italy at 54.0 gallons (204.4 liters) and the United Arab Emirates at 39.7 gallons (150.3 liters). The United States, the largest nation in bottled water consumption by volume, placed tenth in per capita consumption at 28.5 gallons (107.9 liters). In 2000 bottled water was the fifth most popular prepared beverage in the United States, behind carbonated soft drinks, beer, coffee, and milk. By 2008 bottled water had become the second most popular prepared beverage in the United States behind carbonated soft drinks.

■ Impacts and Issues

Bottled water requires a significant amount of energy input for its production and distribution, especially when compared to tap water. According to the U.S. Conference of Mayors, the bottled water industry uses the equivalent of 17 million barrels of oil each year to produce plastic bottles. The U.S. Conference of Mayors estimates that the amount of oil used to produce plastic water bottles each year would provide fuel for one million cars. The production of plastic water bottles produces an estimated 2.5 million tons of carbon dioxide, a major greenhouse gas, each year.

The 17 million barrels of oil cited by the U.S. Conference of Mayors applies only to the production of plastic water bottles. Additional energy input is required to treat the water, fill and cap the bottles, and transport the bottled water from its source to consumers. In an article in the January–March 2009 issue of *Environmental Research Letters*, "Energy Implications of Bottled Water," researchers Peter H. Gleick and Heather S. Cooley found that the U.S. bottled water industry in 2007 required the equivalent energy input of 32 to 54 million barrels of oil. Gleick and Cooley estimated that the global bottled water industry would require approximately three times as much oil as the U.S. industry alone. While Gleick and Cooley's domestic figure only represents about 0.3 percent of the United States' annual energy consumption, the energy used to produce plastic water bottles is largely an unnecessary use of energy. Ultimately, the researchers found that, on average, bottled water production requires 2,000 times the total energy input of municipal tap water.

Although plastic water bottle production consumes a large amount of energy input, most water bottles are high quality, recyclable polyethylene terephthalate, or PET, bottles. Although recycling rates vary greatly by county, the majority of plastic water bottles are not recycled by consumers. According to the Container Research Institute, a non-profit organization that promotes recycling programs and policies,

approximately 80 percent of the almost 35 billion water bottles purchased in the United States are thrown away each year—the equivalent of 877 bottles per second. The International Bottled Water Association, a bottled water trade association, notes that water bottles comprise less than 0.3 percent of all waste produced in the United States in 2005 despite the large number of bottles discarded each year.

Although bottled water production used approximately 52 billion gallons (189 billion liters) of water in 2008, the industry has little impact on increasing water

IN CONTEXT: WHAT'S IN THE BOTTLE?

By 2008 Americans drank an estimated 8.6 billion gallons of bottled water, approximately doubling estimates of consumption made in the late 1990s. By 2009 bottled water grew to be a $11.2 billion industry in the United States.

Despite the popular perception or outright claims that bottled water is always safer and healthier to drink than local tap water, a number of studies and reviews fail to support such assumptions and claims. Moreover, multiple independent studies raise doubts about commercial claims regarding the source and testing of bottled water. Recalls of bottled water contaminated with heavy metals, chemical cleaning solvents, and bacteria also raise concerns about blind confidence in bottle water purity and safety.

Because bottled water is considered a food, it is regulated by the Food and Drug Administration (FDA). The Environmental Protection Agency (EPA) regulates pollution and testing standards for tap water. In 2008 and 2009, the Environmental Working Group (a nonprofit research and advocacy organization) and the U.S. Government Accountability Office (GAO), respectively, published reports that raised questions about whether the FDA and EPA devoted adequate resources and personnel to testing and whether the division of regulatory and oversight responsibility created quality assurance gaps for consumers. At a minimum, government, health, and environmental experts broadly argued that water bottling companies should be held to the same disclosure standards as local municipal water suppliers with regard to sources, contaminants, and the potential health impacts of contaminants. In addition, critics argued that bottled water claims should be independently verified and tested by independent certified laboratories. In 2009 the GAO once again urged for implementation of requirements that labels more fully disclose bottled water sources, testing methods, and safety measures, and Congress held hearings addressing the matter.

In September 2009 new FDA regulations required bottlers to report test results that meet criteria establishing a serious health threat, and by 2010 manufacturers were required to ensure that products were free of *E. coli* contamination. Critics continue to push for stricter standards, more complete disclosure, and enhanced enforcement.

A man cycles next to bottled water left on a sidewalk outside of a water depot in Beijing, China, 2007. China's food safety watchdog promised to probe a report that more than half of the water coolers in Beijing use counterfeit branded water. According to a report in the *Beijing Times*, the water is either tap water or purified water from small suppliers put into the water jugs and sealed with fake quality standard marks.   *AP Images.*

usage around the world. In the United States, the world's leading consumer of bottled water, the bottled water industry uses less than 0.02 percent of the nation's total groundwater withdrawals. Furthermore, water withdrawals used by the bottled water industry do not necessarily increase water usage or consumption. Consumers typically drink bottled water in place of another beverage, such as tap water or carbonated beverages.

IN CONTEXT: BISPHENOL A (BPA)

In April 2008 Canada's government became the first to declare that the chemical bisphenol A (BPA) is a toxin. In particular, it has been shown to have teratogenic effects in animal studies. BPA, which is not regulated in the United States, is used in many plastic food containers, baby bottles, and water bottles. The U.S. Centers for Disease Control said in 2007 that it had found BPA in 93 percent of Americans over five years old, with the highest levels in women and children. Studies of BPA's effects on animals have found that the chemical can disrupt hormone function, especially in fetuses and infants; may alter development of sexual organs and the nervous system; and may trigger obesity or early puberty. In 2008 the U.S. National Toxicology Program said that there was "some concern" about exposure of human infants and children to BPA. The chemical industry insisted that there was no evidence of danger, but after the Canadian announcement some manufacturers of water bottles and baby bottles began to remove BPA from their products voluntarily.

In January 2010 the U.S. Food and Drug Administration (FDA) raised concern over the safety of BPA. The FDA statement was a change from an earlier report asserting that the small amounts of BPA were not dangerous.

Since 2009 several countries have banned or restricted use of BPA. The World Health Organization (WHO) and the Food and Agriculture Organization (FAO) issued a joint study raising concerns over use of BPA, but neither organization issued explicit warnings because they did not want to exacerbate malnutrition or starvation in areas were people depended on infant formula or food from cans lined with BPA without more definitive scientific evidence that the chemical causes harm.

SEE ALSO *Bisphenol A; Ethical Issues in Food Aid; Food Fads; Food Packaging; Water; Water Scarcity.*

BIBLIOGRAPHY

Books

Gleick, Peter H. *Bottled and Sold: The Story behind Our Obsession with Bottled Water.* Washington, DC: Island Press, 2010.

Royte, Elizabeth. *Bottlemania: Big Business, Local Springs, and the Battle over America's Drinking Water.* New York: Bloomsbury, 2009.

Periodicals

"Bottled-Water Industry—Tap v. Bottle." *The Economist* 388, no. 8589 (2008): 85.

Mooney, Chris. "Things Can Get Pretty Murky When You Start Thinking about the Virtues of Bottled Water." *New Scientist* 2659 (June 7, 2008): 49.

Ward, Lorna A., et al. "Health Beliefs about Bottled Water: A Qualitative Study." *BMC Public Health* 9 (June 19, 2009): 196.

Web Sites

"Bottled Water." *National Resources Defense Council.* http://www.nrdc.org/water/drinking/qbw.asp (accessed September 5, 2010).

"Bottled Water: Get the Facts." *Food and Water Watch.* http://www.foodandwaterwatch.org/water/bottled/ (accessed September 5, 2010).

Joseph P. Hyder

Botulism

■ Introduction

Botulism is a disease that is caused by a bacterial toxin released by the bacterium *Clostridium botulinum*. Botulism toxins are powerful neurotoxins; they affect nerves and can produce paralysis. *C. botulinum* are commonly found in soil and can be present on vegetables and other food grown in soil. The bacteria are ingested when contaminated vegetables and other foods are not properly washed.

In the soil and on the surface of growing foods, conditions where oxygen is present, the bacteria do not produce the toxin and so are harmless when eaten. The toxin is produced when the bacterium grows in the absence of oxygen. Growth of the bacteria in, for example, the low-oxygen and slightly acidic environment of some canned foods can, however, also produce sufficient toxin to cause illness and death. With foodborne botulism, growth of the bacteria in the food may occur, but is not mandatory for developing botulism, as the presence of the toxin alone is sufficient to cause illness. Because the toxin causes the illness, foodborne botulism often is described as a food intoxication.

Botulism is a rare illness: Most cases occur because of improper canning of foods at home. Normally, the mature adult digestive system can handle typical amounts of exposure to the bacterium *C. botulinum*. In infants, however, a form of botulism poisoning termed infant botulism causes severe illness in about 100 infants per year in the United States. Infant botulism occurs as a result of infants harboring the bacterium in their digestive system.

Paralysis from botulism affects the functioning of organs and tissues, and when botulism is fatal, it is usually due to failure of the respiratory muscles. Botulism is not a contagious disease—it cannot be spread from person to person.

■ Historical Background and Scientific Foundations

Botulism was first described in 1735 in an illness outbreak that was traced to the consumption of contaminated German sausage. Indeed, the word botulism was derived from the Latin word *botulus*, meaning sausage.

Growth of the bacteria in a low-oxygen and slightly acidic environment (the bacteria cannot grow above pH 5) is associated with the production of gas. Canned foods can bulge due to the build-up of the gas. For this reason, experts recommend discarding unopened cans of food if they are bulging.

The toxin is one of seven types (A-G) made and released by the bacterium *Clostridium botulinum*. Botulism toxin types A, B, E, and F cause botulism in humans. Another bacterium called *Clostridium baratii* can also produce a disease-causing toxin, but this bacterium is rarely encountered and is responsible for far fewer cases of botulism compared to *C. botulinum*.

Although unrelated directly to food, botulism can result from an infection of *C. botulinum* in an open wound. Growth of the bacteria deep in the tissues leads to the production of the toxin, which then spreads via the bloodstream.

Symptoms of botulism are produced when the toxin enters the bloodstream. The toxin blocks the production of a neurotransmitter called acetylcholine, a chemical that bridges the physical gap between nerve cells and aids in the transmission of impulses from nerve to nerve. As nerves are affected and paralysis occurs, a person experiences difficulty seeing, talking, and swallowing, and can become nauseous.

C. botulinum is one of a few types of bacteria that can produce a structure known as a spore. A spore is a form of the bacterium that is non-growing but can persist in that form for a long time despite conditions of excessive heat, dryness, and other harsh environments that would kill the normally growing cell. The spore form enables the organism to survive inhospitable conditions and then, when conditions improve, such as in canned food or inside the body, the bacteria can resume growth, division, and toxin production.

The different forms of the botulism toxin display some differences in their geography. In the United States, type A botulism, which is the most severe, occurs most often in western regions, particularly in the Rocky Mountains. Type B toxin, the symptoms of which tend to be less severe, is more common in the eastern United States. Type E toxin is found more in the bacteria that live in freshwater sediments. The reason for their different distributions is not clear.

Botulism also has significance in its potential as a bioterrorist threat. The potent killing power of the *Clostridium* neurotoxins has been recognized for decades. During World War II (1939–1945) several nations, including the

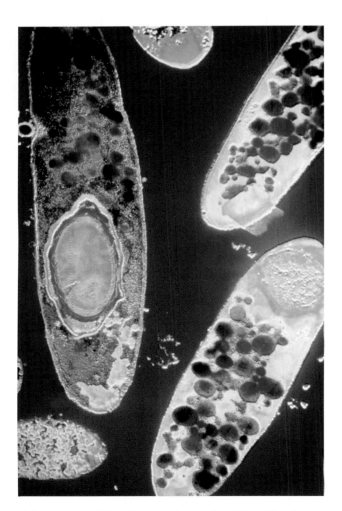

Colorized transmission electron micrograph of *Clostridium butyricum* bacteria showing spores and granules. Less common than other *Clostridia*, it causes an intoxication syndrome known as botulism that sometimes taints canned foods. © *Phototake / Alamy.*

WORDS TO KNOW

NEUROTOXIN: A poison that interferes with nerve function, usually by affecting the flow of ions through the cell membrane.

SPORE: A dormant form assumed by some bacteria, such as anthrax and *Clostridium botulinum,* that enables the bacteria to survive high temperatures, dryness, and lack of nourishment for long periods of time. Under proper conditions, the spore may revert to the actively multiplying form of the bacteria.

United States and Canada, experimented with the development of botulism toxin-based weapons. Sprays that contained the spore form of *C. botulinum* were developed and tested. The idea was that inhalation of the spores would lead to resumed growth of the bacteria and production of the lethal neurotoxin. The sprays were never used in battle.

Botulinum toxin A is exploited cosmetically as a means of lessening wrinkles. Injection of Botox® relaxes muscles, which can produce a more youthful appearance. The American Society of Aesthetic and Plastic Surgery (ASAPS) estimates that the worldwide market for Botox® is around 900 million dollars annually, and more than two million Botox® procedures are performed per year. Botulinum toxin A has also shown promise in lessening dystonia (muscle spasms) that occur in cerebral palsy and in treating strabismus (crossed eyes).

Detection

Diagnosis involves the detection of the botulinum toxin in blood samples, which can be accomplished using specific immune components, or antibodies. An antibody to the specific botulinum toxin will react with the toxin, producing a visible clump of material. As well, sometimes living bacteria can be recovered from the feces.

Treatment for botulism often involves the administration of an antibody-containing antitoxin that blocks the binding of the toxin to the nerve cells. With time, paralysis fades. However, recovery can take many weeks. If botulism is suspected soon after exposure to the bacteria, the stomach contents can be emptied to remove potentially contaminated undigested food. When lung muscles have been affected, a patient may need mechanical assistance in breathing.

■ Impacts and Issues

A century ago, botulism was frequently a death sentence—one of every two people who became ill with it died. By 2010, according to the Centers for Disease Control and Prevention (CDC), only about 3–5 percent of affected people die, and less than 150 cases are

IN CONTEXT: SODIUM NITRATE USE

In low doses, sodium nitrate is used to cure meats and prevents the growth of the bacterium *Clostridium botulinum* and thereby the subsequent release of botulism-causing toxin. However, in higher doses nitrite poisoning can oxidize the iron in hemoglobin from the normal ferrous form to the ferric form, thereby changing hemoglobin to methemoglobin. The methhemoglobin form loses hemoglobin's ability to bind and carry oxygen. Characteristic signs of nitrite poisoning are dyspnea (a shortness of breath), cardiac arrhythmias (irregular heartbeats or rhythm), convulsions, and in the most severe cases, coma or death.

reported in the United States to the CDC each year. Only 15 percent of those cases are from foodborne botulism (65 percent were from infant botulism, and the remaining 20 percent were wound botulism). In contrast to some other diseases that take a toll on the underdeveloped areas of the world, botulism is more prevalent in developed regions, particularly where food is processed, canned, and sold. However, economies in transition, especially those with lax regulatory oversight, have observed spikes in cases of botulism.

Diagnosis of botulism is complicated by the fact that the disease is infrequently seen. A physician may have little experience in dealing with the illness. As well, in its early stages, botulism has symptoms that are similar to other ailments such as Guillain-Barré syndrome and stroke. Both of these considerations sometimes lead to a delayed diagnosis of botulism.

In 1976 a form of botulism was recognized in infants in the United States that stemmed from babies ingesting *C. botulinum* spores that colonized their intestinal tract (an infant's intestinal tract is less acidic than that of an adult) and eventually produced botulinum toxin. Evidence indicated that honey was linked with both the reservoir of the bacteria and the resulting disease. Since that time, honey-linked infant botulism has been reported in other countries, prompting recommendations from the American Academy of Pediatrics for all infants less than 12 months of age not to receive foods containing honey.

Because botulism is a rare occurrence, The Centers for Disease Control and Prevention (CDC) maintains a central supply of antitoxin against botulism. State health departments consult with the CDC for release of the antitoxin when a case has been reported to them. Fast action is essential, because the antitoxin reduces the severity of the symptoms only if given soon after symptoms develop.

When a food source of botulism is discovered, the Food and Drug Administration (FDA) usually issues a class-1 recall of the product. Class-1 recalls are reserved for dangerous or defective products that could cause serious health problems or death and involve communication between the FDA, manufacturer or supplier, and the public to remove the product from the market or remove the food source from the food supply. Manufacturers may also issue voluntary recalls if there is a possibility of contamination. For example, in February 2007 the FDA issued a warning against consumption of an organic baby food because of the risk of contamination with *Clostridium botulinum*. The manufacturer initiated a recall of the food, and working in conjunction with the FDA, removed the potentially contaminated baby food jars from store shelves, began an awareness campaign, and tracked and corrected the source of the contamination. There were additional voluntary recalls of organic baby food products in 2008 and 2010. There were no verified reports of illness or death.

Recent U.S. manufacturer recalls related to potential *Clostridium botulinum* contamination include a diverse array of products such as fish, bean salad, chili sauce, and Italian olives.

SEE ALSO *Center for Food Safety and Applied Nutrition; Consumer Food Safety Recommendations; Food Inspection and Standards; Food Preparation Methods; Food Recalls; Food Safety and Inspection Service; Foodborne Diseases.*

BIBLIOGRAPHY

Books

Emmeluth, Donald. *Botulism (Deadly Diseases and Epidemics)*. New York: Chelsea House Publications, 2005.

Web Sites

"Botulism." *Centers for Disease Control and Prevention (CDC)*. http://www.cdc.gov/nczved/divisions/dfbmd/diseases/botulism/ (accessed October 8, 2010).

"Botulism." *World Health Organization (WHO)*. http://www.who.int/entity/mediacentre/factsheets/fs270/en/index.html (accessed October 8, 2010).

Brian Hoyle

Breastfeeding

■ Introduction

From a low of 28 percent of babies being breastfed in 1972 to a high in 2008 of 78 percent, breastfeeding rates in the United States have fluctuated wildly since the early 1960s. This same trend appears in many developed countries. Research that demonstrates nutrition and health benefits to both mother and infant, public health campaigns promoting breastfeeding, and laws and policies to help protect breastfeeding mothers' rights have all contributed to the increase in breastfeeding.

The World Health Organization (WHO) began tracking data on breastfeeding in various countries in 1991. The WHO Global Data Bank on Infant and Young Child Feeding and UNICEF note that worldwide, 39 percent of newborns are breastfed initially, with a widely divergent range of 85 percent in Honduras down to 17 percent in Serbia.

Breast milk composition provides the most nutritionally complete substance for the infant, changing the ratio of fats, sugars, and water throughout the day to meet the infant's specific needs at any time. Breastfeeding is often at the nexus of public health campaigns, social debate over privacy and public actions, policy and law for working mothers, and food and medical research worldwide.

■ Historical Background and Scientific Foundations

Shortly before or after giving birth, a woman's breast milk glands begin to produce colostrum, a pre-milk substance that contains nutrients to sustain the newborn before the milk glands begin full breast milk production, which typically happens between two and four days after birth. Mammals sustain their infant young via breastfeeding, and infants who cannot gain access to breast milk or a nutritionally-acceptable substitute will not survive.

Throughout history, women breastfed their young through the first and second years of life and often beyond. Social patterns vary widely from culture to culture: During the Middle Ages in parts of Western Europe, nursing until the "milk teeth" (toddler molars) came in was a typical pattern. In modern-day Afghanistan more than 30 percent of two-year-olds breastfeed. American anthropologist Kathryn Dettwyler (1955–) notes in her book *Breastfeeding: Biocultural Perspectives* that "in societies where children are allowed to nurse as long as they want they usually self-wean, with no arguments or emotional trauma, between three and four years of age."

In developing societies with poor water supply and public health conditions, breastfeeding provides a filter for the infant, protecting the baby from harmful bacteria that could lead to death. Breastfeeding on demand is common in these societies, and breastfeeding tends to last longer.

Wet nursing, common in all societies but phased out in the developed world after the introduction of artificial baby milk in the late 1800s, involves a lactating woman stepping in to breastfeed as a stand-in for the biological mother. Wet nurses were hired for pay or could be relatives or volunteers. The practice of hiring wet nurses declined dramatically as infant formula became available in the 1860s. Modern milk banks accept donated breast milk from women. The milk is pasteurized and used for medically needy infants.

If a wet nurse was not available, the last resort for infant feeding was cow's milk or goat's milk. By the mid-1800s scientists knew that the protein load in these animal milks was too high for infant kidneys. In 1867 German confectioner Henri Nestlé (1814–1890) and German chemist Justis von Liebig (1803–1873) invented infant formula, a powder that balanced fats, carbohydrates, and sugars to more closely resemble breast milk.

The introduction of formula led to a gradual decline in breastfeeding rates in developed countries and among the middle and upper classes, who could

WORDS TO KNOW

DRY NURSING: The term for the feeding of infants during the 1800s and 1900s, via spoon, finger, or bottle, any mixture of animal milk and other foods as a substitute for breast milk.

LA LECHE LEAGUE INTERNATIONAL: Founded in 1956 in Franklin Park, Illinois, at a time when breastfeeding rates were close to 20 percent in the United States, La Leche League International supports on-demand breastfeeding for mother and child pairs, with monthly meetings for women seeking breastfeeding support in 68 countries.

WET NURSING: A term for a woman, not an infant's biological mother, who breastfeeds an infant due to the biological mother's inability to breastfeed. Wet nurses were typically women who had recently had an infant, whose infant died, or women who maintained lactation easily and charged a fee for wet nursing services to provide economic support for their families.

afford to buy this new product. A 2001 article in *The Journal of Nutrition* by Anne L. Wright and Richard J. Schanler, "The Resurgence of Breastfeeding at the End of the Second Millenium," argues that breastfeeding rates also dipped as a result of intensive management of labor and childbirth from a medical perspective. Hospital births and the use of analgesia to induce "twilight sleep" from the 1930s through 1960s during labor and delivery, combined with advice from nurses to adhere to strict feeding schedules that are not conducive to on-demand breastfeeding, created barriers to breastfeeding. The authors note that breastfeeding rates began to increase in the early 1970s among well-educated, "prepared childbirth" advocates who ignored schedule advice in favor of perceived natural childbirth and feeding methods.

Since 1972, breastfeeding rates in the United States have been on the rise, with the exception of a small dip in the late 1980s. The current rate of initiation of breastfeeding at birth in the United States is 78 percent, whereas 21 percent of babies are still breastfed at age one.

■ Impacts and Issues

In 2003 Australian Parliament member Kirstie Marshall (1969–) was ejected from the floor of Parliament for bringing her 12-day-old daughter, who was breastfeeding, with her. Marshall argued that the nursing pair needed to be together for the baby's feedings, whereas Standing Order 30 of the House rules states that "strangers" cannot be present for parliamentary proceedings. Marshall's ejection made headlines worldwide and gained the attention of lactivists (breastfeeding activists), prompting the Australian Speaker of the House to create facilities for female MPs who are breastfeeding to use while conducting business.

The much-debated 2010 health care reform bill in the United States included a little-discussed provision requiring employers to give lactating mothers paid breaks and acceptable facilities for pumping breast milk and storing it. Federal law protects the right of women to breastfeed their children on federal property. Laws in 44 states and Washington, DC, protect the right to breastfeed.

The presence of polybrominated diphenyl ethers (PBDE) and polychlorinated ethyls (PCB) in breast milk has gained media attention throughout the first decade of the twenty-first century. These environmental toxins are the subject of research on breast milk levels in arctic Inuit women; studies find that infants receive harmful doses of PDBEs and PCBs from breast milk found in women from the Arctic Circle down to California. A fertile area for ongoing research, public health authorities caution mothers that the PCB/PDBE issue is not a reason to avoid breastfeeding, because the same chemicals are found in the animal milks used in many commercial infant formulas, and that the benefits of breast milk outweigh the harm from PCB/PDBE.

Wet nursing gained some media attention when WHO, UNICEF, and the Pan American Health Organization issued a joint statement encouraging lactating women in Haiti to help breastfeed orphaned infants after the January 10, 2010, earthquake that hit Haiti killed many nursing mothers. Wet nursing, also referred to as shared nursing or cross nursing, is considered to be the safest feeding option for infants during crisis situations in which a stable water supply is not available for infant formula preparation and serving.

■ Primary Source Connection

Mercy Corps began over 30 years ago, and its mission is to find local solutions to local problems around the world involving issues such as poverty, armed conflict, natural disasters, and political changes in more than 40 countries. Approximately 95 percent of the team members are citizens of the country in which they are working.

Annalise Briggs, author of the following primary source—an Internet commentary or "blog" entry—served as Marketing Officer for Mercy Corps. Her blog entry illustrates the increasing openness about the benefits of breastfeeding as well as the increasing awareness that issues formerly classified as "women's issues" are really social issues of broad concern requiring contributions to solutions from all members of the community.

More than 500 mothers breastfeed their children of different ages during the Second Synchronized Breastfeeding Worldwide Saturday, October 11, 2008, in Marinkina City, Philippines. Held in different parts of the country, the event links thousands of Filipino mothers with mothers in other countries in a global effort to educate people on the benefits of breastfeeding. *AP Images.*

The Drawbacks of Women's Equality

Diba, a communications officer for Healthy Start—Mercy Corps' breastfeeding program in Jakarta—is one of these powerhouse women. (I am convinced women like this have more chemicals in their brain which I lack and have always envied.) She's a single mother, works full time and is going to school for her Master's degree. Diba's eyes light up when she talks about her job.

"I never thought I would find an NGO with a breastfeeding program!" she exclaims to me as we drive to the health clinic. I have never met someone so enthusiastic and heartfelt about their job. This is her passion, and you can see it in the way she describes the program details, talks with field staff, volunteers, midwives and mothers.

Breastfeeding—or lack their of—is a huge challenge in Jakarta. Breastfeeding has numerous health benefits and can prevent malnutrition and child mortality. Drug companies push formulas on doctors, health clinics and midwives—many mothers aren't even aware of their basic right to breastfeed. In the hospitals after delivery, the babies are taken from their mothers and bottle fed without the mother's permission. Baby formula is expensive and mothers often times dilute it with dirty water—the only thing available—which can cause diarrhea and illness.

Healthy Start is working with health care providers, midwives, community leaders and government workers to educate and support women and their right to breastfeed. I sat in on a mothers' support group where women asked questions—and not just about breastfeeding.

"When can I introduce solid foods?"

"When I have leg cramps [from pregnancy] what is the least painful way to get up?"

"When will my baby's teeth come in?"

The irony is that breastfeeding is not just a women's issue in Jakarta. It takes the entire community to mobilize to learn about the benefits of breastfeeding and support these mothers. Many of the Healthy Start facilitators are men and most of the government leaders that Mercy Corps works with are men.

Annalise Briggs

MERCY CORPS. ANNALISE BRIGGS'S BLOG. "THE DRAWBACKS OF WOMEN'S EQUALITY." HTTP://WWW.MERCYCORPS.ORG/ANNALISEBRIGGS/BLOG/16757 (ACCESSED NOVEMBER 5, 2010).

SEE ALSO   *Changing Nutritional Needs throughout Life; Infant Formula and Baby Food; Lactose Intolerance; UN Millennium Development Goals; Vitamins and Minerals.*

BIBLIOGRAPHY

Books

Lawrence, Ruth A., and Robert M. Lawrence. *Breastfeeding*. St. Louis, MO: Elsevier Mosby, 2005.

Palmer, Gabrielle. *The Politics of Breastfeeding: When Breasts Are Bad for Business*. London: Pinter & Martin, 2009.

Sullivan, Dana, and Maureen Connolly. *Unbuttoned: Women Open Up about the Pleasures, Pains, and Politics of Breastfeeding*. Boston: Harvard Common Press, 2009.

Wolf, Joan B. *Is Breast Best?: Taking on the Breastfeeding Experts and the New High Stakes of Motherhood*. New York: New York University Press, 2011.

Periodicals

"Breastfeeding—Still Not Reaching the Target." *Public Health Nutrition* 13, no. 6 (2010): 749–750.

"Protection, Promotion and Support of Breast-Feeding in Europe: Progress from 2002 to 2007." *Public Health Nutrition* 13, no. 6 (2010): 751–759.

Purdy, Isabell B. "Social, Cultural, and Medical Factors That Influence Maternal Breastfeeding." *Issues in Mental Health Nursing* 31, no. 5 (2010): 365–367.

"The Risks of Not Breastfeeding." *Journal of Acquired Immune Deficiency Syndromes: JAIDS* 53, no. 1 (2010): 1–4.

Web Sites

"Breastfeeding." *World Health Organization.* http://www.who.int/topics/breastfeeding/en/ (accessed October 8, 2010).

"Breastfeeding: Impact on Child Survival and Global Situation." *UNICEF.* http://www.unicef.org/nutrition/index_24824.html (accessed October 8, 2010).

Gates, Melinda. "Celebrating the Simple, Lifesaving Act of Breastfeeding." *Bill & Melinda Gates Foundation.* http://www.gatesfoundation.org/foundationnotes/Pages/melinda-gates-100830-celebrating-breast-feeding.aspx (accessed October 8, 2010).

Melanie Barton Zoltan

Building Better Ovens

■ Introduction

More than three billion people, nearly half of the global population, rely on some type of cooking fire, open hearth, or traditional stove without a chimney for cooking. Cooking and heating fires fueled by coal or biomass fuels (dung, plant waste, or wood) fill dwellings with dust, smoke, and soot, polluting indoor air and causing illness.

Worldwide, one death every 20 seconds is linked to cooking technology. Indoor air pollution, primarily attributable worldwide to cooking fires, hearths, and traditional stoves, kills 1.6 million people each year. Open-hearth or traditional means of cooking and heating can produce indoor air conditions that exceed acceptable levels of small particulate matter (primarily soot) by 100-fold. The World Health Organization (WHO) estimates that indoor smoke from cooking and heating is responsible for 2.7 percent of the global disease burden, and for increasing the incidence of pneumonia, bronchitis, lung cancer, and other respiratory diseases.

The polluting effects of cooking fires are not limited to indoors. Cooking fires send black carbon emissions into the atmosphere, significantly contributing to global climate change.

■ Historical Background and Scientific Foundations

In developing nations, reducing black carbon emissions and indoor air pollution associated with open-hearth cooking requires the development and implementation of improved cooking technologies—better stoves and ovens—that are durable, easy to maintain, desirable to use, produce good tasting food, and are low in cost. Developers of new portable cookstoves seek to replace traditional open-hearth cooking practices with solar stoves, alternative fuel stoves, or stoves that consume less of the same fuel as traditional hearths.

Researchers and nongovernmental organizations (NGOs) have deployed various models of improved stove technologies in developing regions since the 1970s. The early generation of stoves sought to improve indoor air quality by venting smoke out of homes. Stoves equipped with chimneys replaced open hearths. Cookstove developers and the NGOs with which they were partnered found that less than 20 percent of the homes where new stoves had been installed were properly maintaining their stoves. Some had abandoned using them entirely; others misused them in a manner that exacerbated indoor air pollution.

In 1992 the WHO declared indoor air pollution from cooking and heating smoke one of the world's most pressing health problems. That same year, the WHO released a synthesis of studies that linked acute respiratory infections, chronic bronchitis, and chronic obstructive pulmonary disease (COPD) in women and young children in developing nations with cooking smoke. Indoor cooking fires were also linked to carbon monoxide poisoning, low birth weights, reproductive problems, vision problems, and severe headaches. In 1997 less than 20 percent of homes studied in Brazil and Mexico had an indoor air quality that met WHO safety standards. Subsequent studies also noted that stove replacement programs needed to improve the rates at which households were using new cookstoves two years after obtaining them. In some areas, use after two years was as little as 30 percent.

The earliest stoves did not take into account cultural cooking preferences, another barrier to their implementation. Whereas a stove may have been efficient in terms of requiring less fuel to operate and venting smoke out of the home, it could not satisfactorily cook frequent diet staples such as tortillas or whole animal roasts. Cookstove designers thus shifted their focus from developing one cookstove that could work worldwide to tailoring multiple versions of cookstoves to specific regions or foods. For example, stoves intended to replace open fire cooking in Ethiopia are designed to cook injera, a spongy flat bread, whereas stoves intended for distribution in parts of India are designed to accommodate bowls of cooking stews or curries.

■ Impacts and Issues

The adoption of cleaner and greener cooking technologies has immediate, beneficial yields. Indoor air quality immediately improves. Residents of households formerly filled with smoke from cooking and heating show improved lung function and greater resistance to respiratory infection in as little as six weeks. Likewise, mass adoption of cleaner cooking technologies could have dramatic effects on outdoor air quality. Unlike carbon dioxide emissions, which have an atmospheric lifetime of 40 to 100 years, black carbon remains in the atmosphere for only 10 to 40 days on average. Climate researchers thus assert that reductions in black carbon emissions from cooking and heating fires could help abate some of the earliest effects of climate change, including glacial melt and global warming.

Emission savings vary by the type of new cookstove introduced in a region. Solar stoves and ovens operate with zero emissions, but they are often costlier and limited in their use by weather. Extended cooking times and the inability to cook some types of foods also affect their usefulness. Improved stoves that burn traditional fuels more efficiently offer 50 to 80 percent reductions in emissions when compared with traditional cooking technologies. These types of stoves are typically more readily accepted by local populations. In areas where traditional fuels are threatened or increasing in expense, new alternative fuel stoves offer the chance for households to reduce energy expenses while reaping environmental and health benefits.

The quest to supply greener cooking technologies to developing regions not only promises to improve health and environment, it also offers to reduce household work burdens. Women and children are primarily responsible for cooking-related tasks, from gathering and preparing fuel to making meals. Family members in developing nations who cook on open hearths spend

A cook prepares food using a charcoal stove in the kitchen of a small restaurant, in Mumbai, India. Up to 3 billion people worldwide rely on solid fuels such as wood, coal, crop waste, or animal dung for indoor cooking and heating. The resulting household smoke ranks as the fourth biggest health risk in the poorest countries, yet it's typically overlooked. *AP Images.*

Nathan Lorenz, vice president of engineering for Envirofit, a nonprofit company that builds clean-burning cook stoves for underserved global markets, examines a Envirofit clean cook stove. The stoves represent a solution to indoor air pollution, reducing toxic emissions by 80 percent, while also using 50 percent less fuel and providing an affordable product. *AP Images.*

an average of 120 to 200 percent more time doing cooking-related household tasks than households that cook on portable cookstoves using the same fuels. The labor and resource-saving properties of greener cookstoves can help alleviate household poverty, allowing families to spend less time maintaining subsistence and leaving more time for school or money-generating tasks.

On September 21, 2010, the United States and several international partners announced the Global Alliance for Clean Cookstoves. The initiative combines private-industry development of new cooking technologies with the foreign aid and development of capabilities of national governments and international NGOs to increase the use of new cleaner and greener cookstoves worldwide. The initiative aims to enable 100 million households to adopt better cooking technology. The U.S. government pledged over $53 million toward the project.

SEE ALSO *Agroecology; Climate Change and Agriculture; Cooking, Carbon Emissions, and Climate Change; Women's Role in Global Food Preparation.*

BIBLIOGRAPHY

Periodicals

Denton, Fatma. "Climate Change Vulnerability, Impacts, and Adaptation: Why Does Gender Matter?" *Gender & Development* 10, no. 2 (2002): 10–20.

Duflo, Esther, Michael Greenstone, and Rema Hanna. "Cooking Stoves, Indoor Air Pollution and Respiratory Health in Rural Orissa." *Economic and Political Weekly* 43, no. 32 (2008): 71–76.

Mishra, Vinod, Xiaolei Dai, Kirk R. Smith, and Lasten Mika. "Maternal Exposure to Biomass Smoke and Reduced Birth Weight in Zimbabwe." *Annals of Epidemiology* 14, no. 10 (2004): 740–747.

Venkataraman, C., et al. "The Indian National Initiative for Advanced Biomass Cookstoves: The Benefits of Clean Combustion." *Energy for Sustainable Development* 14, no. 2 (2010): 63–72.

Web Sites

"Black Carbon Implicated in Global Warming." *Science Daily,* July 30, 2010. http://www.sciencedaily.com/releases/2010/07/100729144225.htm (accessed November 2, 2010).

Global Alliance for Clean Cookstoves. http://cleancookstoves.org/ (accessed November 2, 2010).

"Indoor Air Pollution and Cookstove Efforts at NIH." *John E. Fogarty International Center, National Institutes of Health.* http://www.fic.nih.gov/news/resources/cookstoves.htm (accessed November 2, 2010).

Adrienne Wilmoth Lerner

Bushmeat

■ Introduction

Bushmeat is meat obtained from wild animals for human consumption or trade. In Africa, remote forests are also known as the bush, and bushmeat is taken from hunted or trapped wildlife within these forest habitats. Whereas many species of wild vertebrate animals are hunted for their meat, populations of forest primates in Africa are especially vulnerable to bushmeat hunters. Wildlife experts identify the chimpanzee in Sierra Leone and the mountain gorilla, lowland gorilla, and bonobo in the Democratic Republic of Congo as species especially at risk for decimation from poachers and bushmeat traders.

Although hunting and trade in bushmeat is illegal in most of the countries where it occurs, and both export and import of bushmeat is also illegal in most countries, bushmeat has made its way into the markets of large cities in both Europe and Asia. As populations of vulnerable wildlife dwindle and bushmeat hunting only increases, some scientists suggest that developing a regulated, sustainable bushmeat hunting strategy, along with taxing the hunters and marketers, is the only

---

WORDS TO KNOW

CITES: The Convention on International Trade in Endangered Species of Wild Fauna and Flora, often known as the CITES agreement, is a voluntary international agreement to restrict trade in animal or plant products from endangered or threatened species.

POACHING: Illegal hunting and killing of animals, often to sell their meat, skins, tusks, or other parts.

ZOONOTIC DISEASE: A disease transmitted from animals to humans.

---

readily available way to preserve ape populations, to reduce zoonotic disease transmission, and to allow local communities to sustain their livelihoods and traditions of consuming bushmeat.

■ Historical Background and Scientific Foundations

Bushmeat has long been a nutritional staple among forest-dwelling people in Sub-Saharan Africa and in tropical regions of Central America, South America, and Asia. Historically, meat from both small and large animals was a dependable source of protein for people living in small communities in areas rich in biodiversity. Traditional hunting, a localized activity that occurred in vast forests, was accomplished using mostly spears, pits, or arrows, and was a less efficient process, that took the lives of fewer animals, than poaching for bushmeat does in the twenty-first century.

As colonialism spread rapidly through Central Africa during the nineteenth century, traditional hunting techniques gave way to more efficient means, including firearms and weatherproof snares made from wire, then eventually nylon. Later, mechanized winches and trucks enabled hunters to transport large sport game and bushmeat efficiently. After colonialism was replaced by independence, during the mid-twentieth century many nations in Africa experienced a rise of civil war and tribal conflict. Millions of people fled the countryside for burgeoning cities in search of opportunity and in order to escape conflict. In these cities, the market for bushmeat remains high. Industry, meanwhile, pushed deeper into the forest in search of natural resources, destroying animal habitats along the way and coming into increasing contact with animals that were used to supply the demand for bushmeat in growing cities. Thus, the quest for bushmeat became an organized trade as well as a local subsistence measure.

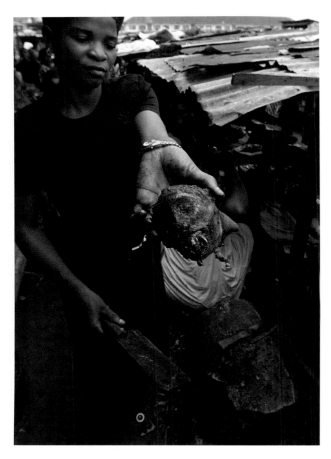

A woman in Kisangani, Democratic Republic of Congo, holds up the head of a monkey who she just decapitated behind the bar at Mama Ekila's Inzia restaurant, where African bushmeat is flown in for diners looking for the illegal meats. *AP Images.*

■ Impacts and Issues

Growing African mega-cities continue to spread into nearby forests, placing millions of people nearer to wildlife habitats and providing avenues for poachers to bring bushmeat to larger markets. Whereas the bushmeat from mother apes is often sold at markets, for example, the young are often carried to larger markets alive, where babies command attention and a high price. The bushmeat trade has even reached European capitals: After confiscating 51 kg (112 pounds) of bushmeat in one suitcase during a 2010 study in Paris's Roissy-Charles de Gaulle airport, French customs officials, along with additional study authors from the Zoological Society of London (ZSL), the Royal Veterinary College (RVC), and the National Veterinary School and Natural History Museum of Toulouse, concluded that almost 5 tonnes (5.5 tons) of illegal bushmeat is smuggled into Europe each week in personal luggage through Charles de Gaulle airport alone. More than one third of the confiscated bushmeat was derived from endangered species protected under the International Convention for the Trade in Endangered Species (CITES) agreement.

Deforestation in tropical areas is causing hunters increasingly to come into contact with wildlife, and with this contact comes the chance for humans to acquire a zoonotic disease from their prey. The Amazon basin, and West and Central Africa, are areas of great biodiversity and also areas of increasing deforestation. The demand for bushmeat in West and central Africa, however, is four times greater than in the Amazon basin. Deforestation in African tropical forests is mainly the result of the timber industry, with countries including Cameroon, Congo, the Democratic Republic of Congo, Gabon, Ghana, Ivory Coast, and Liberia supplying the bulk of African tropical timber.

As logging industries press into the forests to find new areas to harvest, they build roads, where loggers often set up camps. The roads fragment and disturb nearby animal habitats, and the logger camps provide a ready market for selling the bushmeat killed by local inhabitants. Some logging companies have also encouraged their employees to kill wildlife for meat rather than employ the logistics necessary to deliver food to their workers deep into the forest.

As the habitat for the animals becomes more fragmented, and their populations decrease due to poaching or inability to move freely, the pathogens (disease-causing organisms) that normally inhabit them find new hosts. Scientists consider this environment to be highly favorable for the emergence of new zoonotic diseases, especially viral diseases. Much of the time, viruses can be traded back and forth between humans and animals causing minimal spread of disease, and this is termed "viral chatter" by scientists. Occasionally, a virus that inhabits an animal and then a human becomes capable of causing disease and also capable of being transmitted from person to person. Zoonotic viral diseases that previously emerged to affect humans in a similar fashion include Ebola and human immunodeficiency virus (HIV), the virus that causes acquired immunodeficiency syndrome (AIDS).

Despite laws that prohibit hunting wildlife, in many developing countries poverty and necessity play roles

---

IN CONTEXT: BUSHMEAT CONSUMPTION

Experts estimate that the trade and regional consumption of wild animal meat in Central Africa is more than 2.2 billion pounds (1 billion kg) per year, and estimates for consumption in the Amazon Basin are in the range of 220 million pounds (100 million kg) annually. For mammals, this amounts to 6.4 million to 15.8 million individual animals slaughtered for bushmeat each year.

IN CONTEXT: BUSHMEAT BAR CODES

In 2009 a new tool was developed in the international fight against the illegal trade of bushmeat. Researchers from the University of Colorado at Boulder and the American Museum of Natural History sequenced DNA barcodes for 25 species of wildlife—Old World monkeys, alligators, crocodiles, antelopes, and wild pigs—targeted by illegal hunters. The researchers used a region of the mitochondrial gene COX1 to generate the barcodes, which can identify tissues or meat from an animal. This relatively small gene segment was selected because its rate of mutation is rapid enough to distinguish between closely related species but slow enough to ensure that individuals of the same species have similar barcodes. The real value of the DNA barcodes lies in their precision at the species level. The processed meats, hides, and other wildlife products sold in markets are often unidentifiable, but the availability of DNA barcodes enables laboratory analysis and species-level identification of some of these products. An open-access online repository provides barcode information to scientists worldwide. The ultimate goal is to sequence DNA barcodes for every animal on Earth.

in the inclusion of bushmeat in the diet. One study showed that in Cameroon poor families rely on bushmeat for almost 20 percent of the meat they consume. In addition, organized bushmeat traders often enrich the coffers of West and Central African warlords, tribal leaders, and corrupt governmental officials. Bushmeat gained by any means, however, results in the loss of an animal, and in areas where threatened species are involved, some researchers support limited, legal hunting for animals in the wild in order to dissuade poachers from hunting on reserves where the animal populations are intended for protection. According to the International Union for Conservation of Nature and Natural Resources (IUCN), there are about 172,700 to 299,700 chimpanzees left in the wild worldwide, and their population is decreasing to a point at which they are classified as endangered; about 100,000 lowland gorillas remain, and they are considered critically endangered; less than 600 endangered mountain gorillas remain; and 29,500 to 50,000 endangered bonobos are left in the wild. The bushmeat trade, along with disease and habitat loss, are the largest threats to the sustainability of these species.

■ Primary Source Connection

Bushmeat is not found just in the rural areas of developing countries. As this Associated Press article of 2010 details, major urban cities such as Paris, France, receive

tons of illegally imported bushmeat each week. Disease is a major concern, because there are no regulations or inspections of this meat, and there have been reports that some consumers of bushmeat have been exposed to an HIV-like virus. The potential for other diseases, including Ebola and salmonella, is worrisome. Cultural issues are also complicating this issue. African immigrants are accustomed to bushmeat as part of their diet. Most investigations reveal that the meat goes into the luxury market.

Bushmeat Smuggling Widespread in Paris; 5 Tons Smuggled in Weekly

PARIS—The traders sell an array of bushmeat: monkey carcasses, smoked anteater, even preserved porcupine.

But this isn't a roadside market in Africa—it's the heart of Paris, where a new study has found more than five tons of bushmeat slips through the city's main airport each week.

Experts suspect similar amounts are arriving in other European hubs as well—an illegal trade that is raising concerns about diseases ranging from monkeypox to Ebola, and is another twist in the continent's struggle to integrate a growing African immigrant population.

The research, the first time experts have documented how much bushmeat is smuggled into any European city, was published Friday in the journal Conservation Letters.

"Anecdotally we know it does happen . . . But it is quite surprising the volumes that are coming through," said Marcus Rowcliffe, a research fellow of the Zoological Society of London and one of the study's authors.

In the Chateau Rouge neighborhood in central Paris, bushmeat is on the menu—at least for those in the know.

Madame Toukine, an African woman in her 50s, said she receives special deliveries of crocodile and other bushmeat each weekend at her green and yellow shop off the Rue des Poissonieres market. She wouldn't give her full name for fear of being arrested.

"Everyone knows bushmeat is sold in the area and they even know where to buy it," said Hassan Kaouti, a local butcher. "But they won't say it's illegal."

For the study, European experts checked 29 Air France flights from Central and West Africa that landed at Paris' Roissy-Charles de Gaulle airport over a 17-day period in June 2008.

Of 134 people searched, nine had bushmeat and 83 had livestock or fish.

The people with bushmeat had the largest amounts: One passenger had 112 pounds (51 kilos) of bushmeat—and no other luggage. Most of the bushmeat was smoked and arrived as dried carcasses. Some animals were identifiable, though scientists boiled the remains of others and reassembled the skeletons to determine the species.

Experts found 11 types of bushmeat including monkeys, large rats, crocodiles, small antelopes and pangolins, or anteaters. Almost 40 percent were listed on the Convention on International Trade in Endangered Species.

Based on what officials seized—414 pounds (188 kilos) of bushmeat—the researchers estimated that about five tons of bushmeat gets into Paris each week.

They also noted that penalties for importing illegal meats are light and rarely imposed. Under French law, the maximum penalty is confiscation of the goods and a $556 (450 euro) fine. Of the passengers searched in the study, only one person with bushmeat actually was fined.

Bushmeat is widely eaten and sold in Central and West Africa, with Central African Republic, Cameroon and Republic of Congo being the main sources. It varies whether it is legal. It is typically allowed where people are permitted to hunt, as long as their prey aren't endangered and they can prove the animals were killed in the wild.

A bushmeat ban is enforced in Kenya, but it is legal in most parts of the Republic of Congo, where hunters may stalk wildlife parks that aren't heavily guarded. Even after several outbreaks of the deadly Ebola virus linked to eating bushmeat, the practice remains widespread.

Scientists warned eating bushmeat was a potential health hazard.

"If you have intimate contact with a wild animal—and eating is pretty intimate contact—then you could be exposed to all kinds of diseases," warned Malcolm Bennett, of Britain's National Centre for Zoonosis Research at the University of Liverpool, who was not linked to the study.

Bennett said bushmeat had a higher risk of bacteria like salmonella and might also be carrying new diseases. The virus that causes AIDS originated in monkeys, and the global 2003 SARS outbreak was traced to a virus in bats and civets.

Nina Marano, chief of the quarantine unit at the U.S. Centers for Disease Control and Prevention, said similar underground markets for bushmeat exist across America.

"We have to be culturally sensitive and recognize this is important for some African communities," she said. "But there are no regulations for the preparation of meat from wildlife to render it safe."

The scale of Europe's illicit bushmeat trade suggests the emergence of a luxury market. Prices can be as high as $18 per pound (30 euros per kilo), double what more mundane supermarket meats cost.

"It's like buying the best cut of organically grown beef," Rowcliffe said, adding that bushmeat like giant rats and porcupine, which he has tasted, has a strong, gamey flavor.

Maria Cheng
Christina Okello

CHENG, MARIA. AND CHRISTINA OKELLO. "BUSHMEAT SMUGGLING WIDESPREAD IN PARIS; 5 TONS SMUGGLED IN WEEKLY." *ASSOCIATED PRESS*, JUNE 19, 2010. AVAILABLE ONLINE AT HTTP://WWW.HUFFINGTONPOST.COM/2010/06/19/TONS-OF-BUSHMEAT-IN-PARIS_N_618299.HTML (ACCESSED NOVEMBER 4, 2010).

SEE ALSO *Agricultural Deforestation; Biodiversity and Food Supply; Climate Change and Agriculture; Ecological Impacts of Various World Diets; Population and Food.*

BIBLIOGRAPHY

Books

Davies, Glyn, and David Brown. *Bushmeat and Livelihoods: Wildlife Management and Poverty Reduction.* Oxford, UK: Blackwell, 2007.

Gaynup, Sharon. *State of the Wild 2006: A Global Portrait of Wildlife, Wildlands, and Oceans.* Washington, DC: Island Press, 2005.

The Bushmeat Trade. London: Parliamentary Office of Science and Technology, 2005.

Periodicals

Bennett, Elizabeth, L., et al. "Hunting for Consensus: Reconciling Bushmeat Harvest, Conservation, and Development Policy in West and Central Africa." *Conservation Biology* 21, no. 3, (2006): 884–887.

Wolfe, Nathan D., et al. "Bushmeat Hunting, Deforestation, and Prediction of Zoonotic Disease." *Emerging Infectious Diseases* 11, no. 12 (2005): 1822–1827.

Web Sites

Bushmeat Crisis Task Force. http://www.bushmeat.org/ (accessed October 30, 2010).

"Chimpanzees and Bushmeat 101." *Jane Goodall Institute.* http://www.Janegoodall.org/Chimpanzees-And-Bushmeat-101 (accessed October 30, 2010).

"Illegal Bushmeat Trade Rife in Europe, Research Finds." *Science Daily*, June 18, 2010. http://www.sciencedaily.com/releases/2010/06/100617210641.htm (accessed October 30, 2010).

Brenda Wilmoth Lerner

Caffeine

■ Introduction

One of the most widely used drugs, caffeine is part of an array of foods and beverages consumed daily by 90 percent of the world's people. Evidence of its use dates to the origins of human culture, and it is a common ingredient in coffee, tea, and soft drinks. Caffeine is also consumed in snacks such as chocolate candy or as a component in medications.

Caffeine is present in coffee, tea, and chocolate. These plant-derived beverages and foods also contain the other methylxanthines, which some scientists say serve as defense chemicals for leaves and berries produced in climates where there are no winter temperatures to kill populations of chewing bugs. Tea contains mostly caffeine, with small amounts of theophylline and theobromine, but tea is a weaker plant extract than the stronger brew, coffee. Theobromine is the primary methylxanthine found in cocoa, which also contains a small amount of caffeine per cup. Caffeine content generally ranges from as little as 5 mg in a cup of hot cocoa to 300 mg in 6 oz (177 ml) of espresso. Colas generally have about 50 mg per 12 fl oz (355 ml).

■ Historical Background and Scientific Foundations

Caffeine, the active substance responsible for the stimulant effect of the coffee plant's berry, is a methylxanthine, one of the family of stimulants present in more than 60 species of plants. The pure chemical forms white, bitter-tasting crystals, which were first isolated from coffee in 1820. Other family members are theophylline, found in tea leaves, and theobromine, found in the cacao pods that are ground to make chocolate. The most potent component in the coffee family by unit weight is theophylline, whereas theobromine, the weakest component by unit weight, stays in the body longer than does caffeine.

Caffeine is also a trimethylxanthine, which is made up of three methyl groups. Efforts by the liver to deactivate caffeine at first appear counterproductive. Liver enzymes usually detoxify potentially harmful chemicals obtained through food or those naturally present in the body. But what is left after the liver initially removes a methyl from caffeine are theophylline and paraxanthine, both of which are still active. Only when the final methyl is stripped away is the chemical inert. This production of active metabolites is why the stimulant lasts a relatively long time. It is also why people with liver disease, or those who consume other drugs that engage the liver enzymes, cannot efficiently clear caffeine from their body. Impaired caffeine metabolism is also evident in women taking estrogen for birth control or who are at the high estrogen phase of their monthly cycle. Newborn babies, whose livers are not yet fully developed, also break down caffeine more slowly until the enzymes are fully activated.

The robusta strain of coffee plant cultivated in Indonesia and Africa contains about 2.2 percent caffeine, whereas the arabica variety, grown in Central and South America, contains half that concentration. The caffeine in tea was purified in 1827, and it was initially given its own name of theine, as chemists of the day thought it different from the caffeine in coffee.

The kola nut, source of some of the flavoring of cola drinks, also has a bit of caffeine. About 5 percent of the 35 mg in a 9.5 oz (280 ml) serving of cola is naturally present from the kola nuts. The remaining caffeine in sodas is added by the manufacturer.

Caffeine is available by prescription as a solution of caffeine citrate. Caffeine is also an active ingredient in many headache medicines, both by prescription and sold over the counter, as well as in nonprescription aids and herbal preparations for alertness and dieting. Caffeine is added intentionally to energy drinks, including some bottled waters. Some drugs, both legal and illegal, contain caffeine either for added effect or as a filler, often mixed in powder form.

A functional magnetic resonance imaging (MRI) study of the brain can actually determine between the regular and the occasional coffee drinker. Caffeine consistently slows blood flow by 25 percent to the gray matter of the brain, which contains the cells, and by 20 percent to the white matter, which contains the connecting nerve fibers. Heavy users of caffeine show more blood flow in the gray matter in the front of the brain when they had abstained for 30 hours, compared to those who infrequently ingest caffeine. With fMRI, the doctor can look inside the brain and observe the phenomenon of caffeine withdrawal in action.

Within minutes of consumption, a caffeinated beverage will cause the drinker to feel more alert. Simple intellectual tasks are performed more readily, as are physical jobs that require endurance. However, while reaction time is shortened by caffeine, fine motor control suffers, perhaps due to the slight tremor that becomes more pronounced with higher doses of caffeine. Larger doses of caffeine, especially for people who do not use it regularly, cause headache and nervousness.

Caffeine decreases the duration of slow waves in the electroencephalogram (EEG) for about five hours after it is ingested. Taken near bedtime, caffeine will delay the time it takes for the consumer to fall asleep and will reduce the depth and quality of sleep. Sleepers will also

move more and waken more easily. These effects are evident with the amount of caffeine present in a cup or two of coffee, approximately 75–150 mg.

A policewoman helps unidentified diplomats examine packs of caffeine before incineration during a ceremony to destroy narcotic drugs in Kyaing Tong, in eastern Shan State of Myanmar, 2009. *AP Images.*

IN CONTEXT: CAFFEINE AND COMPETITION

IN CONTEXT: CAFFEINE AND COMPETITION

Caffeine has a proven positive effect on the function of the body in endurance sports. The ingestion of caffeine increases the level of circulating fatty acids in the bloodstream, which permits these fat stores to be oxidized, or burned, as fuel. Accessing these fatty acids as fuel means that the body's stores of energy (known as glycogen), created through the processes that convert it from food carbohydrates, will not be exhausted in long competition. Marathon runners, long-distance cyclists, and cross-country skiers have been established as prime benefiaries of caffeine when it is consumed approximately one hour before competition.

The effect of caffeine on the conversion of fatty acids to energy is further enhanced if the athlete is not a regular coffee drinker or does not consume caffeine products. In an alternative to the pre-competition consumption of caffeine by endurance athletes, further research has demonstrated the efficacy of caffeine in sports drinks. The carbohydrates in the caffeine-enhanced sport drinks were found to be absorbed by the body at a rate 26 percent faster than the rate achieved without caffeine. The ability of the body to utilize this portable energy source effectively saved bodily stores of energy.

Caffeine is considered an illegal, performance-enhancing substance in Olympic competition only if found in an athlete's system in levels in excess of 12 mcg/ml (micrograms/milliliter)—an amount that is the rough equivalent to the caffeine contained in eight to ten 6-oz (175 ml) cups of coffee—consumed within two hours of testing. In 2004 the World Anti-Doping Agency (WADA) removed caffeine from its list of prohibited substances. It is unlikely that an athlete could ingest caffeine in excess of the Olympic standard without causing an adverse impact upon the body's renal (kidney) and urinary systems, as the diuretic impact of high levels of caffeine will reduce hydration and stimulate urine production.

Frankly toxic effects, such as persistent insomnia and anxiety, only become evident when people drink more than eight or nine cups of coffee or tea per day. Convulsions and delirium can follow enormous doses, and a near-fatal dose can induce a state similar to that of a diabetic person lacking insulin. Blood sugar surges, and ketones appear in the urine. The lowest recorded fatal dose of caffeine was 3200 mg, which was given by accident directly into the bloodstream. It takes the equivalent of 40 cups of coffee consumed by mouth in a short interval for caffeine to kill a person.

Most studies find that moderate use of caffeine does not impair fertility, risk miscarriage, or increase the chance of having a baby with birth defects. Caffeine can enter the milk of mothers. Babies younger than six months cannot metabolize caffeine as well as do adults. Mothers are advised, however, that small or modest amounts—up to three cups of coffee or several cans of soda—can be consumed without passing caffeine on to their nursing infants.

The American Cancer Society states that there does not seem to be any relationship between caffeine and cancer. However, other adverse effects for women remain a concern, such as the possibility that large amounts of caffeine could contribute to osteoporosis (thinned and fragile bones), particularly in elderly women. As caffeine is a diuretic, which increases loss of fluids and electrolytes in the urine, it could rob the body of calcium. Nevertheless, a study published in 2001 concluded that the net effect of carbonated sodas on the body's calcium is negligible, and that the loss of calcium in urine due to carbonated drinks is too small to affect calcium balance.

In 1979 a Swiss company developed a new distillation method to remove the caffeine from coffee, creating decaffeinated coffee. The Swiss water process proved popular among young urban professionals as it was considered to make a more natural-tasting product by contrast to the earlier method of making decaffeinated coffee, which used chemicals such as methylene chloride. The Swiss method also retained more of the flavorful oils residing in the coffee bean. Caffeine-free versions of colas soon followed.

■ Impacts and Issues

Both health claims and controversies have followed caffeine through the centuries. By the 1960s, health concerns over coffee use were raised in the medical literature as well as the popular press. Research linked coffee consumption to medical conditions such as pancreatic cancer, breast lumps, and elevated levels of cholesterol. Most follow-ups to earlier studies warning of the adverse effects of caffeine have failed to duplicate the initial findings, especially for the moderate use of caffeine.

In 1980 the Food and Drug Administration (FDA) proposed to remove caffeine from its Generally Recognized As Safe list. But the FDA concluded in 1992 that, after reviewing the scientific literature, no harm is posed by a person's intake of up to 100 mg per day. As of 2009, the American Heart Association stated that moderate consumption of caffeine was not harmful.

In 1997 the Food and Drug Administration (FDA) required labeling of the caffeine content of foods and drinks. Prior to 2004 some body builders used a combination of caffeine with the herbal stimulant ephedra. However, ephedra was linked to several deaths, and subsequently the FDA banned the sale of ephedra-containing diet aids in 2004. In 2001 the U.S. military endorsed the usefulness of caffeine, recommending it as a safe and effective stimulant for its soldiers.

The therapeutic treatment of obesity with caffeine remains a controversial area of interest. Many over-the-counter diet aids include caffeine, but it has not yet been determined whether there is a medically safe way to universally use caffeine as a diet aid. For example, green tea with caffeine is a popular alternative diet aid. As of 2010, studies do not yet create a complete testing picture, proponents arguing that caffeine—through the action of phosphodiesterase enzymes—indirectly boosts the adrenergic signals. However, there is no direct evidence that green tea successfully allows people to lose weight and keep it off.

Legally, caffeine is not regulated as a dangerously addictive substance. Yet withdrawal from caffeine is documented as a recognized set of symptoms in the medical literature. Many people who regularly consume caffeine and then suddenly stop will experience headache, irritability, muscle aches, and lethargy, including impaired concentration.

The extent to which people suffer withdrawal from caffeine use remains controversial. Published studies show that a small percentage of people report withdrawal symptoms following a halt to their normal caffeine intake. Few claim their symptoms interfered with daily living. Multiple studies treat caffeine withdrawal as an established and well-documented phenomenon. A major symptom of abrupt cessation of caffeine use is a headache of moderate to severe intensity that generally begins within 18 hours of the last dose. It peaks at about three to six hours of onset. The feeling is of fullness in the head that continues to a diffuse, throbbing pain and is worsened by physical activity. Sadness and mild nausea are also reported by a quarter of those who show the withdrawal headache. Those who chronically consume 500 to 600 mg of caffeine per day are more likely to experience withdrawal if they suddenly cease their habit.

In recent years new "energy" drinks are purposely formulated to contain higher amounts of the mild stimulant. Critics of drinks with elevated caffeine levels argue that the higher caffeine and sugar content pose a potential risk of dehydration for athletes and that they could also pose a significant danger for adverse effects on the heart. In addition, these high-caffeine drinks are increasingly used as mixer beverages for alcohol, combining a mild stimulant (caffeine) with a mild central nervous system depressant (alcohol), a potentially dangerous combination. Critics are especially vocal about sales of mildly addictive caffeine (usually in soft drinks) to minors in school settings.

SEE ALSO *Bottled Water; Chocolate; Coffee; Diet and Heart Disease; Diet and Hypertension; Fair Trade; Food Additives; Food as Celebration; Food Preparation Methods; French Café Culture; Tea.*

BIBLIOGRAPHY

Books

Chambers, Kenneth P. *Caffeine and Health Research.* New York: Nova Biomedical Books, 2009.

Clark, Taylor. *Starbucked: A Double Tall Tale of Caffeine, Commerce, and Culture.* New York: Little, Brown, 2007.

Health Canada. *Caffeine.* Ottawa: Health Canada, 2007.

Heiss, Mary Lou, and Robert J. Heiss. *The Story of Tea: A Cultural History and Drinking Guide.* Berkeley, CA: Ten Speed Press, 2007.

National Library of Medicine (U.S.), and National Institutes of Health (U.S.). *Caffeine.* Medline Plus health topics series. Washington, DC: U.S. National Library of Medicine, 2000. Also available at http://www.nlm.nih.gov/medlineplus/caffeine.html (accessed October 19, 2010).

Nehlig, Astrid. *Coffee, Tea, Chocolate, and the Brain.* Nutrition, brain, and behavior, vol. 2. Boca Raton, FL: CRC Press, 2004.

Rosbottom, Betty. *Coffee.* San Francisco, CA: Chronicle, 2007.

Smith, Barry D., Uma Gupta, and Bhupendra S. Gupta. *Caffeine and Activation Theory: Effects on Health and Behavior.* Boca Raton, FL: CRC Press, 2007.

Spiller, Gene A. *Caffeine.* Boca Raton, FL: CRC Press, 1998.

Weinberg, Bennett Alan, and Bonnie K. Bealer. *The World of Caffeine: The Science and Culture of the World's Most Popular Drug.* New York: Routledge, 2001.

Web Sites

"Caffeine—What's the Buzz?" *National Geographic Society.* http://science.nationalgeographic.com/science/health-and-human-body/human-body/caffeine-buzz.html (accessed October 19, 2010).

Calories

■ Introduction

In common usage by nutritionists and others in the food industry, the calorie is a unit of measurement for heat energy obtained from the digestion of foods. It is also used to measure the amount of heat energy expended by the human body when performing various activities.

The calorie is technically defined as the metric unit of measurement for energy. In most fields, the calorie has been superseded by the joule, the SI unit (French for Système International d'Unités, [International System of Units]) for energy.

■ Historical Background and Scientific Foundations

In the human body energy is not a substance and cannot be transferred; it is a function of state that can be raised or lowered by the ingestion and biochemical transformation of food. When the human body eats food, the caloric intake is an indirect indication of the potential increase in the internal energy state of the body (the capacity to do work ranging from basic physiologic processes to the most complex human

behaviors). The particular amount of increase in the internal energy state depends on the specific foods ingested, along with physiologic factors that may vary slightly among individuals.

More specifically, the food calorie—sometimes also called the nutritional or dietary calorie—is usually stated simply as the calorie. It is equivalent to the kilogram calorie (kcal), or kilocalorie. The kilogram calorie, or the large calorie, is defined as the heat energy necessary to increase the temperature of one kilogram of water by one degree within the Celsius temperature scale. It is equivalent to about 4.185 kilojoules (where one kilojoule is equal to 1,000 joules). Further, the gram calorie, or the small calorie, is the amount of heat energy necessary to raise the temperature of one gram of water by 1° Celsius. Thus, one food calorie is equal to one kilogram calorie, which is equal to 1,000 gram calories. When a label on food reads 4.5 calories, these 4.5 food calories are the same as 4.5 kilogram calories, or 4,500 gram calories.

Food calories are not technically measured as amounts of heat energy, but rather as approximate comparisons of the energy density (in units of kilocalories per gram) for a large number of different food samples. Generally, a food product is first analyzed by separating it into its constituent parts (carbohydrates, proteins, fats, sugars, etc.). The results are then compared to standardized chemical tests in order to estimate the product's digestible constituents. The results are converted into an equivalent energy value based on an internationally approved conversion table for energy densities of predetermined food samples. For instance, fats have an energy density of 9 kilocalories per gram (kcal/g), which is an especially high value. Proteins and carbohydrates have a value of 4 kcal/g. Then, special metabolic equipment can be used to evaluate the

---

WORDS TO KNOW

GRAM CALORIE: The small calorie; the amount of heat energy necessary to raise the temperature of one gram of water by one degree Celsius.

KILOGRAM CALORIE: The heat energy necessary to increase the temperature of one kilogram of water by one degree Celsius.

caloric output (consumption) that occurs when performing specific physical activity such as running and walking.

■ Issues and Impacts

Many industrialized countries worldwide require their food manufacturers to label the caloric content of their products. Since 1994 the United States Food and Drug Administration (FDA)—through the Nutrition Labeling and Education Act (NLEA) of 1990—has required that most packaged food products contain a nutritional facts label. The FDA mandates that food manufacturers abide by these NLEA-stated guidelines with respect to the presentation of these labels, being regulated primarily by the type of food and its serving size. Some of the information found on these labels includes total calories, calories from fat, total fat (and saturated fat), cholesterol, trans fats, sodium, total carbohydrates, dietary fiber, sugars, protein, vitamin A, vitamin C, calcium, and iron. Other nations have differing labeling laws: Some are based on kilocalorie standards whereas others use calories as the standard measure.

Proposed improvement of changes to labeling laws can spur intense debate. Several cities and states within the United States have passed legislation requiring restaurants to disclose the caloric and nutritional value of foods served.

Although the calorie is used as the unit for comparing foods consumed, it is not the only measure of the importance or use of food by the human body. Foods contain other substances that are required to maintain

IN CONTEXT: CALORIC "BURNS"

The amount of energy that the human body uses during a specific activity is known as caloric output (commonly called the caloric burn). The size and weight of a person and the amount of effort and time needed for a particular activity affect the specific amount of caloric output. For the most part, more energy is required as the intensity and strenuousness of the sport increases. The average food caloric output for a 150-lb (68-kg) person in various sports activities is the following:

- golf: 270 calories per hour
- ice skating (leisurely): 300 calories per hour
- walking on a level surface: 360 calories per hour
- water skiing: 390 calories per hour
- bicycling at 10 mph (16 km/h): 420 calories per hour
- racquetball: 540 calories per hour
- swimming (recreationally): 600 calories per hour
- running at 7.5 mph (12 km/h): 750 calories per hour
- walking upstairs: 1,050 calories per hour

In any sport, food calories are an important part of how well an athlete trains and ultimately competes. Eating a balanced diet is critical to sports nutrition. The correct combination of fuel (calories) from carbohydrates, proteins, and fats provides the increase in energy needed for top performance.

heath. Some nutrients are needed because the body does not produce them or produces them in amounts that are too minute. These so-called essential nutrients are

Calorie labeling on a menu board in a Panera bread store in Massachusetts in March 2008. Panera became one of the first food chains to post calories on menus nationally. *AP Images.*

IN CONTEXT: COMMON FOOD CALORIE VALUES

The average number of food calories for a few commonly eaten foods and drinks include:

- coffee (one coffee cup, 0.46 pint; 220 ml): 15.4 calories
- apple (4 oz; 112 g): 53 calories
- brown bread (one medium slice): 74 calories
- orange juice (one drinking glass, 0.42 pint; 200 ml): 88 calories
- American cheese (1.5 oz; 42.5 g): 110 calories
- doughnut (1.7 oz; 49 g): 140 calories
- almonds (1 oz; 28 g): 171 calories
- chicken breast (7.1 oz; 200 g): 342 calories
- chocolate (3.5 oz; 100 g): 530 calories

obtained from food sources such as carbohydrates, fats, minerals, proteins, vitamins, and water. Nonessential nutrients are those nutrients that are already manufactured in the human body and thus are not necessary to be acquired from the intake of food. One such nonessential nutrient is cholesterol. Each person requires various amounts of essential nutrients depending on such factors as age, gender, health, and certain other conditions. Specific health conditions such as illness, pregnancy, and breastfeeding often increase the need for certain essential nutrients. There is no linear relationship between calories and essential nutrients. Some foods, especially so called "junk foods," can be high in calories yet low in essential nutrients.

Every person has different caloric requirements depending on such attributes as age, body size, health, and activity level. If a person is within his or her ideal weight range, then that individual is probably getting the correct amount of calories in his or her diet. However, the nutritional value of the foods eaten must also be monitored to maintain a healthy diet.

The recommended daily energy intake for adult men in the United States commonly ranges from 1,700 to 2,800 kcal depending on size, age, and weight. For women in the United States, the most common range is between 1,300 to 2,100 kcal.

SEE ALSO *Changing Nutritional Needs throughout Life; Dietary Guidelines for Americans; Dietary Reference Intakes; Food Packaging; Protein and Carbohydrate Metabolism.*

BIBLIOGRAPHY

Books

Benardot, Dan. *Advanced Sports Nutrition.* Champaign, IL: Human Kinetics, 2006.

Bender, David A. *A Dictionary of Food and Nutrition.* New York: Oxford University Press, 2009.

Berdanier, Carolyn D. *CRC Desk Reference for Nutrition.* Boca Raton, FL: CRC/Taylor & Francis, 2006.

Chen, Nancy N. *Food, Medicine, and the Quest for Good Health: Nutrition, Medicine, and Culture.* New York: Columbia University Press, 2008.

Claybourne, Anna. *Healthy Eating: Diet and Nutrition.* Chicago: Heinemann Library, 2008.

The Japan Society of Calorimetry and Thermal Analysis, ed. *Comprehensive Handbook of Calorimetry and Thermal Analysis.* Hoboken, NJ: John Wiley & Sons, 2004.

Joint FAO/WHO/UNU Expert Consultation on Human Energy Requirements (2001: Rome, Italy). *Human Energy Requirements: Report of a Joint FAO/WHO/UNU Expert Consultation: Rome, 17–24 October 2001.* Rome: Food and Agriculture Organization of the United Nations, 2004.

Kohlstadt, Ingrid, ed. *Scientific Evidence for Musculoskeletal, Bariatric, and Sports Nutrition.* Boca Raton, FL: CRC/Taylor & Francis, 2006.

Larson-Meyer, D. Enette. *Vegetarian Sports Nutrition.* Champaign, IL: Human Kinetics, 2007.

MacClancy, Jeremy, and Helen Macbeth. *Researching Food Habits: Methods and Problems.* The Anthropology of Food and Nutrition, Series 5. New York: Berghahn Books, 2004.

Medical Economics Company. *PDR for Nutritional Supplements.* Montvale, NJ: Thomson Reuters, 2008.

Web Sites

"Make Your Calories Count." *U.S. Food and Drug Administration (FDA).* http://www.fda.gov/Food/LabelingNutrition/ConsumerInformation/ucm114022.htm (accessed October 9, 2010).

"Nutrition." *Centers for Disease Control and Prevention (CDC).* http://www.cdc.gov/nccdphp/dnpa/nutrition.htm (accessed October 9, 2010).

"Nutritional Support." *National Institutes of Health (NIH), U.S. Department of Health and Human Services.* http://health.nih.gov/topic/Nutritional Support (accessed October 9, 2010).

William Arthur Atkins

Cannibalism

■ Introduction

The human preoccupation with cannibalism is universal. All cultures have stories about people who eat human flesh, and in the past cannibalism was an important part of the ritual and religion of many different societies. This fascination helps account for the enduring popularity of narratives of some very different types of cannibalism: psychopathic cannibalism, survival cannibalism, myths and fairy tales of human-eating monsters, and sensationalized accounts of more academic examinations of culturally sanctioned anthropophagy.

Anthropologists have focused on the symbolic importance of cannibalism and its role in colonial history. Cannibalism is also relevant to examinations of racism, social order, and the construction of savage or exotic types of "the other" in anthropology. This other type of humanity may include such popular stereotypes as the inhabitants of the Marquesas Islands, who called human flesh "long pig"; bloodthirsty Aztec priests; Neanderthals who smashed their enemies' skulls and ate their brains; and Native peoples who consumed their dead relatives. Although the study of cannibalism as part of a religious system remains fundamental, other researchers are attempting to document why, how, when, and where people ate other people, and how cannibalism relates to prion diseases such as kuru and variant Creutzfeldt-Jakob Disease (vCJD).

■ Historical Background and Scientific Foundations

The word *cannibal* comes from the Spanish word *Caribal* and refers to the island natives who also gave their name to the Caribbean. Although documents from Christopher Columbus' second voyage to the New World in 1493 describe the discovery of human bones in a Native house, the Europeans did not actually witness cannibalism at this time; its existence was taken for granted. As William Arens argued in *The Man-Eating Myth* in 1979, many European (and later American) descriptions of cannibalism were almost certainly exaggerated. It is clear that cannibalism—sometimes falsely attributed—was an important colonial justification for appropriating Native lands and enslaving or marginalizing indigenous peoples in the Caribbean, Mexico, South America, Africa, and the Pacific. This does not mean that cannibalism did not ever occur there: Good evidence exists for different types of cannibalism in many of these places. Perhaps most famously, large-scale exocannibalism of war captives and slaves was practiced by the Aztec nobility as part of their state religion. Endocannibalism, especially as part of funeral ritual, was widely practiced, most notably in New Guinea, where it was finally discontinued in 1959. Both types of institutionalized cannibalism may include a gustatory appreciation of human meat along with a belief in its sacred meaning, but it was apparently more common (though very rare) for people to be killed explicitly in order to be eaten in societies with exocannibalism.

Cannibalism as a desperate means of survival and as an expression of mental illness belong in a different category from culturally sanctioned anthropophagy. People in all cultures may resort to eating the dead when faced with starvation. Many people were engrossed by lurid accounts of the members of the Donner Party in northern California in 1846 and the story of the survivors of a Uruguayan plane crash in the Andes in 1972.

Stories about cannibals exist in so many cultures, in so many places, that it is likely both the actual practice and its symbolic importance in human culture have great antiquity. Chimpanzees occasionally kill and eat each other, and archaeologists have found butcher marks on the bones of human ancestors that were discarded with other animal bones almost 800,000 years ago at Gran Dolina, a cave in Spain. Similarly, smashed skulls and long bones were found mixed with animal bones at

WORDS TO KNOW

ANTHROPOPHAGY: Cannibalism; eating humans.

ENDOCANNIBALISM: Eating people from within one's own group, usually as part of a religious rite involving dead ancestors. In contrast, exocannibalism is defined by eating outsiders, usually the enemies of the one's group.

GUSTATORY: Relating to taste. Gustatory cannibalism refers to the practice of eating human flesh as another kind of meat and is often used in contrast to ritual cannibalism. Even in those cultures in which human flesh was allegedly enjoyed as a food, however, it carried more symbolic meaning than other kinds of meat.

KURU: An incurable, degenerative type of TSE (Transmissable Spongiform Encephalopathy), a fatal brain disease transmitted by infection with prions. Kuru is found in New Guinea and was mainly contracted by the Fore people during endocannibalistic funeral rituals. A gene protecting its carriers from kuru (and possibly other TSE diseases) has been discovered among the Fore.

PRION: A proteinaceous infectious particle, or prion, is a deformed protein that converts other proteins into the same form, resulting in a buildup of abnormal proteins causing one of several types of TSE, a type of fatal brain disease, such as BSE (bovine spongiform encephalopathy, or "mad cow disease"), scrapie in sheep and goats, and Creutzfeldt-Jakob Disease (CJD) in humans. Variant CJD (vCJD) is usually contracted by human consumption of BSE-infected beef.

TSE: Transmissable Spongiform Encephalopathies, or prion diseases, are incurable brain diseases transmitted by contact with prions.

Member of the Korowai tribe in Indonesia. Korowai in nearby in West Papua are among the last humans known to practice cannibalism. © *Danita Delimont / Alamy.*

Moula-Guercy, a French cave occupied by Neanderthals about 100,000 years ago.

More recent evidence for prehistoric cannibalism is controversial, as it is often difficult to distinguish between rituals that involved dismembering and defleshing human bodies, as opposed to those in which dismemberment was followed by consumption. Furthermore, the descendants of people said to be cannibals often take offense at allegations of ancestral cannibalism. Archaeological evidence for cannibalism at several ancestral Pueblo sites in the southwestern United States (dating between 1000–1400 AD) have been fiercely debated for decades. Although human myoglobin was found on the inside of a ceramic cooking pot at one Anasazi Pueblo site, along with a human coprolite (preserved fecal matter) containing the same human protein, it is not clear which Native group was actually responsible for this, and cannibalism does not appear to have been particularly widespread in the Southwest at this time.

■ Impacts and Issues

Cannibalism continues to be an important literary and cultural trope, as it has since Michel de Montaigne's essay "Of Cannibalism" in 1580 and the publication of *Robinson Crusoe* in 1719. It also continues to inspire anthropological debate, especially when it comes to explanations for its importance and meaning. Although most anthropologists no longer argue that institutionalized cannibalism can be explained as a response to environmental conditions or protein deficiency, they are still divided when it comes to explaining the evolutions of both exo- and endocannibalism and documenting their historic and prehistoric occurrences.

In the 1990s endocannibalism was discovered to be the cause of kuru, a fatal disease found among the Fore people of New Guinea. Kuru is transmitted by the consumption of prions, and like other TSE diseases such as BSE (mad cow disease) and variant Creutzfeldt-Jakob Disease (vCJD), it has a very long incubation period—up to 25 years. Ritual consumption of the dead, including victims of kuru, was apparently common among the Fore through the 1950s. The cannibalistic mortuary ritual not only made kuru endemic, but led researchers to the discovery of a gene variant that protected its carriers from kuru. Although some scientists argued that the existence of this gene proved that prion diseases and cannibalism were important in human evolution, further genetic research did not support this hypothesis. More recent research on the "anti-kuru" gene variant indicated that it probably evolved rapidly during the last century. Scientists hope that more research on the genetics of the few remaining living cannibals and their descendants in New Guinea will provide a way to protect people and animals from deadly prion diseases. BSE and related animal diseases have already cost affected nations hundreds of millions of dollars, and hundreds of people have died from vCJD and kuru.

SEE ALSO *Foodborne Diseases; Humane Animal Farming; Mad Cow Disease and vCJD.*

BIBLIOGRAPHY

Books

Anderson, Warwick. *The Collectors of Lost Souls: Turning Kuru Scientists into Whitemen.* Baltimore, MD: Johns Hopkins University Press, 2008.

Avramescu, Catalin. *An Intellectual History of Cannibalism.* Princeton. NJ: Princeton University Press, 2009.

Peck, Pamela. *Tales from Cannibal Isle: The Private Journals of an Anthropologist in Fiji.* Bloomington, IN: Trafford On Demand, 2010.

Travis-Henikoff, Carole A. *Dinner with a Cannibal: The Complete History of Mankind's Oldest Taboo.* Santa Monica, CA: Santa Monica Press, 2008.

Werth, Nicolas. *Cannibal Island: Death in a Siberian Gulag.* Princeton, NJ: Princeton University, 2007.

Periodicals

Bergstresser, Sara M. "Cannibal Talk: The Man-Eating Myth and Human Sacrifice in the South Seas." *Ethos* 38, no. 1 (2010): 1–3.

Collinge, John, et al. "Kuru in the 21st Century—an Acquired Human Prion Disease with Very Long Incubation Periods." *Lancet* 367, no. 9528 (2006): 2068–2074.

Lindenbaum, Shirley. "Cannibalism, Kuru, and Anthropology." *Folia Neuropathologica* 47, no. 2 (2009): 138–144.

Milius, Susan. "Cannibal Power." *Science News* 169, no. 9 (2006): 131–132.

Reinhard, Karl J. "A Coprological View of Ancestral Pueblo Cannibalism." *American Scientist* 94, no. 3 (2006): 254–261.

Web Sites

Phillips, Melissa Lee. "No Cannibalism Signature in Human Gene." *The Scientist,* January 9, 2006. http://www.the-scientist.com/templates/trackable/display/news.jsp?type=news&o_url=news/display/22927&d=22927 (accessed October 14, 2010).

Salisbury, David. F. "Exploration: Brief History of Cannibal Controversies." *Vanderbilt University,* August 15, 2001. http://www.vanderbilt.edu/exploration/news/news_cannibalism_pt2.htm (accessed October 14. 2010).

Sandra L. Dunavan

Cartagena Protocol on Biosafety (2000)

■ Introduction

The Cartagena Protocol on Biosafety is a supplementary agreement to the Convention on Biological Diversity that regulates trade of living modified organisms (LMOs) among countries. An international agreement, it was adopted at a meeting of members of the Convention on Biological Diversity (CBD) on January 29, 2000, and entered into force on September 11, 2003. The Convention on Biological Diversity, an international treaty adopted in 1992, promotes the conservation and sustainable use of biological diversity and its components. The Cartagena Protocol addresses the impact that LMOs, a subtype of genetically modified organisms (GMOs), might have on biodiversity, particularly on conventional plants and animals used in agriculture.

The Cartagena Protocol utilizes the precautionary principle in its regulation of LMOs. The precautionary principle states that a new product, action, or process suspected of posing a risk to the public or environment should not be introduced in the absence of scientific consensus that the product, action, or process is safe. The burden of proof falls on the party wishing to introduce the new product, action, or process to prove that their actions are safe. The Cartagena Protocol enables countries to prohibit the importation of LMOs that the country argues to be a threat to its biodiversity. The Protocol also requires strict labeling of LMOs and establishes a center for sharing scientific and technical information about LMOs.

■ Historical Background and Scientific Foundations

A genetically modified organism (GMO), including an LMO, is created through genetic engineering. Genetic engineering is a process in which genetic material is altered or added to an organism's genome. Genetic engineering generally involves the use of recombinant DNA (rDNA) technology. Recombinant DNA is an artificial strand of DNA formed by combining two or more genetic sequences into a sequence that normally would not occur. The use of rDNA technology enables geneticists to modify an organism in such a way that it expresses desired traits that otherwise would not be expressed within that organism.

The genetic sequences used in rDNA technology may either be from the same species, from closely related species, or from different species. GMOs that use DNA from the same or closely related species are referred to as cisgenic organisms. GMOs created from the genetic material of two more differing species are referred to as transgenic organisms.

For centuries humans have influenced the traits of plants and animals used in agriculture through selective breeding. Farmers produced hybrid plants with greater yields and resistance to drought and pests by cross breeding related species. Cross breeding also produced livestock that supplied more milk, yielded more meat, and adapted more easily to harsh climates.

Following the discovery of the double helix structure of DNA in 1953, geneticists theorized about the ability to identify and splice genes from one organism to another. In 1973 American scientists Herbert Boyer (1936–) and Stanley Cohen (1935–) created the first recombinant DNA organism, a transgenic *Escherichia coli* bacterium. In 1992, Calgene, a U.S. agricultural biotechnology company, received approval for the Flavr Savr tomato, the world's first commercially produced, genetically engineered whole food crop. The Flavr Savr tomato featured increased rot resistance.

■ Impacts and Issues

The Conference of the Parties to the Convention on Biological Diversity adopted the Cartagena Protocol on Biosafety on January 29, 2000. The Cartagena Protocol

Activists in Mexico City, Mexico hold ears of corn in a protest against importing genetically modified corn and seeds. Under the Cartagena Protocol on Biosafety, countries may ban the importation of living modified organisms if product safety is in question. *AP Images.*

addresses the concerns that many parties to the CBD expressed about potential threats posed by LMOs. The Protocol primarily seeks to protect biological diversity from any potential risks posed by GMOs.

Many nations participating in the CBD expressed concerns about imported transgenic crops cross-pollinating with native species. Cross-pollination of native or hybrid species with transgenic species could reduce genetic diversity if the dominant genes within the transgenic crop are expressed in the resulting hybrid. Because wind and insects may spread pollen over great distances, a single farmer raising transgenic crops potentially could affect the conventional crops of farmers located far away.

The threat posed to local farmers by transgenic crops became greater with the invention of so-called "terminator" gene technology. Terminator genes are genes inserted into a transgenic crop that prevent the crop from producing seeds that may be planted the following year. Terminator technology ensures that farmers growing genetically modified crops will buy seeds from the seed producer each year, which is usually required

under that farmer's contract with the seed producer. If the terminator genes cross-pollinate with a neighboring farmer's conventional crops, the conventional farmer's crops could produce sterile seeds.

The Cartagena Protocol employs several mechanisms that give nations control over protecting conventional species from any potential threats posed by living modified organisms. The establishment of the Biosafety Clearing-House under the Protocol allows nations to exchange scientific and technical data on LMOs. Nations may use this data to make decisions regarding any threats to biodiversity or public health posed by a particular LMO.

The Protocol also requires exporters of LMOs to seek permission of the target nation before the first shipment of a new LMO is introduced in the importing nation. This advance informed agreement (AIA) enables nations to chose which genetically modified seeds, plants, fish, animals, or microorganisms might pose a threat within their country.

The Cartagena Protocol also mandates specific labeling of shipments of genetically modified commodities, such as corn or soybeans, intended for direct use as food, feed, or processing. Shipments composed in whole or part of LMO commodities must state that the shipment "may contain" LMOs and are "not intended for intentional introduction into the environment."

Because the Cartagena Protocol is concerned with biodiversity issues, the agreement does not address issues involving genetically modified foods or food safety. The import and export requirements of the Cartagena Protocol only apply to LMOs, not to food produced using LMOs. Any non-living food derived from genetically modified plants or animals, including milled grains and processed foods, are not subject to the Cartagena Protocol.

SEE ALSO *Biodiversity and Food Supply; Commission on Genetic Resources for Food and Agriculture; Consumer Food Safety Recommendations; Convention on Biological Diversity (1992); Ethical Issues in Agriculture; Genetically Modified Organisms (GMO); Political Food Boycotts; Truth in Labeling.*

BIBLIOGRAPHY

Books

Convention on Biological Diversity. *Handbook of the Convention on Biological Diversity: Including Its Cartagena Protocol on Biosafety.* Montreal: Secretariat of the Convention on Biological Diversity, 2005.

Thomson, Jennifer A. *Seeds for the Future: The Impact of Genetically Modified Crops on the Environment.* Ithaca, NY: Comstock Publishing Associates, 2007.

Periodicals

Koester, Veit. "The Compliance Mechanism of the Cartagena Protocol on Biosafety: Development, Adoption, Content and First Years of Life." *Review of European Community & International Environmental Law* 18, no.1 (2009): 77–90.

Web Sites

"The Cartagena Protocol on Biosafety." *Convention on Biological Diversity.* http://bch.cbd.int/protocol/ (accessed August 1, 2010).

Joseph P. Hyder

Celebrity Chef Phenomenon

■ Introduction

The celebrity chef phenomenon refers to the fame gained by certain chefs, either by unique talent, personality, or by media exposure. Fueled by the surge of interest in food and cooking, the phenomenon is apparent in mainstream media as well as food-oriented media companies such as cooking magazines and culinary television channels. While the rise of celebrity chefs follows closely with the creation of other media fame of the early twenty-first century, celebrity status for chefs puts them in a precarious position in which a change in public opinion could cause the sudden rise or sudden collapse of a restaurant.

■ Historical Background and Scientific Foundations

As cooking techniques have become more refined and the associated level of artistry and talent needed to become a chef has risen, more attention has been paid to the individuals who stand out as notable chefs. Talented chefs have become well known and respected for their abilities. Perhaps the earliest celebrity chef is Marie-Antoine Carême (1784–1833), who worked in France in the early sixteenth century. Carême was well known for his *pièces montées*, large elaborate centerpieces that he would make for banquets and dinners. Another celebrity chef from around the same time is Alexis Soyer (1810–1858), who in addition to being a famous chef, invented a tabletop stove called "Soyer's Magic Stove" that he began to market in 1849. However, before mass communication outlets such as newspapers with widespread circulation and television existed, most chefs were known only to their local customers. This started to change in 1900, when the Michelin brothers (of the Michelin tire company) started publishing a guidebook known as the *Michelin Guide*. The guide listed hotels, gas stations, and restaurants to assist motorists touring France. Eventually the Michelin guide added stars to identify the best restaurants. Because many tourists had no local knowledge and trusted completely in the guide's ranking, a Michelin star quickly became an important and sought-after sign of quality that could greatly increase a restaurant's number of guests. At first the guide simply placed a star next to certain restaurants; it later introduced a zero-to-three star ranking system.

The Michelin guide is still published and remains influential, with guides available for many countries, including Spain, Germany, Italy, and Great Britain, as well as several city guides for major metropolitan areas in the United States such as New York and Los Angeles. Among chefs, one means to celebrity status is achieved with the gaining of a Michelin star. The purpose of the Michelin guide was to single out the chefs and restaurants that were the best, but it had another unintentional effect: By naming the best restaurants, the Michelin guide also promoted the concept that exceptional restaurants and chefs should be publicized. With the development of mass media outlets such as radio and newspapers, along with the increase in advertising during this time period, unique restaurants and chefs eventually became famous names.

A more recent phenomenon is the celebrity chef TV personality. Many consider Julia Child (1912–2004) and James Beard (1903–1985) to be the first chefs to become famous in the United States due to their early appearances on television, where they explained and demonstrated classic French and continental cuisine techniques to American television viewers. Although some TV chefs have extensive restaurant experience and others do not, television chefs often become famous for their on-screen personas. As chefs appear more often on television and the Internet, the name of a famous chef can be interpreted as a symbol of quality, as the familiarity of a name that a diner recognizes from a TV show or website could attract guests to a restaurant. The result is a culture in which fame and critical acclaim in the media become important coins in the public opinion, and the eventual success of a restaurant or celebrity chef-endorsed products may depend on the popularity of a chef's television persona.

■ Impacts and Issues

In the modern culinary world, celebrity status for chefs often takes on an entirely new and non-traditional role for a chef. Today's celebrity chefs are expected to be multi-talented businesspeople in addition to simply being accomplished chefs. Celebrity chefs must write cookbooks, appear on cooking programs on television, give interviews, or have their image marketed for lines of cooking products such as cookware, knives, or name-brand spice mixes. Some current celebrity chefs, such as Mario Batali (1960–), Cat Cora (1967–), Paula Deen (1947–), Sara Moulton (1952–), Jamie Oliver (1975–), Gordon Ramsay (1966–), and Michael Symon (1969–), after proving their talents in the kitchen, transfer to careers as hosts of cooking television shows. New York chef Anthony Bourdain (1956–) became as well known for his travel writing and *No Reservations* television program as for his culinary talents. The branching out of a celebrity chef into other fields can be an extremely lucrative venture, as the chef's endorsement of a product can bring with it trust and name recognition, thus greatly adding to the product's popularity.

Some television celebrity chefs, despite being popular, have received much criticism. The primary job of a television personality is to provide entertainment and generate advertising revenue through high ratings, and there are times when a TV chef will simplify

Julia Child (1912–2004) poses with Emeril Lagasse (1959–) on the set of Lagasse's show in New York in 2000. Child, the original TV chef, is featured in "Julia Child's Kitchen Wisdom," a PBS two-hour retrospective. Lagasse and fellow chefs Jacques Pepin (1935–), Alice Waters (1944–), and Martha Stewart (1941–) are among the Julia Child fans in the special, praising her for blazing the food-television trail they have all traveled. A replica of Child's kitchen is in the Smithsonian Museum in Washington, DC. *AP Images.*

Celebrity chefs Gordon Ramsay (1966–) and Anthony Bourdain (1956–) talk in the new kitchen of "The London," Ramsey's Manhattan restaurant. Ramsay is a working chef and star of several restaurant and chef themed reality shows in the United States and United Kingdom. Bourdain, once a chef at "Les Halles" in New York, is an author, food writer, and host of an international travel-food program. © *Neville Elder / Corbis.*

a recipe or modify a technique in order to fit the model of their program. Though it may serve the purpose of entertainment, culinary critics argue that anyone watching the show searching for education could come away misinformed.

Another critique of TV celebrity chefs arises when restaurants are opened under a famous chef's name and guests choose the restaurant based on name recognition independent of the actual quality of the food. Chefs who are celebrities but do not appear on television often have become famous because they have a unique or innovative cooking style and recipes. There are many fine chefs throughout the world who prepare well known dishes with skill, but the review system in most media is geared to notice the new and innovative chefs rather than the talented traditionalists. Those who prefer tried and true cuisine very rarely reach celebrity status. Whereas often the new and innovative chefs are considered more exciting, there exists a question of whether or not they are better or more praiseworthy than those who strive for perfection in classic cuisine.

The celebrity chef phenomenon has impacted the responsibilities of a successful chef. Now in addition to managing the menu, business, and operation of his or her restaurant, a successful chef must also be aware of public relations and the marketing of his or her own name.

SEE ALSO *Alice Waters: California and New American Cuisine; Culinary Education; Food and the Internet; Food Critics and Ratings; Food Fads; Gastronomy; Michael Pollan: Linking Food and Environmental Journalism; Movies, Documentaries, and Food; Television and Food.*

BIBLIOGRAPHY

Books

Cowen, Ruth. *Relish: The Extraordinary Life of Alexis Soyer, Victorian Celebrity Chef.* London: Phoenix, 2007.

Periodicals

"Food: Celebrity-Chef Endorsements: Are Brand Ambassadors Losing Their Cachet?" *Marketing* (May 19, 2010): 16.

"Gordon Ramsay Shares a Few Choice Words on Becoming a Celebrity Chef." *People Weekly* (July 24, 2006): 67.

Web Sites

Abend, Lisa. "The Cult of the Celebrity Chef Goes Global." *Time,* June 21, 2010. http://www.time.com/time/magazine/article/0,9171,1995844,00.html (accessed October 6, 2010).

Shapiro, Ari. "Americans' Insatiable Hunger for Celebrity Chefs." *NPR: National Public Radio,* March 5, 2005. http://www.npr.org/templates/story/story.php?storyId=4522975 (accessed October 6, 2010).

Sherman, Lauren. "Up-And-Coming Celebrity Chefs." *Forbes.com,* April 1, 2008. http://www.forbes.com/2008/04/01/chef-celebrity-food-forbeslife-cx_ls_0401food.html (accessed October 6, 2010).

David Brennan Tilove

Center for Food Safety and Applied Nutrition

■ Introduction

Part of the Food and Drug Administration (FDA), the Center for Food Safety and Applied Nutrition (CFSAN) oversees food, dietary supplements, and cosmetics regulations for the FDA. Charged with a wide range of responsibilities for regulating food safety and cosmetics quality, CFSAN is concerned with all aspects of the nation's food supply except meat and poultry, which are managed by the U.S. Department of Agriculture (USDA). As noted on the FDA's CFSAN website, a partial list of foods and substances for which CFSAN handles quality assurance includes biological pathogens, naturally-occurring toxins, dietary supplements, pesticides, heavy metals, allergens, nutrient issues, and product tampering.

When the federal government issues a recall for food or cosmetics it is CFSAN that works behind the scenes to verify problems, troubleshoot causes, and create remedy plans, public education campaigns, and ongoing safety plans to prevent future food supply contamination. The Center for Food Safety and Nutrition regulates more than $536 billion worth of food, cosmetics, and dietary supplements each year.

■ Historical Background and Scientific Foundations

The Federal Food and Drugs Act of 1906, also known as the Pure Food and Drug Act, created the agency that was later named the Food and Drug Administration (FDA), and was sparked in part by Upton Sinclair's novel *The Jungle*, a fictionalized account of meatpacking plant conditions in Chicago that highlighted extreme food safety issues as well as worker injuries and deaths resulting from lack of regulation. Some form of food and chemical regulation had been in place by federal authorities since the 1840s, because the Department of Agriculture was involved with light regulation of chemicals used

in farming. From 1879 to 1906 more than 200 bills were proposed in both houses of Congress to establish varying degrees of pure food and drug regulations; the 1906 Pure Food and Drug Act passed the Senate by a vote of 63 to 4 and the House by a vote of 241 to 17. The creation of what became the FDA was the culmination of decades of work to establish some degree of quality product assurance with government regulations developed to guide private industry.

The gradual evolution of food, chemical, and drug safety regulation on the part of the federal government increased through the 1930s. The 1938 Federal Food, Drug and Cosmetics Act replaced the original 1906 Food and Drug Act with a series of sweeping reforms that gave the federal government the most comprehensive oversight over the nation's food supply to that date. The 1938 budget for the FDA was $1,750,000; by 1945 the budget increased by more than 80 percent to $3,278,000. The rapid rise came about in part as a response to wartime demands for safety and reliability in the nation's limited food supply, but also with industry support following the 1943 Supreme Court decision in *US. v. Dotterweich*, which held that corporations and their officers were legally responsible for selling contaminated or tainted products, even when ignorant of safety violations. Initially the FDA used a "top down" approach to regulations, but by the late 1960s and 1970s began to assume a consumer-education approach, working to make consumers informed customers and soliciting input from the public to manage food, drug, and cosmetics issues.

The Center for Food Safety and Applied Nutrition, as one of the six subdivisions within the FDA, gained more public attention as food and drug recalls became better publicized through mass media. In 1963 the Codex Alimentarius Commission, a United Nations commission, was formed in conjunction with various UN member countries' food regulatory bodies to promote food, drug, and chemical safety across borders and to

WORDS TO KNOW

CODEX ALIMENTARIUS COMMISSION: Formed as a joint effort between the Food and Agriculture Organization of the United Nations and the World Health Organization in 1963, the Codex Alimentarius Commission works to supervise international cooperation for safe food practices across borders.

PURE FOOD AND DRUG ACT OF 1906: This Act created the agency that is now known as the Food and Drug Administration; CFSAN operates under the authority of the FDA.

RECALL: In a recall, CFSAN asks the public to return products from a specific batch produced by a manufacturer, for reasons such as contamination or food-borne illness. Most CFSAN-originated recalls are voluntary recalls, in which the manufacturer works proactively with CFSAN to remove a product from shelves and to educate consumers to return or destroy defective products.

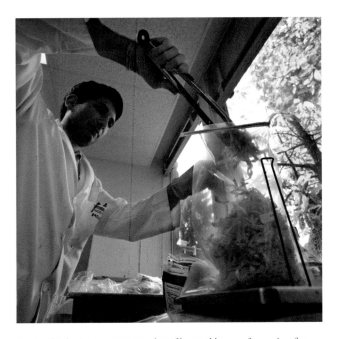

A microbiologist prepares samples of bagged lettuce for testing for salmonella and several versions of *E. coli* in May 2010. After investigators saw illness tied to a bacteria strain that federal inspectors and food manufacturers did not normally test for in the U.S. food supply, the Centers for Disease Control called for additional testing. The Center for Food Safety and Applied Nutrition is a part of the Food and Drug Administration that is responsible for ensuring that "the nation's food supply is safe, sanitary, wholesome, and honestly labeled," including testing for and research on foodborne pathogens. *AP Images.*

develop internationally recognized standards. CF-SAN works with Codex Alimentarius and other international food safety organizations.

CFSAN and the FDA operate under the authority of various laws giving the agency regulatory authority, and CFSAN uses a wide range of tools to manage and enforce regulations, including inspecting establishments, collecting samples for analysis, monitoring imports, tracking adverse effects and consumer complaints, conducting market research with consumers, laboratory testing, and education and outreach.

■ Impacts and Issues

CFSAN provides the research and the inspections that drive many food, supplement, and cosmetics recalls. The 1994 Dietary Supplement Health and Education Act (DSHEA) altered the way that the FDA and CFSAN handled dietary supplements, no longer requiring that dietary supplements be treated as a food. Dietary supplement manufacturers do not need to prove that the supplement is safe, as is the case with prescription and over-the-counter drugs. Infant formula falls under CFSAN's purview because it is considered a food, but it also has specific nutrient supplement requirements; a 2007 recall of Abbott Similac infant formula was initiated by CFSAN research and monitoring of the product.

CFSAN's Adverse Events Reporting System (CAERS), launched in 2003, enables the agency, private companies, non-profit groups, and public sector agencies and employees to report contaminants and food-related pathogens to CFSAN for tracking. This highly-efficient computerized system works to catch problems with food, dietary supplements, and cosmetics as early as possible to prevent illness and injury.

CFSAN was instrumental in two recent high-profile food recall cases in the United States: peanut butter and eggs. In 2007 and in 2009 two separate salmonella contamination incidents involving peanut butter—Peter Pan brand and Peanut Corp. brand, respectively—prompted consumer education campaigns from CFSAN in conjunction with widespread recalls. A 2010 recall that fell under CFSAN's regulation was prompted by salmonella contamination that sickened hundreds of consumers in the United States. The case involved more than 500 million eggs produced by two Iowa manufacturers and sold under numerous brand names. These highly publicized cases triggered significant public outcry regarding food safety standards and manufacturing and farming practices. CFSAN's operating budget for fiscal year 2009 was $182 million, out of a total $2.7 billion FDA budget for that same year.

SEE ALSO *Food, Drug, and Cosmetic Act of 1938; Food Inspection and Standards; Food Irradiation; Food Safety and Inspection Service; Foodborne Diseases; Import Restrictions; Meat Inspection Act of 1906; Pure Food and Drug Act of 1906; U.S. Food and Drug Administration (FDA).*

BIBLIOGRAPHY

Books

Center for Food Safety and Applied Nutrition. *100 Years: Working to Keep Food and Cosmetics Safe and Promote Good Nutrition*. Washington, DC: Food and Drug Administration, Center for Food Safety and Applied Nutrition, Department of Health and Human Services, 2006.

Pampel, Fred C. *Threats to Food Safety*. New York: Facts On File, 2006.

Periodicals

Miglierini, Giuliana. "Regulatory Focus—Center for Food Safety and Applied Nutrition (CSFAN)." *Agrofoodindustry Hi-Tech* 16, no. 1 (2005): 6.

Web Sites

"About the Center for Food Safety and Applied Nutrition." *U.S. Food and Drug Administration (FDA)*. http://www.fda.gov/AboutFDA/CentersOffices/CFSAN/default.htm (accessed August 30, 2010).

Melanie Barton Zoltan

Changing Nutritional Needs Throughout Life

■ Introduction

The human body requires regular intake of six nutrient groups. The macronutrients, required in substantial quantities, are carbohydrate, protein, and fat. The micronutrients, as vitamins and minerals are known, are needed in only small quantities. In addition, the body is about 65 percent water by weight; an adequate fluid intake, of about two liters per day, is necessary to keep it functioning correctly. These nutrients have a range of functions, including fueling the body, growth and repair, and driving metabolism by building thousands of different enzyme molecules that the cells need for biochemical reactions. The amount of each nutrient group required by an individual depends upon his or her gender, age, and activity level. Governments make detailed recommendations on how to get an adequate intake of nutrients through a balanced diet. Some groups, such as pregnant women, teenagers, and the elderly, have specific requirements for certain nutrients. For instance, people in nursing homes may rarely venture outside and may develop vitamin D deficiency, which can increase the risk of falls and injuries. Many people eat either too much food, which increases the risk of obesity, or an unbalanced diet, which may lead to deficiency disease such as anemia.

■ Historical Background and Scientific Foundations

Dietary guidelines for Americans have been issued by the United States Department of Agriculture (USDA) and Health and Human Services (HHS) every five years since 1980. They have evolved as the state of scientific knowledge on nutrition has advanced. Research entities such as the Centers for Disease Control and Prevention (CDC) conduct studies, e.g. the National Health and Nutrition Examination Survey, to provide ongoing monitoring of how the population measures up

regarding these dietary recommendations. According to the guidelines, a balanced diet includes a regular intake of foods that provide the major nutrient groups and the daily calorie allowance to meet the body's energy needs. Daily calorie intake varies with the size of the body and the level of physical activity. A person with a physically demanding job such as an athlete or soldier in combat will require far more calories than a person in a sedentary job. Infants need between 650 and 850 calories (kcal) per day, whereas teenagers require between 1,300 and 2,000. The adult daily intake should be between 2,200 and 2,900 calories, with women's requirements being less than those of men.

Protein is necessary for growth and repair of body tissues. Humans need about 0.8 grams of protein per kilogram of body weight. Teenagers require proportionally more protein than adults, because they are still growing. Protein should be eaten in the form of lean meat, poultry, beans, eggs, or fish. Fat is important for dissolving fat-soluble vitamins, for building cell membranes, for insulation against cold temperatures, and to synthesize some hormones. Butter and oils provide fat in the diet. Carbohydrates supply the body's immediate energy needs for cells, tissues, and organs. There are two types of carbohydrates: complex and simple. Complex carbohydrates are found in whole grains, starchy vegetables, and legumes. Simple carbohydrates come from fruits, milk products, and refined sugars. Some simple carbohydrate sources offer nutritional benefits, though products made with refined sugars have little nutritional value and should be limited. Fruits and vegetables provide essential minerals, and low-fat dairy products are a good source of calcium for strong bones and teeth. Fruits, vegetables, and whole grains also provide fiber, which helps with weight control and gastrointestinal health.

As humans grow and age, the body's nutritional needs, across many of the different nutrients, change. During infancy and childhood, requirements for calories and nutrients are higher because of rapid growth. Water

A staff member at a nursing home serves an elderly woman a lunch that is formulated to meet the dietary requirements of the elderly. *AP Images.*

■ Impacts and Issues

Many Americans consume more calories than they need without meeting recommended intakes for a number of nutrients. In 2009 more than 25 percent of the population was obese in the majority of states. Obesity, defined as body mass index of 30 or more, is associated with increased risk of heart disease, some cancers, and diabetes. Most age groups are at risk of obesity through excessive calorie consumption. The exception is the elderly, who often do not eat or absorb enough food because of lack of appetite, difficulty in getting to shopping areas, difficulty with cooking food and eating, or illness.

Dietary surveys have also shown that some groups are not getting enough of specific nutrients. Many adults, children, and adolescents may be short on fiber, calcium, potassium, and vitamins A, C, and E. This could be remedied easily by eating five or more portions of fruits and vegetables daily, but a survey by the U.S. Centers for Disease Control and Prevention (CDC) reports that only around a third of the population actually does so.

Older people may be at risk of falls and fractures if they lack vitamin D. A poor diet, coupled with lack of sun exposure may lead to lower than optimal levels of this vitamin. The importance of vitamin D and calcium in the diet of the elderly was underlined in a recent review study. This found that supplementation of both vitamin D at 700–800 IU per day and calcium at 500–1,200 mg/day decreased the risk of falls, fractures, and bone loss among elderly people in the 65–85 age group. Fractures in an older person often lead to loss of independence and even premature death, so vitamin D and calcium supplementation are simple, often-recommended steps to take to protect health and quality of life in later years.

requirements are also higher, and children are therefore at higher risk of dehydration than are adults. Apart from a higher intake of protein and calories to meet growth needs, nutrients for adolescents are similar to those for adults. It is in the older age group that nutritional needs begin to change again. As older people tend to be less active, muscle mass declines, and fewer calories are required. If calorie intake is not adjusted accordingly, weight gain may occur. Protein needs stay the same, but issues like difficulty in chewing meat could reduce intake. Iron needs decline for older women, because after the menopause they no longer lose iron during menstruation. The need for vitamin D actually increases in later life in order to maintain normal levels of calcium and phosphorus for bone health.

In a balanced diet, whatever one's age or sex, foods should be nutrient, rather than energy, dense. That is why it is inadvisable to eat too many fatty or fried foods, because they provide more than twice as many calories as the same weight of carbohydrates, and exceeding recommended calorie intake without increasing activity levels will lead to weight gain. The guidelines also advise against excessive consumption of added sugars, which provide calories but no other nutrients, and excessive salt and saturated fats, which may harm health.

Women of childbearing age tend to run short of iron and need to eat either meats, iron-rich plant foods, or iron-fortified foods with an enhancer of iron absorption, such as vitamin C-rich foods. Furthermore, women who are planning a pregnancy or who are pregnant already need to consume adequate folic acid daily; some may benefit from fortified foods or supplements, in addition to food forms of folate from a varied diet. Very few people are short of food in developed countries but they may not always make the choices that best meet their individual nutritional needs. However, information is increasingly available on food labels, which can help consumers assess the calorie content and overall nutritional value of the food they buy and eat.

SEE ALSO *Breastfeeding; Calories; Dietary Changes in Rapidly Developing Countries; Dietary Guidelines for Americans; Dietary Reference Intakes; Dietary Supplement Health and Education Act of 1994 (DSHEA); Edible Schoolyard Movement; Family Meal Benefits; Food and Body Image; Improving Nutrition for America's Children Act of 2010; Nutrient Fortification of Foods; Nutrition; Nutrition and U.S. Government Food Assistance; Protein and Carbohydrate Metabolism; School Lunch Reform; Undernutrition; USDA Food Pyramid; Vitamins and Minerals; Women's Role in Global Food Preparation.*

BIBLIOGRAPHY

Books

Bernstein, Melissa, and Ann S. Luggen. *Nutrition for the Older Adult.* Sudbury, MA: Jones and Bartlett, 2010.

Brancato, Robin F. *Food Choices: The Ultimate Teen Guide.* Lanham, MD: Scarecrow, 2010.

Sharlin, Judith, and Sari Edelstein. *Essentials of Life Cycle Nutrition.* Sudbury, MA: Jones and Bartlett, 2011.

Sorte, Joanne, Inge Daeschel, and Carolina Amador. *Nutrition, Health, and Safety for Young Children: Promoting Wellness.* Boston: Pearson, 2011.

Walker, Marsha. *Breastfeeding Management for the Clinician: Using the Evidence,* 2nd ed. Sudbury, MA: Jones and Bartlett, 2011.

Walker, W. Allan, and Courtney Humphries. *The Harvard Medical School Guide to Healthy Eating during Pregnancy.* New York: McGraw-Hill, 2006.

Periodicals

Bales, Connie W. "What Is the 'Right Diet' for a Healthy Old Age?" *Journal of Nutrition for the Elderly* 29, no.1 (2010): 2–3.

Bowne, Mary. "A Comparative Study of Parental Behaviors and Children's Eating Habits." *ICAN: Infant, Child, & Adolescent Nutrition* 1, no.1 (2009): 11–14.

Collison, Kate S., et al. "Sugar-Sweetened Carbonated Beverage Consumption Correlates with BMI, Waist Circumference, and Poor Dietary Choices in School Children." *BMC Public Health* 10, no. 234 (2010): 34ff.

Schooler, Deborah. "Real Women Have Curves." *Journal of Adolescent Research* 23, no. 2 (2008): 132–153.

Snyder, Carolyn, and Tandalayo Kidd. "Quality of Life Factors Influencing Health Behaviors in Young Adult Families." *Journal of Nutrition Education and Behavior* 42, no. 4 (2010).

Web Sites

U.S. Department of Agriculture. "Life Stages." *Nutrition. gov.* http://riley.nal.usda.gov/nal_display/index. php?info_center=11&tax_level=1&tax_subject=395 (accessed August 30, 2010).

Susan Aldridge

Chocolate

■ Introduction

Chocolate comes from the beans of the Theobroma cacao tree. Cacao, or cocoa, beans are 50 percent fat, made of palmitic and stearic acids, both saturated fatty acids, and oleic acid, a monounsaturated fatty acid. The cocoa bean contains vitamins A, B1, B2, B3, B5 and E, and the minerals magnesium, manganese, copper, calcium, iron, zinc, and potassium. When mixed with sugar and other flavorings, chocolate becomes a tasty treat as well as big business: Worldwide sales for chocolate products topped $52.3 billion in 2005. In the United States in 2008, the average person spent $55 per year on chocolate, whereas the highest per-capita spending on chocolate products occurs in Switzerland, at $206 per person per year.

Medical and nutrition researchers have zeroed in on the health benefits of chocolate consumption, but for the most part people eat chocolate because it tastes good. Chocolate is made by mixing ground cacao beans with a sugar base and adding a variety of ingredients, such as nuts and nut butters, fruits, berries, cream fillings, and more. The quality of chocolate depends on its cacao content. Most commercial chocolate products from large corporations such as Nestlé, Hershey's, and Cadbury contain relatively low cacao amounts, higher milk fats, and higher sugar levels. Dark chocolate and bittersweet chocolates have gained popularity in the United States and Western Europe because reports in the late 1990s and early 2000s from medical researchers indicated that dark chocolate has antioxidant properties. In 2006 sales of dark chocolate in the United States increased by 40 percent, a dramatic change in consumer behavior sparked by media reports of medical research.

■ Historical Background and Scientific Foundations

Central America is the home to the Theobroma cacao tree, and the first recorded use of chocolate made from grinding cacao beans comes from Olmec culture, around 1500 BC. Archaeologists have found residue from the cacao bean on pottery in Honduras from 1400 BC, and theorize that the cacao beans were used to create a fermented chocolate drink. By the time the Mayans were at their peak, from AD 300 to 900, cacao beans were ground and made into a thick, unsweetened drink, sometimes flavored with spicy chili peppers. This mixture was reserved for consumption by the elite in society, and often used in religious ceremonies. By the fourteenth century, the Aztecs had adopted the use of this chocolate, called "xocoatl," much as the Mayans had, for use only by priests and royalty.

Europe learned about chocolate from the Aztecs. As Hernán Cortés (1485–1547) and his band of conquistadors defeated the Aztec emperor Montezuma II (c.1466–1520) in Mexico in 1520, they brought not only "gold, God, and glory" back to Europe, but also chocolate. Prince Philip of Spain (1527–1598) drank Aztec chocolate in 1544 at court, and soon Spain developed cacao tree colonies in the Philippines. The European elite rejected the bitter, spicy version of chocolate favored by the Aztecs, removing the chili and adding honey or sugar to the ground cacao beans. By the 1600s chocolate was a fashionable luxury for the wealthy. Chocolate was consumed for its medicinal properties, and some considered it an aphrodisiac as well.

The Theobroma cacao tree can grow only within 10 to 20 degrees latitude of the Equator, so cacao bean cultivation is limited by climate. In the 1500s Spain developed cacao plantations in the Philippines, while the French formed Caribbean cacao plantations. The tree was brought to Europe, and cacao colonies were formed in Africa as well. Most cacao bean production in the twenty-first century takes place in Africa, southeast Asia, and central and northern South America. There are three main types of cacao beans: Forastero, Criollo, and Trinitario. More than 90 percent of all cacao beans are Forastero, but the Criollo cacao bean is a delicacy, produced mainly on small farms in Venezuela. A 2005 report from the Food and Agriculture Organization of

Workers in Pedregal, Venezuela, break open the cacao pods to retrieve the cocoa beans. The cocoa beans are fermented, roasted, milled and transformed into high-quality chocolate. *AP Images.*

the United Nations notes that the top cacao bean producer worldwide is Cote d'Ivoire, Africa, producing more than 1.3 million metric tons of beans per year. Ghana, Africa, is a distant second at 736,000 metric tons. Nearly 70 percent of all cacao beans are grown in west Africa.

■ Impacts and Issues

Media reports of the health benefits of chocolate, from information about theobromine as an aphrodisiac to its stimulation of the brain and neutralization of free radicals in the body, have all helped boost the sale of raw cocoa and cacao nibs. Raw food diet proponents tout the benefits of raw cocoa over processed cocoa, claiming its high protein content (5 grams per ounce) and high fiber content (7 grams per ounce), along with the antioxidant properties and high iron counts, make raw cocoa a "superfood" for optimal health. Cacao nibs, which are chunks of broken cacao beans, became a food fad in the middle of the first decade of the 2000s. Sold as raw nibs to be consumed raw, or as chocolate-covered treats, these cacao nibs carry the purported benefits of raw cocoa powder and are touted as vegan, gluten free, dairy free, organic, and raw, with premium pricing in specialty stores and online.

Fair trade issues permeate the global trade and sale of chocolate, much as fair trade has been an issue in the coffee industry for decades, but the cacao bean industry also includes allegations from some advocacy groups that cacao beans from west Africa are harvested by workers who are treated as slaves. Major manufacturers and importers of cocoa worldwide signed the Harkin-Engel protocol of 2001, which outlined a series of steps to reduce, then eliminate, child labor and slave labor used for cacao farming and production. The use of slave and exploitative child labor in cocoa production has become so pervasive that some companies, such as Trader Joe's, Green and Black's, Equal Exchange, and

San Francisco Chocolate Factory have created publicity campaigns and labeling to declare their chocolate products "slave free." Slave-Free Chocolate is also the name of an advocacy group that works to reduce and/or eliminate slavery for labor in the cocoa industry. The International Labor Rights Forum noted that major cocoa manufacturers and producers failed to meet 2005 and 2008 benchmarks for slavery reduction set forth in the Harkin-Engel protocol.

A 2008 study by researchers in Italy published in the journal *Nutrition* concluded that eating one 20-gram square of dark chocolate every three days reduces C-reactive protein (CRP) in the body. CRP is a marker for inflammation, and the data collected from more than 4,800 study participants showed that eating this small amount of dark chocolate reduced heart attack risk by one-third for women and one-fourth for men in the study. The study also concluded that these health benefits are negated by the intake of extra calories and fat if individuals eat more than 20 grams of dark chocolate every three days.

Throughout 2009 and 2010, news outlets and marketing analyses reported that chocolate sales rose in spite of economic recessions in many countries; U.S. dark chocolate sales were up by 9 percent in 2009. Media reports zeroed in on consumers' turning to chocolate as an affordable and healthful small luxury.

SEE ALSO *Advertising Food; Aid and Subsidies to Promote Agriculture and Reduce Illicit Drug Production; Confectionery and Pastry; Fair Trade; Indigenous Peoples and Their Diets; Wage Slavery in Food Production.*

BIBLIOGRAPHY

Books

Aaron, Shara, and Monica Bearden. *Chocolate: A Healthy Passion.* Amherst, NY: Prometheus, 2008.

Beckett, Stephen T. *The Science of Chocolate.* Cambridge, UK: RSC Publishing, 2008.

Dreiss, Meredith L., and Sharon Greenhill. *Chocolate: Pathway to the Gods.* Tucson: University of Arizona Press, 2008.

Grivetti, Louis, and Howard-Yana Shapiro. *Chocolate: History, Culture, and Heritage.* Hoboken, NJ: Wiley, 2009.

Off, Carol. *Bitter Chocolate: The Dark Side of the World's Most Seductive Sweet.* New York: New Press, 2008.

Periodicals

Bone, Eugenia. "Sweet Temptations—What Goes into Our Passion for Chocolate?" *Forbes* 39 (2006): 162.

Chin, Gilbert. "Dark Chocolate." *Science* 329, no. 5989 (2010): 259.

"Chocolate Helps Your Brain." *Psychology Today* 40, no. 4 (2007): 54.

"Lose Weight with Chocolate?" *Health* 20, no. 1 (2006): 114.

"Power from Chocolate—the Mighty Bean." *The Economist* 390, no. 8624 (2009): 50.

Rose, Natalie, Sabrina Koperski, and Beatrice A. Golomb. "Mood Food: Chocolate and Depressive Symptoms in a Cross-Sectional Analysis." *Archives of Internal Medicine* 170, no. 8 (2010): 699–703.

Web Sites

Branson, Kyle. "Slave-Free Chocolate." *Stop Chocolate Slavery.* http://vision.ucsd.edu/~kbranson/stopchocolateslavery/main.html (accessed October 23, 2010).

"Organic Chocolate." *organic-nature-news.com.* http://www.organic-nature-news.com/organic-chocolate.html (accessed October 23, 2010).

Melanie Barton Zoltan

Cholera

Introduction

Cholera is an acute intestinal infection caused by the bacterium *Vibrio cholerae*. It can cause very rapid dehydration of the body, which can be fatal. Cholera is transmitted by contaminated food and water.

Cholera is endemic—that is, present all the time—in countries where there is inadequate access to clean water. Treatment of cholera is simple and relies on restoring the fluids lost by the body. However, even this simple treatment may not be available in very poor countries. The best approach to preventing cholera lies in better sanitation—improving public health through adequate sanitation and assuring clean water for drinking, food preparation, and washing. In poor and developing countries, this is a difficult challenge to meet, because it requires political stability and increased investment in the national infrastructure.

Historical Background and Scientific Foundations

Cholera is one of the great killers of all time. The characteristic symptoms of the disease were described by the Greek physician Hippocrates (c.460–c.357 BC), and the disease is also mentioned by early Indian and Chinese writers. Epidemic cholera was first described in 1563 by Garcia del Huerto, a Portuguese physician working in Goa, India. The natural "home" of cholera appears to be the Ganges plain and delta in northern India and Bangladesh. From here, it spread along trade routes, although for many centuries the disease was generally confined to India. Beginning in the nineteenth century, cholera began to spread around the world as trade expanded. Between 1817 and 1923, there were six pandemics. It was the second pandemic, beginning in 1824, that brought cholera to England (1831), North America (1832), and the Caribbean and Latin America (1833).

The seventh pandemic of cholera, caused by the *El Tor* serotype, began in 1961 and affected the Far East, although most of Europe was spared. During the 1980s, outbreaks of cholera were common in refugee camps and city slums in famine and war-stricken countries such as Ethiopia and Sudan. The disease returned to the Western Hemisphere in the early 1990s, beginning in Peru—where it had been absent for more than 100 years—and spreading outwards through Latin America. In 1992 a large epidemic in Bangladesh was attributed to the newly identified 0139 serotype.

The rapid onset and high mortality of cholera brought great fear to populations during the nineteenth century, as it affected many areas for the first time. Many people thought the cause of cholera—and other diseases—was "miasma" or "bad air." Therefore, the standard treatment was to burn huge bonfires to cleanse the air. However, some blamed cholera on low morals and drunkenness. The belief that "cleanliness is next to Godliness" at least led to the beginnings of an interest in public health in England and America. Social reformers began to campaign for piped water, drains, and proper sewage disposal. Although these changes took many years to bring about, they eventually made a significant contribution towards cutting the death toll from cholera and many other infectious diseases.

It was English physician John Snow (1813–1858) who suggested that contaminated water, rather than bad air, caused the transmission of cholera. He carried out a serious scientific investigation during the 1848 epidemic in London. His classic work on the subject is titled "On the Mode of Communication of Cholera." In August 1854 there was a fresh outbreak of cholera in and around Broad Street, near Snow's own home. He suggested removing the handle from the Broad Street pump, because this was the probable source of the outbreak. This was done and thereafter there were no more major cholera outbreaks in London.

Snow also accepted the germ theory of disease, put forward by Louis Pasteur (1822–1895) and Robert Koch (1843–1910). In 1882 Koch discovered the bacillus that causes tuberculosis—also a major killer—and the following year, working in Egypt, he identified *V. cholerae* as the cause of cholera.

Thanks to Snow, Koch, and other researchers, cholera is now a well understood disease in scientific and clinical terms. The causative agents have been discovered, an effective cure is known, and there are vaccines against the disease. Its continuing existence is not due to a lack of scientific understanding or effective treatment and prevention options but to the economic and political factors in many countries that affect their level of development.

V. cholerae belongs to the *Vibrio* genus of Gram-negative bacteria. The term Gram-negative refers to the way in which a bacterium absorbs visualizing stains under a microscope for identification purposes. *Vibrio* species exist as straight or curved rods in watery environments. These bacteria use a whiplike projection called a flagellum to propel themselves. (The flagellum is an extension to the bacterial cell body.) *Vibrio* species prefer marine environments and grow best in the presence of salt. They are one of the most common organisms in the surface waters of the world.

There are 139 serotypes of *V. cholerae*—they are basically all the same species, but are distinguished by the number and type of antigen (protein) molecules on their cell surfaces. Most cholera infections are caused by the *V. cholerae* 01 serotype, but others have been found in specific outbreaks or epidemics. For instance, the *El Tor* serotype was first isolated in the quarantine station of the same name in Sinai in 1906, and was linked to an outbreak among pilgrims returning from Mecca. It seems to survive for longer than the 01 serotype, which is killed by 15 minutes of heating. In 1992 the 0139 serotype was first identified in Madras and was responsible for outbreaks in Bangladesh and Thailand during the following year.

Scope and Distribution

Cholera affects many countries around the world. According to the latest data from WHO, there were 131,943 cases reported in 2005 (the latest published data as of September 2010), including 2,272 deaths, in 52 countries. This represents a 30 percent increase over 2004, although the number of countries reporting cholera was down from 56. The 2005 increase can be largely accounted for by a series of outbreaks in 14 countries in West Africa, including Senegal, Guinea-Bissau, Ghana, Guinea, and Mauritania. The latter, and Gambia, had previously been free from cholera for more than a decade, so this is a downturn for them. Indeed, Africa accounted for about 95 percent of all cholera cases, although the number of cases from Asia increased by 18 percent. The Indian subcontinent accounted for nearly half of all the Asian cases. There were 12 cases in the United States—four of them related to Hurricane Katrina—and ten in Europe. Globally, WHO admits that the toll from cholera is much higher, because surveillance

---

WORDS TO KNOW

ELECTROLYTES: Compounds that ionize in a solution; electrolytes dissolved in the blood play an important role in maintaining the proper functioning of the body.

FECAL-ORAL ROUTE: The transmission of minute particles of fecal materia from one organism (human or animal) to the mouth of another organism.

---

and reporting systems are far from perfect. Some countries only report laboratory-confirmed cases, and there is often confusion over what is and is not cholera.

Cholera often is a seasonal disease, occurring each year during the rainy season. For example, in Bangladesh, where it is endemic, cholera comes after the monsoons. This is related to an increase in the growth of algae during the rainy season in the watery environment inhabited by *V. cholerae*. The algae and the bacteria form a symbiotic (mutually beneficial) relationship, which enables the bacteria to survive indefinitely in contaminated water. Cholera is also associated with floods and cyclones and often spreads in times of war, especially in refugee camps, because upheaval and overcrowding cause the breakdown of basic facilities, such as water supply. For example, about 45,000 people died of cholera in refugee camps during the war in Rwanda in 1994.

Symptoms

Most people infected with *V. cholerae* do not actually become ill, although the bacterium is present in their feces for 7–14 days, which means they may contaminate food or water.

However, *V. cholerae* 01 and a few other serotypes produce a potent toxin that affects the mucosal lining of the small intestine, causing severe diarrhea, with very rapid onset. The incubation period of *V. cholerae* ranges from just a few hours to five days. In most cases, the illness is difficult to distinguish from other diarrheal diseases. But in severe cholera, the diarrhea is copious—the patient may lose more than a quart (liter) of fluid every hour. Microscopic examination of stool samples reveals the presence of *V. cholerae* as "shooting stars"—as the bacteria use their flagella to dart through the sample. Pathologists may call a sample "rice-water stool" due to its appearance—clear, but flecked with mucus and cells. The diarrhea may be accompanied by vomiting, but pain and fever are minimal and certainly not comparable to the severity of the diarrhea.

Severe cholera can lead to dehydration, through a combination of diarrhea and vomiting. The patient may enter a state of shock due to massive fluid loss and electrolyte imbalance, suffering seizures, kidney failure, heart rhythm abnormalities, and unconsciousness. Death from

A young girl carries buckets along a garbage-filled canal to fetch water in an impoverished area of Antananarivo, Madagascar, in 2000. Poor hygiene and squalid living conditions make the area a breeding ground for cholera. *AP Images.*

dehydration and shock may occur within hours. As a result, cholera is always considered a medical emergency and, indeed, it is one of the most rapidly fatal illnesses ever known. Left untreated, severe cholera has a death rate of 30 to 50 percent, but when treated promptly, mortality falls to less than one percent of cases.

Transmission

Transmission of *V. cholerae* is through the fecal-oral route, which, in practical terms, means the consumption of, or contact with, contaminated food and water. *V. cholerae* is hard to avoid in places where sanitation is poor and access to clean water for drinking or washing is limited or non-existent. Imported foodstuffs are only a rare cause of cholera, and the risk can be kept at bay through high standards of food handling hygiene.

Cholera is rare in areas where basic hygiene standards can be assured. However, there has been a source of cholera present in the Gulf of Mexico since at least 1973. This has led to sporadic cholera cases in Texas, Louisiana, Georgia, and Florida, linked to eating crabs,

shrimp, or oysters that were not properly cooked or stored.

Prevention and Treatment

Clean water and effective sanitation are the most effective preventive measures against cholera. Chlorination of water, boiling of water in households, and the construction and maintenance of latrines are basic measures that can help achieve these goals. High standards of personal hygiene and food preparation can also reduce the spread of the disease. Accurate and ongoing surveillance of outbreaks and epidemics can help reduce the toll from cholera.

As of 2010, there is an oral vaccine for cholera available outside the United States. The Centers for Disease Control and Prevention (CDC) does not, however, recommend vaccination for travelers.

The most important treatment for cholera is fluid and electrolyte (salt) replacement to treat the losses caused by diarrhea and vomiting. Oral rehydration fluid, containing glucose and salt dissolved in water, is the most convenient form of this treatment. Eighty percent of all cases of cholera can be treated in this way, and the treatment needs to be continued until the diarrhea stops. Intravenous administration of rehydration fluid sometimes may be necessary. In countries where oral rehydration fluid is not available, water in which rice has been boiled provides a good alternative. When antibiotic treatment is needed, tetracycline is the drug of choice and has been shown to shorten the duration of the disease. Ampicillin is a suitable alternative for children and pregnant women.

■ Impacts and Issues

As of 2010, the World Health Organization (WHO) states that most developing countries face the threat of a cholera outbreak or epidemic. According to WHO and its Global Task Force on Cholera Control, improvements in sanitation and access to clean water represent the only sustainable approach to cholera prevention and control. These factors are more important than drugs to treat the disease or vaccines to protect against it. In areas of the world afflicted by poverty or war (or both), the high standards of public health that are taken for granted in the West are too often hard to achieve and sustain.

The response to cholera is too often reactive—that is, dealing with an outbreak or epidemic once it has occurred. Fighting the threat of cholera requires a multidisciplinary approach involving a country's agriculture, water, health, and education sectors. Investment in infrastructure, including construction of water and sewage treatment plants, is key to improving public health. Long-term planning is needed so that attention is given not only to responding to cholera when it happens—although that is important—but also to prevention and surveillance. There is a need for far more openness and transparency on surveillance and reporting. Some countries fear that reporting a cholera outbreak will lead to travel and trade restrictions that will hurt their economies.

Because the above goals may be difficult to achieve in many countries, especially in urban slums and in crisis situations, the use of oral cholera vaccines as a complementary management tool is becoming more popular. For example, in 2002–2003 a mass vaccination campaign—the first in an endemic setting—was carried out in Beira, Mozambique, where there are yearly outbreaks. Vaccinated people were shown to have a high level of protection from cholera. Other mass vaccinations have been carried out in emergency settings—in Darfur in Sudan in 2004, for example. These campaigns are challenging, because they are costly and hard to implement, but WHO regards the experience gained as encouraging.

The Global Task Force on Cholera Control has been considering how to improve the use of vaccination as a control tool. It is looking for ways to identify the

IN CONTEXT: FOOD SAFETY: BOIL IT, COOK IT, PEEL IT, OR FORGET IT

The Division of Bacterial and Mycotic Diseases at the Centers for Disease Control and Prevention (CDC) states that "when simple precautions are observed, contracting the disease (cholera) is unlikely" and offers guidelines for travelers to lower their risk of cholera.

All travelers to areas where cholera has occurred should observe the following recommendations:

- Drink only water that you have boiled or treated with chlorine or iodine. Other safe beverages include tea and coffee made with boiled water and carbonated, bottled beverages with no ice.
- Eat only foods that have been thoroughly cooked and are still hot, or fruit that you have peeled yourself.
- Avoid undercooked or raw fish or shellfish, including ceviche [raw seafood marinated with citrus juice].
- Make sure all vegetables are cooked. Avoid salads.
- Avoid foods and beverages from street vendors.
- Do not bring perishable seafood back to the United States.

A simple rule of thumb is "Boil it, cook it, peel it, or forget it."

SOURCE: Centers for Disease Control and Prevention (CDC).

populations most at risk and protocols for proper use of vaccines in complex emergency settings.

SEE ALSO *Extreme Weather and Food Supply; Foodborne Diseases; Water; Water Scarcity.*

BIBLIOGRAPHY

Books

Hempel, Sandra. *The Strange Case of the Broad Street Pump: John Snow and the Mystery of Cholera.* Berkeley: University of California Press, 2006.

Web Sites

Centers for Disease Control and Prevention (CDC), Division of Foodborne, Bacterial and Mycotic Disease. http://www.cdc.gov/nczved/dfbmd/disease_listing/cholera_gi.html (accessed September 7, 2010).

"Cholera." *World Health Organization (WHO).* http://www.who.int/entity/mediacentre/factsheets/fs107/en/index.html (accessed September 7, 2010).

"Global Task Force on Cholera Control." *World Health Organization (WHO).* http://www.who.int/entity/cholera/en (accessed September 7, 2010).

Susan Aldridge

Climate Change and Agriculture

■ Introduction

Global climate change presents one of the greatest threats to agriculture and food security in the twenty-first century. For centuries humans have developed agricultural practices that maximize production by tailoring those practices to the local environment and climatic conditions. Global climate change, however, threatens to alter these environmental and climatic conditions through increased average temperatures in most regions, temperature extremes, changes in precipitation patterns, lengthened growing seasons, decreased availability of freshwater, desertification, extreme weather, and drought.

The impacts of global climate change could vary greatly across the globe. Mild to moderate global climate change could result in increased agricultural production in temperate areas and decreased agricultural production in equatorial regions. Severe climate change could reduce agricultural production in almost all regions. Humans will have to adapt agricultural practices to the changing climate within regions in order to maintain global food security. Many of the areas that are likely to suffer the greatest negative effects of global climate are in developing nations, which have little economic, political, or technical ability to implement climate change adaptation initiatives.

■ Historical Background and Scientific Foundations

The Earth's climate is not static. Data taken from core ice samples from polar regions reveal a dynamic climate that slowly changes over millennia, resulting in prolonged warmer and cooler periods. A variety of factors, including solar variation, volcanism, plate tectonics, orbital variations, and variability in ocean circulation, account for the Earth's changing climate. Since the beginning of the Industrial Revolution in the eighteenth century, however, human activities, including the burning of large quantities of fossil fuels and deforestation, have also contributed to changes in the Earth's climate.

Greenhouse gases (GHGs) absorb and emit radiation within the thermal infrared range. Heat leaving the surface of the Earth is absorbed by these GHGs and reemitted—including back towards the surface—instead of escaping into space. This so-called greenhouse effect increases the surface temperature. Without any GHGs in the atmosphere, the surface of the Earth would be about 59.4°F (33°C) cooler, which would make the Earth virtually uninhabitable by current flora and fauna.

Burning fossil fuels, including coal, natural gas, and oil, releases carbon dioxide (CO_2) and other GHGs into the atmosphere. Burning other biomass fuels, such as wood, also releases GHGs. The accumulation of GHGs in the atmosphere has exacerbated the atmospheric greenhouse effect, resulting in anthropogenic global climate change. Anthropogenic climate change refers to the effect that humans have had on climate over natural climate variations that would be expected in the absence of human activity. According to the Fourth Assessment Report (AR4) of the United Nations Intergovernmental Panel on Climate Change (IPCC), human activities over the last 200 years have resulted in higher atmospheric CO_2 concentrations than experienced at any time within the last 650,000 years. Furthermore, deforestation has hampered the Earth's ability to remove CO_2 from the atmosphere. Through a process called respiration, vegetation removes CO_2 from the air and produces oxygen. The excess carbon is stored in the plant's biomass.

The increase of atmospheric GHGs produced by human activities has had a profound effect on global surface temperatures. According to the IPCC, global surface temperatures increased by 1.33 ± 0.32 degrees Fahrenheit (0.74 ± 0.18 degrees Celsius) between 1906 and 2005. The IPCC projects that global surface temperatures will increase by an additional 2 to 11.5 degrees Fahrenheit (1.1 to 6.4 degrees Celsius) by 2100.

■ Impacts and Issues

According to the IPCC's AR4, the effects of global climate change on agriculture will vary considerably among regions. Generally, the IPCC asserts that global climate change will increase crop yields slightly in mid- to high-latitude regions of the globe, with local temperature increases between 1.8–5.4 degrees Fahrenheit (1–3 degrees Celsius). For low latitude regions, however, the IPCC anticipates crop productivity likely will decrease even with only moderate local temperature increases of 1.8–3.6 degrees Fahrenheit (1–2 degrees Celsius). Declining yields will be a particular concern in tropical and seasonally dry low latitude regions.

Changing precipitation patterns will have a significant impact on agricultural production in the twenty-first century, particularly in some of the world's most vulnerable and food insecure regions. Declining seasonal rainfall and more frequent droughts are expected to result in some regions. In addition to exposing 75 to

Red grapes are agitated to aid the fermenting process at Denbies Wine Estate in Dorking, southern England. In recent years, aided by milder springs and autumns, a few British wineries have revived a red winemaking tradition that died around 600 years ago. © *STR/Reuters/Corbis.*

200 million Africans to water stress by 2020, changing precipitation patterns may produce a 50 percent reduction in rain-fed crop production in some African nations by 2020. Furthermore, the IPCC expresses a high confidence that changes in precipitation will result in a 5–8 percent increase in unproductive, arid, and semi-arid land in Africa by 2080. Climate change will likely pose a significant threat to food security in Africa throughout the twenty-first century.

Other regions of the world may experience similar negative effects on agriculture caused by global climate change. In Latin America, the production of several important crops and livestock could decrease, leading to an overall increase in hunger in the region. Increased drought could decrease agricultural production in parts of Australia and New Zealand. Higher temperatures and increased drought, meanwhile, will likely threaten crop productivity in southern Europe. The more temperate regions of Eurasia, however, likely will experience an overall increase in crop yields, although changing precipitation patterns may decrease yields in a few areas. In North America, one of the world's leading agricultural exporting regions, the IPCC expects overall crop production to increase during the first decades of the twenty-first century. Some areas of North America will experience declines in production, however, particularly areas that grow crops at the warm end of the crops' productive range.

In order to maintain or optimize agricultural production in the twenty-first century, regions will be challenged to adapt to the effects of global climate change, including changes in temperature, vegetative cover, and precipitation patterns. Climate change adaptation refers to altering prevailing social, economic, political, and agricultural practices and thinking in order to minimize the negative effects of climate change or enhance benefits. Many of the negative impacts of global climate change on agricultural production will occur in developing nations that lack financial capacity to formulate and implement an adequate response. Global assistance for climate change adaptation projects in developing nations has been a focus of international negotiations on a comprehensive climate change treaty to replace the Kyoto Protocol, which was a part of the United Nations Framework Convention on Climate Change treaty that was adopted on December 11, 1997, in Kyoto, Japan, which has been highly controversial and divisive, mainly between developed nations, which have the highest emissions and tougher emissions standards, and developing nations, which state they need time to and funds to assist them in moving away from traditional energy sources and curbing emissions. As of October 2010, the Kyoto Protocol had been signed and ratified by 191 states and the EU; it was signed by the United States in 1998 but never ratified. Rounds of talks about a successor treaty were held in Copenhagen, Denmark in 2009, Cancun, Mexico in 2010, and were planned for South Africa in 2011.

Even nations that expect to experience an overall increase in agricultural production will need to employ climate change adaptation strategies to maximize production. Increased temperatures will likely decrease yields of crops grown at the warm end of their productive ranges. Areas that cultivate crops at the warm end of their ranges will require transition to crops that grow in warmer temperatures or can tolerate higher temperature extremes. Some countries could also place land into agricultural production in areas that currently are too cold to sustain agriculture.

SEE ALSO *Agricultural Deforestation; Agricultural Demand for Water; Biodiversity and Food Supply; Cooking, Carbon Emissions, and Climate Change; Desertification and Agriculture; Famine; Famine: Political Considerations; Hunger; Malnutrition; Population and Food; Rome Declaration on World Food Security (1996); Sustainable Agriculture; Undernutrition; Water; Water Scarcity.*

BIBLIOGRAPHY

Books

Bals, Christoph, Sven Harmeling, and Michael Windfuhr. *Climate Change, Food Security and the Right to Adequate Food.* Stuttgart, Germany: Diakonisches Werk der Evangelischen Kirche, 2008.

Brown, Lester R. *Outgrowing the Earth: The Food Security Challenge in an Age of Falling Water Tables and Rising Temperatures.* New York: W.W. Norton & Company, 2004.

Collin, Robin M., and Robert W. Collin. *Encyclopedia of Sustainability.* Santa Barbara, CA: Greenwood Press, 2010.

European Union Director General for Agriculture. *Climate Change: The Challenges for Agriculture.* Luxembourg: EUR-OP, 2008.

Periodicals

Rosenberg, Norman J. "Climate Change, Agriculture, Water Resources: What Do We Tell Those That Need to Know?" *Climatic Change* 100, no. 1 (2010): 113–117.

Trevors, Jack T. "Climate Change: Agriculture and Hunger." *Water, Air & Soil Pollution* 205, no. S1 (2010): 105.

Web Sites

"Climate Change and Food Security: A Framework Document." *Food and Agriculture Organization of the United Nations (FAO).* http://www.reliefweb.int/rw/lib.nsf/db900sid/PANA-7KADCQ/$file/fao_may2008.pdf?openelement (accessed October 27, 2010).

"Climate Change: Food Security." *Food and Agriculture Organization of the United Nations (FAO).* http://www.fao.org/climatechange/49357/en/ (accessed October 27, 2010).

Darwin, Roy. "Climate Change and Food Security." *U.S. Department of Agriculture Economic Research Service (USDA/ERS).* http://www.ers.usda.gov/publications/aib765/aib765-8.pdf (accessed October 27 2010).

Joseph P. Hyder

Codex Alimentarius

■ Introduction

Codex Alimentarius is a Latin phrase meaning "food code." In the broadest terms, the codex or food code, adopted by the Food and Agriculture Organization (FAO) of the United Nations (UN) and the World Health Organization (WHO), is designed to develop, refine, and implement a uniform set of worldwide standards, based on scientific principles, for all aspects of food safety.

A central purpose of the food code is to ensure that products produced in-country, as well as those imported from other nations, are safe, healthy, and appropriate for consumption by the general public. The food code is also designed to create standards relating to the specific means of safe transport of food in order to protect the public from foodborne risk factors, whether parasites, bacteria, dangerous additives, or chemical or genetic adulterations. In addition to setting standards for keeping food safe in transport and consumption, the codex sets guidelines for food growers and producers in order to protect their industries, as well as the economies of the individual food item producing nations.

The Codex Alimentarius Commission was created subsequent to the Eleventh Session of the Conference of the FAO of the UN in 1961 and the Sixteenth World Health Assembly in 1963. The purpose of the commission is to embody the mission of the Codex by developing and implementing standards for food production, transport, and distribution among member nations worldwide. The compiled standards are published in the Codex Alimentarius. Another important task of the commission is the creation of fair trade practices in the food industry, bolstered by the global implementation of co-ordinated, uniform standards. The FAO and WHO also established sets of statutes and rules of procedure for the commission in carrying out its mission. The statutes provide the legal framework for the commission; the rules of procedure set the standards and create the infrastructure within which the commission does its work.

■ Historical Background and Scientific Foundations

The concept of a food code as a means of protecting public health, ensuring safety of food preparation and transport, and as a means of regulating food-related trade predates written history and likely can be traced back to the earliest organized societies. Some of the earliest writings of the Assyrians and the Egyptians specified the procedures for accurate weight and measurement of food, as well as for the labeling of consumables. The ancient Greeks documented systems for food inspection in order to verify product safety.

During the past two centuries, food laws were formalized and adopted and mechanisms for oversight of quality control standards for maintenance of food safety were implemented. As technology burgeoned and the sciences rapidly evolved, food science came into being. At the same time, it became progressively more possible to move foods and food products internationally, necessitating the development of standards and practices for the regulation of the food industries in order to assure public health and safety as well as to regulate fair trade practices.

The model for the evolution of the Codex Alimentarius was provided by the Codex Alimentarius Austriacus, developed during the Austro-Hungarian Empire. It was created as a means of setting standards for specific foods as well as determining acceptable ingredients for different food products. It was used for guidance only, and did not have legal authority. At the beginning of the twentieth century, the International Dairy Federation created a set of international standards for milk and other dairy products. The FAO was codified in 1945 and was tasked with setting international food and nutrition standards. Three years later WHO was created, bearing broad-based responsibilities for health maintenance. In 1961 the FAO Conference established the Codex Alimentarius as an outgrowth of the European Codex developed in Austria during the 1950s, with the goal of expanding it to a global level. The Codex

WORDS TO KNOW

BIG PHARMA: This refers to the largest multinational pharmaceutical companies, often reported in the media as having the financial ability to exert considerable influence on governments and other decision-making bodies.

HARMONIZATION OF FOOD STANDARDS: Harmonization occurs when all member nations adopt the same standards to the same degree.

NONGOVERNMENTAL ORGANIZATION (NGO): This generally refers to organizations that are created and directed outside of any governmental affiliation. Often, NGOs are involved with human rights and health-related issues. They are typically dedicated to development and service.

Commission was created during the same year. In 1963 the World Health Assembly ratified the statutes of the Codex Alimentarius and approved the establishment of a joint FAO/WHO Food Standards Programme.

■ Impacts and Issues

The Codex Alimentarius Commission meets biannually (every two years) and alternates between the commission's main offices in Rome, Italy, and those of WHO in Geneva, Switzerland. The chair- and vice chairpersons are drawn from among the member nations. In 2010 there were 185 member nations. Attendance at commission meetings is drawn from developed and developing countries, with the latter steadily outnumbering the former. Although only national delegations to the commission can engage in decision-making, representatives of governmental and non-governmental organizations (NGOs) may attend as observers.

The legal means by which the commission operates is specified in the *Codex Alimentarius Procedural Manual.* It delineates the processes and procedures by which the Codex standards may be created. There are two types of standards: general and commodity. General standards are applicable to all aspects of food production, whereas commodity standards refer to specific foods or food groups. Creation or revision of a standard is a multi-stage and quite specific process. Because the process of creating a standard is both rigorous and complex, it typically takes more than a year to develop, codify, and adopt a single standard. Every standard is based upon the best available, most current, scientific research and knowledge. As new information is developed and adopted by acknowledged scientific subject matter experts, standards are proposed for change.

A goal of the Codex is harmonization, or universal adoption, of all Codex standards. Codex's General

Chinese law enforcement officers check edible oil at a supermarket after China's Health Ministry launched a crackdown on food safety in 2008 following a melamine-tainted milk scandal in which six infants died and another approximately 300,000 infants and children required medical treatment. Two milk suppliers were subsequently executed and 19 other people sentenced to lengthy prison sentences for their roles in a scheme to illegally add melamine (a chemical used in fertilizers and plastics production) to milk powder in order to artificially raise the protein levels in products derived from milk to increase profits. China enacted new food safety laws in 2009 intended to bring China into closer compliance with FAO/WHO *Codex Alimentarius* rules. Despite government efforts, melamine-tainted milk power resurfaced in 2010, but investigators initially attributed the tainted products to ingredients contaminated during the 2008 scandal. *AP Images.*

Principles stipulate that each member country has the option to accept standards along a continuum, ranging from full acceptance to acceptance with minor deviations to free distribution. The use of the continuum, specified in the General Principles of the Codex, varies depending on whether it relates to a general standard, a commodity standard, or involves food additives, veterinary drug residues, or allowable pesticide levels.

In making decisions about the extent to which Codex standards are embraced and adopted, each nation's political, financial, and socio-economic structure must be considered. In struggling developing nations, where infrastructure and financial systems are unstable or not fully in place, it is unlikely that full adoption of Codex would be possible or practical.

There is much information in the global electronic community suggesting that implementation of the Codex philosophy and values would be detrimental to world health. Some assert that the expert opinions offered to and by the Commission are not unbiased and may be influenced in their decision-making by multinational corporations and "big pharma." One such site claims that full implementation of the Codex will have a dramatic and negative impact on public health, by eliminating natural medicine products. Others have suggested that the goal of Codex is to limit population growth, cause mass starvation, and dramatically reduce the size of the world's population. Still others argue that implementation of the Codex will constitute the ultimate invasion of privacy by government and will completely eliminate personal choice in health and food-related decision-making.

Historically, the United States has participated in the Codex process on many important levels, although full acceptance of the standards has not been mandated. On June 10, 2010, President Barack Obama signed into law Executive Order 13544, "Establishing the National Prevention, Health Promotion, and Public Health Council." There has been considerable electronic debate regarding whether this mandates full acceptance of Codex, whether it aligns the United States more fully with the FAO/WHO Programme, or whether it is a further step toward implementation of national healthcare initiatives.

SEE ALSO *Biodiversity and Food Supply; Convention on Biological Diversity (1992); Dietary Changes in Rapidly Developing Countries; Food and Agriculture Organization (FAO); Food Inspection and Standards.*

BIBLIOGRAPHY

Books

Codex Alimentarius Commission. *Codex Alimentarius.* Rome: Food and Agriculture Organization of the United Nations, 2009.

Codex Alimentarius Commission. *Codex Alimentarius Commission: Strategic Plan 2008–2013.* Rome: Food and Agriculture Organization of the United Nations, World Health Organization, 2007.

Codex Alimentarius Commission. *Understanding the Codex Alimentarius.* Rome: World Health Organization, 2006.

Masson-Matthee, Marielle D. *The Codex Alimentarius Commission and Its Standards.* The Hague, The Netherlands: T.M.C. Asser Press, 2007.

Web Sites

"Codex Alimentarius." *Codex Alimentarius Commission.* http://www.codexalimentarius.net/web/index_en.jsp (accessed October 16, 2010).

Food Safety and Inspection Service. "Codex Alimentarius." *U.S. Department of Agriculture (USDA).* http://www.fsis.usda.gov/codex_alimentarius/index.asp (accessed October 16, 2010).

Pamela V. Michaels

Coffee

■ Introduction

Coffee sales worldwide top $70 billion each year. From coffee shops to offices to the morning brew at home, people around the world in nearly every culture drink coffee in some form. Coffee is the second most-traded commodity in the world (petroleum is first), and the International Coffee Organization (ICO), created in 1963 with United Nations cooperation, manages the flow of the coffee trade worldwide through voluntary agreements.

According to the ICO more than 25 million families worldwide in 60 countries rely on coffee farming for their livelihoods. Coffee cherries grow on coffee plants; these bright red seeds are harvested, dried, and then sold as unroasted green coffee beans, named for their grayish-green color. Green coffee has a long shelf life, but the beans must be roasted, ground, then brewed with hot water for coffee to be produced. The amount of time green coffee beans are roasted helps to determine caffeine content: Lighter roasts have a higher caffeine content, whereas darker roasts have less caffeine.

■ Historical Background and Scientific Foundations

According to legend, sometime in the eighth or ninth century an Ethiopian goatherd named Kaldi noticed some of his goats eating red berries from a bush and behaving excitedly. Kaldi tried some of the red berries and experienced a similar euphoria. A monk from a nearby monastery witnessed Kaldi and his goats and plucked some of the berries to share with his fellow brothers. The monks were able to stay up all night in alert prayer. Coffee brewed from roasted beans first appeared around AD 1000. By the fourteenth century, Arabs cultivated coffee plants and historical records indicate that trade within the Middle East had begun.

Middle Eastern coffee houses became popular by the fourteenth century, in part due to the prohibition of alcohol under Islam. Coffee and the caffeine within it that acted as a stimulant was permitted, and Muslim men gathered in *qahveh khaneh* (coffee houses) to drink, chat, smoke, play chess, listen to music, and at times attend speeches by religious figures.

Trade outside of the Middle East also was flourishing in the thirteenth century, with Arab trade routes delivering green coffee to Africa and parts of the Mediterranean. In the 1600s an Indian named Baba Budan allegedly smuggled coffee seeds out of the city of Mecca, the seeds taped to his belly, to take back to India to plant and cultivate coffee. Coffee reached Europe via Venice in the early 1600s, and by the end of the seventeenth century the Dutch used the colony of Indonesia to produce coffee beans as an export crop.

Whereas tea had long been popular in Europe, imported from Asia, coffee took hold quickly. By the early 1700s coffee was cultivated in the Caribbean and in northern Latin America. The market for coffee in the United States expanded dramatically after the War of 1812 between the United States and Britain; the British refused to sell tea to the Americans, and coffee filled the void. By the early 1800s Brazil's coffee crop was so large that prices dropped, enabling the masses to afford the crop, and the market expanded worldwide.

Coffee was banned for various reasons by different groups, starting with the Eastern Orthodox Church in the twelfth century. In the sixteenth century Muslim scholars banned it for a short time, and followers of the Church of Jesus Christ of Latter-Day Saints, or Mormons, to this day do not consume coffee: The religion has banned it since 1833.

■ Impacts and Issues

Since about 1990 the coffee trade has focused on the concept of fair trade, paying coffee farmers a fair price for their crops. The International Coffee Association formed as a reaction to volatile coffee prices worldwide. From 1930 to 1960 coffee prices fluctuated dramatically, leaving millions of farmers in Africa, Latin America, and parts of southeast Asia at the mercy of mercurial markets. The ICO manages agreements between coffee-producing countries, with a goal of "strengthening the economies of the coffee producing countries and the development of international trade and cooperation."

The Fair Trade movement began in the 1960s, but gained momentum in specialty coffee markets in the 1980s. As coffee prices dropped dramatically in the mid-1980s, in some instances as much as 60 percent, coffee producers scrambled to avoid starvation. Coffee crops can take from three to seven years to mature, and extreme drops in prices may come at the same time as a bounty harvest, further decreasing prices. Fair trade spread as the corporate coffeehouse chains grew in the United States and worldwide, spearheaded by Starbucks, but also including Dunkin Donuts, Peet's Coffee, and Seattle's Best. According to corporate statistics, Starbucks purchased 367 million pounds of coffee in 2009; 40 million pounds were fair trade certified. Despite the trend towards fair trade in the coffee market, the majority of coffee is still not considered fairly traded. Advocates for fair trade continue to push for better

WORDS TO KNOW

FAIR TRADE: A process that incorporates equitable distribution of profit, environmental, ecological, human rights, and cultural issues into capitalist markets. In the late twentieth century, advocacy groups pushed for fair trade in the coffee industry.

GREEN COFFEE: The dried berries from the coffee bush. Green coffee has a long shelf life, and beans are sold in large volume as green coffee. Coffee cannot be brewed until the green coffee beans are roasted and ground; leaving the beans in their green state prolongs the life of the berries.

INTERNATIONAL COFFEE ORGANIZATION (ICO): Founded in 1963, the ICO works to coordinate coffee trade worldwide, and to set industry standards for farmers, middlemen, and large manufacturers. The ICO has a loose association with the United Nations.

quality control, more equity for farmers, and for larger corporations and individual consumers to purchase fair trade products.

A worker is paid for the coffee he picked, as others wait in line at the end of the day, on a coffee plantation outside Belen, Costa Rica, in 2002. *AP images.*

IN CONTEXT: CIVET CAFÉ

Some gourmet coffee, espresso-based coffee drinks, and high-end coffees such as Jamaican Blue Mountain and Hawaiian Kona have become luxury items. Jamaican Blue Mountain coffee can cost as much as $60 per pound, with pure Kona a close second in price at $40. Kopi Luwak, civet coffee, made headlines in the first decade of the 2000s, with prices generally exceeding $100 per pound and in some cases reaching $1,000 per pound.

Kopi Luwak is coffee made from coffee cherries scavenged from the feces of the civet, a lemur-like creature in Indonesia and Malaysia. The animals eat coffee cherries for their fruity flesh, and the beans make their way through the animals' digestive systems. According to preliminary research from scientists at the University of Guelph in Canada, digestive enzymes affect the coffee beans, creating a unique taste after the beans have been retrieved from the feces, carefully washed, roasted, ground, and then brewed. *The New York Times* reported market prices of $150–227 per pound in April 2010. Coffee farmers report receiving $9 per pound for the "cat dung" coffee, approximately five times the rate for traditionally-grown coffee in the region. Coffeehouses in Europe, the United States, and Australia serve this delicacy in house, charging a premium as high as 79 U.S. dollars per cup.

■ Primary Source Connection

Mary Frances Kennedy Fisher (1908–1992) was a prolific author who wrote in a variety of genres, but is best known for her literary essays on various aspects of cuisine and the culinary arts. Fisher wrote more than 20 books throughout her career, and her essays and short stories appeared many different food and literary magazines, including *Gourmet*, *The New Yorker*, *House Beautiful* and *Atlantic Monthly*. Her first book, *Serve it Forth*, was published in 1937.

Though most of M.F.K. Fisher's writing is about cooking and eating, many times cuisine merely serves as a metaphor for Fisher's exploration of topics like philosophy, psychology, culture, and social issues. She did much of her writing in the 1930s and 1940s, during the Great Depression and World War II—two experiences in deprivation that helped form her philosophy of "living agreeably in a world full of an increasing number of disagreeable surprises."

M.F.K. Fisher's essay, "Coffee," an ode to the best and the worst of coffee experiences, first appeared in *Atlantic Monthly* magazine in 1945.

Coffee

Comparisons are odious, of course. They are also difficult, especially when they are concerned with such a complex question as the worst coffee of my life.

While I think of the coffee I drank one night in the railway station at Valence, while I waited for the Paris express to stop for me and three Spahis in their long, scarlet-lined capes, I am sure it was the worst. Over the greasy steamed window of the café the rain dripped interminably down, and I thought of how cool and clean it must taste, I was cold and tired and shy. The pale, stinking brew I swallowed offered me a kind of sensory comfort, upon which my throat muscles closed like the oar of an outraged snake. The Spahis spat out their first mouthful and matter-of-factly filled the nasty thick-grimed glasses with rum, and I watched them, wishing I could be as easy in my white skin as they seemed to be in their shining dark ones.

Coffee almost as hideous was brewed every few hours in a big hotel in Cornwall. Perhaps the fact that is happened more than once was the most unpleasant thing about it.

I would smell it, slithering and sneaking up the elevator shaft like the gray-brown ghost of a long-dead, forgotten scrubwoman. I would know that after the interminable dinner with its pink fish sauce and its limp savory, after the last tipple of digestive or purgative tonics, the other solemn souls and I would sit in the drawing room, politely vying for places near the tiny fire and wait impatiently for the waiter to come with his tray of small cups. "Black or white, Madam?" he would ask, bending over the sweetened grayish brew, "Black," I would say stubbornly, hating the implication of his description, and wondering each time if I could swallow what I chose.

It has a burned taste to it: that was what I smelled always a few hours before its appearance. And there was a disgusting fatness about it, like ancient boiled mutton. I thought perhaps the dripping pans were charred and then rinsed out to color it. But as in Valence, in the station café, it was hot—and I was very cold.

It is surprising to me that in a country as standardized as ours we still manage to make our coffee in almost as many ways as there are people to make it. It comes in uniform jars, which we buy loyally according to which radio program hires the best writers, so that whether the label is green or scarlet the contents are safely alike, safely middling. Once in the pot, however, its individuality becomes evident, a watery monster full of venom or sweet promise, as the case may be. Coffee in a roadside waffle joint may outdo the nectar, and some made most carefully, measured and boiled just so and with the pot heated and swabbed and such according to directions, may be a loathsome brew in my best friend's kitchen.

There are vintners who believe that certain human beings have a chemical (or spiritual?) aura about them which will make wine turn over and mope in the bottles. Perhaps it is true that some people breed trouble in the fragile oils of roasted coffee beans. I have at least three familiars who could no more make a potable cup

Coffee

of coffee than they could walk upon waters. They have tried too—and even wept at their defeat.

Methods can be amusing or merely finicky—elaborate or as simple as spilling some grounds into boiling water and letting them settle, unmeasured, unhindered by directions. And what people want is even plainer. First of all, coffee must be hot, they say—all except a stern old man I once knew who frowned on "stimulants" but drank quarts of cold black coffee every day, instead of water. And then coffee must be fresh, made shortly before its drinking and made only once. (In Cornwall, water was boiled twice or more over the same sad grounds, in defiance of counsel I found in an old cookery book. "Dried coffee, once used, is best employed as filling for pincushions, and will not pack down nor rust the needles.")

And some people like a light delicate brew and others, equally firm about the freshness of their grinding, and the rest, will settle for strength or nothing. Their coffee, like tea for the Irish lady, must be strong enough to trot a mouse upon.

I like to lead strangers and intimates, in that order, to tell me the only right way to do a thing, their way. Scrambled eggs, reducing, surrealism, are all good gambits, but coffee making is the best.

One woman who lived for years in Guatemala will grow soft-eyed and gentle in the telling, over and over, of the way coffee smells in the air down there, dark and sweet with the sugar that is stirred into the pan of green beans in the oven. It turns black finally, in a kind of glaze, and when the beans are ground they have a fine richness about them.

A tall man, usually preoccupied with such things as laparotomies and the tightrope balance between death and life in the "closed" wards, will discuss with voluptuous candor how to blend and boil true Turkish brew. It is an elaborate ritual, like part of a ballet, and he the *premier danseur.*

A woman now more remote from the present than the past will tell me, had her voice becomes younger in the telling, of the coffee at Aunt Annie's, in the days of Sam Ward and Diamond Jim and all the gilt-edged gluttons.

It came every week from Park and Tilford, freshly roasted, and cost fifteen cents a pound. It was from Maracaibo. It was ground in the kitchen by a big hand-mill, two pounds at a time, and mixed into a paste with four beaten eggs. Then, spread thinly on a pan, it dried out in a slow oven until it could be broken up into a powdery mess again, while the whole of the great house was perfumed by its tantalizing fresh, strong smell. And it was used like any other coffee: a heaping tablespoonful for each cup of water, and one-plus for the pot. But I can never tire of hearing, and believing, that is was the best ever made. Maracaibo—the word is magic, as that weary woman says it, as I listen.

Of course I have my own formula, less charmed but more misquoted. At least ten philosophers from half as many countries have claimed it as their own, so why not me? Coffee, I say, should be

Fresh as the springtime,
Black as death,
Strong as a long going lover's arms,
And hot as hell.

Then, whether it be shipped, a bag of green beans, from some foreign port, or true-test roasted, be poured from a vacuum-sealed, dealer-dated jar, it will be good. It will, being good at all, be perfect.

M.F.K. Fisher

FISHER, MARY FRANCES KENNEDY. "COFFEE" IN *A STEW OR A STORY: AN ASSORTMENT OF SHORT WORKS,* EDITED BY JOAN REARDON. EMERYVILLE: SHOEMAKER & HOARD, 2006.

SEE ALSO *Agriculture and International Trade; Caffeine; Fair Trade.*

BIBLIOGRAPHY
Books

Clark, Taylor. *Starbucked: A Double Tall Tale of Caffeine, Commerce, and Culture.* New York: Little, Brown, 2007.

Coffee, Neil. *The Commerce of War: Exchange and Social Order in Latin Epic.* Chicago: University of Chicago Press, 2009.

Cycon, Dean. *Javatrekker: Dispatches from the World of Fair Trade Coffee.* White River Junction, VT: Chelsea Green, 2007.

Jaffee, Daniel. *Brewing Justice: Fair Trade Coffee, Sustainability, and Survival.* Berkeley: University of California Press, 2007.

Jolliffe, Lee. *Coffee Culture, Destinations and Tourism.* Bristol, UK: Channel View Publications, 2010.

Wild, Antony. *Coffee: A Dark History.* New York: W.W. Norton, 2005.

Periodicals

"Fuelled by Coffee." *Economist* 390, no. 8621 (2009).

Lee, Thomas H. "Good News for Coffee Addicts." *Harvard Business Review* 87, no. 6 (2009): 22–24.

Lopez-Garcia, Esther, et al. "The Relationship of Coffee Consumption with Mortality." *Annals of Internal Medicine* 148, no. 12 (2008): 904–914.

Web Sites

"Coffee Production." *Coffee Science Information Center.* http://www.cosic.org/background-on-coffee/coffee-production (accessed October 15, 2010).

Hensrud, Donald. "Coffee and Health: What Does the Research Say?" http://www.mayoclinic.com/health/coffee-and-health/AN01354 (accessed October 15, 2010).

Melanie Barton Zoltan

Commission on Genetic Resources for Food and Agriculture

■ Introduction

The Commission on Genetic Resources for Food and Agriculture (CGRFA), a commission within the Food and Agriculture Organization (FAO) of the United Nations, works to conserve biodiversity within agriculture. The CGRFA promotes biodiversity conservation in order to preserve global food security and promote sustainable development for the current and future generations of farmers, livestock breeders, and consumers.

The CGRFA works with farmers, breeders, and seed curators to conserve agricultural diversity and share the benefits of biodiversity. Under the International Treaty on Plant Genetic Resources for Food and Agriculture, member nations recognize the rights of farmers to access genetic resources, participate in policymaking, and use, save, and sell seeds. To further these goals, the CFRFA implemented a Multilateral System that allows access to and benefit sharing of the 64 crops deemed most important for guaranteeing food security.

■ Historical Background and Scientific Foundations

In 1983 the Food and Agriculture Organization (FAO), an agency of the United Nations dedicated to agriculture and world hunger issues, adopted the International Undertaking on Plant Genetic Resources. The International Undertaking resolved to ensure that plant genetic resources of economic and social value are preserved for future generations and made available for breeding and scientific research.

To further the FAO's goal of preserving plant genetic diversity, the International Undertaking authorized the FAO to establish the Commission on Plant Genetic Resources (CPGR), the predecessor to the CGRFA. The CPGR addressed many important issues regarding plant genetic diversity, including the rights of plant breeders and farmers, the roles of developed and developing nations in conserving plant biodiversity, and the sovereign rights of nations over their plant genetic diversity.

In 1992 the United Nations adopted the Convention on Biological Diversity and Agenda 21 at the Earth Summit in Rio de Janeiro, Brazil. The Convention on Biological Diversity called for the conservation of biological diversity, the sustainable use of biodiversity's components, and a fair and equitable sharing of benefits derived from genetic resources. Chapter 14 of Agenda 21, an action plan for sustainable development and environmental conservation issues, calls for expanding and strengthening the FAO's plant genetic diversity program to bring it in line with the biodiversity demands of the Convention on Biological Diversity. In 1995 the FAO created the CGRFA, which expanded the CPGR's mandate to cover issues involving animal, marine life, microorganism, and invertebrate genetic diversity.

The CGRFA seeks to halt the loss of genetic diversity of species used for food and agriculture. The CGRFA also seeks to ensure food security by conserving genetic resources that might be utilized to produce disease resistant or more productive crops in the future. Conservation of these genetic resources is particularly important in light of growing agricultural challenges presented by global climate change, desertification, and regional water scarcity. In 2001 the FAO Conference adopted the International Treaty on Plant Genetic Resources for Food and Agriculture, a binding treaty under international law. The treaty establishes a system to facilitate international access to plant genetic resources used in food and agricultural production. The treaty also promotes the CGRFA's goal of fairly and equitably sharing benefits derived from the use of genetic resources.

■ Impacts and Issues

The work of the CGRFA in preserving the genetic diversity of agricultural plants, livestock, aquaculture, and agriculturally useful microorganisms and

Several varieties of potatoes are sold at a market in the Andean town of Arequipa, Peru. Approximately 3,000 varieties of potatoes exist in the Andes. © *Paul Kingsley / Alamy.*

invertebrates attempts to avoid problems related to the loss of agricultural biodiversity. The preservation of agricultural genetic diversity ensures food security by conserving species of plants and animals that might produce higher yields or be resistant to unknown or mutated diseases.

Despite the importance of biological diversity, the world has lost a tremendous amount of agricultural diversity over the last century. Over thousands of years, humans cultivated more than 7,000 species of plants and hundreds of thousands of distinct varieties. The FAO estimates that in the early twenty-first century, 30 species of crops provide 95 percent of human food energy requirements. Four species—maize, potatoes, rice, and wheat—fulfill 60 percent of human calorie needs. Within these important crops, preservation of genetic diversity is of paramount importance. Fortunately, thousands of distinct varieties of crops exist within each species. Several gene banks and seed banks worldwide maintain a safehold of distinct species of crop species, including the Svalbard Global Seed Vault, located in Norway

above the Arctic Circle, which stores more than 500,000 samples of seed.

The rise of industrialized farming in the twentieth century and a focus on increased yields resulted in farmers relying heavily on only a few varieties of each species. This reliance on only a few crops over a wide area, known as monoculture, diminishes genetic diversity, often with severe consequences. By the 1970s Asian farmers relied on only a few varieties of high-yield rice. A virus known as rice grassy stunt virus (RGSV) decimated Asian rice production. Scientists discovered a single, long-forgotten variety of rice resistant to RGSV and hybridized the variety's disease resistance with other types of rice.

Modern livestock breeding practices also threaten genetic diversity among livestock. According to the FAO, approximately 1,500 livestock breeds out of the 7,600 breeds reported are either at risk of extinction or already extinct. The FAO estimates that more than 60 breeds of livestock became extinct between 2001 and 2006. Overfishing also threatens the genetic diversity of the world's marine life: Approximately 75 percent of the world's marine fish stocks are fully exploited, overexploited, or depleted. The CGRFA works with its member nations to ensure that these genetic resources are available for future generations.

SEE ALSO *Agenda 21; Biodiversity and Food Supply; Food and Agriculture Organization (FAO); Food Security; Genetically Modified Organisms (GMO); UN Millennium Development Goals; Undernutrition; Water Scarcity.*

BIBLIOGRAPHY

Books

Food and Agriculture Organization. *International Treaty on Plant Genetic Resources for Food and Agriculture: A Global Treaty for Food Security and Sustainable Agriculture.* Rome: Food and Agriculture Organization of the United Nations (FAO), 2002.

Food and Agriculture Organization. *Livestock Keepers: Guardians of Biodiversity.* Rome: Food and Agriculture Organization of the United Nations (FAO), 2009.

Food and Agriculture Organization. *World Food Security: The Challenges of Climate Change and Bioenergy.* Rome: Food and Agriculture Organization of the United Nations (FAO), 2008.

Tansey, Geoff, and Tasmin Rajotte. *The Future Control of Food: A Guide to International Negotiations and Rules on Intellectual Property, Biodiversity and Food Security.* London: Earthscan, 2008.

Periodicals

Holt, Robert D. "Ecology: Asymmetry and Stability." *Nature* 442, no. 7100 (2006): 252–253.

Tirado, Reyes, and Paul Johnston. "Food Security: GM Crops Threaten Biodiversity." *Science* 328, no. 5975 (2010): 171–172.

Web Sites

"About the Commission." *Commission on Genetic Resources for Food and Agriculture.* http://www.fao.org/nr/cgrfa/cgrfa-about/cgrfa-history/en/ (accessed September 14, 2010).

"Biodiversity for a World without Hunger." *Commission on Genetic Resources for Food and Agriculture. UN Food and Agriculture Organization (FAO).* http://www.fao.org/fileadmin/templates/nr/documents/CGRFA/commissionfactsheet.pdf (accessed September 14, 2010).

Joseph P. Hyder

Women look at produce at a farm stand that distributes member's community supported agriculture (CSA) allotments or shares each week at a local farmers' market. *K. Lee Lerner / Lerner & Lerner / LernerMedia Global Photos*

issue for CSA farmers to weigh against the potential increase in customers.

CSA membership increased in the wake of several high-profile food recalls in 2007 and 2008, with a notable focus on buying local produce sparked by a massive recall of packaged spinach that contained *E. coli* O157:H7. Consumers turned to farmers' markets and CSAs as the media chronicled the contamination issues associated with agribusiness from the factory farm through manufacturing to the grocery store, helping to bring CSAs into the media spotlight as a local food source alternative.

A 2008 report from the Rodale Institute notes the growing trend of CSAs that accept food stamps as partial or full payment for farm shares. Many food stamp recipients use their benefits to pay part or all of the share fee and combine the federal food benefit with a work-share program, volunteering an agreed-upon number of hours as farm labor. Just Food, a New York City non-profit organization, trains CSA farmers in the bureaucratic process required to accept food stamps. Farmers who learn this process can also accept food stamps at farmers' markets and for other retail sales of foods that qualify under the program. The food stamp initiative is part of a larger movement to make local produce

available to all income levels, because CSA share costs have historically been high enough to be an obstacle for lower-income consumers.

SEE ALSO *Agribusiness; Agroecology; Alice Waters: California and New American Cuisine; Ethical Issues in Agriculture; Factory Farming; Farm-to-Table Movement; Food Recalls; Locavore; Organic Foods Production Act of 1990; Organics; Slow Food Movement; Sustainable Agriculture.*

BIBLIOGRAPHY

Books

Adam, Katherine L. *Community Supported Agriculture.* Fayetteville, AR: National Sustainable Agriculture Information Service, 2006.

Cotler, Amy. *The Locavore Way: Discover and Enjoy the Pleasures of Locally Grown Food.* North Adams, MA: Storey, 2009.

Gregson, Bob, and Bonnie Gregson. *Rebirth of the Small Family Farm: A Handbook for Starting a Successful Organic Farm Based on the Community Supported Agriculture Concept.* Austin, TX: Acres U.S.A, 2004.

Henderson, Elizabeth, and En R. Van. *Sharing the Harvest: A Citizen's Guide to Community Supported*

Agriculture. White River Junction, VT: Chelsea Green, 2007.

Smith, Jeremy N., Chad Harder, and Sepp Jannotta. *Growing a Garden City: How Farmers, First Graders, Counselors, Troubled Teens, Foodies, a Homeless Shelter Chef, Single Mothers, and More Are Transforming Themselves and Their Neighborhoods through the Intersection of Local Agriculture and Community—and How You Can, Too.* New York: Skyhorse Publishing, 2010.

Periodicals

Brown, Cheryl, and Stacy Miller. "The Impacts of Local Markets: A Review of Research on Farmers Markets and Community Supported Agriculture (CSA)." *American Journal of Agricultural Economics* 90, no. 5 (2008): 1296–1302.

Schnell, Steven M. "Food with a Farmer's Face: Community-Supported Agriculture in the United States." *Geographical Review* 97, no. 4 (2007): 550–564.

"Talking Pictures—Community Supported Agriculture." *World Watch* 22, no. 3 (2009): 18–19.

Web Sites

"Community Supported Agriculture." *Local Harvest.* http://www.localharvest.org/csa/ (accessed October 16, 2010).

"Community Supported Agriculture." *National Agricultural Library, U.S. Department of Agriculture (USDA).* http://www.nal.usda.gov/afsic/pubs/csa/csa.shtml (accessed October 16, 2010).

Melanie Barton Zoltan

Confectionery and Pastry

■ Introduction

Confections include all types of candy, pastries, chewing gum, mints, deserts, chocolate, and ice cream. The term *confectionery* is used to refer to the entire spectrum of confections, whereas *a confectionery* is the establishment in which confections are sold. Confections are ubiquitous: They are a part of every culture in the world in which some form of sugar or sweetener is found. *Confectionery* also refers to sweets made with fruit or nuts, such as marzipan, Halvah, and fruitcake. Although confections are generally thought to be sweets that can be eaten without utensils (i.e., just by using the hands), there are notable exceptions, such as ice cream and several varieties of meringue.

Food historians suspect that some confections got their start in the medicinal realm, as a treatment for coughs, sore throats, and digestive issues. Those early remedies were the precursors to contemporary mints, cough drops, and throat lozenges. The first candies were made from fruits, flowers, seeds, and plant stems coated with honey as a means of preserving them. Confections were a global phenomenon even in antiquity: Ancient Greek, Roman, Indian, Egyptian, Middle Eastern, and Chinese histories all make mention of the honey-coated fruits and nuts used as sweet treats, in ritual, and in ceremonies.

The art of pastry-making is thought by food historians to be as old as that of candy-making. The ancient Egyptians are argued to have been the first to wrap meats in a paste made from water and flour in order to absorb the juices during cooking. They also made sweet pastries using dough made from flour, water, or oil and honey. Often, the dough was stuffed with fruit or nuts.

In a world growing increasingly overweight, the practice of overindulgence in sweets is a significant concern. So, too, is the incidence of dental caries associated with the ingestion of excessive amounts of sugar.

■ Historical Background and Scientific Foundations

Assorted confections and preserves (fruit preserved with sugars) were served at the most elaborate ancient Greek and Roman celebrations. After the demise of those cultures, little is written about confections until sweets resurfaced during the Middle Ages in Europe, where they were used primarily for medicinal purposes. At a time when people were prone to unhealthy diets and excessive eating, sweetmeats composed of spices and sugars were used to aid digestion. In the New World, confections were called candy rather than sweetmeats. Boiled sugarplums were popular sweets in both the Old and the New Worlds in the seventeenth century. At that time, maple-syrup candy and treats made from sesame seeds were very popular in the New World. Caramels and lollipops were invented in the 1800s; lemon and peppermint hard candies debuted early in the nineteenth century. The creation of solid milk chocolate in Switzerland in 1875 set the stage for the explosion of American candy bars that began in the nineteenth century and continues unabated.

Boiling sugar in order to make hard candy dates to antiquity. Sugar syrup is heated to different temperatures in order to achieve different concentrations of sugar syrup. The higher the temperature, the more water will boil off and evaporate and the denser the concentration of sugar to water in the syrup. At sea level, water boils at 212°F (100°C). At slightly higher temperatures (around 215–235°F, 101.6–112.7°C), the sugar water mixture forms long threads when tiny amounts are dropped into cold water. This low-density mixture can be used for making some icings and syrups. At 235–240°F (112.7–115.5°C), the soft-ball stage occurs. When a bit of syrup is dropped into cold water, it forms a soft ball that flattens on removal from the water. Soft-ball stage syrup is used in making cream candies such as buttercream and peppermint creams, as well as fudge and fondant.

WORDS TO KNOW

HALVAH: A Middle Eastern and Mediterranean confection made by grinding almonds into a sweet paste and combining them with other ingredients and flavorings.

MARZIPAN: A type of confection made from almond paste. It is often made into fruit or animal shapes as a standalone treat. It can also be used as a topping for cakes and pastries.

Heating the mixture another 5 to 10 degrees Fahrenheit moves the syrup into the firm-ball stage, wherein the ball formed when dropping some syrup into water no longer compacts when it hits the air, although it can be compacted by squeezing. Firm-ball stage syrup is used in the making of caramels. Hard-ball stage syrup occurs at around 250–265°F (121–129°C) and is quite concentrated. The mixture forms a hard ball in cold water and maintains its shape on removal. Hard-ball syrup is used to make rock candy, gummy candies, nougat, and marshmallows. At the hard-crack stage, reached at temperatures of 300–335 degrees Fahrenheit (149–168°C), the concentration of sugar to water is 99 to 1. This is the highest temperature used in candy-making. It is appropriate for making hard candies, toffee, brittles, and butterscotch. When a small amount of hard-crack syrup is dropped into very cold water, it forms hard threads that break easily when bent.

Pastry-making is thought to date back to ancient Egypt, where it was used as a wrapping for meats, in order to seal in juices during cooking. Egyptian bakers also used a mixture of flour, oils, and wild honey in order to make sweet pastries, which were often filled with fruit. The ancient Greeks distinguished between bakers and pastry-makers. Pastry-makers used combinations of honey, oil, flour, spices, and aromatic herbs. Pastry was either fried or cooked under coals (akin to baking). Various nuts and seeds were used either in the dough mixture or as fillings. The art of pastry-making was given impetus during the Crusades of the Middle Ages, when travelers were exposed to sugar cane and puff pastry on journeys to the East. By the mid-fifteenth century, the professions of baker and pastry-cook had been delineated, although there was still some overlap.

A confectionery displays its wares in La Boqueria market in Barcelona, Spain. *Image copyright Philip Large, 2010. Used under license from Shutterstock.com.*

French pastries are displayed in a cake shop in the town of Metz, France. *Image copyright Carole Castelli, 2010. Used under license from Shutterstock.com.*

Choux pastry is reported to have been created in the mid-1500s. Pate Choux is a very light French pastry used with cream fillings. The center of the pastry, which is eventually filled with cream, is initially hollow. The dough is made by boiling butter with a mixture of water and milk, then adding flour. Eggs are added to the beaten mixture, which is poured into a forcing bag and extruded in rounds that are baked in a very hot oven. After baking and cooling, the pastry has to be vented to allow the steam to escape. The light pastry is then sliced open and filled.

Puff pastry had its genesis during the Renaissance of the sixteenth century. It is made by mixing a dough of flour, salt, and water, and then folding and rolling so as to create a large number of layers of dough and fat—typically butter. This layering process results in an extremely light, fluffy, airy pastry. When the folding and rolling process is carried out correctly, the dough and fat layers remain separate. When the dough is baked in a very hot oven, water steams off from the dough layers and migrates into the fat layers, causing the pastry to vastly inflate, or puff, to as much as eight to ten times its original height.

Pâte brisée and pâte sucrée are often used to make pie and tart crusts. If the dough is made with very little sugar, it is called pâte brisée; if made with egg and sugar, it is called pâte sucrée.

■ Impacts and Issues

In a world growing increasingly overweight, there is much public and governmental effort aimed at reducing excessive consumption of both confections and pastry. Commercially-produced candy is typically made with highly processed ingredients, colorings, flavorings, and preservatives, leading to issues around not only the long-term weight-related health consequences of overindulgence, but concerns about the impact of artificial ingredients and chemical additives on the quality of the human lifespan.

In an effort to highlight the epidemic of overweight and obesity among contemporary American children

IN CONTEXT: FLAVONOIDS

After years of research on the levels of antioxidants in selected fruits, scientists at Cornell University published a study in the *Journal of Agricultural and Food Chemistry* establishing that strawberries have high levels of phenolic compounds, including flavonoids, which pack a potent antioxidant punch. The published studies also showed a correlation between gross levels of phenolics and the powerfully antioxidant flavonoids (such as the red pigmented anthocyanins). Strawberries are not the only berries in the patch that turn out to have antioxidant potency: Other studies have indicated that blueberries provide phenolic antioxidants linked to processes protective of neural tissues in animals. And, in a boost for chocolate makers, several studies, including one from the University of California—San Francisco, found that the cocoa in dark chocolate is also high in flavonoids.

In chemistry, antioxidant molecules are those that prevent or slow the breakdown of other substances by oxygen. In biochemisty, antioxidants scavenge free radicals—a class of small, highly reactive molecules with one or more unpaired electrons—that react rapidly with other molecules in processes of oxidation. Free radicals are a normal product of metabolism, and their levels are usually controlled by the antioxidants produced by the body or taken in as nutrients. Within cells, antioxidants include intracellular enzymes such as superoxide dismutase (SOD), catalase, and glutathione peroxidase. Extracellular antioxidants are found in vitamins such as ascorbic acid (vitamin C), tocopherol (vitamin E), and vitamin A. Free radicals serve a normally useful purpose as they aid in the natural breakdown of damaged cells or in fighting infectious substances. In order to maintain a healthy balance of free radicals, enzymes in the body carefully regulate their production.

Although the scientific evidence remains contradictory and inconclusive, a number of health advocates promote antioxidants as remedies or supportive treatment for a wide range of diseases and conditions, including—but not limited to—aging, stress, pollution "cleansing," smoking addiction, obesity, some forms of cancer, macular degeneration, and an array of other problems.

In addition to contradictory evidence regarding the value of flavonoid-rich foods, however, studies have also shown that combinations of certain foods may negate potential benefits. For example, one study published by researchers with the National Institute for Food and Nutrition Research suggested the milk components in milk chocolates may inhibit the absorption and use of antioxidants. Although a seeming boost for dark chocolates, current evidence remains thin that dark chocolates should be considered a "health food," especially when other health factors such as obesity are considered.

There are also lingering questions as to whether antioxidants in the form of dietary supplements provide benefits equal to those derived from a healthy diet. Some studies show that supplements may interfere with the body's own healthy production of antioxidants. Natural antioxidant food sources also contain additional beneficial nutrients, contributing to an overall healthy diet.

and youth, President Barack Obama (1961–) and his family made a public gesture by handing out fruit to Halloween trick-or-treaters at the White House in 2010.

Many schools across America have banned the custom of bringing cakes, candy, ice cream, and cupcakes to elementary school classrooms for birthday celebrations. Instead, they are recommending bringing fruits and other healthy snacks—or skipping the food entirely and donating a special book to the school library in the name of the birthday child.

Much has been made of the growing problem of environmental and ingredient sensitivities and allergies—many people are unable to ingest nuts safely as well as non-nut-containing products manufactured in plants where nuts are sometimes present. This has led to labeling of many non-nut-containing food items, which informs the public of the presence of nuts in confectionary and pastry-making facilities.

In the most recent movie adaptation of Roald Dahl's "Charlie and the Chocolate Factory," mention is made of a gum that carries the flavors of consecutive courses in a meal. Researchers at the Institute of Food research in Norwich (United Kingdom) have developed a technology that would allow different flavors to be time-released in chewing gum, potentially making real the fantasy of the Willy Wonka character. An initial flavor could be released when the gum is initially moistened by saliva in the mouth; a second flavor could come forth after a specific amount of chewing and a final flavor might release after a specific chewing intensity, according to the October 2010 report in the UK's *Telegraph*. A group of American scientists at the University of Massachusetts is using nanotechnology as a means of placing flavor layers in gum. In addition to the entertainment value, this could quickly become adopted as a diet aid: chewing meal-replacement gum as an alternative to overeating.

SEE ALSO *Chocolate; Dietary Guidelines for Americans; Food as Celebration; French Paradox; Obesity; Oral Health and Diet; School Lunch Reform; Sugar and Sweeteners.*

BIBLIOGRAPHY

Books

Cahill, Jamie. *The Patisseries of Paris: Chocolatiers, Tea Salons, Ice Cream Parlors, and More.* New York: Little Bookroom, 2007.

Off, Carol. *Bitter Chocolate: The Dark Side of the World's Most Seductive Sweet.* New York: New Press, 2008.

Parkinson, Eleanor. *The Complete Confectioner, Pastry-Cook, and Baker.* Charleston, SC: BiblioLife, 2010.

Periodicals

"Bob Hartwig: Bob Hartwig, Chef Instructor at the French Pastry School in Chicago, Gives His Take on Industry Trends, Pastry versus Confectionery and the Trials of Making Chocolate." *Candy Industry* 174, no. 3 (2009): 20–23.

"The Future of Confectionery Lies in Chocolate." *Food Manufacture* 84, no. 12 (2009): 43.

Moore, Simon C., Lisa M. Carter, and Stephanie van Goozen. "Confectionery Consumption in Childhood and Adult Violence." *The British Journal of Psychiatry* 195, no. 4 (2009): 366–367.

"Organic Confectionery Market." *Candy Industry* 169, no. 12 (2004): 40–46.

"Sweeteners Focus: Opportunities in Sugar-Free Confectionery Market." *Food Manufacture* 82, no. 11 (2007): 69–70.

Tarantino, Maria, and Sabina Terziani. "A Journey into the Imaginary of Sicilian Pastry." *Gastronomica: The Journal of Food and Culture* 10, no. 3 (2010): 45–51.

Web Sites

Horovitz, Bruce. "Pepsi Is Dropping Out of Schools Worldwide by 2012." *USA Today*, March 17, 2010. http://www.usatoday.com/money/industries/food/2010-03-16-pepsicutsschoolsoda_N.htm (accessed November 4, 2010).

Luchetti, Emily. "The Life of a Pastry Chef." *SFGate*, July 21, 2010. http://insidescoopsf.sfgate.com/eluchetti/2010/07/21/the-life-of-a-pastry-chef/ (accessed November 4, 2010).

"Slave-Free Chocolate." *Stop Chocolate Slavery.* http://vision.ucsd.edu/~kbranson/stopchocolateslavery/main.html (accessed November 4, 2010).

"Top Issues Today." *National Confectioners Association.* http://www.candyusa.com/PublicPolicy/IITopIssueToday.cfm?navItemNumber=2671 (accessed November 4, 2010).

Wrigt, Andy. "Finally, Candy Makers Market Directly to Women with Food Issues." *Mother Jones*, February 13, 2009. http://motherjones.com/media/2009/02/finally-candy-makers-market-directly-women-food-issues (accessed November 4, 2010).

Pamela V. Michaels

Consumer Food Safety Recommendations

■ Introduction

Consumer food safety recommendations include a variety of recommendations for home cooks on proper food storage, handling, and preparation. The goal of food safety recommendations is to reduce the number of foodborne illnesses caused by the consumption of improperly prepared food. All food contains millions of microorganisms, including bacteria, viruses, and parasites, on the surface and within the food item. Whereas most of these microorganisms are harmless, several varieties of microorganisms may cause illness or even death in humans if they exist in sufficient numbers and are not killed.

Common causes of foodborne illnesses include the pathogens *E. coli*, *Salmonella*, *Campylobacter jejuni*, *Clostridium perfringens*, and *Trichinella spiralis*. Proper refrigeration or freezing slows the reproductive rate of most foodborne bacteria, and cooking food to proper temperatures kills most bacteria and other pathogens. Virtually all food poisoning may be prevented if proper storage, handling, and preparation standards are observed. Governments and organizations that promote consumer food safety, therefore, must clearly define these standards and effectively educate the public.

■ Historical Background and Scientific Foundations

Safe preservation, storage, and preparation of food has been a vital health concern throughout human history. Although humans did not realize fully the role that bacteria and other microbes play in causing illness until the nineteenth century, they have long known that spoiled or improperly prepared food may cause illness or death. Historically, people have relied on their senses, including sight and smell, to determine whether food is safe to eat. Visual inspection reveals the presence of mold, maggots, rot, or other indicators that food may be past its prime. Smelling food reveals whether dairy products have turned rancid or meat has begun to spoil. Food laws and regulations were seldom in place or enforced, although the Roman empire and several medieval European countries had laws to regulate the safety of certain products.

Until the late eighteenth and early nineteenth centuries, most people consumed food that was grown and preserved on their own farms or in the surrounding countryside. Traditional preservation techniques, such as salting and curing, were used to preserve meat, and root vegetables were stored in underground root cellars. During the Industrial Revolution, companies began to mass process and package food. Unscrupulous food manufacturers would include unhealthy or inedible additives to processed foods. These practices raised consumer interest in the foods they purchased and how they prepared foods at home. By the late nineteenth century, governments began investigating food production and preparation practices. To promote food safety, governments adopted food safety laws or regulations. The Codex Alimentarius Austriacus, a document created by food industry experts and universities in Austria-Hungary in the late 1800s and early 1900s, focuses on food purity and production standards. It was one of the most comprehensive collections of food safety recommendations of the time and the basis for later standards and laws throughout the world.

Recommendations aimed at consumers regarding the safe handling and preparation of food in the home are relatively recent developments. Throughout the 1950s through 1970s, most textbooks used in university-level food science classes in the United States did not address food safety. By the 1980s, the U.S. Food and Drug Administration (FDA) noted in consumer publications that raw meat could contain *Salmonella*. The FDA gave little advice to avoid contracting foodborne illnesses beyond taking general precautions, including cooking food thoroughly and refrigerating promptly. By the 1990s, however, the U.S. Department of Agriculture (USDA) had adopted and began promoting specific consumer food safety guidelines, including internal cooking temperatures of meat and maintaining refrigerator temperatures at 40°F (4.4°C) or below. Many governments followed the FDA and USDA and began promoting consumer food safety recommendations.

■ Impacts and Issues

All consumer food safety recommendations are intended to prevent illness or death from foodborne diseases from bacteria or parasites, such as *E. coli*, *Salmonella*, or *Trichinella spiralis*, by promoting proper food storage, handling, and preparation in the home. Many consumer food safety recommendations factor human error into their calculations of cooking temperatures and times. The USDA, for example, recommends cooking ground beef to an internal temperature of 160°F (71.1°C) in order to kill *E. coli* bacteria, a common source of foodborne illness. Cooking meat to 155°F (68.3°C), however, is sufficient to kill *E. coli*. The USDA accounts for human error or inaccurate thermometers by recommending that people cook meat 5°F (2.8°C) beyond the temperature required to kill *E. coli*.

Like the United States, Canada actively promotes consumer food safety though both Health Canada, the

national government's health ministry, and the Canadian Food Inspection Agency. The Canadian government has also partnered with the Canadian Partnership for Consumer Food Safety Education to promote consumer food safety through the organization's "Be Food Safe" campaign.

A cook uses a meat thermometer to ensure that meat is cooked to the recommended temperature. *Image copyright Alexey Stiop, 2010. Used under license from Shutterstock.com.*

Most other nations, however, have not made consumer food safety recommendations a priority, preferring instead to focus on food safety regulations for the food production and restaurant industries. The European Union (EU) does not have a vigorous consumer food safety campaign, but the EU has implemented the EU Hazard Analysis and Critical Control Point (HACCP). HACCP applies to the manufacture, processing, transportation, and storage of food in the EU. HACCP sets standards and establishes a technique for anticipating where in the supply chain a problem may occur. Many of the regulations contained in HACCP, including food preparation and storage temperatures, could be adopted by home cooks.

The World Health Organization (WHO) notes that food safety in Africa is of vital importance for a number of factors, including the high percentage of persons living with HIV/AIDS, the large number of malnourished children, and a lack of access to clean drinking water in many areas. When dealing with immunocompromised or malnourished persons, food safety avoids placing additional stress on their already weakened immune systems. The lack of clean water or basic sanitation facilities demands that additional steps and care be given to properly store, handle, or prepare food. In 2005 representatives from the Food and Agriculture Organization (FAO) of the United Nations, WHO, and other interested parties attended the Regional Conference on Food Safety for Africa. The conference largely addressed food safety issues involving the production, processing, and distribution issues. The Strategic Plan of Action for Food Safety in Africa adopted at the conference, however, also addressed the need for increased consumer food safety education.

SEE ALSO *Center for Food Safety and Applied Nutrition; E. Coli Contamination; Food Recalls; Food Safety and Inspection Service; Foodborne Diseases; Norovirus Infection; Salmonella; Staphylococcal Food Poisoning.*

BIBLIOGRAPHY

Books

Hoffmann, Sandra A., and Michael R. Taylor. *Toward Safer Food: Perspectives on Risk and Priority Setting.* Washington, DC: Resources for the Future, 2005.

Sherrow, Victoria. *Food Safety.* New York: Chelsea House, 2008.

Periodicals

Godwin, Sandria, Richard Coppings, Leslie Speller-Henderson, and Lou Pearson. "Scholarship—Study Finds Consumer Food Safety Knowledge Lacking." *Journal of Family and Consumer Sciences* 97, no. 2 (2005): 40–44.

Jevsnik, Mojca, Valentina Hlebec, and Peter Raspor. "Consumers' Awareness of Food Safety from Shopping to Eating." *Food Control* 19, no. 8 (2008): 737–745.

Kosa, Katherine M., Sheryl C. Cates, Shawn Karns, Sandria L. Godwin, and Delores H. Chambers. "Consumer Food Safety and Home Refrigeration Practices: Results of a Web-Based Survey." *Journal of the American Dietetic Association* 106, no. 8 (2006): A68.

May, Kidd. "Food Safety—Consumer Concerns." *Nutrition & Food Science* 30, no. 2 (2000): 53.

Web Sites

"Food Safety Education: Be Food Safe." *U.S. Department of Agriculture (USDA).* http://www.fsis.usda.gov/Be_FoodSafe/index.asp (accessed October 19, 2010).

"Foodborne Illness: What Consumers Need to Know." *Food Safety and Inspection Service, U.S. Department of Agriculture (USDA).* http://www.fsis.usda.gov/Fact_Sheets/Foodborne_Illness_What_Consumers_Need_to_Know/index.asp (accessed October 19, 2010).

Joseph P. Hyder

Convention on Biological Diversity (1992)

■ Introduction

The Convention on Biological Diversity is an international treaty that addresses the conservation of biological diversity and the sustainable use of biological resources. Biological diversity, also referred to as biodiversity, denotes the variety of species that exist in the world. The exploitation and destruction of biological diversity through human action prompted the international community to address issues surrounding conservation and sustainable development. In the late 1980s the United Nations Environment Programme (UNEP) convened a panel of experts and policymakers to address these issues. Their efforts produced the Convention on Biological Diversity, which was opened for signatures at the United Nations Conference on Environment and Development, also called Earth Summit, in June 1992. The convention entered into force on December 29, 1993.

Article 1 of the Convention on Biological Diversity states that the goals of the treaty are "the conservation of biological diversity, the sustainable use of its components and the fair and equitable sharing of the benefits arising out of the utilization of genetic resources." The Convention on Biological Diversity seeks to balance conservation of biodiversity with the need of humans to utilize natural resources for agriculture and industry. The treaty supports the use of natural resources in a sustainable manner while using the precautionary principle as a guide. The precautionary principle states that an action, product, or policy should not be introduced into an environment in the absence of scientific consensus regarding the safety of that action to the environment and public health.

■ Historical Background and Scientific Foundations

The wide array of biological diversity in the world supplies humans with all needed resources—from plants and animals for food to raw materials for the production of an array of goods from building materials to pharmaceuticals. Without this range of natural resources, humans would not have the necessities of life, including food to eat and materials for shelter and clothing. According to UNEP, scientists have identified only about 1.75 million species out of an estimated 13 million species, although estimates range from 3 million to 100 million species.

Biodiversity is lost when species become extinct. Extinction occurs naturally through changing conditions on Earth and through mass extinction events. Although scientists cannot accurately determine the number of species that have become extinct over the years due to deficiencies in the fossil record, mathematical modeling shows that approximately 99.9 percent of all species that have ever existed are now extinct.

Over the last several millennia, however, the actions and impacts of humans have accelerated the extinction of numerous species. Human impact has contributed to the ongoing Holocene extinction, a sharp rise in extinctions that began approximately 11,000 to 12,000 years ago at the end of the last glacial period. Over the last 500 years, the International Union for Conservation of Nature and Natural Resources (IUCN) has documented the extinction of fewer than 900 species. Because most extinctions are not documented—with fewer than half of all species identified—the actual extinction rate is much higher. Under the species-area theory, a mathematical examination of the relationship between species and their habitat, up to 140,000 species may become extinct annually.

■ Impacts and Issues

Human actions that affect biodiversity include destruction of habitat, hunting and fishing, pollution, introduction of non-native species, and anthropogenic contributions to global climate change. Humans can also diminish agricultural biodiversity by favoring certain species for cultivation or breeding. Modern agriculture has favored certain species for desired characteristics, such as disease resistance

WORDS TO KNOW

BIODIVERSITY: The variety of living organisms within a given ecosystem or the world as a whole.

EXTINCTION: The state or process of a species or larger taxonomic group ceasing to exist.

MONOCULTURE: The agricultural practice of cultivating only a specific crop within a given area.

PRECAUTIONARY PRINCIPLE: The principle that any product, action, or process that might pose a threat to public or environmental health should not be introduced in the absence of scientific consensus regarding its safety.

SPECIES: A taxonomic group of living organisms capable of exchanging genes or interbreeding.

Monoculture also has significant, and potentially disastrous, consequences. Monoculture makes the crop yield over a large area susceptible to destruction if a destructive disease or pest emerges. The Irish potato famine of 1845 to 1852 resulted in the deaths of approximately 1 million people and forced another million to emigrate. The severity of the Irish potato famine was exacerbated by the small number of potato species used in agriculture, all of which were susceptible to potato blight. In the 1970s, rice grassy stunt virus (RGSV) decimated rice harvests across Asia, because the region's rice production relied on only a few high-yield strains of rice. Only one species out of nearly 6,300 known varieties of rice exhibited resistance to RGSV. This variety has now been hybridized to produce high-yield, RGSV-resistant varieties.

The Convention on Biological Diversity seeks to conserve biodiversity by developing and implementing national biodiversity conservation and sustainable use strategies. It achieves these goals by providing scientific and technical assistance, promoting access to technology, educating the public on biodiversity issues, distributing financial resources to parties, assessing the impact and success of conservation initiatives, and providing incentives for conservation. In the area of agricultural biodiversity, the parties to the Convention on Biological Diversity also have established a program

and increased yield. Monoculture, the production of a single crop over a wide area, has distinct advantages. Species of crops are typically grown in an area that will produce the greatest yield for the least input of labor or resources. This system has produced greater crop yields, which has decreased famine and increased standards of living.

A worker on Réunion Island butchers endangered green sea turtles (*Chelonia mydas*) for sale. The actions of humans, such as hunting, continue to accelerate the extinction of numerous species, reducing biodiversity on the planet. © A & J Visage / Alamy.

to address the environmental, cultural, and socio-economic dimensions of biodiversity and sustainable agriculture. The program provides financial and technical assistance for farmers to engage in sustainable agriculture.

SEE ALSO *Biodiversity and Food Supply; Cartagena Protocol on Biosafety (2000); Climate Change and Agriculture; Commission on Genetic Resources for Food and Agriculture; Ecological Impacts of Various World Diets; Food and Agriculture Organization (FAO); Sustainable Agriculture.*

BIBLIOGRAPHY

Books

Andrée, Peter. *Genetically Modified Diplomacy: The Global Politics of Agricultural Biotechnology and the Environment.* Vancouver: UBC Press, 2007.

Convention on Biological Diversity. *Handbook of the Convention on Biological Diversity: Including Its Cartagena Protocol on Biosafety.* Montreal: Secretariat of the Convention on Biological Diversity, 2005.

Jarvis, Devra I., and Christine Padoch. *Managing Biodiversity in Agricultural Ecosystems.* New York: Columbia University Press, 2007.

Periodicals

Adam, R. "Missing the 2010 Biodiversity Target: A Wake-Up Call for the Convention on Biodiversity?" *Colorado Journal of International Environmental Law and Policy* 21, no. 1 (2010): 123–166.

Web Sites

"The Cartagena Protocol on Biosafety." *Convention on Biological Diversity.* http://bch.cbd.int/protocol/ (accessed August 1, 2010).

Joseph P. Hyder

Cooking, Carbon Emissions, and Climate Change

■ Introduction

Cooking, the preparation of food to render it safe to eat or improve its flavor, is a universal human activity. It occurs daily worldwide, employing a wide variety of technologies ranging from open fires to highly engineered commercial stoves. Like almost all human activities, the production, transport, and preparation of food can negatively affect the local and global environment. Cooking can be the direct cause or end result of agricultural chemical use, air pollution, deforestation, climate change, fossil fuel use, industrial production and waste, land degradation, and mining.

For most of the modern era, the world's industrialized nations were the leading producer of black carbon. However, by the start of the twenty-first century, developing nations were the largest black carbon contributors. A significant portion of that pollution is derived from cooking over open fires and on biomass-burning stoves.

Black carbon is a pollutant emitted during the burning of biomass, biofuels, and fossil fuels. Soot, a particulate matter, and black carbon are commonly found in smoke from slash-and-burn agriculture, home chimneys, and cooking stoves. The use of diesel and other fossil fuels also contributes to the presence of black carbon air pollution. The presence and accumulation of black carbon and soot in Earth's atmosphere has been linked to global climate change, especially warming temperatures and glacial melt.

Unlike carbon dioxide emissions, which have an atmospheric lifetime of 40 to 100 years, black carbon remains in the atmosphere for only 10 to 40 days on average. Climate researchers thus assert that reductions in black carbon emissions could have immediate effects in mitigating the effects of climate change. Soot and other particulate air pollutants also have negative health impacts, contributing to respiratory illness.

■ Historical Background and Scientific Foundations

In 2007 an Intergovernmental Panel on Climate Change (IPCC) report estimated that black carbon emissions trail only carbon dioxide emissions as the largest contributor to global warming. A 2008 study published in *Nature Geoscience* concluded that black carbon soot from cooking and diesel exhaust, especially in Asia, likely played a more significant role in global climate change than was previously assumed. The study noted that coal and animal waste biomass (dung fuel) fueled cookers in China and India produced one-third of Earth's atmospheric concentrations of black carbon.

Soot and other types of black carbon equal approximately 60 percent of the world's warming effects from all carbon emissions. Experts estimate that reducing cooking related emissions could eliminate as much as 25 to 33 percent of the net observed effects of global warming.

The largest sources of black carbon emissions attributable to cooking are Asia, Latin America, and Africa. The type and amounts of cooking emissions vary by region and prevalent cooking technologies. The United States, for example, emits about 20 percent of the world's total carbon dioxide, but only 6 percent of the world's soot. Stricter emissions controls and the prevalence of in-home electric or gas-fueled food preparation technologies (refrigerators, stoves, ovens, crock pots, immersion circulators, and microwaves) reduce overall soot pollution despite increasing average household energy use. In South Asia, biomass-fueled cooking is more prevalent, whereas in eastern Asia, coal stoves or electric kitchen appliances (powered by coal-sourced energy) are common. Africa has the largest population of people who cook over open fires.

Although black carbon emissions are predominantly associated with open fire and biomass fueled cookstoves in developing regions, cooking in industrialized nations carries a carbon emissions footprint that also contributes to climate change. The modern kitchen comprises a significant portion of home energy use. Twenty minutes of cooking on a gas stove, one hour of cooking on an electric stove, and six days of refrigerating food all emit about one kilogram of carbon dioxide. Researchers in the United Kingdom determined that an average of 58 percent of carbon dioxide emissions linked to the use of potatoes occurs during the cooking of the potato. Preparing the potato by boiling produces more emissions than the average; microwaving the potato whole produces fewer emissions than the average by consuming less energy.

Whereas cooking is the end preparation for food, the production and transport of food also carry a carbon footprint worldwide in both developing and developed nations. Slash-and-burn land clearing in order to increase available farmland produces black carbon and soot. Tractors, agricultural machinery, and transport vehicles (trucks, trains, and boats) use fossil fuels and produce carbon emissions. Processed foods and exotically-sourced fresh foods carry increased carbon footprints from manufacture and transport long before they are prepared in home kitchens.

WORDS TO KNOW

BIOMASS: Plant material, agricultural debris, or animal waste that is used as a fuel or energy source, most commonly by burning.

BLACK CARBON: A pollutant emitted during the burning of biomass, coal, diesel, and other fossil fuel; a component of soot.

SOOT: A particulate air pollutant, primarily composed of carbon, produced by the incomplete combustion of biomass and fossil fuels.

■ Impacts and Issues

In order to reduce emissions, fight air pollution, and combat the effects of global climate change, environmental and development advocates favor a global

Urban administration officers prepare to destroy confiscated coal-fire stoves in Beijing, China, in February 2008. Officials attempted to eliminate the use of coal within Beijing's Third Ring Road, as part of an effort to reduce the city's notorious air pollution before the opening of the 2008 Olympic Games. The stoves, which use circular coal bricks, are commonly used for cooking and heating in older homes and restaurants. *AP Images.*

greening of foodways (peoples' eating habits) and food preparation technologies. The greening of agricultural production—especially the reduction of slash-and-burn land clearing in Asia, Africa, and South America, the world's black carbon hot spots—could help eliminate one quarter to half of all localized black carbon emissions in some regions. Developing alternative green fuels for agricultural machinery would also lower the carbon footprint of food. Choosing foods to cook that are locally grown decreases a meal's final carbon footprint by reducing transportation-related emissions. Cooking with less meat or fewer processed foods, which take more energy to produce, and an industry-wide reduction in the use of ozone-depleting gasses as food preservatives could also improve the environmental impacts of cooking.

Greening kitchens in industrial nations requires changing the energy demands of cooking appliances or changing people's methods of cooking. More efficient kitchen appliances lower household energy costs, moderate household energy use, and therefore reduce household emissions. Choosing to cook foods with microwaves or crock pots uses less energy than ovens and stoves. Eco-cooking methods, such as passive heat—heating up food on the stove, turning off the burners, and then leaving the food to finish cooking with the remnant heat—also save energy and lower the total emissions of cooking. Critics note that eco-cooking methods may not be safe for all foods and that microwaves

produce less desirable tasting foods than more energy-intensive cooking methods such as pan-searing, broiling, and grilling, making people less likely to choose the energy saving-alternative.

In developing nations, reducing black carbon emissions associated with open-hearth cooking depends on the development of better stoves that are durable, easy to maintain, desirable to use, produce good-tasting food, and are low cost. Developers of new portable cookstoves seek to replace traditional cooking practices with solar stoves, alternative fuel stoves, or stoves that consume less of the same fuel as traditional cookers. Black carbon and soot savings vary by the type of new cookstoves deployed. Solar stoves produce zero emissions, but are generally costlier and are limited in use by weather and extended cooking times. Fuel-burning stoves and ovens (usually improved efficiency coal or other biomass cookers) demonstrate 50 to 80 percent reductions in emissions when compared with traditional cooking methods and technologies.

Taste criticisms are not unique to industrialized kitchens. Adoption of cleaner cookstoves by local populations often is hampered by a preference for the taste of food cooked over open fires or on traditional stoves that produce more black carbon emissions.

■ Primary Source Connection

The widespread use of open fires for cooking food in underdeveloped areas has been found to be a significant contributor to global climate change, as well as a serious threat to the health of those who spend several hours of their day exposed to harmful wood smoke. A few non-governmental organizations, companies, and development and public health agencies have tried to replace these traditional stoves with cleaner alternatives, so far meeting with only isolated successes.

In her 2009 article for *Gourmet Magazine*, "Asia's Dirty Little Secret," Karen Coates explores first-hand some of the main issues and obstacles involved with the efforts to clean up cooking fires in southern Asia.

Karen Coates, an American journalist and author, has covered food, environmental, and social issues across Asia for publications around the world for more than a decade. She is author of *Cambodia Now: Life in the Wake of War* (2005), and co-author of *Pacific Lady: The First Woman to Sail Solo across the World's Largest Ocean* (2008). Karen served as *Gourmet's* Asia correspondent until the magazine's demise in 2009, and currently is a Ted Scripps Fellow in Environmental Journalism at the University of Colorado at Boulder.

Asia's Dirty Little Secret

A few years ago, I visited the cramped wooden hut of a Lahu tribal elder named Jamor, who lived high in the

A woman cares for her baby while preparing an earthen furnace to cook in one of the slums of Kolkata, India. *AP Images.*

hills of northern Thailand. It was a hot, dry day with a crisp, blue sky and brilliant light outside. But we stepped inside to a world of black, a house so caked in soot from years of endless cooking fires it looked as though the walls had been lacquered. The scene could have been anywhere in rural Asia. A fire smoldered in a rectangular pit. "I don't need a kitchen," Jamor said. "I cook here and eat here. The fire keeps insects away." I imagined Jamor's lungs to be as black as the walls.

Researchers have recently determined that soot, or black carbon, is a huge contributor to global climate change. That same indoor air pollution kills up to 1.6 million people a year, according to the World Health Organization. Women and children are most susceptible because they spend the most time around the cooking fire. This predicament has sent scientists, agencies, and institutes scrambling to supply the developing world with more efficient cooking stoves that save trees and emit fewer harmful particles. Some of the newfangled stoves rely on solar power, others turn trash into fuel, and still more simply burn wood more efficiently.

All good news, but a few key issues remain. Price is one of them. And some of these stoves cost S20—easily a month's wages for many of the world's poorest people. Other folks rely on donations or subsidies (and stove parts that must be imported), which is not necessarily sustainable. At least one solar-stove project aims to use carbon credits to fund fuel-efficient stoves, thereby making them free for their users. That might work in some places—when it's sunny—but what about those six months of monsoon rains? (Plus, this particular stove isn't powerful enough to fry food.)

A smokeless stove also leads to a critical question about taste and tradition. Many cooks swear by the flavor of fire. Smoke is an ancient ingredient in numerous Asian cuisines, which is precisely what a young Burmese woman announced to a large crowd gathered at an April Earth Day celebration at the American Center in Yangon, Myanmar. When the subject of cooking fires came up, she said she had a hard time persuading her relatives to abandon smoky stoves. Fire is tradition, and it's available. She noted another problem: Most locals have no idea what "environmental awareness" means. Her country's government doesn't exactly welcome education, nor are NGOs visiting the poorest, most remote regions. That means it's up to the Burmese people to work individually, using their own time and money to make small changes, step by step. It's slow, but sometimes it works.

That was the only surefire solution to come from the conversation: empathy and effort. Fourteen years ago, author C. J. Jepma pointed out in *Tropical Deforestation: A Socio-Economic Approach* that successful fuel conservation projects are those in which the people who design new gadgets work with—not just in the name of—the people who use them. Common sense, right? That means Jamor needs better protection from malaria-carrying mosquitoes before he gets rid of the fire that keeps the insects away. And it means his family needs a new way to cure the meats and dry the vegetables that normally hang above the family fire. I'm betting Jamor wouldn't forgo smoked pork for carbon credits. But he might for an empathetic friend who drinks his tea and listens to his stories.

Karen Coates

COATES, KAREN. "ASIA'S DIRTY LITTLE SECRET." *GOURMET* (SEPTEMBER 2009). HTTP://WWW.GOURMET.COM/TRAVEL/2009/09/KITCHEN-SMOKE-ASIA (ACCESSED NOVEMBER 29, 2010).

SEE ALSO *Agricultural Deforestation; Agroecology; Building Better Ovens; Climate Change and Agriculture; Women's Role in Global Food Preparation.*

BIBLIOGRAPHY

Books

Heyhoe, Kate. *Cooking Green: Reducing Your Carbon Footprint in the Kitchen: The New Green Basics Way.* Cambridge, MA: Da Capo Lifelong, 2009.

Rodger, Ellen. *Reducing Your Foodprint: Farming, Cooking, and Eating for a Healthy Planet.* St. Catherines, Ontario, Canada: Crabtree, 2010.

Periodicals

Dullo, Esther, Michael Greenstone, and Rema Hanna. "Cooking Stoves, Indoor Air Pollution and Respiratory Health in Rural Orissa." *Economic and Political Weekly* 43, no. 32 (2008): 71–76.

Mishra, Vinod, Xiaolei Dai, Kirk R. Smith, and Lasten Mika. "Maternal Exposure to Biomass Smoke and Reduced Birth Weight in Zimbabwe." *Annals of Epidemiology* 14, no. 10 (2004): 740–747.

Web Sites

"Black Carbon Implicated in Global Warming." *Science Daily*, July 30, 2010. http://www.sciencedaily.com/releases/2010/07/100729144225.htm (accessed November 1, 2010).

Global Alliance for Clean Cookstoves. http://cleancookstoves.org/ (accessed November 1, 2010).

Adrienne Wilmoth Lerner

Cooking Fats

■ Introduction

The use of fats and oils in cooking adds to the texture, flavor, and enjoyment of food. Oils lubricate food so it does not stick to the cooking vessel and allow cooking to take place at a much higher temperature than does boiling or steaming, because oils have higher boiling points than water. At higher cooking temperatures more complex chemical reactions occur between the food molecules, which promote the development of flavor. A higher cooking temperature also enables a crisper texture.

There is a wide range of cooking fats, which impart character to a region's cuisine. For instance, people in some parts of France cook mainly with butter, whereas in other regions olive oil is more popular. For health reasons, it is preferable to cook with monounsaturated fats such as olive oil, or polyunsaturated fats such as safflower oil. Saturated fats, which come mainly from animal sources but are also found in tropical fats including coconut oil and palm oil, raise cholesterol levels and may increase the risk of heart disease. Trans fats, found in margarine and in many baked goods, act like saturated fats, and many manufacturers are trying to eliminate them from their products. Fats in general are high in calories, providing about 9 calories per gram of fat.

■ Historical Background and Scientific Foundations

Cooking oils have been known for thousands of years but it is not clear how long they have been used in cooking. However, the Old Testament Book of Leviticus does make a distinction between bread baked in the oven and bread cooked in a griddle or pan. The frying of eggs is mentioned by Roman authors in the first century, and writers in the Middle Ages make frequent references to the frying of food. Fats and oils are complex mixtures of triglycerides, which consist of fatty acids chemically

bonded to a glycerol backbone. As such, they do not have a sharply defined melting point: Their structure weakens gradually from a firm solid to a spreadable material as different triglyceride components melt. Once liquid, a cooking fat can be heated to a high temperature that efficiently transfers heat to a food during the frying process. However, the cooking temperature is limited by the smoke point of the cooking fat. Ghee, a clarified butter that is often used in Indian cuisine, has a higher smoke point (375–485°F, 190–250°C depending on its purity) than does butter at 350°F (177°C). Extra virgin olive oil has a relatively low smoke point of 320°F (166°C). Frying can be either shallow, in which the cooking fat forms a thick layer on the surface of the cooking vessel with which the food comes into contact; or deep, which is popular for cooking fish: The food is immersed in hot oil.

The appeal of frying as a cooking method is that cooking fats collect heat gradually from the source; they can be kept easily at a constant temperature for consistent results; and the fats stay fluid so they can penetrate the food. The higher temperatures of cooking fat allow browning reactions to occur. Browning includes far more than just imparting a brown color to foods: It consists of many chemical processes related to the caramelization of the sugar content of a food and also the reaction between proteins and sugars in the food. The result is the availability of many hundreds of flavor compounds that add depth to the taste of fried foods. The higher the temperature of cooking, the more browning takes place. The lower limit for browning is 250°F (120°C), which is why it cannot occur during boiling but can during frying.

Cooking fats also play an important role in baking. Pastries, cakes, and cookies have a rich flavor and texture because of added fat. The fat stops water from hydrating the gluten protein molecules in the flour of the baking mixture. The gluten strands are therefore shorter, which is why fat in baking is sometimes known as shortening. The higher the fat content, the richer, flakier, and more tender a baked good will be. There is marked difference in a pie crust made with lard, which is 100 percent fat, rather than with butter or margarine, which are around 80 percent fat. Low-fat spreads, which contain a lot of water, are not suitable for baking. Moreover, solid fats hold air bubbles in a baking mixture and help aerate a cake, giving it a light texture. Fat also transports flavor molecules, many of which are fat soluble, to taste receptors in the mouth, so helps enhance the experience of consuming baked goods.

■ Impacts and Issues

There are two main categories of cooking fats. Saturated fats, such as butter and lard, generally come from animal sources, whereas unsaturated fats, such as corn, olive, and other vegetable oils, are derived from plant sources. Healthy eating advice recommends minimizing consumption of fried and baked goods because they are high in calories and, if made with saturated fat, will contribute to

The chef and owner of Sylvia's restaurant in New York cooks southern fried chicken using a soybean oil that doesn't contain trans fats. The New York City Board of Health voted December 5, 2006, to make New York the nation's first city to ban artificial trans fats at restaurants. *AP Images.*

WORDS TO KNOW

MONOUNSATURATED OIL: Oil with a fatty acid carbon chain containing one double or triple bond per molecule. Peanut oil, canola oil, and olive oil are examples of monounsaturated oils, which are thought to help lower LDL cholesterol levels in the blood.

OIL: A fat that is liquid at room temperature. Oils generally come from vegetable sources, and a wide range of oils are available for cooking.

POLYUNSATURATED OIL: Oil with a fatty acid carbon chain that contains multiple double or triple bonds in each molecule. Corn oil, safflower oil, soybean oil, and sesame oil are examples of polyunsaturated oils. Polyunsaturated oils are thought to help reduce LDL cholesterol levels in the blood.

SATURATED FAT: Fat in which the fatty acid chain contains only single bonds between carbon atoms in each molecule. Saturated fats are usually obtained from animal products, including lard and butter, but are also derived from plants, such as coconut oil and palm oil. Saturated fats are thought to increase LDL cholesterol levels in the blood.

SMOKE POINT: The temperature at which a cooking fat breaks down into visible gaseous products.

raised cholesterol levels in the blood. In recent years, attention has focused upon the health hazard posed by excess consumption of trans fatty acids. When it became apparent that saturated fat was associated with high cholesterol, manufacturers started to look for ways of substituting for it with healthier unsaturated fats. But unsaturated fats are not very stable, which is a drawback in processed goods intended to have a longer shelf life. Manufacturers began to hydrogenate these fats in an attempt to make them more stable. It is these partially hydrogenated fats that contain trans fatty acids, which are not found in nature.

Clinical studies showed that the sudden introduction of trans fatty acids into the human diet was linked to increased cholesterol and increased heart disease risk. Any product containing partially hydrogenated vegetable oils will have trans fatty acid in it. Typical products with trans fatty acids include solid margarines, high-fat baked goods such as donuts, French fries, and corn chips. Some manufacturers of processed foods have voluntarily removed trans fats from their products, and laws have been enacted against trans fats in some areas of the United states, including restaurants in the city of New York and in the state of California. Restaurant foods also must be free of trans fats by law in Switzerland and Denmark. Several additional nations are pursuing controls on foods containing trans fats.

IN CONTEXT: SATURATED FATS AND HEART DISEASE

In March 2010, a Harvard Medical School report that synthesized eight prior clinical studies concluded that replacing saturated fats with polyunsaturated fats can reduce the risk of heart disease by 20 percent in some people. Polyunsaturated fats are usually found in fish and vegetable derived oils. The study recommended that the normal healthy adult diet should restrict saturated fats that raise the levels of low-density lipoprotein cholesterol (LDL cholesterol), more commonly known as "bad cholesterol," that can block arterial flow to the heart and other organs. Many laboratory studies have shown that polyunsaturated fats promote high-density lipoprotein (HDL) or "good cholesterol" levels. The reductions in heart disease were observed in subjects who also avoided trans-fats substitutions for saturated fat. The report did not specifically address the impact of using monounsaturated fats (commonly found in oils such as olive oil) in comparison with polyunsaturated fats as a saturated fats substitute. In many cultures, olive oil routinely replaces butter as a source of fat in the daily diet.

In the meantime, evidence in support of the beneficial effects of a Mediterranean diet that emphasizes the use of olive oil has been accumulating. A 2004 summary by the U.S. Food and Drug Administration (FDA) concluded that olive oil, when substituted calorie-for-calorie for other cooking fats in the diet, has a protective effect against heart disease. Studies have also shown that olive oil consumption likely plays a large role in the lower incidence of breast and colon cancers occurring in the Mediterranean region, where olive oil is the primary fat in the diet. Current studies are under way to investigate a possible link with extra-virgin (first-pressed) olive oil consumption and increased longevity, along with reduced rates of Alzheimer's disease.

■ Primary Source Connection

Proctor & Gamble introduced Crisco to the American market in 1911. Advertised as more economical than lard, the 100 percent vegetable product was a revolutionary way to bake and fry foods. Proctor & Gamble created cookbooks and used home economists in cooking schools to spread the word of the ease and benefits of using Crisco.

Marion Harris Neil wrote and edited numerous cookbooks including *How to Cook in Casserole Dishes* published in 1912, and wrote the following article endorsing the use of Crisco in 1913. The claims made in the source below must be considered in the context of the fact that it is an advertisement for a product introduced almost 100 years ago. The formula for the product, which was originally made from hydrogenated cottonseed oil, has

changed several times since its arrival on the market, including a 2007 reformulation to remove trans fats.

The Story of Crisco

The culinary world is revising its entire cook book on account of the advent of Crisco, a new and altogether different cooking fat.

Many wonder that any product could gain the favor of cooking experts so quickly. A few months after the first package was marketed, practically every grocer of the better class in the United States was supplying women with the new product.

This was largely because four classes of people—housewives—chefs—doctors—dietitians—were glad to be shown a product which at once would make for more digestible foods, more economical foods, and better *tasting* foods.

. . .

It seems strange to many that there can be anything better than butter for cooking, or of greater utility than lard, and the advent of Crisco has been a shock to the older generation, born in an age less progressive than our own, and prone to contend that the old fashioned things are good enough.

But these good folk, when convinced, are the greatest enthusiasts. Grandmother was glad to give up the fatiguing spinning wheel. So the modern woman is glad to stop cooking with expensive butter, animal lard and their inadequate substitutes.

And so, the nation's cook book has been hauled out and is being revised. Upon thousands of pages, the words "lard" and "butter" have been crossed out and the word "Crisco" written in their place.

. . .

Man's Most Important Food, Fat

No other food supplies our bodies with the *drive,* the vigor, which fat gives. No other food has been given so little study in proportion to its importance.

Here are interesting facts, yet few housewives are acquainted with them:

Fat contains more than twice the amount of energy-yielding power or calorific value of proteins or carbohydrates. One half our physical energy is from the fat we eat in different forms. The excellent book, "Food and Cookery for the Sick and Convalescent," by Fannie Merritt Farmer, states, "In the diet of children at least, a deficiency of fat cannot be replaced by an excess of carbohydrates; and that fat seems to play some part in the formation of young tissues which cannot be undertaken by *any other constituent of food.* . . ."

The book entitled "The Chemistry of Cooking and Cleaning," by the two authorities, Ellen H. Richards and S. Maria Elliott, states that the diet of school children should be regulated carefully with the fat supply in view. Girls, especially, show at times a dislike for fat. It therefore is necessary that the fat which supplies their growing bodies with energy should be in the purest and most inviting form and should be one that their digestions *welcome,* rather than repel.

The first step in the digestion of fat is its melting. Crisco melts at a lower degree of heat than body temperature. Because of its low melting point, thus allowing the digestive juices to mix with it, and because of its vegetable origin and its purity, Crisco is the easiest of all cooking fats to digest.

When a fat smokes in frying, it "breaks down," that is, its chemical composition is changed; part of its altered composition becomes a non-digestible and irritating substance. The best fat for digestion is one which does *not* decompose or break down at frying temperature. Crisco does not break down until a degree of heat is reached *above* the frying point. In other words, Crisco does not break down at all in normal frying, because it is not necessary to have it "smoking hot" for frying. No part of it, therefore, has been transformed in cooking into an irritant. That is one reason why the stomach welcomes Crisco and carries forward its digestion with ease.

A part of the preliminary work done in connection with the development of Crisco, described in these pages, consisted of the study of the older cooking fats. The objectionable features of each were considered. The good was weighed against the bad. The strength and weakness of each was determined. Thus was found what the ideal fat should possess, and what it should *not* possess. It must have every good quality and no bad one.

After years of study, a process was discovered which made possible the ideal fat.

The process involved the changing of the composition of vegetable food oils and the making of the richest fat or solid *cream.*

The Crisco Process at the first stage of its development gave, at least, the basis of the ideal fat; namely, a purely *vegetable* product, differing from all others in that absolutely no animal fat had to be added to the vegetable oil to produce the proper stiffness. This was but one of the many distinctive advantages sought and found.

· · ·

It was the earnest aim of the makers of Crisco to produce a strictly *vegetable* product without adding a hard, and consequently indigestible animal fat. There is today a pronounced partiality from a health standpoint to a vegetable fat, and the lardy, greasy taste of food resulting from the use of animal fat never has been in such disfavor as during the past few years.

So Crisco is absolutely *all* vegetable. No stearine, animal or vegetable, is added. It possesses no taste nor odor save the delightful and characteristic aroma which identifies Crisco, and is suggestive of its purity.

· · ·

The shortening fat in pastry or baked foods, is merely distributed throughout the dough. No chemical change occurs during the baking process. So when you eat pie or hot biscuit, in which animal lard is used, *you eat raw animal lard.* The shortening used in all baked foods therefore, should be just as pure and wholesome as if you were eating it like butter upon bread. Because Crisco digests with such ease, and because it is a pure vegetable fat, all those who realize the above fact regarding pastry making are now won over to Crisco.

A hint as to Crisco's purity is shown by this simple test: Break open a hot biscuit in which Crisco has been used. You will note a sweet fragrance, which is most inviting.

A few months ago if you had told dyspeptic men and women that they could eat pie at the evening meal and that distress would not follow, probably they would have doubted you. Hundreds of instances of Crisco's healthfulness have been given by people, who, at one time have been denied such foods as pastry, cake and fried foods, but who *now* eat these rich, yet digestible Crisco dishes.

You, or any other normally healthy individual, whose digestion does not relish greasy foods, can eat rich pie crust. The richness is there, but not the unpleasant after effects. Crisco digests *readily.*

A good digestion will mean much to the youngster's health and character. A man seldom seems to be stronger than his stomach, for indigestion handicaps him in his accomplishment of big things.

As more attention is given to *present* feeding, less attention need be given to *future* doctoring. Equip your children with good stomachs by giving them wholesome Crisco foods—foods which digest with ease.

They may eat the rich things they enjoy and find them just as digestible as many apparently simple foods, if Crisco be used properly.

They may eat Crisco doughnuts or pie without being chased by nightmares. Sweet dreams follow the Crisco supper.

· · ·

Crisco is being used in an increasing number of the better class hotels, clubs, restaurants, dining cars, ocean liners.

Crisco has been demonstrated and explained upon the Chautauqua platform by Domestic Science experts, these lectures being a part of the regular course.

Domestic Science teachers recommend Crisco to their pupils and use it in their classes and lecture demonstrations. Many High Schools having Domestic Science departments use Crisco.

Crisco has taken the place of butter and lard in a number of hospitals, where purity and digestibility are of *vital* importance.

Crisco is Kosher. Rabbi Margolies of New York, said that the Hebrew Race had been waiting 4,000 years for Crisco. It conforms to the strict Dietary Laws of the Jews. It is what is known in the Hebrew language as a "parava," or neutral fat. Crisco can be used with both "milchig" and "fleichig" (milk and flesh) foods. Special Kosher packages, bearing the seals of Rabbi Margolies of New York, and Rabbi Lifsitz of Cincinnati, are sold the Jewish trade. But all Crisco is Kosher and all of the same purity.

Marion Harris Neil

NEIL, MARION HARRIS. *THE STORY OF CRISCO.* CINCINNATI: PROCTOR & GAMBLE CO., 1913.

SEE ALSO *Dairy Products; Diet and Cancer; Diet and Heart Disease; Dietary Changes in Rapidly Developing Countries; Hydrogenated Fats and Trans Fats; Mediterranean Diet.*

BIBLIOGRAPHY

Books

Gursche, Siegfried. *Good Fats and Oils: Why We Need Them and How to Use Them in the Kitchen.* Summertown, TN: Alive Books, 2007.

Yellow Fats, Butter and Spreads. London: Mintel International, 2006.

Periodicals

Angell, Sonia Y., et al. "Cholesterol Control beyond the Clinic: New York City's Trans Fat Restriction." *Annals of Internal Medicine* 151, no. 2 (2009): 129–134.

Chen, Guanyi, Ming Ying, and Weizhun Li. "Enzymatic Conversion of Waste Cooking Oils into Alternative Fuel-Biodiesel." *Applied Biochemistry and Biotechnology* 132, no. 1–3 (2006): 129–132.

Kontogianni, Meropi D., et al. "The Impact of Olive Oil Consumption Pattern on the Risk of Acute Coronary Syndromes: The Cardio2000 Case-Control Study." *Clinical Cardiology* 30, no. 3 (2007): 125–129.

La Vecchia, Carlo. "Association between Mediterranean Dietary Patterns and Cancer Risk." *Nutrition Reviews* 67, suppl. 1 (May 2009): 126–129.

Sanders, Tom A. B. "The Role of Fat in the Diet—Quantity, Quality, and Sustainability." *Nutrition Bulletin* 35, no. 2 (2010): 138–146.

Zevenbergen, Hans, et al. "Foods with a High Fat Quality Are Essential for Healthy Diets." *Annals of Nutrition & Metabolism* 54, suppl. 1 (2009): 15–24.

Web Sites

Bliss, Rosalie Marion. "Molecular Biology Provides Clues to Health Benefits of Olive Oil." *U.S. Department of Agriculture (USDA),* June 28, 2010. http://www.ars.usda.gov/is/pr/2010/100628.htm (accessed September 22, 2010).

Susan Aldridge

Corn

■ Introduction

Corn, or maize, is a coarse grain used to feed people and livestock. It has a wide variety of shades, most commonly yellow or white, although some varieties are orange, blue, and other shades. The annual corn harvest outweighs that of any other grain. Corn is made into a wide variety of processed foods, industrial products, and livestock feeds. The United States is both the largest producer and the largest exporter of corn in the world. For this reason, policy actions by the United States that affect corn have an impact on international prices of corn and of all coarse grains.

■ Historical Background and Scientific Foundations

Corn is the world's most harvested grain by weight. Also called field corn or maize, corn is a staple food in the diet of many people in the world, especially in the Americas and in Sub-Saharan Africa. Corn was first harvested in what is now Mexico and Central America around 10,000 years ago, although the biological and archeological records are largely incomplete. The Maya and Aztec civilizations at the time used corn extensively for food, and corn appears to have been traded very early in its history. With the arrival of European settlers and trade between the Americas and the Old World, corn spread to all regions of the globe, where it replaced other cereals such as millet in the local diets; the younger ears, known as sweet corn or dessert corn, were consumed as a fresh starchy vegetable. Hybrid varieties of corn were developed from various existing types of corn, also called landraces, beginning in the late nineteenth century, and hybridization remains a primary strategy for increasing yields.

During the Green Revolution starting in the 1940s, higher-yielding varieties of corn became available. Unlike the dwarf varieties of crops such as wheat, rice, and sorghum that emerged during the Green Revolution, corn was reduced only to a stalk of 8.2 feet (2.5 meters), though some landraces can grow stalks of up to 23 feet (7 meters).

In 1996 genetically modified (GM) corn became available in the United States. Corn is the third most dominant GM crop in the world following soybeans and cotton, and GM corn took up 26 percent of the world's planted area in 2009 according to GMO Compass. GM corn predominates in the United States and Argentina, where it comprised 85 percent of planted area in 2009. GM corn is one reason corn production has expanded greatly in the twenty-first century. According to the U.S. Department of Agriculture's Foreign Agricultural Service (USDA/FAS), coarse grains such as corn expanded only 1.6 percent in area planted between 2001 and 2009, though production expanded 23 percent.

The grain of corn is found on what is called an ear, on which the grains surround a cob, an inedible hard center. The ear is surrounded by a husk like other grains, but beneath the husk, small strands of fiber called silk are found. Cornhusks are used in some cuisines as wrappers for preparing foods for steaming or baking. Young corn can be eaten as a vegetable, and sweet corn like this is canned, frozen, cooked fresh, or served raw in many parts of the world. Sweet corn and processed corn have been incorporated into many cuisines, and some varieties of sweet corn have been bred to be sweeter. In general, the sweeter corn has a shorter stalk than field corn used as a grain. Like many fresh vegetables, sweet corn remains sweeter by reducing the time between when it is harvested and eaten or processed. Field corn is processed in one of two ways. Wet millers process field corn grains to produce high fructose corn syrup and other sweeteners, corn oil, corn starch, fuel ethanol, and a wide variety of other alcohols both for human consumption and for industrial uses. Dry millers process corn grains to produce breakfast cereals such as corn flakes, corn grits widely used as a porridge and for use in producing beer, corn flour, and cornmeal.

Livestock on feed lots or in concentrated animal feeding operations (CAFOs) are fed most of the corn and coarse grains produced in the United States. Corn is also fed to pastured livestock as winter or off-season feed, as well as supplemental feed. Corn is by far the most common coarse grain, accounting for around 75 percent of traded coarse grain. Other coarse grains include oats, rye, barley, and sorghum. Corn is a high-protein ingredient in many commercially produced livestock feeds. Corn, including the entire stalk, can be dried or can be stored wet and fermented to produce silage, a high-nutrient feed stock for livestock that is easy for ruminants such as cows, goats, and sheep to digest. Because corn is commonly used as a feed grain, sometimes coarse grains are called feed grains.

■ Impacts and Issues

The United States produces more corn and exports more corn than any other country in the world, supplying around 60 percent of traded corn from 2003 to 2008, according to the U.S. Department of Agriculture's Economic Research Service (USDA/ERS). However, within the United States, exports of corn are only one source of demand. Exports only make up between 15 and 20 percent of use in any given year for the United States. For this reason, economists state that the United States has market power; in other words, the actions of corn producers and consumers in the United States have a large influence on the price in the world market by changing the size of supply and demand. As the United States makes up a majority of the world market, but the world market does not constitute a majority of the U.S. market for domestic corn producers, market conditions in the

Several varieties of native maize from Venezuela illustrate a biodiversity that is being lost with new hybrids and genetically modified corn increasing in popularity and creating monoculture crops for global production. © *Jacques Jangoux / Alamy.*

United States drive corn prices worldwide. As corn predominates within traded coarse grains, because corn is a substitute for other coarse grains, the price of corn has an influence on the price of other coarse grains. Corn has, historically, experienced a natural stabilization of supply.

The second largest exporter of corn is the South American country of Argentina. Because the Southern hemisphere's season for planting corn in Argentina follows the vast majority of the harvest in the United States, Argentinean farmers can substitute corn for other crops when prices are high or when there is a reduced supply from the United States. Other countries including Brazil, Romania, South Africa, and Ukraine also appear to respond to higher prices or lowered U.S. supplies by exporting more corn. The largest corn import markets are Japan and South Korea, both of which produce very few coarse grains even though they have expanding livestock sectors.

The market power of the United States in corn has been one factor in food price crises. For example, in the 1970s U.S. corn exports grew by huge amounts. In 1970, 13 million metric tons of corn were exported, but by 1980, 63 million metric tons were being exported. One factor in this hugely increased demand was that at the time, the former Soviet Union, instead of reducing animal stocks in response to grain shortfalls, decided to import American corn as livestock feed. However, the hugely increased profits and rising prices for commodities such as corn, along with hefty subsidies of corn and low interest rates, caused many farmers in the United States in corn-producing regions to bid these profits into acquiring more land. In the 1980s, as a result of the increased land values, but rising interest rates and falling corn prices, many farmers faced a mortgage crisis: They owed more money for their land than the land was then worth.

U.S. subsidies are heavily concentrated in a few commodities such as corn. According to the Environment Working Group (EWG) using data from USDA, corn is the most subsidized crop in the United States: Corn subsidies between 1995 and 2009 totaled almost 74 billion U.S. dollars, dwarfing subsidies for wheat (31 billion dollars), cotton (30 billion dollars), soybeans (23 billion dollars), and rice (13 billion dollars), or peanuts (3 billion dollars). However, other subsidies for corn occur outside the farm policy environment.

Due to energy demand for corn ethanol, mostly a response to monetary incentives and other U.S. government policies, corn prices shot up dramatically in 2007 and 2008. From 2004 to 2006, the price of corn increased 54 percent according to USDA/ERS. The price rose again in 2007 and 2008 by a further 28 percent. Part of this rise in price was rise in demand for corn in the United States for use in corn ethanol as a biofuel. Also, demand continued to grow from developing countries. Other than the United States, the other country whose agricultural policies influence the international

IN CONTEXT: RESTRICTIONS ON GENETICALLY MODIFIED CORN

In 1998, MON 810 Bt maize, a genetically modified maize that contains a gene from a bacteria that creates a toxin deadly to certain caterpillars, became the only genetically modified (GM) crop approved by the European Union (EU) for commercial use. Despite this approval, current EU law allows individual countries to bar GM crops. In April 2009 Germany banned the cultivation and sale of Monsanto's MON 810, joining France and several other European nations that had already banned the same type of genetically modified maize over environmental and human health concerns. Monsanto filed a lawsuit against Germany several days after the ban was announced, but lost the case in May 2009 after an administrative court in Brunswick sided with the German government, stating that there was sufficient evidence of environmental risks. Monsanto stated it would consider further legal action. The European Union Food Safety Authority stated in June 2009 that the maize was safe and "unlikely to have any adverse effects on the environment."

price of corn is China. In some seasons China imports corn and in others it exports corn, and has done so in quantities large enough to become the second largest exporter some years. These swings largely depend on tax policy and export subsidies, as China maintains a domestic price for corn above that found on international markets through its policies. Therefore, both U.S. biofuel policy and Chinese demand for coarse grains both contributed to the dramatic price rises in 2007 and 2008.

SEE ALSO *Agribusiness; Biofuels and World Hunger; Ethical Issues in Agriculture; Factory Farming; Food Price Crisis; Free Trade and Agriculture; Genetically Modified Organisms (GMO); Grains; Green Revolution (1943); Latin American Diet; Subsidies.*

BIBLIOGRAPHY

Books

Danforth, Arn T. *Corn Crop Production: Growth, Fertilization and Yield.* New York: Nova Science Publishers, 2009.

Fitting, Elizabeth M. *The Struggle for Maize: Campesinos, Workers, and Transgenic Corn in the Mexican Countryside.* Durham, NC: Duke University Press, 2011.

Nassauer, Joan I., Mary V. Santelmann, and Donald Scavia. *From the Corn Belt to the Gulf: Societal and Environmental Implications of Alternative Agricultural Futures.* Washington, DC: Resources for the Future, 2007.

NGCA. *Corn: Nature's Sustainable Resource.* Washington, DC: National Corn Growers Association, 2006.

Samuelson, Sheila, and Ed Williams. *The Feel-Good Heat: Pioneers of Corn and Biomass Energy.* North Liberty, IA: Ice Cube Press, 2007.

Staller, John E., Robert H. Tykot, and Bruce F. Benz. *Histories of Maize in Mesoamerica: Multidisciplinary Approaches.* Walnut Creek, CA: Left Coast Press, 2010.

Watts, Martin. *Corn Milling.* Oxford, UK: Shire, 2008.

Periodicals

"Kill King Corn." *Nature* 449, no. 7163 (2007): 637.

Web Sites

"Briefing Rooms: Corn: Trade." *U.S. Department of Agriculture Economic Research Service (USDA/ERS).* http://www.ers.usda.gov/Briefing/corn/trade.htm (accessed November 15, 2010).

"Corn." *U.S. Department of Agriculture Economic Research Service (USDA/ERS).* http://www.ers.usda.gov/Briefing/Corn/ (accessed October 23, 2010).

"Corn Cam." *Iowa Farmer Today.* http://www.iowafarmertoday.com/corn_cam/ (accessed October 23, 2010).

Kleim, Brandon. "Fast Food Just Another Name for Corn." *Wired Science*, November 10, 2008. http://www.wired.com/wiredscience/2008/11/fast-food-anoth/ (accessed October 23, 2010).

Podmolick, Mary Ellen. "Trade Group Seeks Name Change for High-Fructose Corn Syrup." *Los Angeles Times*, September 15, 2010. http://articles.latimes.com/2010/sep/15/business/la-fi-corn-sugar-20100915 (accessed October 23, 2010).

Blake Jackson Stabler

Culinary Education

Introduction

For most of history, cooking techniques and recipes were primarily an oral tradition. People were either born into cooking because that was their family's trade, or it was one of the few options available to their social class. With the emergence of restaurants and hotels as independent businesses, however, cooking became a viable career option, and individuals interested in cooking began to seek culinary education. For most of the nineteenth century the only cooking instruction available was apprenticeship, in which an apprentice worked with a master cook to learn the trade before striking out on his or her own. However, in 1895, with the founding of Le Cordon Bleu cooking school in Paris—the first culinary school to gain notoriety internationally—culinary education began to codify into a more regimented and organized system.

Historical Background and Scientific Foundations

It is impossible to discuss the development of culinary education without discussing the French chef Georges-Auguste Escoffier (1846–1935). Escoffier studied under some of the most eminent chefs of his day, but his crowning achievement was writing *Le Guide Culinaire*, which codified and organized French cooking techniques. *Le Guide Culinaire* is still in print and remains part of the curriculum of most major culinary education programs in the early twenty-first century. In addition, Escoffier developed what is called *the brigade system*, which is a hierarchical arrangement that assigns specific tasks to certain cooks in a kitchen. Before the brigade system, the kitchen operated as a single chef and a group of assistants, all of whom simply responded to the orders of the chef as needed. Under the brigade system, a chef is still in charge of the kitchen as a whole, but every other person in the kitchen has a specific set of

tasks upon which to focus. Classic positions in the brigade system are the *saucier*, who makes sauces for all the dishes, the *poissonier*, who is responsible for cooking fish and seafood, and the *grillardin*, who operates the grill, among others. While not all restaurants need every position included in the classic brigade system, some form of this basic structure is still the most common organization for modern kitchens.

These two contributions helped to lay the foundation for formal culinary education. *Le Guide Culinaire* helped by giving culinary educators around the world a reference standard for most major techniques and recipes. The brigade system altered the former apprenticeship model by introducing the concept of a *commis*, or an assistant for each station, who studied under a more experienced cook to learn the station before moving up in responsibility.

When Le Cordon Bleu cooking school opened in Paris in 1895, it was the first school to offer classes on culinary arts to gain international renown. Culinary art schools quickly replaced the apprenticeship model as the primary style of culinary education, and currently there are culinary programs offered at many secondary education institutions worldwide. Most culinary schools provide a two-year Associate's degree, with many offering a Bachelor's degree as well.

Impacts and Issues

The impact of formalized culinary education on the foodservice industry has been a flood of qualified, educated workers on the market, aspiring to make a working wage. Under the old system, a novice chef would work up through all the stations in a kitchen, and then eventually move on to start a kitchen of his or her own. The advantage of this program was that by the time the apprentice started a restaurant or became the chef of a hotel or other establishment, he or she would have years of hands-on experience. The downside was that the student knew only the methods and techniques of one

WORDS TO KNOW

BRIGADE SYSTEM: A system of kitchen organization in which each person in the kitchen is assigned a specific station and task.

COMMIS: The assistant to a cook in the brigade system, who acts as apprentice and understudy to the cook.

STAGE: To work in a kitchen for no wages to gain experience.

particular master chef. Unless one is fortunate enough to find work in restaurants of drastically different styles, it is difficult to reproduce the broad scope of techniques, styles, and ideas presented in culinary programs. Attending a modern culinary school exposes students to many different cooking styles and techniques, but can provide only a limited amount of hands-on experience. In fact, many culinary schools state that graduating from their program will not make one a great chef, but it will give them the tools they need in order to become great chef.

In the early twenty-first century, there exists some occasional industry backlash against culinary school graduates versus cooks that start working in kitchens early and gain hands-on experience in lieu of attending school. Some workers in the food service industry consider culinary graduates stereotypical graduate cooks: arrogant, inexperienced, and difficult to work with. Many culinary schools are working against this stereotype by reminding their students of the importance of real life experience. Also, many culinary school graduates have debt in student loans and therefore require a higher starting wage than most new employees in the restaurant industry. For these reasons, some chefs prefer to staff their kitchens with experienced workers who did not attend culinary school. Historically, in some major cities with large immigrant populations, many find work in restaurant kitchens. Although these employees lack the range of knowledge of a culinary education, they have both the necessary years of hands-on experience and require less monetary compensation than culinary graduates. Also, it is not uncommon for high-end restaurants to require new cooks to *stage* for a few weeks prior to being hired, or work without wages to gain experience in a particular restaurant.

Although modern cooking schools have become more popular than the old apprentice system in developed countries, hands-on experience remains vital to the study of culinary arts. It is very rare for a graduate of

Students prepare Gâteau Saint Honoré in their baking and pastry class at the newly renamed International Culinary Schools at The Art Institutes, in Pittsburgh, Pennsylvania, 2007. *AP Images.*

culinary school to immediately become a successful independent chef without several years of industry experience. Rather, in a variant of the old apprentice system, it is common for most culinary school graduates to spend a few years working in various restaurants to gain experience before branching off on their own. In some cases, aspiring chefs will travel to foreign countries to study under chefs native to the cooking style they favor with the goal of taking their experience home to open their own restaurant.

The global interest in culinary arts is an increasing trend, and there is a growing level of culinary education being offered to the general public in developed nations. Most kitchen supply stores have public cooking or technique classes available, and many companies offer in-home lessons for private parties or events. Some of the large culinary education institutions have started to offer short basic cooking programs to the public as well. The growing popularity of private cooking classes for non-professionals is expanding the career field for culinary educators, to the point that it has become possible to study cooking with the intent of becoming a private culinary instructor. The creation of new job categories in the culinary field is important, because with each graduating class from culinary schools there is another group of aspiring chefs and restaurateurs seeking opportunities.

SEE ALSO *Celebrity Chef Phenomenon; Food and the Internet; Food Critics and Ratings; Food Styling; Gastronomy; Gourmet Hobbyists and Foodies; Immigration and Cuisine.*

BIBLIOGRAPHY

Books

Darling, Katherine. *Under the Table: Saucy Tales from Culinary School.* New York: Atria Books, 2009.

Eguaras, Louis, and Matthew Frederick. *101 Things I Learned in Culinary School.* New York: Grand Central Pub, 2010.

Periodicals

Müller, Keith F., Dawn VanLeeuwen, Keith Mandabach, and Robert J. Harrington. "The Effectiveness of Culinary Curricula: A Case Study." *International Journal of Contemporary Hospitality Management* 21, no. 2 (2009): 167–178.

Tumlison, Katie M., Margaret Harris, Reza Hakkak, and Polly A. Carrol. "Student Behavior Outcomes of an Expanded Nutrition Curriculum in Culinary School of Apprenticeship." *Journal of the American Dietetic Association* 107, no. 8 (2007): A56.

Web Sites

"Ecosystems: Agroecosystems: Agriculture." *United States Environmental Protection Agency (EPA).* http://www.epa.gov/ebtpages/ecosagroecosystemsagriculture.html (accessed September 17, 2010).

The Journal of Culinary Education. http://culinaryeducation.org/ (accessed September 17, 2010).

David Brennan Tilove

Cult Diets

Introduction

Diets promising quick and easy weight loss have been part of American culture for more than a century, but an increase in obesity and the knowledge of weight-related diseases and disorders has brought them renewed notoriety. More people than ever diet in an attempt to lose weight, while others diet to improve their health, cure specific illnesses, detoxify themselves, and develop their spirituality. Doctors and nutritionists warn of the health risks associated with some unconventional, nutritionally unbalanced dietary regimes, and social scientists are intrigued by dieters' lifestyles and what their behavior reveals about their cultures, their personal relationships with food, and their mental health.

Some diets may described as cults. One common definition of a cult is a group of people who follow an ideology that is seen as extreme or outside the mainstream, often with excessive devotion to a charismatic and authoritarian leader. As with any religion or ideology, disciples hold certain principles sacred and must perform distinctive rituals. Another definition of a cult is a system for the cure of a disease based on dogma set forth by a practitioner, as in a health cult. Although most popular diets do not explicitly include a spiritual component (though there are exceptions, including the Hallelujah diet, some raw food diets, and some versions of macrobiotics), religions often do include dietary restrictions, and the symbolic nature of food lends itself easily to cult-like behavior. Most people, however, maintain that it is the zeal with which a popular or fad diet is practiced that makes it a cult, and not the nature of the diet plan itself. Individual obsession with a diet may also be seen as a condition called orthorexia.

Historical Background and Scientific Foundations

Dietary advice promising weight loss and freedom from disease was common well before scientists discovered calories or carbohydrates. In the 1830s, Presbyterian minister Sylvester Graham (1794–1851) traveled the United States promoting unleavened bread (and Graham crackers) as part of a diet that reduced intemperance, gluttony, and lust. In the 1850s, Seventh Day Adventists touted the advantages of a vegetarian diet from their headquarters in Battle Creek, Michigan, and in 1876 the American physician John Harvey Kellogg (1852–1943), an ardent Grahamite, became the director of an Adventist health center in Battle Creek later known as the Battle Creek Sanitarium or The San. The Sanitarium catered to wealthy patients with diverse therapies including regular enemas, exercise, and abstinence from sexual relations, along with a strict diet emphasizing fiber, whole grains, and nuts. Meat, alcohol, and spices were discouraged. The San and its alternative diets for the upper class flourished for more than 50 years.

Meanwhile, English coffin and cabinet maker William Banting (1797–1878) published the first bestselling diet plan, his *Letter on Corpulence: Addressed to the Public*, in 1863. In his pamphlet, Banting shared the diet that was prescribed by his physician to help Banting lose almost 50 pounds. The diet excluded starchy foods, butter, sugar, and beer. The "Banting system" became popular in both Europe and America, and the popular mystery writer Agatha Christie (1891–1976) was still writing about women who were "banting" in 1927. A German physician promoted the first low-carbohydrate diet in the 1880s, and near the turn of the twentieth century, corpulent American businessman Horace Fletcher (1849–1919) recommended more thorough chewing—typically 32 times per mouthful or 100 times per minute—as the preferred way to reduce weight and improve vitality. Fletcherism was promoted at the Battle Creek Sanitarium, and like the Banting and German low-carbohydrate diets, was widely popular with magazines and celebrities of the day.

It is notable that a newspaper article on "39 False Food Fads" had already been published by *The Washington Post* in 1910, declaring that among other things, it was wrong that "prolonged mastication should be made a cult." This negative press did not change public attitudes towards the new diets, nor notably lessen the likelihood that people would try them. The 1920s saw the beginning of calorie counting and weight-reducing diets based on spinach, or lamb chops with pineapple. The 1930s ushered in the mostly meat Arctic diet (which resembled current Paleolithic diets), weight loss pills such as dinitrophenol and amphetamines, the Hay diet, the natural hygiene movement, and a banana-skim-milk diet. In the 1940s Hollywood celebrities did the "Master Cleanse" (popularized again as pop star Beyonce's maple-syrup-lemonade-cayenne-pepper fast in 2006), and the mostly grapefruit "Mayo Clinic Diet" (not endorsed by the Mayo Clinic). The following decades saw the waxing and waning popularity of thousands of diet books, programs, and products, including raw food diets, the Rice Plan, the Weston A. Price Foundation's "traditional foods" diet, macrobiotic diets, Weight Watchers, Atkins, South Beach, Scarsdale, Rockefeller, Pennington, Fit for Life, and the Zone diets, blood type diets, cabbage soup regimes, baby food diets, liquid protein diets, the HCG diet, and primal living and Paleolithic lifestyle plans. Some diet organizations, such as Weight Watchers, that are based upon nutritionally balanced weight reduction, continue to devote resources to encouraging members to make food choices based upon fact rather than fad or popularity.

At its most extreme, diet and food can be used as a measure of exerting control on vulnerable members of a cult-like group. In Australia during the 1990s, for example, an organization that promoted a diet called the Vibrational Individuation Program targeted pregnant women and their babies to receive specialized and restrictive diets based upon the movements of their various muscle groups. Clients paid for repeated "food tests" and for variations of a diet that usually included only five or six foods and always included supplements of offal. Members resided at a group home while participating in parts of the diet. Shortly after the program caught the attention of Australian authorities in 2000, hundreds of participating babies and children were identified as underweight or malnourished.

■ Impacts and Issues

Any fashionable diet can be classified as a fad, and any diet that is followed with excessive devotion by numerous people will probably be called a cult. Neither classification necessarily makes a particular diet unhealthy, but as American physician Steven Bratman pointed out in *Health Food Junkies* in 2000, diets with certain philosophical and spiritual ideologies lead to orthorexia or cult-like behavior more easily than others. These are often the same diets to which people can become truly committed, and that work well for them. Although some of these diets are balanced and nutritious, many lack sufficient protein, particular vitamins, fiber, or calories for long-term use. Very rapid weight loss weakens the immune system and can cause muscle loss and permanent damage to the heart and blood vessels. Crash dieting (non-nutritionally sound

rapid weight loss) may also lead to heart arrhythmia, dehydration, kidney damage, and, paradoxically, an increase in weight after the diet is discontinued, commonly known as rebound or yo-yo weight gain.

In addition to examining how well diets supply basic nutritional needs, some other aspects of popular diets demand scrutiny. Diets that make unrealistic claims, promising results within days or weeks, or with little effort, and purport to cure everything from dandruff to cancer should be viewed with skepticism, regardless of the personal testimonials that accompany them. Diets that require expensive products, especially those sold exclusively by their promoters, are also suspect. Diets that categorize common nutritious foods along with the people who eat them as virtuous or evil, exaggerate the benefits of a single food, or draw simplistic conclusions from complicated scientific studies (or especially a single study) should also be viewed critically. Many cult diets share similarities with conspiracy theories as well as with social or religious cults: They claim to possess secret knowledge, often from the past or from some exotic part of the world, and their promoters and followers are said to be subject to persecution by "diet dictocrats" or sadly misunderstood by the nutritional establishment. If a diet doesn't work, or someone stops practicing it for some other reason, the person may be characterized as weak for not properly following the dietary rules, addicted to SAD (the Standard American Diet), or a victim of brainwashing by corporate agribusinesses or another less enlightened food ideology.

In general, doctors continue to emphasize that weight loss can be healthfully achieved and sustained only by restricting calories and increasing activity in relation to calories consumed. However, some fad diets are promoted by individual doctors in advertisements and in

Various diet books are displayed at a bookstore. Advocates of the South Beach and Atkins diets want the public to give their approaches a try, saying they are not that different from the official recommendations from the United States government. Critics note that both diets involve giving up essential food groups. *AP Images.*

media interviews, who claim them to be proven effective, causing consumers to be understandably confused. A recent survey of popular diet books' claims found that more than half of the nutrition "facts" presented were not supported by the peer-reviewed medical literature.

SEE ALSO *Eating Disorders; Food and Body Image; Food Fads; Food Phobias.*

BIBLIOGRAPHY

Books

Hesse-Biber, Sharlene N. *The Cult of Thinness.* New York: Oxford University Press, 2007.

Lankford, Ronald D. *Can Diets Be Harmful?* Detroit: Greenhaven Press, 2007.

Periodicals

Anderson-Fye, Eileen P., and Jielu Lin. "Belief and Behavior Aspects of the Eat-26: The Case of Schoolgirls in Belize." *Culture, Medicine, and Psychiatry* 33, no. 4 (2009): 623–638.

Drummond, Sandra. "Bringing the Sense Back into Healthy Eating Advice." *The Journal of Family Health Care* 16, no. 5 (2006): 143–145.

Lee, Jennifer, et al. "Beyond the Hazard: The Role of Beliefs in Health Risk Perception." *Human and Ecological Risk Assessment: An International Journal* 11, no. 6 (2005): 1111–1126.

"The Simplicity Diet Fad—After a Variety of Hot Diet Books Extolling Extreme Nutritional Approaches, Common Sense Returns to the Table." *Publishers Weekly* 252, no. 45 (2005): 28.

Van Horn, Linda. "Nutritional Research: The Power behind the Fad-Free Diet." *Journal of the American Dietetic Association* 107, no. 3 (2007): 371.

Web Sites

Howard, Mike. "Is Your Diet a Cult?" *Dietblog.* http://www.diet-blog.com/08/is_your_diet_a_cult.php (accessed September 6, 2010).

Sandra Dunavan

Dairy Products

■ Introduction

The unique physical and chemical composition of milk has enabled the manufacture of several foods that play an important role in human nutrition and enjoyment of food. Milk and its associated products are called dairy products and are now the output of a highly complex food industry, although they have been produced by hand for thousands of years. Milk itself is the food of baby mammals; humans are unusual in consuming the milk of other species into adult life. The fat in milk can be concentrated to form various types of creams that are valued in cuisine for their texture. Churning milk solidifies its fat globules to make butter. The action of bacteria on milk can be exploited to produce yogurts and a very wide range of cheeses with different flavor and texture characteristics. Dairy products are nutritious because they provide calcium, protein, and energy. But many people in less developed countries cannot break down the lactose sugar in milk. Furthermore, milk proteins may cause allergies, and some dairy products, such as butter and certain cheeses, are high in saturated fat so ought to be consumed in moderation for health.

■ Historical Background and Scientific Foundations

Humans probably began drinking the milk of other mammals, and making products from it, sometime after the dawn of agriculture, about 12,000 years ago. At first the animals were valued mainly for milk and skins. There are rock paintings from the Sahara dated around 6,000 years ago that show evidence of dairying activities. There is also evidence of cheese making in Egyptian tombs dating back to 2,800–3,000 years ago. It is likely that fermentation processes leading to bread, cheese, wine, and beer were all discovered around the same time. Random microbial action upon milk led to the first dairy products, and their manufacture was manual until the development

of mechanized methods in the nineteenth century. Around this time, advances in microbiology by French microbiologist Louis Pasteur (1822–1895) and others led to more controlled microbial cultures for the production of cheese and yogurt.

Milk is a complex fluid that is the primary food of a baby mammal. Produced by the mother's breast, its composition makes it a complete food for the first months of life. Milk contains carbohydrates in the form of lactose, or milk sugar, along with a wide range of proteins, vitamins, and minerals. Its fat content enables it to carry fat-soluble vitamins and minerals. It is therefore often fortified with vitamins A and D. Because milk is so nutritious, it is very attractive to bacteria, which will feed off the lactose sugar, turning it into lactic acid. Therefore, milk will readily sour if left at room temperature for even a few hours. Most milk intended for human consumption is pasteurized to reduce its bacterial content, but even pasteurized milk contains millions of bacteria, so it must be considered perishable.

Milk can readily be made into other foods, known as dairy products. Milk has about four percent fat but can be transformed into creams having up to 40 percent fat by centrifugation, which separates the fat into two layers, with the watery portion of the milk in the bottom layer. Cream is useful in cooking because it can form a foam in which the fat globules trap air, lending texture to dishes such as mousses. Whipping cream creates this foam but if the whipping is overdone, lumps form, which are a crude type of butter. Churning milk produces the solid fat called butter, in which the fat particles coagulate. Butter has probably been made for as long as animals have been milked. It keeps longer than either fresh milk or cream. In ancient Rome, butter was the only fat allowed on meat abstention days. Butter is, technically, a water-in-oil emulsion in which the oil or fat particles predominate. The fat content of butter is between 36 and 44 percent and it adds richness, texture, and flavor to sauces and dishes.

Milk can also be fermented to produce yogurt, long valued for its health giving properties, and cheese, which

WORDS TO KNOW

HOMOGENIZATION: Milk is an emulsion of fat in water, and if left standing will separate into two layers. Homogenization involves passing the milk through a fine nozzle, which breaks up its fat globules into smaller particles that form a uniform liquid with the watery component of milk.

LACTOSE: The sugar in milk, lactose, is not found in any other food. It is a disaccharide made up of glucose and galactose and requires the enzyme lactase to break it down into molecules that the body can utilize as fuel.

PASTEURIZATION: The process of heating milk to kill off any contaminating organisms. Raw, unpasteurized milk is used to make some cheeses but may pose a health risk. Pasteurization was invented by the French scientist Louis Pasteur, who discovered that bacteria can make milk and wine sour by their action.

is an important part of many countries' cuisine. Acid-loving bacteria such as lactobacilli solidify milk to produce yogurt, and the populations of these microbes in the resulting product may help promote immunity and

gastrointestinal health. Making cheese involves using enzymes or acids, or both, to coagulate the major milk protein, casein, to make a soft curd that traps the milk's fat particles. Often this coagulation is done with an enzyme called rennin, which is obtained from the stomach of a calf. This is used in the manufacture of many traditional cheeses such as Italian parmesan. However, some North American cheeses are made with an equivalent enzyme called chymosin, which is produced from genetically modified bacteria. The source of the milk and the way its curd is aged contributes to the wide variety of cheeses around the world, many of which are central to a country's culinary culture.

■ Impacts and Issues

Humans are the only species that consumes the milk of another species, and this imposes some biological burdens. Levels of the enzyme lactase fall dramatically after the time when a human infant is dependent upon its mother's milk. Therefore the majority of the human adult population is lactose intolerant and cannot properly digest milk. Undigested lactose passes into the intestines where bacteria feed on it, causing pain and

A man hand-pokes holes into aging rounds of blue cheese to allow for the development of desired molds. *Adrienne Lerner / Lerner & Lerner / LernerMedia Global Photos.*

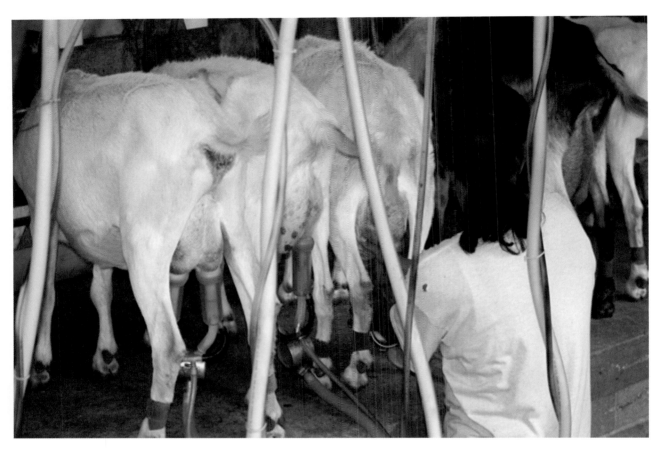

A dairy worker uses mechanized pumps to milk dairy goats. The goats live in spacious pastures on the site of Sweet Grass Dairy, a family-owned artisan cheese maker. *Adrienne Lerner / Lerner & Lerner / LernerMedia Global Photos.*

bloating. The widespread nature of lactose intolerance was not recognized until the 1960s, perhaps because Northern Europeans and Americans have learned to tolerate lactose because of the prevalence of dairy products in their diet. For other nations, consuming dairy products remains problematic, which is why shipping dried milk to famine-stricken countries is not a good way of alleviating their nutritional status. However, dairy products such as cheese are relatively free of lactose and are a good source of calcium and protein. Low- or no-fat versions are recommended, because the saturated fat in dairy products can raise cholesterol levels and may pose a risk of heart disease.

The raw milk movement argues that consumers are missing out on many of the nutritional benefits of milk because of the pasteurization process. Raw milk comes straight from the cow and is not pasteurized, treated, or processed in any way. Its advocates say that pasteurization destroys many valuable enzymes, proteins, and friendly bacteria. Consuming raw milk is said to boost immunity and protect against asthma and other allergies, while the good bacteria improve digestion by balancing the gut flora. The raw milk movement is, however, at odds with the Food and Drug Administration regulations, which demand that all milk sold between states be pasteurized, a rule in place since 1987. The Centers for Disease Control and Prevention have also linked consumption of raw milk with several cases of food-borne illness, although the movement disputes that the milk is the cause.

■ Primary Source Connection

"The Cheese Poet" James McIntyre (1828–1906) was a Canadian citizen living most of his life in Ingersoll, Ontario, a small farming community known for its dairies and cheese making. Although he was a furniture manufacturer by trade, his love was poetry, and he frequented the local social scenes, composing poetry for all sorts of events: from business meetings to weddings.

In 1894 *Musings on the Banks of Canadian Thames* was published and in 1889 he published *Poems of James McIntyre*. He was most known for his dairy and cheese poems, and many would argue that he has earned the title of Canada's Worst Poet. He died in 1906, but his poetry was rediscovered in the 1920s when his poems appeared in the Toronto newspaper *The Mail and Empire* and its successor *the Globe and Mail*. Some of his poems were reprinted in anthologies in 1979 and 1999.

DAIRY ODE

Our muse it doth refuse to sing
Of cheese made early in the spring,
When cows give milk from spring fodder
You cannot make a good cheddar.

The quality is often vile
Of cheese that is made in April,
Therefore we think for that reason
You should make later in the season.

Cheese making you should delay
Until about the first of May.
Then cows do feed on grassy field
And rich milk they abundant yield.

Ontario cannot compete
With the Northwest in raising wheat,
For cheaper there they it can grow
So price in future may be low.

Though this a hardship it may seem,
Rejoice that you have got the cream,
In this land of milk and honey,
Where dairy farmers do make money.

Utensils must be clean and sweet,
So cheese with first class can compete,
And daily polish up milk pans,
Take pains with vats and with milk cans.

And it is important matter
To allow no stagnant water,
But water from pure well or stream
The cow must drink to give pure cream.

Canadian breeds 'tis best to pair
With breeds from the shire of Ayr,
They thrive on our Canadian feed
And are for milking splendid breed.

Though 'gainst spring cheese some do mutter,
Yet spring milk also makes bad butter,
Then there doth arise the query
How utilize it in the dairy:

The milk it floats in great spring flood
Though it is not so rich and good,
Let us be thankful for this stream
Of milk and also curds and cream.

All dairymen their highest aims
Should be to make the vale of Thames,
Where milk doth so abundant How,
Dairyland of Ontario.

James McIntryre

MCINTYRE, JAMES. *POEMS OF JAMES MCINTYRE.*
INGERSOLL, ONTARIO, 1889.

SEE ALSO *Factory Farming; Foodborne Diseases; Humane Animal Farming; Lactose Intolerance; Nutrient Fortification of Foods; Organics; Pasteurization; Raw Milk Campaign.*

BIBLIOGRAPHY

Books

Clark, Stephanie, Michael Costello, and Maryanne Drake. *The Sensory Evaluation of Dairy Products*, 2nd ed. New York: Springer, 2009.

Farrell-Kingsley, Kathy. *The Home Creamery.* North Adams, MA: Storey Pub, 2008.

Mattila-Sandholm, Tiina, and Maria Saarela, eds. *Functional Dairy Products*, 2 vols. Cambridge, UK: Woodhead, 2003 and 2007.

Miller, Gregory D., Judith K. Jarvis, and Louis D. McBean. *Handbook of Diary Foods and Nutrition*, 3rd ed. Boca Raton, FL: CRC Press, 2007.

Park, Young W. *Bioactive Components in Milk and Dairy Products.* Ames, IA: Wiley-Blackwell, 2009.

Rathore, Narendra S. *Consumer Awareness for Food & Dairy Products.* Udaipur: Apex Pub. House, 2006.

Tamime, Adnan Y. *Structure of Dairy Products.* Oxford, UK: Blackwell Pub, 2007.

Periodicals

Lanou, Amy J., Susan E. Berkow, and Neal D. Barnard. "Calcium, Dairy Products, and Bone Health in Children and Young Adults: A Reevaluation of the Evidence." *Pediatrics* 115, no. 3 (2005): 736–743.

Levin, Susan. "Dairy Products and Bone Health." *Journal of the American Dietetic Association* 107, no. 1 (2007): 35.

Paxon, Heather. "Post-Pasteurian Cultures: The Microbiopolitics of Raw-Milk Cheese in the United States." *Cultural Anthropology* 23, no. 1 (2008): 15–47.

West, Harry G. "Food Fears and Raw-Milk Cheese." *Appetite* 51, no. 1 (2008): 25–29.

Web Sites

"What's Healthier: Raw Milk or Regulation?" *All Things Considered, National Public Radio (NPR)*, March 5, 2005. http://www.npr.org/templates/story/story.php?storyId=128912799 (accessed September 2, 2010).

Susan Aldridge

Decollectivization

■ Introduction

Collectivization of agriculture refers to a method of agricultural production wherein several farmers or families work together to farm a large piece of land. Collective agriculture typically entails state ownership and control of the means of agricultural production, including arable land. Collective agriculture became a prevalent method of agricultural production in the twentieth century, when many communist states collectivized agriculture within their nations. Many nations adopted collectivized agriculture as a means to increase agricultural productivity or to serve a political ideology that called for eradicating the role of capital in the economy.

By the end of the twentieth century, however, many of these nations decollectivized agriculture by privatizing ownership of land or by relinquishing state control of the agricultural sector. The fall of communism in the Soviet Union and Eastern Europe prompted these nations to decollectivize agriculture, which no longer served those nations' ideological objectives. Other nations, including China, decollectivized agriculture in order to transform their economies or to increase agriculture production following disastrous collectivization programs.

Despite the state-controlled model of collective agriculture that was dominant in the last century, not all forms of collective agriculture involve government ownership or control of the means of agricultural production. In Israel, Jewish individuals and families combined socialist and Zionist principles to create kibbutzim, or collective communities that have traditionally focused on agriculture. Each kibbutz involves individuals and families jointly participating in farming or other activities for the benefit of the whole community. Approximately 270 kibbutzim exist in Israel.

■ Historical Background and Scientific Foundations

Prior to the twentieth century, collective agriculture generally occurred only within small tribal groups. Collective agriculture enabled these communities to pool labor and resources to produce crops and livestock for the benefit of the tribe. In the twentieth century, numerous countries implemented national collective agriculture campaigns. These nations, guided by communist principles, imposed collective agriculture on their citizens as a means of bringing agricultural production under state control.

Following the Russian Civil War (1917–1923), Vladimir Lenin (1870–1924), the leader of the newly formed Soviet Union, abolished the private ownership of land but allowed peasants to farm equal land shares privately. The government divided the large pre-war farms that had provided the urban population with food and redistributed the land to peasants. Within a few years, grain production returned to pre-war levels. Food shortages occurred in the cities, however, because peasants consumed the excess food rather than sell it. Josef Stalin (1878–1953), Lenin's successor, authorized the government to seize excess grain from farmers. Grain production declined rapidly, and in response the government began a program to collectivize agriculture. Following World War II (1939–1945), the Communist-controlled Eastern European nations that fell under the Soviet Union's sphere of influence, with the exception of Poland, also implemented collective agriculture programs.

In the 1940s and 1950s, China conducted a forced collective agriculture program in order to increase agricultural production. The collectivization program, which accelerated under the Great Leap Forward initiatives of Chairman Mao Zedong (1893–1976), produced a disastrous decline in agricultural production. Widespread

WORDS TO KNOW

COLLECTIVE AGRICULTURE: The organization of agricultural production wherein farmers jointly work on a large farm. Collective agriculture typically involves state ownership of the means of production, including the land.

DECOLLECTIVIZATION: The process of moving from collective agriculture to private land ownership or removing state control over agriculture.

MARKET ECONOMY: An economy that permits the open exchange of goods and services and relies on market forces to determine price, production, investment, and savings without government intervention.

famine resulted in the deaths of between 20 and 48 million people. The Chinese government estimates that 14 million people died as a result of famine during the Great Leap Forward, but scholars reject this official estimate. Despite the failure of China's collectivization

Collective farm workers fill sacks with maize at the 21st Collective Congress farm near Donetske, Ukraine, USSR, in 1989. © *Mike Goldwater / Alamy.*

campaign, other communist nations in Asia, including North Korea and Vietnam, also implemented forced collectivization campaigns.

Following China's disastrous collectivization campaign under the Great Leap Forward, agricultural production managed to keep pace with China's growing population but did not produce much above subsistence levels. Deng Xiaoping (1904–1997), who took over as China's leader in 1978, also sought to transform the Chinese from an agricultural economy to an industrial economy, which would require additional labor in the cities. In order to increase agricultural production, in 1982 and 1983 the government abolished the communes that guided and implemented the nation's collective agriculture program. The government retained ownership of agricultural land but allowed peasant families to work small plots. The government also retained ownership of collective assets, such as farm equipment, which were leased to farmers.

The Soviet Union and its Eastern European satellite states did not begin decollectivization until after the fall of Communism in the late 1980s and early 1990s. Decollectivization within the former sphere of Soviet influence has yielded mixed results. The complete privatization of land has come slowly in the former Soviet states of Russia, Ukraine, and Belarus. Within these nations, most agricultural production has remained on large, collective farms. Although land ownership has been privatized in these countries, the majority of private landowners still hold their land rights in common with other landowners on collective farms.

The former Soviet states of Armenia, Azerbaijan, and Georgia have made a more complete and smoother transition towards privatization of land and a move towards a market economy within the agricultural sector. The former Soviet Baltic states—Estonia, Latvia, and Lithuania—merely restituted land to former owners or their heirs. Much land remained unclaimed, however, which led to a decline in production. Most of the unclaimed land in Estonia remained in collective-style farms. The Baltic states have implemented plans to sell the land and return it to production.

The former Communist countries of Eastern Europe had a relatively easy transition to private ownership of land and restructuring the agricultural sector. Bulgaria and Romania, like the Baltic states, restituted land to former owners or their heirs. Hungary imposed a scheme to compensate former owners or their heirs for confiscated land. Hungary's agricultural land was then auctioned off, redistributed to landless collective farmers, and maintained as collective farms. The Czech Republic, Slovakia, and Slovenia did not expropriate all agricultural land during collectivization. Under collectivization in these countries, individuals could retain ownership, but the state seized the right to allow cooperative farms to work the land. After the fall of Communism, these states restored ownership and use of the land

A Chinese farmer plants rice in a paddy in Guangxi province, China. The Central Committee of Chinese Communist Party (CPC) approved key land reforms that will allow farmers to trade and mortgage their land rights. The reforms aim to spur economic growth in the countryside. *Image copyright Hung Chung Chih, 2010. Used under license from Shutterstock.com.*

to owners or their heirs or provided restitution to owners that had surrendered their land to the state. Albania, Poland, and the former Yugoslav republics—Bosnia and Herzegovina, Croatia, Macedonia, Montenegro, Slovenia, and Serbia—generally retained private ownership and agricultural production throughout the Cold War. Since the early 1990s the agricultural sectors in these countries have been marked by difficulties in transitioning from a command economy to a market economy, not by privatization and agricultural restructuring.

■ Impacts and Issues

Decollectivization entails either the privatization of state-owned land or the relinquishment of state control over agricultural production on state-owned land. The post-Communist experience of the former Soviet Union and Eastern Europe highlight several of the difficulties of decollectivization, including compensation of former owners and restructuring the agricultural sector. Easy access to credit, which allows farmers to purchase farm equipment, fertilizers, pesticides, seed, and other goods, is also an issue when nations decollectivize the agricultural

sector. Following decollectivization in Russia in the 1990s, farmers were allowed to own and work their own land. The relatively large size of the privatized farms in Russia—approximately 40 hectares (100 acres)—forced farmers to purchase their own machinery and other goods required to run such a large farm. The unavailability of credit for Russian farmers compelled most of them to remain on state-owned collective farms.

Decollectivization may produce environmental degradation and agricultural stagnation if not implemented responsibly. The decollectivization of Chinese agriculture to small, family-operated farms initially increased productivity. The new agricultural system, however, encouraged farmers to overwork their land. Within years of decollectivization, poor land management degraded the land and led to stagnation in agricultural production. Chinese farmers also depleted several of China's most important aquifers in their quests to meet production quotas. Consequently, by 2000 China became a net importer of grain.

Decollectivization may also produce social and political discontent. Resentment over compensation for land, loss of employment, and other factors may upset landowners or agricultural workers. Decollectivization in

China, for example, has produced a large and potentially destabilizing class of landless peasants. Although agricultural production has stagnated in China, additional labor cannot cure the environmental problems that trouble China's agricultural sector, causing the country to be faced with approximately 70 million landless peasants. Many of these peasants work seasonally as factory workers along China's industrial coast. Whether and how these people are permanently integrated into China's economy could have a significant impact on China's future political stability and economic growth.

SEE ALSO *Agricultural Land Reform; Ethical Issues in Agriculture; Food Security; Food Sovereignty; Free Trade and Agriculture; Subsistence Farming.*

BIBLIOGRAPHY

Books

Cheung, Sidney C. H., and Chee Beng Tan. *Food and Foodways in Asia: Resource, Tradition and Cooking.* London and New York: Routledge, 2007.

Lipton, Michael. *Land Reform in Developing Countries: Property Rights and Property Wrongs.* London and New York: Routledge, 2009.

Periodicals

Gillespie, Gilbert W. "2009 AFHVS Presidential Address: The Steering Question: Challenges to Achieving Food System Sustainability." *Agriculture and Human Values* 27, no. 1 (2010): 3–12.

Grimond, John. "China's Peasants Look to the Skies." *Economist* 395, no. 8683 (May 22, 2010).

Petrick, Martin, and Michael R. Carter. "Critical Masses in the Decollectivisation of Post-Soviet Agriculture." *European Review of Agricultural Economics* 36, no. 2 (June 2009): 231–252.

Rowe, William. "Agrarian Adaptations in Tajikistan: Land Reform, Water and Law." *Central Asian Survey* 29, no. 2 (2010): 189–204.

Saar, Ellu, and Marge Unt. "Falling High: Structure and Agency in Agriculture during the Transformation." *Journal of Baltic Studies* 41, no. 2 (2010): 215–235.

Tiwari, Rakesh, et al. "Land Use Dynamics in Select Village Ecosystems of Southern India: Drivers and Implications." *Journal of Land Use Science* 5, no. 3 (2010): 197–215.

Trang, Tran T. T. "Social Differentiation Revisited: A Study of Rural Changes and Peasant Strategies in Vietnam." *Asia Pacific Viewpoint* 51, no. 1 (2010): 17–35.

Web Sites

"Rapid Growth of Selected Asian Economies: Lessons and Implications for Agriculture and Food Security." *Regional Office for Asia and the Pacific, Food and Agriculture Organization of the United Nations (FAO).* http://www.fao.org/docrep/009/ag087e/AG087E00.htm (accessed August 24, 2010).

Joseph P. Hyder

Desertification and Agriculture

■ Introduction

Desertification refers to the process by which fertile land is degraded and turns into desert. Whereas desertification typically changes semi-arid shrublands into desert, the process may also transform semi-arid land into non-native grasslands incapable of supporting a wide variety of flora and fauna. Desertification may occur in any area where the evapo-transpiration rate is 70 percent or greater of total precipitation.

Both naturally occurring and anthropogenic factors contribute to desertification. Overgrazing, overcultivation, poor water management, and deforestation are major contributing factors to desertification. Climate change has influenced the expansion and contraction of deserts for eons. Variations in annual precipitation by only a few centimeters can transform drylands that support flora and fauna into degraded, arid deserts. In areas undisturbed by humans, the deserts return to drylands when precipitation levels increase. Over the next century, however, anthropogenic global climate change and population growth could accelerate desertification in many areas.

■ Historical Background and Scientific Foundations

Beginning in the early Holocene, human actions began to affect the environment. The rise of agriculture, including cultivation and animal husbandry, placed increased pressure on the land and water supplies. Crop cultivation requires clearing land for planting and tilling the soil. Improper plowing and irrigation techniques increase soil erosion. When nutrient-rich topsoil erodes, farmers move on to a new parcel of land, which degrades additional land. Livestock also degrade the land by grazing. When livestock graze on dryland vegetation, the soil is exposed to the wind. Through a geological process known as saltation, wind blows the exposed soil and sand over increasingly large areas. Again, when the land degrades, humans must move livestock to other grazing areas, degrading them also and accelerating desertification.

The removal of topsoil through saltation and erosion contributes to other processes that increase the rate of desertification, including higher evaporation rates and greater soil salinity. Once vegetation is removed, the soil becomes exposed to the sun, which quickens evaporation of water from the top layer of soil. With little moisture remaining on the top layer of soil, naturally occurring vegetation struggles to take root, so the land remains devoid of vegetation. Increased evaporation rates at the soil surface prevent precipitation from seeping deep into the ground. Salts contained in rain remain near the surface of the soil. Furthermore, if the water table is within 6.6–9.8 feet (2–3 m) of the soil surface, salts may move from the water table to the surface through capillary action. High soil salinity prevents new vegetation from growing.

By the 1970s the occurrences of famine and other effects of desertification prompted the international community to act. A major famine affected the Sahel, a semi-arid transition region of Africa between the Sahara desert and the African savanna, from the late 1960s through the early 1980s. The famine killed more than 100,000 people and forced an additional 750,000 in Mali, Niger, and Mauritania to rely on food aid. In 1977 the United Nations (UN) convened the United Nations Conference on Desertification (UNCOD) in Kenya to address desertification in the Sahel and other areas.

International efforts following the UNCD resulted in the United Nations Convention to Combat Desertification (UNCCD), which entered into force in December 1996. Recognizing the environmental, economic, and social problems associated with desertification, the UNCCD seeks to combat the problem by working with national governments to establish national action programs and other long-term efforts to minimize or reverse desertification, improve agricultural practices, and decrease the effects of drought.

WORDS TO KNOW

DESERTIFICATION: The process by which fertile land, typically semi-arid dryland, degrades and turns into arid desert.

DRYLAND: Arid desert or semi-arid xeric shrubland biomes.

EVAPO-TRANSPIRATION: Loss of water through both evaporation from the surface and the transpiration of moisture from the aboveground parts of plants.

HOLOCENE: The current geological epoch, which began approximately 12,000 years ago.

SALTATION: The process by which sand or soil particles move across an uneven surface when carried by the wind.

■ Impacts and Issues

Drylands occupy approximately half of the world's total land area, and between 10 and 20 percent of the world's drylands are already degraded. Degraded drylands may become either arid desert or non-native grasslands incapable of supporting a wide range of flora and fauna. Population growth, which places an additional burden on the land and water resources, threatens to degrade even more of the world's drylands over the next century. Global climate change may also accelerate desertification in some areas, while potentially providing relief in others. Whereas poor agricultural practices are a driving force behind desertification, the implementation of good agricultural practices may slow, or even reverse the condition and produce enough food to sustain growing local populations.

Between 2010 and 2050, the world's population will grow from 6.9 billion people to approximately 9.2 billion people, a 33 percent increase. This rapid population growth, much of which will occur in developing countries affected by desertification, will necessitate the expansion of land cultivation and grazing. The desertification rate likely will increase if farmers in drylands do not adopt sustainable agricultural practices designed to minimize desertification.

Global climate change will affect the desertification rate in drylands over the next century. While climate change may increase precipitation in some regions, the Intergovernmental Panel on Climate Change's (IPCC) *Fourth Assessment Report: Climate Change 2007* states that scientists have "high confidence" that global climate change will result in many semi-arid areas suffering a decrease in precipitation in the coming decades. Africa, for example, will experience a 5 to 8 percent increase in

Villagers build a vegetable greenhouse in China's Gansu province on April 16, 2007. Located beside the Tenggeer Desert and the Badain Jaran Desert, it is one of the most severely deserted places in the arid region. *AP Images.*

semi-arid areas by 2080 based on current climate change patterns. Droughts in many semi-arid areas will increase, which will contribute to desertification of these areas.

Even with population growth and global climate change, the desertification rate may be slowed, stopped, or even reversed with sound policies and practices. Desertification prevention is preferable to rehabilitating degraded land, which is a difficult and expensive undertaking. Soil fixation is a major tool to prevent desertification. Soil fixation involves planting trees or shrubs to serve as a buffer zone and windbreaker to reduce soil erosion and evapo-transpiration. Enriching the soil with nitrogen-fixing legumes or synthetic fertilizers may also encourage plants to root and grow. These plants may then fixate the soil. Even educating farmers about proper plowing and irrigation techniques may prevent soil erosion and extend the productive life of a field.

■ Primary Source Connection

James Fairhead and Melissa Leach have written two books about the African rainforest and the changes that have occurred over time. They suggest that some of the reductions to the rainforest areas are due to climate changes over many years and not necessarily due to human exploitation. In fact they suggest that small-scale farming has actually increased the health of some rainforests and enhances rainforest regeneration.

Enriching the Landscape: Social History and the Management of Transition Ecology in the Forest—Saving the Mosaic of the Republic of Guinea

. . . . The striking presence of dense semi-deciduous rainforest patches in an otherwise open woodland savanna landscape, and the sharp boundary between the these vegetation forms, has intrigued observers and invited considerable ecological debate as to the origin and evolution of this vegetation mosaic. In Kissidougou prefecture of the Republic of Guinea this issue is not merely academic: theoretically derived interpretations of forest-savanna transition are orienting external perceptions of local land use and driving environmental policy.

The predominant view, shared by most outside observers of Kissidougou at all dates, considers the patches of forest island around villages and gallery forests to be relics of the original, and formerly much more extensive, dense humid forest cover (e.g. Valentin, 1893; Adam, 1948; Schnell, 1952; Guinée, 1988). Human impact is seen as destructive of forest, causing progressive conversion to grassland as a result of shifting cultivation and the lighting of bush fires (e.g. Aubréville, 1949; Keay, 1959;

Gayibor, 1986; Jean, 1989). Thus the 'pre-forest' zone, spatially, is portrayed as temporally ex-forest, or 'derived' savanna. Climate (e.g. annual rainfall levels in excess of 1,600 mm) and the presence of humid forest species and associations, are taken as proof of high forest potential and indicative of the past existence of actual forest. The mixed forest-savanna species composition sometimes found at the boundaries of forest patches is taken as evidence of savanna encroachment (Adam, 1968).

A second view, initially outlined for Nigeria in an article in *Africa* by Morgan and Moss (1965; Moss and Morgan, 1970; cf. Avenard *et al.,* 1974, for Côte d'Ivoire), considers the forest-savanna mosaic as a relatively stable vegetation pattern, principally reflecting edaphic differentiation (i.e. variations in soil conditions, but also in water table and drainage). Only certain soils and sites can support forest, and inhabitants of the mosaic use and maintain the diversity of its vegetation types (Moss, 1982; Blanc-Pamard, 1978). This position is not necessarily incompatible with the first, where analysts recognise stability in a residual mosaic following savannisation (e.g. Adejuwon and Adesina, 1992). Research in Côte d'Ivoire has modified the argument for edaphic stability, showing the forest to be advancing into savanna areas (Asjanohoun, 1964; Miège, 1966; sf. Aubréville, 1962, for Gabon). And explaining this is the context of climatic rehumidification of the Upper Guinea Coast region. This is the consensus of climate historians, who argue that dryer climate conditions than the present prevailed at various periods: between 700 BP and 150 BP in the recent past (Brooks, 1986; Nicholson, 1979); between 4,500 and 3,500 BP in the medium term (Lézine and Casanova, 1989; Talbot *et al.,* 1974).

Both the 'derived savanna' and 'edaphic mosaic' arguments consider forest patches as 'natural' and 'original', whether as relics or as stable patches. There is a third possibility, however: that forest patches in savanna result from human disturbance and the people's activities actually encourage the formation of forest vegetation. This possibility carries very different implications for assessments of human interaction with other ecological variables in the shaping of the forest-savanna mosaic, and hence for environmental policy. A few studies of fallow dynamics show how certain local agricultural practices encourage the regeneration of secondary forest in savanna (Amanour, 1994; Guelly *et al.,* 1993). Inhabitants in one area—the Baoulé 'V' of Côte d'Ivoire—themselves suggest that 'where one cultivates, the forest advances' (Spichiger and Blanc-Pamard, 1973). Our study in Kissidougou suggests that local practices which enhance forest regeneration may be of more general significance in accounting for the long-term evolution of the forest-savanna mosaic. . . .

James Fairhead
Melissa Leach

FAIRHEAD, JAMES, AND MELISSA LEACH. "ENRICHING THE LANDSCAPE: SOCIAL HISTORY AND THE MANAGEMENT OF

TRANSITION ECOLOGY IN THE FOREST—SAVING THE MOSAIC OF THE REPUBLIC OF GUINEA." *AFRICA: JOURNAL OF THE INTERNATIONAL AFRICAN INSTITUTE* 66 (1996). EDINBURGH, UK: EDINBURGH UNIVERSITY PRESS, 1996.

SEE ALSO *Agricultural Deforestation; Agricultural Demand for Water; Agroecology; Biofuels and World Hunger; Climate Change and Agriculture; Food Security; Land Availability and Degradation; Livestock Intensity and Demand; Subsistence Farming; Sustainable Agriculture; U.S. Agency for International Development (USAID); Water; Water Scarcity.*

BIBLIOGRAPHY

Books

Newson, Malcolm D. *Land, Water and Development: Sustainable and Adaptive Management of Rivers.* London: Routledge, 2009.

Pearce, Fred. *When the Rivers Run Dry: Water, the Defining Crisis of the Twenty-First Century.* Boston: Beacon Press, 2006.

Zdruli, P. *Land Degradation and Desertification: Assessment, Mitigation and Remediation.* Dordrecht, The Netherlands: Springer, 2010.

Periodicals

Dregne, Harold E. "Land Degradation in the Drylands." *Arid Land Research and Management* 16, no. 2 (2002): 99–132.

Pengue, Walter. "Agrofuels and Agrifoods." *The Bulletin of Science, Technology & Society* 29, no. 3 (2009): 167–179.

Slegers, Monique F., and Leo Stroosnijder. "Beyond the Desertification Narrative: A Framework for Agricultural Drought in Semi-Arid East Africa." *Ambio* 37, no. 5 (2008): 372–380.

Web Sites

"Desertification." *Food and Agriculture Organization of the United Nations (FAO).* http://www.fao.org/desertification/default.asp?lang=en (accessed October 15, 2010).

"Sustainable Agriculture Will Help Stop Desertification, UN Agency Says." *UN News Center,* June 17, 2008. http://www.un.org/apps/news/story.asp?NewsID=27048&Cr=desert&Cr1 (accessed October 15, 2010).

Joseph P. Hyder

Diet and Cancer

■ Introduction

Around one quarter of all deaths from cancer are related to either poor diet or obesity. But the human diet is so complex that it is difficult to define which components prevent cancer and which promote it. Not only do foods themselves contain thousands of compounds, but people in different groups may consume very different diets. Research has established that there are links between certain cancers and diet. The evidence is strongest for bowel, stomach, mouth, esophageal, and breast cancer. Based upon what is known from scientific evidence, the best way to prevent cancer is to eat plenty of fruits and vegetables and fiber but to cut down on processed and red meats, saturated fats, and salt. Whereas compounds within certain foods, such as lycopene in tomatoes, have been said to have a strong anti-cancer effect, the evidence from actual human diets is lacking. Most of this type of information comes from exposure of cells or laboratory animals to single compounds in foods. Therefore, there is no one compound that, taken as a supplement, has been shown to reduce the risk of cancer. The best approach in cancer prevention is as for health in general, to have a balanced diet with a wide range of foods.

■ Historical Background and Scientific Foundations

The National Institute of Environmental and Health Sciences has been looking at the role of dietary aflatoxins in promoting liver cancer since the early 1960s. Aflatoxins are carcinogens that are produced by molds that can grow on many foods including corn, rice, wheat, nuts, and spices. Other known carcinogens occur in charred or blackened foods, such as barbecued meats. Humans ingest literally thousands of different compounds in their daily diet, and it is challenging to link exposure to any of these to a cancer that may develop many years later.

Cancer is a disease of genes and cells, which progresses through a complex, step-wise process. Establishing a clear cause and effect relationship between a food compound and a cancer is, therefore, complicated.

However, scientific research has established at least some guidelines on cancer prevention and diet. Much of this information comes from the European Prospective Investigation of Cancer (EPIC) study, which is a prospective study involving half a million people in 10 countries throughout Europe. Previous work on diet and cancer has involved groups of people that were too small, given the complexity of the human diet, to give meaningful results.

Eating foods rich in fiber can protect against the risk of bowel cancer, according to EPIC, which found that people eating the most fiber had a 25 to 40 percent lower risk of bowel cancer compared to those eating least. Other studies have backed up this finding. Fiber interacts with bacteria in the bowel to produce substances that exert an anti-cancer effect. It also speeds waste through the bowel, which minimizes contact between the bowel and any harmful substances in the waste. EPIC also confirmed the value of fruits and vegetables in the diet, showing that a high intake reduces the risk of mouth, esophageal, and lung cancers, although it has little impact on other cancers.

Many studies have shown that eating a lot of red or processed meats increases the risk of bowel cancer. Red meat is any type of lamb, beef, or pork, whereas processed meats include bacon, ham, salami, and sausages. According to the EPIC study, eating just two portions per day of these meats can increase the risk of bowel cancer by as much as one third. Red and processed meat has also been linked to an increased risk of pancreatic and stomach cancer. But there is no evidence that consumption of white meats such as chicken is linked to an increased risk of cancer. Red and processed meats also contain heme, a red pigment that can stimulate the bacteria in the gut to produce carcinogenic chemicals called N-nitroso compounds.

Some studies, including EPIC, have suggested that a high consumption of saturated fat is linked to an increased risk of breast cancer. This may be through increasing levels of estrogen and other hormones that stimulate the growth of breast cancer cells. Also, eating a lot of salt or salty foods is linked to stomach cancer. In Asian countries such as Japan, people tend to eat salty foods often and their rate of stomach cancer is much higher than in the West. At the same time, Asian women have very low rates of breast cancer. They eat few, if any, dairy products and their diet is higher in soy proteins that contain compounds that provide some protection against estrogen-dependent tumors.

■ Impacts and Issues

The search for the specific compounds in fruits and vegetables that can help prevent cancer is ongoing. Often a compound such as lycopene in tomatoes, or polyphenols in green tea, will be found to have the ability to kill cancer cells in the laboratory. But such findings do not translate to the everyday human diet. Although it may be worthwhile to include tomatoes and green tea in the

Cyclist Lance Armstrong (center), a cancer survivor, prepares to start a Livestrong bicycle race. The Lance Armstrong Foundation's Livestrong website provides online diet and nutrition resources for cancer survivors and people living with cancer. © *Sol Neelman/Corbis.*

diet, buying supplements containing these compounds is not guaranteed to prevent cancer. Indeed, studies of antioxidants that are common in fruits and vegetables, such as vitamins A, C, and E, have shown that they do not prevent cancer when taken as supplements, and in some studies they have even been shown to increase risk.

There is also an indirect link between diet and cancer in that eating too much and gaining weight increases the risk of certain cancers. Research conducted since the year 2000 has shown that obesity increases the risk of breast, endometrial, colon, kidney, and esophageal cancers. The reason may be that fat tissue has its own metabolic activity and produces hormones, such as estrogen, that can promote the growth of cancer cells. Going forward, more clinical trials are needed to find out whether losing weight and increasing exercise can reduce the risk of cancer.

SEE ALSO *Dietary Guidelines for Americans; Dietary Reference Intakes; Functional Foods; Macrobiotics; Mediterranean Diet; Nutrient Fortification of Foods; Obesity; Pesticides and Pesticide Residue; Phytochemicals (Phytonutrients); Preservation; Processed Foods; Salt, Nitrites, and Health; Therapeutic Diets; Vitamins and Minerals.*

BIBLIOGRAPHY

Books

American Cancer Society. *American Cancer Society's Complete Guide to Cancer and Nutrition.* Atlanta, GA: American Cancer Society, 2008.

Knasmüller, Siegfried. *Chemoprevention of Cancer and DNA Damage by Dietary Factors.* Weinheim, Germany: Wiley-VCH, 2009.

Lutz, Carroll A., and Karen R. Przytulski. *Nutrition & Diet Therapy: Evidence-Based Applications.* Philadelphia: F.A. Davis Co., 2006.

Shaw, Clare. *Nutrition and Cancer.* Chichester, West Sussex, UK: Blackwell, 2011.

Periodicals

Cade, Janet E., E. Faye Taylor, Victoria J. Burley, and Darren C. Greenwood. "Common Dietary Patterns and Risk of Breast Cancer: Analysis from the United Kingdom Women's Cohort Study." *Nutrition and Cancer* 62, no. 3 (2010): 300–306.

Dias-Neto, Marina, Mariana Pintalhao, Mariana Ferreira, and Nuno Lunet. "Salt Intake and Risk of Gastric Intestinal Metaplasia: Systematic Review and Meta-Analysis." *Nutrition and Cancer* 62, no. 2 (2010): 133–147.

Hu, Jinfu, et al. "Nutrients and Risk of Prostate Cancer." *Nutrition and Cancer* 62, no. 6 (2010): 710–718.

Martinez, Maria E., James R. Marshall, and Edward Giovannucci. "Diet and Cancer Prevention: The Roles of Observation and Experimentation." *Nature Reviews. Cancer* 8, no. 9 (2008): 694–703.

McCullough, Marjorie L., and Edward L. Giovannucci. "Diet and Cancer Prevention." *Oncogene* 23, no. 38 (2004): 6349–6364.

Pelucchi, Claudio, et al. "Selected Aspects of Mediterranean Diet and Cancer Risk." *Nutrition and Cancer* 61. no. 6 (2009): 756–766.

Willett, Walter C. "Diet and Cancer: An Evolving Picture." *Journal of the American Medical Association* 293, no. 2 (2005): 233–234.

Williams, Christina D., et al. "Associations of Red Meat, Fat, and Protein Intake with Distal Colorectal Cancer Risk." *Nutrition and Cancer* 62, no. 6 (2010): 701–709.

Web Sites

"ACS Guidelines on Nutrition and Physical Activity for Cancer Prevention." *American Cancer Society.* http://www.cancer.org/Healthy/EatHealthyGetActive/ACSGuidelinesonNutritionPhysicalActivityforCancerPrevention/acs-guidelines-on-nutrition-and-physical-activity-for-cancer-prevention-diet-cancer-questions (accessed September 6, 2010).

Clifford, Carolyn, et al. "Diet and Cancer Risk." *National Cancer Institute.* http://rex.nci.nih.gov/NCI_Pub_Interface/raterisk/risks73.html (accessed September 6, 2010).

Susan Aldridge

Diet and Diabetes

■ Introduction

In the past, diabetes was invariably a fatal disease because lack of the hormone insulin (or unresponsiveness to insulin) meant that the body's cells starved for lack of glucose fuel. Modern understanding of the cause of diabetes and the development of treatments such as injected insulin mean that in the early twenty-first century a person with diabetes can expect to live a normal lifespan. However, diabetes is a progressive disease that requires vigilant control, without which complications such as heart disease may occur. These problems arise from the presence of excess glucose in the blood that is not transported to the body's cells. Therefore it is important for a person with diabetes to keep blood sugar levels as close to normal limits as possible. This means matching insulin production or intake with dietary intake of the carbohydrates that break down to glucose in the blood. A diet rich in complex carbohydrates, which break down slowly, is one key to good blood glucose control.

Diabetes is on the increase both in the United States and around the world. Growing levels of obesity are a major contributory factor, so plenty of exercise and a healthy diet are the main elements of diabetes prevention.

■ Historical Background and Scientific Foundations

The symptoms of diabetes, with its characteristic weight loss and frequent urination, are first mentioned in an Egyptian papyrus dating back to 3,500 years ago. The Greek physician Aretaeus (30–90 AD) first named the disease. Thereafter it rarely appears in medical texts: It was not until the 1920s that the cause of diabetes was recognized as a lack of insulin secreted by the pancreas. The hormone was discovered by the Nobel Prize-winning Canadian physician, Frederick Banting (1891–1941).

With his co-worker, Charles Best (1899–1978), he worked on purifying insulin and bringing it into use for patients. Before insulin, patients with diabetes would invariably die, quite probably with their illness unrecognized.

Without insulin, as in type 1 diabetes, or with insulin that does not work properly, as in type 2, the body is unable to extract nourishment from food, because glucose is not passed to the cells that need it. Because glucose is the body's fuel, this means that cells are being starved of energy; instead, the glucose is excreted in the urine. The full name for diabetes is diabetes mellitus. The word *mellitus* means sweet and refers to the taste of diabetic urine.

Insulin, and newer drugs that help control blood glucose, are life-saving but their optimal use presents some challenges. The amount of insulin a person with diabetes takes must be matched carefully with the amount of glucose that is taken in with diet. If insufficient insulin is taken to cope with the amount of glucose flooding the blood after a meal, blood glucose levels will remain high. Over time, the presence of excess glucose in the blood damages many organs and leads to the well-known complications of diabetes, which include heart disease, kidney disease, and blindness. If too much insulin is taken, and insufficient food, then levels of glucose in the blood will fall too low, possibly leading to an episode of hypoglycemia, accompanied by feelings of faintness, dizziness, and other unpleasant symptoms. Left untreated, an episode of hypoglycemia may lead to coma or even death. During a hypoglycemic episode, a diabetic may pose a danger to themselves and others if he or she is driving or operating machinery.

Therefore, individuals with diabetes must take special care with their diet if they are to achieve good blood glucose control with their insulin or other medication. Glucose comes from the breakdown of carbohydrate molecules. Carbohydrates fall into two main categories. Complex carbohydrates, including whole grain foods and potatoes, consist of large molecules called polysaccharides, such as starch. They are broken down slowly into glucose in the blood so levels do not rise so rapidly after a meal. Simple carbohydrates are composed of either one sugar unit (monosaccharide) or two sugar units (disaccharides). Glucose itself is a monosaccharide, whereas sucrose is a disaccharide. Simple carbohydrates, found in fizzy drinks, sweets and baked goods, raise blood glucose levels very rapidly after being ingested. It is easier for insulin to deal with a gradual rise in blood glucose than a rapid one. Therefore, a diet with complex, rather than simple, carbohydrates, is better for the long-term health of a person with diabetes.

The American Diabetic Association (ADA) previously advised diabetics to avoid sugar at all costs. It was then realized that sugar does not raise blood glucose any more than other carbohydrates, so in 1994 the ADA lifted the sugar ban and began to focus more upon controlling carbohydrate intake. Those on insulin found it easier to control their blood glucose, also known as glycemic control, and therefore their diabetes, if they were eating roughly the same amount of carbohydrate at each meal. The ADA's exchange approach involves lists of foods and their carbohydrate content in grams and allows for more individualized and flexible meal planning. If one is allowed 60 grams of carbohydrate at breakfast, for example, it does not mean having the same breakfast each day: A fruit juice could be exchanged for a cereal, or a slice of toast for a bagel, so long as the carbohydrate count still totals 60 grams. In more recent years, the ADA has modified the exchange approach and now recommends a more general healthy eating plan, emphasizing fruits and vegetables, whole grains, low-fat dairy products, and fish.

Some people with diabetes have found it useful to plan their eating around the glycemic index (GI) of different foods. GI is a measure of how rapidly a food raises blood glucose. Foods with GI less than 55 are considered low GI and foods with a GI greater than 70 are classified as high GI. Examples of low GI foods include beans and most fruit and vegetables, except parsnips (GI 97) and watermelon (GI 72). Pastries and certain types of breads and breakfast cereals have high GI: For instance, a serving of a baguette has a GI of 95 and a bowl of cornflakes has a GI of 83.

The insulin index is similar to the GI but relates to the amount of insulin a food releases rather than how much it raises blood glucose. The higher the sugar and carbohydrate in a food, the higher the insulin index; and the higher the fat and protein content, the lower the insulin index. People with diabetes may achieve better glycemic control by sticking with foods of low GI and low insulin index.

There is also evidence that a high-fiber diet can help those with type 2 diabetes achieve better glycemic control. In 2000 the ADA began to recommend increasing fiber intake from 20 grams per day to 35 grams per day, but this was mainly because increased fiber lowers cholesterol. Around this time, a study in the *New England*

WORDS TO KNOW

DIABETES: Type 1 diabetes is caused by a lack of insulin and usually starts at an early age. Type 2 diabetes is more likely to start in middle age and is characterized by insufficient insulin or insulin resistance.

GLUCOSE: A type of sugar that serves as the body's fuel. Other sugars include sucrose (or table sugar), lactose, and fructose.

INSULIN: A hormone produced by the pancreas after eating that carries glucose in the blood to muscle, liver, and fat cells after a meal. Too much insulin makes blood glucose levels too low, whereas insufficient insulin results in high blood sugar that is stored as excess glucose. The right amount of insulin is needed to keep blood glucose levels under control.

Journal of Medicine showed beneficial effects of a high fiber diet, emphasizing soluble fiber such as oats, on a group of people with type 2 diabetes that had developed after the age of 40. Their mean and daily glucose, and daily insulin levels were decreased compared to a control group who consumed an ADA recommended diet. Their lipid profiles, including cholesterol levels, were also improved.

Much has been learned since the discovery of the cause of diabetes on how to manage the condition through diet. Indeed, in the early stages of type 2 diabetes, management by diet and other lifestyle changes alone is possible, although many people will need medication eventually because diabetes is a progressive disease. A person with diabetes needs a healthy balanced diet with a good balance between carbohydrate and fat. Monounsaturated fats, such as olive oil, are recommended over saturated fats such as butter, and a portion of oily fish should be eaten at least twice per week. Regular meals are very important for diabetics. These should be based on starchy complex carbohydrates such as bread, pasta, potatoes, noodles, rice, and cereals. Sweets and other sugary foods are to be minimized. Diabetics are also advised to eat plenty of fruits and vegetables. Those who are overweight or obese should make efforts to lose some weight as this can help slow the progress of diabetes or even stop it developing in the first place.

■ Impacts and Issues

Diabetes is a growing public health problem in the United States, with most of the increase occurring in type 2 diabetes, in which symptoms develop gradually compared to type 1. According to a Gallup-Healthways survey, 11.3 percent of American adults had diabetes in 2009, which is an increase of 10 percent over the previous year. That means that about 26 million Americans

An elderly male diabetic checks his blood sugar level and prepares to give himself an insulin shot.   © *Baron Bratby / Alamy.*

have diabetes. And according to the Centers for Disease Control and Prevention, about one in five of those who have diabetes do not realize their condition, leaving it to worsen without any treatment. If current trends continue, there will be more than 37 million Americans with diabetes by the end of 2015.

One reason for the rise in diabetes is the accompanying rise in overweight and obesity. Studies show that excess weight is a potent risk factor for diabetes and, conversely, cutting body weight by even 10 percent can reduce the risk. Exercise is a particularly helpful way of reducing diabetes risk through weight control. There has been an increasing focus upon prevention of diabetes. A condition called pre-diabetes, in which blood glucose levels are elevated but are not high enough to diagnose diabetes, has been identified. People with pre-diabetes are known to be at risk of developing type 2 diabetes. However, a simple blood test will identify those with pre-diabetes and, with a healthy diet and more exercise, they stand a good chance of warding off the development of diabetes.

SEE ALSO *Diet and Heart Disease; Diet and Hypertension; Dietary Guidelines for Americans; Nutrition; Protein and Carbohydrate Metabolism; Therapeutic Diets.*

BIBLIOGRAPHY

Books

American Diabetes Association. *What to Expect When You Have Diabetes: 170 Tips for Living Well with Diabetes* Intercourse, PA: Good Books, 2008.

D'Amore, Joseph, and Lisa D'Amore-Miller. *Just What the Doctor Ordered Diabetes Cookbook: A Doctor's Approach to Eating Well with Diabetes.* Alexandria, VA: American Diabetes Association, 2010.

Periodicals

Chiu, Ching-Ju., and Linda A. Wray. "Factors Predicting Glycemic Control in Middle-Aged and Older Adults with Type 2 Diabetes." *Preventing Chronic Disease* 7, no. 1 (2010).

"Diabetes and Cancer: A Dietary Portfolio for Management and Prevention of Heart Disease." *Proceedings of the Nutrition Society* 69, no. 1 (2010): 39–44.

Psaltopoulou, Theodora; Ioannis Ilias; and Mana Alevizaki. "The Role of Diet and Lifestyle in Primary, Secondary, and Tertiary Diabetes Prevention: A Review of Meta-Analyses." *Review of Diabetic Studies* 7, no. 1 (2010): 26–35.

Reisin, Efrain. "The Benefit of the Mediterranean-Style Diet in Patients with Newly Diagnosed Diabetes." *Current Hypertension Reports* 12, no. 2 (2010): 56–58.

Ruxton, Carrie H. S.; Elaine J. Gardner; and Helene M. McNulty. "Is Sugar Consumption Detrimental to Health? A Review of the Evidence 1995–2006." *Critical Reviews in Food Science and Nutrition* 50, no. 1 (2010): 1–19.

"The Use of Low-Glycemic Index Diets in Diabetes Control." *British Journal of Nutrition* 104, no. 6 (2010): 797–802.

Web Site

"What Can I Eat?" *American Diabetes Association.* http://www.diabetes.org/food-and-fitness/food/what-can-i-eat/ (accessed October 6, 2010).

Susan Aldridge

Diet and Heart Disease

■ Introduction

Diet plays an important role in both promoting and preventing coronary heart disease, which is the most common form of heart disease. Around half a million people die from heart disease each year, making it the most common cause of death, although mortality rates from heart disease have fallen in recent years. A diet rich in animal fats raises cholesterol and triglyceride levels, which is a potent risk factor for heart disease, because it leads to fatty plaque blocking the arteries. Conversely, a diet with plenty of fruits, vegetables, and fish provides both antioxidants and omega-3 fatty acids, which help prevent inflammation and free radical damage, both of which are thought to play a role in heart disease.

This knowledge of how components of the diet affect heart health is a result of many years of study of the diets and heart disease rates of populations of different countries. In the Mediterranean region heart disease rates are low, and research has shown that these peoples' diets—rich in fruit, vegetables, fish, whole grains, and olive oil—sprotect the heart. Unfortunately, the typical American diet, which is high in animal fat, has the opposite effect. It is not just what is eaten, but the amount, which is important. Obesity is a known risk factor for heart disease.

■ Historical Background and Scientific Foundations

The American physiologist Ancel Keys (1904–2004) was stationed in Italy during the 1940s and was struck by the observation of a colleague that Italians rarely get heart disease. This led him to set up the Seven Countries Study, in which 12,000 men from rural populations in countries with widely differing diets were monitored over a number of years. Participants from countries where much animal fat, including milk, meat, and cheese, was consumed, were more likely to die of heart disease than those from Mediterranean countries such as Greece and Italy, where fish, fruit, and vegetables were the staples of the diet. The link between diet and heart disease was cholesterol. Keys found higher cholesterol levels in the participants with the diets richer in animal fat, as well as higher levels of heart disease.

These studies led Keys to develop and popularize the idea of the Mediterranean diet in the 1960s and 1970s. The Mediterranean approach is based upon fruits, vegetables, nuts, seeds, fish, olive oil, bread, and a modest amount of wine. Animal fats are restricted. This is similar to the diet that the American Heart Association (AHA) currently recommends for heart health. Further studies have shown the value of the Mediterranean diet. For example, the Lyon Diet Heart Study was concerned with secondary prevention in people who had already had a heart attack. One group followed a modified Mediterranean diet, and, rather than using butter, substituted a spread with a fat composition such as olive oil, but with added alpha-linolenic acid. The other followed a typical Western diet. The Mediterranean diet group had a 50–70 percent decreased risk of having a second heart attack compared to the control group.

Research has also focused upon the benefits of omega-3 fatty acids in heart disease prevention. One of the first studies, in 1989, involved men with heart disease and found that those who ate extra fish had a 29 percent reduced risk of a recurrence. Omega-3 fatty acids stop the blood from thickening, stabilize the heart rhythm, and prevent inflammation. There is mounting evidence that inflammation plays a role in many diseases, including heart disease. Therefore, the AHA recommends eating two portions of oily fish such as salmon or tuna each week to get these benefits. The AHA does caution that some types of fish may contain high levels of mercury, PCBs (polychlorinated biphenyls), dioxins and other environmental contaminants, so eating certain fish such as shark, swordfish, and mackerel should be limited, especially by children and pregnant women, but that generally the positive benefits of fish in the diet outweigh any risks.

■ Impacts and Issues

Whereas heart disease remains the leading cause of death in the United States, mortality rates have more than halved since the late 1970s. This is true of all industrialized nations. Though it is likely that increased awareness of the importance of a healthy diet has had an influence, there are other factors involved. Treatment of heart disease has improved dramatically, which would have contributed to the improved survival rates. Unhealthy diets, obesity, lack of exercise, high blood pressure, and smoking, all of which lead to an increased heart disease risk, are still all too common in the United States.

In developing nations, changing life patterns among people who move from the countryside into burgeoning cities are also contributing to increased risks for heart disease. Diets of the new city dwellers change to more processed and fatty foods instead of their usual agrarian fare and bring about higher rates of obesity. Coupled with having less exercise compared to tending their farmland and livestock in their former rural homes, and walking shorter distances in the city, heart disease rates of residents in the mega cities of Africa are increasing.

WORDS TO KNOW

CHOLESTEROL: A waxy lipid found in animal foods and also produced in the body by the liver. Cholesterol is needed for essential bodily functions such as synthesis of cell membranes and hormones. Excess cholesterol may clog the arteries and lead to coronary heart disease and stroke.

CORONARY HEART DISEASE: In atherosclerosis, which is the main cause of coronary heart disease, fatty material, including cholesterol, forms a deposit called plaque on the inner walls of the arteries. This causes them to narrow—slowing or even stopping the flow of blood to the heart.

TRIGLYCERIDES: The chemical name for the form in which most fats exist both in the body and in foods. Higher levels of triglycerides in the blood, resulting from a high fat diet, are a known risk factor for coronary heart disease.

Cholesterol and triglycerides remain an important heart disease risk. However, cholesterol and triglyceride levels can often be lowered to within a healthier range

A field of canola, a rapeseed cultivar. Canola oil is recommended for people with heart disease, because it is low in saturated fat and high in monounsaturated fat. *Image copyright ncn18, 2010. Used under license from Shutterstock.com.*

by either drugs or by functional foods. Functional foods, sometimes known as nutraceuticals, have been manufactured to have a specific health benefit. A simple example would be vitamin C-fortified orange juice or margarine with vitamin D. Functional foods containing modified phytosterols, cholesterol-like compounds found in small amounts in many fruits, vegetables, nuts, seeds, legumes, vegetable oils, and other plant sources, have long been known to be capable of lowering low-density lipoprotein (LDL, or "bad" cholesterol) blood cholesterol levels. Consuming two to three grams per day of phytosterols in these products has been shown to lead to a significant lowering of LDL levels, which could possibly translate, in the long-term, into a reduction of about 25 percent in the risk of coronary heart disease. Levels of protective high-density lipoproteins (HDL, or "good" cholesterol) can also be raised by consuming phytosterols and other components of the Mediterranean diet, as well as exercise.

This knowledge has led to the development of a range of functional foods containing modified phytosterols. These compounds have been incorporated into spreads, breads, cereals, low-fat milk, low-fat cheese, yogurt, yogurt drinks. and orange juice. The products have the added bonus of being healthier alternatives to foods such as full-fat cheese and butter that are high in saturated fat and high in LDL cholesterol.

SEE ALSO *Cooking Fats; Diet and Hypertension; Dietary Changes in Rapidly Developing Countries; Dietary Guidelines for Americans; Dietary Reference Intakes: Fast Food; Functional Foods; Mediterranean Diet; Monounsaturated and Polyunsaturated Oils; Obesity; Salt, Nitrites, and Health; Standard American Diet and Changing American Diet.*

BIBLIOGRAPHY

Books

American Heart Association. *An Eating Plan for Healthy Americans: Our American Heart Association Diet.* Dallas: American Heart Association, 2005.

Beck, Leslie, and Michelle Gelok. *Heart Healthy Foods for Life: Preventing Heart Disease through Diet and Nutrition.* Toronto: Penguin Canada, 2009.

Smith, Elspeth. *Healthy Heart.* London: Simon & Schuster, 2005.

Periodicals

"The Effects of a Mediterranean Diet on Risk Factors for Heart Disease." Summaries for Patients. *Annals of Internal Medicine* 145, no. 1 (2006): 1–11.

Esposito, Katherine, Miryam Ciotola, and Dario Giugliano. "Low-Carbohydrate Diet and Coronary Heart Disease in Women." *The New England Journal of Medicine* 356, no. 7 (2007): 750–752.

Fung, Teresa T., et al. "Adherence to a Dash-Style Diet and Risk of Coronary Heart Disease and Stroke in Women." *Archives of Internal Medicine* 168, no. 7 (2008): 713–720.

Harris, William. "Omega-6 and Omega-3 Fatty Acids: Partners in Prevention." *Current Opinion in Clinical Nutrition and Metabolic Care* 13, no. 2 (2010): 125–129.

Kummerow, Fred A. "The Negative Effects of Hydrogenated Trans Fats and What to Do about Them." *Atherosclerosis* 205, no. 2 (2009): 458–465.

Lichtenstein, Alice H. "Diet, Heart Disease, and the Role of the Registered Dietitian." *Journal of the American Dietetic Association* 107, no. 2 (2007): 205–208.

Roehm, Eric. "The Evidence-Based Mediterranean Diet Reduces Coronary Heart Disease Risk, and Plant-Derived Monounsaturated Fats May Reduce Coronary Heart Disease Risk." *The American Journal of Clinical Nutrition* 90, no. 3 (2009): 697–698.

Shute, Nancy. "The Scoop on Carbs and Fats. A New Study Tries to Make Sense of Diet and the Risk of Heart Disease." *U.S. News & World Report* 141, no. 19 (2006): 89–90.

Van Horn, Linda. "Diet and Heart Disease: Continuing Contributions." *Journal of the American Dietetic Association* 108, no. 2 (2008): 203.

Web Sites

"Diet and Lifestyle Recommendations." *American Heart Association.* http://www.heart.org/HEARTORG/GettingHealthy/Diet-and-Lifestyle-Recommendations_UCM_305855_Article.jsp (accessed September 10, 2010).

"Fish and Omega-3 Fatty Acids." *American Heart Association.* http://www.americanheart.org/presenter.jhtml?identifier=4632 (accessed September 10, 2010).

Susan Aldridge

Diet and Hypertension

■ Introduction

Salt is found in most foods, and it is essential to human health. The common name for sodium chloride, salt has long been prized for its role in flavoring foods, and most chefs continue to regard it as an essential additive to their dishes. However, too much salt in the diet can lead to hypertension, although research into the reasons why this is so remains ongoing. Many people eat more salt than is necessary for normal bodily functioning because it is present in a wide range of foods. Hypertension increases the risk of many diseases, but excess salt is not the only cause: Other factors contributing to hypertension include obesity, excess alcohol consumption, and lack of exercise. Genetic differences probably account for why some people are more sensitive to salt than others. There is evidence from long-term clinical trials that following a low-salt diet can reduce the risk of heart disease, which is a complication of high blood pressure. Moreover, the Dietary Approaches to Hypertension diet, which emphasizes a high intake of fruits and vegetables, nuts, and olive oil, has been shown in several recent studies to not only reduce hypertension, but also the risk of associated complications.

■ Historical Background and Scientific Foundations

"Too much salt in food endangers the heart," according to the *Yellow Emperor's Classic of Internal Medicine*, which dates back around 2,000 years. Salt is cheap and widely available in the early twenty-first century, but in the Old Testament it was prescribed as an offering to God. Roman soldiers were given a special allowance called a salarium to buy salt with, which is the origin of the word salary. Other phrases such as "salt of the earth" and "worth his salt" show the esteem in which this common mineral was once held.

Salt, also known as sodium chloride, has long played a role in food and cuisine. It is an essential ingredient in cheese making because it dehydrates the curd as well as controls the ripening process. It is used in preserving foods and also as a flavor ingredient in many dishes and sauces. The body needs the sodium in salt for transmission of nerve impulses, for muscle contraction, and in fluid balance. The chloride component is also required in fluid balance and is a component of stomach acid.

Most people on a Western diet eat far more salt than is needed to maintain good health. The recommended limit of refined salt limit is six grams per day, which corresponds to about 2.4 grams of sodium. The American Heart Association recommends less that 3000 mg of sodium per day. Average intakes of ten grams (10,000 mg) per day or more are not uncommon in industrialized countries worldwide, because salt is found in widely eaten foods such cheese, bread, cereals, and many other processed products. However, studies of the Yanomamo Indians of the Amazonian rainforest, who traditionally consume less than a half gram of salt per day, conclude that good health can be maintained with minimal salt intake. Hypertension is unknown among the Yanomamo. The so-called INTERSALT studies included this group as well as participants whose salt intake was much higher than this. A link between salt intake and hypertension was thus established. This is important because hypertension is a potent risk factor for stroke, heart disease, and kidney disease.

Around one third of the American population has hypertension. Because it usually does not give rise to symptoms, many do not realize that their blood pressure is raised. Hypertension can be controlled by lifestyle changes, which include reducing salt, but also keeping to a healthy weight, reducing alcohol intake, and engaging in more exercise. Hypertension can also be treated with medication Studies have shown that a low salt diet, kept up for many years, can reduce the risk of heart disease by up to 25 percent.

WORDS TO KNOW

BLOOD PRESSURE: The pressure exerted by circulating blood upon the walls of the blood vessels. Blood pressure is measured in millimeters of mercury (mm Hg) and a reading is composed of two figures. The lower figure is the diastolic blood pressure, which corresponds to blood pressure in the resting phase of a heartbeat. The higher figure, the systolic blood pressure, is the blood pressure when the heart is actually contracting.

HYPERTENSION: Also known as high blood pressure, hypertension is defined as having systolic blood pressure greater than or equal to 140 and/or diastolic blood pressure greater than or equal to 90, or the state of being on medication for hypertension.

PREHYPERTENSION: A term that reflects increased risk through mildly raised blood pressure. Prehypertension is defined as having systolic blood pressure greater than or equal to 120 and/or diastolic blood pressure greater than or equal to 80.

■ Impacts and Issues

The link between salt intake and hypertension has always been controversial, with the food industry sometimes accusing the researchers of overstating their case. However, a number of manufacturers have committed to reducing the salt content of their products. Some people seem to be more sensitive to salt than others, owing to genetic differences. Salt is lost through urine and sweat and must be replaced in the diet. When salt was scarce, people with genes that helped them hang onto their body's salt in hot climates would have had a survival advantage. Modern genetic studies are uncovering some of these salt-related genes. For instance, researchers at the University of Chicago have been looking at a gene called CYP3A5 that acts in the kidney to retain salt. A variant of this gene produces a non-functioning protein that does not retain salt. The variant was least common in some natives of sub-Saharan Africa, but common in Europe and Asia, suggesting the survival advantage of holding onto salt in earlier times.

Dietary advice to reduce the risk of hypertension has gone beyond mere reduction of salt intake. The United States National Heart, Blood, and Lung Institute devised the Dietary Approaches to Stop Hypertension (DASH) diet in the early 1990s. DASH is high in fresh fruits and vegetables, whole grains, nuts, fish, and olive oil. It also includes low-fat dairy products. Several clinical trials have shown that those following the DASH diet not only reduce their blood pressure, but also their risk of heart disease.

A researcher with Campbell Soup Co. tastes several of Campbell's reduced sodium soups. *AP Images.*

SEE ALSO *Diet and Heart Disease; Dietary Changes in Rapidly Developing Countries; Dietary Guidelines for Americans; Dietary Reference Intakes; Fast Food; Preservation; Processed Foods; Salt; Salt, Nitrites, and Health; Therapeutic Diets; USDA Food Pyramid; Vitamins and Minerals.*

BIBLIOGRAPHY

Books

Anderson, Jennifer E. L., L. Young, and E. Long. *Diet and Hypertension.* Fort Collins: Colorado State University, Cooperative Extension, 2005.

Anderson, Patricia, Nancy Clark, and Jan Temple. *Eating Well—Moving More for Healthier Blood Pressure, Blood Cholesterol, and Weight: I Lowered My Blood Pressure, So Can You.* Ames: Iowa State University, 2008.

Black, Henry R., and William J. Elliott. *Hypertension: A Companion to Braunwald's Heart Disease.* Philadelphia: Elsevier Saunders, 2007.

Periodicals

Elias, Merrill F., and Amanda L. Goodell. "Diet and Exercise: Blood Pressure and Cognition: To Protect and Serve." *Hypertension* 55, no. 6 (2010): 1296–1298.

Nauänez-Caordoba, Jorge M., et al. "The Mediterranean Diet and Incidence of Hypertension." *American Journal of Epidemiology* 169, no. 3 (2009): 339–346.

Srinath, Reddy K., and Martin B. Katan. "Diet, Nutrition and the Prevention of Hypertension and Cardiovascular Diseases." *Public Health Nutrition* 7 (2004): 167–186.

Svetkey, Laura P., Denise G. Simons-Morton, et al. "Effect of the Dietary Approaches to Stop Hypertension Diet and Reduced Sodium Intake on Blood Pressure Control." *Journal of Clinical Hypertension* 6, no. 7 (2004): 373–381.

Web Sites

"Your Guide to Lowering Your Blood Pressure with DASH." *National Institutes of Health, U.S. Department of Health and Human Services.* http://www.nhlbi.nih.gov/health/public/heart/hbp/dash/new_dash.pdf (accessed September 1, 2010).

Susan Aldridge

Dietary Changes in Rapidly Developing Countries

■ Introduction

Diets are changing in the rapidly developing countries of Asia and Latin America. According to Engel's Law, increased income leads to a reduced proportion of income spent on food but to real increases in food spending. As countries' incomes increase, their populations' spending on food increases also, and the composition of that spending changes. Globalization influences dietary changes in the rapidly developing countries by providing convenience foods, various new choices in supermarkets, and new foods available from trade. Urbanization drives demand for convenience food as increases in women's workforce participation may decrease the time women have available for traditional food preparation practices. Whereas changing diets do not necessarily lead to poor nutritional outcomes, it appears the rapidly developing countries are consuming more calories, more meat, and more fat. Health problems associated with obesity are becoming more common as a result of these changing diets.

■ Historical Background and Scientific Foundations

Engel's law states that as income rises, the income earner will spend proportionally less income on food. However, while the proportion of income dedicated to food will fall, the real amount of spending will increase. Developing world consumers appear to be following Engel's law by buying more convenient forms of food, spending on more meals away from home, or simply buying more food or more expensive foods. Generally, more affluent consumers will spend, to a point, more on fruit, vegetables, meat, and dairy products compared to less affluent consumers. The per-capita income in developing countries tripled between 1970 and 2005. This has led to a shift in dietary choices towards increased consumption of meat, dairy, and other foods. Whereas lower income, middle income, and higher income countries all devote from 22 and

25 percent of food spending to meat and meat products, these constitute only 4 percent of total calories consumed for lower income countries. However, for middle-income countries, which include the rapidly developing countries, meat contributes between 7 and 11 percent of total calories. This figure rises to 13 percent of calories for upper income countries according to data from Euromonitor for 2006 as analyzed by the U.S. Department of Agriculture's Economic Research Service (USDA/ERS). So, following Engel's law, consumers start consuming more expensive forms of caloric intake such as more meat and dairy and more processed foods as their incomes increase. Engel's law is one factor in the changing diets of the rapidly developing countries.

Globalization and convergence in the food industry also appear to be a factor in dietary decisions. For example, in Latin America before the early 1980s, supermarkets appeared primarily in affluent neighborhoods. Their share of food sales was between 15 and 30 percent of total retail food sales in the 1970s, according to data cited by USDA/ERS. By 2001 supermarkets accounted for 50 to 70 percent of retail food sales in Latin America. Fast food outlets have also increased their presence and sales in the rapidly developing countries: In China, for example, sales at fast food outlets doubled from 1999 to 2005. The growing similarity between rich country food markets and those in rapidly developing countries is referred to as convergence. Multinational corporations involved in the food industry tend to invest in supermarkets, fast food, the snack food industry, and the soft drink industry all over the world. However, unlike other forms of foreign direct investment (FDI) from the developed world to the developing world, the food industry tends to expand through horizontal integration. Instead of vertically integrating by buying farms to provide ingredients, running food processing facilities, and owning retail sales outlets, food industry multinationals invest in a single step in the value chain across many different countries. For example, a worldwide brand such as Coca-Cola is bottled in many different countries with partial control at the local level. In addition to the increase in FDI in these countries, some foods enter via trade.

From 1970 to 2005, highly processed foods such as prepared breakfast cereals and wine increased in trade volume 500 percent worldwide, according to data from the Food and Agriculture Organization of the United Nations (FAO) analyzed by USDA/ERS. Bulk commodities are also traded, which is one contributing factor to the global fall of real food prices. Using prices adjusted for inflation, known as real prices, the prices of sugar, rice, and soybean oil were less than 40 percent of their 1970 price levels in 2000. Through 2008, food prices, for the most part, remained below 1970 levels when adjusted for inflation. Following the laws of supply and demand, the lower price of food will lead to increased demand for these foods by consumers.

Urbanization also influences consumers' food choices. Urban consumers may seek more convenient foods including ready-to-eat foods, partially prepared foods, fast food, and food from restaurants, street food vendors, and carry-outs. They also tend to participate in less physical activity than their rural counterparts. As the likelihood of women in urban areas working outside of

WORDS TO KNOW

ENGEL'S LAW: As a household's income increases, it will spend a lower percentage of income on food though its actual food expenditures may increase. The increase in spending is due to a shift in the diet away from grain to more expensive foods such as meat, dairy, fruits, and vegetables. Engel's law is named after Ernst Engel (1821–1896), the German economist and statistician who first wrote about it.

HORIZONTAL INTEGRATION: Controlling a single step or stage of a value chain.

MIDDLE-INCOME COUNTRY (MIC): A country that when compared to other countries in the world is neither very poor nor very rich. According to the World Bank, a middle-income country has a per capita gross national income (GNI) between 996 and 12,195 U.S. dollars. In 2010 middle income countries included Botswana, Brazil, Chile, China, Fiji, India, Indonesia, Jordan, Kazakhstan, Mexico, Nigeria, Russia, Senegal, South Africa, Thailand, and Turkey, among others.

People buy sweets at a shop in New Delhi, India, in preparation for Diwali celebrations. In recent years, however, a surge in obesity and diabetes rates in India among the middle class has led many Indians to turn to more healthful alternatives for celebrations. *AP Images.*

the home increases, they may devote less time for traditional food preparation practices. The increased income from women's participation in the formal workforce drives both demand for convenience food and provides some of the income to purchase these foods. From 1975 until 2005, the rate of urbanization in all developing countries outpaced the population growth rate by two to three times, according to USDA/ERS.

■ Impacts and Issues

The increased caloric consumption resulting from rising incomes may not result in improved nutrition. High-income and some middle-income countries had similar caloric consumption rates of around 3,300 calories per day per capita, according to a study by USDA/ERS in 1997. Consumption rates do not measure caloric intake because some food is wasted or unusable at all income levels. Urbanization rates play a role in food choice, as it appears more urbanized populations consume food higher in fat content. While having similar per capita incomes in 2005, Mexico is only 67 percent urban compared to Uruguay, a country in South America where 92 percent of the population is in urban areas. Mexicans consume one-half the fat of Uruguayans, according to a study by USDA/ERS in 2008. Culture and food preferences also play a role: Whereas Japan had the highest per capita gross domestic product (GDP) in 1997, it had the lowest caloric consumption rate of any higher income country at 2,900 calories daily compared to, for example, Ireland's consumption of 3,837 calories or the United States figure of 3,732 calories. The Japanese diet also remains heavily tilted towards vegetables, which comprise up to 80 percent of consumption. The example of Japan shows that higher income does not necessarily lead to poor dietary choices.

In 2008 the International Food Policy Research Institute (IFPRI) estimated there were one billion overweight people worldwide, a growing number of these in middle-income countries. Associated health problems from being overweight and obese include hypertension, diabetes, and coronary disease. The incidence rate for hypertension increased 12 percent in China between 1991 and 2002 according to the World Health Organization. Other middle income countries such as Thailand, Mexico, and Tunisia have seen rises in the rate of diabetes, which may affect 25 to 50 percent of their populations according to the World Health Organization (WHO). Health systems designed to deal with infectious diseases and widespread undernutrition may be unprepared for the consequences of high incidence of these new diseases caused by changing diets.

Some countries with highly unequal income distributions experience both widespread undernutrition and rising rates of obesity simultaneously. For example, in Guatemala, a country in Central America, the poorest

20 percent of the population receives 3 percent of the total income. These people only eat enough to meet 75 percent of recommended caloric intake and are at risk of malnutrition and undernutrition. At the same time, the most affluent 20 percent of the population receives 64 percent of the country's income and consumes 30 percent above the recommended caloric intake. This part of the population is more at risk of obesity than undernutrition. How to deal with these dietary changes and associated health problems will remain a challenge for both middle-income and higher-income countries.

■ Primary Source Connection

The U.S. Department of Agriculture (USDA) publishes a journal called *Amber Waves* dedicated to the "Economics of Food, Farming, Natural Resources, and Rural America." It is published four times a year. The following article from *Amber Waves* addresses global trends in people's food choices and expenditures and was the feature article of the February 2008 issue.

Converging Patterns in Global Food Consumption and Food Delivery Systems

Income growth, which is associated with increased demand for higher valued foods, is a primary force driving convergence in global diets. Consistent with Engel's Law, for a given change in income, lower income consumers make bigger changes in food expenditures than do higher income consumers. For example, a 10-percent increase in income is estimated to increase meat expenditures by 1 percent for the average U.S. consumer, but 7 percent for a consumer in a middle-income country such as Thailand.

Larger income-induced changes in lower income countries drive the food consumption trend toward convergence. The term convergence implies a dynamic process—movement from different starting levels toward some common outcome. In the case of food consumption, the common outcome is some universal "ceiling" or "saturation" level of demand for a particular food or food group, which is achieved at high income levels. Convergence can be statistically estimated as the speed of food expenditure changes over time across countries. This speed varies considerably—growth in food expenditures between 1998 and 2005 was as low as 14 percent in Japan and more than 100 percent in Indonesia.

Regression analyses conducted on food expenditure changes point to a high degree of convergence between middle- and high-income countries, particularly for total food expenditures and meat expenditures. Although actual food spending levels are higher in wealthier countries, middle-income countries show faster growth in expenditures. Middle-income countries thus appear to be "catching up" to countries with higher expenditure levels, leading to convergence (low-income countries had to be excluded from this analysis due to lack of reliable data).

Globalization of the food industry, as measured by the expansion of multinational retail and food service chains, is also contributing to converging trends. The last decade has witnessed an unprecedented rise in standardized retail outlets such as supermarkets, convenience stores, and large discount stores in developing countries. For example, supermarkets accounted for 15 to 30 percent of national retail sales of food in Latin America before the 1980s, but 50 to 70 percent in 2001, registering in two decades the level of growth experienced in the U.S. in five decades. The food retail structure in Asia is undergoing similar rapid changes.

Similarly, Western-style restaurants and fast food chains are becoming more prevalent in middle-income countries, where increasingly urban and dual-income household demand for convenient food supports expansion of these outlets.

Whereas local tastes and diets typically determine what products are sold, consumer choices are also being influenced by products sold in these standardized retail and foodservice outlets, which are often owned by multinational companies operating in several countries. As a result, the evolving food delivery system is also contributing toward converging trends in global food consumption patterns. . . .

In summary, income growth and globalization of the food retail and foodservice industry are giving rise to increasingly similar food consumption patterns across the world. Food consumption patterns of middle- and high-income countries, as indicated by their food spending across different food types over time, are converging. The expansion of Western-style retail and foodservice outlets is modernizing the food marketing sector in developing countries. At the current rate, ERS estimates that in about 20 years, food purchases in middle-income countries through Western-style grocery stores will approach 50 percent of the level of the sales in higher income countries. Convergence in the foodservice sector is moving faster, with expenditures in middle-income countries expected to reach 50 percent of the level of high-income countries within a decade. However, given ERS research showing that the foods U.S. consumers choose to eat away from home, on average, are higher in calories but lower in nutrients than foods eaten at home, these trends have important implications for obesity and health in developing countries.

"CONVERGING PATTERNS IN GLOBAL FOOD CONSUMPTION AND FOOD DELIVERY SYSTEMS." *AMBER WAVES,* FEBRUARY 2008. HTTP://WWW.ERS.USDA.GOV/AMBERWAVES/ FEBRUARY08/FEATURES/COVERGINGPATTERNS.HTM (ACCESSED NOVEMBER 4, 2010).

SEE ALSO *Agriculture and International Trade; Asian Diet; Biodiversity and Food Supply; Biofuels and World Hunger; Diet and Cancer; Diet and Diabetes; Diet and Heart Disease; Diet and Hypertension; Ecological Impacts of Various World Diets; Ethical Issues in Agriculture; Ethical Issues in Food Aid; Fair Trade; Food and Agriculture Organization (FAO); Food Security; Food Sovereignty; Free Trade and Agriculture; International Fund for Agricultural Development; Street Food; U.S. Agency for International Development (USAID); Women's Role in Global Food Preparation; World Food Programme; World Trade Organization (WTO).*

BIBLIOGRAPHY

Books

Caballero, Benjamin, and Barry M. Popkin. *The Nutrition Transition: Diet and Disease in the Developing World.* Amsterdam: Academic Press, 2006.

Hartog, Adele P., Wija A. Staveren, and Inge D. Brouwer. *Food Habits and Consumption in Developing Countries: Manual for Field Studies.* Wageningen, The Netherlands: Wageningen Academic, 2006.

Wang, Wuyi, Thomas Krafft, and Frauke Kraas. *Global Change, Urbanization and Health.* Beijing: China Meteorological Press, 2006.

Periodicals

Ebrahim, Shah, et al. "The Effect of Rural-to-Urban Migration on Obesity and Diabetes in India: A Cross-Sectional Study." *Plos Medicine* 7, no. 4 (2010): e1000268.

Tuei, Vivian C., Geoffrey K. Maiyoh, and Chung-Eun Ha. "Type 2 Diabetes Mellitus and Obesity in Sub-Saharan Africa." *Diabetes Metabolism Research and Reviews* 26, no. 6 (2010): 433–445.

Web Sites

"The Developing World's New Burden: Obesity." *Food and Agriculture Organization of the United Nations (FAO),* January 2002. http://www.fao.org/FOCUS/E/ obesity/obes1.htm (accessed October 15, 2010).

Smith, David. "Change Beckons for Billionth African." *Guardian co.uk,* December 28, 2009. http://www.guardian.co.uk/world/2009/ dec/28/billionth-african-future (accessed October 15, 2010).

Blake Jackson Stabler

Dietary Guidelines for Americans

■ Introduction

The dietary guidelines for Americans grew out of a report published by U.S. Senator George McGovern (1922–) and the Senate Select Committee on Nutrition and Human Needs in 1977. That first report was entitled *Dietary Goals for the United States*. The report made a number of specific dietary recommendations. It was not well-received by the scientific, nutrition, agricultural, and food service industries because the recommendations were based primarily on scientific and literature review rather than on dedicated research.

In an effort to address the many concerns, the Department of Health, Education, and Welfare (since renamed the Department of Health and Human Services) and the United States Department of Agriculture (USDA) were tasked with the creation of nationwide scientific panels, drawn from their respective departments, to create evidence-based guidelines for health and nutrition for the American public. This led to the publication, in 1980, of *Nutrition and Your Health: Dietary Guidelines for Americans*, issued jointly by the two departments. Also in 1980, the Senate Committee on Appropriations mandated that a federal advisory committee be created to remain abreast of nutritional and scientific developments in order to issue periodic revisions to the *Dietary Guidelines for Americans*.

The overarching goal of the dietary guidelines is to advise the American public above the age of two years on how best to consume adequate nutrition and maintain an appropriate degree of physical activity in order to achieve and maintain good health, as well as how to reduce risk for a variety of severe and chronic illnesses. As they have evolved, the dietary guidelines have become the foundation for many federal nutritional, educational, and dietary programs.

■ Historical Background and Scientific Foundations

After the initial publication of the controversial *Dietary Goals for the United States* in 1977 and the subsequent creation of the joint task force by the Departments of Health, Education, and Welfare and Agriculture, respectively, to create the initial edition of *Nutrition and Your Health: Dietary Guidelines for Americans* in 1980, an advisory committee composed of subject matter experts was impaneled in 1983 through 1984 in order to review critically the existent scientific data and research on nutrition and physical activity so as to be able to make recommendations for revisions to the first edition of the *Nutrition and Your Health: Dietary Guidelines for Americans*. The committee was composed of nine scientists from around the country who were not directly affiliated with any government agencies. They reported their findings to the two federal departments tasked with the production of the guidelines. The second edition of the *Nutrition and Your Health: Dietary Guidelines for Americans* was published in 1985 and was met with widespread professional and public approval.

In 1987 the *Conference Report of the House Committee on Appropriations* stated that the United States Department of Health and Human Services (DHHS), in collaboration with the USDA, "shall establish a Dietary Guidelines Advisory Group on a periodic basis. This Advisory Group will review the scientific data relevant to nutritional guidance and make recommendations on appropriate changes to the Secretaries of the Departments of Agriculture and Health and Human Services."

In 1989 the second federal advisory committee was convened in order to make recommendations for revision of the 1985 dietary guidelines, and in 1990 the third edition of *Nutrition and Your Health: Dietary Guidelines for Americans* was published. This edition was the first to look at recommendations for diet as a whole, rather than at key nutrients or specific foods. It was the first edition to specify recommended daily fat intake by type and amount.

In the same year, the 1990 National Nutrition Monitoring and Related Research Act was passed into federal legislation, mandating that new or revised editions of *Nutrition and Your Health: Dietary Guidelines for Americans* be published no less frequently than every five years and that every federal publication involving dietary guidance for the American general public be reviewed jointly by the USDA and DHHS. In every case, there is an advisory committee created two to three years before the publication of an edition of the guidelines. They complete their research and issue a report to the two federal departments, which then compile and create the subsequent edition of the dietary guidelines.

In 1993 the 11-member advisory committee for the revision of the third edition of the guidelines was appointed; in 1995 the fourth edition was published. This edition contained the first major additions to the guidelines: the Food Guide Pyramid, delineating types and amounts of nutrition recommended for daily consumption; nutrition facts labels required on packaging of prepared foods; charts quantifying three weight ranges by height; and suggestions for specific types of food consumption in order to obtain naturally the recommended amounts of essential nutrients.

The next advisory group was selected in 1997, leading to the publication of the fifth edition of the dietary guidelines in 2000. This edition marked the expansion of dietary recommendations from seven to 10. The initial recommendations were: "Eat a variety of foods; maintain a desirable weight; avoid too much fat, saturated fat and cholesterol; avoid too much sugar; avoid too much sodium; and, if you drink alcoholic beverages, do so in moderation." The expanded recommendations, published in 1995, were: "Balance the food you eat with physical activity—maintain or improve your weight; choose a diet with plenty of grain products, vegetables and fruits; choose a diet low in fat, saturated fat and cholesterol; eat a variety of foods; choose a diet moderate in salt and sodium; choose a diet moderate in sugars; and if you drink alcoholic beverages, do so in moderation." The expanded recommendations were divided into three areas. "Aim for fitness, aim for a healthy weight, and be physically active each day. Build a healthy base: Let the Pyramid guide your food choices; choose a variety of grains daily, especially whole grains; choose a variety of fruits and vegetables daily; and keep food safe to eat. Choose sensibly: Choose a diet that is low in saturated fat and cholesterol and moderate in total fat; choose beverages and foods to moderate your intake of sugars; choose and prepare foods with less salt; and, if you drink alcoholic beverages, do so in moderation."

WORDS TO KNOW

EVIDENCE-BASED: Using scientific method and research studies to determine the best practice in a specific discipline.

OBESITY EPIDEMIC: The steadily increasing self- and medically-documented incidence of obesity among Americans, both adults and children.

The 13-member advisory committee chosen in 2003 took a very strong data quality and evidence-based approach to scientific literature review, considering roughly 40 questions related to nutrition, wellness, physical activity, disease prevention, and wellness enhancement as a basis for guidelines revision and development. They reviewed the Institute of Medicine's Dietary Reference Intake reports, World Health Organization reports, and numerous Agency for Healthcare Research and Quality publications. The Committee also received guidance from acknowledged subject matter experts worldwide. The goal was the creation of a wholly data-based set of guidelines relevant to the diversity of the American population. In addition to the publication of the sixth edition of the *Nutrition and Your Health: Dietary Guidelines for Americans* in 2005, the departments also issued an 80-page policy piece.

The 13-member advisory committee for the seventh edition of the dietary guidelines was developed in 2008. They submitted their report to the two federal department secretaries in June 2010. Their work, researching the 180 scientific questions developed for the seventh edition of the dietary guidelines, utilized meta analysis of existing scientific data and data gleaned from the USDA's Nutrition Evidence Library as well as Institute of Medicine Reports, food pattern modeling through the use of the MyPyramid Food Guidance System developed for the 2005 edition, and public commentary gathered from a database developed specifically for this purpose.

■ Impacts and Issues

The purposes of the dietary guidelines are health improvement and promotion, along with reduction of risk for the development of severe and chronic illness. The information contained in each edition of the guidelines is used by a variety of federal agencies in their development of national food programs, nutrition education modules, and public information pieces. Federal law stipulates that the *Dietary Guidelines for Americans* must be "promoted by each Federal agency in carrying out any Federal food, nutrition, or health program." They inform the specific content of the National School Lunch Program; the educational modules used within the Women, Infants and Children Special Supplemental

Nutrition Program, in the development of the goals and objectives of the national Healthy People program, and in the creation of myriad public service announcements and publications related to diet and exercise for the American general public.

Based on data published by the Centers for Disease Control and Prevention, in the August 3, 2010, edition of the *Morbidity and Mortality Weekly Report*, the self-disclosed obesity prevalence in the United States in 2009 was 26.7 percent, with the highest rates of obesity self-reported among African Americans (36.8 percent), Hispanic-Americans (30.7 percent), individuals who did not complete high school (32.9 percent), individuals between the ages of 50 and 59 years (31.1 percent) and those between 60 and 69 years of age (30.9 percent). Despite six editions of dietary guidelines aimed at risk prevention and health promotion spanning 30 years, the American public has become steadily more obese and suffers from a myriad of illnesses related to what has been colloquially termed "the obesity epidemic in America." The dietary guidelines provide a broad base of information from which Americans can tailor their nutritional and physical activity choices in order to improve health and decrease risk of many types of preventable chronic and serious illness, yet the health of America (overall) continues to decline.

The dietary guidelines are not without controversy. There is much concern about the growing number of significantly to morbidly obese Americans, as well as the concomitant increase in serious, chronic, and life-threatening illnesses throughout the American population.

The October 2010 issue of the journal *Nutrition* contains an article that takes specific issue with the 2010 Dietary Guidelines Advisory Committee Report. The authors assert that information contained in the Report "is not based on sound scientific principles and demonstrable results. Reforming the food environment must begin with a re-evaluation of 30 y(ears) of nutritional policy that was originally implemented without a thorough and unbiased evaluation of the science." Essentially, the authors report that the American public has largely followed the recommendations made in the guidelines, while becoming increasingly more obese and experiencing progressively greater incidence of the health problems associated therewith. They suggest that a more responsible means of developing comprehensive dietary guidelines for the American public might be for a wholly neutral panel to be created from subject matter

Workers at a doughnut shop in North Carolina remove doughnuts from the production line. The *Dietary Guidelines for Americans* recommends a significant reduction of intake of foods that contain added sugar and solid fats. © *Jeff Greenberg / Alamy.*

expert scientists, drawn from fields apart from nutritional policy, who are tasked with the creation of impartial recommendations based on scientific principles and evidence-based research and practice.

SEE ALSO *Changing Nutritional Needs Throughout Life; Dietary Reference Intakes; Improving Nutrition for America's Children Act of 2010; Malnutrition; Nutrient Fortification of Foods; Nutrition; USDA Food Pyramid; Vitamins and Minerals.*

BIBLIOGRAPHY

Books

Duyff, Roberta L. *American Dietetic Association Complete Food and Nutrition Guide.* Hoboken, NJ: John Wiley & Sons, 2006.

Farrell, Marian L., and Jo A. L. Nicoteri. *Nutrition.* Sudbury, MA: Jones and Bartlett Publishers, 2007.

Nestle, Marion. *What to Eat.* New York: North Point Press, 2006.

U.S. Department of Agriculture (USDA) and U.S. Department of Health and Human Services. *Nutrition and Your Health: Dietary Guidelines for Americans,* 6th ed. Washington, DC: U.S. Government Printing Office, 2005.

Periodicals

Fite, Adele H., et al. "In the Face of Contradictory Evidence: Report of the Dietary Guidelines for Americans Committee." *Nutrition* 26, no. 10 (2010): 915–924.

U.S. Centers for Disease Control and Prevention. "Vital Signs: State-specific Obesity Prevalence among Adults—United States, 2009." *Morbidity and Mortality Weekly Report (MMWR)* 59 (August 3, 2010): 1–5.

Web Sites

"Dietary Guidelines for Americans." *U.S. Department of Health and Human Services.* http://www.health.gov/dietaryguidelines/ (accessed October 19, 2010).

Pamela V. Michaels

Dietary Reference Intakes

Introduction

Micronutrients, or vitamins and minerals, are essential to human health in many ways. For instance, calcium is needed for bone health and vitamin A for good vision. Dietary Reference Intakes (DRIs) are a guide to what constitutes sufficient intake of micronutrients in the diet to prevent vitamin and mineral deficiency and ensure good health. They reflect what is known of the impact of nutrition on health and are constantly being revised in light of new evidence. DRIs are specified for different age groups in the population, ranging from infants to the elderly and may also differ for men and women. Increasing awareness of DRIs has led to a thriving dietary supplements industry, which enables people to ensure they get their DRIs when their diet may be deficient or in cases of illness. Supplements ought not to be necessary if the diet provides all the micronutrient DRIs and may even be harmful if a person takes too much of an individual vitamin or mineral.

Historical Background and Scientific Foundations

The first recommended daily allowances (RDAs) for vitamins and minerals were published by the Food and Nutrition Board of the National Academy of Science in 1941, following advances in nutritional research in the 1920s and 1930s. The RDAs were intended to prevent obvious deficiency diseases such as pellagra (vitamin B3), night blindness (vitamin A), and rickets (vitamin D). The advent of RDAs led to food fortification to eliminate these diseases. RDAs were reviewed every five years in the light of the most recent research. Multivitamin and mineral dietary supplements have been popular for many years. In the 1980s the range of dietary supplements was expanded to include single vitamins. In 1997 the Institute of Medicine of the National Academy of Sciences began to replace RDAs with DRIs; a similar development occurred in Canada.

The DRI is not just one figure, but rather a set of values. The estimated average requirement (EAR) is the average daily intake of a vitamin or mineral that will meet the nutritional needs of 50 percent of a group. Meanwhile, the recommended daily allowance (RDA) is defined as the daily intake that will meet the nutritional needs of 98 percent of all healthy individuals in a group. The RDA, which is the figure most people will look at when planning their diet, is calculated from the EAR. Sometimes the EAR is unknown so the average intake, which is an estimate, is given instead. This also is meant to meet the needs of the majority of the group. DRIs go beyond the RDA because they include lower limits, below which deficiency will occur, and upper limits (ULs), above which harm from overdose may result. For carbohydrates, proteins, and fats, also known as the macronutrients, recommendations are given as Acceptable Macronutrient Distribution Ranges rather than DRIs. These are expressed as a percentage of the total calorie intake.

Although DRIs apply to daily intakes, their impact on health will be apparent only over time. On a daily basis, most people are likely to get either more or less of a specific micronutrient depending on what they eat on that day. DRIs are intended for healthy people and for groups within a population, rather than for the individual. Thus there are DRIs for children in various age bands, for adolescents, and for adults. The adult group is divided into men and women and further into pregnant and breastfeeding women. For some micronutrients, there may be specific requirements for older adults.

Impacts and Issues

DRIs are still a relatively imperfect tool for planning a diet for optimal health, mainly because of gaps in scientific knowledge on the impact of nutrition and health. For example, knowledge on upper limits is still incomplete, and those who use high-dose vitamin or mineral supplements, particularly of fat-soluble vitamins, could be at risk. There is also no distinction made between acute and chronic vitamin or mineral overdose problems. DRIs also do not take the issue of bioavailability into account, which can make it challenging for consumers to know which foodstuffs to eat to get their requirements. Nor do DRIs take account of genetic diversity within the population. Some groups within the age group bands may need more or less of a specific micronutrient because of their genetic background. At present, little is known of how genetic factors influence dietary needs but the field of nutrigenomics is a fast-growing one, so DRIs may become more tailored to the individual genotype in years to come.

DRIs are also meant for healthy people. Those who are ill may need more or less of specific micronutrients and may benefit from supplementation or dietary advice from a healthcare professional. But knowledge in this area is still limited. Moreover, supplements may interact with one another and with prescribed and

A woman runs during a cross country race. Daily activity level, along with gender, age, height, and weight, affects an individual's personalized Dietary Reference Intake recommendations. *Image copyright Shawn Pecor, 2010. Used under license from Shutterstock.com.*

WORDS TO KNOW

BIOAVAILABILITY: The degree to which an ingested substance, including a vitamin or mineral, can be absorbed and used by the body. For instance, iron in meat is more bioavailable than iron in spinach, although both foods are rich in the mineral.

DIETARY REFERENCE INTAKES: Developed by the Institute of Medicine of the National Academy of Sciences, Dietary Reference Intakes are intended to plan and assess nutrient intake for healthy people. DRIs include the recommended daily allowance (RDA) and also the tolerable upper intake level (UL), which is the maximum daily intake unlikely to result in adverse health effects. The DRIs are intended to plan and assess nutrient intake for healthy people.

DIETARY SUPPLEMENT: A product, such as vitamin, mineral, or herb, that is intended to be consumed in addition to the regular diet in the expectation that it will improve health.

over-the-counter drugs. Such interactions are not well understood but may alter the absorption, utilization, and excretion of various vitamins and minerals in ways that mean the person needs either more or less of a particular micronutrient.

Also, evidence of what constitutes an excessive amount is still lacking for many vitamins and minerals. DRIs for some micronutrients, such as vitamin D, may be in need of revising upwards in the light of emerging evidence on how diet can prevent chronic disease rather than just remedy obvious deficiency disease.

SEE ALSO *Changing Nutritional Needs throughout Life; Dietary Guidelines for Americans; Dietary Supplement Health and Education Act of 1994 (DSHEA); Nutrient Fortification of Foods; Nutrition; Nutrition's Role in Human Evolution; Vitamins and Minerals.*

BIBLIOGRAPHY

Books

Devaney, Barbara L. *Review of Dietary Reference Intakes for Selected Nutrients: Challenges and Implications for Federal Food and Nutrition Policy.* Washington, DC: USDA Economic Research Service, 2007.

Hewlings, Susan J., and Denis M. Medeiros. *Nutrition: Real People, Real Choices: Food Composition Table and Dietary Reference Intakes (DRIs): Recommended Intakes for Individuals of Elements.* Upper Saddle River, NJ: Pearson Prentice Hall, 2009.

Otten, Jennifer J., Jennifer P. Hellwig, and Linda D. Meyers. *DRI, Dietary Reference Intakes: The Essential Guide to Nutrient Requirements.* Washington, DC: National Academies Press, 2006.

Periodicals

Hambidge, K. M. "Micronutrient Bioavailability: Dietary Reference Intakes and a Future Perspective." *American Journal of Clinical Nutrition* 91, no. 5 (2010): 1430S–1432S.

Yetley, Elizabeth A., et al. "Dietary Reference Intakes for Vitamin D: Justification for a Review of the 1997 Values." *The American Journal of Clinical Nutrition* 89, no. 3 (2009): 719–727.

Web Sites

"Dietary Guidance." *Food and Nutrition Information Center, U.S. Department of Agriculture (USDA).* http://fnic.nal.usda.gov/nal_display/index.php?info_center=4&tax_level=2&tax_subject=256&level3_id=0&level4_id=0&level5_id=0&topic_id=1342&&placement_default=0> (accessed September 29, 2010).

"Dietary Reference Intakes (DRIs): Recommended Intakes for Individuals, Vitamins." *Food and Nutrition Board, National Institute of Medicine, U.S. Department of Agriculture (USDA).* http://iom.edu/en/Global/News%20Announcements/~/media/Files/Activity%20Files/Nutrition/DRIs/DRISummaryListing2.ashx (accessed September 29, 2010).

Penland, James G. "Dietary Reference Intakes (DRIs)—New Dietary Guidelines Really Are New!" *U.S. Department of Agriculture (USDA).* http://www.ars.usda.gov/News/docs.htm?docid=10870" (accessed September 29, 2010).

Susan Aldridge

Dietary Supplement Health and Education Act of 1994 (DSHEA)

■ Introduction

The Dietary Supplement Health and Education Act of 1994 (DSHEA) is an amendment to the Federal Food, Drug, and Cosmetic Act that establishes standards and regulations with respect to dietary supplements. DSHEA defines a dietary supplement as a "product . . . intended to supplement the diet" that contains one or more of the following: a vitamin, a mineral, an herb or other botanical, an amino acid, a dietary substance used to supplement the diet by increasing the total dietary intake, or a concentrate, metabolite, constituent, or extract that contains any combination of the preceding ingredients.

DSHEA contains a provision under which the U.S. Food and Drug Administration (FDA) may regulate dietary supplements. The FDA must regulate dietary supplements as a food: The FDA is not required to approve dietary supplements before sale, and the manufacturer does not have to prove that the supplement is safe or effective. The lack of robust safety regulations over dietary supplements has caused concern in the medical community and among consumer protection organizations.

■ Historical Background and Scientific Foundations

The FDA and similar drug and food regulatory agencies around the world recommend the intake of certain levels of vitamins and minerals to maintain health. People who do not obtain enough of a particular vitamin or mineral from diet often take dietary supplements containing the vitamin or mineral. Increasingly, however, consumers have turned to dietary supplements containing herbs or other substances derived from natural sources that are not recommended by the FDA, the World Health Organization (WHO), or Food and Agriculture Organization (FAO) of the United Nations for maintaining health. Some nations regulate dietary supplements as food, whereas other nations regulate dietary supplements as drugs or health products.

In the early 1990s the U.S. Congress considered legislation that would have strengthened the power of the FDA and the Federal Trade Commission (FTC) to regulate dietary supplements. One bill would have increased the power of the FDA to enforce the provisions of the Food, Drug, and Cosmetic Acts and increased penalties for violations. A separate bill would have made it illegal to advertise nutritional or therapeutic claims if the Food, Drug, and Cosmetic Act would bar placing such claims on the labels of dietary supplements. The dietary supplement industry responded to the proposed legislation by lobbying Congress and urging consumers to contact Congress over the proposed legislation.

The dietary supplement industry's lobbying and public action campaign was effective and resulted in Congress passing DSHEA. Under DSHEA, the FDA classifies dietary supplements as food, not as drugs. The Food, Drug, and Cosmetic Act and subsequent FDA regulations require pharmaceutical companies to obtain FDA approval for a drug before the drug may be sold. Pharmaceutical companies must undergo a lengthy process to prove the efficacy and safety of new drugs. Under DSHEA, however, dietary supplement manufacturers are not required to register a dietary supplement with the FDA or obtain FDA approval prior to sale. If a dietary supplement contains a new dietary ingredient, dietary supplement companies only need to inform the FDA that they will be selling the product.

■ Impacts and Issues

The most significant issue surrounding DSHEA is its lack of requirement of FDA approval before a company may manufacture and sell dietary supplements. The responsibility of proving that a dietary supplement is safe before being sold to the public lies solely with the company selling the product. The company must also self-report to the FDA

WORDS TO KNOW

DIETARY SUPPLEMENT: Any nutrient or combination of nutrients taken to supplement nutritional requirements, although legally the term may refer to herbs or other botanicals, amino acids, or other substances.

EPHEDRA: An herbal supplement, derived from the plant *Ephedra sinica*, which is a stimulant that may increase blood pressure and heart rate.

FOOD AND DRUG ADMINISTRATION: The U.S. federal agency that regulates, inspects, and approves the release of new foods and health-related products; often known as the FDA.

that the product is safe, but DSHEA does not require a particular process to evaluate the supplement's safety or effectiveness. Once a dietary supplement is on the market, the FDA may investigate reports of complications related to a particular supplement or category of supplements.

In the late 1990s and early years of the twenty-first century, the deaths of several people linked to the consumption of ephedra-based dietary supplements highlighted the potential dangers of the lack of regulation and oversight of the dietary supplement industry. Metabolife International, Inc., an American corporation, marketed an ephedra-based dietary supplement as a diet aid and realized annual sales of approximately $1 billion. Ephedra, an herbal extract, is a stimulant that increases blood pressure and heart rate.

The consumption of ephedra-based supplements produced by Metabolife and other companies resulted in thousands of incidents of serious adverse events, including at least 100 deaths. The FDA banned the sale of ephedra-based dietary supplements in 2004. The U.S. Department of Justice charged Michael Ellis, the founder of Metabolife, with eight counts of making false statements to the FDA about the health risks associated with ephedra. Ellis was sentenced to six months in prison after pleading guilty to one count of lying to the FDA.

DSHEA also regulates statements that a dietary supplement company may make about its products. DSHEA allows dietary supplements to bear statements of nutritional support, which claim a benefit related to nutrient deficiencies or describe how a substance affects the body. A dietary supplement may not contain claims that suggest that the product may be used to prevent or treat a disease. Statements of nutritional support also may not be misleading.

A pharmacy shelf displays dietary supplements.   © *Jeff Greenberg / Alamy.*

Congress has considered several proposals that would impose additional regulations on dietary supplement companies or increase the penalties for violating DSHEA or other food laws. In 2010, U.S. Senators John McCain ([1936–]; R-AZ) and Byron Dorgan ([1942–]; D-ND) introduced the Dietary Supplement Safety Act of 2010. The bill would have required dietary supplement manufacturers to register their products with the FDA and disclose all of the ingredients contained in the supplement. The law also would have granted the FDA the power to issue mandatory recalls of supplements found to be unsafe. The FDA, with its limited powers under DSHEA, took over a decade to ban ephedra after the reports of ephedra-related deaths. In May 2010, Senator McCain withdrew his sponsorship of the bill and announced that he would work with Senator Orrin Hatch ([1934–]; R-UT), an author of DSHEA, on a new bill to increase transparency and safety within the dietary supplement industry.

Also in 2010 the Consumers Union, a U.S. consumer protection organization, published a report in its periodical *Consumer Reports* evaluating dietary supplements. An examination of dietary supplements revealed that some supplements were contaminated with heavy metals, pesticides, or prescription drugs. The report stated that only one-third of more than 54,000 dietary supplements listed in Natural Medicines Comprehensive Database had scientific evidence to support their safety or efficacy.

SEE ALSO *Center for Food Safety and Applied Nutrition; Food Safety and Inspection Service; Functional Foods; Herbs and Spices; Nutrient Fortification of Foods; U.S. Food and Drug Administration (FDA).*

BIBLIOGRAPHY

Books

Bass, Scott. *The Dietary Supplement Health and Education Act: Regulation at a Crossroads.* Boston, MA: American Society of Law, Medicine & Ethics (ASLME); Boston University School of Law, 2005.

Hurley, Dan. *Natural Causes: Death, Lies, and Politics in America's Vitamin and Herbal Supplement Industry* New York: Boradway, 2006.

Williams, Elizabeth M., and Stephanie J. Carter. *The A–Z Encyclopedia of Food Controversies and the Law.* Santa Barbara, CA: Greenwood, 2010.

Periodicals

Geraghty, Maureen E., Jody Bates-Wall, and Christopher A. Taylor. "The Factors Associated with Dietary Supplement Use in College Students." *Journal of the American Dietetic Association* 108, no. 3 (2008): A29.

Mehta, Darshan H., Paula M. Gardine, Russell S. Phillips, and Ellen P. McCarthy. "Herbal and Dietary Supplement Disclosure to Health Care Providers by Individuals with Chronic Conditions." *Journal of Alternative and Complementary Medicine* 14, no. 10 (2008): 1263–1269.

Saldanha, Leila. "The Dietary Supplement Marketplace: Constantly Evolving." *Nutrition Today* 42, no. 2 (2007): 52–54.

Web Sites

"Dietary Supplement Health and Education Act of 1994." *Office of Dietary Supplements, National Institutes of Health.* http://ods.od.nih.gov/About/DSHEA_Wording.aspx (accessed September 26, 2010).

"Dietary Supplements." *U.S. Food and Drug Administration (FDA).* http://www.fda.gov/food/dietary-supplements/default.htm (accessed September 26, 2010).

"Tips for the Savvy Supplement User: Making Informed Decisions and Evaluating Information." *U.S. Food and Drug Administration (FDA).* http://www.fda.gov/Food/DietarySupplements/ConsumerInformation/ucm110567.htm (accessed September 26 2010).

Joseph P. Hyder

Disasters and Food Supply

■ Introduction

Disaster preparedness, response, and recovery: These are the basic elements of disaster or emergency management. Disaster management incorporates anticipating, dealing with, and minimizing risks. Preparedness is an investment against human-caused and natural disasters, which can include plans for use and deployment of resources, human and financial. In food supply terms, preparedness may include stockpiling at local or national levels, obtaining financial commitments, fostering local organization, and creating policy focusing on differing probabilities of "what if" scenarios for disaster occurrences.

The response is the set of actions put into place when the disaster hits. At that point, the clock starts ticking; time is an essential enemy of the response. Being as prepared as possible helps, but an accurate anticipation of likely future events and how these might unfold can be complex and makes the process of preparedness very challenging.

Surveillance and mitigation planning are also invaluable in reducing the impacts of disastrous events on food supplies. Through the lens of food supply, predictability and scale of a disaster will define the extent of its impact on populations. Seasonal drought, for example, tends to be more predictable, whereas hurricanes tend to have much shorter lead warning times. Human-caused disasters that could affect food supplies include hazardous material spills, infrastructure failure, and bioterrorism, as well as war and conflict. Since 1990 the proportion of short and long-term food crises that can be attributed to human causes has more than doubled, rising from 15 percent to more than 35 percent, many triggered by conflicts.

■ Historical Background and Scientific Foundations

Within the United Nations (UN), responsibility for emergency response rests with the Resident Coordinator within the affected country. At the international level, disaster response is coordinated by the UN Office for the Coordination of Humanitarian Affairs (UN-OCHA), when requested by the affected country's government.

Other main players in international emergency response include the National Red Cross/Red Crescent societies, which often have pivotal roles in responding to emergencies; the World Bank, which has approved more than 500 emergency response operations since 1980 for both response and mitigation efforts; regional governments, such as the European Union; and nongovernmental organizations (NGOs) that may also play a role.

In developed countries, national organizations formulate and manage the country's emergency preparedness and response. Since the end of the Cold War in the early 1990s, the term *emergency management* has largely eclipsed *civil defense*, in which the original focus was protecting civilians from military attack. The term *civil protection* is widely used within the European Union for response to both natural and human-made disasters. Whatever the terminology, emergency management depends on local economic, social, and environmental conditions.

■ Impacts and Issues

According to the World Food Programme (WFP), after a disaster, "whether refugees are fleeing war, floods are washing away homes, or drought is destroying farmland, hunger is often the first emergency." Time saved can mean lives saved. The challenge for global organizations such as the WFP is meeting the time demands. They must assess the needs in the local area, which means deployment of assessment teams and planning the response, from how much food is needed to the logistics of how it can be delivered to the hungry.

When food stocks are deployed from international sources, which is often the case, it is necessary to identify which agencies serve the area, which transport corridors are intact, and which will lead to the crisis zone. The formal response plan then enables a formal appeal for funds to the international community. After the 2004 Indian Ocean tsunami, for example, the WFP demonstrated its ability to mobilize people and provisions by being one of the first humanitarian agencies at the heart of the worst hit areas.

As funds and food start to flow, food is transported to crisis zones using ships, planes, helicopters, and trucks. Sometimes, before the aid can reach its country of destination, logistics experts need to upgrade ports and secure warehouses.

When the food reaches designated distribution sites, such as refugee camps, therapeutic feeding centers, and other emergency shelters, governments and NGOs help deliver food to the hungry. The WFP works with about 3,000 international and local NGOs to distribute food aid. At this stage, local community leaders work closely with the WFP to ensure rations reach the people who need it most: mothers, pregnant women, children, the injured, and the elderly.

Pakistan Case Study

Over the course of the 2010 monsoon season, Pakistan battled an unprecedented catastrophe when it was hit by the worst floods in its history. Heavy rainfall, flash floods, and riverine floods combined to create a moving

---

WORDS TO KNOW

DISASTER RECOVERY: Distinct from disaster management, disaster recovery encompasses the process, policies, and procedures related to preparing for recovery or continuation of technology infrastructure critical to an organization after a natural or human-induced disaster.

EMERGENCY RELIEF: The aspect of humanitarian assistance that seeks to directly preserve life, health, and safety and directly protect livelihoods and dignity.

RECOVERY: The aspect of humanitarian assistance that seeks to prevent further deterioration of and restoring basic living conditions, services, livelihoods, security and rule of law, and national capacities.

---

body of water equal in dimension to the land mass of the United Kingdom, according to the UN emergency response plan report. The floods affected 84 of 121 districts in Pakistan and more than 20 million people (one-tenth of Pakistan's population), devastating homes and farmlands from the Himalayas to the Arabian Sea.

The scale of the disaster multiplied the complexities of the response. In food aid requirements alone, the

Pallets of food and water are air delivered to the outskirts of Port-au-Prince, Haiti, following the earthquake of January 12, 2010.
© *Stocktrek Images, Inc. / Alamy.*

IN CONTEXT: FOOD NEEDS DRIVE AND DIVERT HAITIAN EARTHQUAKE RECOVERY EFFORTS

Following the devastating January 2010 earthquake in Haiti, relief agencies raced to repair destroyed transportation infrastructure and replenish decimated emergency food supplies that would be needed during a hurricane evacuation. UN World Food Programme and other relief agency officials and workers struggled to balance daily needs against the need to set aside rations sufficient to sustain people in camps and shelters in the event of tropical weather. The race was made more urgent by predictions of a highly active 2010 hurricane season. By August, more than 2 million meals were diverted to shelters scattered across the island. Knowing that food distribution would be critical, officials also dedicated recovery resources to the construction of a special barge service connecting Haitian ports that could be used to move food supplies if the still fragile road system were to be blocked by storm damage.

response plan identified 10 million people in need of food rations who were unable to meet their immediate food needs or rebuild their livelihoods. But in any disaster, food aid cannot be examined in isolation.

The concurrent and interrelated issues include health and nutrition related issues, especially for children and mothers; displacement of people from their schools, jobs, and farms; and social unrest from which the most vulnerable need protection. Setting up refugee camps requires extensive resources, including necessities from tents, bedding, mats, and kitchen sets to latrines, safe drinking water, and hygiene kits. Delivery of food aid and other resources in the case of Pakistan was exacerbated by the loss of logistical corridors, particularly roads. And contingency planning for the risk of an early winter put even greater time pressure on the response.

The agricultural response is always critical in rural regions. In the case of the Pakistan floods, the vulnerable included smallholder farmers, landless agricultural workers and sharecroppers, and women-headed households who were either displaced or badly affected by the floods. The food aid response also aims to help these farmers and farm workers to resume productive agriculture activities and contribute to livelihood recovery. They are provided with agricultural inputs such as seeds or fertilizers to help revive and restore productive agricultural activities, as well as with livestock support such as animal feed.

The single biggest issue facing disaster response, whether in developing or developed countries, is sufficient, timely, and appropriate mobilization of resources—financial, human, and otherwise. In Pakistan

the floods presented a massive economic challenge: By September 2010, the UN had raised close to 70 percent of the $460 million appeal, but oftentimes pledges are slow to be mobilized, especially when the disaster fades from the media spotlight.

After the 2010 Haitian earthquake, for example, numerous national governments from around the world pledged to coordinate and send humanitarian aid to the Haitian people affected by the disaster. However, more than six months after the quake, less than one-tenth of the money that was pledged by foreign governments to the UN fund for the Haitian earthquake was actually received.

Failures within a disaster response stem from many factors, both controllable and uncontrollable. The challenge of multi-agency coordination means inefficiencies and ineffectiveness will be inevitable in parts of the response. Poor risk assessment also lays the foundation for poor preparation, a reason many people attribute to the response failures during hurricane Katrina that devastated the U.S. Gulf Coast in 2005, including the inability to provide food and water to residents trapped at the New Orleans Superdome. In contrast, the U.S. Coast Guard mounted a rapid and efficient response to the disaster, saving countless people trapped on roofs and in trees during the height of the flooding in New Orleans and delivering them to shelters where clean water and food were available.

Reducing Risk

Risk mitigation can be an elusive challenge, as most people are not inclined to take steps to reduce risk if it means, for example, moving from their homes. In fact, most disaster preparedness still focuses on how to manage when populations end up in harm's way, rather than on preventing people from being in harm's way. In the United States, officials urge each household to maintain a three-day supply of food and water for all family members in order to be self sufficient in the early days of a disaster while help strategies are formulated and mobilized.

SEE ALSO *African Famine Relief; Bioterrorism: Food as a Weapon; Famine; Food and Agriculture Organization (FAO); Food Security; Hunger; International Food Aid; International Fund for Agricultural Development; U.S. Agency for International Development (USAID); World Food Programme.*

BIBLIOGRAPHY

Books

Doornbos, Martin R. *Complex Emergencies, Food Security and the Quest for Appropriate Institutional Capacity.* The Hague, The Netherlands: Institute of Social Studies, 2006.

Fountain, Brent J. *Disaster Relief: Facts about Food & Floods.* Starkville: Mississippi State University Extension Service, 2008.

Maxwell, Daniel. *Emergency Food Security Interventions.* London: Humanitarian Practice Network, 2008.

United Nations World Food Programme: Indian Ocean Tsunami Emergency Operation. Colombo: UNWFP, 2006.

Periodicals

Brodie, Mollyann, et al. "Experiences of Hurricane Katrina Evacuees in Houston Shelters: Implications for Future Planning." *American Journal of Public Health* 96, no. 8 (2006): 1402–1408.

Dalton, Craig B., Michelle A. Cretikos, and David N. Durrheim. "A Food 'Lifeboat': Food and Nutrition Considerations in the Event of a Pandemic or Other Catastrophe." *The Medical Journal of Australia* 188, no. 11 (2008): 679.

Jayatissa, Renuka, Aberra Bekele, C. L. Piyasena, and S. Mahamithawa. "Assessment of Nutritional Status of Children under Five Years of Age, Pregnant Women, and Lactating Women Living in Relief Camps after the Tsunami in Sri Lanka." *Food and Nutrition Bulletin* 27, no. 2 (2006): 144–152.

Liu, Yifan, and Lawrence M. Wein. "Mathematically Assessing the Consequences of Food Terrorism Scenarios." *Journal of Food Science* 73, no. 7 (2008): 346–353.

MacDonald, Rhona. "Save Somalia!" *Lancet* 373, no. 9682 (2009): 2184.

Singh, Neeta. "Expert System Prototype of Food Aid Distribution." *Asia Pacific Journal of Clinical Nutrition* 16 (2007): 116–121.

Web Sites

"Chadians Face a Threefold Emergency of Hunger, Floods, and Cholera." *Médecins Sans Frontières (Doctors without Borders),* October 4, 2010. http://www.msf.org/msf/articles/2010/10/chadians-face-a-threefold-emergency-of-hunger-floods-and-cholera.cfm (accessed October 15, 2010).

"Pakistan Emergency." *World Food Programme.* http://www.wfp.org/crisis/pakistan (accessed October 15, 2010).

Melissa Carson

E. Coli Contamination

■ Introduction

Escherichia coli is a common and widespread bacterial species found in the environment and as a commensal organism associated with humans and other animals. Normally, *E. coli* performs a beneficial role in the digestive tract by preventing the growth of harmful organisms and by synthesizing vitamins.

Thousands of genetically distinct strains or serotypes of *E. coli* are known, but of these only a few are pathogenic. Some serotypes have gained the ability to invade healthy cells and cause diseases of varying severity. Bacteriological studies during the early- and mid-twentieth century identified some strains of *E. coli* that were implicated in gastroenteritis. Two of the early-known strains, which were called enteropathogenic because they caused disease in the intestines, were O111 and O55.

A newer and more dangerous strain called O157:H7 (O157 for short) emerged in the 1970s in the United States. O157 produces verotoxin or shiga-like toxins, which are also produced by the pathogenic bacterium *Shigella dysenteriae*. These toxins are damaging to the intestinal lining.

■ Historical Background and Scientific Foundations

E. coli O157 is dangerous because of genetic changes that have transformed it into a pathogen; its common presence in and around cattle living in crowded conditions; an ability to survive outside of its natural enteric environment; and a low infectious dose, possibly as low as ten organisms.

Young children, the elderly, and immunocompromised individuals (persons with weakened immune systems) are more at risk for the lethal form of the disease than healthy adults are. In most cases, O157 strains cause mild diarrhea, which is usually self-limiting to within a week to ten days. If the infection enters a more acute phase called hemorrhagic colitis, the watery stool becomes infused with blood. Other symptoms of infection include abdominal pain and vomiting. Fever is usually low-grade or absent.

If untreated, the bacteria can spread from the digestive system to colonize other organs of the body. Death can occur rapidly. In children especially, there is a risk of contracting hemolytic uremic syndrome (HUS), which damages the kidneys and causes loss of red blood cells (hemolytic anemia). Hemolytic anemia can lead to heart failure and is especially dangerous for those with preexisting heart, vascular, or renal conditions. Up to 15 percent of children infected with O157 go on to develop HUS. Elderly patients are also at risk for HUS and an additional neurological condition called thrombotic thrombocytopenic purpura (TTP). This complication results in fever and low platelet count caused by the formation of small blood clots throughout the body that are visible as purple lesions under the skin. The mortality rate of elderly TPP sufferers is as high as 50 percent.

The onset of hemorrhagic colitis usually results in a trip to the hospital and should trigger a rapid diagnostic response from health care providers. The presence of pathogenic *E. coli* is detected by the isolation of the O157 serotype in patient stool samples. Some labs are able to directly test stool samples for verotoxin, which results in more rapid diagnosis than a culture test. If O157 or another verotoxin producing strain is confirmed, a search for the organism is then made to find the source, which is usually a contaminated food. It is possible to suffer from an O157 event and not become seriously ill. For this reason, it is likely that cases of O157 are underreported.

Normally, *E. coli* inhabits the human gut without causing harm. However, O157 has obtained a suite of genes via the horizontal transfer of virulence factors. At the chromosomal level, O157 is essentially identical to any other *E. coli* strain. It is when the DNA on smaller non-chromosomal DNA (plasmids) is analyzed that the

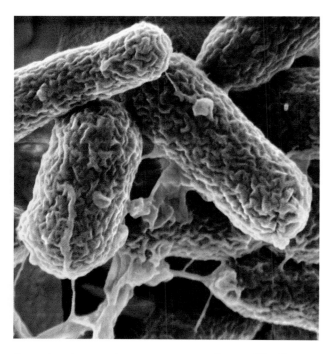

A scanning electron microscope captures an image of *E. coli* bacteria. © *PHOTOTAKE Inc. / Alamy.*

virulence genes are detected. Molecular studies suggest that the O157:H7 serotype arose quite recently by transduction, wherein foreign DNA is introduced by the infection of a bacterium by a virus.

■ Impacts and Issues

Recorded outbreaks of disease caused by the earlier known pathogenic strains of *E. coli*, O55 and O111, occurred in Scotland in the 1940s, in Indonesia in 1960, and the United States and Canada in the 1970s. These strains use the same molecular mechanism for adhering to cells as does O157, but they lack the ability to produce shigatoxins. It has been proposed that O55 is a direct descendant of O157, with anecdotal evidence indicating that O157 originated in Argentinean cattle during the 1960s.

The first outbreaks of illness linked to O157 occurred in the United States in the early 1980s, although a retrospective study done by the Centers for Disease Control and Prevention identified a previous case from a sample collected from a patient in 1975. The complete genome sequence of an O157 strain was first reported in 2001, although it has not yielded as much information as was hoped that would be useful in creating better preventions or treatments for infections.

By far the greatest risk of exposure to enteropathogenic bacteria comes from contaminated food. Sources typically implicated in outbreaks include undercooked hamburger, unpasteurized juices and milk, and vegetables that have been field irrigated with sewage-contaminated water. Cattle manure is a rich source of

E. coli bacteria, and any product contacting cattle waste (which is also composted to make an excellent fertilizer) can potentially be exposed to O157. Hamburger is the most commonly contaminated meat to cause widespread illness, because a small introduction of bacteria into a processing plant is efficiently spread to the plant's entire output by the grinding and mixing process.

Although the consequences of *E. coli* contamination are serious, the food processing industry has been resistant to increased monitoring. This is because of the costs associated with additional testing. The cost of product recalls and legal settlements paid to harmed consumers may eventually bring about a change.

In 2001 a two-year-old Colorado boy named Kevin Kowalcyk died after eating a hamburger contaminated with O157:H7. Since then, his mother, Barbara Kowalcyk, has worked to get the U.S. Congress to pass what is known as "Kevin's Law" (originating as the Meat and Poultry Pathogen Reduction Act of 2003). The original bill and several subsequent versions have not made it out of committee for consideration by the full congress. As of August 2010, no version of the bill was pending action.

New serotypes of *E. coli* continue to arise, some of which are pathogenic. A May 2010 outbreak of bloody diarrhea in the northeastern United States has been linked to a new shiga-toxin producing strain identified as O145. Of the 30 patients exhibiting symptoms, 40 percent required hospitalization. The source of the bacteria was shredded lettuce from a single processing facility. Another hemorrhagic strain called O26 was found in ground beef in August of 2010.

It is somewhat of a paradox that a well-studied organism such as *E. coli* presents such medical and food safety challenges. Most knowledge about the species has

IN CONTEXT: AVOIDING *E. COLI* CONTAMINATION AND EXPOSURE IN FOOD

To avoid *E. coli* O157:H7 contamination and exposure resulting in potential infection, the U.S. Department of Agriculture's Food Safety and Inspection Service and the Centers for Disease Control and Prevention (CDC) recommend that people:

- Cook all ground beef and hamburger thoroughly. Because ground beef can turn brown before disease-causing bacteria are killed, use a digital instant-read meat thermometer to ensure thorough cooking. Ground beef should be cooked until a thermometer inserted into several parts of the patty, including the thickest part, reads at least 160°F (71.1°C). Persons who cook ground beef without using a thermometer can decrease their risk of illness by not eating ground beef patties that are still pink in the middle.

- If served an undercooked hamburger or other ground beef product in a restaurant, send it back for further cooking. It would be prudent to ask for a new bun and a clean plate, too.

- Avoid spreading harmful bacteria in the kitchen. Keep raw meat separate from ready-to-eat foods. Wash hands, counters, and utensils with hot soapy water after they touch raw meat. Never place cooked hamburgers or ground beef on the unwashed plate that held raw patties. Wash meat thermometers in between tests of patties that require further cooking.

- Drink only pasteurized milk, juice, or cider. Commercial juice with an extended shelf-life that is sold at room temperature (e.g. juice in cardboard boxes, vacuum sealed juice in glass containers) has been pasteurized, although this is generally not indicated on the label. Juice concentrates are also heated sufficiently to kill pathogens.

- Wash fruits and vegetables under running water, especially those that will not be cooked. Be aware that bacteria are sticky, so even thorough washing may not remove all contamination. Remove the outer leaves of leafy vegetables. Children under 5 years of age, immunocompromised persons, and the elderly should avoid eating alfalfa sprouts until their safety can be assured. Persons at high risk of complications from foodborne illness may choose to consume cooked vegetables and peeled fruits.

- Make sure that persons with diarrhea, especially children, wash their hands carefully with soap after bowel movements to reduce the risk of spreading infection, and that persons wash hands after changing soiled diapers. Anyone with a diarrheal illness should avoid swimming in public pools or lakes, sharing baths with others, and preparing food for others.

SOURCE: *Centers for Disease Control and Prevention (CDC).*

been gained through study in the artificial environment of the laboratory and not in the complex natural environment, which includes populations of both humans and cattle.

SEE ALSO *Center for Food Safety and Applied Nutrition; Consumer Food Safety Recommendations; Factory Farming; Food Inspection and Standards; Food Recalls; Food Safety and Inspection Service; Foodborne Diseases; Humane Animal Farming; Livestock Intensity and Demand; Meat Inspection Act of 1906; Meats; Pure Food and Drug Act of 1906; Raw Milk Campaign; Staphylococcal Food Poisoning; Wholesome Meat Act of 1967.*

BIBLIOGRAPHY

Books

Lew, Kristi. *Food Poisoning: E. Coli and the Food Supply.* New York: Rosen, 2011.

Pennington, Thomas Hugh. *When Food Kills: BSE, E. Coli, and Disaster Science.* Oxford and New York: Oxford University Press, 2003.

Periodicals

Groves, Rachel M. "E. Coli Outbreak." *The American Journal of Nursing* 107, no. 10 (2007): 16.

Pearson, Helen. "The Dark Side of E. Coli." *Nature* 445, no. 7123 (2007): 8–9.

Tyagi, Sanjay. "E. Coli, What a Noisy Bug." *Science* 329, no. 5991 (2010): 518–519.

Web Sites

"*Escherichia coli* O157:H7." *National Center for Zoonotic, Vector-Borne, and Enteric Diseases, U.S. Centers for Disease Control and Prevention (CDC).* http://www.cdc.gov/nczved/divisions/dfbmd/diseases/ecoli_o157h7/ (accessed September 1, 2010).

U.S. National Library of Medicine. "E. coli Enteritis." *Medline Plus.* http://www.nlm.nih.gov/medlineplus/ency/article/000296.htm (accessed September 1, 2010).

Philip McIntosh

Eating Disorders

■ Introduction

An eating disorder is defined as any pattern of consuming food, or intentionally refusing to consume food, that interferes with a person's physical, psychological, and/or emotional health. Anorexia nervosa involves intentional restriction of food for weight loss; patients lose anywhere from 15 to 60 percent of their body weight, and the mortality rate is estimated between 4 and 18 percent, the highest of all psychiatric disorders. Patients with bulimia nervosa alternate between episodes of anorexia and binge-purge cycles. A bulimic typically binges—consumes extremely large amounts of food in one sitting—then purges the food through forced vomiting, diuretic, and laxative use, or through extreme exercise designed to burn off the number of calories consumed. Binge eating disorder involves only the binge in bulimia, and not the purging behavior.

Orthorexia nervosa, while not an officially recognized psychiatric diagnosis, shares many characteristics with eating disorders, and describes people who seek perfection in the food they consume in terms of specific micronutrients, organic or local produce, or balance of calories between fats, carbohydrates and proteins. Orthorexia takes healthy eating to disordered extremes, often leading to the emaciation seen in anorexia.

■ Historical Background and Scientific Foundations

While there had been documented cases of "holy anorexia"—intentional self-starvation for religious purity means—by women such as Catherine de Siena (1347–1380) in fourteenth-century Europe, anorexia gained wider notice in 1868 when British Physician Sir William Whitney Gull (1816–1890) noted self-starvation in teenage female patients. A French contemporary, Charles Lasègue (1816–1883), documented anorexia cases he observed, but also wrote about patients with disordered eating who purged in an effort to control weight. He used the term "cynorexia" to describe what is now known as bulimia nervosa.

During the Victorian era anorexia was understood to be a psychological disorder, with the social and cultural aspect of food part of the disease; patients exhibiting this behavior were referred to as "the fasting girls." Rejecting or severely limiting food was considered not simply part of self-control, but a rejection of the social context of food and often of the mother, who represents and provides food in most families and cultures.

By the 1920s anorexia was incorrectly viewed as an endocrine disorder, and food shortages during the Great Depression (1929–1941) led to a perceived decline in eating disorders. In the 1970s these eating disorders gained new attention, but in the United States it was the 1983 death of singer Karen Carpenter (1950–1883), of the hit music group The Carpenters, that brought anorexia and bulimia into the media spotlight. Carpenter died of heart failure at the age of 33 after spending half her life battling eating disorders, and her death triggered a wave of media coverage and public health campaigns on anorexia and bulimia.

Although anorexia, bulimia, and binge eating appear in all cultures, races, and across all socio-economic classes, these eating disorders appear disproportionately in developed countries among the middle-class and upper classes. A 2003 study of nearly 990,000 Swedish residents indicated that sociocultural context, rather than medical or genetic triggers, is the most crucial risk factor for developing anorexia and attendant eating disorders. Wealthy, white women have the highest rates of this disorder. The reference for psychiatric diagnosis, *DSM-IV*, notes that people with eating disorders tend to come from backgrounds with high levels of chaos, low levels of nurturing, and patients who feel that they had little control over their lives before beginning disordered eating.

Orthorexia involves many of the same behaviors found in anorexia, but the orthorexic patient is focused not on food restriction for weight loss, but for purity.

WORDS TO KNOW

ANOREXIA NERVOSA: An eating disorder in which the patient intentionally restricts eating to the point of near starvation with the purpose of weight loss and control over weight.

BINGE EATING: Considered a separate disorder from bulimia by some eating disorder specialists, binge eating occurs when a person consumes extraordinarily large amounts of food in one sitting, but does not purge.

BULIMIA NERVOSA: An eating disorder in which the patient eats large volumes of food ("binge eating") and later purges the food via forced vomiting, the use of diuretics and/or laxatives, and/or excessive exercise.

ORTHOREXIA: A condition first described in 1997 in which the patient's obsession with eating the purest or healthiest foods leads to near starvation, weight loss, and general signs of anorexia nervosa.

An anorexic young woman, who is 5 feet 4 inches (1.63 meters) tall and weighs 75 pounds (34 kilograms), sits on a swing. *AP Images.*

In orthorexia the patient wishes to attain the perfect diet, incorporating organic vegetables, fruits, grains, and meats into the diet, drinking purified water, taking specific supplements, and exhibiting health behaviors aimed at a perceived goal of ultimate fitness or perfection. As with anorexia or bulimia, behaviors fall on a continuum, and otherwise health-promoting behaviors tip over into dysfunction when the patient cannot bring himself or herself to break away from the perfection, even when it results in self harm. Orthorexia is a fairly new and controversial diagnosis that is not in the DSM-IV and has not been introduced into the forthcoming DSM-V, although it is emerging as a recognizable pattern among physicians who treat persons with eating disorders.

■ Impacts and Issues

A 2008 survey by the University of North Carolina and Self Magazine revealed that 10 percent of women in the United States identified themselves as having anorexia nervosa, bulimia nervosa, or a binge eating disorder. An additional 65 percent of women claimed to have experienced "disordered" eating patterns at some point in life. Eating disorders have been documented in medical literature for more than 150 years in western society, with a sharp increase in attention, research, and treatment since the late 1970s.

In a society where food is all-pervasive and social and family activities often revolve around food, disordered eating not only causes physical and psychological harm to the patient, but can be a serious impediment to social interactions and can lead to increased isolation, reinforcing the eating disorder over time. Genetic research reveals familial patterns with eating disorders, and researchers have isolated specific genes that may be related to anorexia. Eating disorders have obsessive-compulsive

behavior patterns as well. Food is necessary for survival, so treatment for eating disorders involving obsessive-compulsive (OCD) traits or addictive behaviors can be challenging; the Cleveland Clinic estimates that short-term treatment helps 50 to 70 percent of bulimics, but the 6-month relapse rate can be as high as 50 percent. People with bulimia have higher rates of long-term recovery than anorectics.

While eating disorders tend to be found predominately among women, approximately 14 percent of patients are men. Male anorectics and bulimics tend to be athletic and channel their disordered eating patterns through extreme dietary and exercise habits.

Message board culture on the Internet along with social media outlets have helped to give rise to the "pro-Ana" movement, a loose culture of people with anorexia and bulimia who use internet message boards for support and advice for extreme weight loss and managing anorexia without overcoming it. On these message boards "Ana" and "Mia" personify "anorexia" and "bulimia," turning the disorders into a lifestyle not lived in isolation, but in solidarity online, with tips on the best laxatives and diuretics, meal plan exchanges, exercise ideas, and weight tracking for extreme losses. This trend alarms eating disorder professionals, who fear the dual impact of social isolation in real life and the reinforcement online of a social network devoted to enhancing the dysfunction.

As a February 12, 2010, article in *Time* magazine notes, orthorexia is often mistaken for anorexia, and doctors who are unaware of an orthorexic's motivation may mistakenly encourage the patient to eat a healthier diet, reinforcing the disorder rather than helping the patient to get proper treatment. Orthorexia's exclusion from the DSM makes it difficult for U.S. patients to receive treatment, because health insurance companies often refuse coverage for mental health conditions without a DSM diagnosis.

■ Primary Source Connection

This excerpt from "Anorexia Nervosa" by Sir William Withey Gull, published in *Transactions of the Clinical Society of London* in 1874 shows us that anorexia nervosa is not a new health issue, or a new diagnosis. In modern society, analysts and commentators are often quick to blame the media for its depiction of the slim and super slim as the ideal body form as contributing to the rise of people diagnosed with anorexia nervosa. In 1874, however, the stereotypical ideal woman was considerably heavier than today's popular fashion and style celebrities.

Anorexia nervosa is an eating disorder characterized by unrealistic fear of weight gain, self-starvation, and conspicuous distortion of body image. The name comes from two Latin words that mean nervous inability to eat. Eating disorders have been part of many cultures since antiquity. Ancient Romans invented the *vomitorium*, a place to purge bloated stomachs during multi-day feasts so that celebrants could return to consume more food, while religious ascetics had long used fasting as a ritual to help gain spiritual purity. Gull's writing linked patients' "want of appetite" to an "hysterical" mental state.

At the same time, French physician Charles Lasègue found that girls suffering from anorexia went through three phases during their illness. First, they used alleged discomfort after eating as an excuse to reduce consumption. Second, they became preoccupied with weight loss and food. In the third stage, they entered into an emaciated and compromised state that led to death unless medical experts intervened. Despite the risk of death, Lasègue noted, the girls continued to starve themselves, against logic. In addition to self-starvation, Lasègue noted that patients who were force-fed as part of their treatment often vomited deliberately afterward. In the late 1860s, physicians referred to this as cynorexia; people who binged and then purged themselves by vomiting were called cynorexics; the modern term for this eating disorder is bulimia nervosa.

Cases of anorexia and bulimia dot medical literature from the late 1860s onward. In the late 1970s in the United States, various dieting fads took hold; fashion magazines idolized rail-thin women as the female ideal. While this was not new—the 1960s had established the

model Twiggy as an ideal—the trickle-down effect of these fashion trends to teen and preteen readers affected ideals of the female body. Books such as Hilde Bruch's *The Golden Cage: The Enigma of Anorexia Nervosa* came to public attention. By the 1980s, eating disorders had become a major social and medical concern.

Researchers estimate that as many as one in four women exhibit some eating disorder behavior at some point in time, generally during the late teens and early twenties. While most pass through this phase quickly, at least six percent of all women develop a clinical eating disorder. Approximately twenty percent of all people with eating disorders die as a direct result of eating disorder behaviors or from medical complications related to anorexia or bulimia.

Anorexia Nervosa

As a further illustration, I may add the following correspondence on one of these cases with Dr. Anderson, of Richmond.

Miss C, aet. 15 years 8 months, was sent to me in April 1873. The clinical history was that she had been ailing for a year, and had become extremely emaciated. (Woodcut, Miss C, No. 1.) The catamenia had never appeared. Pulse C4, reps. 16. Very sleepless for six months past. All the viscera healthy. Urine normal. Lower extremities edematous. Mind weakened. Temper obstinate. Great restlessness. No family history of disease beyond the fact that the maternal grandmother had had peculiar nervous symptoms. I wrote the following letter to Dr. Anderson: —

'Dear Dr. Anderson, — I saw Miss C. to-day. The case appears to be an extreme instance of what I have proposed to call "Apepsia hysterica," or "Anorexia nervosa." (See "Address on Medicine at Oxford," 1868.) I believe it to be essentially a failure of the powers of the gastric branches of the pneumogastric nerve. It differs from tuberculosis, though that state may subsequently arise, by the pulse, which I found to be 64 by the breathing, 16, the cleanness of the tongue, &c. In fact, the disease will be most correctly interpreted if it is remembered that no symptom more positive than emaciation is presented in and throughout its course.

'I would advise warm clothing, and some form of nourishing food every two hours, as milk, cream, soup, eggs, fish, chicken. I must only urge the necessity of nourishment in some form, otherwise the venous obstruction, which has already begun to show itself by oedema of the legs, will go on to plugging of the vessels. With the nourishment I would conjoin a dessert-spoonful of brandy every two or three hours. Whilst the present state of weakness continues, fatigue must be limited, and if the exhaustion increases beyond its present degree the patient should for a time to kept in a warm bed. I do not at present prescribe medicines, because the nursing and the food are more important than anything else. Such cases not unfrequently come before me; but as the morbid state is not yet generally recognised, I should be glad if you would second my wish of having a photograph taken of Miss C. in her present state, that we may compare it with some later one, if, as I hope, our plan of treatment is successful, as in my experience it generally is. I would, as I say, enclose a prescription, but I feel it most unnecessary to insist on food and stimulants, at least for a time.

Yours truly,

April 30, 1873.

On May 24 I received the following note from Dr. Anderson: —

'Dear Sir William, — I enclose photograph of Miss C. . . . There is rather an improvement in one respect, viz. there is less aversion to food. Want of sleep and swelling of the feet are the two great troubles. You have given us all new hope, however, and I trust I may one day send you a plump photograph, like what she was two years ago. With renewed thanks, I am, dear Sir William, yours very truly,'

On Oct. 23, 1873, I received a further report.

'Dear Sir William, — Miss C. is now at Shanklin, but returns very soon. I hear she is much better. She had a bad slough on the leg near the ankle, from persisting in wearing a tight boot.

'The great difficulty was to keep her quiet, and to make her eat and drink. Every step had to be fought. She was most loquacious and obstinate, anxious to overdo herself bodily and mentally. I will give you particulars when they return, but I am told she is much improved. Rest, and food, and stimulants as prescribed, undoubtedly did her a great deal of good. She used to be a nice, plump, good-natured little girl. Believe me, &c.'

The last report I received was on April 15, 1874.

'Dear Sir W., — I am sure you will be delighted to hear that Miss C, in whose case you were so kindly interested, . . . has now made a complete recovery, and is getting plump and rosy as of yore . . . .' (Vide Woodcut, Miss C., No. 2.)

William Withey Gull

GULL, WILLIAM. "ANOREXIA NERVOSA." *TRANSACTIONS: CLINICAL SOCIETY OF LONDON. LONDON:* LONGMAN, GREENS, AND CO., 1874. AVAILABLE VIA GOOGLE BOOKS AT HTTP://BOOKS.GOOGLE.COM/BOOKS?ID=CIXQUHBDVUWC&PG=PA22&LPG=PA22&DQ=CLINICAL+SOCIETY+LONDON+ANOREXIA+NERVOSA+GULL&SOURCE=BL&OTS=53CXLA7N5O&SIG=DJ0OUOOPHDCDYQBSHJVLXMFSXVM&HL=EN&EI=YYVRTJTD4GBLAEFVRW9DA&SA=X&OI=BOOK_RESULT&CT=RESULT&RESNUM=2&VED=0CBCQ6AEWAQ#V=ONEPAGE&Q&F=FALSE.

SEE ALSO *Changing Nutritional Needs throughout Life; Cult Diets; Diet and Heart Disease; Dietary Guidelines for Americans; Dietary Reference Intakes; Food and Body Image; Obesity; Undernutrition; Vitamins and Minerals.*

BIBLIOGRAPHY

Books

Arnold, Carrie, and B. T. Walsh. *Next to Nothing: A Firsthand Account of One Teenager's Experience with an Eating Disorder.* Oxford: Oxford University Press, 2007.

Costin, Carolyn. *The Eating Disorder Sourcebook: A Comprehensive Guide to the Causes, Treatments, and Prevention of Eating Disorders.* New York: McGraw-Hill, 2007.

Grilo, Carlos, and James E. Mitchell. *The Treatment of Eating Disorders: A Clinical Handbook.* New York: Guilford, 2010.

Gura, Trisha. *Lying in Weight: The Hidden Epidemic of Eating Disorders in Adult Women.* New York: HarperCollins, 2007.

Mitchell, James E. *Binge-eating Disorder: Clinical Foundations and Treatment.* New York: Guilford, 2008.

Saxen, Ron. *The Good Eater: The True Story of One Man's Struggle with Binge Eating Disorder.* Oakland, CA: New Harbinger, 2007.

Siegel, Michele, Judith Brisman, and Margot Weinshel. *Surviving an Eating Disorder: Strategies for Families and Friends.* New York: Collins Living, 2009.

Periodicals

Borzekowski, Dina L. G., Summer Schenk, Jenny S. Wilson, and Rebecka Peebles. "E-ana and E-Mia: A Content Analysis of Pro-Eating Disorder Web Sites." *American Journal of Public Health* 100, no. 8 (2010): 1526–1535.

"Could You Have an Eating Disorder? Learn the Signs—and Get the Help You Need." *Seventeen* (August 2008): 158.

Liu, Aimee. "The Perfect Pantomime: What Is Our Body Telling Us When We Have an Eating Disorder?" *MS New York* 19, no. 2 (2009): 74–78.

Pope, Harrison G., et al. "Binge Eating Disorder: A Stable Syndrome." *The American Journal of Psychiatry* 163, no. 12 (2006): 2181–2183.

Wilson, G. Terence, Denise E. Wilfley, W. Stewart Agras, and Susan W. Bryson. "Psychological Treatments of Binge Eating Disorder." *Archives of General Psychiatry* 67, no. 1 (2010): 94–101.

Web Sites

"Eating Disorders." *National Institute of Mental Health.* http://www.nimh.nih.gov/health/publications/eating-disorders/complete-index.shtml (accessed October 8, 2010).

National Eating Disorder Association (NEDA). http://www.nationaleatingdisorders.org/index.php (accessed October 8, 2010).

Melanie Barton Zoltan

Ecological Impacts of Various World Diets

■ Introduction

The production of food has become increasingly efficient with techniques such as crop rotation, animal and mechanical powered plowing, the use of fertilizers and pesticides, and the development of disease-resistant plant and animal hybrids. Populations have been able to consume larger quantities of fish and other seafood with the use of sophisticated boats, large nets, and by growing seafood on fish farms. The improvements in technology have allowed food production to increase with population, as well as enabled a rise in the quantity of food consumed per person. This intensification has introduced a variety of ecological concerns, including soil erosion, desertification, pollution of waterways, depletion of groundwater, air pollution, exhaustion of fish stocks, and losses of biodiversity. Wealthier modern societies tend to consume larger quantities of animal products, which exacerbate environmental concerns. In some parts of the world, the consumption of wild game, or bushmeat, threatens endangered species. The variety of modern diets influence the extent to which food-related ecological impact occurs.

■ Historical Background and Scientific Foundations

The human population existed primarily as hunter-gatherers until approximately 10,000 years ago, when societies shifted to more stationary agricultural-based communities. The development of a wide variety of environment-changing technologies including irrigation, terracing, drainage of wetlands, and reclaiming seas to expand cultivation enabled the growth of human populations. The development of efficient food production technologies has been particularly strong in the last 100 years, allowing many wealthier societies to consume more food energy per person than their ancestors. This is primarily due to a more regular consumption of meat, eggs, dairy, and other animal-based products.

Modern industrialized agriculture production in North America, Europe, and other parts of the world typically focuses on one or several monoculture crops. This enables farmers to meet the consumer demand for low-cost corn, wheat, fruit, vegetables, and other foods desired in a modern diet. Achieving high food yields requires the use of large amounts of synthetic chemical fertilizer and pesticides, which can have a negative long-term impacts on soil quality. Approximately 10 to 20 percent of global dry land areas suffer from some level of land desertification or degradation as a result of agriculture production, partly due to heavy chemical use. Runoff from farms is a cause of pollution, as excess pesticide and fertilizer flows into nearby streams, rivers, lakes, and eventually oceans. This puts aquatic ecosystems at risk for eutrophication. Intensive agriculture methods necessitate large quantities of water, which often comes from scarce underground and surface sources. Many modern farmers also plant genetically modified crops that have inherent resistance to pests, as well as faster growth rates. There is a risk of genetically modified crops cross passing their engineered genes to naturally occurring organisms, altering the genetic biodiversity of ecosystems that have evolved over thousands of years.

■ Impacts and Issues

The consumption of meat products has a larger impact on the environment than plant foods, as the growth of animal feed uses fertilizers, pesticides, and other resources that otherwise could be used to produce vegetables and grains consumed directly by people. Additionally, the grazing of animals has increased pressure on deforestation. Approximately 70 percent of previously forested land in the Amazon is used for animal production. Conversion of land for grazing has a large impact on biodiversity, as wildlife habitat is diminished. Livestock production produces 18 percent of the world's

WORDS TO KNOW

ANTHROPOGENIC: Being caused by, or coming from, human activities.

EUTROPHICATION: The depletion in water of oxygen available for fish and other animals resulting from the rapid growth of algae and other organisms in the presence of excess nutrients in the water system.

MONOCULTURE: Growing a considerable quantity of one crop over a large area.

Vegan activists in London, England, encourage the public to eliminate meat consumption to reduce carbon dioxide emissions, which contribute to global climate change. © *Mark Boulton / Alamy.*

greenhouse gases, which is a larger amount than the use of cars, boats, and planes combined. Converting land to grazing and the growth of feed crops is responsible for 9 percent of human-caused carbon dioxide generation. Animal production is responsible for 37 percent of anthropogenic methane, released by cattle and other ruminants, and 65 percent of anthropogenic nitrous oxide, which comes primarily from animal manure. Animal production uses 8 percent of the world's freshwater, primarily for the growth of animal feed crops. Animal waste going into lakes and rivers pollutes water systems, particularly when many animals are raised in small areas. This waste is associated with a large portion of the ammonia released into the environment, causing acid rain and the acidification of ecosystems.

Many of the world's peoples include a portion of seafood in their diets. This demand has caused 25 percent of fish stocks in oceans and freshwater systems to be overexploited and depleted, while another 52 percent are nearing overexploitation. Of particular concern are the diminishing populations of keystone species, or those species that play a critical role in maintaining the structure of an ecosystem. An example is salmon, a fish in declining numbers that carries marine nutrients to less productive streams and rivers, and provides food for a number of other animals, such as bears and eagles. Diminishing numbers of salmon may disrupt these natural ecosystems. Sea turtles, sharks, dolphins, sea birds, and other organisms, many of which are keystone species, are killed unintentionally as fish are harvested. Such fishing methods have the potential to disrupt the entire food chain. The amount of farm-raised fish has grown as the numbers of wild fish have declined. Although the techniques vary greatly, the excess food and fish waste from aquaculture can be a source of water pollution.

There is an observable pattern of increasing demand for animal-based products as the income of societies and individuals increases. In westernized developed countries, the large increase in animal products has occurred with the growth of fast food restaurants. Even in poorer developing countries, families shift from diets based on the regular consumption of vegetables and grains to diets including more frequent consumption of dairy products, eggs, and meat. The consumption of wild animals, or bushmeat, is common practice in many parts of the world, particularly in Africa, Asia, and South America. Animals, including primates, antelope, wild birds, and bears are regularly consumed. Approximately 1 million metric tons of bushmeat is traded each year in the central part of Africa, where 80 percent of residents rely on wild game for a critical source of protein. The often-illegal trade and consumption of these animals, particularly those threatened and endangered, drives these species closer to extinction. Balancing people's nutritional needs and protection of the environment is a challenge.

Some environmentalists promote the consumption of non-meat vegetarian diets as a method to reduce the impact from the production and consumption of food. Vegan diets go further, promoting the complete removal of animal products, including milk and eggs, from the diet. Other individuals choose to eat organic and ecologically friendly products, which use fewer synthetic fertilizers and pesticides. These diets may include less frequent consumption of unsustainably grown animal products. Ecological farming techniques are concerned with the appropriate carrying capacities for animals, and managing pollution generated from food production, so they are less likely to impact the environment. Governments have passed some regulations for farmers that aim to address the environmental impacts from modern diets.

SEE ALSO *African Famine Relief; Agricultural Deforestation; Agricultural Demand for Water; Agricultural Land Reform; Agroecology; Biodiversity and Food Supply; Biofuels and World Hunger; Commission on Genetic Resources for Food and Agriculture; Desertification and Agriculture; Ethical Issues in Agriculture; Extreme Weather and Food Supply; Factory Farming; Family Farms; Food, Conservation, and Energy Act of 2008; Food Security; Food Sovereignty; Free Trade and Agriculture; Genetically Modified Organisms (GMO); Green Revolution (1943); Hydroponics; International Federation of Organic Agriculture Movements; International Fund for Agricultural Development; Land Availability and Degradation; Livestock Intensity and Demand; Organics; Pesticides and Pesticide Residue; Shark Harvesting; Sustainable Agriculture; UN Millennium Development Goals; Veganism; Vegetarianism; Whaling; World Food Programme.*

BIBLIOGRAPHY

Books

Hahlbrock, Klaus. *Feeding the Planet: Environmental Protection through Sustainable Agriculture.* London: Haus, 2009.

Horsfield, Alan, and Elaine Horsfield. *Talking about Food and the Environment.* New York: Gareth Stevens, 2010.

Periodicals

Pollock, Chris, and Jules Pretty. "Farming Could Destroy Earth Unless We Rethink What 'Sustainable' Agriculture Is." *New Scientist* (April 21, 2007): 18–19.

Sachs, Jeffrey D. "The Promise of the Blue Revolution: Aquaculture Can Maintain Living Standards While Averting the Ruin of the Oceans." *Scientific American* 297, no. 1 (2007): 37–38.

Web Sites

"Livestock Impacts on the Environment." *Food and Agriculture Organization of the United Nations (FAO),* 2006. http://www.fao.org/ag/magazine/0612sp1.htm (accessed October 15, 2010).

Sustainable Table. http://www.sustainabletable.org/issues/ (accessed October 15, 2010).

"Why Vegan?" *Vegan Outreach.* http://www.veganoutreach.org/whyvegan/ (accessed October 15, 2010).

Steven Joseph Archambault

Edible Schoolyard Movement

Introduction

The edible schoolyard (ESY) is a school garden program originally founded at Martin Luther King Jr. Middle School in Berkeley, California, in 1995 by Alice Waters, the chef and owner of Chez Panisse restaurant. In 2005 an affiliate ESY garden was begun in New Orleans, and since then ESY gardens have been created in San Francisco; Los Angeles; Greensboro, North Carolina; and Brooklyn, New York. The Smithsonian Folklife Festival featured an edible schoolyard display on the National Mall in Washington, DC, which was visited by more than one million people. The edible schoolyard is just one particularly high profile school garden project, however: School gardens of many different types have become increasingly popular since the early 1990s as parents and educators have become more concerned with children's health and nutrition, environmental literacy, experiential learning, and the importance of local food networks.

Although the ESY movement has been subject to some criticism, especially by the American social commentator and writer Caitlin Flanagan, school gardens have proliferated in many states, especially California. Despite some severe budget cutbacks in public education, most school gardens remain successful, although finding appropriate staff to maintain gardens and integrate garden work with educational curricula can be problematic.

Historical Background and Scientific Foundations

Even though school gardens are once again a hot topic in the news and on the bookshelf, the idea is definitely not new. In the mid 1800s, several European nations required schools to have gardens to improve agricultural education and food security. By the late nineteenth century, school reformers and devoted gardeners in the United States endorsed the idea of school gardens as a way to cultivate American virtues along with flowers and vegetables. School gardens were an important part of the North American nature-study movement of the early twentieth century, and the United States School Garden Army was created in 1917 by the U.S. Board of Education with funding from the War Department to urge children and teachers to grow food in urban and suburban areas during World War I (1915–1918). Similar programs were developed in Europe and Australia in the late nineteenth and early twentieth centuries.

Many American schools planted victory gardens during World War II (1939–1945), but despite the efforts of John Dewey (1859–1952) and Maria Montessori (1870–1952), two prominent educators who promoted school gardens, educational reform in the 1950s and 1960s emphasized knowledge acquired in the classroom and school gardens became rare. This began to change in the 1970s as teachers returned to experiential education, and concerns with fresh, sustainably raised food and other environmental issues became more important to the public. Several horticultural organizations began promoting school gardens in the 1980s, and news stories featuring schools with gardens began to appear again regularly for the first time since World War II. The edible schoolyard project brought new publicity to school gardens in 1995, and the years since then have seen a huge increase in "edible education," as Waters calls it, and in innovative ways of integrating gardens and produce into school programs and lunches.

Impacts and Issues

School garden advocates maintain that students who get their hands dirty working in gardens are more motivated and enthusiastic about school in general. They praise the different garden programs' effects on student teamwork, self-esteem, individual responsibility, community-building, and parental involvement, and claim that gardens are linked to an increase in academic progress, mostly in math and science but sometimes in health, social studies, writing, and history. Some educators also assert that students reap health benefits—both physically and psychologically—from garden work, and argue that growing food leads to better nutrition and an appreciation for environmental connections. Special education teachers also find numerous sensory and occupational benefits in school gardens.

Given the advantages attributed to school gardens, it is not surprising that they have become so popular in the last few decades, especially in areas with long growing seasons. Texas, California, and New York all provide public schools with a state-sponsored school garden curriculum, and Florida, Louisiana, and South Carolina have state programs promoting school gardens. Botanical gardens, horticultural societies, and agricultural extension offices also sponsor or assist schools with thousands of gardens in many different states and in Canada, Australia, and the United Kingdom. "Good Food for All Kids: A Garden at Every School" was one of the top ten winning "Ideas for Change" in 2010 on a website pitching social change for the administration of U.S. President Barack Obama. First lady Michelle Obama's

garden on the White House lawn involves children from several different Washington, DC, schools in gardening and cooking, and the garden is used to publicize recent child nutrition legislation, sustainable agriculture, and the anti-obesity Let's Move initiative.

The most outspoken critic of school gardens—and especially the edible schoolyard, with its emphasis on gastronomy, ecology, and slow food—is Caitlin

Flowers and garlic plants grow in the organic garden at Martin Luther King Jr. Elementary School in Berkeley, California. The garden is part of the Edible Schoolyard Project founded by chef and restaurateur Alice Waters. © *Karen Huntt/Corbis.*

School children dig up vegetables in a garden plot at a Herefordshire primary school in England.　© *Simon Hadley / Alamy.*

Flanagan (1961–), whose article entitled "Cultivating Failure: How School Gardens Are Cheating Our Most Vulnerable Students" in *The Atlantic* magazine in 2010 prompted a torrent of angry responses. Flanagan suggested that school gardens were "a cruel trick" played on minority students by "an agglomeration of foodies and educational reformers who are propelled by a vacuous, if well-meaning ideology that is responsible for robbing an increasing number of American schoolchildren of hours they might otherwise have spent reading important books or learning higher math." She argued that during tough economic times, garden programs were especially frivolous, and stated that there is no evidence that "classroom gardens help students meet the state standards for English and math." Her article struck a chord with those who agree that school gardens are "one manifestation of the way the new food hysteria has come to dominate and diminish our shared cultural life" and with those who argue that only parents should be responsible for children's food.

As Flanagan's critics were quick to point out, however, most edible schoolyards are privately funded by groups like the Chez Panisse Foundation. There is also a growing body of evidence that school gardens

do produce measurable, positive increases in academic achievement and that students make better nutritional choices after gardening at school. Quite a bit of qualitative and anecdotal evidence for positive social and behavioral changes in students who garden has been collected by the California Department of Education and the Cornell Garden-Based Learning program. Many programs also claim that students show a much greater concern for environmental issues and an appreciation for the natural world at a time when children in general are spending less time than ever outdoors.

Research also shows that if school gardens are going to be educationally effective and nutritionally productive, programs need to be administered by dedicated and knowledgeable staff, which are in short supply in some districts. Volunteer contributions by parents, local chefs, and food enthusiasts may fill in some of the holes left by funding cutbacks, and help with gardens during summers when schools are typically closed, but programs need to be tailored to regional populations to be successful. If current levels of support and interest continue, however, school gardens in the twenty-first century may endure longer than the ones planted at schools few generations ago.

SEE ALSO *Alice Waters: California and New American Cuisine; Farm-to-Table Movement; Improving Nutrition for America's Children Act of 2010; Locavore; School Lunch Reform; Slow Food Movement; Sustainable Agriculture; Sustainable Table; Urban Farming/Gardening.*

BIBLIOGRAPHY

Books

Bucklin-Sporer, Arden, and Rachel Pringle. *How to Grow a School Garden: A Complete Guide for Parents and Teachers.* Portland: Timber Press, 2010.

Louv, Richard. *Last Child in the Woods: Saving Our Children from Nature-Deficit Disorder*, updated and expanded. Chapel Hill, NC: Algonquin Books, 2008.

Waters, Alice. *Edible Schoolyard: A Universal Idea.* San Francisco: Chronicle Books, 2008.

Periodicals

Blair, Dorothy. "The Child in the Garden: An Evaluative Review of the Benefits of School Gardening." *Journal of Environmental Education* 40, no. 2 (2009): 15–38.

Klemmer, Cynthia D., Tina M. Waliczek, and Jayne M. Zajicek. "Growing Minds: The Effect of a School Gardening Program on the Science Achievement of Elementary Students." *HortTechnology* 15 (2005): 448–452.

Web Sites

Bennett, Lisa. "The School Garden Debate: To Weep or Reap?" *Center for Ecoliteracy.* http://www.ecoliteracy.org/essays/school-garden-debate-weep-or-reap (accessed July 11, 2010).

Desmond, Daniel, James Grieshop, and Aarti Subramanian. "Revisiting Garden Based Learning in Basic Education: Philosophical Roots, Historical Foundations, Best Practices and Products, Impacts, Outcomes, and Future Directions." *United Nations Food and Agriculture Organization (FAO).* http://www.fao.org/sd/2003/kn0504_en.htm (accessed July 10, 2010).

Flanagan, Caitlin. "Cultivating Failure: How School Gardens Are Cheating Our Most Vulnerable Students." *The Atlantic,* January/February 2010. http://www.theatlantic.com/magazine/archive/2010/01/cultivating-failure/7819 (accessed July 10, 2010).

Genauer, Ethan. "Good Food for All Kids: A Garden at Every School." *Ideas for Change in America,* January 25, 2010. http://www.change.org/ideas/view/good_food_for_all_kids_a_garden_at_every_school_2 (accessed July 20, 2010).

"A Healthy Nutrition Environment: Linking Education, Activity, and Food through School Gardens." *California Department of Education.* http://www.cde.ca.gov/LS/nu/he/gardenoverview.asp (accessed July 20, 2010).

Sandra L. Dunavan

Eggs

Introduction

No one knows when a human ate an egg as a food for the first time, but scholars do have a general idea of the timeline for intentional domestication of birds for use of eggs. Archaeologists and anthropologists have uncovered evidence of bird domestication in India and China dating back to 3000 BC and possibly as far back as 6000 BC, whereas Persians used colored eggs by 3000 BC to signify the first day of Spring, a forerunner to the current practice of coloring Easter eggs in some cultures.

The egg includes a protective eggshell that is made of minerals such as calcium; a clear, gelatinous albumin commonly called the egg white; and yellow-orange vitellus known as the egg yolk. Chicken eggs are the most widely-consumed eggs worldwide, and eggs provide protein, vitamin A, choline, and fat. The egg white contains the majority of the egg's protein, whereas the yolk contains the fat. The color of the yolk is dependent on the foods the hen consumes. Unfertilized eggs do not require refrigeration and remain safe to cook for one to two weeks, and sometimes longer. This quality has made eggs a standard part of diets worldwide for millennia, although modern food safety standards and Food and Drug Administration recommendations in the United States strongly advise that eggs remain refrigerated at all times to prevent *Salmonella* caused illness.

Historical Background and Scientific Foundations

By 1500 BC, chickens were domesticated and used for eggs and meat in parts of southern Europe and north Africa. Evidence of domesticated fowl and egg consumption can be found in Roman, Greek, and western European ruins and art dating back more than 2000 years. Domesticated fowl were brought to the Americas by Christopher Columbus (1451–1506) on his 1493 voyage.

Chicken eggs are the most widely-consumed egg, but humans eat eggs from turtles, quail, ostrich, emu, ducks, and geese—nearly any animal that lays an egg.

Although eggs can be eaten raw, *Salmonella* transmission is a major concern, with the bacteria forming on the outside of the shell and also on the inside. Cooking eggs before consuming is the safest measure, and for as long as humans have been eating eggs they have been cooking them as well, either plain or as a binding and rising agent in other foods. Scholars have found evidence of baked goods that use eggs in foods given to Egyptian pharaohs and recipes calling for eggs in a cake in ancient Rome. Eggs have been such a mainstay of the diet in baked goods that during World War I and World War II, when eggs were in short supply and rationed in the United States and parts of Europe, a new culinary trend—the eggless cake—emerged as an anomaly, driven by necessity and scarcity.

All humans cannot safely consume eggs; the egg is the second-most common source of food allergies in children, trumped only by milk. A 2007 research study by the American Academy of Allergy, Asthma and Immunology shows that 50 percent of children with egg allergies outgrow the allergy by age 17. Egg allergies can have an adverse effect on receiving immunizations, as many vaccines are incubated in chicken eggs. People with egg allergies may not be able to tolerate receiving these immunizations, placing them at greater risk for contracting vaccine-preventable illnesses.

Impacts and Issues

In recent years, egg producers have developed "designer eggs" to market to consumers looking for a better nutritional boost from eggs. Hens fed diets high in flaxseed and other omega-3-rich foods produce eggs that are rich in omega-3 fatty acids, leading to a more expensive product that consumers view as healthier. These

Two hens sit with an egg. *Image copyright mocagrande, 2010. Used under license from Shutterstock.com.*

omega-3-rich eggs sell for up to twice the price of regular eggs; marketing campaigns for omega-3 versions claim that the omega-3 helps to counteract some of the cholesterol in eggs, a claim disputed by groups such as the Center for Science in the Public Interest. Research has shown, however, that consumption of omega-3 fatty acids does provide an overall benefit in reducing health threats including heart disease, stroke, and hypertension.

Investigative journalists turned their attention to concentrated animal feeding operations, or CAFOs, and egg production in the late 1990s and the first decade of the 2000s. Books such as Michael Pollan's (1955–) *The Omnivore's Dilemma*, Eric Schlosser's (1959–) *Fast Food Nation*, and David Kirby's (1960–) *Animal Factory* focused on the details and the impact of factory farming on animals and the food supply. The movie documentary *Food, Inc.* paid special attention to poultry farming, revealing animal abuses and food supply chain contamination.

Calls for free-range eggs (eggs laid by hens free to roam and eat a natural diet rather than raised in cramped, dark quarters and fed a substandard diet that often includes ground-up chicken parts), as well as organic eggs, fueled a shift in consumer behavior. In the United Kingdom free-range egg sales increased by 8.4 percent in 2008, with continued growth for this sector in the United States as well. In the United States there is no set standard for the term *free range*, leaving consumers in a potentially vulnerable position, paying a premium for a product perceived to be healthier or more humane, but that does not carry any guarantee of having a set definition for quality or production.

The "urban chicken" movement in the United States has led to a small but steady increase in the number of families in urban and suburban areas who keep small chicken coops in backyards. Many towns, home owner associations (HOAs), and cities have codes against backyard chicken coops, leading some homeowners to violate the law in order to maintain home-grown chickens, whereas older towns and cities tend to have provisions for urban chicken farming. Owners claim they keep these flocks to make fresh, free-range eggs easily available and to increase access to locally-grown food. A 2008 report from WorldWatch Institute indicates that chicken owners are gaining success in changing city and local ordinances to allow the urban chicken and egg movement to grow.

In August 2010, in the United States, the egg became a reportable food and the subject of one of the largest food recalls in history, with more than 550 million eggs recalled for *Salmonella* contamination. The center of the recall involved two egg factories in Iowa owned by a group that had a history of violations dating back 35 years, according to *New York Times* reports. The *Salmonella* outbreak sickened more than 1,600 people throughout the United States and provoked a sharp rise in demand for local eggs produced by small farmers.

Different types of eggs—including aged and tea-soaked eggs prized as delicacies—line the shelves of a market stall in China. *Joseph Hyder / Lerner & Lerner / LernerMedia Global Photos.*

SEE ALSO *Center for Food Safety and Applied Nutrition; Consumer Food Safety Recommendations; Diet and Heart Disease; Diet and Hypertension; Dietary Guidelines for Americans; Dietary Reference Intakes; Factory Farming; Poultry; Salmonella; Urban Chicken Movement.*

BIBLIOGRAPHY

Books

Hosking, Richard. *Eggs in Cookery: Proceedings of the Oxford Symposium of Food & Cookery 2006.* Totnes, UK: Prospect, 2007.

Mead, Geoffrey C. *Microbiological Analysis of Red Meat, Poultry and Eggs.* Boca Raton, FL: CRC Press, 2007.

Wright, Simon, and Diane McCrea. *The Handbook of Organic and Fair Trade Food Marketing.* Oxford, UK: Blackwell Pub, 2007.

Periodicals

"Green Eggs and *Salmonella*?" *Smithsonian* (June 2010): 92.

Harmon, Katherine. "Shelling Out for Eggs." *Scientific American* 301, no. 5 (2009): 20–21.

McLaren, Anne. "Free-range Eggs?" *Science New York Then Washington* 316, no. 5823 (2007): 339–339.

Web Sites

"Poultry and Eggs." *U.S. Department of Agriculture Economic Research Service (USDA/ERS).* http://www.ers.usda.gov/Briefing/Poultry/ (accessed October 19, 2010).

"Tips to Reduce Your Risk of Salmonella from Eggs." *Centers for Disease Control and Prevention (CDC).* http://www.cdc.gov/Features/SalmonellaEggs/ (accessed October 19, 2010).

Melanie Barton Zoltan

Embargoes

Introduction

An embargo is an imposed prohibition of sales or exports to a particular country. Some embargoes involve blockading ports and the ending of all trade, although this measure is relatively difficult to enforce. Embargoes typically have political goals or health and safety goals instead of being merely an economic tool. Export and import embargoes can also be used as sanitary and phytosanitary (SPS) controls to prevent the spread of plant, animal, and human diseases. Trade in food and medicine is often allowed to continue under an embargo. Embargoes and other export restrictions may have contributed to rising prices for many food commodities in 2007 and 2008. One example of a long embargo that has both included and excluded food trade is the embargo by the United States on Cuba that began in 1958.

Historical Background and Scientific Foundations

An embargo limits trade. The earliest recorded embargoes, in ancient times, were enforced by blocking ships from entering port. Often, the purpose of an embargo is to force change or surrender by cutting off a city or country from the products of rest of the world. In this way, an embargo is both an act of war and an economic sanction. During the Civil War in the United States (1861–1865), an embargo by the Union against the Confederacy made it difficult for the Confederacy to ship and import goods to and from other countries. Embargoes are one of the ways in which the United Nations (UN) Security Council (SC) can sanction a country and are generally considered an option to be explored before the use of force. Embargoes, sanctions, and various trade restrictions that are undertaken for political reasons, not for economic reasons or for other goals, are broadly referred to as economic statecraft. These economic tools are used by countries to influence policies in countries that they cannot otherwise influence.

Embargoes are calculated to produce outrage or provide moral authority, so they may only be symbolic, with little if any effect on actual trade or prices. As the tools of economic statecraft involve the whole country, and not just its leadership, they have been criticized on humanitarian grounds as being harmful to helpless populations or populations already suffering from war, disaster, or lack of economic growth.

In the twentieth and early twenty-first centuries, both food and medicine have often been excluded from embargoes. In other words, countries could continue to sell food or medicine to a sanctioned country despite an embargo. The reasoning for this common exclusion is that cutting off food or medical supplies does great harm to the population, does not seem to influence the decisions of the leadership of the country, and contravenes other international agreements regarding humanitarian protections. For these and other reasons, most embargoes in the late twentieth century and early twenty-first century have been attempts to target the leadership of a country or certain groups of people: They are limited to arms, energy supplies, or key commodities that are argued to fund war or weapons. In some cases where there are embargoes in place during conditions of famine, even countries participating in the embargo may continue to bring in food aid. The United States provided the majority of food aid to North Korea in the late 1990s and the first decade of 2000s despite having an embargo on other forms of trade.

The term *embargo* is also used to describe the action when a country decides to cut off its exports to the rest of the world and not just to a specific country or group of people. During the food price crisis in 2007 and 2008, fourteen countries, including China, Vietnam, and India, halted exports of rice in an attempt to save their entire crop for domestic consumption and stockpiling. Fifteen countries, including Argentina and Kazakhstan, suspended exports of wheat to do the same. These rice and wheat embargoes may have contributed to rising prices for those commodities during that year. In 2010 Russia announced an embargo on wheat exports in reaction to a drought in key production regions. Because Russia was expected to be a major wheat exporter in 2010, the shortfall and trade restrictions will likely contribute to reduced supply in world markets. This reduced supply, according to classical economic theory, will increase price as long as demand remains the same. Following the announcement of the embargo, there was a 5 percent increase in world food prices from July to August of 2010, according to a report by the Food and Agriculture Organization (FAO) of the United Nations. These trade restrictions or embargoes on exporting can be used as a form of economic statecraft, but they are also conducted to calm consumers or producers within a country and keep domestic prices lower. The World Trade Organization (WTO) permits embargoes to prevent critical shortages.

Embargoes are also used to contain disease. Sanitary and phytosanitary (SPS) measures can include the use of embargoes, especially during an outbreak or epidemic. A country can voluntarily cut off exports of a food product that may carry disease or, more often, other countries can place an embargo on imports of affected food products. Bovine spongiform encephalopathy (BSE) is a disease of cattle (also called mad cow disease) that can affect humans who consume meat or meat products from an infected cow. Following an outbreak in the United Kingdom in 1996, the European Union (EU) and many countries outside of the EU imposed embargoes on beef and beef products from the

United Kingdom. The United Kingdom took steps to contain and limit the spread of disease in its cattle herd, and by 2005 the European Union lifted the embargo. The embargo successfully prevented BSE from spreading to other countries and may have prevented a worldwide outbreak of the disease.

Whereas BSE represents a human health risk, countries also use embargoes to protect their livestock, their forests, and their crops from disease. For example, foot and mouth disease (FMD; also called hoof and mouth disease) affects cattle and other livestock with hooves. Although meat or other animal products from these animals present little or no health risk to humans, the disease could spread quickly through a region's livestock herd. Countries in which FMD is present may be unable to export animal products until the outbreak has been controlled. To make these embargoes fair, and prevent countries from using them as a form of economic statecraft, many countries are members of the World Organization for Animal Health (OIE, after the organization's older name in French) to which a country reports outbreaks, receives lists of contagious animal disease status in other countries, and receives training and assistance in control and prevention of livestock disease. The WTO allows embargoes as an SPS measure to contain diseases of humans, animals, and plants.

■ Impacts and Issues

In 1958 the United States first launched an embargo on arms to Cuba in reaction to the Cuban revolution. In 1960, following the nationalization of property of U.S. citizens by the new communist government, more goods were prohibited from export, and Cuba's quota for sugar export to the United States was reduced. The embargo was further strengthened in 1962 following the Cuban Missile Crisis, limiting most forms of trade. However, in 1992 the Cuban Democracy Act in the U.S. Congress limited the ability of firms from the United States to transship food to Cuba through a third country and severely limited flows of medicine and medical devices. A 1997 report by the American Association for World Health (AAWH) reports a drop in caloric intake in Cuba of 33 percent between 1989 and 1993, partially as a potential result of the strengthening of the embargo. This outright ban on sales of food was lifted in 2000 by the Trade Sanctions Reform and Export Enhancement Act, which allows sales of food and medicine to Cuba. Cuba began to import food from the United States in 2001, as typically around 60 percent of food consumed in Cuba is imported. U.S. food sales to Cuba reached 710 million U.S. dollars in 2008, though they fell in 2009 and 2010.

Not even all proponents of using economic statecraft measures such as embargoes find that embargoes are an effective way to influence a decision in a country. Whereas

Farmers harvest sugar cane in Valle de los Ingenios, Cuba. The U.S. embargo against Cuba prohibits the import of Cuban sugar and other goods. © *Peter M. Wilson / Alamy.*

embargoes, such as those by many countries against South Africa, were credited with being one factor that ended apartheid in 1993, some embargoes appear to be relatively ineffective. For example, the United States launched an embargo against the Soviet Union in 1980 that cancelled U.S. grain shipments, but this embargo failed to end the invasion of Afghanistan: The Soviet Union continued to occupy Afghanistan until 1988. Embargoes are difficult to enforce, and the exclusion of food and medicine may actually weaken the efficacy of the embargo.

Economists point out that some commodities are fungible. This means that one unit of a commodity is absolutely indistinguishable from another. The source of a barrel of oil or a bushel of wheat cannot be known just by looking at it. Because agricultural commodities and many raw materials are fungible, they are hard to exclude from trade. Fungible goods that are smuggled around an embargo are difficult to catch later in the value chain because they are indistinguishable from legally purchased commodities. Also, if food trade is allowed, it can serve as a way to trade money around the embargo or as a source of trains, trucks, boats, and containers to use for smuggling. Even highly monitored embargoes that include exceptions for food, such as the oil-for-food program for Iraq from 1996 until 2003, provide some room for smuggling and the diversion of funds.

SEE ALSO *Agriculture and International Trade; Banana Trade Wars; Fair Trade; Food Inspection and Standards; Food Safety and Inspection Service; Import Restrictions; Mad Cow Disease and vCJD; Subsidies; World Trade Organization (WTO).*

BIBLIOGRAPHY

Books

Erlich, Reese W. *Dateline Havana: The Real Story of U.S. Policy and the Future of Cuba.* Sausalito, CA: PoliPoint, 2009.

United Nations. *Necessity of Ending the Economic, Commercial and Financial Embargo Imposed by the United States of America against Cuba: Report of the Secretary-General.* New York: United Nations, 2004.

Periodicals

Dupin, Chris. "Finding a Way into Cuba: Despite Embargo, U.S. Is Cuba's Largest Supplier of Food Products." *American Shipper* 48, no. 10 (2006): 73–79.

"EU Embargo Jolts South American Beef Trade." *Food Chemical News* 49, no. 51 (2008): 17.

"International—Six More Brazilian States Escape Russia's Meat Embargo." *Food Chemical News* 47, no. 5 (2005): 17.

"UK Beef Embargo to Be Lifted." *Fleischwirtschaft International* 1 (March 2006): 8–9.

Wieck, Christine, and David Holland. "The Economic Effect of the Canadian BSE Outbreak on the US Economy." *Applied Economics* 42, no. 8 (2010): 935–946.

Web Sites

al-Mughrabi, Nidal. "Israel Eases Gaza Embargo to Allow Snack Food in." *Reuters,* June 9, 2010. http://www.reuters.com/article/idUSTRE65820E20100609 (accessed October 25, 2010).

"Companies Send Goods to Cuba under Embargo Exception." *NewsMax.com,* July 26, 2004. http://archive.newsmax.com/archives/articles/2004/7/25/174317.shtml (accessed October 25, 2010).

"It's Over: France Lifts 'Illegal' Embargo on British Beef." *Food Navigator.com,* October 3, 2002. http://www.foodnavigator.com/Legislation/It-s-over-France-lifts-illegal-embargo-on-British-beef (accessed October 25, 2010).

Blake Jackson Stabler

Ethical Issues in Agriculture

■ Introduction

Ethical issues in agriculture stem from several types of ethical principles. Ethics involves studying concepts of how people should behave, so ethical issues are situations in which principles of right and wrong are invoked. Issues of rights such as human rights, women's rights, land rights, and animal rights pervade discussions of ethical controversies and of the ethics of various actions in agriculture. Also, new technology often faces a variety of protests based on the new technology's juxtaposition to nature or the natural order. One aspect of this argument is that those who oppose the new technology often invoke the precautionary principle and stress the risks posed by the new technology. Lastly, ethical controversies in agriculture often deal with issues of equity and justice. Inequalities between farmers, between countries, and between men and women are questioned on ethical grounds. One timely set of ethical issues involves women's role in developing world agriculture. Both women's rights and issues of equity influence ethical concerns about women's roles in these rural economies.

■ Historical Background and Scientific Foundations

Until the late 1990s, use of the term ethics was relatively rare in the hallways of the Food and Agriculture Organization (FAO) of the United Nations in Rome, the capital of Italy. However, when founding a program of study and publications on ethics in food and agriculture in 2001, researchers interviewing FAO staff discovered that many arguments used at FAO and much of the logic used to justify FAO actions and FAO programs were based on ethical foundations. For example, any argument about rights, whether they be land rights, rights of indigenous peoples, women's rights, children's rights, intellectual property rights (IPR), or animal rights

is based in ethics. FAO's "right to food" approach to hunger alleviation, then, is supported by the ethical argument that all people deserve access to adequate food. A variety of arguments about rights are found in ethical controversies in agriculture, and rights arguments seek to appeal to what proponents usually label as universal, ethical principles.

Opposition to new technologies in agriculture is a common area in which ethical arguments can be heard. New technologies in agriculture have been opposed, for various reasons, since at least the introduction of extensive aqueducts for irrigation during the Roman Empire during the first century BC. Apprehension concerning a new agricultural technology usually is based on the idea that the new technology violates nature and thus has unidentified negative consequences. Whereas there is an ethical aspect of opposing various new technologies, part of the logic of opposition to new technologies stems from contrasting views of risk. Some people are comfortable with risk taking or taking a scientific approach based on a risk analysis. Risk analysis calculates the likelihood that a specified risk might actually manifest. Others invoke what is known as the precautionary principle: that scientific risk assessment or willingness to take risks resembles gambling because the potential long-term loss may be far more likely than the potential short-term benefit. They want the risks and the long-term effects of a technology to be fully understood. Under the logic of the precautionary principle, many new technologies are simply too risky.

Biotechnology, especially transgenic crops (also known as genetically modified crops), is one area in which the argument that the technology opposes the natural order is heard. Using the precautionary principle, opponents of transgenic crops argue the unknown long-term effects of these crops are potentially harmful to human health, the environment, and livestock. Proponents of these crops argue the risks appear to be minimal on the basis of both field trials and the experience of those farmers who already grow them. Some proponents of this

WORDS TO KNOW

INTELLECTUAL PROPERTY RIGHTS (IPR): Rights to produce or reproduce intangible property such as music, written words, ideas, or processes that are protected through patents, copyrights, and other means. In agriculture, recent disputes in IPR include controversies surrounding patenting genes or seeds in biotechnology and the effort to grant IPR to indigenous or traditional knowledge.

INTERGENERATIONAL EQUITY: The principle that actions of one generation must take into account their impact on subsequent generations and that some resources must be preserved for use by future generations.

PRECAUTIONARY PRINCIPLE: In a case of uncertainty, taking into account potential long-term effects and the level of uncertainty to guide decisions related to risk.

Fair trade cocoa farmers in the Dominican Republic carry bags of cocoa beans. Fair trade attempts to address the rights of small farmers in the developing world and to increase their bargaining power in a global marketplace. © *Simon Rawles / Alamy.*

technology state that opposition to the spread of these crops limits options for farmers, or rather limits the right of farmers to choose the crops they deem most profitable to grow on their land.

In addition to ethical arguments based on rights and based on the precautionary principle, another area of ethical practice in agriculture comprises the appeals to equity and justice. Equity between farmers in different countries surrounds many concerns about agricultural subsidies, international trade, and the rights of the poor. The issues of equity between farmers in the same country or between landowners and sharecroppers spark ethical controversies about land reform, land rights, and land access.

Most environmental arguments also have an ethical component, and movements for sustainability often appeal to intergenerational equity, the concept that each generation has a right to have access to some of the earth's resources. If the current generation abuses its rights by irrevocably harming the environment, the harm is passed on to future generations. The equity between the present and the future is stressed under this principle, sometimes called sustainability. In perhaps the most famous appeal for sustainability, the Brundtland Report, published by the United Nations-sponsored World Commission on the Environment and Development in 1987 under the title *Our Common Future*, sustainability is defined using principles of intergenerational equity as "the ability to meet the needs of the present without compromising the ability of future generations to meet their needs." However, some critics of sustainability will point to inequities in the present, such as between developed and developing nations, as a greater form of injustice; they argue efforts to rectify present inequities are undermined by a focus on intergenerational equity.

■ Impacts and Issues

One area in which ethical arguments are often invoked in agriculture is the role of women in agriculture in the developing world, especially in Africa. According to the FAO, women in rural areas of Sub-Saharan Africa carry eight times more fuel, water, and farm produce than men. Women average an hour per day gathering fuel and water for preparing meals, and in some areas these tasks may occupy up to four hours per day. Women also work an average of thirteen hours more per week than men. At the same time, women provide 70 percent of agricultural labor and produce 90 percent of food from their agricultural activities. These inequities between women and men are argued to be an ethical issue. Some analysts see women's inequality as not only a problem in itself, but an issue of intergenerational equity: Because women tend to bear primary responsibility for feeding and raising children, if their unequal work burdens lead to poor nutritional status of their children, those children may not reach their potential. The ultimate result of overworked, overburdened women, then, is the perpetuation of poverty in future generations.

Whereas women's unequal work burden and unequal status is a major ethical issue, other forms of ethical arguments can also be heard in calls to improve women's status. Proposals for legal reform often rest on granting women new rights or on strengthening existing rights. These would include land rights so that women who are abandoned, widowed, or divorced can maintain access to agricultural land. The issue of access to land for women-headed households may be growing in importance because, at least in Sub-Saharan Africa, the number of such households is increasing due to the death of males in violent conflicts, increasing prevalence of divorce, male labor migration, and men dying from illnesses such as acquired immunodeficiency syndrome (AIDS). FAO estimates that as many as one in five farms in the world may be woman-headed, heralding a trend known as the feminization of agriculture and as the feminization of poverty. The diversity of ethical issues in agriculture remains large, and many times various sides in a controversy will use appeals to ethical principles in support of their position.

SEE ALSO *African Famine Relief; Agricultural Deforestation; Agricultural Land Reform; Agriculture and International Trade; Agroecology; Aid and Subsidies to Promote Agriculture and Reduce Illicit Drug Production; Biodiversity and Food Supply; Biofuels and World Hunger; Decollectivization; Ethical Issues in Food Aid; Factory Farming; Fair Trade; Family Farms; Famine; Famine: Political Considerations; Food and Agriculture Organization (FAO); Food Security; Food Sovereignty; Gender Equality and Agriculture; Genetically Modified Organisms (GMO); Indigenous Peoples and Their Diets; International Food Aid; International Fund for Agricultural Development; Land Availability and Degradation; Livestock Intensity and Demand; Migrant Labor, Immigration, and Food Production; Organics; Pesticides and Pesticide Residue; Population and Food; Rome Declaration on World Food Security (1996); Slow Food Movement; Subsidies; Subsistence Farming; Sustainable Agriculture; Truth in Labeling; UN Millennium Development Goals; U.S. Agency for International Development (USAID); U.S. Department of Agriculture (USDA); Wage* *Slavery in Food Production; Women's Role in Global Food Preparation.*

BIBLIOGRAPHY

Books

Genetic Engineering and Food Sovereignty: Sustainable Agriculture Is the Only Option to Feed the World. Bonn: Evangelischer Entwicklungsdienst (EED), 2009.

Hahlbrock, Klaus. *Feeding the Planet: Environmental Protection through Sustainable Agriculture.* London: Haus, 2009.

Hatfield, Jerry L., ed. *The Farmer's Decision: Balancing Economic Agriculture Production with Environmental Quality.* Ankeny, IA: Soil and Water Conservation Society, 2005.

Thomson, Jennifer A *Seeds for the Future: The Impact of Genetically Modified Crops on the Environment.* Ithaca, NY: Comstock, 2007.

World Commission on Environment and Development. *Our Common Future.* New York: Oxford, 1987.

Periodicals

Trentmann, Frank "Before 'Fair Trade': Empire, Free Trade, and the Moral Economies of Food in the Modern World." *Environment and Planning D: Society & Space* 25, no. 6 (2007): 1079–1102.

Web Sites

"Agriculture: Fairer Markets for Farmers." *World Trade Organization (WTO).* http://www.wto.org/english/thewto_e/whatis_e/tif_e/agrm3_e.htm (accessed September 30, 2010).

"FAO and the Eight Millennium Development Goals." *Food and Agriculture Organization of the United Nations (FAO).* http://www.fao.org/mdg/en/ (accessed September 30, 2010).

"Land Tenure." *Food and Agriculture Organization of the United Nations (FAO).* http://www.fao.org/nr/tenure/lt-home/en/ (accessed September 30, 2010).

"Women, Agriculture, and Food Security." *Food and Agriculture Organization of the United Nations (FAO).* http://www.fao.org/worldfoodsummit/english/fsheets/women.pdf (accessed September 30, 2010).

Blake Jackson Stabler

Ethical Issues in Food Aid

■ Introduction

The humanitarian aims of food aid are about providing food and related assistance to tackle hunger, either in emergency situations or to help with deeper, longer-term hunger alleviation and achieve food security. Structurally it is a voluntary transfer of resources from one country to another to directly or indirectly supply food to people suffering from a shortage of food. Given that there are still so many people that go hungry around the world, however, food aid efforts to date could be considered enormously ineffective.

The criticism of food aid in mainstream media tends to be directed towards corrupt government practices in many developing countries, which often result in diversion of aid funds, food, and other resources. Food aid can also create cycles of dependency in regional populations. Critics closest to the food aid system additionally focus on food aid donors, some of whom they claim are aligning their actions with their own foreign policy agendas. While development objectives are not overlooked, these are not necessarily at the heart of the agenda. Herein lies the crux of the ethical dilemma of food aid.

Although corruption, inefficiencies, and dependencies in the recipient country are certainly significant ethical issues, the lesser publicized ethical considerations of donor country interests in food aid also exist. The United States is the world's largest provider of international food aid, supplying nearly half of all food aid, or about 4 million metric tons of food per year. Whereas food aid from any country can come under criticism, U.S. policy with respect to food aid differs from most other donor countries and tends to be most heavily criticized in this context.

■ Historical Background and Scientific Foundations

The modern practice of food aid at the global level stems from the devastation after the twentieth-century World Wars, when rebuilding had economic, political, and humanitarian benefits for both donors and recipients of alike. During and after World War II (1939–1945), the United States and others increased and formalized food aid efforts and saved thousands of lives as famine spread throughout Europe. The Marshall Plan (officially the European Recovery Program, ERP) totaled nearly $13 billion in aid and focused on economic recovery, rebuilding infrastructure and feeding victims of the war in Western Europe and Japan.

Food aid may be said to have been formally established in the United States in 1954 with Public Law 480 (PL480). But the move to a more multilateral approach was launched in 1961 with the establishment of the United Nation's World Food Programme (WFP). By the 1970s the WFP was a major player, and in the early twenty-first century it handles 99 percent of multilateral food aid, coordinating donations and delivery around the world.

In 1967 the Food Aid Convention (FAC) provided a set of policies for the donor countries; FAC is monitored by the Consultative Sub-Committee on Surplus Disposal (CSSD). The CSSD's primary purpose is to ensure that food aid does not affect commercial imports and local production in recipient countries.

Early on, the United States and Canada accounted for more than 90 percent of global food aid flows. By 2009, according to the WFP report *2009 Food Aid Flows*, 55 donor governments (including the European Commission, which includes all European Union countries) provided 89 percent of all global food aid. According to the report, of the funding contributed by donor governments, the United States provided 51 percent of funding, followed by the European Union countries in aggregate at about 17 percent, Japan at 7 percent, and Canada and Saudi Arabia at 4 percent each. Other countries contributed about 9 percent of the total donor government total, with the United Nations contributing the remaining 8 percent. In total, 76 countries were donors in 2009. The remaining donations were received from financial institutions and private donors.

■ Impacts and Issues

The primary ethical criticisms of food aid revolve around domestic agricultural policy benefits of food aid to domestic farmers through dumping (when free, subsidized, or below market price food undercuts local farmers); tied aid; creating and building domestic economies; ensuring shipping and packaging are from domestic corporations; and local impacts such as the depression of local market prices.

As currently implemented, critics say that U.S. food aid profits American agribusiness and the shipping industry. Under existing rules, for example, a minimum of 75 percent of the food contributed as food aid by the United States must be grown and packaged in the United States, and shipped using U.S. vessels.

The United States has also been criticized for insisting on giving in-kind donations rather than cash. Achieving the humanitarian aims of food aid, according to some aid organizations, can be twice as effective if aid is in cash rather than food. Cash donations allow for greater flexibility in meeting needs and much faster response times. With cash donations, foods can also be purchased locally, which has numerous benefits, from infusing local markets with money to ensuring that the right foods are supplied for the local diet and nutritional needs.

WORDS TO KNOW

AID: Aid (also known as international aid, overseas aid, or foreign aid, especially in the United States) is a voluntary transfer of resources from one country to another, given at least partly with the objective of benefiting the recipient country.

DUMPING: Food aid that consists of free, subsidized, or below market price food, which undercuts local farmers and can lead to the destruction of local farming and economies and lead to an ongoing cycle of poverty and hunger.

FOOD AID: Food aid is given to countries in urgent need of food supplies, especially if they have just experienced a natural disaster. Food aid can be provided by importing food from the donor, by buying food locally, or by providing cash.

FOOD ASSISTANCE: Any intervention to address hunger and undernutrition (e.g., food stamps, WIC, food subsidies, food price stabilization, etc.). It is distinct from food aid in that it is not related to international sourcing of resources tied to the provision of food, whether by a donor or to a recipient.

IN-KIND DONATIONS: Donations that are made in goods and services rather than money (or cash).

A man in Cochabamba, Bolivia, carries boxes of food aid donated by the United States government and distributed by the World Food Programme. © *frans lemmens / Alamy.*

IN CONTEXT: FOOD SECURITY AS A BASIC HUMAN RIGHT

Recognition that food supplies are adequate but that millions of people remain hungry has led to a new emphasis on food security as a human right. At the 1996 World Food Summit, the United Nations World Food Programme, along with governmental and nongovernmental organizations, committed to the goal of enforcing the fundamental right of everyone to be free from hunger.

In-kind donations can also take months to arrive to the populations in crisis, and sometimes then clash with local harvests, rather than bridging the gap between harvests. In disaster response, timeframes become even more important, as opposed to longer-term food aid projects. Not only are timeframes shorter with cash donations for disasters, but food experts argue that more relevant needs can be met with cash donations. They say that what people often need is simply buying power, perhaps for food, but also for soap or kerosene. Often the challenge they face is an inability to buy local food because of losing their means of making a living. And if food prices have spiked because of a disaster, buying power becomes all the more relevant.

The United States also sells a portion of its food aid to recipient governments, or it allows it to be monetized. Monetization, usually under the umbrella term of program food aid, is a process by which food aid can be sold by recipients to generate proceeds for whatever purpose, whether for development projects or simply to provide budgetary relief for recipient governments.

In practice, when subsidized food aid is sold through local markets, it is typically done at prices under the cost of production, undermining local competition. This then depresses prices at which local farmers can sell their produce, discouraging production and possibly casting them into crisis, bankruptcy, and economic and physical dislocation.

The human rights group Madre, the small-farmer advocacy organization Institute for Agriculture and Trade Policy (IATP), and other organizations advocate food for populations in crisis being sourced as locally as possible. Ironically, this is becoming increasingly challenging in many areas, Haiti being a prime example.

Haiti, a once largely rural, agriculture-based country, suffered from a food crisis after the earthquake of 2010. Since 1980 it has been flooded with cheap, subsidized food imports, primarily rice from the United States. As a result, economic opportunity in agriculture dwindled, the urban population swelled, and due to many ongoing issues (deforestation, build-up of urban slums), local food supply chains also dwindled.

Finally, an emerging ethical issue for food aid centers around genetically modified organisms (GMOs). Many governments in Africa, South America, and the European Union have banned all or certain types of GMO crops. Famously, in 2002, a U.S. donation of 10,000 tons of GMO maize intended for Zimbabwe was not accepted by the Zimbabwean government and was sent elsewhere because it came in whole kernels, which if used as seed could have spread GMO varieties locally. The event piqued international interest, because Zimbabwe's policy against GMO foods was not waived even as almost half of the population was facing famine due to political problems, drought, and floods.

SEE ALSO *African Famine Relief; Agroecology; Biofuels and World Hunger; Dietary Changes in Rapidly Developing Countries; Disasters and Food Supply; Famine: Political Considerations; Food and Agriculture Organization (FAO); Food Price Crisis; Food Security; Heifer International; Hunger; International Food Aid; International Fund for Agricultural Development; Malnutrition; Population and Food; Subsistence Farming; Sustainable Agriculture; UN Millennium Development Goals; Undernutrition; U.S. Agency for International Development (USAID).*

BIBLIOGRAPHY

Books

Calaguas, Belinda. *Failing the Rural Poor: Aid, Agriculture, and the Millennium Development Goals.* Johannesburg: ActionAid International, 2008.

De Waal, Alex. *Famine That Kills: Darfur, Sudan.* Oxford, UK: Oxford University Press, 2005.

Fraser, Evan D. G., and Andrew Rimas. *Empires of Food: Feast, Famine, and the Rise and Fall of Civilizations.* New York: Free Press, 2010.

Haggard, Stephan, and Marcus Noland. *Famine in North Korea: Markets, Aid, and Reform.* New York: Columbia University Press, 2007.

Periodicals

Brett, John. "The Political-Economics of Developing Markets versus Satisfying Food Needs." *Food and Foodways* 18, nos. 1–2 (2010): 28–42.

Marchione, Thomas, and Ellen Messer. "Food Aid and the World Hunger Solution: Why the U.S. Should Use a Human Rights Approach." *Food and Foodways* 18, nos. 1–2 (2010): 10–27.

Rublin, Lauren R. "A Special Report on Philanthropy—Animal Spirits—Through the Gift of Livestock, Heifer International Nurtures Self-Reliance." *Barron's* (December 1, 2004): 26.

Web Sites

"2009 Food Aid Flows." *World Food Programme.* http://home.wfp.org/stellent/groups/public/documents/newsroom/wfp223562.pdf (accessed October 20, 2010).

"What Is Food for Peace?" *United States Agency for International Development (USAID).* http://www.usaid.gov/our_work/humanitarian_assistance/ffp/ (accessed October 15, 2010).

World Food Programme. http://www.wfp.org/ (accessed October 15, 2010).

Melissa Carson

Extreme Weather and Food Supply

■ Introduction

Weather, as distinct from climate, is the state of the atmosphere as measured on a scale of hot or cold (temperature), wet or dry (rainfall and humidity), calm or storm (atmospheric pressure and wind), clear or cloudy (atmospheric particle count), and other meteorological elements. Climate is the condition of these same elements in a given region over long periods of time. Extreme weather phenomena are those at the extremes of the historical distribution, especially severe or unseasonal weather. These are, by definition, rare.

In food production terms, extreme weather events have both primary (immediate and delayed) and secondary effects. Extreme weather events that have an immediate effect on food production, crops, or livestock, are events that exceed a critical physiological or physical threshold that the crop/livestock can endure, such as a cold snap or a hurricane. These events can damage or destroy entire crops or herds over a short period of time. Prolonged extreme weather, such as severe drought or storms resulting in flooding or continued soil wetness, can directly destroy crops and the habitats of both land and marine life.

■ Historical Background and Scientific Foundations

Extreme weather events such as drought, flooding, hurricanes, and severe storms are naturally occurring events and have wreaked havoc on food production since the beginning of time. The exodus of early humans out of Africa around 135,000 years ago has been attributed to drought, and stories of a great flood sent to destroy civilization (and food supplies) are featured in the mythology of many cultures.

Cold waves, or cold snaps, as defined by the U.S. National Weather Service, are rapid falls in temperature within a 24-hour period requiring substantially increased protection to agriculture, industry, commerce, and social activities. Cold waves can cause death to livestock and wildlife, typically due to hypothermia or starvation, and they often necessitate the purchase of additional fodder for livestock at considerable cost to farmers. Cold waves that bring unexpected freezing and frost can kill plants during the growing season, especially during the early and most vulnerable stages of growth.

Heat waves, long periods of abnormally high temperatures, can destroy vegetation and lead to deaths among livestock and wildlife, typically due to dehydration or heat stroke. Wildfire outbreaks can increase in frequency as dry vegetation becomes more susceptible to igniting. Excessive evaporation from bodies of water can also devastate marine populations as their habitats shrink and nutrients in the water are reduced.

Drought is an extended period of months or years of consistently below-average precipitation. In many regions, farmers can effectively mitigate the impact of drought through irrigation and crop rotation, but failure to develop adequate drought mitigation strategies carries a grave human cost and is exacerbated by ever-increasing population densities. Subsistence farmers, for example, are more likely to migrate during drought because they do not have alternative food sources, and these areas are the most vulnerable to drought-triggered famine.

Drought has further reaching consequences as well. It can reduce water quality as lower flows reduce the dilution of pollutants and increase contamination of remaining water sources. It can lower the carrying capacity of the land for livestock and lead to erosion of the landscape and, in prolonged drought, to desertification of the land.

Floods are caused by many different weather phenomena including monsoonal rain, hurricanes and tropical cyclones (in coastal areas), severe thunderstorms and rapid snow melt (in river basins), and also unexpected drainage obstructions such as landslides, ice, or debris. The damage to physical infrastructure can significantly disrupt food supplies. Entire harvests can be lost, and livestock may drown or become vulnerable to waterborne disease. However, floods are sometimes a benefit to food production: Lowlands near rivers often depend on seasonal flooding. River silt deposited by floods adds nutrients to the local soil and replenishes groundwater.

In many countries, rivers prone to flooding are carefully managed with defenses such as levees, reservoirs, and weirs. Coastal flooding defenses have been addressed with sea walls, beach nourishment, and barrier islands. The designation of wetlands, a strategy used in the United States after the 1993 flood across the Midwest, helped to prevent further disasters by allowing the wetlands to act as a sponge in storms. Flood diversion areas such as these are used in many countries.

■ Impacts and Issues

Weather extremes place a heavy strain on food production, and with the complexity of coincident pressures on the global food chain, food supply has become an increasingly sensitive system. The coincident pressures

are many and global in scale, including population growth, economic growth that leads to changing diets and increased consumption, pollution, and the reliance on energy for both production and transport. The physical limits of the planet are being tested, too: The United Nations Environment Program stated in 2007 that the planet's water, land, air, plants, animals, and fish stocks were all in "inexorable decline."

Heavy rains flood a farm in Connecticut.   *Image copyright Laura Stone, 2010. Used under license from Shutterstock.com.*

IN CONTEXT: EXTREME WEATHER IMPACTS ON EMERGING DISEASES

Weather can influence the evolution and spread of viruses. In April 2010, researchers published an analysis of changes in wild bird migration patterns during the unusually cold European winter of 2005–2006. The report concluded that the extreme cold altered migration routes and caused unique aggregations of birds that were associated with observed transmission of highly pathogenic avian influenza virus (HPAIV) H5N1. In particular, waterbird species were forced to concentrate in smaller areas where lakes and ponds remained at least partially unfrozen. The wild birds also remained in more densely concentrated populations for longer than normal, and such conditions enabled a faster—and ultimately broader—spread of the virus. The HPAIV H5N1 virus emerged from Asian avian populations in 2005 to spread from Southeast Asia into poultry and wild birds in Africa, the Middle East, and Europe. Researchers continue to study the role of wild bird populations in the spread of avian viruses.

The spread of disease in wild birds is important because they can act as carriers of viruses with the potential to infect domesticated flocks and poultry farms. The result of such contamination is often massive culling of birds and a loss of consumer confidence in avian food products.

Food supply fluctuations often result in food price hikes. Episodes of skyrocketing food prices, such as those seen in 2007 and during the global food crisis in 2008, when bad weather resulted in poor crop production at the same time as a spike in oil prices, are predicted to become more frequent. Whether extreme weather events are on the rise or not, they will have increasing impact on the ever more sensitive global food supply system.

Effects of extreme weather on food supply also often include food supply management and environmental issues. Severe drought over the summer of 2009 in Mongolia, for example, resulted in lower crop production and prevented the stockpiling of food for livestock that typically would ensure the livestock's survival during the cold winter months. More than one million livestock were lost over the following winter, which devastated the poor, landlocked regions of this country. Equally, environmental impacts include water quality or disrupted patterns of pest migration. Watersheds, for example, are at risk of pollution through normal rain cycles, but are at much greater risk after prolonged rains and flooding as surface runoff flushes pollutants from poorly managed agricultural fields. In Pakistan, unprecedented monsoonal rains beginning in July 2010 gave rise to extreme flooding, first in the country's

northern provinces and then spreading to affect more than 25 percent of the country. More than 21 million people have been displaced or otherwise affected; wheat harvests were decimated by more than one million tons; and the region remains at risk for prolonged, severe food shortages.

There is almost no reference to extreme weather effects on food production in the media that does not cite a trend of increasingly frequent incidents of extreme weather events and attribute this trend to climate change. But in the scientific community, whether climate change accounts for changes in frequency to weather extremes is hotly debated, and there continues to be disagreement on whether the frequency and scale of extreme weather events is on the increase or simply part of a natural cycle. However, both the World Meteorological Organization of the United Nations and the U.S. Environmental Protection Agency, among many others, report a clear increase in the number of extreme weather events directly linked to climate change. In particular, they anticipate an increase in the frequency of heat waves in areas affected by drought, increased intensity in tropical cyclone activity, and rising sea levels.

The Intergovernmental Panel on Climate Change (IPCC) stated in its 2007 report that "increased frequency of heat stress, droughts, and floods negatively affect crop yields and livestock beyond the impacts of mean climate change, creating the possibility for surprises [i.e., extreme weather events], with impacts that are larger, and occurring earlier, than predicted using changes in mean variables alone. This is especially the case for subsistence sectors at low latitudes. Climate variability and change also modify the risks of fires, pest and pathogen outbreak, negatively affecting food, fiber, and forestry."

SEE ALSO *Agroecology; Climate Change and Agriculture; Desertification and Agriculture; Famine; Food and Agriculture Organization (FAO); Food Security; International Food Aid; International Fund for Agricultural Development; Water; Water Scarcity.*

BIBLIOGRAPHY

Books

Intergovernmental Panel on Climate Change (IPCC). *Climate Change 2007: Synthesis Report.* Geneva: IPCC, 2008.

Singh, Satya Narayan. *Climate Change and Crops.* Berlin: Springer, 2009.

United Nations. *Extreme Weather Events, Water, and Health.* Geneva: United Nations ECE Secretariat, 2005.

Periodicals

Haile, Menghestab. "Weather Patterns, Food Security and Humanitarian Response in Sub-Saharan Africa."

Philosophical Transactions: Biological Sciences 360, no. 1463 (2005): 2169–2182.

Zarocostas, John. "New Network of Weather Stations in Africa Aims to Improve Food Security and Health." *BMJ* (clinical research ed.) 338 (2009): b2555.

Web Sites

"Climate Change—Health and Environmental Effects: Agriculture and Food Supply." *U.S. Environmental Protection Agency (EPA)*. http://www.epa. gov/climatechange/effects/agriculture.html (accessed October 1, 2010).

The Earth Institute. "Toll of Climate Change on World Food Supply Could Be Worse Than Thought; Predictions, Already Daunting, Fail to Account for Extreme Weather, Disease and Other Complications." *Columbia University*. http://www.earth.columbia. edu/articles/view/2001 (accessed October 1, 2010).

Melissa C. Carson

Factory Farming

■ Introduction

Factory farming is industrial-scale agriculture that depends upon rearing animals in large numbers, usually in confined spaces. It has become increasingly popular because technology has found ways of rearing animals for eggs, milk, and meat on a larger scale. The addition of vitamins to feed, so animals could be reared all year long indoors, and the routine use of antibiotics to stop the spread of infection in crowded conditions have been important landmarks in the development of the factory farm. Mechanization also helps factory farming run smoothly and boosts productivity. Factory farms differ in many ways from traditional agriculture, with their main aim being to produce as much food as possible at the lowest possible cost. Whereas intensive farming of this kind may help meet the growing demand for food, the continued existence of malnutrition around the world suggests it is not a complete solution.

Factory farming raises many animal welfare issues, with animals sometimes being mutilated to adapt them to their unnatural conditions of confinement. Use of antibiotics increases antibiotic resistance in humans. Factory farming also uses chemicals such as pesticides and fertilizers, which, along with animal waste, form a major pollution problem. In addition, factory farming concentrates food production in the hands of a few powerful multinational companies. Critics of factory farming suggest that buying local, free-range produce from family farms that are sustainable is the better, more environmentally friendly way of feeding the world.

■ Historical Background and Scientific Foundations

Factory farming originated in the 1920s and was a spin-off of the discovery of vitamins A and D. It was realized that if these vitamins were added to animal feed, then large numbers of animals could be raised indoors all year round. However, such overcrowding increased the spread of disease. This problem was dealt with by routine dosing with antibiotics, once these drugs became available in the 1940s and 1950s. Further major developments of the factory farm included the use of mechanization and assembly line technology. In the early twenty-first century, factory farming is an intensive industry and far removed from the traditional image of agriculture.

The Environmental Protection Agency (EPA) defines a large factory farm, or concentrated animal feeding operation (CAFO) as one that has 1,000 cattle, 700 dairy cattle, 2,500 pigs over 55 pounds weight, or 125,000 chickens. A medium sized CAFO has between 300 and 999 cattle, or between 200 and 699 dairy cattle, 750 to 2,499 pigs, or between 37,500 to 124,999 chickens. What these facilities share is that they contain many animals in a confined space, often with little or no access to sunlight or fresh air. There is a danger that animals might fight one another, being in such close proximity. They are adapted to their conditions by modifications such as cutting off the beaks of chickens and turkeys, and amputating the tails of cows and pigs. Animals are fed low doses of antibiotics on a regular basis to ward off infection. They are also given hormones to promote rapid growth. The animals' waste may be handled with a liquid manure system, in which their urine and feces are mixed with water and held under the farm facility or outside in open-air lagoons. The main animals found in factory farms are cows, pigs, chickens, and turkeys, as well as sheep, goats, and rabbits.

Broiler chickens are raised in closely confined broiler houses instead of cages, and these are often unlit to discourage fighting among the birds. They grow at a very rapid rate, reaching their market weight in just a few weeks. These birds are selectively bred to be so heavy that it often is difficult for them to stand. Layer chickens supply about 95 percent of eggs in the United States. They are usually held in battery cages that are very small, with slanted wire floors. Greater egg production is encouraged by constant exposure to light. Meanwhile, around 90 percent of all pigs raised for food are confined at some point in facilities that have automated water, feed, and waste removal. Dairy cows are often injected with bovine growth hormone, which increases their rate of milk production. They are often impregnated continuously to keep up the flow of milk.

■ Impacts and Issues

Advocates of factory farming consider these approaches necessary to meet the growing demand for food. Factory farming, however, raises several animal welfare issues. Confining animals and depriving them of light and freedom is considered by many to be inhumane. There are also health issues in the repeated dosing of animals with antibiotics. In the United States, almost half of all antibiotics are used in factory farming. This practice has been linked to the spread of antibiotic resistance among humans. The presence of antibiotics in food creates a selective pressure, which favors the emergence of resistant strains of bacteria.

Factory farming also creates environmental problems because the liquid manure system is a pollution source. International exports from factory farms also increase carbon emissions, contributing to accelerating climate change. Finally, factory farming puts food production in the hands of relatively few large multinational companies.

Intensive poultry farming. *Image copyright nikkytok, 2010. Used under license from Shutterstock.com.*

Critics of factory farming advocate consumers looking for free-range products, such as eggs, which have come from operations that have higher standards of animal welfare. They also advocate buying local produce from organic and smaller, more sustainable family-run farms, which try to avoid the use of chemicals such as fertilizers, pesticides, hormones, and antibiotics. Factory farms are geared almost exclusively towards production of animal protein, which requires more resources than production of plant protein. Overall reduction of meat consumption may be a more realistic way of feeding the world than intensive factory farming.

SEE ALSO *Agribusiness; Dairy Products;* E. Coli *Contamination; Eggs; Ethical Issues in Agriculture; Family Farms; Farm-to-Table Movement; Food Recalls; Head-to-Tail Eating; Humane Animal Farming; Livestock Intensity and Demand; Meat Inspection Act of 1906; Meats; Organics; Poultry; Sustainable Table; Veganism; Vegetarianism.*

BIBLIOGRAPHY

Books

Baur, Gene. *Farm Sanctuary: Changing Hearts and Minds about Animals and Food.* New York: Simon & Schuster, 2008.

Crocombe, Angela. *Ethical Eating: How to Make Food Choices That Won't Cost the Earth.* Camberwell, Victoria, Canada: Penguin Books, 2008.

Miller, Frederic P., Agnes F. Vandome, and John McBrewster. *Industrial Agriculture: Factory Farming, Livestock, Aquaculture, Agribusiness, Monoculture, Agroecology, Organic Farming, Urban Agriculture.* Beau Bassin, Mauritius: Alphascript Publishing, 2009.

Nierenberg, Danielle, and Lisa Mastny. *Happier Meals: Rethinking the Global Meat Industry.* Washington, DC: WorldWatch Institute, 2005.

Periodicals

Holdrege, Craig. "Blame Factory Farming, Not Organic Food." *Nature Biotechnology* 25, no. 2 (2007): 165–166.

Pluhar, Evelyn B. "Meat and Morality: Alternatives to Factory Farming." *Journal of Agricultural and Environmental Ethics* 23, no. 5 (2010): 455–468.

Web Sites

Becker, Jeffrey S. "Humane Treatment of Farm Animals: Overview and Issues." *U.S. Department of Agriculture (USDA).* http://www.ncseonline.org/nle/crsreports/08Sept/RS21978.pdf (accessed October 19, 2010).

Dr. Temple Grandin's Web Page: Livestock Behavior, Design Facilities, and Humane Slaughter. http://www.grandin.com/index.html (accessed October 19, 2010).

"Factory Farming." *HFA: The Humane Farming Association.* http://www.hfa.org/factory/index.html (accessed October 19, 2010).

Susan Aldridge

Fair Trade

■ Introduction

In economics, fair trade involves changing trade rules between countries or allowing countries to protect certain interests through trade barriers. In marketing, fair trade refers to a group of practices intended to protect the interests of small producers in the developing world from what are considered unfair prices paid for tropical commodities and goods by companies from the developed world. Fair trade is an attempt to address the price problem that small farmers in the developing world face in that they have no market power so they are price takers. Marketing cooperatives, marketing boards, and a variety of other measures have been utilized in the past in attempts to secure higher prices for small farmers. Some of these practices are based in dependency theory, an economic theory that states tropical countries face declining terms of trade for their bulk commodities. Fair trade employs third-party certification to gain access to fast growing, high value markets. Critics of certified fair trade state that small farmers' rights continue to be violated or that free trade would offer more benefits for small farmers in the developing world.

■ Historical Background and Scientific Foundations

Fair trade certification has emerged since the 1960s as one way to address the problem that small producers face because they lack market power. Certified fair trade's advocates claim that small farmers in the developing world receive unfairly low prices for their cash crops. Small producers face perfectly competitive markets in that they have little or no influence over who will purchase their goods and what price will be paid. Because each small farmer has a minimal volume of production compared to the size of the market, no one small farmer will be missed if those goods are not brought to the market. Since the late nineteenth century, some groups of farmers

have formed producer cooperatives or marketing cooperatives in an attempt to gain market power. For example, many small almond producers banded together to form associations, and nine of these associations linked to form the California Almond Growers Exchange (CAGE) in 1910. In 1986 this producer cooperative was renamed the Blue Diamond Growers, and this cooperative is the world's largest processor of tree nuts. By controlling a large or merely a substantial volume of production, producer cooperatives and associations gain market power and some room to negotiate prices. Also, cooperatives may run their own processing facilities or their own brands, like Blue Diamond Growers, in order to further gain profits from different stages in the value chain.

In dependency theory, as first outlined by Raúl Prebisch (1901–1986), an Argentine economist who was the founding secretary of the United Nations Conference on Trade and Development (UNCTAD) from 1964 to 1969, declining terms of trade hurt tropical products produced by small farmers in developing nations. Bulk commodities such as mined minerals or tropical agricultural products such as coffee experienced declining terms of trade over time. This means the price of these commodities would fall over time compared to the price of the manufactured goods the developed countries exported to the developing world. In dependency theory, the tropical countries depend on manufactured goods from the developed countries whereas the developed countries are dependent on the tropical countries as a source of raw materials and bulk commodities.

To combat declining terms of trade, several strategies were used by developing countries based on dependency theory in the 1960s and 1970s. One strategy was to form single window export boards or marketing boards. Many developing countries established marketing boards for agricultural products such as coffee, peanuts, cocoa, and tea to try to achieve higher prices in world markets. Marketing boards achieve higher prices through price discrimination. In a spot market or at an exchange, prices may simply be asked of buyers and seller or prices in some markets may be posted or reported daily. A marketing board, such as the Wheat Boards of Canada or Australia, does not publish prices. Then the board charges each customer based on what the consumers are willing to pay, not a single price for all customers. The failure of the tropical marketing boards stems from several reasons. First, they failed to control enough of world trade because many countries produce tropical commodities. Second, corruption within the marketing boards led some of them to pay low prices to the small farmers and charge high prices to customers without adequately improving the quality of the commodity. This extra covered other government expenses or simply was pocketed as graft. Third, unlike the Canadian Wheat Board, which has improved many qualities of the wheat sold over time, the boards failed to improve the quality of the commodities produced. Countries discontinued these boards for the most part as they liberalized their economies in the 1980s and 1990s. For example, Tanzania, a country in East Africa, dissolved its coffee export board in 1990. However, some marketing boards remain in 2010, such as the Grain Marketing Board, which continues to operate in Zimbabwe, a land-locked country in Southern Africa.

Based on the experience of churches in the 1940s and 1950s selling handicrafts at church fairs and on the successful experience of certified organic goods, fair trade has many of the same objectives of increasing the amount paid to small producers for tropical agricultural goods. Using the success of the organic foods model, special trade fairs or specialized stores emerged to offer fair trade goods. Later, third party certification was employed so that fair trade goods could enter other market channels such as supermarkets, coffee shops, and other major retailers. A certification body inspects and controls for quality across many small producers so that consumers can be confident that the products contain a trait that they cannot, at home, find in the product with their senses. The traits for fair trade goods are: the company marketing the good paid a higher price for the raw material from small farmers, and a variety of other labor, environmental, and community objectives were met. Many fair trade models remain based on producer cooperatives and the principles of cooperative development, but they have borrowed heavily from the marketing techniques used by certified organic production to enter high value markets in developed countries, with the largest markets being in Europe.

Coffee bag labeled fair trade sustainable from Monteverde, Costa Rica. © *Loetscher Chlaus / Alamy.*

■ Impacts and Issues

Certified fair trade goods have grown to a larger marketplace in the developed countries since they were first introduced. However, fair trade certified products tend to be traditional tropical agricultural goods such as coffee, tea, bananas, cocoa, sugar, and cotton, according the Fairtrade Labeling Organization (FLO). In 2009 FLO reported 3.4 billion euros in sales using its certification system. This represents a 15-percent growth rate from 2008 during a worldwide economic slump. For the previous five years, FLO estimated an annual growth rate of 40 percent of sales. The World Fair Trade Organization (WFTO) estimates that one and a half million workers and producers participate in fair trade in the developing countries. Some critics note that fair trade production in Asia and Latin America is more common than in Africa, which still faces disadvantages even in accessing these preferential markets that are designed to benefit small farmers.

Certified fair trade goods face criticisms from two major groups. One group of critics argues that fair trade has not pushed hard enough for the rights of the farmers involved. They would like to see fair trade institute higher standards for health, worker protection, educational access, and other benefits for workers and producers participating in fair trade. They accuse fair trade organizations of seeking growth of the industry before providing the actual benefits to the small farmers. Others see fair trade certification as opposed to free trade and as an impediment for further trade liberalization. They argue that free and open trading systems will benefit all producers by the removal of trade barriers and better market access. Solutions that connect these small producers to developed world markets at prices above the world market price fail to address the issues of trade diversion and the influence of agricultural subsidies and preferential trading agreements on agricultural commodity prices. They state that allowing true free trade and removing trade distorting subsidies will have far more benefits for poor, small farmers in the developing world than the small projects involved in fair trade production.

SEE ALSO *Agribusiness; Agriculture and International Trade; Banana Trade Wars; Chocolate; Coffee; Ethical Issues in Agriculture; Food Sovereignty; Free Trade and Agriculture; Sustainable Agriculture; World Trade Organization (WTO).*

BIBLIOGRAPHY

Books

Jaffee, Daniel. *Brewing Justice: Fair Trade Coffee, Sustainability, and Survival.* Berkeley: University of California Press, 2007.

Lyon, Sarah, and Mark Moberg. *Fair Trade and Social Justice: Global Ethnographies.* New York: New York University Press, 2010.

Moberg, Mark. *Slipping Away: Banana Politics and Fair Trade in the Eastern Caribbean.* New York: Berghahn Books, 2008.

Nicholls. Alex, and Charlotte Opal. *Fair Trade: Market-Driven Ethical Consumption.* London: Sage, 2008.

Raynolds, Laura T., Douglas L. Murray, and John Wilkinson. *Fair Trade: The Challenges of Transforming Globalization.* London: Routledge, 2007.

Stiglitz, Joseph E., and Andrew Charlton. *Fair Trade for All: How Trade Can Promote Development.* Oxford, UK: Oxford University Press, 2005.

Wright, Simon, and Diane McCrea. *The Handbook of Organic and Fair Trade Food Marketing.* Oxford, UK: Blackwell Pub, 2007.

Periodicals

Besky. Sarah. "Can a Plantation Be Fair? Paradoxes and Possibilities in Fair Trade Darjeeling Tea Certification." *Anthropology of Work Review* 29, no. 1 (2008): 1–9.

"Fair Trade?" *Nature* 455, no. 7216 (2008): 1008.

Getz, Christy, and Aimee Shreck. "What Organic and Fair Trade Labels Do Not Tell Us: Towards a Place-Based Understanding of Certification." *International Journal of Consumer Studies* 30, no. 5 (2006): 490–501.

Shreck, Aimee. "Resistance, Redistribution, and Power in the Fair Trade Banana Initiative." *Agriculture and Human Values* 22, no. 1 (2005): 17–29.

Web Sites

Fairfood International. http://www.fairfood.org/?gclid=COG0l8WCyqQCFcTt7Qod9VcqDA (accessed October 19, 2010).

Fairtrade Foundation. http://www.fairtrade.org.uk/products/default.aspx (accessed October 19, 2010).

Blake Jackson Stabler

Family Farms

Introduction

The family farm has long been the basic unit of agriculture. It may have been in a family for generations, the land being handed down from parents to children. In developing countries, the family farm is still the norm and the majority of farms in the United States are also family owned. The family farm is in direct contrast to the factory farm, which is a large-scale industry, often with a strong focus upon rearing and maintaining animals for slaughter, eggs, or milk in closely confined conditions. It is often assumed that the factory farm is more productive because it achieves economies of scale that are not possible for most family farms. However, larger family farms actually account for most agricultural product sales in the United States. The family farm also more easily serves the growing trend towards local and organic produce. When a family farm uses agro-ecological techniques, including organic methods, the environment benefits. There has been a small increase in the number of family farms in recent years. But most of these new farms are very small and may not be sustainable. Indeed, the traditional family farm is in danger of dying out, as its owners age and cannot rely on handing their operation on to the next generation.

Historical Background and Scientific Foundations

The family farm has been the norm since the start of agriculture, and it is still important all around the world. In many traditional social structures, the farm is maintained by the oldest man and oldest sons, while the women in the family take care of child rearing, housework, and financial matters. Women are increasingly becoming involved, however, in farm management and marketing of the product. The family farm may specialize in growing crops, trees, or other plants, or in raising animals, or a mixture of all of these.

According to a survey carried out by the USDA in 2007, 96 percent of the total of 2,204,792 farms in the United States are family farms. They are classified as very large, large, or small family farms, and this is done on the basis of gross annual sales, rather than size, because it is hard to compare productivity of farms in different locations on the basis of the number of acres. An acre of non-irrigated land in an arid region may be far less productive than one in a more temperate region with plenty of rainfall. A very large family farm is one with gross annual sales of more than $500,000, whereas a large family farm has gross annual sales of between $250,000–500,000. A small family farm is one with gross annual sales of less than $250,000.

Large and very large family farms produce more than 63 percent of the value of all farm products sold in the United States, according to the USDA. This is despite the fact that they account for only around 9 percent of all farms. Non-family farms, including factory farms, account for 21 percent of products, and two million or so small family farms account for the rest.

It is often argued that family farms are not as productive as factory farms. However, productivity often comes at the expense of biodiversity and environmental degradation, particularly in the tropical rain forests. A study by researchers at the University of Michigan suggests that small, diversified farms are more likely to help to preserve biodiversity in tropical regions that are undergoing deforestation. The researchers examined case studies from Costa Rica, El Salvador, Panama, Argentina, and Brazil and found that small family-owned farms come closer than factory farms in mimicking the natural forest habitat and create corridors that allow plants and animals to migrate between remaining forest fragments. This is especially so if the farm is using agro-ecological techniques that are sensitive to the environment, such as biological controls instead of pesticides and compost or other organic matter instead of chemical fertilizers. These tropical family farms are also able to integrate well into the rainforest environment by growing crops under a canopy of trees or perhaps growing crops mixed with fruit trees such as mango or avocado.

The researchers concluded that it would be beneficial to split up large-scale farms in the tropics into smaller units. They cited the 2009 "International Assessment of Agricultural Knowledge, Science, and Technology for Development" synthesis report, which concludes that small-scale sustainable farms are the best way to tackle world hunger, rather than large industrial-scale factory farms.

■ Impacts and Issues

After a period of decline, the number of family farms in the United States is increasing again, by around 4 percent per annum, according to the latest USDA figures. This growth probably is due to the increased popularity of local produce and farmers' markets as a reaction against factory farming. However, it is not clear how sustainable these new farms are, as most have a very small volume of sales and may find it hard to survive in a harsh economic climate. Another issue threatening the survival of family farms is the aging of their owners: Around 70 percent of family farms are due to change hands over the next 20 years because their owners will be retiring. Most of these family farms will either go out of business, be sold to other families, be converted to non-farm use, or become part of a bigger farming operation.

A man purchases tomatoes from the farm stand of a local farm. Products from family farms are enjoying a resurgence in popularity in developed countries whose agriculture is dominated by large corporate farms. Consumers cite a variety of reasons for eschewing grocery store produce aisles for direct from the farm produce including supporting a local business, desiring more sustainable food products, preferring the taste, and reduced cost. *Ellie Lerner / Lerner & Lerner / LernerMedia Global Photos.*

Driving a tractor used by his father, a farmer feeds cattle on his farm near Greenleaf, Kansas. As the overall population of farmers in the United States ages, passing on the family farm is becoming a growing concern. *AP Images.*

SEE ALSO *Agribusiness; Agroecology; Biodiversity and Food Supply; Community Supported Agriculture (CSAs); Ethical Issues in Agriculture; Factory Farming; Farm-to-Table Movement; Foodways; Genetically Modified Organisms (GMO); Humane Animal Farming; Locavore; Neighborhood Food Cooperatives; Sustainable Agriculture; Sustainable Table; U.S. Department of Agriculture (USDA).*

BIBLIOGRAPHY

Books

Gregson, Bob, and Bonnie Gregson. *Rebirth of the Small Family Farm: A Handbook for Starting a Successful Organic Farm Based on the Community Supported Agriculture Concept.* Austin, TX: Acres, 2004.

Pyle, George. *Raising Less Corn, More Hell: The Case for the Independent Farm and against Industrial Food.* New York: Public Affairs, 2005.

Strange, Marty. *Family Farming: A New Economic Vision.* Lincoln: University of Nebraska Press, 2008.

Tamayo, Efren J. *America's Family Farms.* New York: Nova Science Publishers, 2010.

Periodicals

Carnegie, Michelle. "Reviews: Family Farms: Survival and Prospect. A World-Wide Analysis." *Geographical Research* 47, no. 3 (2009): 339–340.

Darnhofer, Ika. "Strategies of Family Farms to Strengthen Their Resilience." *Environmental Policy and Governance* 20, no. 4 (2010): 212–222.

Peck, Jason. "The Courage of Farmers: In Our Transient Society, Few People Stay Put in One Place." *The Piedmont Virginian* 2, no. 4 (2008): 54–60.

Web Sites

Hoppe, Robert A., David E. Banker, and James M. MacDonald. "America's Diverse Family Farms, 2010 ed." *U.S. Department of Agriculture (USDA).* http://www.ers.usda.gov/publications/eib67/ (accessed October 19, 2010).

"The Issues: Family Farms." *Sustainable Table.* http://www.sustainabletable.org/issues/familyfarms/ (accessed October 19, 2010).

National Family Farm Coalition. http://www.nffc.net/ (accessed October 19, 2010).

Susan Aldridge

Family Meal Benefits

■ Introduction

When families come together to eat meals they share more than just food. Family mealtime is when social interactions occur among family members and when role-modeling of eating behaviors takes place. Parents are able to catch up on the lives of their children and assess how they are doing emotionally and physically. Evidence shows that consistent family meals can actually improve the diets of children, help them to do better in school, and reduce their risk of abusing drugs. A 2000 study in the *Archives of Family Medicine* showed that adolescents consumed more fruits, vegetables, and dairy foods when their parents were present at an evening meal.

Beyond the nutritional benefits of eating meals together, anthropologists assert that there is substantial value in the making of the food and the ritual of family members coming together to share a common table. The *Journal of the American Dietetic Association's* article entitled "Adolescent and Parent Views of Family Meals" acknowledges that shifts in family structure, living arrangements, increased after-school activities, and the availability of more convenient foods has negatively impacted opportunities for family meals over the years. Whereas the protective properties of family meals are more widely known, the exact reasons for these benefits are still unclear.

■ Historical Background and Scientific Foundations

Although eating patterns are always changing, anthropologists explain the history of mealtime as a constant vehicle for the integration of children into the social order of their particular community. Both mealtime communication and commensality are described as fostering the family as a social unit. The ethnographic examples discussed in *New Directions for Child and Adolescent Development* show how mealtimes can reinforce gender roles, social orders, and food distribution. The children of the Micronesian island of Fais are taught that food sharing is the basis of the family unit through participation in multiple household visits that involve making, offering, and eating food with others. In China, children can be excluded from the dining table, and older family members take food before the younger members in a household on special occasions. A study involving Italian family mealtimes showed that when distributing food, parents usually favored their children over themselves. Parents in the United States tend to promote equal distribution of food and teach children that they should not take food at the expense of other members of the family. Whether children are expected to be silent during meals, to eat separately, or to receive the largest portion of food, the objective during these mealtimes is for the child to gain sociocultural knowledge by watching and listening to other family members at the table. While the characteristics of mealtimes vary from society to society, the goal is shared.

■ Impacts and Issues

Research has shown that family meals contribute greatly to the general health and well-being of children and adolescents. When families share food and strengthen family ties, they are influencing their child's performance in school, affecting the child's likelihood of developing a chronic disease, and preventing unhealthy weight control behaviors. The development of eating disorders such as anorexia nervosa, bulimia, and binge-eating typically occur between the ages of 14 and 18 years. An alarming conclusion in a 2004 study in the *Archives of Pediatrics and Adolescent Medicine* is that girls who ate alone might be at a greater risk of developing an eating disorder, whereas girls who ate with their parents consumed up to 14 percent more calories than they did when they ate alone. The study also found that young girls who did

WORDS TO KNOW

ADOLESCENT: A person who has started puberty and continues to mature by experiencing a period of physical and psychological development. Also known as a transitional period of development between youth and maturity, this period usually starts at age 12 or 13 and lasts until 18 or 19 years of age. This time period, adolescence, is informally referred to as the teenage years.

COMMENSALITY: The act of eating with other people.

EATING DISORDERS: Several conditions whereby a person is constantly preoccupied with food and weight. This preoccupation leads to an extreme change in eating habits and at its most severe can be life-threatening. The three main types of eating disorders are anorexia nervosa, bulimia nervosa, and binge-eating disorder. Both females and males can have eating disorders but females seem to suffer from them more often. Treatments for eating disorders can involve psychotherapy, nutrition education, family counseling, medications, and hospitalization.

EATING HABITS: Describes what foods people eat, why and how people eat, and with whom they eat. Individual, social, cultural, religious, economic, and environmental factors can influence people's eating habits. Acceptable and learned eating behaviors can vary by cultural group and are reflected in a person's meal and snack patterns, portion sizes, and food combinations.

MEALTIME: The period of time at which a meal is habitually or customarily eaten. All meals, whether at home or in a restaurant, are usually structured events. Current standard meals include breakfast, lunch, and dinner. The components of a meal vary across cultures, but generally include the consumption of two or more foods.

OBESITY: A condition caused by the over-consumption of foods that are nutrient-poor and high in fat or sugar, combined with low levels of physical activity. Obesity is a risk factor for developing heart disease, high blood pressure, high cholesterol, type 2 diabetes, and other chronic diseases.

A family enjoying an alfresco meal. Studies have shown both medical and social benefits are gained from frequent family meals, including higher nutritional intake, less snacking, improved communication skills, and higher scholastic scores among students who regularly eat meals with their families as opposed to eating alone. © *Cephas Picture Library / Alamy.*

not have regular family meals and ate alone consumed more soft drinks and ate less fruits, vegetables, and calcium-rich foods.

The influence of family meals on adolescents has been the focus of numerous studies in the United States and many other developed countries over the years. This attention is a result of the surge in childhood and adolescent obesity rates. Obesity can put a person at a greater risk for developing chronic diseases such as high blood pressure, diabetes, and heart disease. Many argue that healthier eating habits can help prevent these diseases, and information about what to eat and how much to eat is usually gleaned at home. Researchers also began to question whether family meals result in healthier eating habits or if it is a coincidence and children from more

health-conscious families also tend to eat meals together because their parents are health-conscious. A 2004 study at the University of Minnesota worked to find the answer to this question by measuring the psychological health of a family or "family connectedness" and analyzing the relationship between kids eating more healthful foods, doing better in school, and their risk of drug and alcohol use. What this study found is that the absence or presence of family connectedness was less important than consistently eating together. By eating together regularly, children of families with or without family connectedness made healthier food choices, did better in school, and had a lower risk of engaging in risky behaviors with drugs and alcohol.

SEE ALSO *Changing Nutritional Needs throughout Life; Dietary Guidelines for Americans; Eating Disorders; Foodways; History of Home Cooking; Nutrition's Role in Human Evolution; Women's Role in Global Food Preparation.*

BIBLIOGRAPHY

Books

Procter, Sandy. *Everyone to the Table: Family Meals Serve Us Well.* Manhattan: Kansas State University, 2007.

Weinstein, Miriam. *The Surprising Power of Family Meals: How Eating Together Makes Us Smarter, Stronger, Healthier and Happier.* Campbell, CA: Paw Prints, 2010.

Periodicals

Eisenberg, Marla E., et al. "Correlations between Family Meals and Psychosocial Well-being among Adolescents." *Archives of Pediatrics & Adolescent Medicine* 158, no. 8 (2004): 792–796.

Fulkerson, Jayne A., et al. "Adolescent and Parent Views of Family Meals." *Journal of the American Dietetic Association* 106, no. 4 (2006): 526–532.

Ochs, Elinor, and Merav Shohet. "The Cultural Structuring of Mealtime Socialization." *New Directions for Child and Adolescent Development*, no. 111 (2006): 35–49.

Web Sites

Gibbs, Nancy. "The Magic of the Family Meal." *Time*, June 4, 2006. http://www.time.com/time/magazine/article/0,9171,1200760,00.html (accessed October 1, 2010).

Purdue University Center for Families. "Promoting Family Meals." *Purdue University.* http://www.cfs.purdue.edu/cff/promotingfamilymeals/ (accessed October 1, 2010).

Tiffany Imes

Famine

■ Introduction

A famine is a rapid reduction in the availability or supply of food that may be linked to a crop failure or to changing economic conditions. Every reduction in food supply or rapid change in food prices does not necessarily lead to famine. Famine occurs when food supply has been reduced to the point that some residents of an area are unable to feed themselves sufficient amounts of food, and these people suffer from hunger, malnutrition, disease, and even starvation. A famine's duration tends to be short and no longer than a few years. This distinguishes famine from long-term problems such as chronic malnutrition or endemic hunger. Famines are also limited in their geography: The areas of impact tend not to affect entire countries or regions. A single state or province of a country may be affected by famine while nearby areas are not. Natural triggers of famine include droughts, floods, earthquakes, blights, other plant diseases, pest infestations, and other natural disasters or perils. A natural disaster, however, rarely causes a famine on its own. While localized, not all residents of an area will necessarily suffer during a famine, as some residents will find new sources of food or be able to purchase food from outside of the area of famine. Thus, a famine occurs only if the poor and often marginalized residents of the area affected are unable to secure food from outside the area.

■ Historical Background and Scientific Foundations

From the historical record, famines appear to have occurred all over the globe during all periods of history. Advances in agricultural technology, increasing ability to trade food, and the accumulation of wealth by an increasing number of people have made famine much less common in the twenty-first century. Modern ideas and theories about famine often are shaped by the experience of the Irish potato famine, which occurred from 1845 until 1852. The potato blight that affected Ireland, an island just northwest of Europe, caused several years of near total crop loss for poor farmers with small farms who primarily grew potatoes. The huge drop in self-supplied food and the sudden drop in income led to undernutrition and malnutrition, with approximately one million people dying from associated diseases and from starvation. Another million people emigrated from Ireland at least in part in search of food.

Many observers at the time and since have proposed that overpopulation of Ireland was the cause of the famine. Drawing upon the work of British economist Thomas Robert Malthus (1766–1834), these observers proposed that Ireland's population had grown too quickly, and that a population that cannot be supported is naturally prone to famine, blight, and other dramatic events that limit population. Arguments along these lines about famines or other events that cause depopulation are referred to as Neo-Malthusian. Other scholars of famine have pointed to the role of poverty in famines. The reduced purchasing power of Ireland explains, then, why food products continued to be exported from Ireland to England, both areas within the United Kingdom: Ireland's rural residents could not afford food at the prevailing rising prices, whereas England's could. While not particularly successful at limiting the scope of the famine, the government of the United Kingdom did attempt several relief measures. These programs became standard models of mitigating the effects of famine during the twentieth century. Food relief by distributing imported corn into Ireland was attempted. Also, programs of public paid work for the unemployed were established.

In the twentieth century, famines occurred in many parts of the world for a wide variety of reasons. However, most attention to famine and studies of famine focus on recurrent famines starting in 1968 in some regions of the African countries of the Sahel, a dry land region just south of the Sahara desert, and also in some regions of the countries of the Horn of Africa starting in 1973. In 1984 drought hit Ethiopia, a country on the Horn of Africa, in the provinces of Wollo, Tigray, Gojjam, and Hararghe in the northern part of the country and in what is now the independent country of Eritrea, an African country on the Red Sea. Media efforts around the world highlighted the famine and brought it to the attention of the West. Having been dealing with famines in this region, the U.S. Agency for International Development (USAID) set up the Famine Early Warning System (FEWS) in 1985 to better be able to predict the onset of famine and to react more quickly to famine. Later this program was renamed the Famine Early Warning Systems Network (FEWSNet). Using satellite data, weather data, price data on key crops, and information from social science surveys, FEWSNET is one famine early warning system, more broadly called a food security monitoring system. Advances in technology such as using satellite images to predict crop yields and using computers to process large amounts of data from many sources have enabled a more comprehensive approach to predicting famine and being able to mitigate some of its effects.

WORDS TO KNOW

BLIGHT: A plant disease inflicted by a pathogen that causes the plant to brown, wither, and die.

CARRYING CAPACITY: The ability of an ecosystem to sustain a certain population of a species. The carrying capacity defines the maximum load of population the ecosystem can support without disrupting other species' populations

FAMINE: A rapid reduction in the availability or supply of food that may be linked to a crop failure or to changing economic conditions.

UNDERNUTRITION: The chronic condition of not consuming sufficient calories or not consuming sufficient fat or protein in a diet to lead a healthy, active life. Undernutrition is sometimes referred to as hunger or as protein-energy malnutrition (PEM). Most definitions of undernutrition are based on estimates that adults need between 1,800 and 2,000 calories per day.

Two women gather some precious grains of corn that fell to the ground at the food station at Serewa. Rain has been missing from the region since 2007, causing a major famine to occur. Because of the remoteness of the area and bad infrastructure, the UN World Food Programme has had difficulties regularly transporting food and other kinds of aid to the area. © *Kai-Otto Melau / Alamy.*

■ Impacts and Issues

Probably the most contentious issue in famine studies is the role that population and population growth may play in making an area susceptible to famine. Drawing on the work of Malthus, population growth may lead to decreased wages due to the larger labor supply. Some theorize that as an already poor population becomes increasingly impoverished, nature works to eliminate the overpopulation through famine, among other means. The overpopulation argument states that land has a limited carrying capacity for humans who will necessarily suffer consequences if they overpopulate an area.

Critics of neo-Malthusian arguments employ several counterarguments. First, some economists point out that food can be traded so that many areas with very little agricultural production support large populations. Second, they point to the role that improvements in agricultural technology can play in accommodating a growing population. Lastly, some critics, including Amartya Sen (1933–), an Indian economist who won the Nobel Prize for Economics in 1998, state that famine is primarily the result of political failure to prevent famine during a decline in food production or supply. Famine is not a result of the relationship between population and the land but rather a failure of a population to have an entitlement to food. Critics of neo-Malthusian arguments challenge the idea of an absolute carrying capacity for land.

■ Primary Source Connection

Written in 1847 and published in Dublin, this was penned in the midst of the "Great Famine." From 1845 to 1852 approximately one million people died of starvation in Ireland.

During the late eighteenth and early nineteenth centuries, the population of Ireland expanded rapidly but the country was still predominantly rural, lacking the large-scale industrial development that had supported population growth in England. The potato was the staple food crop for the Irish people, many of whom were poor farmers forced to pay high rents for their farms and properties to rich landowners. When they could not pay, they were often evicted from their homes, and their possessions were taken by the landlord.

Disaster struck when the whole potato crop was blighted by disease in 1845, and a potato famine spread through the country during the following year. To make matters worse, the harvest failed again in 1848. Tens of thousands of people died from starvation or from the many diseases which spread among a population weakened by hunger, including a cholera epidemic in 1948.

A famine and poverty-driven mass emigration from Ireland in the mid-nineteenth century left the country in a severe state of population decline, which it would not recover from until well into the twentieth century, and which affected its economic progress for many decades. However, the longer-term impact of the famine and mass emigration did bring about land reform in Ireland, as the remaining farmers were gradually able to add to and consolidate their holdings, while the landlords lost much of their power.

The mass migration from Ireland also had a lasting influence on the ethnic and national compositions of the major American cities where many of the emigrants settled, with the Irish accounting for up to twenty percent of the population of some American cities by the mid-1850s. In 1850 alone, an estimated 370,000 immigrants entered the United States from Ireland and other European countries, the highest rate of immigration in America's history. The surge in numbers gave rise to concern about the impact of immigration on the native-born population and eventually resulted in the passing of laws in the late nineteenth century and early twentieth century that banned certain categories of immigrants. Until the passing of the Immigration Act of 1924, however, immigration restrictions were limited, and high levels of immigration continued to boost America's population.

THE SONG OF THE FAMINE

Want! want! want!
Under the harvest moon;
Want! want! want!
Thro' dark December's gloom;
To face the fasting day
Upon the frozen flag!
And fasting turn away
To cower beneath a rag.

Food! food! food!
Beware before you spurn,
Ere the cravings of the famishing
To loathing madness turn;
For hunger is a fearful spell,
And fearful work has done,
Where the key to many a reeking crime
Is the curse of living on!

For horrid instincts cleave
Unto the starving life,
And the crumbs they grudge from plenty's feast
But lengthen out the strife—
But lengthen out the pest
Upon the fostid air,
Alike within the country hut
And the city's crowded lair.

Home! Home! Home!
A dreary, fireless hole—
A miry floor and a dripping roof,
And a little straw-its whole.

Only the ashes that smoulder not,
Their blaze was long ago,
And the empty space for kettle and pot,
Where once they stood in a row!

Only the naked coffin of deal,
And the little body within,
It cannot shut it out from my sight,
So hunger-bitten and thin;—
I hear the small weak moan—
The stare of the hungry eye,
Though my heart was full of a strange, strange joy
The moment I saw it die.

I had food for it e'er yesterday,
But the hard crust came too late—
It lay dry between the dying lips,
And I loathed it—yet I eat.
Three children lie by a cold stark corpse
In the room that's over head—
They have not strength to earn a meal,
Or sense to bury the dead!

And oh I but hunger's a cruel heart,
I shudder at my own,
As I wake my child at a tearless wake,
All lightless and alone!
I think of the grave that waits
And waits but the dawn of day,
And a wish is rife in my weary heart—
I strive and strive, but it won't depart—
I cannot put it away.

Food! food! food!
For the hopeless days begun;
Thank God there's one the less to feel!
I thank God it is my son!
And oh! the dainty winding-sheet,
And oh ! the shallow grave!
Yet your mother envies you the same
Of all the alms they gave!

Death! death! death!
In lane, and alley, and street,
Each hand is skinny that holds the bier,
And totters each bearer's feet;
The livid faces mock their woe,
And the eyes refuse a tear;
For Famine's gnawing at every heart,
And tramples on love and fear!

Cold! cold! cold!
In the snow, and frost, and sleet,
Cowering over a fireless hearth,
Or perishing in the street.
Under the country hedge,
On the cabin's miry floor,
In hunger, sickness, and nakedness,
It's oh I God help the poor.

It's oh I if the wealthy knew

A tithe of the bitter dole
That coils and coils round the bursting heart
Like a fiend, to tempt the soul!
Hunger, and thirst, and nakedness,
Sorrow, and sickness, and cold,
It's hard to bear when the blood is young,
And hard when the blood is old.

Death! death! death!
Inside of the work-house bound,
Where maybe a bed to die upon,
And a winding-sheet is found.
For many a corpse lies stiff and stark—
The living not far away—
Without strength to scare the hateful things
That batten upon their prey.

Sick! sick! sick!
With an aching, swimming brain,
And the fierceness of the fever-thirst,
And the maddening famine pain.
On many a happy face To gaze as it passes by—
To turn from hard and pitiless hearts,
And look up for leave to die.

Food! food! food!
Through splendid street and square,
Food! food! food!
Where is enough and to spare;
And ever so meagre the dole that falls,
What trembling fingers start,
The strongest snatch it away from the weak,
For hunger through walls of stone would break—
It's a devil in the heart!

Like an evil spirit, it haunts my dreams,
Through the silent, fearful night,
Til I start awake from the hideous scenes
I cannot shut from my sight;
They glare on my burning lids,
And thought, like a sleepless goul,
Rides wild on my famine-fevered brain—
Food! ere at last it come in vain
For the body and the soul!

Anonymous

"THE SONG OF THE FAMINE." *THE DUBLIN UNIVERSITY MAGAZINE*, VOL. 671. WM. S. ORR AND COMPANY, 1847.

SEE ALSO *African Famine Relief; Agricultural Deforestation; Agroecology; Biofuels and World Hunger;
Climate Change and Agriculture; Desertification
and Agriculture; Dietary Changes in Rapidly
Developing Countries; Disasters and Food Supply; Ethical Issues in Agriculture; Ethical Issues in
Food Aid; Famine: Political Considerations; Food
and Agriculture Organization (FAO); Food Price
Crisis; Food Security; Heifer International; Hunger;*

International Food Aid; International Fund for Agricultural Development; Malnutrition; Population and Food; Subsistence Farming; Sustainable Agriculture; UN Millennium Development Goals; Undernutrition; U.S. Agency for International Development (USAID).

BIBLIOGRAPHY

Books

De Waal, Alex. *Famine That Kills: Darfur, Sudan.* Oxford, UK: Oxford University Press, 2005.

Fraser, Evan D. G., and Andrew Rimas. *Empires of Food: Feast, Famine, and the Rise and Fall of Civilizations.* New York: Free Press, 2010.

Haggard, Stephan, and Marcus Noland. *Famine in North Korea: Markets, Aid, and Reform.* New York: Columbia University Press, 2007.

Seekamp, Gail, and Pierce Feiritear. *The Irish Famine.* Phibsboro, Dublin: Pixie Books, 2008.

Stanford, Claire, ed. *World Hunger.* New York: H. W. Wilson, 2007.

Veryha, Wasyl. *A Case Study of Genocide in the Ukrainian Famine of 1921–1923: Famine as a Weapon.* Lewiston, NY: Edwin Mellen, 2007.

Periodicals

Woo, Jean, Chi Shun Leung, and Yeung Shan Samuel Wong. "Impact of Childhood Experience of Famine on Late Life Health." *The Journal of Nutrition, Health, and Aging* 14, no. 2 (2010): 91–95.

Web Sites

Famine Early Warning Systems Network (FEWS-Net). *U.S. Agency for International Development.* http://www.fews.net/Pages/default.aspx (accessed September 9, 2010).

Medecins sans Frontieres (Doctors without Borders). "Starved for Attention." *StarvedforAttention.org.* http://www.starvedforattention.org/ (accessed September 9, 2010).

"Oxfam Calls for Radical Shake-Up of Aid System to Break Cycle of Hunger in Ethiopia." *Oxfam International,* October 22, 2009. http://www.oxfam.org/en/pressroom/pressrelease/2009-10-22/aid-system-break-cycle-hunger-ethiopia (accessed September 9, 2010).

Blake Jackson Stabler

Famine: Political Considerations

■ Introduction

A famine is a rapid reduction in the availability or supply of food that may be linked to a crop failure or to changing economic conditions. Every reduction in food supply or rapid change in food prices does not necessarily lead to famine, however, and because of this, some social scientists have proposed that famines should be understood in their political context, which may play a larger role in bringing about famine than the agricultural context. The political causes of famine may be ineffective land and agricultural policies, intentional use of famine as genocide, or the failure of governments to react to stop an imminent famine. Famines in the Soviet Union in the 1930s, China during 1958–1961, and North Korea in the 1990s may have been caused by agricultural and governmental policies rather than simply by crop failures. According to Amartya Sen (1933–), an Indian-born economist who won the Nobel Memorial Prize in Economic Sciences in 1998 and teaches at Harvard University, all famines are caused by a failure of the population to command an entitlement to food. Sen also hypothesizes that democracy and famine are mutually exclusive.

■ Historical Background and Scientific Foundations

Famine has long been associated with drought, blight, floods, and other natural disasters that may trigger widespread crop failure or a destruction of food stocks. However, examinations of the largest scale famines of the twentieth century reveal that the political regime influences the scope of the famine. In some cases, critics propose that governments intentionally cause famines with their policies to target particular ethnic or racial groups as an act of genocide. In a different account of why famines occur, governments may not take the necessary actions to stop the deaths that stem from famine once a crop failure or other potential cause of famine is imminent.

Whereas there are many examples of famines made more severe by political indifference or famines induced by failed agricultural policies, two of the most severe famines of the twentieth century occurred in the context of regimes radically reshaping agriculture under avowed Marxist regimes, occurring in the Soviet Union in the 1930s and later in China in 1958–1961. Under Joseph Stalin (1878–1953), the Georgian leader of the Soviet Union from 1924 until 1953, the Soviet Union, a twentieth-century state that included present-day Russia along with additional areas in both Europe and Asia,

WORDS TO KNOW

ENTITLEMENTS APPROACH: An approach to understanding famine, hunger, malnutrition, and poverty based on understanding how a population acquires food and on what resources a population has available to acquire food. Pioneered by Amartya Sen, the approach looks at the right to food and other goods and to changes in exchange conditions to explain sudden deprivation events such as a famine.

GENOCIDE: According to the United Nations (UN) Convention on Genocide of 1948, "any of the following acts committed with intent to destroy, in whole or in part, a national, ethnical, racial or religious group, as such: killing members of the group, causing serious bodily or mental harm to members of the group, deliberately inflicting on the group conditions of life calculated to bring about its physical destruction in whole or in part, imposing measures intended to prevent births within the group, or forcibly transferring children of the group to another group."

NO ACCESS—NO FOOD: The principle that humanitarian food aid will be distributed only under regimes in which the distribution and storage can be monitored by humanitarian relief workers, usually by foreign humanitarian relief workers. Food refers to food aid, and access refers to the ability to travel to the locations where food aid is stored and distributed.

Memorial to the 1932–1933 famine in USSR in Obukhow, Kiev region, Ukraine. Historians estimate that approximately 5 to 10 million people died during the Great Famine (Holodomor), which began after Josef Stalin began collectivization policies. *Image copyright Sergey Kamshylin, 2010. Used under license from Shutterstock.com.*

experienced a famine in the early 1930s alongside its campaign to collectivize its agriculture. The Soviet Union was in the process of collectivizing its farms, which meant relocating many farmers and confiscating their land, equipment, and livestock to newly formed collective and state farms. Drought, grain shortfalls, the killing of livestock instead of turning them over to the new farms, and other difficulties caused severe food shortages from 1932 to 1934. Estimates often fall in the range of 5 million to 10 million deaths resulting from the famine.

In China, in relationship to Mao Zedong (1893–1976) and his program of the Great Leap Forward, there was a severe famine in China from 1958 to 1961. This famine may have been the most severe in recorded history, and estimates generally range up to 30 million deaths as a result. This famine, like the earlier Soviet famine, may have resulted from ineffective agricultural policies related to collectivization, or in the case of China, to moving peasants into people's communes. A locust outbreak, flooding, drought, and a policy of grain

export to pay government debts also contributed to the food shortages. Other famines caused by government indifference, ineffective reaction to natural disaster, or by poor agricultural policies as opposed to food unavailability, may have also occurred in the Wollo famine of 1973 and 1974 in Ethiopia, the Bangladesh famine of 1974, and the Ethiopian famine of 1984 and 1985.

The famine in North Korea in the 1990s is another candidate for being politically induced. Because North Korea depended heavily on trade with and assistance from the Soviet Union, the collapse of the Soviet Union in 1991 led to lack of key agricultural inputs such as fertilizer in North Korea. Heavy rains and floods in 1995 led to further reductions in production of the key grains of rice and corn. The North Korean government initially reacted in 1992 by instituting a program encouraging families to consume only two meals per day instead of three. Unable to feed its population, North Korea eventually called for international humanitarian assistance in the form of food aid in 1995. The World Food Programme, a United Nations agency that administers food aid programs, was allowed to distribute food to lessen the suffering of those affected by the famine. However, many critics accused the North Korean government of using the food aid to feed its army instead of the rural poor. As many as 3 million people died in North Korea during the famine of the 1990s.

A South Korean activist holds a sign that features children allegedly suffering from famine in North Korea. *AP Images.*

In 1998 the World Food Programme and its largest donor, the United States, insisted on a more conditioned food aid program. Under the principle of no access—no food, the World Food Program's staff must be able to visit storage and distribution points for monitoring in order for North Korea to receive food aid. Additional crop failures, also potentially related to changes in income levels and in agricultural and land policies in North Korea, had some humanitarian agencies worried about a return of famine to North Korea in 1999, 2003, 2006, 2007, and 2010.

■ Impacts and Issues

In one of the most complete examinations of famine, Sen has proposed that all famines are, in a sense, political events. Using a framework he calls the entitlement approach, Sen examines how famine victims obtain food. How the population receives its entitlement to food is key to understanding how famines occur, according to Sen, and more importantly, is key to understanding how famines can be prevented. Whereas famine may be triggered by natural disaster or a sudden, unexpected change

in market conditions. Sen does not propose these events are sufficient to result in famine. Instead, certain segments of the population must experience a failure in their entitlement to food, not merely a change in their income or in the conditions of their key markets. This approach helps explain how famine would occur during periods of peak food availability, such as the 1974 famine in Bangladesh. It also helps explain why famine in the Horn of Africa, in Sudan, and Ethiopia occurred in the early 1980s despite drops in production of as little as 11 percent. Countries in Southern Africa at the time, such as Zimbabwe and Botswana, experienced more severe drops of food production of 38 percent and 17 percent respectively, but had no widespread famine due to effective government relief policies according to Sen. In Sen's theory, because of the population's ability to continue to command an entitlement to food, a drop in food production or income will not necessarily lead to famine.

Perhaps the most controversial aspect of Sen's work is his hypothesis that famine does not occur in democracies. Democratic participation and a free press, he states, prevent famines from occurring. According to Sen, a government that faces elections at some point cannot be indifferent to the level of suffering found during

Internally displaced women and a child are seen at the Action Against Famine's Feeding Center in North Darfur, Sudan, in 2005. By 2010, the number of internally displaced persons in Sudan had risen to over 4 million people. Most of these people experience food shortages and/or famine due to continued intra-tribal and militia violence, along with lack of civil infrastructure. *AP Images.*

a famine. A press serves to alert the electorate and politicians about a famine that is occurring. Sen's most striking example is that China experienced one of the worst famines in history from 1958 to 1961 while India has not had a famine since it gained independence from Great Britain in 1947 despite experiencing multiple droughts, typhoons, floods, and a variety of other disasters causing food shortages in some states. Although China has been more effective at improving general health indicators such as life expectancy than India, Sen states that democracy in India prevents short-term severe deprivation of the type that leads to famine.

SEE ALSO *African Famine Relief; Biofuels and World Hunger; Disasters and Food Supply; Ethical Issues in Agriculture; Ethical Issues in Food Aid; Famine; Food and Agriculture Organization (FAO); Food Security; Hunger; International Food Aid; International Fund for Agricultural Development; Population and Food; UN Millennium Development Goals; U.S. Agency for International Development (USAID); World Food Day; World Food Programme.*

BIBLIOGRAPHY

Books

Bayart, Jean-Francois. *The State in Africa: The Politics of the Belly.* Cambridge: Polity, 2009.

De Waal, Alex. *Famine Crimes: Politics & the Disaster Relief Industry in Africa.* London: African Rights, 2006.

Devereux, Stephen. *The New Famines: Why Famines Persist in an Era of Globalization.* London: Routledge, 2007.

Gill, Peter. *Famine and Foreigners: Ethiopia since Live Aid.* Oxford, UK: Oxford University Press, 2010.

Holden, Stacy E. *The Politics of Food in Modern Morocco.* Gainesville: University Press of Florida, 2009.

Thaxton, Ralph A. *Catastrophe and Contention in Rural China: Mao's Great Leap Famine and the Origins of Righteous Resistance in Da Fo Village.* Cambridge, UK: Cambridge University Press, 2008.

Periodicals

Brown, David, J. Christopher, and Scott Desposato. "Who Gives, Who Receives, and Who Wins?" *Comparative Political Studies* 41, no. 1 (2008): 24–47.

Dowlah, Caf. "The Politics and Economics of Food and Famine in Bangladesh in the Early 1970s—with Special Reference to Amartya Sen's Interpretation of the 1974 Famine." *International Journal of Social Welfare* 15, no. 4 (2006): 344–356.

Jabs, Lorelle. "Where Two Elephants Meet, the Grass Suffers." *American Behavioral Scientist* 50, no. 11 (2007): 1498–1519.

Web Sites

Gambrell, John. "10 Million Face Famine in West Africa." *The Independent,* May 30, 2010. http://www.independent.co.uk/news/world/africa/10-million-face-famine-in-west-africa-1986875.html (accessed October 17, 2010).

Haggard, Stephen, and Marcus Noland. "Hunger and Human Rights: Politics and Famine in North Korea." *U.S. Committee for Human Rights in North Korea.* http://www.hrnk.org/download/Hunger%20and%20Human%20Rights.pdf (accessed October 17, 2010).

Makabila, Stephen. "Politics of Relief Food Get Worse as Famine Strikes." *The Standard,* October 2, 2010. http://www.standardmedia.co.ke/InsidePage.php?id=2000019547&cid=4 (accessed October 17, 2010).

Blake Jackson Stabler

Farm-to-Table Movement

■ Introduction

The farm-to-table movement, also referred to as the farm-to-fork movement, promotes the consumption of fresh, local, seasonal produce and meat. This grassroots movement traces its origin to the late 1960s and early 1970s, when a small cadre of consumers, chefs, and restaurateurs in California began a movement that encouraged the use of organic, fresh food. Essentially, the farm-to-table movement encourages people to return to the eating patterns that existed before the development of modern industrialized agriculture.

The farm-to-table movement spread slowly among chefs who focused on fresh, local ingredients to create better tasting dishes. Over the years, consumers and chefs expressed a desire for more flavorful, seasonal ingredients. Proponents of farm-to-table eating argue that the movement strengthens the connection between consumers and the land. Legislation in the United States, however, threatens the economic viability of the movement in that country.

■ Historical Background and Scientific Foundations

Since the rise of agriculture, most people have practiced farm-to-table eating. Early farmers had to rely on the plants, fish, and animals that existed in the region in which they lived. Early European farmers cultivated wheat, peas, onions, cabbage, and fava beans. North Asian farmers relied on cabbages, soybeans, millet, and tree fruits, while South Asians cultivated rice, yams, coconuts, bananas, and citrus. Native African crops included yams, millet, rice, and sorghum. Indigenous American peoples—separated from Eurasia and Africa by two oceans—relied on crops distinct to the Americas, including corn, potatoes, beans, tomatoes, and squashes.

Early livestock breeds also developed from native animals. Mesopotamians domesticated wild sheep as early as 9000 BC. People in Southeast Asia domesticated the chicken—which lived wild in the jungles of Southeast Asia—before 7500 BC. The use of domesticated chickens for both meat and egg production spread throughout Asia and reached the Middle East and North Africa by 1500 BC and Southeastern Europe by 800 BC. People in both the Middle East and India domesticated wild aurochs around 8000 BC. These early domesticated cattle eventually evolved into distinct European cattle breeds and the zebu of southern Asia. People of the Tibetan plateau also domesticated the yak around the same time.

The cultivation of native plants and domestication of native animals led humans to rely on locally sourced food. The lack of good transportation and reliable preservation techniques meant that produce, meat, and dairy products could not be shipped over long distances. Except for a few spices that could be dried and stored for long periods, people had to eat produce and meat that was produced nearby. The lack of safe preservation techniques, especially for vegetables, meant that humans had to eat seasonally as well.

During the Industrial Revolution of the late eighteenth and early nineteenth centuries, people in Europe and the United States began moving to cities to seek work in factories and other urban jobs. By the mid-nineteenth century, the development of railroad networks and canning enabled companies to preserve and ship vegetables and meat to urban dwellers. The development of refrigeration, including refrigerated railcars, in the late nineteenth century made it possible for producers to ship fresh vegetables and meat across long distances. The industrialization of food production intensified in the mid-twentieth century as consumers expressed a preference for processed foods that could be prepared quickly to accommodate busy modern lifestyles.

WORDS TO KNOW

AUROCHS: Aurochs, or urus (*Bos primigenius*) is a species of wild cattle that existed across Eurasia and North Africa, from which modern cattle breeds were derived. Humans hunted wild aurochs into extinction, with a hunter killing the last known aurochs in Poland in 1627.

FOODBORNE ILLNESS: An illness caused by the consumption of improperly stored, handled, or prepared food.

U.S. FOOD AND DRUG ADMINISTRATION (FDA): The Food and Drug Administration (FDA) is an agency of the U.S. Department of Health and Human Services (HHS) that is responsible for regulating and ensuring the safety and effectiveness of food, drugs, cosmetics, tobacco, and other products.

■ Impacts and Issues

The quest for flavorful food remains one of the driving forces behind the farm-to-table movement. Many chefs, including Alice Waters (1944–) of Chez Panisse restaurant in Berkeley, California; David Link of Cochon in New Orleans; and Dan Barber (1969–) of Blue Hill in New York City, assert that local, fresh produce and meats taste superior to processed foods or food picked and shipped before ripeness. These chefs and hundreds of others have forged relationships with local farmers and livestock producers to supply their restaurants with local, seasonal produce.

Advocates of farm-to-table eating also promote the movement as a way to increase the connection between consumers and the land. With modern production and shipping methods, grocery stores in developed countries have a supply of most fruits and vegetables almost year round. The farm-to-table movement seeks to educate consumers about seasonality and the length of growing seasons—information that slipped from the consciousness of people in industrialized countries generations ago.

Many advocates of the farm-to-table movement in the United States fear that the U.S. Congress may pass laws that impair the ability of small farms to compete in agricultural markets. The Food and Drug Administration (FDA) Food Safety Modernization Act (FFSMA) would amend the Federal Food, Drug, and Cosmetic

People visit an organic apple farm to pick their own fruit, including apples of many varieties, at the University of Paris South.
© *Directphoto.org / Alamy.*

The Texas Farm-to-Table Café features locally grown produce. © *M. Timothy O'Keefe / Alamy.*

Act, the law that grants the FDA most of its authority. The FFSMA would apply to virtually all agricultural producers in the United States. The FFSMA seeks to protect consumers by strengthening food production regulations designed to prevent food contamination and the outbreak of foodborne illnesses in the United States.

Farm-to-table movement proponents argue that disease prevention is a legitimate objective, but that the FFSMA should focus on large-scale producers, which have been responsible for most of the recent foodborne illness outbreaks in the United States. Instead, the FFSMA would apply to small-scale bakers, jam producers, and farms that minimally process food for sale to consumers, restaurants, grocery stores, or food co-operatives. The enhanced regulations of the FFSMA would place a financial burden on small farms that would decrease their ability to compete in the marketplace or even put some producers out of business altogether.

SEE ALSO *Agroecology; Alice Waters: California and New American Cuisine; Community Supported Agriculture (CSAs); Edible Schoolyard Movement; Family Farms; Locavore; Organics; Slow Food Movement; Sustainable Agriculture; Sustainable Table.*

BIBLIOGRAPHY

Books

Burnside, Robin. *Farm to Table.* Salt Lake City, UT: Gibbs Smith, 2010.

Holthaus, Gary H. *From the Farm to the Table: What All Americans Need to Know about Agriculture.* Lexington: University Press of Kentucky, 2006.

Manning, Ivy. *The Farm to Table Cookbook: The Art of Eating Locally.* Seattle: Sasquatch Books, 2008.

Parsons, Russ. *How to Pick a Peach: The Search for Flavor from Farm to Table.* Boston: Houghton Mifflin, 2007.

Periodicals

Cassel, Chris, Joseph Miller, Todd Biddle, and Michael Benner. "Food to Me: A Farm-to-Table Program for Middle School Children." *Agricultural Education Magazine* 77, no. 1 (2004): 19–22.

Hinderliter, Justine D. "From Farm to Table: How This Little Piggy Was Dragged through the Market." *University of San Francisco Law Review* 40, no. 3 (2006): 739–768.

Web Sites

Farm to Table. http://www.farmtotablenm.org/ (accessed October 23, 2010).

Farm to Table: The Emerging American Meal. http://www.farmtotableonline.org/ (accessed October 16, 2010).

Stein, Joel. "Extreme Eating." *Time*, January 10, 2008. http://www.time.com/time/magazine/article/0,9171,1702353,00.html (accessed October 16, 2010).

Joseph P. Hyder

Fast Food

■ Introduction

Fast food is popular the world over because it is easy, inexpensive, and filling. It appeals especially to families, busy people, and those living on their own because it is both speedy and practical. The most familiar fast foods are probably hamburgers and hot dogs, which first appeared in the United States at the turn of the twentieth century. The sandwich, which is known the world over, has been around since the nineteenth century. Different countries have different kinds of fast food, some of which, such as noodles, sushi, or falafel, are specialties of a particular culture's cuisine. Many fast food franchises have become global brands. Fast food is often equated with junk food, because it tends to be high in fat, sugar, and salt. Consuming a lot of fast food may, therefore, contribute to obesity, particularly childhood obesity. Traditional fast food does not usually equate with healthy eating guidelines, because fast food meals are low in fruits, vegetables, and fiber. Fast food may also contribute significant carbon emissions and waste. These concerns have led to an interest in slow food, which emphasizes the pleasure and traditions of food, as well as respecting the environment. Some fast food franchises have also made concessions by introducing some healthier choices and trying to cut back on packaging.

■ Historical Background and Scientific Foundations

People have always eaten fast food. Stalls selling bread and wine were popular in ancient Rome, and pies and pasties were sold on the streets in Europe and elsewhere in the Middle Ages. Street food such as samosas and falafels have long been popular in India and the Middle East, respectively. But modern fast food probably began in England, with the invention of the sandwich by Lord Sandwich (1718–1792), who reportedly placed meat between two slices of bread to save having to leave his desk for dinner. The United States is often regarded as the fast food capital of the world, and it all began with the hot dog. A German butcher, Charles Feltman (1841–1910), opened the first hot dog stand in Brooklyn in 1867. The first fast food restaurant opened in 1912, in New York City. The trend soon caught on and these restaurants, sometimes known as automats, had spread around the United States by the 1920s. As cars became more affordable, drive-in restaurants became popular. The White Castle hamburger chain, set up in 1916, was the forerunner of McDonald's, which was founded as a barbecue drive-in in 1940 by brothers Dick and Mac McDonald. Burgers proved more popular than barbeque so they re-opened as a chain selling burgers, fries, and drinks in paper wrappings and cups. The term *fast food* first entered the dictionary in 1951.

There are many different types of fast food besides hot dogs and burgers, including crisps, pot noodles, the British favorite fish and chips, kebabs, pizza, and chicken. Fast food is available from many types of outlets, including shops, restaurant franchises, garages, and street stalls. Author Eric Schlosser (1959–) highlights the love American people have of fast food in his popular 2005 book *Fast Food Nation*. He points out that Americans spend about 110 billion dollars per year on fast food and one quarter of the population eats fast food every day. Fast food is popular because it saves time in preparing and cooking food; it is filling; and, above all, it is relatively inexpensive. Added to this, many fast food restaurants are clean, warm, and welcoming to families, often providing treats and playgrounds for children. Fast food also enables busy people to eat on the run. For those living alone, it is often more economical to buy takeout than cooking from scratch, because food in supermarkets generally comes in bigger packages.

■ Impacts and Issues

Fast food has become synonymous with unhealthy food, and it is often known as junk food. Regular consumption has been blamed for rising levels of obesity. Several

WORDS TO KNOW

FAST FOOD: Food that can be prepared and served rapidly, usually involving precooked or preheated ingredients. Fast food is usually taken away, rather than eaten where it is prepared.

FRANCHISE: Many restaurants and other outlets serving fast food are franchises, or branches, of a chain where the food is delivered from a central location and is standardized.

SLOW FOOD MOVEMENT: Founded by the Italian writer Carlo Petrini (1949–) in 1989, the international Slow Food Movement acts as an antidote to fast food, with its campaigning for the pleasure of food, preservation of traditional dishes, and respect for community and environment.

researchers at the New York City Department of Health and Mental Hygiene concluded that much fast food, and fried chicken meals in particular, contains more than the recommended daily intake of salt, which increases the risk of high blood pressure.

Childhood obesity is a particular problem arising from fast food consumption. Reared on fast food, children learn to prefer French fries to vegetables, which are normally available only as a salad garnish on a burger. *Fast Food Nation* reports that teenage boys can be getting up to ten percent of their daily calories from sodas, rather than from more nutritious foods. Traditional fast foods are high in fat, salt, and sugar and, to compound the problem, are often available in large portions. But fast food need not be unhealthy. Some franchises have begun to cut salt intake in their products, and many display nutritional labels to help consumers make more educated choices. There is also an increasing interest in home cooking, slow food, buying local, and eating organic, all of which counter the fast food trend.

Fast food is linked to a number of environmental issues. In 2000, researchers at Stockholm University and the Swiss Federal Institute of Technology analyzed the various energy inputs that are associated with a single cheeseburger and concluded that it was responsible for an extra 2.2–7.7 pounds (1–3.5 kg) of carbon emissions. Fast food

research studies back this finding. For instance, a 15-year study of 3,000 Americans showed that people who consume fast food on a regular basis over a long time do have a greater tendency towards obesity and developing type-2 diabetes. Those who reported eating fast food meals more than twice per week weighed an average of 10 pounds more than those who rarely ate fast food. A study from

In-N-Out Burger signs fill the skyline in Baldwin Park, California, in June 2010. Amid complaints of obesity and lines of idled cars stretching into neighborhood streets, this blue-collar town is banning new drive-throughs in hopes of shedding its reputation as a haven for convenient, fatty foods. (AP Photo/Adam Lau) *AP Images.*

also increases the carbon footprint because of fuel consumption involved in their distribution. Finally, fast food creates local pollution problems through the amount of polystyrene packaging used. However, some companies are attempting to reduce their packaging and McDonalds, for instance, has implemented the use of recycled materials in some of its food containers. The consumer can help by recycling fast food containers such as cardboard pizza boxes.

SEE ALSO *Advertising Food; Alice Waters: California and New American Cuisine; Diet and Cancer; Diet and Diabetes; Diet and Heart Disease; Diet and Hypertension; Dietary Changes in Rapidly Developing Countries; Ecological Impacts of Various World Diets; Edible Schoolyard Movement; Farm-to-Table Movement; Foodways; Obesity; Processed Foods.*

BIBLIOGRAPHY

Books

Espejo, Roman. *Fast Food*. Detroit: Greenhaven Press, 2009.

Schlosser, Eric. *Fast Food Nation: The Dark Side of the All-American Meal*. New York: Harper Perennial, 2005.

Spurlock, Morgan. *Don't Eat This Book: Fast Food and the Supersizing of America*. New York: G. P. Putnam's Sons, 2005.

Periodicals

"Fast Food: Good and Hungry." *Economist London Economist Newspaper Limited* 395, no. 8687 (June 19, 2010): 65.

Klass, Perri. "The Fast-Food Fund." *The New England Journal of Medicine* 360, no. 3 (2009): 209–211.

Web Sites

"Fast Food Nutrition Facts." *FastFoodNutrition.org*. http://www.fastfoodnutrition.org/ (accessed October 17, 2010).

Susan Aldridge

Fermentation: Alcohol

■ Introduction

Some alcoholic beverages, notably beer and wine, are produced by the process of fermentation. At its simplest, fermentation occurs when sugar is added to yeast causing a chemical reaction that leads to the production of carbon dioxide and ethyl alcohol. An enzyme in yeast called zymase catalyzes the chemical reaction and leads to fermentation.

The three types of sugar most often used at the start of the wine fermentation process are grape sugars, fruit sugars, and cane sugars. Cane sugar can be chemically changed into fruit sugar; fruit sugar can be converted to grape sugar; and grape sugar can be fermented to produce wine. In making beer, yeast is mixed with the natural sugars present in malt. Fermentation occurs without the presence of air and is therefore said to be an anaerobic process. Correct temperature is critical and varies by type of beverage to be created. Basically, the warmer the temperature, the faster fermentation occurs. However, if the temperature is too high, the ferment and yeast will be killed, and the process will stop. Red wine ferments best between 70–90°F (21.1–32.2°C). Optimal temperature for white wine fermentation is between 55–60°F (12.8–15.5°C). In general, beer ferments best at around 80°F (26.6°C).

Alcoholic beverages, used to excess, can create numerous problems for drinkers. Young people, particularly males below the age of 24, are most likely to abuse alcohol. Alcohol dependence is a global concern, and is the focus of much research and treatment development. Driving while under the influence of alcohol is also a worldwide problem; the World Health Organization has created the Global Road Safety Partnership in an effort to assist policy-makers and governments to enact effective programming and legislation in this area.

■ Historical Background and Scientific Foundations

Although there is a lack of agreement concerning the date on which the first beer was brewed, there is consensus that it occurred between 6,000 and 10,000 years ago, and may have predated bread as a food staple. Despite its alcohol content, beer was the beverage of choice during the Middle Ages, due to lack of potability of water. It remains the third most popular beverage worldwide after water and tea.

The general formula for fermentation is sugar (glucose) plus yeast, which yields carbon dioxide plus ethanol. The carbon dioxide is allowed to escape into the air during the chemical reaction, leaving ethanol and water. The fermentation process for beer progresses through several stages. Beer always contains at least four ingredients: barley (or other grain), water, hops, and yeast. Beer brewing begins with the malting process, during which the barley grain is germinated by soaking it water for several days, then draining and chilling it for five additional days. The husk of the barley opens and the grain begins to sprout. During early germination, some of the starch in the grain is converted to sugar by enzymes already present in the barley. The temperature of the malt is slowly increased, and the malt is dried. At the conclusion of the malting process, any roots that began forming during germination are removed. Next, the malt is milled: The grain undergoes a cracking process. The cracked grain is mixed with water and heated to specific temperatures for discrete periods of time (time and temperature depend on the type of beer to be brewed). This process is called mashing, and it causes enzymes to activate and convert the starch remaining in the grain to sugars that can be fermented. At the end of the mashing process, the material is divided into a sugar and water mixture, called wort, and grain husks. The method for accomplishing this is called sparging, which entails rinsing the grains with very hot water in order to extract as much sugar as possible.

Hops are then added to the wort, which is then boiled for between one and two hours. Hops are the flower of the hop vine, which is a member of the hemp family. Hops are characteristically bitter, with a specific scent and flavor. Their bitterness is used to balance the sweetness of the wort. After boiling, the wort is placed in a cooler, which rapidly lowers its temperature to around 80°F (26.6°C), the optimal temperature for fermentation. The wort is then transferred to be fermented, at which point yeast is added. If the beer to be brewed is an ale, a top fermenting yeast is added; if it is going to be a lager, a bottom fermenting yeast is used. During initial, or primary, fermentation occurring over a period of three to seven days, the yeast digests the sugar and produces alcohol and carbon dioxide. The settled yeast is then drained from the bottom of the tank. If the brew is to be a lager, it is placed in cold storage for several weeks. Lagers can be bocks, doppelbocks (or double bocks), Munichs, Viennas, Marzens, and Pilsners. If it is an ale, it is kept at a warmer temperature for a shorter time period. Ales include pale ales, porters, stouts, barley wines, trappists, and alts. In both cases, this is referred

to as secondary fermentation and results in carbonation and maturing of the brewed beer. Then, the beer is filtered for improved appearance and prepared for commercial distribution.

Draft and keg beer is unpasteurized and unfiltered; it has a very limited shelf life. It is safe to drink for only about six weeks after brewing before it is at risk of microbial contamination. Bottled beer is pasteurized using

Fermenting pinot noir grapes and must with thermometer in Burgundy, France. © *Per Karlsson, BKWine 2 / Alamy.*

An artisan liquors expert pours a sample of a Scotch liquor at Demijohn's, a shop in Edinburgh, Scotland, that features artisan liquors made by micro-distilleries in Scotland and England. Scotch whisky has been produced in Scotland for hundreds of years. *Joseph Hyder / Lerner & Lerner / LernerMedia Global Photos.*

a rapid heat treatment, extending its shelf life to around three months. Beer in brown bottles lasts longer than beer in clear or other colored bottles. Canned beer is filtered and then pasteurized after canning.

Craft beers are produced in breweries with an annual production of less than 2 million barrels. Although they are made with the four traditional basic ingredients, craft brewers often add unique ingredients to create highly specialized tastes (e.g., seasonal beers such as pumpkin ales). They tend to be small, locally-owned businesses, rather than branches of large international corporations. Microbreweries are the smallest producers, with less than 10,000 barrels made annually. They rarely export their products beyond the local area and often conduct all sales on-site.

■ Impacts and Issues

Beer is the third most popular beverage in the world after water and tea. In 2010 Asia became the world's largest producer of beer, followed by Europe and North America. The ten countries with the largest average per person consumption of beer are the Czech Republic with 159.9 liters; Ireland, 131.1 liters; Germany, 115.8 liters; Australia, 109.9 liters; Austria, 108.3 liters; the United Kingdom, 99 liters; Belgium, 93 liters; Denmark, 89.9 liters; Finland, 85 liters; and Luxembourg, 84.4 liters. The United States ranked 13th, with 81.6 liters. According to the World Health Organization, the United States is the third heaviest country in the world, with 66.7 percent of the population considered overweight; Germany is number four at 66.5 percent; and the United Kingdom is tenth, at 61.9 percent overweight. The *Internet Journal of Nutrition and Wellness* posits a positive relationship among college students between alcohol consumption and likelihood of being overweight.

The first arrest and conviction for drunk driving occurred in the United Kingdom in 1897: George Smith was the individual's name and he was 25 years of age. The first drunk driving law in America was enacted in 1917, although it was not assiduously enforced. In 1938 the United States National Safety Council set legal limits for intoxication, which were made part of nationwide drunk driving laws. In May of 1980, Mothers Against Drunk Driving (MADD) was incorporated. The organization's stated purpose was "to stop drunk driving, to reduce alcohol-related deaths and injuries and to offer support and services to the victims of drunk or drugged drivers and to prevent underage drinking." American activist Candy Lightner (1946–) founded MADD after she lost her 13-year old daughter in an automobile accident that was the fault of a repeat drunk driving offender with a blood alcohol level of 0.20. In 1984 President Ronald Reagan (1911–2004) recommended that the legal drinking age in America be raised to 21. Throughout the first decade of the twenty-first century, drunk driving laws were strengthened across America, which maintains blood alcohol levels of 0.08 to 0.10 as the legal limit for intoxication.

The World Health Organization's Global Road Safety Partnership (GRSP) has created a publication entitled *Drinking and Driving: A Road Safety Manual for Decision-Makers and Practitioners*, designed to facilitate the creation of programs designed to reduce the global incidence of drunk driving and related motor vehicle accidents. Consumption of alcohol, even at very low levels, negatively affects judgment, task performance, concentration, and decision-making abilities. This increases with continued drinking. Although each country has the right to set individual blood alcohol concentration limits, the European Union has recommended 0.05. Japan has zero tolerance for drinking and driving, followed by Estonia, Sweden, and the Russian Federation, with legal limits of 0.02. The United States of America has the second highest allowable BAC, with rates varying by state between 0.08 and 0.10. Uganda has the highest BAC reported by the GRSP at 0.15.

Statistically, teenaged drivers, inexperienced young adult drivers, and young adults in general are at highest risk of having a motor vehicle accident while driving when impaired or intoxicated. Underage drinking and binge drinking (generally defined as consuming five or more alcoholic drinks in a row) have also been the focus of much concern, particularly in the United States. In the 1980s the drinking age was raised nationally to 21 in an effort to reduce fatalities among the nation's youth. Longitudinal data collected over nearly three decades on underage drinking by the National Survey on Drug Use and Health (formerly called the National Household Survey on Drug Abuse or NHSDA) revealed that underage drinking and binge drinking have sharply declined among under-21 males who do not attend college, but has remained stable for male college students. In 2007 a group of more than 100 college presidents formed a group called the Amethyst Initiative, arguing that the current drinking age renders most college students unable to purchase alcohol legally and leads them to drink out of the public eye, making binge and underage drinking more likely. The members of MADD and similar groups disagree, asserting that

colleges and universities should be doing a more effective job of creating prevention initiatives.

IN CONTEXT: FERMENTATION AS AN ANCIENT ART

Because grains and fruits ferment naturally, it is likely that the earliest civilizations knew how to make alcoholic beverages. Wild yeasts, for example, collect on the skin of grapes and other fruits, causing fermentation. Ancient pottery shards show the presence of tartrates, a byproduct of fermentation, indicating that the Chinese were brewing a drink made of rice, honey, and fruit as early as 7000 BC. Centuries later, they developed a process to break down complex sugars in rice to simple sugars such as glucose, which were then fermented to make rice wine. The first stage in this process is carried out by a mold called *Aspergillus oryzae*, which is then followed by a sake strain of *S. cerevisiae*.

Wine was also produced 8,000 years ago in Caucasus Mountain settlements, as well as in ancient Iran. Sumerians in ancient Babylonia (modern Turkey) considered beer a divine drink; they worshipped Ninkasi, the goddess of beer and alcohol, composing a hymn to her 4,000 years ago. In the Gilgamesh epic (c.3000 BC), Gilgamesh's boon companion, the bestial Enkidu, was "civilized" by learning to eat bread and beer, the two main products of Babylonian fermentation.

■ Primary Source Connection

Studies of historical artifacts indicate that humans began to ferment beverages as early as 10,000 BCE. Ancient Egyptians made at least 24 different wines and more than 17 varieties of beer. While they may not have fully understood the chemical processes of fermentation, ancient civilizations knew the ingredients and conditions needed for successful brewing.

In this article, published in 1909, French chemist and microbiologist Louis Pasteur explains how and why fermentation takes place.

On the Relations Existing Between Oxygen and Yeast

IT is characteristic of science to reduce incessantly the number of unexplained phenomena. It is observed, for instance, that fleshy fruits are not liable to fermentation so long as their epidermis remains uninjured. On the other hand, they ferment very readily when they are piled up in heaps more or less open, and immersed in their saccharine juice. The mass becomes heated and swells; carbonic acid gas is disengaged, and the sugar disappears and is replaced by alcohol. Now, as to the question of the origin of these spontaneous phenomena, so remarkable in character as well as usefulness for man's service, modern knowledge has taught us that fermentation is the consequence of a development of vegetable cells the germs of which do not exist in the saccharine juices within fruits; that many varieties of these cellular plants exist, each giving rise to its own particular fermentation. The principal products of these various fermentations, although resembling each other in their nature, differ in their relative proportions and in the accessory substances that accompany them, a fact which alone is sufficient to account for wide differences in the quality and commercial value of alcoholic beverages.

Now that the discovery of ferments and their living nature, and our knowledge of their origin, may have solved the mystery of the spontaneous appearance of fermentations in natural saccharine juices, we may ask whether we must still regard the reactions that occur in these fermentations as phenomena inexplicable by the ordinary laws of chemistry. We can readily see that fermentations occupy a special place in the series of chemical and biological phenomena. What gives to fermentations certain exceptional characters of which we are only now beginning to suspect the causes, is the mode of life in the minute plants designated under the generic name of *ferments*, a mode of life which is essentially different from that in other vegetables, and from which result phenomena equally exceptional throughout the whole range of the chemistry of living beings.

The least reflection will suffice to convince us that the alcoholic ferments must possess the faculty of vegetating and performing their functions out of contact with air. Let us consider, for instance, the method of vintage practised in the Jura. The bunches are laid at the foot of the vine in a large tub, and the grapes there stripped from them. When the grapes, some of which are uninjured, others bruised, and all moistened by the juice issuing from the latter, fill the tub-where they form what is called the *vintage*—they are conveyed in barrels to large vessels fixed in cellars of a considerable depth. These vessels are not filled to more than three-quarters of their capacity. Fermentation soon takes place in them, and the carbonic acid gas finds escape through the bunghole, the diameter of which, in the case of the largest vessels, is not more than ten or twelve centimetres (about four inches). The wine is not drawn off before the end of two or three months. In this way it seems highly probable that the yeast which produces the wine under such conditions must have developed, to a great extent at least, out of contact with oxygen. No doubt oxygen is not entirely absent from the first; nay, its limited presence is even a necessity to the manifestation of the phenomena which follow. The grapes are stripped from the bunch in contact with air, and the must which drops from the wounded fruit takes a little of this gas into solution. This small quantity of air so introduced into the must, at the commencement of operations,

plays a most indispensable part, it being from the presence of this that the spores of ferments which are spread over the surface of the grapes and the woody part of the bunches derive the power of starting their vital phenomena. This air, however, especially when the grapes have been stripped from the bunches, is in such small proportion, and that which is in contact with the liquid mass is so promptly expelled by the carbonic acid gas, which is evolved as soon as a little yeast has formed, that it will readily be admitted that most of the yeast is produced apart from the influence of oxygen, whether free or in solution. We shall revert to this fact, which is of great importance. At present we are only concerned in pointing out that, from the mere knowledge of the practices of certain localities, we are induced to believe that the cells of yeast, after they have developed from their spores, continue to live and multiply without the intervention of oxygen, and that the alcoholic ferments have a mode of life which is probably quite exceptional, since it is not generally met with in other species, vegetable or animal.

Another equally exceptional characteristic of yeast and fermentation in general consists in the small proportion which the yeast that forms bears to the sugar that decomposes. In all other known beings the weight of nutritive matter assimilated corresponds with the weight of food used up, any difference that may exist being comparatively small. The life of yeast is entirely different. For a certain weight of yeast formed, we may have ten times, twenty times, a hundred times as much sugar, or even more decomposed, as we shall experimentally prove by-and-by; that is to say, that whilst the proportion varies in a precise manner, according to conditions which we shall have occasion to specify, it is also greatly out of proportion to the weight of the yeast. We repeat, the life of no other being, under its normal physiological conditions, can show anything similar. The alcoholic ferments, therefore, present themselves to us as plants which possess at least two singular properties: they can live without air, that is without oxygen, and they can cause decomposition to an amount which, though variable, yet, as estimated by weight of product formed, is out of all proportion to the weight of their own substance. These are facts of so great importance, and so intimately connected with the theory of fermentation, that it is indispensable to endeavour to establish them experimentally, with all the exactness of which they will admit.

Louis Pasteur
PASTEUR, LOUIS. "ON THE RELATIONS EXISTING BETWEEN OXYGEN AND YEAST." *THE PHYSIOLOGICAL THEORY OF FERMENTATION.* HARVARD CLASSICS: 1909–1914.

SEE ALSO *Agribusiness; Agriculture and International Trade; French Paradox; Gastronomy; Mediterranean Diet; Viniculture.*

BIBLIOGRAPHY

Books

Bird, David. *Understanding Wine Technology: The Science of Wine Explained*, 3rd ed. San Francisco: Wine Appreciation Guild, 2005.

Goldammer, Ted. *The Brewer's Handbook: The Complete Book to Brewing Beer*. Clifton, VA: Apex, 2008.

Hornsey, Ian S. *The Chemistry and Biology of Winemaking*. Cambridge, UK: Royal Society of Chemistry, 2007.

Iverson, Jon. *Home Winemaking, Step-by-Step: A Guide to Fermenting Wine Grapes*. Medford, OR: Stonemark, 2000.

Marczinski, Cecile A., Estee C. Grant, and Vincent J Grant. *Binge Drinking in Adolescents and College Students*. Hauppauge, NY: Nova Science, 2009.

Nossiter, Jonathan. *Liquid Memory: Why Wine Matters*. New York: Farrar, Straus and Giroux, 2009.

Ogle, Maureen. *Ambitious Brew: The Story of American Beer*. Orlando: Harcourt, 2006.

Periodicals

Betts, Bryan. "Beer Comes Clean. Brewing Processes Old and New." *Engineering and Technology* 5, no. 10 (2010): 59–61.

Geraci, Victor W. "Fermenting a Twenty-First Century California Wine Industry." *Agricultural History* 78, no. 4 (Autumn 2004): 438–465.

Plahuta, Primo, Zora Korosec-Koruza, Peter Stanovnik, and Peter Raspor. "Current Viticulture and Winemaking Technology versus GMO Viticulture and Winemaking Technology." *Journal of Wine Research* 17, no. 3 (2006): 161–172.

Ramirez, W. Fred, and Jan Maciejowski. "Optimal Beer Fermentation." *Journal of the Institute of Brewing* 113, no. 3 (2007): 325–333.

Spitz, Janet. "CEO Gender and the Malt Brewing Industry: Return of the Beer Witch, Ale-Wife, and Brewster." *Forum for Social Economics* 39, no. 1 (2010): 33–42.

"United States—Winemaking—the French Touch." *The Economist* 379, no. 8478 (2006): 51.

Web Sites

"Craft Beer: Celebrating the Best of American Beer." *Brewers Association.* http://www.craftbeer.com/ (accessed November 3, 2010).

"Fermentation Process." *Virtual Wine.com.* http://www.virtualwine.com.au/wine-making/fermentation.asp (accessed November 3, 2010).

"Global status Report on Alcohol 2004." *World Health Organization.* http://www.who.int/substance_abuse/publications/globalstatusreportalcoholchapters/en/ (accessed November 3, 2010).

"The History of Beer." *Beer Brewing.org.* http://www.beerbrewing.org/the-history-of-beer/ (accessed November 3, 2010).

MADD. http://www.madd.org/ (accessed November 3, 2010).

National Institutes of Health, National Institute on Alcohol and Alcoholism, College Drinking—Changing the Culture. "A Snapshot of Annual High-Risk College Drinking Consequences." *CollegeDrinkingPrevention.gov.* http://www.collegedrinkingprevention.gov/StatsSummaries/snapshot.aspx (accessed November 3, 2010).

Wineculture: A Hip Guide to Wine on the Web. http://www.wineculture.com/home.html (accessed November 3, 2010).

Pamela V. Michaels

Food Additives

■ Introduction

In modern industrialized societies, individuals are not often directly involved in the cultivation, harvesting, or processing of the foods they consume. Whole foods such as fruits and vegetables are usually transported considerable distances from their place of origin to their ultimate consumers. Prepared food ingredients require careful attention throughout processing to ensure they remain free from contamination or spoilage. For these reasons food additives are an indispensable component of most commercial food preparation processes. Food additives are broadly defined as chemical substances that are added to food products—at any time between their natural state and final consumption—to alter or enhance a specific food characteristic. Additives are a means to achieve what mainstream modern cultures prize as ideal consumer food attributes—the combination of taste and aesthetic appeal with indefinite shelf life.

Food additives are subject to a significant degree of government regulation in many jurisdictions. The United States Food and Drug Administration (FDA) is the primary American processed food additives regulator. A food additive possesses one or more of the following characteristics: food preservative; taste enhancer; maintainer of desired shape, consistency, or density; and enhancer or sustainer of desired product color. Additives are distinct from the ingredients used in food manufacture. Vitamin or mineral supplements added to food and beverage products are not generally regulated as additives. Some ingredients added for taste also have secondary preservative properties. Salt, sugar, and corn syrup are among the most widely used additives in cooked or prepared foods.

■ Historical Background and Scientific Foundations

Food additives have been a feature of human food storage and preparation since prehistoric times. Pure salt (sodium chloride, NaCl) was used as a meat and fish preservative in ancient Greece and the later Roman Empire. By the fifteenth century, European sailing fleets that pursued the rich codfish stocks off the Grand Banks of Newfoundland relied on salt as the means to preserve their catches. Once dried and salted, the cod could be safely transported long distances with little deterioration in its quality for domestic sale and consumption.

Pure salt is an effective preservative due to its antibacterial properties. Salt dehydrates any surface to which it is applied, thus inhibiting moisture accumulation that tends to promote destructive bacterial growth. "Curing" is the traditional process in which salt is used as a beef or pork preservative; modern meat curing often includes the use of nitrates as additional preservatives that also help to restore the natural color of the product removed by the curing process.

The science of food preservation expanded after 1900 to include the development of chemical compounds designed to enhance taste, stabilize food composition, or achieve greater visual consumer appeal. MSG became the most popular taste enhancement additive in the world. Artificial sweeteners such as aspartame (the aspartyl-phenylalanine-1-methyl ester, $C_{14}H_{18}N_2O_5$, a non-carbohydrate additive), were popularized as means to improve taste without increasing calorie intake for consumers.

Carotene compounds used to stimulate desired product surface color and ascorbic acid (a synthetic form of vitamin C), a powerful antioxidant that delays food spoilage, have been formulated for use as food additives. These substances are structurally identical to naturally occurring chemicals present in most fruits and vegetables. Given their similarity to natural substances, these additives have tended to attract a lesser number of health concerns.

The relationship between food additives and human health effects was not a public concern until the early 1800s when the sale of adulterated foods proliferated in Europe and North America—foods that were dishonestly represented as to their content, such as "beef" made from horse meat or animal byproducts. Great Britain was the first jurisdiction to enact legislation to regulate the types of additives permitted in food. The 1958 amendments to the U.S. Food and Drug Act mandated testing of all new food additives for the first time. Current American law provides that two types of additives are exempt from confirmatory safety testing. Substances listed as GRAS ("generally recognized as safe"), including widely used flavoring and preservatives, are those that through extensive usage have proven to be safe for consumer use. The second group is composed of "substances with prior sanction," the additives approved for use in the United States prior to 1958 that may be subject to removal at a future time if they are revealed to be dangerous. Nitrates used in meat curing are a notable example of the prior sanction group.

■ Impacts and Issues

The issues surrounding food additive safety have assumed a prominent place in global public health debates. Chemical food additives have attracted particular attention as consumer and regulatory concerns have mounted over the long-term effects of these substances on human health. The oldest form of food additive is a culprit: Notwithstanding salt's preservative and taste enhancing powers, there is conclusive medical evidence that excessive sodium consumption is a key contributing factor to increased rates of high blood pressure and the associated risk of cardiovascular disease.

The nitrates used in conjunction with salt in curing processes have also attracted regulatory scrutiny. Sodium nitrate added to meat can break down into nitrites that produce N-nitroso compounds that have been linked to colon cancer.

A number of additives were developed and used extensively in consumer food products only to be revealed in subsequent scientific investigations as substances that pose serious risks to human health. Some food dyes, such as Red Dye Number 3 (erythrosine), have been identified as a potential carcinogen; the FDA banned its use in many food applications in 1990. Carmoisine, a coal tar derivative that was developed as a sweetener widely used in yogurt and ice cream, has been banned for similar reasons in many Western countries. Aspartame has been the source of continuing public health controversies since it was initially approved for use as a sweetener by the FDA in 1974. From allegations that aspartame was not subjected to an appropriate degree of clinic trial prior to regulatory approval, the compound has been more recently and inconclusively linked to conditions as disparate as cancer and increased obesity rates that are purported to occur because aspartame stimulates appetite. Aspartame has been pronounced safe for human consumption by most national food regulators with the condition that daily intake limits be observed.

WORDS TO KNOW

FOOD EMULSIFIERS: Emulsifiers are the class of chemicals that facilitate the complete mixture of substances that naturally separate when they are added one to another. An attempt to combine oil and water is the classic example of this physical problem. Emulsifiers are molecules that possess hydrophilic (water attracting) and hydrophobic (water repelling) features. When added to mixtures that contain oil and water based substances, the emulsifier molecules bind themselves to both substances to achieve total mixture. The proteins found in chicken eggs and phospholipids (fat soluble phosphates) are natural emulsifiers. Palm oil is a commonly used commercial emulsifier found in products such as salad dressings.

MELAMINE: Melamine ($C_3H_6N_6$) is a synthetic chemical that is primarily used to produce commercial resins, laminates, and glues. Prohibited for use as a food additive, melamine attained world-wide notoriety in 2008 when a number of Chinese milk products were found to contain the chemical. When added to food products, melamine will tend to disguise low levels of protein and other nutrients in milk adulterated by adding water. A number of deaths from kidney failure have been attributed to melamine present in milk products.

MONOSODIUM GLUTAMATE (MSG): Monosodium glutamate (MSG) is one of the best known food additives, used widely as a flavor enhancing agent since the early twentieth century. In addition to the general health concerns associated with excess sodium consumption in modern human diets, such as high blood pressure and increased risk of stroke, MSG symptom complex is a condition experienced by persons who have MSG intolerance. Its symptoms include rapid heartbeat and breathing difficulty (bronchospasm).

Even when hard science has been inconclusive as to the adverse effect of additives on human health, additives have acquired a largely negative connotation in the public consciousness. Fear of the possible long-term health effects associated with additives has contributed to the rapid growth of the whole food movement. Locavore is the contemporary term used to describe a person who seeks out natural, locally grown food sources that do not rely on additives to maintain their freshness, color, or quality.

Food irradiation is an alternative to the use of food additives to combat spoilage and bacterial contamination. Irradiation subjects the food to intense electron beams or x rays that disrupt bacterial formation on the food surface. It is an effective means to protect foods from coliform bacteria that cause food poisoning. These techniques do not alter the chemical or physical properties of the subject food, other than to precipitate texture or color change in some products.

The Food, Drug, and Cosmetic Act of 1938 was strengthened by the 1958 "Delaney Clause" Food Additives Amendment that required FDA approval of food additives including colorings and flavorings. It authorized U.S. government agencies to define and regulate non-nutritional food additives, such as the food colorings contained in this boy's ice cream cone. © *Picture Contact / Alamy.*

SEE ALSO   *Diet and Cancer; Diet and Diabetes; Diet and Heart Disease; Diet and Hypertension; Dietary Guidelines for Americans; Dietary Reference Intakes; Dietary Supplement Health and Education Act of 1994 (DSHEA); Food, Drug, and Cosmetic Act of 1938; Food Irradiation; Food Recalls; Locavore; Preservation; Processed Foods; Salt, Nitrites, and Health; Sugar and Sweeteners; Truth in Labeling; U.S. Food and Drug Administration (FDA).*

BIBLIOGRAPHY

Books

Ash, Michael, and Irene Ash. *Handbook of Food Additives.* Endicott, NY: Synapse, 2008.

Emerton, Victoria, and Eugenia Choi. *Essential Guide to Food Additives.* Surrey, UK: Leatherhead, 2008.

Ettlinger, Steve. *Twinkie, Deconstructed: My Journey to Discover How the Ingredients Found in Processed Foods Are Grown, Mined (Yes, Mined), and Manipulated into What America Eats.* New York: Hudson Street, 2007.

Metcalfe, Dean D., Hugh A. Sampson, and Ronald A. Simon. *Food Allergy: Adverse Reactions to Foods and Food Additives.* Malden, MA: Blackwell, 2008.

Minich, Deanna. *An A–Z Guide to Food Additives: Never Eat What You Can't Pronounce.* San Francisco: Conari, 2009.

Winter, Ruth. *A Consumer's Dictionary of Food Additives.* New York: Three Rivers, 2009.

Web Sites

"Food Additives." *U.S. Food and Drug Administration (FDA).* http://www.fda.gov/food/foodingredi entspackaging/foodadditives/default.htm (accessed October 7, 2010).

"How Safe are Color Additives?" *U.S. Food and Drug Administration (FDA).* http://www.fda.gov/ ForConsumers/ConsumerUpdates/ucm048951. htm (accessed October 7, 2010).

Bryan Thomas Davies

Food Allergen Labeling and Consumer Protection Act of 2004

■ Introduction

Food allergies are immune system reactions to certain foods. Individuals with food allergies who ingest, inhale, or come into contact with foods to which they are allergic experience a wide range of symptoms, most commonly rashes. In the most severe cases, food allergies produce rapid-onset, whole body, life-threatening reactions known as anaphylaxis, which can include constriction of the airways and irregular heart rhythms.

A true food allergy differs from the more common food intolerance. Individuals who have food intolerances are sensitive to certain foods, but those foods do not produce an immune system reaction. Food insensitivity reactions can include throat dryness, intestinal upset, headaches, mild nausea, and other effects.

In 2004 Congress passed the Food Allergen Labeling and Consumer Protection Act (FALCPA). The law went into effect in the United States on January 1, 2006. In order to better inform consumers about the presence of common possible allergens, the law requires that food product labels indicate if the product contains proteins derived from eggs, fish, milk, peanuts, soybeans, tree nuts, wheat, and some shellfish.

■ Historical Background and Scientific Foundations

There is not an accurate measure of food allergies worldwide. In the United States alone, an estimated 12 million people have food allergies. These allergies cause from 120–200 deaths per year, making deaths from food allergies extremely rare. In Western industrialized nations, diagnoses of food allergies are on the rise. Whereas scientists are not sure what has caused the increase in incidence of food allergies in the world's most developed nations, some theories focus on changes in diet, exposure to allergens as an infant, increased use of antibiotic cleaning solutions, or better and more frequent testing

and diagnoses. Comparatively, food allergies are rarely diagnosed or recorded in developing countries. However, rapidly developing countries such as China have also reported increased incidence of food intolerance and food allergies since 2000.

Food allergens pose a greater risk to children overall than adults. Food allergies affect an estimated 8 percent of U.S. children—mostly under the age of three—and less than 4 percent of U.S. adults. Children are most commonly allergic to nuts, meat, milk, and seeds. Roughly half of all children with food allergies outgrow their allergies by age six. Some food allergies are more likely to have life-long effects. Most people allergic to milk proteins can tolerate milk and milk products in baked or highly processed goods. Tree nut allergies are slightly less likely to be outgrown, but the significant majority of childhood peanut allergy sufferers do outgrow their allergy.

Food allergy awareness in communities took hold in the first decade of the twenty-first century largely through grassroots campaigns. Parents of food-allergic children sought bans of peanut butter, peanut oils, and peanut-containing foods from school cafeterias. Schools began to prohibit students from bringing home-prepared baked goods to school to share with classmates. Grassroots groups pushed restaurants to disclose when certain foods or food products were used. Those same groups lobbied legislators at local, state, and federal levels to enact consumer protection laws that mandated warning labels and ingredient lists on processed foods.

In 2004 Congress passed the Food Allergen Labeling and Consumer Protection Act (FALCPA), giving food producers until 2006 to bring their labels into compliance. Under the law, food labels must disclose all source ingredients from the eight foods and food groups covered by the act. If a product contains tree nuts or shellfish, the type of nut and shellfish must be specified. For example, a product's label must denote that the ingredient "nut butter" is indeed "peanut and almond butters" or "nut butter (peanut or almond)." Products

WORDS TO KNOW

ACT: A statute, rule, or formal lawmaking document enacted by a legislative body or issued by a government.

ALLERGEN: A usually harmless substance that causes an adverse immune response or allergic reaction in certain individuals.

ALLERGY: An abnormal immune reaction to an allergen introduced into the body by ingestion, inhalation, or contact with skin. The reaction produced, which can take many forms, is commonly known as an allergic reaction.

ANAPHYLAXIS: A severe, multi-system hypersensitivity reaction requiring immediate treatment to avert life-threatening symptoms such as vascular collapse, respiratory distress, and shock.

FOOD INTOLERANCE: An unpleasant, but not allergic, reaction to a food. Food intolerances do not provoke an immune system response. Gastrointestinal discomfort is the most common symptom of food intolerance.

The law requires food manufacturers to label their foods in one of two clear, plain language ways if one of the eight FALCPA foods or food groups is present in the product. Manufacturers must put the name of the food source of a FALCPA food allergen in parentheses after any ingredient that does not clearly have the allergen in its name. For example, the ingredient albumin should be labeled "albumin (egg)." Alternatively, a second listing of FALCPA foods may appear after the main ingredient list as a warning prefaced by the word "contains" and followed by the specific FALCPA allergens in the product. These warnings are typically listed in their own, bold-faced type paragraph with phrases such as "Contains wheat and milk products." Products that fail to meet FALCP requirements may be subject to recall or prohibited from entering the market until their labels are changed.

■ Impacts and Issues

The foods affected by the FALCP account for 90 percent of all food allergies. However, not all foods linked to higher incidence of food allergies are covered by the act. Sesame seeds, sunflower seeds, corn, yeast, and oats are also linked to higher than average incidence of food allergy reactions but food manufacturers do not have to note their presence on labeling. Highly processed oils also remain exempt from labeling requirements.

that change their ingredients from region to region or among facilities are required to list variant ingredients that could be used in the product. Such warnings often appear as "flour (wheat or soy)" or "product contains wheat and/or soy."

Nutrition Facts
Serving Size 1 tbsp. (15g)
Serving Per Container about 5

Amount Per Serving

Calories 40	Fat Cal. 25

	% Daily Value*
Total Fat 2.5g	4%
Saturated Fat 0g	0%
Trans Fat 0g	
Cholesterol 0mg	0%
Sodium 430mg	18%

Ingredients: chili, garlic, lemongrass, shallot, galangal, coriander leaves, salt, soy bean oil, coriander seeds, kaffir lime skin, coriander root, shrimp paste (shrimp, salt), cumin powder, turmeric.
Contains shrimp and soya.
Manufactured in a facility that processes sesame and peanuts.

Imported by: Cost Plus, Inc.
200 Fourth Street, Oakland, CA 94607 USA

Manufactured by:
Blue Elephant Marketing Co. Ltd,
89/17-18 Donmuang, Bangkok 10210,
Thailand • trade@blueelephant.com
Product of Thailand
Refrigerate after opening.

A label for food imported to and sold in the United States carries a food allergy warning label notifying consumers that the product contains soy, shellfish, and possibly trace amounts of peanut dust. Food allergen warning labels in the United States and Great Britain are most commonly located on food packaging next to the nutrition information. *Ellie Lerner / Lerner & Lerner / LernerMedia Global Photos.*

Food-allergic individuals whose food allergies are not covered by the FALCPA major food allergens warnings should contact a product's manufacturer to obtain a list of all ingredients or inquire about the source ingredients in listed spices, flavorings, and additives.

As of 2010 the FALCPA applies to all commercially salable, packaged foods—whether domestic or imported—that are subject to U.S. Food and Drug Administration (FDA) regulation. Take-away foods and restaurant foods are not covered under the act. Foods regulated by the U.S. Department of Agriculture (USDA), such as meat, eggs, and poultry, are also not covered by the FALCPA. There is no law requiring allergen labeling on these products, but some manufacturers and restaurants have adopted a voluntary labeling scheme to alert consumers of possible food allergen dangers.

A voluntary labeling scheme also exists to warn consumers when a product has been produced in a facility that also processes other foods made with FALCPA covered allergens. These advisory labels commonly read "May contain trace amounts of wheat" or "Processed in a facility that also processes foods that contain tree nuts."

In September 2008 the FDA opened a regulatory comment period and held a public hearing on enacting laws that could amend the FALCPA and require stricter U.S. food allergen warning labels, also known as "may contain," "Processed with," and "possible cross contamination" labels. Over the course of one year, the FDA received more than 200 public comments, the overwhelming majority of which support more expansive food allergen labeling and warnings.

SEE ALSO *Food Allergies; Food Packaging; Truth in Labeling.*

BIBLIOGRAPHY

Books

Albert, Janice. *Innovations in Food Labelling.* Rome: Food and Agriculture Organization of the United Nations; Boca Raton, FL: CRC Press, 2010.

Maleki, Soheila J., A. Wesley Burks, and Ricki M. Helm. *Food Allergy.* Washington, DC: ASM Press, 2006.

Periodicals

Ahn, Sam S., et al. "Consumer Attitudes and Response to New Food Allergen Labeling." *The Journal of Allergy and Clinical Immunology* 121, no. 2, supplement 1 (2008): S182.

Puglisi, Gregory, and Marianne Frieri. "Update on Hidden Food Allergens and Food Labeling." *Allergy and Asthma Proceedings* 28, no. 6 (2007): 634–639.

Soltis, Cassandra A. "FDA Enforcement of the Food Allergen Labeling Law." *Regulatory Affairs Focus* 11, no. 10 (2006): 28–31.

Verrill, Linda, and Conrad J. Choiniere. "Are Food Allergen Advisory Statements Really Warnings? Variation in Consumer Preferences and Consumption Decisions." *Journal of Food Products Marketing* 15, no. 2 (2009): 139–151.

Web Sites

"Understanding FALCPA (Food Allergen Labeling & Consumer Protection Act of 2004)." *Food Allergy Initiative.* http://www.faiusa.org/?page_id=DA172110-99EA-335F-3D2A5BA8DFE1C21D (accessed August 23, 2010).

Adrienne Wilmoth Lerner

Food Allergies

■ Introduction

Food allergy and food intolerance are conditions that may cause a great deal of distress when someone accidentally consumes a food that provokes an adverse reaction. In a true allergy, it is the immune system that responds to a substance, called an allergen, in the foodstuff, whereas in food intolerance, there is some other physiological mechanism at work. The most common foods to which people are truly allergic include peanuts, milk, eggs, shellfish, wheat, and soy. Lactose intolerance is fairly common, particularly in Asian countries. When people come into contact with a food to which they are allergic, various symptoms such as swelling, itching, and stomach cramps may occur. In rare cases, when the allergen enters the bloodstream, a serious reaction called anaphylaxis may provoke a fatal episode of physiologic shock. Avoidance of allergens in food is the best way to deal with a food allergy but it is not always easy: Some food ingredients such as peanut and egg are very widely used, often in trace quantities, in foodstuffs. Food allergies appear to be on the increase, particularly among children, and the reasons why are not clear.

■ Historical Background and Scientific Foundations

The term allergy was first coined in 1906, as researchers began to better understand the workings of the immune system and how the body responds to an outside threat, be it a pathogen or an allergen. Most allergic reactions are to some kind of protein in the food. Exposure to an allergen causes the body to mount a full-blown immune response. This starts with production of antibody molecules in the IgE class that attach themselves to the surface of immune cells called mast cells found in the linings of the lungs, skin, intestines, mouth, nose, and sinuses. The cells thereby become sensitized to the food allergen so the next time the person ingests it, the immune system mounts a full response that involves the release of a chemical called histamine. The symptoms of allergic response, which include itching, breathing difficulty, stomach pain, and rash, are mainly due to the actions of histamine. In rare cases, an allergic response can result in anaphylaxis, which requires prompt administration of epinephrine, through a self-injectible pen device, to prevent potentially fatal shock.

Children are most likely to be allergic to milk, eggs, peanuts, and wheat, and they tend to grow out of their allergies in time. This is not so for adults, whose main allergens are in shellfish, peanuts, fish, and eggs. The range of foods that can provoke an allergy is very wide but some are more common than others. Much depends on the frequency of consuming a particular food in a culture. Rice allergy is therefore much more common in Asia than in Europe and the United States, where wheat and egg allergies are more likely. The body can also have an adverse response to foods through a non-immune mechanism. In food intolerances, such as lactose or gluten intolerance, the enzymes required to break down these components of milk or wheat may be lacking. These are not true allergens. There is no real treatment for food allergy except strict avoidance. However, there has been some research into gradual exposure to the allergen to see if the immune system can be trained not to respond to it. In the future it may be possible to vaccinate at risk individuals against food allergy. People with other allergies, such as asthma and eczema, are more prone to develop food allergies.

■ Impacts and Issues

Food allergy appears to be on the increase in the United States and elsewhere in the western hemisphere. A recent survey by the Centers for Disease Control and Prevention showed an increase of 18 percent in children with food allergy between 1997 and 2007. Meanwhile, there was a threefold increase in children being treated for food allergies between 1993 and 2006. Currently around 6 to 8 percent of children under three are affected by allergies. It is not clear whether this is an increase in the actual prevalence or just that there is increased awareness of food allergy so more people are reporting it. The number of parents believing their children have food allergies tends to be higher than the number of cases confirmed by clinical diagnosis. If it is a real increase, there are several possible causes. One is the so-called "hygiene hypothesis," which means that the immune systems of children are no longer exposed to everyday microbes in the way they used to be because homes are cleaner, and families are smaller. As a result, the immune system tends to overreact to innocent stimuli. Other theories that have been proposed include lack of vitamin D, the increasing use of paracetamol (acetaminophen), or delayed weaning.

Originally it was argued that introducing other foods early alongside breastfeeding increased the risk of food allergy. This has been disproved, and researchers are currently studying whether introducing foods later, at six months, is a risk factor. In the United States, children living further north, who get less sunlight and, therefore, less vitamin D, have more allergies than those in the sunnier south. Poorer diet, with more fast food and fizzy

drinks, could also be a contributor to the rise in food allergies. Additionally, there is likely a genetic predisposition to food allergies, because first-degree relatives of persons with a food allergy, especially peanut allergies, are also more likely to have food allergies. There are many allergy tests offered over the Internet that not reliable. An allergy specialist can confirm a diagnosis of food allergy.

WORDS TO KNOW

ANAPHYLAXIS: A severe response to an allergen that involves the whole body because the allergen has entered the bloodstream. Left untreated, anaphylaxis can lead to a state of collapse, called anaphylactic shock, which may even be fatal.

FOOD ALLERGY: An allergy is an adverse reaction to a substance called an allergen that is usually harmless. In food allergy, the allergen is contained in one or more foodstuffs. Other allergic diseases include asthma, eczema, and hay fever. Allergic reactions always involve the allergen triggering a response from the immune system.

FOOD INTOLERANCE: An adverse reaction to food that does not involve the immune system.

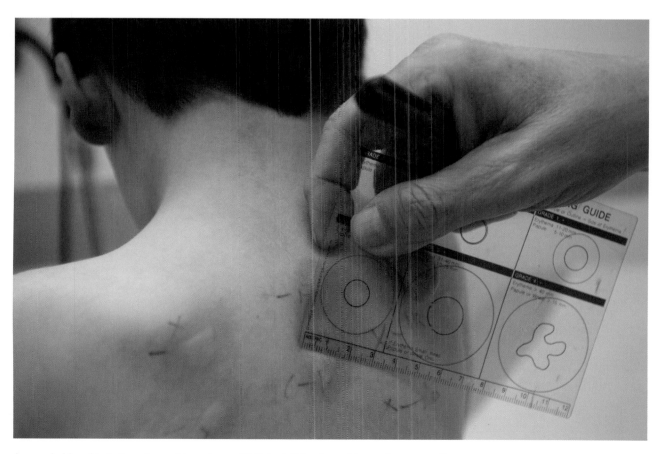

A nurse holds a skin test grading guide against a child's back following a skin test for peanut allergy.   © *Joseph Songco / Alamy.*

The federal Food Allergen Labeling and Consumer Protection Act requires that foods manufactured after January 2006 clearly identify products that contain ingredients from any of the eight major food allergens, along with their source. The eight major food allergens include cow's milk, eggs, soy, wheat, fish, shellfish, tree nuts, and peanuts (which are actually legumes). If a product contains peanuts, for example, the label must state the word "peanut" in at least one of three ways: in the list of ingredients; within parenthesis if the allergen is a derived product, as in "oil (peanut)"; or in a separate statement below the ingredient list that identifies that the product contains the allergen, such as "contains peanuts." Many manufacturers also identify possible exposure with voluntary statements on product packaging such as "produced with machinery that handles nuts, including peanuts" or "may contain trace amounts of peanut."

SEE ALSO   *Center for Food Safety and Applied Nutrition; Consumer Food Safety Recommendations; Food Allergen Labeling and Consumer Protection Act of 2004; Gluten Intolerance; Lactose Intolerance; Truth in Labeling.*

BIBLIOGRAPHY

Books

Chesterton, Carrie M. *Food Allergies: New Research.* New York: Nova Science, 2008.

Richer, Alice C. *Food Allergies.* Westport, CT: Greenwood Press, 2009.

Periodicals

Chang, Huan J., Alison E. Burke, and Richard M. Glass. "Food Allergies." *JAMA: The Journal of the American Medical Association* 303, no. 18 (2010): 1876.

Kuehn, Bridget M. "Food Allergies Becoming More Common." *JAMA: The Journal of the American Medical Association* 300, no. 20 (2008): 2358.

Web Sites

"Allergens." *The Food Allergy & Anaphylaxis Network.* http://www.foodallergy.org/section/allergens (accessed October 2, 2010).

"Healthy Youth! Food Allergies." *National Center for Chronic Disease Prevention and Health Promotion, U.S. Centers for Disease Control and Prevention (CDC).* http://www.cdc.gov/healthyyouth/foodallergies/ (accessed October 2, 2010).

Pittman, Ginevra. "What Do Food Allergy Labels Really Mean?" *Reuters Health,* August 11, 2010. http://www.reuters.com/article/idUSTRE67A4RP20100811 (accessed December 30, 2010).

Susan Aldridge

Food Alliance

■ Introduction

The environmental, or green, movement became increasingly popular beginning in the late 1980s. The advent of factory farming meant that farmers could produce food cheaply with the aid of chemicals and scant regard for the environment, but one of environmental movement's main effects was to make consumers more aware of issues such as the origins of their food. Food Alliance was set up, first on a small scale in the Northwest of the United States, in order to try to reconcile these differences. Producers, like farmers, had to be given some incentive to factor environmental concerns into their practice. Consumers wanted to buy food that had come from sustainable agriculture, so a market existed for environmentally-friendly products. Food Alliance's certification scheme brought the producers and consumers together through creating an environmentally friendly selling point. Food Alliance takes a comprehensive approach in its certification scheme: It looks not just at the produce but also at animal welfare, working conditions, and habitat protection, thereby going further than the organic movement, which is more focused upon the product and whether chemicals have been used in its production. A Food Alliance certification is verified by an independent third party to increase consumer confidence. It can be applied to any operation that involves food, from the farm to the table, and so includes processors, distributors, and food handlers.

■ Historical Background and Scientific Foundations

In 1994 scientists at Oregon State University, Washington State University, and the Washington Department of Agriculture set up an organization called the Northwest Food Alliance, with funding from the W. K. Kellogg Foundation. Their aim was to try to promote sustainable agricultural practice as a viable commercial strategy. Early Alliance projects were focused on improving soil quality and conserving water supplies through, for instance, the use of compost instead of chemical fertilizer. They also commissioned research on consumer attitudes to food and found widespread and growing interest in buying produce grown with more sustainable forms of agriculture. Around this time, interest in so-called green consumerism was germinating both in the United States and in Europe. In 1997 Food Alliance became an independent non-profit organization and began to develop guidelines for fruit and vegetable growers in the Pacific Northwest who wanted to follow a more sustainable path. The Food Alliance certification scheme for farmers was put into operation the following year, and the first certified fruit products appeared in the supermarkets of Portland. Since then Food Alliance has grown nationwide, and it offers certification to farms, ranches, and food handlers for excellence in sustainable agricultural and facility management.

Consumers who choose Food Alliance certified products know they support environmental stewardship, humane treatment of animals, and also safe and fair working conditions. For farms and ranches, and for food packing, processing, and distribution, a Food Alliance certificate is an independent verification of marketing claims that can make the consumer feel confident of the standard of produce they are buying.

Food Alliance offers farmers and ranchers, processors and distributors, and food buyers and handlers (including restaurateurs) a way of adding value to their produce and enhancing their brand. They can address their customers' concerns over social and environmental responsibility and thereby gain their loyalty. A Food Alliance certified business has to be audited by an independent third party inspector to verify that the products do reach the standard required. Criteria for producers include a commitment from the certified party to refrain from use of hormones and non-therapeutic

WORDS TO KNOW

FOOD ALLIANCE CERTIFIED: A comprehensive certification program for sustainably-produced food in North America.

GREEN CONSUMER: A consumer who puts the environment at the top of his or her shopping list by buying products made from natural ingredients that cause minimal or no environmental damage. The term was made popular by a book called *The Green Consumer Guide* written by sustainability pioneers Julia Hailes (1961–) and John Elkington (1949–) in 1987. Green consumers try to eat organic produce and will also use environmentally-friendly household products and perhaps drive a hybrid car to save energy.

ORGANIC AGRICULTURE: Farming carried out without the use of chemicals such as pesticides and fertilizers. There are various schemes for labeling such produce as organic in different countries. Organic produce may be more expensive than that produced by intensive agriculture, and there is no hard scientific evidence that it is actually better for health, although it obviously helps the environment.

antibiotics, to avoid genetically modified crops or livestock, and to reduce pesticide use. A culture of continuous improvement of management practice is also required along with efforts to protect and enhance wildlife habitats, which could otherwise be impacted by operations. Packers, processors, and distributors who are Food Alliance certified are expected to conserve energy and water, reduce and recycle their waste materials, and minimize use of any toxic and hazardous materials in their operations. No artificial flavors, colors, or preservatives are permitted to be added to produce during processing.

■ Impacts and Issues

Food Alliance shares many elements with the organic agriculture movement but the two are not the same. In Food Alliance, synthetic pesticides and fertilizers are allowed where necessary. Both are opposed to the factory farming concept and the industrialization of agriculture. The organic movement preceded Food Alliance, and organic labels continue to be widely respected.

Coffees from Sweetwater Organic Coffee Roasters bear two different trade and growth endorsements intended to help consumers choose products that engage in sustainable harvesting and fair trade practices. There is no international legal standard for sustainable product endorsements, but most certification organizations have adopted similar guidelines and principles. Food Alliance is one of several international organizations that certifies sustainable products. The coffees shown here are endorsed by the Rainforest Alliance. *K. Lee Lerner / Lerner & Lerner / LernerMedia Global Photos.*

However, Food Alliance argues it goes further in addressing other issues in agriculture in its efforts to make it more sustainable. Ensuring good working conditions and protecting wildlife and humane treatment of animals are all part of Food Alliance's tenets, whereas the organic label applies mainly to produce. Originally, organic production was meant to protect the small farmer, but larger organizations are adopting the organic approach and using it in a more intensive, industrialized way that could still harm the environment. It may be time to broaden and redefine organic standards to take account of modern conditions. Food Alliance argues its more holistic and comprehensive approach is more likely to satisfy consumer demand to know the origins and standards of their food and also to protect the environment.

SEE ALSO *Humane Animal Farming; Organics; Sustainable Agriculture.*

BIBLIOGRAPHY

Periodicals

"A Sustainable Ally—Food Alliance Wants to Help Growers Differentiate and Add Value to Their Fruit Crops through Sustainable Agriculture Practices and Certification." *American Fruit Grower* 129, no. 2 (2009): 16–17.

Getz, Christy, Sandy Brown, and Aimee Shreck. "Class Politics and Agricultural Exceptionalism in California's Organic Agriculture Movement." *Politics & Society* 36, no. 4 (2008): 478–507.

Web Sites

"You Are What You Eat!" *Food Alliance.* http://foodalliance.org/information-for/for-consumers (accessed October 17, 2010).

Susan Aldridge

Food and Agriculture Organization (FAO)

■ Introduction

The Food and Agriculture Organization (FAO) of the United Nations (UN) is a specialized UN agency dedicated to reducing hunger and achieving food security around the world. Founded in 1945, in September 2010 the FAO had 192 member states, including two associate members, the European Union and the Faroe Islands. Non-member states include Brunei, Lichtenstein, Singapore, and Vatican City. The Conference of Member Nations, which meets every two years, governs the FAO and appoints a Council to act as an interim governing body. The Conference also elects a director-general to head the agency and manage the daily affairs of the FAO.

The FAO's mandate involves increasing nutrition and standards of living, improving agricultural productivity and distribution, decreasing hunger, and enhancing the condition of rural populations. In addition to agriculture and nutrition, the FAO focuses on forestry, fisheries, and rural development issues in order to achieve its mandate. Instead of direct aid, the FAO generally provides technical assistance to nations or communities. The FAO works with other UN agencies, including the World Food Programme (WFP), to achieve its goals and provide emergency assistance. Over the years, however, the FAO has attracted criticism that the agency is ineffective and has a bloated bureaucracy.

■ Historical Background and Scientific Foundations

In 1896, David Lubin (1849–1919), a Polish-born agriculturalist and merchant, began campaigning for an international organization to assist farmers and other agriculture-related businesses. In May 1908 Lubin, with the support of Italy's king Victor Emmanuel III (1869–1947), opened the offices of the International Institute of Agriculture (IIA) in Rome. The IIA sought to promote the sharing of technical knowledge among farmers, improve agricultural production systems, assist farmers in marketing their products, and establish a cooperative system of rural credit that would allow farmers to purchase equipment and fund their operations.

In 1925 the League of Nations, an intergovernmental organization and precursor to the United Nations, worked with the IIA to produce a report on the global relationship of agriculture, nutrition, and economics. Released in 1928, the joint report was the first assessment of global nutritional needs and the economic aspects of malnutrition. The report's analysis of individual country's nutritional requirements and agricultural production became a valuable resource during World War II (1939–1945) when nations addressed the degree and manner in which to ration food during and after the war. The FAO received some of the IIA's assets and assumed and expanded the IIA's mandate.

In May 1943, representatives from 44 nations attended the United Nations Conference on Food and Agriculture in Hot Springs, Virginia, at the behest of U.S. President Franklin D. Roosevelt (1882–1945).

WORDS TO KNOW

CODEX ALIMENTARIUS: A collection of standards, guidelines, and codes of practices related to food production, hygiene, and food safety produced by the FAO.

FOOD SECURITY: The ability of all people at all times to have both physical and economic access to sufficient food to meet their dietary needs in order to lead a healthy and productive life.

NUTRITION: The process of providing or obtaining the nourishment necessary for health and growth.

UNDERNOURISHMENT: The state of having insufficient food, vitamins, minerals, or other substances necessary for good health.

A teenage boy prepares a field in Senegal for planting based on agricultural self-sufficiency lessons learned from Food and Agriculture Organization experts. © *Dung Vo Trung/Sygma/Corbis.*

Conference representatives agreed that national and global food distribution systems would have to be reorganized in order to supply minimum nutritional requirements to the two-thirds of the world population that faced chronic undernourishment or periodic starvation. The conference declaration states "that the goal of freedom from want of food, suitable and adequate for the health and strength of all people, can be achieved." Conference representatives also noted that improved agricultural production and more efficient distribution would benefit both agricultural producers and consumers.

The Hot Springs Conference recommended the creation of the Food and Agriculture Organization, a new international organization to address issues related to agriculture and nutrition. The United Nations Interim Commission on Food and Agriculture prepared a constitution for the FAO. On October 16, 1945—the first day of the First Session of the Conference of the Food and Agriculture Organization—the requisite number of nations signed the FAO constitution to establish the FAO as a specialized agency of the United Nations.

■ Impacts and Issues

The FAO promotes agricultural and rural development in developing nations through technical assistance projects and advisory services. The organization integrates environmental, economic, and social considerations into technical assistance projects, including crop production, animal production, fisheries management, rural infrastructure, and nutrition programs. The FAO utilizes its vast collection of agricultural, nutritional, forestry, and

fisheries data to develop technical programs that are best suited for a particular nation or area. Sustainable agriculture and rural development have been major priorities of the FAO in recent years, because the agency views development in these areas as a key to long term agricultural success in developing nations.

The FAO also manages consumer protection initiatives, including the promulgation of the *Codex Alimentaris*, a collection of guidelines, standards, and codes of practices related to foods. Created by the FAO in 1963, the *Codex Alimentaris* Commission establishes internationally accepted standards related to food and agriculture to protect human health and promote fair trade of agricultural commodities and goods. The *Codex Alimentaris* focuses on both raw and processed foods and addresses a variety of food issues, including hygiene, food labeling, food additives, and the safety of genetically modified food. The World Trade Organization views the *Codex Alimentaris* as a standard resource in the resolution of international disputes over food safety and consumer protection.

Over the years, many observers have criticized the FAO for being ineffective and for poor use of funds. In response, the FAO commissioned an independent external evaluation of the agency and its actions between 1990 and 2007. The independent external evaluation panel released a critical report, "FAO: The Challenge of Renewal," in September 2007. It called for "reform with growth" and stated that the FAO would have to become more flexible and less risk-averse to achieve its goals. The evaluation also found that the FAO has "a heavy and costly bureaucracy" and "major weaknesses in its organizational structures" which have been "high on costs and low on benefits." The release of the independent external evaluation and subsequent pledges by the FAO to remedy problems have not stemmed criticism of the FAO: In May 2008, President Abdoulaye Wade (1926–) of Senegal called the FAO a "waste of money" and claimed that the FAO was responsible for rising food prices during the food price crisis of 2007 and 2008.

Despite the criticism and calls for reorganization, the FAO continues to address hunger and food security issues. In 2009 the FAO convened the World Summit on Food Security to address threats to global food security, including the high price of food relative to income in developing nations. Representatives from 182 nations unanimously adopted a resolution reaffirming the FAO's goal of halving world hunger by 2015. The FAO estimates that approximately one billion people live in hunger.

SEE ALSO *Codex Alimentarius; Food Security; International Food Aid; International Fund for Agricultural Development; UN Millennium Development Goals.*

BIBLIOGRAPHY

Books

Food and Agriculture Organization of the United Nations (FAO). *The State of Food and Agriculture 2009: Livestock in the Balance.* Rome: FAO, 2009.

Food and Agriculture Organization of the United Nations (FAO). *The State of Food Insecurity on the World: 2009.* Rome: FAO, 2009.

Web Site

Food And Agriculture Organization of the United Nations (FAO). http://www.fao.org/ (accessed September 23, 2010).

Joseph P. Hyder

Food and Body Image

■ Introduction

Standards of beauty, body-size, and shape are increasingly being influenced by what is seen in magazines, in movies, and on television. The power of Western mass media in labeling what is or is not attractive and ideal is negatively impacting self-esteem and body image among both men and women. In a 1992 article in the *Journal of Communication*, it was estimated that on average adolescents see more than 5,260 "attractiveness messages" each year. And according to the American College of Obstetricians and Gynecologists (ACOG) fact sheet "Tool Kit for Teen Care, Second Edition," models are generally 25 percent thinner than the national average weight and represent only 5 percent of the population. The message of such images essentially tells viewers that society values only those who are underweight as physically beautiful. The lack of realistic and diverse images of what is perceived as beautiful in the media has led many to blame media for the increasing number of young people suffering from eating disorders. Many argue that airbrushed and digitally enhanced images in magazines contribute to body dissatisfaction and unhealthy weight control behaviors.

At the same time, rates of overweight and obesity have risen steadily; the Centers for Disease Control National Health and Nutrition Examination Study reports that in the years from 1976–1980 only 6 percent of children ages 2–19 were considered overweight; in 2007–2008 it had risen to 17 percent. During the 2007–2008 NHANES survey of adults, 68 percent of those ages 20–74 were considered overweight or obese compared to 47 percent in 1976–1980. A complicated relationship exists between obesity rates and the prevalence of disordered eating by binging, self induced vomiting, and self-starvation. ACOG states that 54 percent of all females from 12–23 are unhappy with their bodies, and one-third of high-school students think they are overweight even when they are not. The truth is that eating disorders and poor body image are the result of a number of factors, including physical, psychological, and social issues.

■ Historical Background and Scientific Foundations

Standards of female beauty are always changing and have been difficult to achieve throughout history. In the past, when farming and large landholding was dominant, women needed to be both physically strong and fertile in order to manage the daily chores and bear enough children to help with the land and household chores. As the socioeconomic status of landowners shifted away from the farms, so did the ideal woman. It became much more desirable for women to showcase small waists and a fragile state in order to find a suitable partner for marriage. Some decades later, women decided to cut their corsets and flaunt their short hair and pants before shifting back to traditional family and gender roles of the 1950s. Just as it always has, the ideal of beauty, health, and physical attractiveness exists in the second decade of the twenty-first century, but the striking difference is the influence of mass media on these perceptions. According to a 1997 survey by the Commonwealth fund, adolescent girls reported that the majority of their knowledge about women's health issues comes from the media. Television, magazines, movies, and the Internet are powerful tools that advertisers use to sell products.

What researchers have tried to explore over the past few decades is the relationship between mass media and weight control behaviors. A landmark 2002 study entitled "Eating Behaviors and Attitudes Following Prolonged Exposure to Television among Ethnic Fijian Adolescent Girls" was the first work to evaluate the impact of the introduction of television on disordered eating in media-naive populations. Fijian schoolgirls were assessed before and after television was introduced to their island in the mid-1990s. The impact of television on disordered eating attitudes and behaviors was overwhelming, as 83 percent of those interviewed shared that television had made them or their friends to feel

WORDS TO KNOW

ANOREXIA NERVOSA: An eating disorder that usually occurs during adolescence and young adulthood when an individual drastically limits the food that he or she eats; this results in self-starvation. This behavior is sometimes paired with exercising excessively. Women account for more than 90 percent of the cases. Typically those that suffer from this eating disorder are socially withdrawn, irritable, depressed, preoccupied with thoughts about food, and may collect recipes or hoard food. Diagnosis of this disorder is usually made based on a psychiatric examination.

BINGE EATING: An eating disorder that is commonly described as continuously snacking, eating large amounts of food in a short period of time. To be considered binge eating disorder, a person must binge eat two times per week for at least six months. Binge eaters do not try to prevent weight gain by self-induced vomiting, laxative abuse, or use of diet pills. Some, but not all, binge eaters are overweight. Like bulimia and anorexia, women usually suffer from this disorder, but unlike the other two disorders the proportion of men suffering from binge eating is higher.

BULIMIA NERVOSA: An eating disorder that often occurs during adolescence and young adulthood when an individual demonstrates binge eating behaviors followed by self-induced vomiting, abuse of laxatives and diet pills, and sometimes excessive exercising in order to prevent weight gain. Typically those that suffer from this disorder may experience dehydration, an increase in cavities, heart irregularities, and gastrointestinal problems.

EATING DISORDERS: Eating disorders include anorexia nervosa, bulimia nervosa, and binge eating. Individuals suffering from bulimia and anorexia exhibit excessive control over their body weight by controlling their food intake. Anorexia nervosa and bulimia nervosa are disorders that are more prevalent among young women in industrialized countries where food exists in abundance yet there is pressure to diet and to achieve a perceived ideal, thin body.

OBESITY: Possessing accumulated body fat that is excessive enough to have a negative impact on health.

SELF-ESTEEM: A state of being that is grounded in self acceptance and self respect. In the context of body image, a person with high self esteem feels good about his or her body and has a positive self perception about their size and shape. Individuals with low self-esteem will most likely be unsatisfied with their body image and size. Unfortunately this could result in a repetitive pattern of self-deprivation, followed by bingeing, weight gain, and worsening self image.

WEIGHT CONTROL BEHAVIORS: Behaviors exhibited when someone is trying to control his or her body weight. Some of these behaviors include skipping meals, using diet pills, self-induced vomiting, excessive exercise, and dietary restrictions.

dissatisfied with their body shape or weight and 77 percent said that television had impacted their own body image. In another study, published in 2007 in *Pediatrics*, researchers followed girls for a 5-year period and determined that "the frequency of healthy, unhealthy, and extreme weight-control behaviors increased with increasing magazine reading" if the magazines included articles about dieting and weight loss. This included doubling the rates of unhealthy weight control behaviors and tripling the most extreme behaviors such as vomiting and using laxatives by those who read the magazines most frequently when compared to girls who did not read such magazines.

■ Impacts and Issues

For the first time in history, the United States and many other developed countries are experiencing an abundance of food that is readily available and cheaply priced. Oftentimes it is too much of this convenient, affordable, and high-calorie food that is contributing to the obesity epidemic. Yet this abundance of food conflicts with the ideal of thinness.

Rather than healthful means of maintaining body weight, a study in 2006 revealed that self-induced vomiting, use of diet pills, and/or use of laxatives were reported by one-fourth of older adolescent females within the past year. These unhealthy weight control behaviors are not the solution to the increasing rates of obesity in young people. Preventing disordered eating behaviors and obesity in a society that emphasizes thinness and constant dieting is an involved process. The *Journal of Adolescent Health* found that almost half of adolescent girls reported that their mother encouraged them to diet, while 58 percent had been teased about their weight by family members. When parents criticize or over-emphasize weight control behaviors to their children, this is typically associated with unhealthy eating behaviors practiced by the child. One way to address nutrition and promote healthy eating habits is by modeling these behaviors at family meals. Encouraging physical activity by participating in sports or a hobby is also another way to address concerns about obesity in a child or young person.

The illusion of beauty that is seen in magazines, movies, and television is something that probably will remain for some time in Western societies. According to developmental psychologists, the most important thing that a parent, teacher, sibling, or friend of an adolescent person can do to prevent disordered eating behaviors is to reinforce the adolescent's positive self-perceptions, thereby improving their self-acceptance and self-respect.

SEE ALSO *Advertising Food; Eating Disorders; Family Meal Benefits; Food and the Internet; Obesity.*

A British teenage girl with an eating disorder measures her waist. © *Photofusion Picture Library / Alamy.*

BIBLIOGRAPHY

Books

Grogan, Sarah. *Body Image: Understanding Body Dissatisfaction in Men, Women and Children.* New York: Routledge, 2007.

Thompson, Kevin J. *Body Image, Eating Disorders, and Obesity in Youth: Assessment, Prevention, and Treatment*, 2nd ed. Washington, DC: American Psychological Association, 2008.

Periodicals

Derenne, Jennifer, and Eugene Beresin. "Body Image, Media, and Eating Disorders." *Academic Psychiatry* 30 (May–June 2006): 257–261.

Neumark-Sztainer, Diane, et al. "Family Weight Talk and Dieting: How Much Do They Matter for Body Dissatisfaction and Disordered Eating Behaviors in Adolescent Girls?" *Journal of Adolescent Health* 47, no. 3 (2010): 270–276.

Neumark-Sztainer, Diane, et al. "Overweight Status and Weight Control Behaviors in Adolescents: Longitudinal and Secular Trends from 1999 to 2004." *Preventative Medicine* 43, no. 1 (2006): 52–59.

van den Berg, P., D. Neumark-Sztainer, P. J. Hannan, and J. Haines. "Is Dieting Advice from Magazines Helpful or Harmful? Five-year Associations with Weight-control Behaviors and Psychological Outcomes in Adolescents." *Pediatrics* 119, no. 1 (January 2007): e30–37.

Web Sites

American College of Obstetricians and Gynecologists. "Media and Body Image: A Fact Sheet for Parents." *Tool Kit for Teen Care, Second Edition.* http://www.acog.org/departments/adolescent HealthCare/TeenCareToolKit/mediabody_4_parents.pdf (accessed October 20, 2010).

National Women's Health Information Center. "Body Image: Loving Your Body Inside and Out." *womenshealth.gov.* http://www.womenshealth.gov/bodyimage/ (accessed October 9, 2010).

The Nemours Foundation. "Teen's Health: Body Image and Self Esteem." *KidsHealth.org.* http://kidshealth.org/teen/exercise/problems/body_image.html# (accessed October 9, 2010).

Tiffany Middle Imes

Food and the Internet

Introduction

The advent of the Internet has had an enormous impact on the culture and business of food. In addition to the immediate exchange of information and ideas and the wealth of knowledge available on the Internet, it has created new business avenues that previously could not have existed. Whereas the Internet is a relatively new phenomenon, its effect has been immediate and extends throughout the globe.

Historical Background and Scientific Foundations

The Internet is responsible for a great many changes in modern society because it has greatly increased the speed with which people may communicate, as well as providing access to an enormous amount of information. The effect of the Internet on food and cooking has many aspects. One aspect is that as communication between people of various backgrounds increased, people became exposed to a wider array of foods and cuisines. For example, there are many online blogs that enable people to write about their own cooking or restaurants they have visited. Blogs allow people to share their experience with food and give people access to a wider variety of opinions about food and cooking.

As a reference source, the Internet provides access to a seemingly inexhaustible supply of recipes. By simply searching for recipes based upon ingredients that one has available, searching for new recipes in a particular style of cooking, or even searching for recipes from a particular chef, the Internet can serve as a free culinary database that is available to everyone. Previously the only way to access recipes was to purchase a cookbook, watch a demonstration, attend a cooking class, or exchange them among friends.

For small specialty food purveyors, the Internet provides access to the global market. Artisanal producers of items such as olive oil, breads, wine, cheese, soups, sauces, cured meats, and even fresh meats and produce are able to advertise and sell their products online. Previously these producers relied on foot traffic and word of mouth, but with the Internet restaurants and home cooks all over the world gain access to their products. The purveyors of fresh meats and produce also rely on another recent technology: express delivery services and temperature control such as insulated shipping containers and dry ice, which cause shipping time to be much less of a factor in the availability of fresh ingredients than ever before. Aside from the new avenues of business that this has opened, via online communication and express delivery services, regional cuisine is less limited by what ingredients can be used. For example, areas with no access to the sea are able to access freshly caught seafood by having it express-shipped from the coast in an insulated container. Along the same lines, fresh meat, seafood, and produce from opposite sides of the globe can be exchanged in a matter of hours or days. By drastically reducing the time barrier for shipping perishables, the Internet has started a trend of globalization in food and cooking, in which regional cuisines are influencing each other from disparate locations worldwide.

Impacts and Issues

As with any aspect of globalization, there is criticism that it poses a threat to tradition. The free trade between regional cuisines runs the risk of dismantling these same regional cuisines, and critics worry that as new techniques and recipes become popular, older traditional recipes might be forgotten. This is also closely tied in with nationalism, and there are some groups that work to preserve traditional cuisines to ensure they are not lost in the wake of this new trend.

The incredible amount of recipes available online is certainly a great resource for home cooks, but in certain situations the differing information can cause confusion.

Blogger Julia Langbein updates her food blog, "The Bruni Digest," which parodies the reviews of New York Times food critic Frank Bruni, from her home in New York City. *AP Images.*

One can search for a particular recipe and find dozens of conflicting versions. Additionally, the free recipes online compete with sales of cookbooks, which has prompted some cookbook publishers to start expanding into areas beyond simply providing recipes. For example, Thomas Keller's *The French Laundry Cookbook* features many recipes featured at his restaurant, but also includes many passages about the building's history and Keller's philosophy on food to provide insight and background to the development of his dishes. The book *A Return to Cooking* follows the chef Eric Ripert (1965–) along with two photographers, an artist, and a food journalist as they travel to different areas of the world during different seasons. The goal is the study of Ripert's cooking as he explores what it is about food and cooking that he loves. Ripert creates dishes that the photographers shoot, the artist paints, and the journalist documents and interviews Ripert as they travel and watch him work. The end result is a book that not only contains many recipes, but also provides insight into the mind and inspirations of one of the most lauded chefs in the world. Many other cookbooks are breaking away from the traditional

format to try and compete with the multitude of recipes available for free on the Internet.

The combination of the Internet and shipping services has created a grocery shopping model that is an alternative to traditional grocery stores and farmers' markets, particularly in urban areas. There are several companies that enable a consumer to shop for groceries online, and then use refrigerated trucks to deliver the groceries to the shopper's front door. In large cities this is becoming increasingly popular, for although the cost of this service is greater, in many cities it is far easier than attempting to go to a grocery store in person and then carry all the items home. Whereas the traditional answer to this difficulty was small street markets and produce stalls, the internet grocery model provides access to a much wider variety of products, and with the refrigerated delivery the produce is often just as fresh if not fresher than it would be in the store or at the stall.

The Internet is a relatively recent trend, but already it has had enormous impact on the culinary world. It has created business concepts, transferred ideas, and provided access to information that could never before have been so easily available. Although there are critiques of its effect, the popularity of the Internet seems to indicate that it will continue to affect food culture for many years to come.

SEE ALSO *Alice Waters: California and New American Cuisine; Celebrity Chef Phenomenon; Culinary Education; Food Critics and Ratings; Food Fads; Gastronomy; Gourmet Hobbyists and Foodies; Michael Pollan: Linking Food and Environmental Journalism; Movies, Documentaries, and Food; Television and Food.*

BIBLIOGRAPHY

Books

Canavan, Orla; Maeve Henchion; and Seamus O'Reilly. *An Assessment of Irish Speciality Food Enterprises' Use of the Internet as a Marketing Tool.* Dublin: Teagasc, 2005.

Connor, Elizabeth. *Internet Guide to Food Safety and Security.* New York: Haworth Information Press, 2005.

Smith, Drew. *Food Industry and the Internet: Making Real Money in the Virtual World*. Chichester: John Wiley & Sons, Ltd., 2007. Internet resource.

Periodicals

Culp, Jennifer; Robert A. Bell; and Diana Cassady. "Characteristics of Food Industry Web Sites and Advergames Targeting Children." *Journal of Nutrition Education and Behavior* 42, no. 3 (2010): 197–201.

"E-business: Internet Food Sales Rise by 50 Percent at Tesco." *Computer Weekly* (April 22, 2008): 4.

Mauer, Whitney A., et al. "Ethnic-Food Safety Concerns: An Online Survey of Food Safety Professionals." *Journal of Environmental Health* 68, no. 10 (2006): 32–38.

Newell, Alexa. "USDA Launches Searchable Database of Foods." *AWHONN Lifelines / Association of Women's Health, Obstetric and Neonatal Nurses* 10, no. 2 (2006): 167–169.

Weber, Kristi; Mary Story; and Lisa Harnack. "Internet Food Marketing Strategies Aimed at Children and Adolescents: A Content Analysis of Food and Beverage Brand Web Sites." *Journal of the American Dietetic Association* 106, no. 99 (2006): 1463–1466.

Web Sites

Culinary Online: Your Roadmap to the Culinary Internet. http://www.culinary-online.com/ (accessed October 6, 2010).

Escoffier On Line: The Culinary Resource. http://www.escoffier.com/ (accessed October 6, 2010).

Kalins, Dorothy. "The Taste Makers: Artisans: They've Devoted Their Lives to Creating Exquisite Food with the Best Ingredients. Now, Thanks to the Internet, They're Taking Their Passion Nationwide." *Newsweek / msnbc*, September 26, 2005. http://www.msnbc.msn.com/id/9377822/site/newsweek/page/3/print/1/displaymode/1098/ (accessed October 6, 2010).

David Brennan Tilove

Food as Celebration

Introduction

Food has been a central part of celebrations worldwide since the earliest social groupings occurred. Feasts and celebrations traditionally commemorate birthdays, weddings, religious holidays, and days of political or social significance. Foods served vary by country and region as well as event.

Weddings are an exemplary global celebration at which food plays a central role. In many countries, specific traditional dishes are served, holding special meaning regarding happiness, long life together, fertility, or prosperity. In Indonesia it is customary for the entire village to be invited to the wedding reception. In Baltic countries the wedding feast can last for eight hours or more. The tradition of the wedding cake began in Italy in the first century BC: It was customary for a cake of bread to be broken over the head of the bride as a symbol of fertility. In Mexico a papier-mâché piñata filled with candy is hung from the ceiling during the post-wedding fiesta and blindfolded children take turns hitting it with a stick until it breaks and the candy scatters for all to grab. Caribbean Island wedding feasts often last all through the night, with many types of foods served. Curried goat, spicy jerked chicken, and conch fritters are among the more popular feast dishes. The Caribbean wedding cake is called "black cake," and contains flour, brown sugar, butter, eggs, glazed cherries, raisins, prunes, and currents. The dried fruits are soaked in rum for up to a year before the wedding.

Historical Background and Scientific Foundations

The practice of mass cooking in order to feed large groups likely began around 400 BC in China, where large festivals and celebrations necessitated the development of means of feeding and temporarily housing large groups of people. In ancient Greece, Egypt, and Rome, mass cooking was done in order to provide nourishment for traveling military personnel and traders. The practice of public hospitality was not formalized until the ancient Greeks constructed the first inns and hostels. At that time, it was customary to provide food for travelers free of charge.

During the Middle Ages, European catering and hospitality mainly occurred at monasteries, where monks supplied food and accommodations for individuals engaged in religious pilgrimages. As overland trade routes grew in Europe, the need for mass production of food expanded as well. Before the advent of currency, most of the hospitality industries (food and lodging primarily) were either free or offered in exchange for barter. As financial systems developed, catering and hospitality became compensated industries.

Germany was the site of burgeoning service industries during the fourteenth and fifteenth centuries, as the concept of legislation of industry developed. German lawmakers created licenses for the production and public serving of different alcoholic beverages (most notably beer) and foods, and they developed standards and regulations for public lodgings.

The steam catering tray was invented in the eighteenth century, setting the stage for the modern catering industry. As global populations increased and the transportation industry grew, the need for progressively more sophisticated catering/hospitality services evolved. In the early twenty-first century, catering is a full-service industry: Caterers travel to the site of the celebration, bringing everything from food to linens to tents to dance floors. It is no longer a matter of serving a meal, but one of creating an entire event.

Impacts and Issues

Whenever meals are served to large groups of people, food safety is a serious concern. Sanitary procedures and thorough cooking are critical, as is maintenance of correct

WORDS TO KNOW

FEAST: A large and usually elabotate banquet, often prepared for many people, and often in recognition of a celebratory event or religious occasion.

HOSTEL: An informal inn or small hotel that provides overnight lodging and meals for travelers.

VINICULTURE: The science, art, and social customs that surround the practices of growing grapes and making wine.

serving temperature for prolonged periods. Steam trays have made it possible to keep hot foods protected from the open air and at appropriate temperatures in order to prevent bacteria growth. Cold foods are challenging to keep safe, even when they are served and stored over ice.

When large groups of people occupy a confined space for a prolonged period of time, there is an increased risk of foodborne or highly-contagious illness. Norovirus, formerly called Norwalk Virus, is one such sickness: It affects the stomach and intestines, causing vomiting, diarrhea, and cramping. Beginning abruptly and lasting for up to two days, norovirus is most common in areas where there are shared utensils or the space is relatively confined, and many individuals may come into contact with the same surfaces. Norovirus is most frequently reported in college dormitories, nursing homes, following large catered events, and especially aboard cruise ships. Generally, large buffets can be ideal breeding grounds for norovirus. Not all individuals exposed to the virus will get sick, although they may be able to shed the virus and transmit it to others. People remain contagious for up to two weeks after recovery from the illness.

Celebrations of holidays and special occasions with food can have other health effects. The world's population, particularly in developed and developing countries, has become increasingly overweight. As a result, there has been progressive focus on weight loss and healthier eating. Previously, Americans gained an average of five pounds during every winter holiday season, but according to a small-scale research study conducted by the National Institutes of Health, the average individual now gains less than one pound between Thanksgiving and the New Year's holidays.

Birthdays are celebrated around the world, and food typically plays a central role. In many countries, birthday cake is served, generally topped with one candle for each year of life. Candles symbolize transporting birthday wishes to the heavens. Blowing out all of the candles at

Sacred foods are offered to the temple deities for Annakut Darshan, the first day of the Hindu New Year. © *World Religions Photo Library / Alamy.*

Villagers on the Greek island of Sikinos prepare an Easter meal to cook in a communal oven. © *terry harris just greece photo library / Alamy.*

once is said to ensure fulfillment of the birthday wish. In some countries, the birthday child brings treats, cupcakes, or cake to school to share with classmates. Many areas of the United States, with rising concerns about childhood obesity, have ended the practice of bringing sweets into the classroom and are instead suggesting healthy snacks such as fruit or vegetable muffins for birthday celebrations.

Traditionally, many celebrations that involve food, including Thanksgiving in the United States, have brought family and friends together around the time of the harvest. Food festivals around the world that celebrate the harvest of local crops have enjoyed a renewal since the early 1990s, especially with the rise of the organics movement and a renewed worldwide interest in viniculture. After airline fares became less expensive and more competitive beginning in 2000, travel to food festivals became popular destinations and local tourism agencies responded by organizing and promoting them. Grape harvesting festivals along winemaking routes became especially popular, with tours, celebrations, and festivals organized during the September and October grape harvests in Europe, the August through November harvests in California, and the February to April harvests in South America, New Zealand, and South Africa.

SEE ALSO *Confectionery and Pastry; Foodborne Diseases; Foodways; Norovirus Infection; School Lunch Reform; Viniculture.*

BIBLIOGRAPHY

Books

Bhote, Tehmina. *Medieval Feasts and Banquets: Food, Drink, and Celebration in the Middle Ages.* New York: Rosen Central, 2004.

Carey, Diana, and Judy Large. *Festivals, Family and Food. Guide to Seasonal Celebration.* Lansdown, Stroud, UK: Hawthorn Press, 2005.

Morgan, Diane, and Leigh Beisch. *The New Thanksgiving Table: An American Celebration of Family, Friends, and Food.* San Francisco: Chronicle Books, 2009.

Northern Clay Center. *Eat with Your Eyes: A Celebration of the Art and Design and Pleasure of Sharing Food.* Minneapolis: Northern Clay Center, 2007.

Periodicals

Casotti, Leticia. "He Who Eats Alone Will Die Alone? An Exploratory Study of the Meanings of the Food of Celebration." *Latin American Business Review* 6, no. 4 (2005): 69–84.

Einarsen, Kari, and Reidar Mykletun. "Exploring the Success of the Gladmatfestival (the Stavanger Food Festival)." *Scandinavian Journal of Hospitality and Tourism* 9 (2009): 225–248.

Web Sites

"Facts about Noroviruses on Cruise Ships." *U.S. Centers for Disease Control and Prevention (CDC).* http://www.cdc.gov/nceh/vsp/pub/norovirus/norovirus.htm (accessed November 1, 2010).

"Food and Celebrations." *Better Health Channel.* http://www.betterhealth.vic.gov.au/bhcv2/bhcarticles.nsf/pages/Food_and_celebrations (accessed November 1, 2010).

Schulte, Brigid. "Once Just a Sweet Birthday Treat, the Cupcake Becomes a Cause." *The Washington Post,* December 11, 2006. http://www.washingtonpost.com/wp-dyn/content/article/2006/12/10/AR2006121001008.html (accessed November 1, 2010).

Pamela V. Michaels

Food Bans

■ Introduction

The history of food bans stretches back thousands of years to when many of the world's religions imposed sets of dietary laws. Religions enacted these laws as ways to protect human health, signal separation from other cultures, impose moral symbols, and for reasons lost to history. Followers of many of the world's major religions, including Buddhism, Islam, Hinduism, and Judaism, continue to adhere to many of the food bans imposed by their religions.

Religious food bans continue to affect the eating habits of billions of people around the world. In the last century, though, governments have taken an increasingly active role in banning food items. Governments may ban certain food products for a variety of reasons, including health and safety concerns, environmental concerns, animal cruelty prevention, or cultural reasons. The purpose for food bans often sparks debate among competing interests, such as chefs, food producers, consumers, religious leaders, public health advocates, environmentalists, and others.

■ Historical Background and Scientific Foundations

Most laws and rules forbidding the consumption of certain foods were enacted for religious reasons. More than 3,000 years ago, Moses, a Jewish prophet, authored the Torah, which contains numerous dietary laws for Jews, known as kashrut. Foods that conform to kashrut are termed *kosher*. The Torah requires the removal of blood from animals before consumption and prohibits the consumption of pork, rabbit, horse, and shellfish. Jewish dietary laws also prohibit the consumption of fish that do not have fins and scales. Furthermore, meat and dairy products may not be mixed. In addition to prohibited food items, Jewish dietary laws contain a strict set of rules regarding food preparation. Although Jewish

dietary laws were formulated without an understanding of the germ theory of disease, some of the laws appear designed to protect human health. Other laws, however, seemingly do not have a rational explanation.

In the early seventh century, Muhammad espoused dietary laws for Muslims in the *Quran*. Many of Islam's dietary laws closely mirror those of Judaism. The Qur'an specifically forbids the consumption of pork, blood, or any animal that died on its own. In the centuries after Muhammad, Islamic jurisprudence established a broader set of dietary laws. Foods that adhere to Islamic dietary laws are known as *halal*. Islamic dietary laws also seem to prohibit the consumption of alcohol or foods prepared with alcohol.

Modern Hinduism, which arose on the Indian subcontinent between 3,100 and 3,700 years ago, has developed a number of prohibitions on the consumption of certain foods. Cows, which are considered sacred in Hinduism, may not be eaten. According to the *Bhagavad Gita*, a Hindu sacred text, killing a cow will condemn a person to hell without the possibility for atonement. Cow's milk, however, may be consumed. Many doctrines of Hinduism allow for the consumption of meat other than beef. Most Buddhists meanwhile do not consume any meat. Some Buddhist sects eat fish, whereas a few allow adherents to eat all meat.

■ Impacts and Issues

Aside from religious food restrictions, food bans involving public health and safety are perhaps the most common form of food bans. Some governments have banned alcohol for health and safety reasons. Many governments, primarily in Muslim nations, also ban alcohol for religious reasons. In the early twentieth century, many nations banned the sale and distribution of absinthe, an alcoholic spirit with supposed psychoactive properties derived from an infusion of grande wormwood. The temperance movement in the United States and Europe cited alleged crimes and social disorder associated with the consumption of absinthe. In the 1910s and 1920s, the temperance movement succeeded in prohibiting the sale and distribution of all alcoholic beverages in the United States, parts of Canada, Russia (and later the Soviet Union), Iceland, Norway, Finland, and Hungary. Prohibition of alcohol began in the United States in 1919 but ended in 1933. Most of the bans in European and other countries had been lifted by the 1940s.

Most food bans focus on the effects of a food on consumers' health, rather than public safety issues. Fugu, also known as Japanese puffer fish or blowfish, contains neurotoxins in its internal organs that cause paralysis and death if accidentally consumed. In 1603 Japan's Tokugawa shogunate banned the consumption of fugu. Although Japan's fugu ban lasted only until 1868, many nations, including all members of the European Union (EU), prohibit the sale of fugu. In the United States, only specially licensed vendors may sell fugu.

For almost a decade, beef from Britain was banned in many European and other countries after the discovery of an epidemic of bovine spongiform encephalopathy (BSE, or mad cow disease), a progressive infection of the

WORDS TO KNOW

HALAL: Foods that adhere to Islamic dietary laws.

KOSHER: Foods that adhere to Jewish dietary laws.

PRECAUTIONARY PRINCIPLE: The principle that any product, action, or process that might pose a threat to public or environmental health should not be introduced in the absence of scientific consensus regarding its safety.

RECOMBINANT BOVINE GROWTH HORMONE (rBGH): A genetically engineered hormone given to cattle to increase milk production.

brain and nervous system found in cattle. The disease can be transmitted to humans, causing a fatal brain disorder called variant Creutzfeldt-Jakob disease (vCJD). In 2003, 60 nations banned beef from the United States briefly, after one cow with BSE was discovered in Washington state. The bans were later lifted when the cow was traced to a Canadian herd.

Parents and children protest the so-called Bake Sale Ban, New York Department of Education regulation A-812, which restricts the sale of baked goods from schools. Many schools rely on bake sales of home made goods to fund programs that have been affected by the severe budget cuts. In the interest of preventing obesity the regulation bans home-made foods but allows commercially produced snacks such as chips on school campuses. *Richard B. Levine / Alamy.*

A vendor sells pickled tea leaves and beans on a roadside in downtown Yangon, Myanmar. Myanmar's Health Ministry banned the sale of 57 brands of pickled tea leaves, a popular snack food, amidst concerns over chemical dyes and additives. *AP Images.*

Most foods banned for health reasons, however, will not immediately kill consumers but may affect their long-term health. Many nations have placed regulations or bans on the use of foods containing trans fats. Trans fats, a form of unsaturated fat often contained in processed foods and fast foods, have been linked an elevated risk of coronary heart disease and other health problems. In 2003 Denmark passed the first laws to regulate the sale of foods containing trans fats. The restrictions imposed by the Danish law effectively reduce human consumption of trans fats to less than one gram per person per day. Switzerland enacted similar legislation in 2008. Brazil enacted less stringent regulations in 2010. In the United States and Canada, many cities, including New York City, Philadelphia, Boston, and Calgary, have enacted trans fat bans. In 2008 California became the first U.S. state to enact a ban on trans fats, and in 2009 British Columbia became the first Canadian province to ban trans fats.

Countries also impose food bans on products without a proven safety record. Many nations support a precautionary principle approach to food safety. The precautionary principle holds than any product, action, or process that might pose a threat to public or environmentally health should not be introduced in the absence of scientific consensus regarding its safety. In the European Union (EU), genetically modified (GM) foods and the use of recombinant bovine growth hormone (rBGH) are banned. The United States, however, allows the sale and distribution of foods containing GM foods and rBGH.

Governments sometimes ban foods for environmental reasons, particularly in cases in which continued production would endanger the survival of a species. Dozens of nations have banned the import, sale, or distribution of uncertified Patagonian toothfish, also known as uncertified Chilean sea bass. Overfishing has decimated wild populations of the fish to unsustainable levels. In 2005 the United States banned the import of wild beluga caviar from the Caspian Sea, because wild beluga sturgeon populations were becoming endangered. In 2006 the Convention on International Trade in Endangered Species (CITES), an international treaty regulating the trade of endangered plants and animals, banned the sale of sturgeon caviar—beluga, ossetra, and sevruga—from the Black and Caspian Seas. The caviar bans were partially lifted in 2007.

Nations have also banned food products that are perceived as cruel to animals. Animal rights advocacy groups have condemned the production of foie gras, a food product made from the swollen livers of geese or ducks. In order to fatten livers, producers force-feed the ducks and geese by inserting a long tube down their throats—a process known as gavage. Several nations have banned the use of gavage in the production of foie gras, including Argentina, Czech Republic, Denmark, Finland, Germany, Israel, Italy, Luxembourg, Norway, and Poland. Other countries, including Ireland, Sweden, Switzerland, the Netherlands and the United Kingdom, address gavage under their general animal cruelty laws. California and several U.S. cities have also banned foie gras production that utilizes gavage. Consumers in these areas, however, may purchase gavage-produced foie gras originating from areas without production bans. The city of Chicago enacted a ban on the sale of foie gras in 2006, but overturned the law in 2008 following protests from chefs and the mayor.

SEE ALSO *Agriculture and International Trade; Bushmeat; Center for Food Safety and Applied Nutrition; Codex Alimentarius; Commission on Genetic Resources for Food and Agriculture (1995); Embargoes; Ethical Issues in Agriculture; Food Inspection and Standards; Food Safety and Inspection Service; Foodborne Diseases; Genetically Modified Organisms (GMO); Import Restrictions; Mad Cow Disease and vCJD; Paralytic Shellfish Poisoning; Raw Milk Campaign; Religion and Food.*

BIBLIOGRAPHY

Books

Ansell, Christopher K., and David Vogel. *What's the Beef?: The Contested Governance of European Food Safety.* Cambridge, MA: MIT Press, 2006.

Periodicals

"EU—GMOs: Commission Defeated on Food Bans." *Environmental Policy and Law* 35, no.4–5 (2005): 201–202.

"EU Parliament Panel Votes to Ban Food from Clones." *Food Chemical News* 52, no. 9 (2010): 6–7.

"Food Fighter—Jeremy Preston Has Spent His Life Working in the Food Industry and Is Now Defending Its Rights in the Face of Potential Bans." *Marketing* (March 11, 2004): 22.

"Food World—from Stamping Out Counterfeit Food Products, to Lifting UK Beef Bans, Food World Provides a Round Up of News from around the Globe." *Food Processing* 74, no. 12 (2005): 12.

Jochelson, Karen. "Nanny or Steward? The Role of Government in Public Health." *Public Health* 120, no. 12 (2006): 1149–1155.

Resnik, David. "Trans Fat Bans and Human Freedom." *The American Journal of Bioethics* 10, no. 3 (2010): 27–32.

Sturm, Roland, and Doborah Cohen. "Fast-food Bans: The Authors Respond." *Health Affairs* 29, no. 1 (2010): 219.

"Taiwan Bans Food Plastics." *ICIS Chemical Business: Europe, Middle East, Asia* (November 27, 2006): 13.

"USDA—FSIS Permanently Bans Downer Cattle from U.S. Food Supply." *Food Chemical News* 49, no. 22 (2007): 1.

Web Sites

Fox, Nick. "Chicago Overturns Foie Gras Ban." *The New York Times*, May 14, 2008. http://diners journal.blogs.nytimes.com/2008/05/14/chicago overturns-foie-gras-ban/ (accessed November 1, 2010).

Landsberg, Mitchell, and Monte Morin. "School Soda, Junk Food Bans Approved." *The Los Angeles Times*, September 7, 2005. http://articles.latimes. com/2005/sep/07/local/me-junkfood7 (accessed November 1, 2010).

Joseph P. Hyder

Food, Conservation, and Energy Act of 2008

■ Introduction

The Food, Conservation, and Energy Act of 2008, also known as the 2008 Farm Bill, is a comprehensive omnibus bill that set the legal framework for agricultural policy for the United States for a five-year period. The 2008 Farm Bill continues, expands, or eliminates programs and policies contained in its predecessor, the Farm Security and Rural Investment Act of 2002, or 2002 Farm Bill. The 2008 Farm Bill allocates hundreds of billions of dollars of federal spending over the period covering 2008 through 2012.

The 2008 Farm Bill addressed a wide range of topics, including agricultural subsidies, trade, food assistance programs and nutrition, conservation, energy, and rural development. The 2008 Farm Bill, like its predecessors, contains many controversial provisions that have far-reaching effects over agricultural, food, environmental, and trade policy in the United States and around the world. The provisions of the 2008 Farm Bill dealing with agricultural subsidies to American farmers and the expansion of the American biofuel industry attracted the most criticism.

■ Historical Background and Scientific Foundations

According to the National Agricultural Law Center, a leading source on U.S. agricultural law and policy, the Food, Conservation, and Energy Act of 2008 is the sixteenth piece of U.S. legislation that may be called a farm bill. "Farm bill" is a term given exclusively to comprehensive omnibus bills that deal with agricultural and food policy. In recent decades, the U.S. Congress has passed a farm bill approximately every five years to set the nation's agricultural policy and to govern other affairs of the U.S. Department of Agriculture (USDA). Congress may pass additional non-farm bill agricultural legislation to supplement the agricultural and food policy set forth in the governing farm bill.

The Agricultural Adjustment Act of 1933 (1933 Farm Bill) is considered to be the first farm bill. The 1933 Farm Bill was a key component of the New Deal programs and legislation of President Franklin D. Roosevelt (1882–1945). It was passed by the U.S. Congress during the Great Depression (1929–1941) primarily to maintain agricultural commodities prices despite overproduction of those commodities. Congress expanded the purview of subsequent farm bills to cover the use of pesticides, agricultural trade, a variety of subsidies, food assistance and health programs, rural development, energy policy, farm credit, and agricultural taxes.

Congress passed the 2008 Farm Bill to continue, expand, or modify provisions contained in the expiring 2002 Farm Bill. U.S. President George W. Bush (1946–) vetoed the bill, citing its high cost and its impact on small-scale farmers. In an unusual procedural occurrence, 34 pages of the 2008 Farm Bill were omitted when the legislation was transmitted to the President. Because the president vetoed a bill that Congress technically had not passed, Congress had to vote on the 2008 Farm Bill again. President Bush vetoed the new version, too, but Congress overrode his veto in June 2008.

The 2008 Farm Bill allocates approximately $300 billion in spending and contains provisions covering a wide range of agricultural and food issues. The bill expanded agricultural subsidies to include a wider range of specialty fruits and vegetables that were not covered under earlier farm bills. It also created the Average Crop Revenue Election (ACRE) program, a significant reform to the U.S. agricultural subsidy program. ACRE provides better protection for farmers than previous subsidy programs, but ACRE only pays out when farmers have a realized loss of revenue due to crop failure, price fluctuations, or other causes. Analysts argue that ACRE will cut direct subsidy payments by 20 percent. The 2008 Farm Bill also includes massive funding for government food assistance programs and established a program to encourage the development of the biofuel industry.

United States Senator Tom Harkin (D-Iowa) speaks to farmers. Senator Harkin helped craft the Food, Conservation, and Energy Act of 2008, which, among other measures, attempted to limit subsidies to wealthy farmers. © *Mike Voss / Alamy.*

■ Impacts and Issues

As the primary agricultural and food policy legislation for one of the world's largest agricultural producers, the 2008 Farm Bill affects many aspects of global food trade policy from the prices that consumers pay for food at the grocery store to the profits of multi-billion dollar agricultural conglomerates. Various provisions of the 2008 Farm Bill attracted criticism from both liberal and conservative observers in the United States and abroad. More than 1,000 agricultural, consumer, and environmental organizations sent a letter to Congress requesting an override of President Bush's veto of the law. The organizations noted that the 2008 Farm Bill was "by no means perfect" but that the bill was a "carefully balanced compromise of policy priorities that has broad support among organizations representing the nation's agriculture, conservation, and nutrition interests."

Congress allocated almost 75 percent of the 2008 Farm Bill's approximately $300 billion spending to anti-hunger programs, including food stamps and school lunch programs. The bill expanded the coverage of anti-hunger programs, which allows more Americans to receive food assistance. Several Republican legislators, however, asserted that the expansion of anti-hunger

programs was an attempt by Democrats to influence voters during an election year.

The 2008 Farm Bill also expanded or implemented agricultural programs designed to improve the environment. In addition to provisions that financially assist farmers transitioning from conventional to organic farming, the 2008 Farm Bill includes billions of dollars for soil and water conservation and other environmental issues.

The bill contains innovative, market-oriented agricultural subsidies that replace some of the direct subsidies favored in previous farm bills. Analysts estimate that the ACRE program will cover approximately 30 percent of cultivated land in the United States. The program provides a farmer with a subsidy only when the farmer needs it to replace lost revenue. Direct subsidies pay farmers based on politically-influenced target prices for certain commodities. The ACRE program will reduce the effect of subsidies on the commodities market by stabilizing commodity prices and reducing the influence of subsidies on market prices. The ACRE program will also allow the USDA to allocate hundreds of millions of dollars to other programs.

The 2008 Farm Bill did continue the longstanding U.S. policy of providing farmers, including large-scale corporate farms, with subsidies. This policy continuation drew heavy criticism from the international community: The European Union expressed concern to the World Trade Organization, an international organization that resolves regulates international trade and resolves trade disputes, that the farm subsidies contained in the 2008 Farm Bill were a sign of growing protectionism.

Another criticism of the 2008 Farm Bill was in regard to the continuation of funding for the U.S. biofuel industry, particularly corn-derived ethanol producers. At the time Congress passed the 2008 Farm Bill, the world was in the midst of the food price crisis of 2007 and 2008. Between the end of 2006 and 2008, the price of corn increased by 125 percent, and the World Bank and other organizations cited the increase in biofuel production as a major contributing factor to the world food price crisis. The 2008 Farm Bill also maintained protectionist measures, such as high tariffs on sugar cane-derived ethanol from Brazil and other countries. Sugar-derived ethanol is more environmentally friendly, cheaper to produce, and does not require the use of a major grain crop.

SEE ALSO *Agriculture and International Trade; Biofuels and World Hunger; Subsidies.*

BIBLIOGRAPHY

Books

Conner, Mary T. *Farm Bill of 2008: Major Provisions and Legislative Action.* New York: Nova Science Publishers, 2010.

Johnson, Renee, and Geoffrey S. Becker. *The 2008 Farm Bill: Major Provisions and Legislative Action,* CRS Report for Congress, RL34696. Washington, DC: Congressional Research Service, Library of Congress, 2008.

Owens, Jasper T. *The Farm Bill and Its Far-Ranging Impact.* New York: Nova Science Publishers, 2008.

Renewable Energy Programs in the 2008 Farm Bill. Little Rock: University of Arkansas, Division of Agriculture, Public Policy Center, 2009.

Williams, Elizabeth M., and Stephanie J. Carter. *The A—Z Encyclopedia of Food Controversies and the Law.* Santa Barbara, CA: Greenwood, 2010.

Periodicals

"The Farm Bill—A Harvest of Disgrace." *The Economist* 387, no. 8581 (2008): 61.

"The Farm Bill—Long Time in Germination." *The Economist* 386, no. 8573 (2008): 52.

"Farm Bill Reduces Support for Corn Ethanol." *Nature* 453, no. 7193 (2008): 270.

Posey, Lee. "The Farm Bill: Planting Farm, Rural and Food Assistance Policy for America." *Legisbrief* 16, no. 37 (2008).

Web Sites

"2008 Farm Bill Side-by-Side." *U.S. Department of Agriculture Economic Research Service (USDA/ERS).* http://www.ers.usda.gov/FarmBill/2008/ (accessed September 26, 2010).

Joseph P. Hyder

Food Critics and Ratings

Introduction

Since the mid-twentieth century, food reviews have played a prominent role in the success or failure of restaurants. Nearly every major newspaper features restaurant reviews by staff food critics. In the 1980s, restaurant guides, including the *Michelin Guide* and *Gayot*, began to exert greater influence over the culinary scene. In the second decade of the twenty-first century, the success of restaurants and chefs depends largely on food ratings and reviews. Globally, the restaurant industry generates accounts for more than $500 billion in revenue annually.

With differing standards of taste and the ability of restaurant reviews to make or break chefs and restaurants, restaurant reviews and guides have received considerable criticism from chefs, restaurateurs, and gourmets over methodology and perceived bias. Critics of food reviews and guides accuse the publications of showing bias for a traditional cuisine or placing too heavy of an emphasis on décor or service. Some restaurant guides also have been accused of applying different standards in different countries.

Historical Background and Scientific Foundations

The first true restaurants emerged in China in the eleventh century during the Song Dynasty (960–1279). These restaurants, which developed from inns and teahouses visited by travelers, featured a selection of food that diners could chose from written menus. In Europe, inns and taverns continued to provide diners with a single, set-price meal. True restaurants did not develop in Europe and the United States until the late eighteenth and early nineteenth centuries.

The first professionally-written restaurant reviews appeared around the mid– to late nineteenth century. A January 1, 1895, article in *The New York Times*, "How We Dine," details the editor-in-chief tasking an unnamed journalist to dine in New York City's restaurants and write reviews for the newspaper. The journalist dined at both Astor House and Delmonico's for his first assignment. By the late nineteenth century, major newspapers carried at least occasional reviews of local restaurants.

In 1900 André Michelin (1853–1931), co-founder of tire manufacturer Michelin, published a guide for motorists that included locations and information on service stations, mechanics, inns, and restaurants for French motorists. In 1926 the *Michelin Guide* began rating superb restaurants with a star. In the early 1930s the *Michelin Guide* implemented the three-star system still in use in the twenty-first century.

In the second half of the twentieth century, increased ease and frequency of air and road travel raised consumer demand for food guides. In 1965 Henri Gault (1929–2000) and Christian Millau (1929–) launched the *Gault Millau* guide of French restaurants. The *Gault Millau* guide focuses solely on the quality of food and rates restaurants on a scale of one to twenty points. In the United States, André Gayot, who worked with Gault and Millau, launched *Gayot Guides* in 1981. In the 1990s the Internet opened a new venue for food critics and consumers to share restaurant reviews and ratings.

Impacts and Issues

The *Michelin Guide*, the standard bearer for restaurant guides for nearly a century, in particular, has attracted a chorus of criticism since the year 2000. Many chefs and restaurateurs have questioned the *Michelin Guide* over its well-known propensity for secrecy. Whereas secrecy of reviewer's identity is vital for an objective and impartial review, most guides give some indication of the methodology and criteria used to rate restaurants. The *Michelin Guide*, however, does not disclose the criteria used by inspectors to differentiate between one-, two-, and three-star restaurants. Chefs argue that the lack of guidance prevents them from altering their cuisine, décor, or service to satisfy the preferences of Michelin reviewers.

A number of food critics also fault the *Michelin Guide* for perceived bias. Many highly respected restaurants did not receive stars when Michelin released its 2006 New York City guide, the first edition for the city.

New York food critics claimed that the guide was biased towards French cuisine. When Michelin released the first guide for Japan two years later, Japan became the country with the most Michelin stars. Western chefs argued that inspectors used more lax standards in Japan and did not require the same innovative cuisine that inspectors seem to reward in the West.

Many French chefs and gourmets argue that Michelin and other guides favor traditional French cuisine over innovative new French cuisine, leading many of these chefs and gourmets to embrace the Le Fooding movement. Le Fooding is a loosely defined-movement that promotes reinventing French cuisine with innovative techniques adopted from the United States and other countries.

Pascal Rémy, a former Michelin inspector, intensified such criticism with the 2004 release of his book

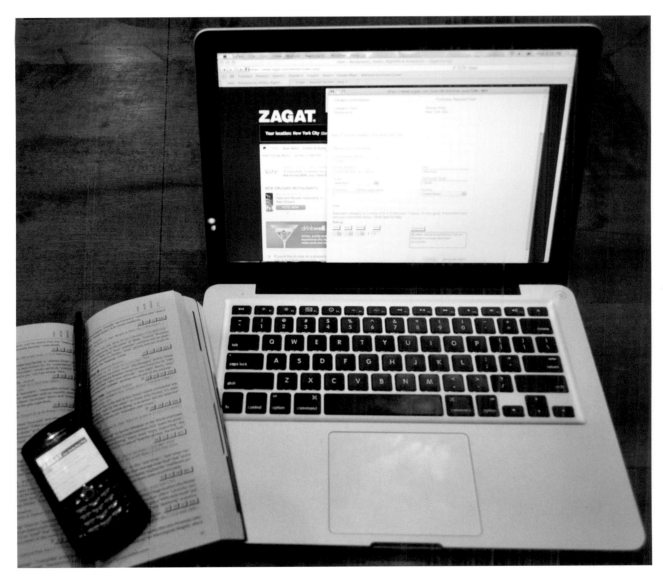

A computer screen shows the website for Zagat, a restaurant review organization, which compiles its reviews and ratings from voluntary public contributors. Diners can complete surveys of restaurants, search reviews, and chat with other reviewers on Zagat's website. Zagat publishes annual city-by-city restaurant guidebooks and mobile applications. *Ellie Lerner / Lerner & Lerner / LernerMedia Global Photos.*

L'Inspecteur se met à table (The inspector sits down at the table), Rémy stated that Michelin reviewers visited restaurants listed in the France guide only once every three and one-half years, not every 18 months as claimed by the Michelin Guide. Rémy also asserted that the Michelin Guide favors certain chefs and restaurants. Later, in an interview, Rémy said that Michelin has used the *Michelin Guide* to raise the company's profile in foreign markets by generously awarding stars. *Michelin Guide* executives deny Rémy's claims.

The rise of consumer-based reviews, however, has diminished the reliance on professional food critic reviews and guides. The *Zagat Survey*, launched in 1979 by Tim Zagat (1940–) and Nina Zagat (1942–), collects restaurant ratings and reviews from customers. Initially the Zagat Survey only covered restaurants in New York City, but as of 2010 Zagat guides collect reviews from more than 375,000 diners and cover more than 100 countries. The Internet has also given consumers another outlet for sharing restaurant reviews: Websites such as Yelp, eGullet, Mouthfuls, and Chowhound enable users to post reviews, rate restaurants, and use social media to communicate with friends and other users.

■ Primary Source Connection

Salon staff writer Dwight Garner interviewed Ruth Reichl about three years into Reichls' career as a restaurant critic at *The New York Times*. Reichl has had a food-related career spanning more than thirty years. Reichl is a published author and also has worked as a food editor.

Palate Revolt

"War of the Times' dining divas." That's the screaming headline the New York Post recently placed atop a "Page Six" item about Ruth Reichl, the current New York Times restaurant critic, and her predecessor Bryan Miller. The Post had obtained a bootleg copy of a letter that Miller—a culinarily conservative Francophile—had written to Reichl's boss at the Times, complaining about her reviews. "How do you think she comes off giving SoHo noodle shops 2 and 3 stars?" Miller wrote. "SHE HAS DESTROYED THE SYSTEM that Craig [Claiborne], Mimi [Sheraton] and I upheld."

Miller's kvetching is fascinating not only because it's great gossip, but because it indicates how wonderfully subversive Reichl's three-year tenure at the Times has been. Gone are the days when only old-school French restaurants such as Lutece, La Grenouille and Aureole ranked highly in the Times' zero-to-four star rating system. Merely by eating the way most food-happy people in New York do—Chinatown one night, a French restaurant the next, a tiny-but-miraculous Greek place in Queens the next—Reichl has been a real democratizing force. "I think everybody knows what a four-star experience is supposed to be," Reichl told Salon in an interview last week. "But the two and three stars are different …It's very hard to compare a great chef in a Chinese restaurant with a great chef in a French restaurant where they're spending $100,000 a year on flowers.…"

DWIGHT GARNER: One of the most remarkable reviews you've written, I think, was of Le Cirque, the well-known French restaurant. It was a kind of dual review, about how you were treated once they recognized you versus how you were treated when they didn't.

RUTH REICHL: Since I wrote that review, I've gotten letters from people saying, "Couldn't you do this for every restaurant in New York?" The reason I did it for Le Cirque is that I'd been coming to New York for years and been treated like dirt there. In the food community, people would say, "Do you want to go to Le Cirque?" And then they would add, "I'm not known there." This happens in a lot of restaurants, but this one was almost proud about it. "We treat the rich better." It was so ridiculous. They just opened themselves up to it.

On one of my visits there, I had dinner with [longtime Times editor and current London Bureau Chief] Warren Hoge, who had hired me, and he said, "I'll make the reservation. They don't know me." So he made the reservation in his own name, and they seated us at this apparently not-good table. Halfway through the meal, Sirio [Maccioni, Le Cirque's owner] came rushing over. He didn't recognize Warren, but somebody had said to him, "That's Warren Hoge." And he wanted to move us. He said, "So-and-so just said, 'How could you seat Warren Hoge behind the glass?'" It was shameless. It was like, "We've given you a bad seat; we've made a terrible mistake; please let us move you."

GARNER: Did you move?

REICHL: We said, "Don't be ridiculous. We're not giving up the table during our dinner." And I thought, well, this is great. Clearly, I'm going to do this. I'm going to go a few times, where he doesn't know me, and I'm going to write about this.

GARNER: That must happen often, where you are recognized mid-meal and the owner's eyes pop open.

REICHL: Yeah, it happens. But people are usually too smart to come rushing over and say, "Oh my God, we've given you the wrong table . . .!"

GARNER: Do you ever walk out of a restaurant just feeling sort of . . . I don't know, debauched?

REICHL: I'll tell you, last night I was at a meal where we had a porterhouse for two for $75 and it came with nothing else. So you're talking about a lot of money. You come outside and you see some homeless person standing on the street, and it doesn't feel great. And I can tell myself, well, I'm just doing my job. Interestingly, people don't say this about fashion. There's some way in which, because it's food, it's very close to the bone. Why aren't people asking that about movies, when each costs $100 million, and an actor is making $20 million in salary? It's precisely because food is so important to us that people are asking these kind of questions, and I think they're legitimate questions. I wouldn't want to be a person who didn't pay attention to it.

Ruth Reichl
Dwight Garner

REICHL, RUTH, INTERVIEW WITH DWIGHT GARNER. "PALATE REVOLT." *SALON.COM*. NOVEMBER 18, 1996. HTTP:// WWW.SALON.COM/NOV96/INTERVIEW961118.HTML (ACCESSED DECEMBER 30, 2010).

SEE ALSO *Advertising Food; Celebrity Chef Phenomenon; Food and the Internet; Food Fads; Foodways; Movies, Documentaries, and Food; Social Media and Food.*

BIBLIOGRAPHY

Books

Blank, Grant. *Critics, Ratings, and Society: The Sociology of Reviews.* Lanham: Rowman & Littlefield, 2007.

Damrosch, Phoebe. *Service Included: Four-Star Secrets of an Eavesdropping Waiter.* New York: William Morrow, 2007.

Greene, Gael. *Insatiable: Tales from a Life of Delicious Excess.* New York: Warner Books, 2006.

Periodicals

Ferguson, Priscilla. "Michelin in America." *Gastronomica: The Journal of Food and Culture* 8, no. 1 (2008): 49–55.

Olson, Kory. "Maps for a New Kind of Tourist: The First Guides Michelin France (1900–1913)." *Imago Mundi* 62, no. 2 (2010): 205–220.

Stringam, Betsy B., John Gerdes, and Dawn Vanleeuwen. "Assessing the Importance and Relationships of Ratings on User-Generated Traveler Reviews." *Journal of Quality Assurance in Hospitality & Tourism* 11, no. 2 (2010): 73–92.

"Taste Everyone's Restaurant Critic on Chowhound." *Maclean's* 123, no. 13 (2010): 62.

Web Sites

Gayot: The Guide to the Good Life. http://www.gayot.com/restaurants/ (accessed October 30, 2010).

"Restaurant Reviews: Personal Experience vs. Professional Opinions." *OpenTable*, May 27, 2009. http://blog.opentable.com/2009/restaurant-reviews-personal-experience-vs-professional-opinions/ (accessed October 30, 2010).

Ruby, Jeff. "Why the Professional Restaurant Critic Will Survive the Age of Yelp." *Chicago Mag.com*, October 2010. http://www.chicagomag.com/Chicago-Magazine/October-2010/The-Professional-Restaurant-Critic-in-the-Age-of-Yelp/ (accessed October 30, 2010).

Zagat. http://www.zagat.com/ (accessed October 30, 2010).

Joseph P. Hyder

Food, Drug, and Cosmetic Act of 1938

■ Introduction

The United States Federal Food, Drug, and Cosmetic Act of 1938 (52 US Stat. 1040, also called FFDCA or FDCA) granted regulatory authority to the U.S. Food and Drug Administration (FDA) to ensure the safety of many foods, medicinal drugs, and cosmetics manufactured or sold within the United States. Although the law has been amended several times since its adoption, the 1938 act established the framework scheme upon which current U.S. food safety laws, regulations, recommendations, and enforcement are built.

FFDCA seeks to make customers better informed about the products they buy and to protect customers against adulterated, impure, or potentially dangerous products. The act requires that product labeling accurately describe the product itself and list most of the product's contents. Labeling requirements also stipulate that consumers be warned if a product contains potentially harmful or reactive substances.

To improve the overall safety and purity of products, the 1938 FFDCA and its subsequent amendments provide for inspections and testing of various products, allowing the FDA to promulgate safety standards for different types of products. The FDA is permitted to regulate hygiene and manufacturing standards for food, drug, and cosmetic producers. It can test various products or mandate that products are verified as safe through a series of scientific trials. If adulterated or contaminated products are located, the act authorizes government regulators to seize or recall the defective products or to oversee a manufacturer's voluntary recall of their products.

■ Historical Background and Scientific Foundations

The United States Federal Food, Drug, and Cosmetic Act of 1938 was a revision of the Pure Food and Drug Act of 1906 (34 Stat. 768), a law enacted on the same day as its companion bill, the Federal Meat Inspection Act. The two pieces of legislation were the first U.S. laws to address the federal government's role in preventing the adulteration of food, addition of intoxicating ingredients, and unsanitary conditions in the food processing industry that had been brought to light by worker strikes, Progressive Era reformers, journalists, and authors. The 1906 act required that all foods and drugs sold across state lines had to carry accurate labels indicating the presence and dosages of then popular medicinal substances including alcohol, cocaine, heroin, morphine, and cannabis (marijuana)—all of which were common additives to popular patent medicines of the day.

The Pure Food and Drug Act of 1906 was amended several times before being replaced. In 1914 the Harrison Act made illegal the sale of several of the narcotic drugs that had been common ingredients in patent medicines. Whereas now-illicit narcotics and stimulants disappeared from commonly sold medicinal remedies, manufacturers continued to use potentially dangerous ingredients without sufficient product testing or consumer warnings.

In 1937 U.S. pharmaceutical corporation S.E. Massengill developed and sold a mixture it called "elixir sulfanilamide" as a readily-available medicinal drug (similar to preparations now considered over-the-counter drugs). Elixir sulfanilamide consisted of flavorings and a sulfa drug dissolved in the colorless, odorless, and sweet-tasting solvent diethylene glycol (DEG). The company performed no tests of the product on animals or humans. No regulations existed mandating per-consumer testing of mass-market remedies.

Within a month of the first sales of elixir sulfanilamide, there were reports of deaths linked to the medicine. The FDA then tested the product and discovered it contained the toxic solvent. More than 100 deaths were attributed to elixir sulfanilamide, though the company chemist who developed the product claimed that he did not know of DEG's toxicity to humans. An investigation and a trial followed the elixir sulfanilamide scandal, and public outrage pushed government officials to consider

WORDS TO KNOW

ACT: A statute, rule, or formal lawmaking document enacted by a legislative body or issued by a government.

COSMETICS: A product that by direct application to the skin, nails, lips, or hair of a person is intended to promote attractiveness by cleansing, enhancing, or otherwise altering appearances.

REGULATION: Controlling behaviors, business practices, or industrial practices through rules restrictions or laws to encourage preferred outcomes or prevent undesired outcomes that may otherwise occur.

SULFA DRUGS: A group of synthetic organic compounds, derived from sulfanilamides, that are limitedly capable of inhibiting bacterial growth. Sulfa drugs were the first and most effective antibiotics used before the discovery and development of the more effective penicillin.

stricter and broader regulation of drugs, food products, and cosmetics.

In 1938 Congress passed New York Senator and homeopathic physician Royal S. Copeland's (1868–1938) proposed Food, Drug, and Cosmetic Act. Among its numerous consumer safety safeguards, the law mandated that companies perform safety tests on their proposed new drugs and submit their findings to the FDA for approval before selling new products marketed as medicines, remedies, or drugs.

Because the 1938 act was adopted after the elixir sulfanilamide incident, Massengill was required to comply only with the weaker provisions of the 1906 act that was then in place. The corporation was fined for calling the mixture an elixir, a term that the 1906 law stipulated was reserved only for preparations containing alcohol.

■ Impacts and Issues

The 1938 version of the FFDCA has been amended several times in the decades following its adoption. However, core elements of the 1938 act remain in place. Almost all amendments to the original FFDCA have strengthened and expanded the role of federal regulations over food, drugs, and cosmetics. Few such products in the twenty-first century enter the stream of commerce—intrastate, interstate, or international—without a significant, science-based demonstration of their overall purity, safety, and efficacy.

The Wheeler-Lea Act, also passed in 1938, granted regulatory authority to the Federal Trade Commission (FTC) to oversee advertising of FDA-regulated products. The FTC continues to promulgate advertising rules that stipulate what companies can truthfully claim about their product's usefulness, purity, and efficacy and in what media they can advertise their products.

The 1951 Durham-Humphrey Amendment classified medications into the now-familiar two categories of legend (prescription) and over-the-counter (OTC). Medications that were habit-forming, contained potentially harmful ingredients, or caused severe negative side effects were prohibited from being dispensed without a doctor's order.

The FDCCA was further strengthened by the 1958 "Delaney Clause" Food Additives Amendment that required FDA approval of food additives including colorings and flavorings. The FDA was prohibited from permitting the sale of any food found to cause cancer in required, preliminary animal testing.

From 1957 until 1961, thalidomide was sold as a sedative and prescribed for pregnant women suffering from severe morning sickness (chronic nausea). The drug, which was heavily used in Europe, was discovered to cause severe birth defects including malformed and missing limbs; it possibly affected up to 20,000 victims. In 1962 an amendment required drug manufacturers to prove that their products were not only safe, but that they were also effective. The law required U.S. manufacturers and importers to evaluate the safety of their products as well as research and disclose their potential side effects before gaining FDA approval for sale.

The FFDCA was also amended in 1997, by which time it covered the regulation of food, food additives, drugs, cosmetics, and also medical devices, biological products (including genetically modified organisms, or GMOs), bottled water, and homeopathic medicines (so long as they are listed in the *Homeopathic Pharmacopoeia of the United States*).

SEE ALSO *Food Inspection and Standards; Pure Food and Drug Act of 1906; Truth in Labeling; U.S. Food and Drug Administration (FDA).*

BIBLIOGRAPHY

Books

Carpenter, Daniel P. *Reputation and Power: Organizational Image and Pharmaceutical Regulation at the FDA.* Princeton, NJ: Princeton University Press, 2010.

Food Litigation & Regulation. Denver, CO: CLE in Colorado, 2007.

Periodicals

Borchers, Andrea T., Frank Hagie, Carl L. Keen, and M. Eric Gershwin. "The History and Contemporary Challenges of the US Food and Drug Administration." *Clinical Therapeutics* 29, no. 1 (2007): 1–16.

Carpenter, Daniel, and Gisela Sin. "Policy Tragedy and the Emergence of Regulation: The Food, Drug, and Cosmetic Act of 1938." *Studies in American Political Development* 21, no. 2 (2007): 149–180.

Web Sites

"The 1938 Food, Drug, and Cosmetic Act." *U.S. Food and Drug Administration (FDA).* http://www.fda.gov/AboutFDA/WhatWeDo/History/ProductRegulation/ucm132818.htm (accessed October 15, 2010).

"Food Standards under the 1938 Food, Drug, and Cosmetic Act: Bread and Jam." *U.S. Food and Drug Administration (FDA).* http://www.fda.gov/AboutFDA/WhatWeDo/History/ProductRegulation/ucm132892.htm (accessed October 15, 2010).

Adrienne Wilmoth Lerner

Food Fads

■ Introduction

Food fads and their attendant folklore are a cultural phenomenon in countries worldwide. Food fads range from fad diets, such as the Grapefruit Diet, macrobiotic diets, the Master Cleanse and fasting regimens, to the popularity of specific foods such as civet coffee, made from coffee beans harvested from the feces of the cat-like civet in southeast Asia. Food fads involving specific trends have focused on processed foods since the mid-twentieth century in developed nations, as new food science processes combine with advertising pushes to create new food memes. Legends surrounding food fads include the (false) concepts that drinking soda pop and while eating either the candy Pop Rocks or Mentos could make the stomach explode.

Food has become a form of entertainment in the United States in the twenty-first century, from the "foodie" movement to the creation of Food Network and the Food Channel, television channels devoted to food topics. Reality television shows about chefs, kitchens, and cooks dominate the airwaves, while food shows and commercials promote food fads such as pancake batter in an aerosol can, supplement-enhanced foods,

and high-protein Greek yogurt. Few food fads convert into mainstream dietary staples; Jell-O's 1918 debut of coffee-flavored Jell-O was among the many unsuccessful products that attempted to enter the market. Advertising in the food industry is part of the impetus for food fad creation, with major food manufacturers and restaurant chains spending more than $11.2 billion in 2004 to promote both new and old products.

■ Historical Background and Scientific Foundations

Food production changed in the 1920s as factory food production, canning, and freezing techniques improved. Advertising expanded as a service to businesses seeking to reach out to new customers and markets. The intersection of improved food production methods and advertising, along with marketing scope expansion, led to the creation of some food products designed to be novelties. For instance, Jell-O debuted new flavors and a range of recipes that were intended to encourage housewives to incorporate the gelatin product into dishes. Jell-O was touted in magazines such as *Ladies Home Journal* in advertisements labeling it "America's most famous dessert," eventually expanding its flavors to include fads such as tomato, celery, Italian, and mixed vegetables. The Jello-mold dessert, in which a Bundt cake pan is used to mix Jell-O and various fruits, vegetables, or other ingredients, was a popular fad food in the 1950s through 1970s.

Processed foods from the 1950s onwards ushered in the era of TV dinners, cheese in a can, flower-flavored PEZ candies, candy cigarettes, and more. In 1953 both Swanson TV dinners and Cheez Whiz hit American grocery store shelves, inspiring a host of imitators. With large advertising budgets and promotion in newspapers and magazines, on radio shows and the newly-emerging television shows, these food fads replaced older staples such as non-processed meats, vegetables, and starches. Frozen, freeze-dried, and compartmentalized meals and foods were also popular, as technologically-altered food products from the American space program made their way into the marketplace. The 1960s also saw the explosion of fast food outlets, initially a fad, that eventually became a staple of the diets of many Americans.

One of the most famous unsuccessful food fads occurred in 1985, when the Coca-Cola company introduced New Coke. The formula made new Coke sweeter, and consumers and critics alike panned the drink, causing a negative media storm that led to New Coke's demise. Coca-Cola's historically savvy advertising department stumbled and, as Michael Blanding notes in his book *The Coke Machine*, "Anguished calls and letters came pouring into Coke headquarters—more than 400,000 by the end of the ordeal." Coca-Cola company executives came to refer to the day New Coke debuted as "Black Tuesday." Responding to public pressure, the company re-introduced the original flavor as Coke Classic, to be sold as an alternative choice alongside New Coke; consumers so overwhelmingly purchased the Classic version, however, that New Coke was limited to sales in selected areas and finally was dropped quietly from the product line in 2004. Five years later the company discontinued the "Classic" moniker, and the last reminder of the product's distinction from New Coke became part of Coca-Cola's storied past.

At the end of the twentieth century and into the second decade of the twenty-first century, food fads focused on novelty, convenience, and health. Pancake batter in an aerosol can—even an organic version—hit supermarket shelves. Frozen crustless peanut butter and jelly sandwiches took the simple PB&J and made it foolproof. Heinz introduced colored ketchup, with purple and green selections; the products were pulled in 2006 due to low sales. Enhanced foods, such as eggs with extra omega-3 fatty acids, additional probiotics in yogurt, or bottled water with vitamins added took the concept of enrichment to extremes by the end of the first decade of the 2000s.

■ Impacts and Issues

Food fads are possible only in countries with an abundance of staple foods and strong food security. Food writer Michael Pollan (1955–) notes that food faddism may be a function of America's immigrant past: Without one unifying food tradition in the United States, the public clings to the latest advertised food product and the popularity of the food fad functions as a substitute for collective dietary traditions. In addition, living in a developed country with economic stability leads to the treatment of food as a frivolous, trivial item to be turned into an object of fun and entertainment.

Anchovy oil in orange juice is just one of the many versions of nutritionally enriched items shoppers can

IN CONTEXT: REDISCOVERED INGREDIENTS BECOME FADS

Chefs, always on the lookout for creative ways to combine new flavors occasionally rediscover and popularize ingredients that have traditionally been overlooked. For instance "ramps," early spring vegetables that are also called wild leeks, have become an extremely popular ingredient to feature on menus while they are in season. In several cities around the globe, as soon as the first harvest of ramps comes in, one can see ramp specials pop up on dozens of menus almost simultaneously. They are so popular that many chefs pickle or otherwise preserve ramps when they are fresh so they can feature ramps on their menu after they have gone out of season and other restaurants stop serving them. As of 2010 this fad is still growing in popularity, perhaps aided by the fact that as ramps are only available in early spring, the public is tiring of the fad more slowly.

IN CONTEXT: TOWERING FOOD

Culinary fads often tend to be subject to a chef's individual methods or styles. One example of such a food fad could be the plating style (how food is arranged on the plate) of many high-end restaurants in the late 1990s. At that time it was very popular for chefs to manipulate their food by raising it as high as possible off of the plate. Using ring molds, piping bags, and other methods, chefs would shape and stack food to give it a tall, artistic look. Some preparations could reach a height of as much as one foot (30.5 cm). This fad did not last long for practical reasons: Plating in this style made the dishes delicate and difficult for the server to carry; they were difficult for the diner to eat; and they were oftentimes expensive to produce.

choose when searching for foods for optimal health. Tropicana's Heart Healthy orange juice includes omega-3 fatty acids via anchovy and sardine oil, whereas Wonder Headstart Bread includes the same fish oil to give consumers a healthy boost from eating bread. Chickens are fed diets rich in flaxseed to produce extra-strong omega-3 eggs, and pasta companies such as Ronzoni add calcium to products to boost nutritional value and gain market share. This recent type of food fad is ever-changing as companies scramble to keep up with the latest nutrition research to introduce products that meet perceived consumer concerns.

Food fads change continually, evolving and declining both rapidly and slowly. In early 2010, bacon-flavored items dominated food shelves, including bacon-flavored salt, bacon-flavored chocolate, "baconnaise," and even

A grocery store in Kailua, Hawaii, displays low carbohydrate products. Low carbohydrate products were popular food fad diet in the early-
and mid-2000s. *AP Images.*

bacon-infused vodka, a trend that waned within the year. Adding the energy drink Red Bull to a flavored vodka was a popular alcoholic drink in the early twenty-first century. Some food fads are inspired by movies: The Harry Potter series launched a real-life candy version of Bertie Bott's Every Flavor Beans, jelly beans with flavors such as booger, grass, soap, vomit, and ear wax. The fictional candy has strong real-life sales and increases in popularity just after the premiere of each new Harry Potter book or movie. In the year after the 2009 debut of the film *Julie and Julia*, French cuisine made at home became a renewed trend, and Julia Child's *Mastering the Art of French Cooking* became a best-seller more than 40 years after its publication.

SEE ALSO *Advertising Food; Celebrity Chef Phenomenon; Fast Food; Food and the Internet; Food Styling; Foodways; Functional Foods; Movies, Documentaries, and Food.*

BIBLIOGRAPHY

Books

Bannerman, Colin. *Seed Cake and Honey Prawns: Fashion and Fad in Australian Food.* Canberra: National Library of Australia, 2007.

Lovegren, Sylvia. *Fashionable Food: Seven Decades of Food Fads.* New York: Macmillan, 1995.

Pollan, Michael. *The Omnivore's Dilemma: A Natural History of Four Meals.* New York: Penguin Press, 2006.

Periodicals

Fitzpatrick, Mike. "Food Fads." *Lancet* 363, no. 9405 (2004): 338.

"Food—the Latest Fad in Healthy Food Additives Is Good Wishes. Can Meals "Embedded" with Love Actually Make You Feel Better?" *Time,* April 6, 2009: 58.

"Gourmet Food Trends: Mighty Special." *The Progressive Grocer* 86, no. 6 (2007): 88–91.

"Health—Got Milk? How Safe Is the Newest Food Fad—Raw Milk?" *Current Science* 93, no. 8 (2007): 10.

Linden, Erik, David McClements, and Job Ubbink. "Molecular Gastronomy: A Food Fad or an Interface for Science-Based Cooking?" *Food Biophysics* 3, no. 2 (2008): 246–254.

Mellentin, Julian. "Why the Beauty Food Fad Is Finished." *Dairy Industries International* 74, no. 3 (2009): 14–15.

"The Top 10 Functional Food Trends." *Food Technology* 62, no. 4 (2008): 24–44.

"The Trends—How the Housewares Show Provokes Food Trends." *Food Processing*, May 2008: 14.

"Trends Food Miles." *Marketing Week*, August 24, 2006: 28–30.

Web Sites

Food Trends. http://www.foodtrends.com/ (accessed October 25, 2010).

Olver, Lynne. "Popular Twentieth-Century American Foods." *Food Timeline*. http://www.foodtimeline.org/fooddecades.html (accessed October 25, 2010).

Steel, Tanya. "Epicurious's Top 10 Food Trends for 2010." *Shine.yahoo.com*, November 30, 2009. http://shine.yahoo.com/channel/food/epicuriouss-top-10-food-trends-for-2010-549297 (accessed October 25, 2010).

Melanie Barton Zoltan

Food First

Introduction

Food First is a movement aiming to eliminate the injustices that cause hunger. The term "Food First" originated from the organization of the same name, also known as the Institute for Food and Development Policy, based in Oakland, California. The Food First idea was predicated on the subject of the organization's first publication, *Food First: Beyond the Myth of Scarcity* (published in 1977), and to this day, the movement continues to assess ways that economic globalization impacts the food system and jeopardizes access to sufficient and nutritional food. By definition, Food First addresses a broad spectrum of issues that hit the food and hunger agenda from policy to practice, technology to trade, and markets to social movements.

Historical Background and Scientific Foundations

Hunger exists everywhere in the world, not only in the poorest countries: Hunger and malnutrition kill a staggering 9 million-plus people worldwide each year. Approximately 1.2 billion others live and suffer from hunger and micronutrient deficiencies. In the United States, the Department of Agriculture (USDA) reported that in 2006, 35.5 million people lived in households considered to be food insecure. By contrast, however, 98 percent of the world's hungry people live in developing countries.

The causes of hunger are far greater than the net difference between the levels of food production and meeting consumption demands in a given region: They are related to the causes of poverty. In fact, one of the major causes of hunger is poverty itself. People living in poverty do not have enough money to buy or produce sufficient food for themselves and their families. In turn, they tend to be weaker and cannot produce enough to buy more food. In short, the poor are hungry and their hunger traps them in poverty.

At the same time, food waste is a shocking 40–50 percent in the United States and 30–40 percent in the United Kingdom. In some parts of Africa, 25 percent of crops go bad before they can be eaten, mainly due to a lack of technology and infrastructure as well as insect infestations, microbial growth, damage, and high temperatures and humidity.

Food First addresses these underlying issues of hunger, poverty, and waste, including globalization, inequitable policies in global trade, insufficient investments in food workers and agricultural infrastructure, and insufficient protection and stewardship of land and nutrition.

Impacts and Issues

Underpinning the central concept of globalization, more and easier access to foreign goods, are a multitude of alterations at the global level including capital expansion, trade expansion or trade liberalization, cultural integration, financial liberalization, increased information and technology flows, increased labor mobility, and changing consumption patterns. It is difficult to disaggregate the various effects of globalization on food and hunger. In developing countries, however, trade liberalization was jumpstarted by structural adjustment policies (SAPs). SAPs are essentially the conditions under which countries secure loans from the International Monetary Fund (IMF) and the World Bank. These conditions (or conditionalities) in principle aim to help reduce the borrowing country's fiscal imbalances and enable the borrowing country to become more market oriented, which in turn boosts the economy. Conditionalities tend to be free market policies and programs such as privatization and deregulation and the reduction of trade barriers. However, critics argue that financial threats to poor countries correlate to blackmail, and that poor nations have no choice but to comply.

Land reform is also an issue in many countries that currently have vast inequities. Whereas there are

A subsistence farmer in Lesotho holds recently harvested carrots. Food First supports subsistence farming efforts around the world. *Kim Haughton / Alamy.*

competing visions for what land reform should look like, grassroots movements across the globe are making some headway to democratize access to land. The land grabs in Africa, which have become a headline issue within the food security arena, have now also raised the profile of land policy issues from the grassroots level to the national and international level. Brazil's Landless Workers Movement, Movimento dos Trabalhadores Rurais Sem Terra (MST), for example, with an estimated 1.5 million landless members from 23 of the 27 states, is one of the largest social grassroots social movements in Latin America. In Brazil almost half of the land on which crops can be grown is controlled by 1.6 percent of the landowners. MST carries out land reform, such as winning land titles for more than 350,000 families in 2,000 settlements.

Unjust policies also impact developed country workers. In the United States, some 17 percent of all jobs are in the food sector, and these tend to be the lowest paid and most under-protected jobs in the nation. Food workers, a significant number of whom are undocumented immigrant workers, subsidize the food industry by paying the social and economic cost of labor injustice. They are sometimes exploited and criminalized, and many go hungry themselves.

In the long-term, improved agricultural output offers the quickest fix for poverty and hunger according to the UN Food and Agriculture Organization (FAO). Food First looks to highlight where this is not being done concurrent with justice and stewardship of the environment, supporting similar social movements from slow food to food sovereignty, and looking to prevent further spreading the roots of hunger.

SEE ALSO *Agricultural Land Reform; Ethical Issues in Agriculture; Food Security; Food Sovereignty; Free Trade and Agriculture; Hunger; Subsistence Farming.*

BIBLIOGRAPHY

Books

Bread for the World Institute. *A Just and Sustainable Recovery: Hunger 2010: 20th Annual Report on the State of World Hunger.* Washington, DC: Bread for the World Institute, 2009.

Desmarais, Annette, Nettie Wiebe, and Hannah Whitman, eds. *Food Sovereignty: Reconnecting Food Nature and Community* Oakland, CA: Institute for Food & Development Policy, 2010.

Food and Agriculture Organization (FAO) of the United Nations. *The State of Food Insecurity in the World 2009: Eradicating World Hunger.* Rome: FAO, 2009.

Stanford, Claire. *World Hunger.* Bronx, NY: H. W. Wilson, 2007.

Web Sites

Food First: Institute for Food & Development Policy. http://www.foodfirst.org/ (accessed October 9, 2010).

"Hunger." *World Food Programme.* http://www.wfp.org/hunger (accessed October 9, 2010).

Melissa Carson

Food Inspection and Standards

■ Introduction

Food inspections in the United States began with meat packing facilities in an attempt to better ensure the safety of processed foods. Inspection seeks to identify dangerous practices or products in a food processing facility. In an effort to improve marketing through product differentiation, food standards (also called grades and standards or sorts) evolved as a way to provide information quickly about food quality to buyers and consumers. These standards are sometimes simply marketing labels and not always an indicator of food safety. Hazard Analysis and Critical Control Point (HACCP) has become the world's primary method of evaluating food safety risks and of implementing solutions and inspections. However, even an excellent food safety system cannot eliminate all risk of foodborne illness. Whereas regulatory authorities and inspectors increasingly rely on HACCP, a wide range of voluntary private sector standards have emerged to assist consumers with choices in the increasingly diverse food marketplace.

■ Historical Background and Scientific Foundations

Food standards serve two purposes. First, they help ensure food safety. Stretching back to the early twentieth century in the United States, standards originally focused on meatpacking plants and slaughterhouses. Partially in reaction to an exposure of the conditions at meatpacking plants in a novel by American novelist Upton Sinclair (1878–1968) titled *The Jungle* published in 1906, the Federal Meat Inspection Act of 1906 established the first mandatory standards and mandatory government inspection for the purpose of food safety in the United States. The system of visual inspection for foreign materials and for sick animals dominated food safety regulation during the twentieth century. The second purpose of food standards is to differentiate and segment markets for food

products, in order to better market the products. Grades and standards, sometimes called sorts, for marketing purposes first appeared in the United States under the Grain Inspection Act of 1916. Currently government-run and private-sector standards help consumers make a wide variety of choices in the food marketplace.

Visual inspection can eliminate some animal disease risk, but many microbial pathogens cannot be seen by the human eye and thus by an inspector. Laboratory tests are necessary to identify these pathogens and their prevalence. In the 1960s, while adapting food to be used by astronauts aboard missions for the National Aeronautics and Space Administration (NASA), the Pillsbury company developed a quality and safety control system that focused on scientific risk analysis, improving performance, and slowly eliminating risk of pathogens. This system became Hazard Analysis and Critical Control Point (HACCP), and as early as 1972 the World Health Organization (WHO) declared HACCP to be the most scientific and rigorous approach to food safety regulation and inspection. The main risks of cross-contamination or of situations that may encourage microbial growth are identified through risk assessment, also called hazard analysis. These critical points in the supply chain or in a processing facility are carefully monitored, and processes are improved to limit risks. For example, if storage temperature is critical, a processor may choose to include in the HACCP plan taking hourly measurements of the temperature in a storage facility and then monitoring samples to ensure that low temperatures eliminate pathogens to an acceptable level of risk. HACCP became mandatory for some processed foods in the European Union starting in 1991 and for meat in the United States in 1996. Many governments use HACCP as their food safety inspection system, but government-mandated HACCP plans are likely only to meet existing food safety standards and not exceed them.

Governments also have a long history of setting standards for use in marketing, though usually producers are not required to follow these; they are strictly voluntary.

Setting standards may not intuitively appear to lead to better prices for food items and higher profits. However, when products are graded, or rather sorted, by size, color, and other characteristics, the higher quality product can then be sold to consumers in retail outlets at a high price with lesser-graded products sold to a processor or kept for consumption by the household. Government-determined grades and standards seek to do the same on a larger scale, and these systems are often voluntary and sometimes paid for by the farmer or processor.

Many different grades and standards are used around the world, including those set by the U.S. Department of Agriculture (USDA), the European Union (EU) standards, the Japanese Standards Association (JIS) standards, and the Gosstandart system used in Russia and some other areas formerly part of the Soviet Union. In an effort to create uniform standards in 1964, the Codex Alimentarius Commission, usually referred to simply as Codex, was established with assistance of the Food and Agriculture Organization (FAO) of the United Nations and the World Health Organization (WHO). Codex is an effort to create a single international set of food

A Chinese woman cries while she struggles with police and officials who are confiscating her equipment during a raid on an illegal bean curd shop, in Wuhan, in central China's Hubei province. European Union officials says that China must take action to lower the number of safety violations among its food exports. Critics assert Chinese officials target small vendors who often do not export their products instead of large corporations. *AP Images*

WORDS TO KNOW

CROSS-CONTAMINATION: The movement of a pathogen or potentially dangerous or uncooked material from one surface to another. For example, if a cook uses the same knife to cut raw chicken and a tomato, the tomato may become cross-contaminated with a pathogen from the raw chicken.

SUPPLY CHAIN: All of the steps between a raw material and the final consumer.

THIRD-PARTY CERTIFICATION: A system in which an organization independent of all the companies in a supply chain certifies that a good complies with particular standards or has particular attributes. Most international organic standards, fair trade standards, claims of being not genetically modified, and a variety of environmental claims are certified using third-party certification.

standards for all nations covering voluntary standards, marketing standards, and food safety standards. Having a single set of standards is intended to facilitate more trade between countries and buyers.

■ Impacts and Issues

Despite inspection systems and food safety standards implemented around the world, foodborne illness remains common. The U.S. Centers for Disease Control (CDC) estimate that 5,000 deaths can be attributed to foodborne illness every year in the United States. A regulatory and inspection system, even a very rigorous HACCP plan, cannot exclude all risks. One hundred percent certainty, also called zero tolerance, of foodborne illness would be enormously expensive. In fact, the safer a system, the more expensive will be the inspection, regulation, and quality control. In addition to the problems posed by inherent risk of foodborne illness, innovation in the food industry creates new challenges for food safety. Foods with a longer shelf life or new ready-to-eat food products pose additional risks that may not be addressed in current standards. However, one of the most significant areas of risks for food safety remains outside of the realm of regulatory inspection and standards: How consumers wash, prepare, and cook foods at home provides plenty of opportunity for cross-contamination, undercooked food, or insufficient cleaning, which fail to eliminate the pathogens that cause foodborne illness. Of course, new pathogens pose new challenges also. For example, bovine spongiform encephalopathy (BSE, also known as mad cow disease) spreads through particular proteins called prions, which are not easy to spot in food processing and cannot be eliminated by good hygienic procedures when preparing beef or beef products at home. Meat from BSE-contaminated animals that made it into the marketplace gave rise to the epidemic of the human form of mad cow disease, called variant Creutzfeldt-Jakob Disease (vCJD), in England beginning in 2000.

While food trends challenge food safety through new products and new venues of food consumption, consumers have started to demand a wide range of food attributes. Standards have been developed for these. Private sector standards, often certified through third-party certification, a voluntary, non-governmental inspector who assures adherence to standards, have proliferated since the 1990s. For example, many supermarkets in Europe use the GlobalGAP standard to increase the quality and safety of the foods they purchase. Products that are certified organic, fair trade, or biodynamic also tend to be done on a voluntary basis with a third party certifier. In addition, businesses around the world have started to become certified as adherents to the International Organization for Standardization (ISO) standards. The proliferation of voluntary, private sector food standards provides more choices and information to consumers, but at the same time, proliferation of standards may confuse consumers who are unaware of what adherence to each standard entails.

SEE ALSO *Center for Food Safety and Applied Nutrition; Consumer Food Safety Recommendations; Food Additives; Food Irradiation; Food Recalls; Food Safety and Inspection Service; Foodborne Diseases; Import Restrictions; Mad Cow Disease and vCJD; Meat Inspection Act of 1906; Pasteurization; Poultry Products Inspection Act of 1957; Produce Traceability; Pure Food and Drug Act of 1906; Reportable Food Registry.*

BIBLIOGRAPHY

Books

Hoffmann, Sandra A., and Michael R. Taylor. *Toward Safer Food: Perspectives on Risk and Priority Setting.* Washington, DC: Resources for the Future, 2005.

Lawley, Richard. *Food Safety and Traceability Strategies: Key Hazards, Risks and Technological Developments.* London: Business Insights, 2010.

Luning, Pieternel A., Frank Devlieghere, and Roland Verhe, eds. *Safety in the Agri-Food Chain.* Wageningen, The Netherlands: Wageningen Academic Publishers, 2006.

Pampel, Fred C. *Threats to Food Safety.* New York: Facts on File, 2006.

Risk-Based Food Inspection Manual. Rome: Food and Agriculture Organization of the United Nations (FAO), 2008.

U.S. Institute of Medicine, Forum on Microbial Threats. *Addressing Foodborne Threats to Health: Policies, Practices, and Global Coordination.* Washington, DC: National Academies Press, 2006.

Periodicals

Chyau, James. "Casting a Global Safety Net—a Framework for Food Safety in the Age of Globalization." *Food and Drug Law Journal* 64, no. 2 (2009): 313–334.

"Food for Thought." *Nature* 445, no. 7129 (2007): 683–684.

Maki, Dennis G. "Coming to Grips with Foodborne Infection—Peanut Butter, Peppers, and Nationwide Salmonella Outbreaks." *The New England Journal of Medicine* 360, no. 10 (2009): 949–953.

"Reforming the Food Safety System: What If Consolidation Isn't Enough?" *Harvard Law Review* 120, no. 5 (2007): 1345–1366.

Web Sites

"Hazard Analysis Critical Control Point System (HACCP)." *World Health Organization (WHO).* http://www.who.int/foodsafety/fs_management/haccp/en/ (accessed September 25, 2010).

International HACCP Alliance. http://www.haccpalliance.org/sub/index.html (accessed September 25, 2010).

USDA: Food Safety and Inspection Service. http://www.fsis.usda.gov/ (accessed September 25, 2010).

Blake Jackson Stabler

Food Irradiation

■ Introduction

Food safety is of concern in both the developed and developing world. Microbial contamination of food can arise from unsanitary or defective food processing or storage, or during preparation. Many commercially prepared food products undergo some treatment to reduce or eliminate potential pathogens. One such process is irradiation.

Food irradiation, although not a widespread practice, is used to treat a variety of processed foods. It is especially effective when a long shelf life without refrigeration is required. In all forms of food irradiation, the product is bombarded with ionizing radiation, which is highly destructive to living cells. Depending on the type of ionizing radiation used, its intensity, and the treatment time, foods may be essentially "pasteurized" (not all organisms are killed) or made sterile.

The kinds of electromagnetic radiation employed for food processing include gamma rays, x rays, and ultraviolet (UV). Electron beams are also used. Which type is chosen for a particular application depends on the physical state, shape, and size of the product, as well as its chemical makeup.

Electromagnetic radiation and electron beams kill cells by disrupting and dislodging the electrons that form chemical bonds in a wide range of biomolecules including DNA. Free oxygen radicals may also be formed, which react rapidly to damage cells they come in contact with.

■ Historical Background and Scientific Foundations

Irradiation as a means of destroying harmful microorganisms in foods has been investigated in the United States since the 1920s, when researchers found it was effective in killing the roundworm Trichinella, the causative agent of trichinellosis in pigs. Milk treated with UV radiation was provided in prisoner-of-war meal packages during World War II. From the early 1960s onward in the United States, more and more foods have been approved for irradiation treatment including wheat flour, white potatoes, herbs and spices, fruits and vegetables, poultry, and other meat products.

Gamma rays are the highest energy and most lethal form of electromagnetic radiation. Their high energy makes gamma rays highly penetrating, capable of processing entire pallet loads of food at once. Although this makes for efficient processing, a radioactive source such as Cobalt 60 or Cesium 137 is required. A radioactive source can never be turned off, so it must remain shielded at all times to protect nearby workers. Heavy shielding is also required around the food product during irradiation.

X rays are also a form of high energy electromagnetic radiation. Only gamma rays are more energetic than x rays. X rays are well absorbed by dense materials, whereas less dense materials allow them to pass. Most foods are relatively transparent to x rays so x rays penetrate deeply to kill microbes. This is convenient for treating foods in bulk quantities. X rays, produced by striking a metal surface with an electron beam, are emitted when electrons in the metal are promoted to higher energy states, and then fall back to their ground state, releasing their energy as x rays. Although no radioactive materials are needed to produce x rays, significant shielding is required to protect workers from operating x ray food processing equipment.

Electron beams consist of electrons accelerated in a vacuum from the tip of a hot filament. Such a beam is easily controlled and involves no radioactivity. A relatively small amount of shielding is needed to protect workers from electrons that may escape the processing chamber. Electron beams kill cells the same way high energy electromagnetic waves do, by collision with the electrons of biomolecules to disrupt chemical bonds and induce abnormal bonding. Unlike gamma or x rays, electrons have relatively low penetrating power and are only effective in cases in which the product is a few centimeters thick. Electron rays are also sometimes used to internally inspect food and food packages for foreign objects or matter.

WORDS TO KNOW

BREMSTRAHLUNG: Electromagnetic energy given off by an electron that passes near a positively charged nucleus.

ELECTROMAGNETIC RADIATION: A phenomenon consisting of oscillating magnetic and electric waves existing at right angles to each other. Waves with shorter wavelengths (higher frequencies) have higher energies.

ELECTRON BEAM: A focused stream of electrons emitted from the hot filament of an electron gun.

GAMMA RAYS: Electromagnetic radiation of wavelengths from about 0.003 to 0.03 nanometers.

ULTRAVIOLET: Electromagnetic radiation of wavelengths from about 100 to 400 nanometers.

X RAYS: Electromagnetic radiation of wavelengths from about 0.03 to 3 nanometers.

One limitation and potential danger of electron beams is the phenomenon known as *bremstrahlung*. *Bremstrahlung* results from the conversion of a portion of a high velocity electron's kinetic energy to electromagnetic energy when the electron encounters a nucleus. This electromagnetic radiation has a very high energy, comparable to that of x rays. The intensity of the *bremstrahlung* increases with both the atomic number of the atoms in the target material and the energy of the electron beam. At energies sufficiently above 1 million electron volts, radioactivity may be induced in the target substance. In practice, beam energies much lower than this are sufficient for processing foods.

Although UV lamps offer a relatively easy and inexpensive method of killing bacteria and other pathogens in food, the low penetrating power of UV rays limit them in practice. Ultraviolet radiation is useful in processing liquid foods that are not too opaque, which can be passed through a treatment chamber in a thin stream (e.g., water, juices, liquid egg whites). One advantage touted by proponents of UV food processing is that it achieves results comparable to pasteurization, without the use of heat, thus better preserving the texture and flavor characteristics of the product.

■ Impacts and Issues

The effectiveness of radiation in killing pathogens in processed foods is not in question. Not all foods can be subjected to ionizing radiation, however, and still remain palatable. Shellfish, meats with high fat content,

The edible, tangy, peach-like, white flesh of a freshly halved mangosteen waits to be eaten. Fresh mangosteens are rare in the United States, as they are difficult to transport ripe from their growing areas in Asia. The United States banned importation of non-irradiated mangosteens over concerns over Asian fruit-flies, but permits irradiated mangosteens from Thailand *Joseph Hyder / Lerner & Lerner / LernerMedia Global Photos.*

A box of Indian mangoes, which are now available on the U.S. market. When an irradiation technique that neutralizes a pest indigenous to Indian mangoes was approved in 2007, the drippingly sweet fruit became available for the first time in U.S. stores. The mangoes must be carefully packed to avoid damage, so the Indian fruit can cost up to five times as much as its Latin American cousin. *Image copyright Sid B. Viswakumar, 2010. Used under license from Shutterstock.com.*

and products containing an appreciable egg white component do not fare well. Irradiation tends to reduce the concentration of some vitamins by a slight amount.

No radioactivity is created in properly irradiated foods, and the destruction of spoilage organisms, along with the primarily targeted pathogens, also increases shelf life. Irradiated foods generally do not contain more hazardous compounds than foods processed in other ways. The act of cooking itself induces profound chemical changes in foods to a much larger degree than does irradiation. Both human and animal studies have revealed no ill effects from consuming irradiated food.

However, the safety of foods that have been bombarded with ionizing radiation remains a concern, more so in Europe than in the United States. The U.S. Centers for Disease Control and Prevention takes the position that irradiated foods do not contain dangerous substances when proper processing procedures are followed (for example, keeping the energy of electron beams below the level that would create *bremstrahlung*-induced radioactivity).

Some foods, especially those that contain a high fat content such as meats, have been found to contain elevated concentrations of 2-alkylcyclobutanones (2-ACBs) after irradiation. The concentration of 2-ACBs is higher when higher energies of radiation are used for processing. Some studies indicate 2-ACBs are carcinogenic in rats. These studies have prompted groups such as Public Citizen and the Center for Food Safety to petition the U.S. Food and Drug Administration to halt further approvals of radiation processing until more research is done. Attempts in the U.S. Congress to pass legislation requiring labeling of irradiated foods have thus far been unsuccessful.

Beginning in 2007, after twenty years of being banned over a concern about seed weevils, the Alphonso variety of mangoes from India started appearing in U.S. grocery stores. It was only after the implementation of radiation treatment that the FDA deemed the mangoes safe for import. Gamma irradiation is effective in killing the larvae of seed weevils, fruit flies, and other pests that may inhabit the fruit. Mango aficionados are not deterred by the "treated by irradiation" stickers that appear on many (but not all) of the mangoes and are pleased to have access to them, as Indian mangoes are considered to be some of the best-tasting in the world. Other consumers are concerned that they may be eating irradiated mangoes without their knowledge.

SEE ALSO *Embargoes; Food Safety and Inspection Service; Free Trade and Agriculture; Produce Traceability; World Trade Organization (WTO).*

BIBLIOGRAPHY

Books

International Atomic Energy Agency (IAEA). *Irradiation to Ensure the Safety and Quality of Prepared Meals: Results of the Coordinated Research Project.* Vienna: International Atomic Energy Agency, 2009.

Sommers, Christopher H., and Xuetong Fan. *Food Irradiation Research and Technology.* Ames, IA: Blackwell, 2006.

Periodicals

"Food Irradiation: A Technology Wasted or Simply Unwanted?" *Food Engineering and Ingredients* 33, no. 2 (2008): 16–19.

"How It Works: Food Irradiation." *Restaurant Business* 106, no. 8 (2007): 74.

Kume, Tamikazu, et al. "Status of Food Irradiation in the World." *Radiation Physics and Chemistry* 78, no. 3 (2009): 222–226.

McCally, Michael, and Martin Donohoe. "Irradiation of Food." *The New England Journal of Medicine* 351, no. 4 (2004): 402–403.

Mostafavi, Hossein A., Hadi Fathollahi, Farahnaz Motamedi, and Seyed M. Mirmajlessi. "Food Irradiation: Applications, Public Acceptance, and Global Trade." *African Journal of Biotechnology* 9, no. 20 (2010): 2826–2833.

Web Sites

"Food Irradiation." *U.S. Centers for Disease Control and Prevention (CDC).* http://www.cdc.gov/ncidod/dbmd/diseaseinfo/foodirradiation.htm (accessed September 11, 2010).

"Irradiation and Food Safety." *Food Safety and Inspection Service, U.S. Department of Agriculture (USDA).* http://www.fsis.usda.gov/Fact_Sheets/Irradiation_and_Food_Safety/index.asp (accessed September 11, 2010).

Roy, Sandip. "Indian Mangoes—Now in America." *National Public Radio (NPR),* June 11, 2009. http://www.npr.org/templates/story/story.php?storyId=104881449 (accessed September 11, 2010).

Philip McIntosh

Food Packaging

Introduction

The majority of food sold to consumers in developed countries is packaged in plastic, glass, metal, paper, or paperboard containers. Food packaging is a convenient way for consumers to purchase food in measured portions. It also provides an easy method by which food producers may transport food products to consumers. Labels attached to food packaging identify food products and communicate information about products, including ingredients, nutrition, and point of origin.

Food packaging serves an important role in decreasing food spoilage rates and preventing contamination, protecting food from chemical and biological agents that cause food to deteriorate more rapidly. Packaging also reduces damage to food from bruising, breakage, and other physical abuse that destroys food or causes it to spoil more quickly. However, food packaging does generate waste that ends up in landfills unless consumers recycle.

Historical Background and Scientific Foundations

Throughout most of pre-industrial history, food was not packaged for sale. People in pre-industrial societies used baskets or jars to store food at home. Although most food was consumed near where it was produced, food producers and merchants used containers, the earliest of which were pottery vessels, to store and transport food. The oldest known pottery vessel was produced in southern China about 18,000 years ago. The invention of the potter's wheel in Mesopotamia between 6000 and 4000 BC facilitated the manufacture of pottery vessels to supply the growing household and commercial demands for pottery in emerging cities.

Around 4800 BC, Chinese potters began to manufacture amphorae—ceramic vessels with two handles and a long, narrow neck. By 3500 BC, amphorae were adopted by traders in the Middle East. The ancient Greeks and Romans used amphorae as the primary means to transport wine, olive oil, and other food products. Amphorae remained an import vessel for food transport until the seventh century AD.

People continued to use jars, typically sealed with cork or wax, as the primary means of food packaging until the late eighteenth century. In 1795 the French army offered a 12,000-franc reward for the development of an improved method of storing and preserving food to feed soldiers, because spoilage and food poisoning had become a major concern. In 1810 the French inventor Nicolas Appert (1749–1841) published an essay describing a method of placing cooked food in glass jars, sealing them, and submerging the jars in boiling water. French Emperor Napoleon Bonaparte (1769–1821) awarded Appert the 12,000 francs for his invention. The boiling-water canning method remains a common form of food preservation, especially among home canners.

Also in 1810, English scientist Peter Durand modified Appert's canning method by replacing fragile glass jars with iron containers. Durand invented a process to rust-proof the iron cans with a thin layer of tin. English industrialist Bryan Donkin (1768–1855) purchased Durand's patent and began producing canned food, primarily for the English army and navy. By the late nineteenth century, improvements in the canning process resulted in canned products that the emerging European and American middle class could afford. Companies, including Nestlé and Heinz, began producing canned products for home consumption. By the early twentieth century, manufacturers began using lighter-weight materials for cans. In the 1960s Reynolds and Alcoa developed processes to manufacture the all-aluminum can still used in the early twenty-first century.

In the middle and late twentieth century, plastic became one of the most important food packaging materials. Although some plastics were developed in the nineteenth century, most plastic products were used primarily by the military. After World War II (1939–1945), improvements in plastics production methods increased

WORDS TO KNOW

CANNING: A method of food preservation in which food is heat processed and sealed in a vessel.

FOODBORNE ILLNESS: An illness caused by the consumption of contaminated food that has usually been improperly stored, handled, or prepared.

POLYETHYLENE TEREPHTHALATE (PET): Also known as PET, polyethylene terephthalate is a lightweight, rigid polymer resin that is widely used for food and beverage containers.

the commercial production of plastics. Jacques Brandenberger (1872–1954), a Swiss scientist, developed cellulose plastic, also known as cellophane, in 1900. Cellophane, which is derived from wood pulp or natural fibers, became a popular food packaging material in the 1950s. In the late 1950s, heat-shrinkable plastic film became a popular choice for "shrink wrapping" meats and other products. In the late twentieth century, food manufacturers began using polypropylene, polyethylene, and polyethylene terephthalate (commonly abbreviated PET or PETE) as food packaging materials.

■ Impacts and Issues

Modern food packaging plays an important role in promoting food safety as many foods are processed and then shipped across great distances to consumers. Food packaging preserves food and ensures that food is safe and wholesome when it reaches the consumers. Foods that are free of contaminants after processing must be placed in packaging that ensures that the food remains contaminate-free for days, weeks, months, or even years. In this regard, food packaging not only maintains food safety, but it also prolongs the shelf life of products. In developing nations where little food is packaged, food loss rates may reach 30 to 50 percent.

Food packaging provides protection from chemical, biological, and physical forces that cause food deterioration. The presence of air, moisture, and light cause many food products to deteriorate more rapidly. Food packaging provides a barrier against these chemical agents, while also preserving food quality by preventing pathogens, insects, and rodents from accessing the food. At the same time, food packaging protects food products from physical damage that may compromise the quality and safety of food products. Fragile food products, such as eggs, fruits, and vegetables, benefit from being transported in food packaging that protects them from

International snack food companies use clearly branded packaging so that their food is recognized worldwide. Aside from label text appearing in the local language, a package of Oreo cookies (shown here) looks largely the same in any country. *Joseph Hyder / Lerner & Lerner / LernerMedia Global Photos.*

A grocery store in Miami, Florida, displays packaged breakfast cereal. Information on the food packaging helps shoppers determine ingredients and nutritional information, but the materials create waste if they are not properly recycled. © *Jeff Greenberg / Alamy.*

physical harm that may increase the rate of spoilage or likelihood of contamination.

Food packaging communicates important information about food products to consumers and health officials. Food package labels identify the food product to consumers, and labels and packaging shapes serve as powerful marketing tools for food producers. Ingredient and nutritional labels on food products, which are required by law in most countries, inform consumers about the ingredients contained in the product and important nutritional information. Labels and stamps on food packages also provide important information that enables health officials to trace a food product to its point of origin. This information is useful for tracing the dissemination of contaminated products and issuing food recalls in the event of an outbreak of foodborne illnesses.

Despite the advantages of food packaging in protecting human health and preserving food, food packaging produces enormous quantities of municipal solid waste that must be recycled or end up in landfills. Almost all packaging materials—glass, metals, plastics, paper, and paperboard—are recyclable. In 2005 U.S. consumers generated approximately 68 million metric

tons (75 million short tons) of containers and packaging. U.S. consumers recycled about 27 million metric tons (30 million short tons) of this waste, while the remaining 41 million metric tons (45 million short tons) went to landfills. Packaging manufacturers have also lightened packaging over the past several decades to save money and lessen the environmental impact of packaging. Since 1975 aluminum beverage cans use more than 25 percent less aluminum, and steel cans use 40 percent less steel than in 1970. Plastic soda bottles and plastic milk jugs have reduced plastic usage by 25 and 30 percent, respectively, since the late 1970s.

SEE ALSO *Bisphenol A; Bottled Water; Diet and Cancer; Food Allergen Labeling and Consumer Protection Act of 2004; Waste and Spoilage.*

BIBLIOGRAPHY

Books

Chiellini, Emo. *Environmentally Compatible Food Packaging.* Boca Raton, FL: CRC, 2008.

Gustafsson, Kerstin *Retailing Logistics & Fresh Food Packaging: Managing Change in the Supply Chain.* London: Kogan Page, 2006.

IN CONTEXT: PACKAGING AND PREVENTION STRATEGIES

The U.S. Food and Drug Administration (FDA) and such agencies as the Centers for Disease Control and Prevention (CDC) collaborate on a variety of issues for which expertise in viral and bacterial identification and in tracking down sources of infection may advance understanding of disease outbreaks and enhance food safety and security. Incidents of product contamination must be investigated to determine whether the tainting is unintentional or the result of deliberate product tampering. In some cases popular, but unintended—and sometimes dangerous—uses of food products occur, and changes to the packaging of a product can become a part of public awareness strategies to overcome such uses.

For example, CDC scientists identified a strain of the bacterium *E. coli* O157:H7 found in contaminated cookie dough that was responsible for an outbreak of disease in the United States in late June 2009. By June 30, 2009, more than 70 people in 30 states were thought to have been infected with *E. coli* O157:H7 derived from the same product source. *E. coli* contamination in food is capable of causing serious illness that can result in kidney failure and death. Officials with the CDC and the FDA warned consumers "not to eat any varieties of prepackaged Nestlé Toll House refrigerated cookie dough due to the risk of contamination with *E. coli* O157:H7." The manufacturer and marketer, Nestlé USA, recalled the cookie dough line. A contaminated sample of the cookie dough was found at Nestlé's facility in Danville, Virginia, on June 25, 2009. Nestlé's Toll House brand products were re-released in August 2009 after testing, cleaning, and monitoring of production facilities. New packaging warns consumers not to eat the product raw, a popular but unintended use of the cookie dough.

Han, Jung H. *Innovations in Food Packaging*. San Diego, CA: Elsevier Academic, 2005.

Hargreaves, Ben. *Eat Me: Delicious, Desirable, Successful Food Packaging Design*. Mies, Switzerland: RotoVision, 2004.

Hargreaves, Ben. *Successful Food Packaging Design*. Crans-Près-Céligny, Switzerland: RotoVision, 2006.

Lee, Dong S., Kit L. Yam, and Luciano Piergiovanni. *Food Packaging Science and Technology*. Boca Raton, FL: CRC Press, 2008.

Morris, Scott A. *Food Packaging Engineering*. Ames, IA: Blackwell, 2006.

Web Sites

"Food Ingredients & Packaging." *U.S. Food and Drug Administration (FDA)*. http://www.fda.gov/Food/FoodIngredientsPackaging/default.htm (accessed October 30, 2010).

Lombardi, Candace. "Compostable Food Packaging on its Way to Europe." *Green Tech*, September 15, 2010. http://news.cnet.com/8301-11128_3-20016471-54.html (accessed October 30, 2010).

Joseph P. Hyder

Food Patents

Introduction

The increasing application of patent law to cover agricultural products and processed foods has become a controversial issue in both agriculture and intellectual property law. A patent is a government grant to an individual or organization that confers an exclusive right to produce, use, or sell an invention for a certain time period. Patents encourage innovation by enabling inventors to recoup their investment in research and development and realize a profit from a new invention.

Standard patent laws cover the use of newly developed processes used to produce food products. Standard patent laws also cover the development of crops or other food products that utilize genetically modified organisms (GMOs). Many nations, including the United States, have implemented laws that also allow for the patentability of plants and cultivars that have existed for centuries. The use of food patents raises a number of issues related to the cross-pollination of conventional crops with GM crops, the patentability of functional foods, and the impact of patented crops on indigenous peoples.

Historical Background and Scientific Foundations

The granting of patents dates to about the fifth century BC, when the Greek city-state Sybaris guaranteed all profits from a new invention to its inventor for one year. In 1474 the Republic of Venice instituted a patent scheme that resembles modern patent systems. The Venetian system required inventors to submit their invention to the government in order to gain the right to exclude others from producing the invention. In 1623 England enacted the Statute of Monopolies, which permitted inventors to receive patents for new inventions. In the early eighteenth century the English government imposed the requirement that patent applicants submit a written description of their invention. Most modern patent statutes retain this requirement.

Despite more than two millennia of patent laws, the first patent for a plant was not granted until the twentieth century. The Plant Patent Act of 1930 allows for the patenting of plants in the United States. The first plant patent was issued to Henry F. Bosenberg of New Brunswick, New Jersey, in 1931 for a climbing rose variety that bloomed throughout the year. U.S. patent law provides for the patentability of plants that have been invented or discovered, reproduce asexually, and represent a new variety of plant. The new plant variety requirement applies to cultivated sports, hybrids, mutants, and newly found seedlings. Tuber-propagated plants and plants discovered in an uncultivated state, however, are not patentable. Patent laws in the United States grant 20 years of exclusive use to the patent holder. Many nations including Australia and European Union (EU) members have plant patent systems similar to that of the Unites States. China, however, does not recognize plant patents.

Although U.S. patent laws do not cover plants that reproduce sexually, the Plant Variety Protection Act of 1970 (PVPA) provides similar protections to breeders of sexually-reproducing plants. The PVPA grants 25 years of exclusive use to breeders of sexually-reproducing plants that are new, distinct, uniform, and stable sexually-reproducing varieties, including tuber-propagated plants.

Patents on food products may also fall under a country's utility patent laws. Generally, in order to receive a patent from a patent granting agency, the inventor must satisfy all of the standards for patentability expressed by law. Most patent laws require the patent applicant to meet four requirements of patentability: The invention must be of patentable subject matter, be novel, be nonobvious, and be useful or have an industrial application. Some nations without specific plant patent laws may regulate the patentability of plants under utility patent laws. These patents also cover the patentability of transgenic and genetically modified (GM) plants. Utility patents also cover special processes used in food production.

WORDS TO KNOW

BIOPIRACY: Claiming patents in existing plant and animal species in order to restrict their use.

FUNCTIONAL FOOD: Also known as nutraceuticals, functional foods are food, beverage, or nutritional supplement products that contain additives with purported medicinal or health benefits.

GENETICALLY MODIFIED FOOD: Genetically modified (GM) foods are foods that contain or are derived from genetically modified organisms (GMOs), or organisms in which genetic material has been manipulated through genetic engineering.

Generally, livestock is not patentable subject matter under patent laws, except for genetically modified organisms (GMOs).

■ Impacts and Issues

The issue of food patents remains a controversial topic because of the potential impact of patent infringement issues on the livelihood of farmers and other food producers. The proliferation of GM foods is the most significant food patent issue to evolve over the last several decades. GM foods are foods that contain or are derived from GMOs, organisms that have had their genetic material manipulated through genetic engineering so that the organism expresses preferred traits, such as drought resistance, increased yields, or herbicide resistance. GM foods were introduced in the early 1990s. Corn, canola, and soybeans are commonly produced GM foods.

Agricultural companies that develop and sell GMOs rely on profiting from their patented product during the protection period granted under patent law. Farmers traditionally save seed to plant the following growing season, but because seed saving would infringe on the GMO manufacturers' ability to sustain profits, GM manufacturers typically prohibit seed saving under licenses that farmers sign when they purchase GM seeds. Under these agreements, farmers have a contractual duty to return or destroy seeds at the end of the season. Such license agreements are legal and valid under both patent and contract law.

Intellectual property issues arise, however, when GM plants from one farmer's field cross-pollinate or drift onto an adjacent farmer's field of conventional crops. Studies indicate that this form of cross-pollination, known as outcrossing, can occur over great distances. In 2007 the U.S. Department of Agriculture (USDA) fined Scotts Miracle-Gro Company when modified genetic material from a new variety of GM grass was discovered in the genetic material of conventional grasses located up to 13 miles (21 km) from the company's testing area.

In 2004 Monsanto Canada, Inc., sued Canadian farmer Percy Schmeiser (1931–) for patent infringement after Roundup Ready Canola, a GM crop produced by Monsanto, was discovered in Schmeiser's field. Schmeiser had discovered the GM plants on his property and saved some of the seeds for the next planting season. The Supreme Court of Canada ruled in favor of Monsanto and determined that Schmeiser had violated Monsanto's right to exclusive use under Canadian patent law.

Patent issues also arise in areas related to the production and sale of functional foods. Functional foods, also referred to as nutraceuticals, are patentable under the patent laws of most countries. Functional foods are food, beverage, or nutritional supplement products that contain additives with purported medicinal or health benefits. The range of functional foods includes probiotics, vitamin- and mineral-fortified products, products that claim to boost metabolism, and digestive aids. Thousands of functional food products have been patented around the world. Roughly one-quarter of all functional food patents are issued in Japan, even though Europe and the United States are larger markets for functional foods. The popularity of Japan for patenting functional foods is related to the relative ease with which Japan issues patents for functional foods. The patent process in Japan typically requires the applicant to make fewer patent claims, which produces a patent that is broader in scope. A patent claim is a statement made on the patent application that is used to define the scope of the patent.

The World Trade Organization (WTO) Agreement on Trade Related Aspects of Intellectual Property Rights (TRIPS) has produced considerable debate in the international community over plant and other food patents. TRIPS is an international agreement that sets minimum standards for intellectual property protections that WTO member states must extend to other members. TRIPS requires nations to extend at least 20 years of patent protection to products and processes patented in another country. Countries may refuse to extend patent protection to a product if the commercial production of the product is contrary to public order or morality in that nation. Countries may also deny patentability to diagnostic, therapeutic, and surgical methods for the treatment of humans or animals.

Perhaps the most significant patentability exception in TRIPS relates to the extension of patent protection to plants and animals. TRIPS states that a country may deny patentability to plants and animals and essentially biological processes for the production of plants or animals. This exception does not apply to microorganisms. However, any country that denies patent protection to plant varieties must provide an effective, unique system of protection. A patent holder who has a patent excluded under this exception may challenge the denial of protection before the WTO.

The TRIPS requirement that nations extend some form of patent protection to plants patented in another

A farmer sprays herbicide on patented, herbicide-resistant corn plants in Rio Grande do Sul, Brazil. © *Sean David Baylis / Alamy.*

WTO country, either under the auspices of TRIPS or through a unique national system, has produced results that infringe on indigenous rights. Large transnational agricultural corporations have patented numerous plant cultivars used for centuries by indigenous peoples in various nations—a practice termed "biopiracy" by indigenous and human rights activists. In 1997 RiceTec, a U.S. company, received patents from the USPTO on numerous basmati rice lines and grains. Following a major diplomatic row between the United States and India, RiceTec lost or withdrew most of its basmati patents. In 1999 the USPTO granted a patent on a variety of Mexican yellow bean, known as the Enola bean. One of the defining characteristics of the Enola bean was its particular shade of yellow. The patent holder sued numerous importers of Mexican yellow beans, resulting in a 90 percent drop in the sale of Mexican yellow beans. The USPTO eventually overturned the patent on the Enola bean. Although many patent-related issues that infringe on indigenous rights are eventually decided in favor of indigenous farmers, years of legal battles and import-export bans place a financial strain on those farmers.

SEE ALSO *Agribusiness; Agriculture and International Trade; Biodiversity and Food Supply; Biofuels and World Hunger; Commission on Genetic Resources for Food and Agriculture; Ethical Issues in Agriculture; Family Farms; Food Sovereignty; Functional Foods; Genetically Modified Organisms (GMO); U.S. Department of Agriculture (USDA); World Trade Organization (WTO).*

BIBLIOGRAPHY

Books

Blakeney, Michael. *Intellectual Property Rights and Food Security.* Wallingford, Oxfordshire, UK: CABI, 2009.

O'Donnell, Ryan W. *Intellectual Property in the Food Technology Industry: Protecting Your Innovation.* New York: Springer, 2008.

Periodicals

"Biotechnology—Key Patent for Roundup Ready Trait Could Be Revoked." *Food Chemical News* 49, no. 6 (2007): 6.

"Dietary Supplements—Patent Protections Called Key to New Dietary Ingredient Safety." *Food Chemical News* 47, no. 14 (2005): 17.

Mitra, Saswata. "Patent & Food Security—Opening the Pandora's Box." *Journals of Intellectual Property Rights* 13, no. 2 (2008): 145–151.

"Monsanto Alleges Patent Infringement in Pioneer GAT Soybeans." *Food Chemical News* 51, no. 9 (2009): 10.

Taylor, Michael R., and Jerry Cayford. "Changing U.S. Biotech Patent Policy Could Bring Food Security to Sub-Saharan Africa." *Resources* 152 (2004): 3.

Wilson, James. "GM Crops—Patently Wrong?" *Journal of Agricultural and Environmental Ethics* 20, no. 3 (2007): 261–283.

Web Sites

"Farmers Protected against GM Patent Lawsuits." *European Public Health Alliance.* http://www.epha.org/a/3404 (accessed October 28, 2010).

Monsanto vs. Schmeiser. http://www.percyschmeiser.com/ (accessed October 28, 2010).

Shah, Anup. "Food Patents—Stealing Indigenous Knowledge?" *Global Issues,* September 26, 2002. http://www.globalissues.org/article/191/food-patents-stealing-indigenous-knowledge (accessed October 28, 2010).

Joseph P. Hyder

Food Phobias

■ Introduction

Cibophobia, also called food phobia, sitiophobia, or sitophobia, involves an abnormal aversion or fear of eating food. Although food phobias can occur across the lifespan, the diagnostic classification is most often used with children from infancy through pre-adolescence who don't readily fit into other eating disorder classifications. Food phobia generally occurs in previously normally developing infants or young children who have not experienced significant trauma or abuse and who have no major medical issues, but who abruptly refuse to eat. Some also refuse to drink liquids and, in extreme cases, will not even swallow their own saliva. Infants and young children with food phobias often have family members who have been diagnosed with anxiety disorders. This syndrome is distinct from any of the anorexic or bulimic disorders, in that the children do not evidence body image or weight control issues. Sometimes they are pre-verbal. Frequently, the onset is preceded by an episode of choking, nausea, vomiting, or allergic reaction involving tongue or throat swelling. Untreated, food phobias can quickly lead to severe malnourishment and dehydration.

Older children or adults who evidence total food or liquid refusal are typically said to have dysphagia or choking phobia. They are generally able to articulate the cause of the phobia, such as an episode of gagging or vomiting subsequent to ingesting a particular type of food or beverage. In the case of total food or liquid refusal, the need for treatment is urgent in order to avert life-threatening complications.

Beyond preschool age, food phobias are more likely to involve circumscribed eating patterns in which persons report an inability to tolerate specific foods, food categories, types, or textures. They may eat or drink only a very limited range of items. This is sometimes called selective eating or restrictive eating. Food avoidance emotional disorder (also called FAED) is another form of food phobia, in which the individual loses weight but does not meet the clinical criteria for a diagnosis of anorexia nervosa. All of these disorders have a significant anxiety component.

■ Historical Background and Scientific Foundations

The term "food phobia" was coined in the United Kingdom in the 1990s by child psychiatrist Bryan Lask and his associate, clinical psychologist Rachel Bryant-Waugh. They sought to describe a phenomenon they were seeing among young patients who abruptly began refusing to eat without underlying physiological cause. In some patients, the refusal extended to drinking and swallowing.

Historically, there has been a lack of scientific agreement on the diagnosis and etiology of eating disorders among very young children. Although estimates vary across the literature, it is generally argued that from 25 to 40 percent of all infants and toddlers experience some form of feeding disturbance. It is typically transient and resolves without formal intervention.

The *Diagnostic and Statistical Manual of Mental Disorders*, Fourth Edition Text Revision (DSM-IV-TR), considered the standard for psychiatric diagnostic classification, lists three categories of childhood eating disorders: pica, which involves eating non-food items (such as paint, hair, or fabric); rumination disorder, characterized by consistently regurgitating and re-eating the same food; and feeding disorder of infancy or early childhood, involving failure to eat enough to maintain or to gain weight. This is often grouped together with a diagnosis of failure to thrive. Food phobias fall under the heading of specific phobias.

There is a developmentally-based diagnostic classification system for children from birth through age three, called *DC Zero to Three*, developed by the American Academy of Child and Adolescent Psychiatry's Task Force for Diagnostic Criteria: Infants and Preschool. The rubric for diagnosis of eating disorders in the very young is similar to that of Lask and Bryant-Waugh in

WORDS TO KNOW

DYSPHAGIA: Dysphagia refers to experiencing difficulty swallowing.

PARENTERAL NUTRITION: Parenteral nutrition is nutritionally complete feeding delivered directly to the stomach, by means of a tube. For short-term nutritional replacement, the tube is generally inserted through the nose. In patients with severe gagging issues, the tube may be surgically placed into the abdomen, connecting directly to the stomach.

PHOBIA: A phobia is a fear of an object or situation that is sufficient in intensity to cause an individual considerable distress and result in avoidance not only of the feared object but of situations associated with it. For example, a person who has a phobia of drowning might initially avoid large bodies of open water and gradually generalize to pools and beaches, eventually being unable even to pass near fountains or take showers or baths. The fear is invariably disproportionate to its object.

SCIENTIFIC RELIABILITY AND VALIDITY: Reliability refers to the consistency or replicability of a measurement across repetition. A reliable instrument is one that gives the same results for the same object measured at different times. Validity is concerned with the accuracy of a measure and the determination of whether a result accurately reflects what was being measured.

A nineteen-month-old prepares to eat a hot chili pepper at home in Denver, Colorado. As research increasingly suggests a child's first experiences with food shape later eating habits, doctors say battling obesity and improving the American diet may mean debunking myths and broadening babies' palates. *AP Images.*

■ Impacts and Issues

Food phobias and feeding disorders have a significant impact not only on the physical well-being of the individual, but on his or her emotional and social health as well. In virtually every socio-cultural group, eating plays a major role. People with significant feeding restrictions are often unable to participate in social activities because of the actual or potential presence of feared foods or choking possibilities. In their nature and course, food phobias and feeding disorders are far more closely aligned with anxiety disorders than they are with the classic eating disorders (anorexic and bulimic syndromes). In infants and very young children, the phobia is likely to be more generalized than it is with verbal individuals, who can distinguish the specific food or activity that triggered the phobic reaction. The very young are most likely to cease eating or drinking entirely subsequent to a strong fear-evoking event because they lack the capacity to fine-tune the experience. For example, an infant who has a frightening episode of projectile vomiting subsequent to a bout of the stomach flu may associate the choking and gagging accompanying the vomiting with the food most recently eaten rather than with the illness, and become unwilling to swallow formula or any other liquid. An older child or adult who experiences the same event may instead become phobic of the last thing eaten before the onset of the illness, such as a peach or other fuzzy-skinned fruit, but may remain able to eat other previously enjoyed foods.

The individual with a feeding disorder experiences great anxiety around the potential for coming across the feared food, being put into situations where intake of

that the disorders are unrelated to illness or trauma. They use the general term "feeding behavior disorder" to refer to a range of feeding abnormalities associated with failure to eat or drink when the brain and body send signals indicating hunger or thirst.

Most of the academic literature describing feeding disorders in infants and children is not rigorously scientifically- or research-based, consisting primarily of individual clinical case studies. This presents a challenge for the creation of diagnostic categories, because the scientific method dictates extensive, repeated research documenting reliability and validity between raters in order to establish a consistent definition of an observed phenomenon.

Food phobias and feeding disorders cross all age, socioeconomic, ethnic, racial, cultural and geographic boundaries and are described in both the popular and scientific press worldwide. In the United Kingdom, several reality shows were created during the first decade of the twenty-first century detailing the lives of adults living with restricted eating, selective eating, food avoidance emotional disorders, and food phobias. In adults, food phobias often occur alongside or as a part of anxiety disorder or obsessive compulsive disorder. Adults with food phobias are often unusually concerned and fearful of expiration dates or achieving a perceived necessary degree of doneness of their food.

A butcher in Venice, Italy, offers fresh and cured horse meat. While horse meat is common in many diets around the world, consumers in the United States and other nations have an aversion to horse meat. © *Danita Delimont / Alamy.*

the food may be required, choking or being unable to swallow, vomiting and possibly becoming sick or dying as a result of exposure to the feared item(s). In infants and very young pre-verbal children, there is a tendency to generalize from one negative food experience to a fear of all foods or liquids, resulting in complete food refusal.

In the case of total food refusal, treatment is often multi-phased, beginning with an emergent inpatient hospital stay for nutritional replacement via the use of parenteral nutrition and intravenous fluids. Once patients are physiologically and nutritionally stabilized, they generally respond well to cognitive behavior treatment involving changing the ways that individuals think about food coupled with systematic desensitization or graduated exposure, along with intensive nutritional counseling and intervention. Systematic desensitization and graduated exposure both involve the gradual, stepwise exposure to the phobic object, beginning with thoughts of the feared item and progressing through exposure to photographs, viewing the actual item at a distance, moving it gradually closer, smelling it, touching it and eventually advancing to placing it in the mouth, chewing, and swallowing it. Rate of progress depends on the comfort level of the individual. If treated early in the food phobia's development, individuals tend to make good recoveries and are unlikely to relapse.

When individuals who experience specific food phobias that fall short of total refusal are left untreated, they are likely to progress in their restricted eating patterns until they subsist on a small number of foods. They are unable to try new foods and gradually restrict their socialization and interpersonal interactions in order to avoid settings or situation in which they might be exposed to feared foods or pressured to eat in different ways. By adulthood, those with untreated food phobias often develop a range of clinically-significant pathological compensatory behaviors in order to avoid triggering situations. This restrictive lifestyle may render them unable to pursue different work environments or social relationships.

SEE ALSO *Changing Nutritional Needs throughout Life; Eating Disorders; Family Meal Benefits; Therapeutic Diets.*

BIBLIOGRAPHY

Books

American Academy of Child and Adolescent Psychiatry: Task Force for Diagnostic Criteria: Infants and Children. *Diagnostic Classification of Mental Health and Developmental Disorders of Infancy and Early Childhood.* Washington, DC: Zero to Three Press, 2005.

American Psychiatric Association. *Diagnostic and Statistical Manual of Mental Disorders*, 4th ed. text revision. Arlington, VA: American Psychiatric Association, 2000.

Jaffa, Tony, and Brett McDermott. *Eating Disorders in Children and Adolescents*. Cambridge, UK: Cambridge University Press, 2007.

Periodicals

Bryant-Waugh, Rachel, Laura Markham, Richard E. Kreipe, and R. Timothy Walsh. "Feeding and Eating Disorders in Childhood." *International Journal of Eating Disorders* 43, no. 2 (2010): 98–111.

Burklow, Kathleen A., and Thomas Linscheid. "Rapid Inpatient Behavioral Treatment for Choking Phobia in Children." *Children's Health Care* 33, no. 2 (2004): 93–107.

Evers, Catharine, F. Marijn Stok, and Denise T. D. de Ridder. "Feeding Your Feelings: Emotion Regulation Strategies and Emotional Eating." *Personality and Social Psychology Bulletin* 36, no. 6 (2010): 792–804.

Gonzalez, Vivian M., and Kelly M. Vitousek. "Feared Food in Dieting and Non-Dieting Young Women: A Preliminary Validation of the Food Phobia Survey." *Appetite* 43, no. 2 (2004): 155–173.

Web Sites

Bays, Jan Chozen. "Mindful Eating: Rediscovering a Healthy and Joyful Relationship with Food: Fear of Food." *Psychology Today*, February 23, 2010. http://www.psychologytoday.com/blog/mindful-eating/201002/fear-food (accessed September 23, 2010).

Lord, Ashley. "Selective Eating May Be a Food Phobia in Disguise." *Tulane University*, February 6, 2003. http://tulane.edu/news/releases/archive/2003/selective_eating_may_be_food_phobia_in_disguise.cfm (accessed September 23, 2010).

Pamela V. Michaels

Food Preparation Methods

■ Introduction

Food preparation methods transform all the foodstuffs people consume, whether meat, fish, grains, fruits, or vegetables, into something edible. Although food preparation usually involves some form of cooking, it also includes non-heating methods such as chopping of raw ingredients or adding dressing to make a salad. Cooking is done to make food taste better by enhancing its texture, flavor, and aroma. It brings out a food's nutritious value and makes it safe to eat by killing bacteria. Cooking is also necessary to make many foods possible to chew and digest. Modern kitchens have an array of equipment for preparing food for cooking, such as knives and bowls, and other equipment for applying heat to it, such as stoves and ovens. A heating method and cooking vessels are among the tools needed to utilize the main cooking methods, which are frying, baking, roasting, boiling, grilling, smoking, steaming, and microwaving. Each cooking method uses a different form of heat transfer, be it conduction, convection, or radiation. The cooking medium, which could be air, fat, or water, influences the time of cooking and the properties of the cooked food. Newer methods of cooking include solar cooking and enzymatic cooking. People who prepare food themselves know what goes into their meals and, if they choose the right cooking method, will be able to extract maximum nutrition from the food they eat.

■ Historical Background and Scientific Foundations

The first known food preparation methods were grilling and roasting, in which foods were put on or in hot coals, which started soon after the discovery of fire. Since then the evolution of food preparation methods has followed the development of cooking utensils: For instance, the use of clay pots around 10,000 years ago enabled food to be boiled. Different types of cookware allow for different methods of food preparation involving moist heat, such as steaming, as well as dry heat food preparation, such as frying. Baking and roasting came later, as the oven is a relatively sophisticated cooking vessel. The first ovens, used for the baking of bread, appeared around 5,000 years ago in Egypt.

All cooking involves one or more of three methods of heat transfer. Conduction is the transfer of heat through a solid from the hotter object to a cooler object, such as from a gas burner on a stove to the base of a saucepan. Convection of heat occurs when a fluid, liquid, or gas carries heat through currents. An example would be hot air conveyed from an oven to a roasting joint of beef. Finally, radiation is the transfer of heat from a source without any intervening medium. An example would be transfer of heat from a grill to a piece of fish. Because radiation is a rather inefficient method of heat transfer, food to be grilled is generally placed as near to the heat source as possible. Microwave cooking also involves heating of food by radiation: Microwaves heat water molecules in food, and they transfer some of their heat energy to the rest of the food. Heat transfer in various food preparation methods can involve a mixture of more than one of these three methods.

Grilling is suitable for foods such as steaks that need browning on the outside and will cook through within 30 minutes. Besides conventional grilling on a cooker, rotisserie and spit roasting are suitable for very large cuts of meat—even whole animals—and use a mixture of convection from surrounding air currents and radiation from the heat source. Grilling and barbecuing are often confused but the latter involves lower heat and longer cooking, which allows time for the connective tissue in barbecued meat to soften and add moisture. In boiling, braising, and stewing, food is heated by convection currents in hot water. The temperature of these moist heat food preparation methods is limited by the boiling point of water (212°F; 100°C) which is too low for browning. That is why a frying step is necessary to brown meat and vegetables before stewing. Despite the upper

WORDS TO KNOW

BROWNING: The color change that occurs when some foods are heated, progressing from yellow to brown, then black. The chemical reactions responsible for this color change produce new flavors. The dehydration of sugars in food, known as caramelization, and the reaction between proteins and sugars, called Maillard reactions, are the two main browning processes.

COOKING: The transfer of heat to a food by conduction, convention, or radiation. The heat brings about chemical reactions between food molecules that transform the food's texture and flavor.

HEAT: A form of energy that makes molecules travel faster. When heat is transferred to a food, it causes physical and chemical changes that transform the food into a palatable dish.

limit of boiling, it is quite an efficient way of cooking because the entire surface of the food is in contact with the water, enabling rapid cooking.

Sauté frying (as opposed to deep-frying) depends on conduction and convection. The layer of oil between pan and food is too thin to allow for much by way of convection currents. The oil helps bring the uneven surface of, say, a lamb chop or an egg, into good contact with the pan by sealing any gaps. It prevents the food from sticking to the pan surface and burning. Oil also adds some of its own flavor, and because its boiling point is well above that of water, it enables browning reactions, with the accompanying delicious flavors, to take place.

In baking, food is surrounded by a hot container and heated by a combination of radiation from its walls and convection currents in the air inside. Although baking temperatures are typically far above the boiling point of water, baking is nowhere near as efficient a cooking method as boiling because the radiation and convection processes at the temperature of an oven are quite slow. Roasting is similar to baking, but relies more upon radiant heat of the oven acting on the surface of the food to make a dark crust.

■ Impacts and Issues

Mastering food preparation methods gives people more control over what they eat compared to relying on prepared, processed, and fast foods. However, it is important to be aware of what particular cooking methods do to the nutrient content of foods, so that the right choice can be made. Frying adds fat and calories to food, and if the cooking fat is high in saturated fat, such as butter or

A roasted pig on a spit in a wood-burning stove.   *Image copyright Mikhail Nekrasov, 2010. Used under license from Shutterstock.com.*

A cook stir-fries a dish of bean curd and vegetables at a street-side restaurant in China. *Adrienne Lerner / Lerner & Lerner / LernerMedia Global Photos.*

lard, this is not ideal for heart health. Grilling is a healthier option for meat and fish.

Boiling fruits and vegetables can leach vitamin C into the cooking water so cooking times should be as short as possible and the minimum amount of water should be used. It is often assumed that fruits and vegetables should be eaten raw whenever possible, to preserve their micronutrient content. An exception is lycopene, a powerful antioxidant found in tomatoes. Levels of lycopene are higher in cooked tomatoes, including tomato sauce and ketchup because it is soluble in oil. In limited research, lycopene from cooked tomatoes was shown to reduce the cell damage that can otherwise lead to certain cancers, especially prostate cancer. However, the U.S. Food and Drug Administration states that such claims of health benefits are premature, given the limited evidence.

Some cooking methods can create health hazards. In grilling and barbecuing, fat dripping from the meat onto the flames may send up a sooty residue that coats the surface of the meat with carcinogenic polycyclic aromatic hydrocarbons. This can be avoided by trimming the fat off the meat first. Browning reactions may also produce carcinogens if meat is allowed to blacken. Also, in developing countries where inefficient wood, dung, or other open-fuel burning cookstoves are used, more than two million people die each year from exposure to pollutants from cookstove smoke. Children are particularly vulnerable to pneumonia caused by fumes from cookstove smoke.

SEE ALSO *Building Better Ovens; Center for Food Safety and Applied Nutrition; Consumer Food Safety Recommendations; Cooking, Carbon Emissions, and Climate Change; History of Home Cooking; Molecular Gastronomy; Raw Foodism; Street Food; Sustainable Table; Women's Role in Global Food Preparation.*

BIBLIOGRAPHY

Books

Rayner, Lisa. *The Sunny Side of Cooking: Solar Cooking and Other Ecologically Friendly Cooking Methods for the 21st Century.* Flagstaff, AZ: Lifeweaver, 2007.

Tiess, Frederick J. *The Culinary Reference Guide: A Quick Resource for Chefs and Apprentices of over 700 Recipes, Formulas, Practical Cooking Methods, Applications and Terminology.* Matthews, NC: Le Guild Culinaire, 2006.

Wrangham, Richard W. *Catching Fire: How Cooking Made Us Human.* New York: Basic Books, 2009.

Periodicals

Miglio, Christina, et al. "Effects of Different Cooking Methods on Nutritional and Physicochemical Characteristics of Selected Vegetables." *Journal of Agricultural and Food Chemistry* 56, no. 1 (2008): 139–147.

See, Siao W., and Rajasekhar Balasubramanian. "Chemical Characteristics of Fine Particles Emitted from Different Gas Cooking Methods." *Atmospheric Environment* 42, no. 39 (2008): 8852–8862.

Tasevska, Natasa. et al. "A Prospective Study of Meat, Cooking Methods, Meat Mutagens, Heme Iron, and Lung Cancer Risks." *The American Journal of Clinical Nutrition* 89, no. 6 (2009): 1884–1894.

Web Sites

Global Alliance for Clean Cookstoves. http://cleancook stoves.org/ (accessed October 2, 2010).

Mayo Clinic Staff. "Healthy Cooking Techniques." *Mayo Clinic.com.* http://www.mayoclinic.com/ health/healthy-cooking/NU00201 (accessed October 2, 2010).

Susan Aldridge

Food Price Crisis

■ Introduction

Between 2004 and 2006, the worldwide price of corn increased by 54 percent. Between the 2006 harvest and 2007, the price of corn rose another 28 percent. By the time a global financial crisis hit in 2008, the prices of corn, wheat, and milk had tripled from their 2003 levels. Rice experienced the most dramatic increase, costing five times its 2003 price by mid-2008. This food price crisis of 2007 and 2008 illuminated the problem of hunger and the volatility of the world's food supply. The varied causes of increased prices included growing purchasing power in larger developing countries, decline in increases in crop productivity, biofuel policy in the United States and the European Union, a decline in the availability of food aid, and droughts in key grain and oilseed production regions in the United States and Australia. However, unlike the food price crisis of the 1970s, multiple famines did not occur. The combined effects of the financial crisis and the food price crisis threatened the food security of many of the world's poor and pushed more households into poverty, but not into a situation of famine.

■ Historical Background and Scientific Foundations

In the early 1970s, a food price crisis occurred with close parallels to the crisis in 2007 and 2008. Stocks of grain, also called grain reserves, were unusually low when droughts hit several parts of the world. A spike in oil prices also helped exacerbate the crisis and contributed to inflation for both food and non-food goods. A series of famines occurred in the developing world. Whereas the reserves, connections to the price of oil, and drought conditions were somewhat similar in 2007 and 2008, there were major differences in how the crisis came about and in how governments reacted to the crisis.

The term *crisis* actually conceals longer-term trends. From 1975 until 2001, prices of grains fell compared to

incomes around the world. However, at the turn of the twenty-first century, prices slowly began to rise and then rose rapidly in 2007 and 2008. Rising prices through 2006 were largely concealed by rising incomes, as even poor households had new sources of income from wage labor or remittances (money sent from migrant laborers back to their home villages or towns). Because grain and vegetable oils make up a larger portion of the diet of the world's poor than of the more affluent, the poor are more vulnerable to the price shocks. The food price shocks caused the crisis in 2007 and 2008 and, together with the financial crisis in 2008, created a dual crisis for the world's poor.

The crisis had several causes, most of them of a longer-term nature. According to classical economic theory, increases in demand or decreases in supply lead to an increase in price. Increasing demand in large developing countries, primarily India and China, helped drive up the cost of food. One factor was that of a growing population consuming a growing amount of food, stimulating demand. Food consumption patterns change as the populations of large developing countries become more affluent. In general, richer populations consume more meat, dairy, fruits, and vegetables instead of primarily consuming grain-based foods. This change in diet is one aspect of what economists refer to as Engel's law. The increase in meat consumption worldwide then further increases the demand for grain to feed livestock, putting more pressure on the grain price to increase.

A variety of other factors unrelated to population growth or Engel's Law drove price increases. Growing demand for biofuels due to policy initiatives in the United States and the European Union (EU) moved food and animal feed crops into the biofuel market and also shifted land to biofuel crops from other crops. Farmers also consume fuel for farm equipment, fuel for shipping, and nitrogen fertilizer made from natural gas. The record high fuel prices and fertilizer prices in 2007 and 2008 were passed on from farmers to consumers in the form of higher prices. Grain stocks or reserves were at their lowest level since the early 1980s, so reserves

WORDS TO KNOW

COPING STRATEGY: The way a household manages an unplanned event or a shock that disrupts income.

ENGEL'S LAW: As a household's income increases, it will spend a lower percentage of income on food though its actual food expenditures may increase. The increase in spending is due to a shift in the diet away from grain to more expensive foods such as meat, dairy, fruits, and vegetables. Engel's Law is named after Ernst Engel (1821–1896), the German economist and statistician who first noted the tendency.

SOCIAL SAFETY NET: A public program designed to prevent households from falling into extreme poverty or reducing their consumption of necessary nutrients, medical services, and education.

productivity gains in the developing world had also been falling. Whereas the developed world increased grain production by 11 percent in response to rising prices, the developing world was only able to increase by 0.9 percent compared to much higher annual increases, averaging 2.7 percent in Sub-Saharan Africa from 1992 until 2003. Also, a few countries actually had production declines: Zimbabwe, for example, a landlocked country in Southern Africa, had once exported large quantities of grain, but its production fell by half between 2000 and 2007. In addition, the parallel financial crisis may have caused investors to move money out of industrial goods and into the already volatile agricultural commodities markets, bidding up the price of commodities. Fortunately, falling oil prices, good harvests, and the drop in worldwide income and demand that followed the worldwide financial crisis in 2008 caused prices of food items to start to decline in the fall of 2008.

■ Impacts and Issues

Unlike the early 1970s crisis, political turmoil appears not to have been a primary result of the food price crisis. Despite many problems, including 61 food price protests

could not be significantly drawn down to help control rising prices. At the same time, food aid flows remained near the same level as those in 1987 despite the growing number of hungry people in the world. Agricultural

Women carrying garlands of vegetables protest against rising food prices in New Delhi, India. *AP Images.*

worldwide, widespread famine or political collapse appears not to have been a result of the crisis, with the possible exception of what some analysts have labeled a famine in Niger, a country in West Africa. Several explanations help explain the differences between the food price crisis of the early 1970s and that of 2007 and 2008. When a poor household faces rising food prices or a possible food shortfall, it employs different strategies to deal with the shock. Poor households often will reduce their overall consumption of food, which can have long-term nutritional and economic consequences, especially for small children and pregnant and lactating women. Other strategies, called coping mechanisms by those who study them, may be selling off assets such as livestock, seeking out additional labor opportunities, drawing down savings accounts, or sending members away as migrant workers. How households cope determines whether a price shock leads to famine, food insecurity, or a more favorable outcome.

Social safety nets are programs that attempt to prevent households from choosing negative coping strategies. Food stamps, which are now known as the Supplemental Nutrition Assistance Program (SNAP) in the United States, and cash transfers in many countries, are two forms of social safety nets (SSNs). SSNs are designed to prevent a reduction in food consumption, health consumption, and educational consumption during an economic shock. In response to the food price crisis, both India and China increased government spending in key areas such as agricultural support and social safety nets. More effective safety nets in many countries, such as the widely praised *Bolsa Familia* program in Brazil, in which government financial aid is given to families who vaccinate their children and keep them in school, may have been one factor in crisis aversion. Also, donor nations and international institutions pledged additional money to assist the poorest countries in their responses to the crisis including funding social safety net programs.

Due to the crisis, the media and the world's governments once again noticed the problems of hunger and food insecurity. Food insecurity had been rising for the decade before the crisis, but the event caused additional exposure of the slowly growing threat. The Food and Agriculture Organization of the United Nations (FAO) reports that hunger increased in every region of the world leading up to the crisis except for Latin America and the Caribbean. As many of the causes of the crisis have not disappeared, a repeat crisis can be avoided most effectively by increasing the food supply for the world's growing population.

■ Primary Source Connection

International Food Policy Research Institute (IFPRI) whose motto is "Sustainable Solutions for Ending Hunger and Poverty," was founded in 1975. It is one of 15 agricultural research centers supported by the Consultative Group on International Agricultural Research (CGIAR). Funding comes from governments, private foundations, and various regional and international organizations. IFPRI research provides policymakers and non-governmental organizations with information to implement food and sustainable development initiatives. IFPRI also conducts programs related to food security, land and water resource management, poverty reduction, and nutrition.

Food and Financial Crises: Implications for Agriculture and the Poor

Even before the world food crisis, the poorest of the poor were being left behind (von Braun and Pandya-Lorch 2007). High and rising food prices further undermined the food security and threatened the livelihoods of the most vulnerable by eroding their already limited purchasing power. Poor people spend 50 to 70 percent of their income on food and have little capacity to adapt as prices rise and wages for unskilled labor fail to adjust accordingly. To cope, households limit their food consumption, shift to even less-balanced diets, and spend less on other goods and services that are essential for their health and welfare, such as clean water, sanitation, education, and health care. It has now become much more expensive to eat nutritious food. For example, in Guatemala, the price of a diet based on corn tortilla, vegetable oil, vegetables, and beans—which supplies key recommended micronutrients—is almost twice as high as the price of a less-nutritious diet based only on tortilla and vegetable oil. In fact, the cost of this balanced diet for just one person is almost three quarters of the total income of a poor household living on one dollar a day. The financial crunch poses additional threats by further lowering the real wages of the poor, and many are now losing their employment altogether. It also limits the funds available for food aid and social protection, which are essential for helping the most vulnerable people avoid malnourishment or even starvation.

Joachim von Braun

VON BRAUN, JOACHIM. *FOOD AND FINANCIAL CRISES: IMPLICATIONS FOR AGRICULTURE AND THE POOR.* WASHINGTON, DC: INTERNATIONAL FOOD POLICY RESEARCH INSTITUTE, 2008.

SEE ALSO *Biodiversity and Food Supply; Biofuels and World Hunger; Ethical Issues in Agriculture; Famine; Famine: Political Considerations; Food Security; Food Sovereignty; Free Trade and Agriculture; Government Food Assistance for Citizens; International Food Aid; International Fund for Agricultural Development; Livestock Intensity and Demand; Population and Food; Rome Declaration on World Food Security (1996); UN Millennium*

Development Goals; U.S. Agency for International Development (USAID); World Food Day; World Food Prize; World Food Programme.

BIBLIOGRAPHY

Books

Food and Agriculture Organization of the United Nations (FAO). *High Food Prices and the Food Crisis: Experiences and Lessons Learned.* Rome: FAO, 2009.

Marsden, Tery. *The New Regulation and Governance of Food: Beyond the Food Crisis?* New York: Routledge, 2010.

Masters, Lesley. *The Global Food Crisis and the Challenge of Food Security.* Pretoria: Africa Institute of South Africa, 2008.

United Nations. *Addressing the Global Food Crisis.* New York and Geneva: United Nations, 2008.

Periodicals

Bourne, Joel K., Jr. "The End of Plenty—Our Hot and Hungry World Could Face a Perpetual Food Crisis." *National Geographic* 215, no. 6 (2009): 26–59.

Butler, Declan. "Food Crisis Spurs Research Spending." *Nature* 453, no. 7191 (2008): 1–2.

"The Food Crisis—Shortages Could Inspire Some Long-Term Solutions." *Business Week* (May 12, 2008): 26.

"International—World Food Prices—Whatever Happened to the Food Crisis?" *The Economist* 392, no. 8638 (2009): 53–54.

Timmer, Peter C. "Staving Off the Global Food Crisis." *Nature* 453, no. 7196 (2008): 722–723.

"World: Food Crisis—The Hefty Dinner Bill." *Time*, May 19, 2008: 34.

Web Sites

"Food Crisis: What the World Bank Is Doing." *The World Bank.* http://www.worldbank.org/foodcrisis/ (accessed September 18, 2010).

"The Global Food Crisis: The Silent Tsunami." *The World Bank.* http://go.worldbank.org/TLTX LXZE00 (accessed September 18, 2010).

"USAID Responds to Global Food Crisis." *U.S. Agency for International Development (USAID).* http://www.usaid.gov/our_work/humanitarian_assistance/foodcrisis/ (accessed September 18, 2010).

Blake Jackson Stabler

Food Recalls

■ Introduction

A food recall is the withdrawal of any food product from further commercial distribution and sale by a government regulator or the product manufacturer. Voluntary food recalls are often instituted by a food manufacturer that becomes aware of a specific health risk posed by a product. Mandatory recalls occur when a government regulatory agency orders a specific food product to be removed from the market.

Modern consumer food production processes require strict measures to reduce inherent health risks posed by both production methods and ingredients used in food manufacture. Foods may contain pathogen-forming substances that are introduced to natural sources during cultivation or harvest. Various chemical additives such as preservatives that are utilized during food processing may create consumer health risks. Foods may also be contaminated by different types of harmful bacteria such as *Salmonella* or *E. coli* during the commercial production cycle that can cause serious illness or death. Usually a food recall is triggered when any of these circumstances are identified in a food production facility or in the subsequent distribution of the product for consumer sale.

Food recalls are distinct from *import bans* imposed by government agencies on specific foods. The 1996 European Union prohibition against imported United Kingdom beef products is a prominent example. UK beef products carried the risk that cattle afflicted with "mad cow disease" (BSE) were used in their preparation. BSE-contaminated beef is linked to an irreversible neurological condition. Whereas an import ban is a peremptory strike to prevent a human health threat, a food recall is the response to a health risk identified after the product is manufactured.

■ Historical Background and Scientific Foundations

Food recalls are a modern phenomenon. As societies moved from agriculture to industrialization, food production became a large-scale commercial activity that did not require the involvement of the ultimate consumer. Food recalls did not exist in earlier times when food was generally harvested, distributed, and sold without significant processing to consumers located near its place of origin. As agriculture was transformed into a large-scale international industry in the twentieth century, there were an increased number of points in the production chain that permitted third-party human contact with manufactured products between the harvest of their raw components and their ultimate consumer consumption.

Strict quality control systems and testing became essential aspects of all food manufacturing, distribution, and storage systems used in food production systems. These systems are designed to ensure that the risks posed by biological contaminants such as *Salmonella* and *E. coli* bacteria are minimized. The safety of the chemical food additives developed to improve shelf life or enhance product quality have also emerged as important considerations in all assessments of the integrity of food production systems. The history of food recalls in the early twenty-first century confirms that the sophisticated monitoring and quality control systems used in North American food processing are not a guarantee that a food product will be safe and not subject to recall.

One of the earliest large-scale food recalls was precipitated in 1982 by a botulism outbreak that originated in canned Alaska salmon. FDA investigators traced the cause to defective machinery that permitted botulism toxins to develop in the salmon after the cans were sealed.

WORDS TO KNOW

E. COLI: *Escherichia coli* is a form of bacteria found in the lower intestine of humans and many warm-blooded animals. Many *E. coli* forms are harmless; the *E. coli* strain O157:H7 is associated with food poisoning, and its presence has precipitated numerous food product recalls in North America and Europe. Dangerous forms of *E. coli* are often present on unwashed vegetables through surface contact with fecal material used as fertilizer. The consumption of improperly cooked meat is also a significant source of *E. coli* strains that cause human illness. Antibiotics used to treat *E. coli* are not always effective due to resistance built up over time in human populations that is attributed to the overuse of antibiotics to treat infection in humans and in the domestic animal populations ultimately used for human food.

FOOD SAFETY MODERNIZATION ACT (FSMA): Passed by the U.S. House of Representatives in 2009, FSMA provides the Food and Drug Administration (FDA) with the power to order the recall of any contaminated foods commercially available in the United States. Under previous legislation, the U.S. Department of Agriculture (USDA) was the only government agency that could exercise the power to recall a food product, and the USDA authority is restricted to meat, eggs, and poultry products. Imported foods in the United States are subject to the same safety standards as domestic food products under the FSMA. The number of mandatory inspections of American food production facilities permitted to FDA regulators is increased under the Act. The FSMA has generated significant controversy in the U.S. agricultural sector as small farmers have expressed concern that the food recall power vested in the FDA will impose an unfair cost burden on smaller-scale producers.

SALMONELLA: The genus *Salmonella* includes more than 2,500 types of bacteria. Salmonellosis, a common form of food poisoning, is the illness that results when food contaminated by this bacterial strain is consumed. *Salmonella* causes a variety of illnesses in humans, animals, and birds; poultry are especially vulnerable to *Salmonella* outbreaks. Salmonellosis is spread among human populations through physical handling of contaminated raw foods or by consumption of *Salmonella* bacteria present in food. Typical Salmonellosis symptoms include diarrhea, stomach cramps, and vomiting. Strict attention to cleanliness in all aspects of food handling, preparation, and storage is essential to reduce the health risk posed by *Salmonella*.

Consumers expect manufacturers to take all reasonable steps to ensure that food products are safe. When recalls are initiated, consumer fears are heightened; the overall security and integrity of the entire modern food production system is often questioned. Public confidence is often a casualty when food products are subject to a recall notice or order. The scale of the following food recalls has reinforced the importance of proper food handling procedures, and the need for ongoing attention to the quality of all ingredients and additives used in commercial food preparations:

1. A suspected *Salmonella* outbreak at production facility in the United Kingdom in 2006 prompted manufacturer Cadbury-Schweppes to recall more than one million chocolate bars in the United Kingdom and Ireland.

2. In 2008 the USDA ordered the recall of 143 million pounds (66 million kg) of processed beef in California. The manufacturer, Westland/Hallmark, had failed to have the cattle used for beef production properly inspected prior to slaughter. The recall was the largest single meat products recall in U.S. history.

3. Maple Leaf Foods, Canada's largest prepared meats producer, voluntarily recalled millions of processed meats and deli foods packages in 2008. Twenty-three people died from the infectious disease Listeriosis that they contracted through eating or handling Maple Leaf products contaminated by the *Listeria* bacterium.

4. In 2010 the manufacturers of the powdered baby formula Similac recalled 5 million containers of the product that were potentially contaminated with insect larvae that the product was exposed to during the manufacturing process.

5. Also in 2010, 500 million American eggs were recalled as a result of a *Salmonella* outbreak that caused more than 1,600 cases of food poisoning. Investigation determined that the outbreak originated with two Iowa egg production operations under the direction of a common corporate owner. *Salmonella enteritidisis* is the specific bacterium associated with egg-based salmonellosis.

■ Impacts and Issues

The observed frequency and scale of food recalls in the early twenty-first century suggests that the producers and regulators are able to address many foodborne illness threats before there is a significant impact on human health such as an epidemic or pandemic occurrence. The proponents of the FSMA argued in the debates prior to the passage of the Act by the House of Representatives that the FDA had to be given the power to order food recalls because the food production system is so important to modern consumer health and national economic well-being that any problems had to be capable of immediate attention.

An important underlying issue that is emerging from the FSMA enactment is the philosophical question

A sheriff's deputy leaves the Peanut Corporation of America processing plant in Blakely, Georgia. In 2009, researchers from the Food and Drug Administration and other agencies pinpointed the peanut processing plant as the source of *Salmonella* contamination that resulted in the largest food recall in U.S. history to that time. *AP Images*

of how much food should cost. Modern food production has reduced the relative cost of food, and it has made food products of all kinds more widely available and more convenient. There is considerable consumer resistance to any measure that would increase food costs.

The larger problem with modern food production that has attracted adverse commentary in the wake of the recent food recalls in North America is whether the scale of agricultural and food manufacturing is worth the increased apparent increased risk to human health. Massive "factory farm" operations permit large volumes of cattle, pigs, and poultry to be raised with maximum efficiency. These operations also raise serious food security and consumer health questions that may not be addressed through greater government regulation alone. *Salmonella* is a primary example of bacteria that tends to proliferate more readily among animals in factory farm settings than it does in smaller scale operations. An

unpalatable solution for many consumers is the prospect of ensuring greater food product safety through smaller, less efficient and more expensive agriculture.

A second concern with modern food recall procedures is the amount of discretion that is left to individual manufacturers and processors concerning whether a voluntary product recall will be instituted. The greatest commercial incentive for food producers to be proactive in initiating voluntary food recalls is the threat of civil liability and expensive claims for negligent product manufacture. In these circumstances, it is open to producers to permit a product to remain commercially available and avoid the cost of a recall if the producer determines that they are prepared to assume such risks.

SEE ALSO *Center for Food Safety and Applied Nutrition; Consumer Food Safety Recommendations;* E. Coli *Contamination; Eggs; Factory Farming; Food Inspection and Standards; Food Safety and Inspection Service; Foodborne Diseases; Infant Formula and Baby Food; Produce Traceability; Reportable Food Registry; Salmonella; U.S. Food and Drug Administration (FDA).*

BIBLIOGRAPHY

Books

Hoeller, Suzie L. *Recall: Food and Toy Safety: An American Crisis.* Charleston, SC: BookSurge, 2007.

Sherrow, Victoria. *Food Safety.* New York: Chelsea House, 2008.

Periodicals

Chyau, James. "Casting a Global Safety Net—a Framework for Food Safety in the Age of Globalization." *Food and Drug Law Journal* 64, no. 2 (2009): 313–334.

"Major North American Pet Food Recall." *Animal Pharm* 610 (March 30, 2007): 8.

Nepusz, Táma, Andrea Petróczi, and Declan P. Naughton. "Worldwide Food Recall Patterns over an Eleven Month Period: A Country Perspective." *BMC Public Health* 8 (2008): 308.

Roth, Aleda V., Andy A. Tsay, Madeline E. Pullman, and John V. Gray. "Unraveling the Food Supply Chain: Strategic Insights from China and the 2007 Recalls." *Journal of Supply Chain Management* 44, no. 1 (2008): 22–39.

Todd, Betsy. "Outbreak: E. Coli O157:h7." *The American Journal of Nursing* 107, no. 2 (2007): 29–32.

Web Sites

"Food Recalls and Alerts." *FoodSafety.gov.* http://www.foodsafety.gov/keep/recalls/index.html (accessed October 10, 2010).

"The Reportable Food Registry, FDA's New Early Detection System Helps Identify 125 Food Safety Problems in First Seven Months." *Center for Food Safety and Applied Nutrition, U.S. Food and Drug Administration (FDA),* August 3, 2010. http://www.fda.gov/Food/NewsEvents/Constituent Updates/ucm220973.htm(accessed October 10, 2010).

Bryan Thomas Davies

Food Rheology

Introduction

An important concept in food science, food rheology relates to how a foodstuff responds with flow to the application of a force. Food materials vary widely as to their physical and chemical nature. They are also submitted to different forces during processing and eating. The baking of bread, for instance, depends upon the network formed by wheat proteins and its ability to be stretched during the kneading process. Foods that are fluids, whether they are simple liquids or dispersions, behave in two different ways when they are subjected to a force. A Newtonian fluid behaves according to the predictable laws of Newtonian physics. A non-Newtonian fluid behaves differently. This distinction is important in determining why foods behave in the way they do. A thicker fluid may sometimes flow more readily than one that is less viscous if the latter follows non-Newtonian behavior. Understanding the science of food rheology is of paramount interest to food scientists. New foods are being developed continuously, but there will be a market for them only if they are good to eat. Texture, which is driven by rheology, is as important an element in taste as flavor. There is a big demand for lower fat or reduced-calorie foods to help people control their weight, and these must have a satisfying texture to be marketed successfully, which is proving to be a challenge for food science.

Historical Background and Scientific Foundations

Food rheology has always been an important element in eating and cooking, although it was not until the seventeenth century that it began to be understood as a branch of physics. An early example comes from baking in ancient Egypt, when the consistency of dough would be assessed by rolling it in the baker's hands before putting into the oven. Food materials experience many different forces during preparation and eating. Depending upon their physical and chemical nature, foodstuffs may flow, bend, stretch, or break when a force is applied. For instance, if a partly used jar of mayonnaise or peanut butter is opened, it tends to retain the shape made by the knife of the last person who used it. But when a jar of honey is opened, the surface is smooth, without a trace of previous use. This means that the mayonnaise does not flow under the influence of the force, but the honey does.

Foodstuffs include a wide range of physical materials. They may be solids, dispersions of liquids in solids, or dispersions of solids in liquids. Some, such as egg white, are foams, which are gases dispersed in a liquid. This means that there is a wide range of rheological properties in foods. The most important difference is probably the viscosity, which, put simply, is the thickness of a food. There is also a difference in behavior of foods when a force is applied. Newtonian fluids, such as water and honey, follow the predictable laws of physics when a force is applied. But non-Newtonian fluids, such as foams and mayonnaise, behave differently. Over the years, scientists have been able to figure out the rules of non-Newtonian rheology, and this has had a big impact upon the food industry, because ultimately food rheology affects the sensory impact of a food through its texture and mouthfeel. It also affects how a food is stored because the rheology and texture of a food can alter over time. Fruits and vegetables go soft, whereas ice-cream can become gritty due to the formation of ice crystals.

Impacts and Issues

Food rheology is a significant factor when it comes to making and marketing new food products. As consumers become more aware of health issues, they are looking for low-fat or even no-fat versions of their favorite foods. The problem is that it is difficult to reproduce the texture and mouthfeel of fat. Modified starches have a smooth mouthfeel and are used in many of the lower fat products,

WORDS TO KNOW

MOUTHFEEL: The textural properties of a food when it is perceived in the mouth. Mouthfeel includes qualities such as crunchiness and creaminess and is an important concept in food technology.

RHEOLOGY: The science of deformation and flow when a force is applied to a material, including a food. Materials vary widely in their rheological behavior.

TEXTURE: The qualities of a food, or other material, that can be felt with the fingers, tongue, palate, or teeth. Foods have many different textures, which contribute to their imparted sensation of taste.

such as yogurts, spreads, and cheeses, but they usually do not impart the same sensory pleasure to the consumer.

Food rheology has also given food scientists a useful tool to help ensure consistency between batches of a food

product. By measuring the viscosity of the food, manufacturers can determine reference points that help ensure consistent performance characteristics such as texture, color, stability, and durability. One practical example of this could be a manufacturer of cake icing, who uses rheological techniques to ensure that each batch of the icing created clings to the side of the cake and has a consistent shelf life.

SEE ALSO *Agribusiness; Cooking Fats; Processed Foods; Tasting Food.*

BIBLIOGRAPHY

Books

Castell-Perez, Elena, Ljubica Dokic, and Petar Dokic. *Rheology Applications to Food Quality and Product Development.* Oxford, UK: Blackwell, 2008.

Fischer, Peter, Philipp Erni, and Erich J. Windhab. *Proceedings of the 4th International Symposium on Food Rheology and Structure.* Zurich, Switzerland: Institute of Food Science and Nutrition, 2006.

Norton, Ian T. *Practical Food Rheology: An Interpretive Approach.* Oxford, UK: Wiley-Blackwell, 2011.

Rao, M. Anandha. *Rheology of Fluid and Semisolid Foods: Principles and Applications.* New York: Springer, 2007.

Sahi, Sarabjit S. *Rheological and Other Techniques and Methods Used in the Characterisation of Food Systems.* Campden, UK: Campden & Chorleywood Food Research Association, 2007.

Sosa-Morales, Maria E., and Jorge F. Vélez-Ruiz. *Food Processing and Engineering Topics.* New York: Nova Science Publishers, 2009.

Periodicals

Mourao, Denise M., Josefina Bressan, Wayne W. Campbell, and Richard D. Mattes. "Effects of Food Form on Appetite and Energy Intake in Lean and Obese Young Adults." *International Journal of Obesity* 31, no. 11 (2007): 1688–1695.

Nishinari, Katsuyoshi. "Rheology, Food Texture and Mastication." *Journal of Texture Studies* 35, no. 2 (2004): 113–124.

Web Sites

Sekuler, Robert. "Texture and Mouthfeel." *Brandeis University.* http://people.brandeis.edu/~sekuler/SensoryProcessesMaterial/rheology.html (accessed October 17, 2010).

Steffe, James D. "Rheological Methods in Food Process Engineering, 2nd ed." *Michigan State University,* 1996. http://www.egr.msu.edu/~steffe/Freebooks/Rheological%20Methods.pdf (accessed October 17, 2010).

Susan Aldridge

Wet curd is poured into moulds at Sweet Grass Dairy in Thomasville, Georgia. The moulds are left to drain, compressing the curd into firmer cheese rounds and dramatically altering its rheology. *Adrienne Lerner / Lerner & Lerner / LernerMedia Global Photos.*

Food Safety and Inspection Service

■ Introduction

Whenever the media announce a food recall of meat, poultry, or eggs, the declaration that a particular lot of food is contaminated and in need of removal from supermarket shelves and the nation's food supply generally comes from the Food Safety Inspection Service (FSIS), a division of the U.S. Department of Agriculture (USDA).

The functions of the FSIS have been provided by the U.S. federal government in some form since 1884. Long before the Pure Food and Drug Act of 1906 passed, creating the forerunner to the Food and Drug Administration (FDA), the USDA worked to ensure the safety of the nation's meat, poultry, and egg supplies.

Over the years the FSIS improved reporting techniques and recall campaigns, using a blend of traditional reporting systems and electronic notification systems. Whereas the FDA's Center for Food Safety and Applied Nutrition (CFSAN) handles food safety issues related to many foods, cosmetics, and dietary supplements, FSIS is part of the USDA. The issue of food safety and eggs is split between the FDA and USDA, however, with the USDA in charge of egg safety at the point of shipment out from breaker plants (egg products processing facilities in which eggs are broken and the liquid is pasteurized for use in other products) that handle large-scale egg processing, and the FDA overseeing these products after they leave the plants and also for egg safety issues for shell eggs.

■ Historical Background and Scientific Foundations

Though the USDA was founded in 1862, the Food Safety and Inspection Service (FSIS) was not created until 1977. During 115 years before its creation, the primary functions of FSIS—food safety management and regulatory enforcement—were performed by different segments of the USDA. In the latter decades of the nineteenth century, the demand for meat soared as refrigerated rail cars and factory slaughterhouse techniques enabled large-scale livestock operations to flourish. Along with this growth came an increase in foodborne illness triggered by the inclusion of diseased or contaminated animals in the food supply. Although some local governments and states worked to regulate the livestock and meatpacking industries, until the establishment of the Bureau of Animal Industry in 1884 no federal agency or law regulated the meat supply in the United States.

Upton Sinclair's novel *The Jungle* provoked public outrage with its depiction of contaminated meat, rodent infestations, and worker abuse and death in the Chicago meat-packing industry. The public outcry, along with more than 25 years of previous legislative lobbying from various members of Congress, led to the passage of the Pure Food and Drug Act in 1906, creating the forerunner of the FDA—the Food, Drug, and Insecticide Administration—which initially operated under the USDA. In 1931 the FDA came under control of the Department of Health and Human Services, and in 1977 the Food Safety and Quality Service, later renamed Food Safety and Inspection Service, was formed to manage all aspects of meat and poultry inspection nationwide.

Food safety regulations were in place, and typically stronger, in Europe and other countries as well, by the post-World War II era, and in 1963 the Food and Agriculture Organization and the World Health Organization of the United Nations jointly formed the Codex Alimentarius Commission to develop food standards and guidelines for international trade. Its standards are voluntary, and most U.S. regulations and products meet these standards, though not all.

For more than 100 years, until 1996, federal inspection of meat and poultry relied on a three-pronged, non-scientific process: sight, touch, and smell. In 1996 the FSIS implemented the Hazard Analysis and Critical Control Point (HACCP) protocol to create decision trees for managing food safety issues on a case-by-case

WORDS TO KNOW

CODEX ALIMENTARIUS COMMISSION: Formed as a joint effort between the Food and Agriculture Organization of the United Nations and the World Health Organization in 1963, the *Codex Alimentarius* Commission works to supervise international cooperation for safe food practices across borders.

FOOD RECALL: In a U.S. recall, the Food Safety Inspection Service (FSIS), a part of the United States Department of Agriculture (USDA), asks the public to return products from a specific batch produced by a manufacturer or farm, for reasons such as contamination by organisms causing foodborne illness. Most FSIS-originated recalls involve voluntary recalls, in which the manufacturer works proactively with government agencies to remove a product from shelves and to educate consumers to return or destroy defective products.

HAZARD ANALYSIS AND CRITICAL CONTROL POINT (HACCP): According to the Food and Drug Administration, HACCP is a "management system in which food safety is addressed through the analysis and control of biological, chemical, and physical hazards from raw material production, procurement and handling, to manufacturing, distribution and consumption of the finished product."

Eggs are inspected after they have been washed on the production line. After the Food Safety Inspection Service investigated a *Salmonella* outbreak in 2010 that sickened thousands of Americans and involved the recall of over 500 million tainted eggs, new regulations were proposed that would require egg farmers to increase sanitation measures and to regularly test their flocks for *Salmonella* bacteria. *AP Images.*

basis, which follows a specific standard rooted in research and focuses on "prevention and reduction of microbial pathogens on raw products that can cause illness," according to agency documents.

A 2002 Health and Human Services report indicated a 23 percent decline in bacterial foodborne illness between 1996 and 2002, attributing much of the decline to the FSIS HACCP program.

■ Impacts and Issues

The FSIS HACCP process manages food safety from harvest to consumption. The agency breaks down the HACCP process by type of food with four divisions: dairy, juice, retail and food service, and seafood procedures. HACCP enables the FSIS to determine the level of hazard in a suspected food safety situation, find critical control points, decide how to monitor the possible contamination, implement corrective actions, verify that the corrective actions worked, and provide records of all actions taken for public health, safety, and future analysis. HACCP is aided by strong integrations with technology tools that enable food manufacturers, agribusinesses, and small farmers to report suspected contamination incidents to FSIS in real time, helping to mitigate a potential food safety crisis and to prompt food recalls if necessary.

Food recalls in 2009 and 2010 initiated by the FSIS and the FDA point to issues of a lack of cohesion within the government's handling of food safety incidents. The FDA and USDA split responsibilities for food, drug, and cosmetics safety, with some items, such as eggs, managed by both agencies. Both agencies provide information to FoodSafety.gov, a website designed to keep consumers informed of the latest food recall issues. With widgets, Twitter feeds, Facebook updates, podcasts, and video downloads, the technology goes far beyond simple articles, email contacts, and telephone numbers to provide the public with a centralized, authoritative communications tool for public health. The divided responsibilities for egg food safety issues prompted calls for the passage of the Food Safety Enhancement Act of 2009, legislation that would consolidate food recall responsibility and give the FDA more authority in these cases.

The widespread *Salmonella enteriditis* contamination that sickened more than 1,400 people from May to the end of August 2010 and led to the removal of more than half a billion eggs from the nation's grocery stores was investigated by FSIS as an agency of the USDA in coordination with other federal and state agencies. New safety rules specifically related to eggs were enacted by the FDA in 2009, but were not required to be implemented until after the outbreak began in 2010.

In September 2010, as part of Food Safety Month, FSIS rolled out a new campaign via its website and social media tools, providing hundreds of documents and outreach materials in Spanish. The campaign includes Spanish-language food safety documents, live chat on the FSIS website with Spanish-speaking service representatives for questions about foodborne illness and food safety, and Twitter and Facebook feeds in Spanish. These features were already established in English; the Spanish translations are part of a broader campaign to improve food safety and increase safe food-handling practices among consumers in the United States and to help reduce further the rate of preventable foodborne illness.

SEE ALSO *Center for Food Safety and Applied Nutrition; Codex Alimentarius; Consumer Food Safety Recommendations; Food, Drug, and Cosmetic Act of 1938; Food Inspection and Standards; Food Recalls; Foodborne Diseases; Meat Inspection Act of 1906; Produce Traceability; Pure Food and Drug Act of 1906; U.S. Department of Agriculture (USDA); U.S. Food and Drug Administration (FDA); Wholesome Meat Act of 1967.*

BIBLIOGRAPHY

Books

Pampel, Fred C. *Threats to Food Safety.* New York: Facts on File, 2006.

U.S. Institute of Medicine. *Addressing Foodborne Threats to Health: Policies, Practices, and Global Coordination.* Washington, DC: National Academies Press, 2006.

Periodicals

Kennedy, Shaun. "Why Can't We Test Our Way to Absolute Food Safety?" *Science* 322, no. 5908 (2008): 1641–1643.

Newbold, K. Bruce; Marie McKeary; Robert Hart; and Robert Hall. "Restaurant Inspection Frequency and Food Safety Compliance." *Journal of Environmental Health* 71, no. 4 (2008): 56–61.

Voelker, Rebecca. "FDA Tries to Catch Up on Food Safety." *JAMA: The Journal of the American Medical Association* 303, no. 18 (2010): 1797.

Web Sites

USDA: Food Safety and Inspection Service. http://www.fsis.usda.gov/ (accessed September 20, 2010).

Melanie Barton Zoltan

IN CONTEXT: FOOD SAFETY: A POLITICAL AND SECURITY CONCERN

Confidence in agricultural systems is essential to food security in developed nations such as the United States because of the great number of food and agricultural products that these nations export worldwide, including the large amount of food donated to areas plagued by hunger or malnutrition. That confidence was tested in the United States in 2008, as large quantities of meat, produce, and animal feed were recalled. After peanut butter and peanut paste were found to be contaminated with the bacteria responsible for *Salmonella*-related illnesses and traced to a processing plant in the state of Georgia, the largest product recall in U.S. history to that point took place, and the contaminated peanut products were implicated in the deaths of nine people.

Tom Vilsack (1950–), then the newly appointed agriculture secretary under U.S. President Barack Obama, called for modernizing and reorganizing the food safety infrastructure in the United States. Food safety in the Unites States is regulated principally by both the U.S. Food and Drug Administration (FDA) and the Food Safety and Inspection Service (FSIS), and Vilsack has suggested the United States consider the creation of a single agency responsible for food safety.

The interrelationship between food security and overall security was cited as a key reason for the nomination of Margaret Hamburg (1955–) as United States Food and Drug Administration (FDA) commissioner. In May 2009 Congress approved Hamburg's nomination by voice vote. Hamburg previously served in the development of U.S. pandemic preparedness plans as New York City health commissioner and was vice president of the Nuclear Threat Initiative's biological program.

Food Security

■ Introduction

Food security refers to the production and supply of affordable food to feed a population, along with the population's ability to access sufficient food. The participants of the 1996 World Food Summit defined food security as a time when "all people have access . . . to sufficient, safe, nutritious food to maintain a healthy and active life." This definition expands the concept of food security to include adequacy of nutrition. Other less commonly applied definitions of food security also consider cultural preferences; for example, refraining from considering meats as available food when assessing the food security of populations who adhere to religious vegetarianism.

Governments and aid organizations assess food security in a given region with three main considerations. Assessment of the physical food availability asks if agriculture is producing enough food and if sufficient amounts of food are available at market. Food access considers whether people have sufficient money or other resources to obtain food and if that food is adequate for a healthy diet. Finally, food use analysis evaluates how populations distribute and consume foods.

Food insecurity, by comparison, refers to an inadequate supply of food or a lack of access to sufficient food resources to maintain health. Hunger is the most commonly known outcome of food insecurity. The United Nations Food and Agriculture Organization (FAO) estimates that more than 1 billion people worldwide go hungry each day. The global population is expected to rise from 6.7 to 9.1 billion by 2050, with most of that growth occurring in developing nations more prone to food insecurity.

■ Historical Background and Scientific Foundations

Food security has been a universal concern throughout history. Local populations were typically dependent on the food they produced, even as global trade expanded.

Crop failures could cause catastrophic local famines and uproot whole populations. The collapse of the potato crop in Ireland during the Great Famine from 1845 to 1852 caused Ireland to lose one quarter of its population to starvation and emigration. The Industrial Revolution and increasing urbanization both increased agricultural productivity and made more people dependent on purchasing food from others rather than growing it for themselves.

During the twentieth century, a modern pattern of food insecurity emerged. Crop failures continued to threaten famine, but so too did political upheaval, conflict, food prices, and trade agreements. The world's poorest regions continued to struggle with endemic food insecurity, whereas the wealthiest nations achieved total food security for most of their citizens. At the close of the century, nutrition had generally improved in most developing nations. However, the abundance of food in wealthy nations–especially manufactured and processed food that did not exist one hundred years earlier–was linked to growing obesity rates and increased health risks.

In the 1940s, famine and food insecurity in Asia, the Pacific Island nations, and parts of the Americas prompted researchers to develop new hardy strains of wheat and rice seeds. The new seeds produced higher yields on existing farmland when coupled with modern agricultural practices such as the use of chemical fertilizers and pesticides. This movement became known as the Green Revolution.

From the 1940s through 1970s, the Green Revolution transformed worldwide agricultural practice. The movement promoted the development and use of hybridized, improved, or genetically altered seeds to prevent crop disease and improve yields. Improved irrigation, better land clearing practices, and mechanization expanded farmlands. From 1965 to 1970, new hybridized crops enabled wheat and rice production in Asia to increase at least two-fold.

Hunger and food insecurity continued even with the yield gains of the Green Revolution. The number of hungry in India alone climbed by an estimated 30 million between 1995 and 2010. As crop yields improved in some places, such as southern Asia, large-scale investment in the form of government incentives and foreign aid declined. Foreign aid for agriculture fell from 18 percent of all aid in 1979 to just over 4 percent in 2009.

In the early twenty-first century, the world's populations most vulnerable to food insecurity and hunger were the those living on less than the equivalent of $2 per day. The world's 1.05 billion poorest citizens are predominantly either recent migrants to urban areas in developing nations or rural smallholders at or near subsistence levels.

■ Impacts and Issues

The consensus of agricultural and economic experts is that enough food is produced worldwide to feed everyone. However, the most efficient food production is often concentrated in nations far away from the world's most insecure regions, challenging food distribution. Factors that contribute to food insecurity—government instability, corruption, warfare, emergencies, and population movement to escape conflict—also threaten the adequate distribution of food. Similarly, the most productive agricultural technologies are concentrated in developed nations, whereas the world's hungry are more likely to reside in developing nations.

Social justice philosophies also address food security. Advocates of food justice assert that access to affordable food is a human right. The movement favors rapid and equitable distribution of food products, especially staple crops such as grains. Food justice advocates state that hunger is not the result of a global lack of food or endemic poverty. Rather, hunger is the result of a lack of political will to distribute food regardless of individuals' or nations' ability to pay. Critics assert that direct food aid programs intend equitable redistribution of food resources. However, distribution is often challenged by external factors such as corruption or emergency in the recipient region.

Global food security is threatened by three main types of problems: environmental stressors, economic stressors, and socio-political stressors. Poverty, an economic stressor, is the primary cause of hunger worldwide. A significant majority of the world's population is not dependent on subsistence farming but is dependent on purchasing most or all of their food. Robust agricultural production helps citizens afford food by stabilizing prices of food at market and preventing food price crises that can trigger famine. Thus, poverty prevents individuals from affording the food they need. Developing nations and regions with high poverty rates are more likely to suffer from food insecurity.

During the food price crisis of 2006–2008, prices of food rose sharply from September 2006 to June 2008. In some places, the price of basic foods nearly doubled.

WORDS TO KNOW

FAMINE: A generalized and extreme scarcity of food; prolonged extreme hunger, undernourishment, or lack of food.

FOOD SECURITY: The production and availability of sufficient food.

NONGOVERNMENTAL ORGANIZATION: A nongovernmental organization, or NGO, is an organization that is not part of, or administered by, any government.

UNDERNUTRITION: A condition that occurs when the body does not get enough nutrients to ensure healthy organ and tissue functions.

YIELD: The amount of a crop produced per planting or per growing season.

By 2009 food prices had dropped worldwide but they remained significantly higher than before the start of the crisis in 2006. Whereas food became more affordable, the global recession in 2008–2009 increased unemployment and drove down wages, again making poorer populations more vulnerable to hunger.

The global food price crisis and the 2008 global economic recession added at least 100 million people to the ranks of the world's hungry. The food price crisis was exacerbated by agricultural subsidies in wealthy nations that drove down the price of their crops on international markets. Similarly, the use of food crops for biofuels and rising fuel costs associated with the harvest and transport of food stressed global food prices. The Food and

IN CONTEXT: MARASMUS

Marasmus is a severe deficiency of all nutrients, categorized along with other protein malnutrition disorders. Meaning "to waste," marasmus can occur at any age but is most commonly found in neonates (children under one year old). Starvation resulting from marasmus is a result of protein and carbohydrate deficiencies. In developing countries and impoverished populations, early weaning from breastfeeding and over dilution of commercial formulas places neonates at high risk for developing marasmus.

Because of the deficiency in intake of all dietary nutrients, growth is severely retarded. Caloric intake is too low to support metabolic activity such as normal protein synthesis or storage of fat. If the condition is prolonged, muscle tissue wasting will result. Fat wasting and anemia are common and severe. Severe vitamin A deficiency commonly results in blindness, although if stopped early this process can be reversed. Death will occur in approximately 40 percent of children with marasmus if left untreated.

Children stand in front of a grain storage building in Kayunga District, Uganda. © *Borderlands / Alamy.*

Agriculture Organization (FAO) of the United Nations notes that populations outside of the wealthiest nations were most likely to experience food insecurity or hunger resulting from spikes in food costs. A food price increase of 2 percent can increase the global population of hungry by 1 percent.

Agriculture remains the largest global employment sector, especially in developing countries. Diminished food prices therefore can also stress food security. Farmers must be able to afford seed and agricultural products for their next crop. They must also have sufficient funds to purchase any food needed to supplement their diet and pay rent or loans on the land that they farm. Surpluses and subsidies that lower the market price of food thus affect the income and food security of food growers.

Socio-political stressors include policy decisions and government actions that influence agricultural production and people's access to food. The factors are wide ranging, encompassing issues from the impacts of warfare to agricultural land ownership, from government corruption to objections to genetically modified crops. Whereas poverty may be the cause of most global incidence of food insecurity, conflict has caused some of the world's most acute food crises. In 2009 the World Food Programme's (WFP) largest aid operation was in the conflict-torn African nation of Sudan where there are

4.9 million internally displaced people (IDPs), a significant portion of whom are dependent on aid delivered to IDP and refugee camps in the region.

Environmental stressors include water deficits, land degradation, and climate change. The United Nations Environment Programme (UNEP) estimates that approximately 40 percent of the world's agricultural land is seriously degraded. Degraded lands typically produce inadequate yields and require greater investment in fertilizers and farming labor.

Climate change poses additional environmental stressors for global food production. Sea-level rise could inundate farmlands and threaten irrigation and freshwater sources. Changing weather patterns may lengthen growing seasons in some places while shortening growing seasons in others. New outbreaks of crop diseases may emerge. Desertification and land degradation may render sterile formerly productive agricultural lands. The effects of climate change on food production are most likely to be felt first in regions such as sub-Saharan Africa that are already struggling with food insecurity.

SEE ALSO *African Famine Relief; Agribusiness; Agricultural Deforestation; Agricultural Demand for Water; Agricultural Land Reform; Agriculture and International Trade; Agroecology; Aquaculture and Fishery Resources; Biodiversity and Food Supply; Biofuels and World Hunger; Bushmeat; Climate Change and Agriculture; Commission on Genetic Resources for Food and Agriculture (1995); Convention on Biological Diversity (1992); Decollectivization; Desertification and Agriculture; Disasters and Food Supply; Ecological Impacts of Various World Diets; Embargoes; Ethical Issues in Agriculture; Ethical Issues in Food Aid; Extreme Weather and Food Supply; Famine; Famine: Political Considerations; Food and Agriculture Organization (FAO); Food First; Food Price Crisis; Food Sovereignty; Free Trade and Agriculture; Gender Equality and Agriculture; Genetically Modified Organisms (GMO); Green Revolution (1943); Heifer International; Hunger; International Food Aid; International Fund for Agricultural Development; Land Availability and Degradation; Livestock Intensity and Demand; Malnutrition; Population and Food; Rome Declaration on World Food Security (1996); Subsistence Farming; Sustainable Agriculture; UN Millennium Development Goals; U.S. Agency for International Development (USAID); Water Scarcity; World Food Day; World Food Prize; World Food Programme.*

BIBLIOGRAPHY

Books

Alinovi, Luca, Günter Hemrich, and Luca Russo. *Beyond Relief: Food Security in Protracted Crises.* Warwickshire, UK: Practical Action Publishing, 2008.

Brown, Lester R. *Outgrowing the Earth: The Food Security Challenge in the Age of Falling Water Tables and Rising Temperatures.* New York: W.W. Norton & Company, 2004.

Food Security: Understanding and Meeting the Challenge of Poverty. Luxembourg: Publications Office of the European Union, 2009.

Guha-Khasnobis, Basudeb, S. S. Acharya, and Benjamin Davis. *Food Security: Indicators, Measurement, and the Impact of Trade Openness.* Oxford, UK: Oxford University Press, 2007.

Lawrence, Geoffrey, Kristen Lyons, and Tabatha Wallington. *Food Security, Nutrition and Sustainability.* Sterling, VA: Earthscan, 2010.

McDonald, Bryan. *Food Security.* Cambridge, UK: Polity, 2010.

Oyeyinka, Banji, and Padmashree G. Sampath. *The Gene Revolution and Global Food Security: Biotechnology Innovation in Latecomers.* Basingstoke, UK: Palgrave Macmillan, 2009.

Shaw, D. John. *World Food Security: A History since 1945.* Basingstoke, UK: Palgrave Macmillan, 2007.

Sinha, Archana, and T. A. John. *Food Security Matters: Social Dynamics and Determinants of Food Security.* New Delhi: Indian Social Institute, 2010.

Tansey, Geoff, and Tasmin Rajotte. *The Future Control of Food: A Guide to International Negotiations and Rules on Intellectual Property, Biodiversity, and Food Security.* London: Earthscan, 2008.

Periodicals

Boddiger, David. "Boosting Biofuel Crops Could Threaten Food Security." *Lancet* 370, no. 9591 (2007): 923–924.

Brown, Molly E., and Christopher C. Funk. "Climate: Food Security under Climate Change." *Science* 319, no. 5863 (2008): 580–581.

Diouf, Jacques. "Food Security and the Challenge of the MDGs—the Road Ahead." *UN Chronicle* 44, no. 4 (2007): 17–18.

Gebbers, Robbin, and Viacheslav I. Adamchuk. "Precision Agriculture and Food Security." *Science* 327, no. 5967 (2010): 828–831.

Lele, Uma. "Food Security for a Billion Poor." *Science* 327, no. 5973 (2010): 1554.

Web Sites

"Food Security." *World Health Organization (WHO).* http://www.who.int/trade/glossary/story028/en/ (accessed October 30, 2010).

"The Future of World Food Security." *International Fund for Agricultural Development (IFAD).* http://www.ifad.org/hfs/ (accessed October 30, 2010).

"Special Programme for Food Security." *Food and Agriculture Organization of the United Nations (FAO).* http://www.fao.org/spfs/en/ (accessed October 30, 2010).

Adrienne Wilmoth Lerner

Food Sovereignty

■ Introduction

Food sovereignty is a movement that aims to put farmers and communities—rather than transnational agribusiness, corporations, and markets—at the heart of agricultural, pastoral, labor, fishing, food, and land policies to suit their own ecological, social, economic, and cultural circumstances. The movement is one that emerged in and focuses on developing countries, or the global south. The term *food sovereignty* was coined by Via Campesina, an international coalition organization of more than 148 organizations founded in 1992, to assist peasant and agrarian movements in places such as South America, Asia, and Africa. It has parallels with, and differences from, the U.S. initiated Food First or food justice movement, which focuses foremost on reduction of hunger.

By empowering farmers and regional populations to make choices about their food production, cuisine, and land use policies, food sovereignty aims to address a variety of social justice issues, from hunger to racism. The tenets of food sovereignty as a social policy include food as a basic human right, agrarian reform, protection of natural resources, ending hunger, social peace, and democratic control.

■ Historical Background and Scientific Foundations

The food sovereignty philosophy was born out of a reaction to the twin curses of hunger and environmental degradation. The international declaration of human rights identifies the right to food, water, and well being, yet estimates from the United Nations Food and Agriculture Organization are 1.04 billion people malnourished and hungry worldwide—a level deemed unacceptable by the food sovereignty movement in a world where, on aggregate, enough food is produced for all.

On the environmental side, the movement is fighting against the damage inflicted by industrial farming on the planet's life supporting ecosystems. Industrial farming uses fossil fuels extensively for fertilizers, agrochemicals, production, transport, processing, refrigeration, and retailing. Agrochemical nutrient pollution, primarily from nitrogen rich fertilizers, causes biological dead zones in areas as diverse as the Gulf of Mexico, the Baltic Sea, and off the coasts of India and China. Also, genetic diversity of both crops and livestock has been lost through the spread of industrial monocultures.

This philosophy also recognizes that food, or the lack thereof, can be used as a weapon and political tool. Food sovereignty organizations advocate for the restoration of power to peasant communities by giving them more control over their lives, and food sovereignty is one way to accomplish this. Landlords with massive holdings of land are discouraged under policies created within the food sovereignty framework, as are outside controls on food production such as dictates from the global market.

■ Impacts and Issues

In February 2007, 500 delegates from more than 80 countries at the Forum for Food Sovereignty in Séingué, Mali, adopted the Declaration of Nyéléni which states in part: "Food sovereignty is the right of peoples to define their own food and agriculture; to protect and regulate domestic agricultural production and trade in order to achieve sustainable development objectives; to determine the extent to which they want to be self reliant; to restrict the dumping (free, subsidized, or below market price food that undercuts local farmers) of products in their markets; and to provide local fisheries-based communities the priority in managing the use of and the rights to aquatic resources. Food sovereignty does not negate trade, but rather, it promotes the formulation of trade policies and practices that serve the rights of peoples to safe, healthy and ecologically sustainable production."

Put simply, the International Assessment of Agricultural Science and Technology for Development (IAASTD),

A Mexican woman displays ears of corn during a protest in Mexico City against imported corn and genetically modified corn seeds. *AP Images.*

an intergovernmental panel, adopted the following definition: "Food sovereignty is defined as the right of peoples and sovereign states to democratically determine their own agricultural and food policies." According to the Food First Information and Action Network (FIAN), "What emerges [from the food sovereignty declaration] is a persuasive and highly political argument for refocusing the control of food production and consumption within democratic processes rooted in localized food systems."

Sustainable Agriculture

Within the food sovereignty approach, environmental ills are avoided by developing production systems that mimic the biodiversity and functioning of natural ecosystems. These systems seek to combine modern science with the experiential knowledge of farmers and indigenous peoples to achieve a more environmentally sustainable approach. This means reducing dependence on expensive external inputs, and reducing cost-price squeezes and debt traps that many of the world's farmers endure.

Such agro-ecological methods include crop rotation, intercropping, natural pest control, use of mulches and compost, terracing, nutrient concentration, water harvesting, and management of micro-environments. Scientists have reported that a series of large-scale experimental projects around the world have yielded excellent results: In southern Brazil, for example, the use of cover crops to increase soil fertility and water retention enabled 400,000 farmers to raise maize and soybean yields by more than 60 percent. Farmers earned more as beneficial soil biodiversity was regenerated.

Trade and Policy

Food sovereignty advocates are not against trade, but the concept does argue for a fundamental shift away from current practices. It emphasizes the need to support domestic markets and small-scale agricultural production. Networks of local food systems are favored because they reduce the distance between producers and consumers, limit food miles (the number of miles a product travels before it is actually consumed), and enhance citizen control and democratic decision-making.

Current trade policies for agriculture are straining the environment and leading to the economic demise of unprecedented numbers of farmers. Food sovereignty calls for new governance systems that stop the negative impacts of international trade such as food dumping, prioritizing local markets, restricting overproduction in commodity agreements, and guaranteeing small-scale producers equitable prices that cover the costs of producing food in socially and environmentally sustainable ways.

Perhaps the biggest challenge to the food sovereignty movement is creating inclusive alliances between farmers, fisher-folk, indigenous peoples, scholars, and other citizens of sufficient influence to exert countervailing power. In principle, governments that fully commit themselves to food sovereignty as a social policy must be prepared to promote the redistribution of land to the control of the people who farm it. Food sovereignty also emphasizes a reconsideration of the way people think about food, encouraging nations to turn away from viewing it as a mere tradable commodity and to promote democratic methods of food production.

In 2008 Ecuador became the first country to adopt food sovereignty in its constitution through a people's vote that recognized peoples' right to sustainable food production, particularly local production by small farmers, and nature's right to remain unexploited. Its new Law on Food Sovereignty, passed in 2009, was not without controversy, as the legislation left the door open to approvals of genetically modified organisms (GMOs) in exceptional cases. However, it put forward many important provisions in support of food sovereignty, protecting many areas of the country, discouraging monoculture, and recognizing the rights of nature. Mali and Bolivia have also adopted the food sovereignty principles as their overarching policy framework for food and farming.

SEE ALSO *Agribusiness; Agricultural Land Reform; Agriculture and International Trade; Agroecology; Decollectivization; Ethical Issues in Agriculture; Food First; Subsistence Farming; Sustainable Agriculture.*

BIBLIOGRAPHY

Books

Agroecology for Food Sovereignty. Cincinnati: Food First Books, 2009.

Food Sovereignty. Warwickshire, UK: Practical Action Pub, 2010.

Majahara, Pharahada. *Food Sovereignty and Uncultivated Biodiversity in South Asia: Essays on the Poverty of Food Policy and the Wealth of the Social Landscape.* New Delhi: Academic Foundation in association with International Development Research Centre, Ottawa, Canada, 2007.

Perfecto, Ivette, John H. Vandermeer, and Angus L. Wright. *Nature's Matrix: Linking Agriculture, Conservation and Food Sovereignty.* London: Earthscan, 2009.

Pimbert, Michel. *Towards Food Sovereignty.* London: International Institute for Environment and Development, 2009.

Schanbacher, William D. *The Politics of Food: The Global Conflict between Food Security and Food Sovereignty.* Westport, CT: Praeger Security International, 2010.

Young, Sophie, and Anuradha Mittal. *Food Price Crisis: A Wake up Call for Food Sovereignty.* Oakland, CA: Oakland Institute, 2008.

Periodicals

Altieri, Miguel A. "Agroecology, Small Farms, and Food Sovereignty." *Monthly Review New York* 61, no. 3 (2009): 102–113.

Patel, Raj. "Food Sovereignty." *Journal of Peasant Studies* 36, no. 3 (2009): 663–706.

Web Sites

"Forging Food Sovereignty for Human Rights and Sustainable Livelihoods." *Food First.* http://www.foodfirst.org/about/programs (accessed October 17, 2010).

Mousseau, Frederic. "Food Aid or Food Sovereignty? Ending World Hunger in Our Time." *Oakland Institute.* http://www.oaklandinstitute.org/pdfs/fasr.pdf (accessed October 17, 2010).

Melissa Carson

Food Styling

■ Introduction

Food styling is the art of preparing food for photography. Often food that has been prepared by a food stylist for a photo shoot is inedible, because food stylists use a wide range of tools, materials, and chemicals to make the food look appealing, some of which would be harmful or distasteful if eaten. Most food stylists have a background in culinary arts as well as design or photography. Food stylists may be independent workers, work for a culinary media company such as a cookbook publisher, or work for a marketing or advertising company that handles foodservice accounts.

■ Historical Background and Scientific Foundations

The history of food stylists can be traced back to the gradual switch in advertisements and books from drawn images to photographs. This took place in the beginning of the twentieth century, as photography technology became cheaper and better. In much the same manner as when photographers realized that professional make-up artists could make people look better in photos, designers with food experience started creating techniques to make food look better in photos as well.

Some of the classic techniques are well known, such as using heavy cream instead of milk when photographing cereal. Because heavy cream is much thicker than milk, it pours more artfully for photos, holds cereal higher in the bowl, and appears much more pure white in the picture. Other classic food stylist techniques are coating strawberries with lipstick to make them brilliant red, and filling the bottom of a bowl of soup with marbles so the meat and vegetables rise up out of the broth. Modern food stylists have a much wider array of tools from which to choose. For meats, the stylist can use browning agents to make them appear perfectly cooked and moist, or employ cool air nebulizers to create the

appearance of steam. As technology has developed food stylists have constantly discovered methods of making food look more appealing in photos, as well as dealing with the constant temperature issues of keeping hot food looking hot and cold food looking cold in long photo sessions. Sometimes these techniques are complicated, such as coating lettuce with chemicals that prevent wilting or creating false steam over a hot dish, and sometimes these techniques are very simple, as with using plastic ice cubes that will not melt or pouring motor oil over a turkey to make it appear roasted.

■ Impacts and Issues

The issues surrounding food styling primarily deal with giving false impressions about the food. For any situation in which the photo or film of the food is being used for advertisement, it becomes subject to the advertising law of the country. In the United States all advertisements are covered by the "truth in advertising" standards of the Federal Trade Commission, which says that any photo used in an ad must show the actual product that is being sold. For example, if a food stylist in the United States were taking photos of cookies and ice cream for an advertisement for the cookies, he or she might replace the ice cream with mashed potatoes to avoid melting. However, if that same photo were to appear on a package in which ice cream will be sold, the photo must be of the actual ice cream. Most countries have a regulatory board that oversees accuracy and truth

---

WORDS TO KNOW

BROWNING AGENT: A chemical that causes food to turn brown to give it the appearance of having been cooked.

A food photographer takes a photograph of an arrangement of peppers.　© *Ryan B. Stevenson / Alamy.*

in advertising, such as the Advertising Standards Authority in the United Kingdom.

There is a general social trend amongst modern food stylists for food photography to be more realistic and genuine, even when there is no legal obligation to do so. For cookbooks there are no regulations regarding truth in food photos because the photos themselves are not advertising a product. The food stylist, therefore, has no legal concerns with enhancing the look of a dish. However, there has been ethical backlash against cookbooks that show images of the food looking far more appealing then what the average cook might produce from that recipe. Most modern cookbooks try to show images of the finished recipes that, while prepared professionally and presented artfully, are reasonably close to what the home cook following the recipe might produce. Also, in several magazine features and films, including the 2009 motion picture *Julie and Julia*, food stylists have presented all-edible foods for the camera that the actors actually eat.

With the efficiency of modern photo-editing software, many pictures can be touched up after photographing, and because of this ability the requirements for food stylists are changing. Many of the tricks used in the past to adjust color, shine, and the appearance of moisture can be duplicated on the computer and do not need to be manufactured in front of the camera. Although it is still important that a food stylist have a culinary background, a strong knowledge of modern photography and computer editing skills are also required in order to compete for jobs.

SEE ALSO *Advertising Food; Food and the Internet; Movies, Documentaries, and Food; Television and Food.*

BIBLIOGRAPHY

Books

Custer, Delores. *Food Styling: The Art of Preparing Food for the Camera.* Hoboken, NJ: Wiley, 2010.

Web Sites

Severson, Kim. "Film Food, Ready for Its 'Bon Appetit.'" *The New York Times,* July 28, 2009. http://www. nytimes.com/2009/07/29/dining/29movie.html (accessed September 28, 2010).

David Brennan Tilove

Food Webs and Food Chains

■ Introduction

Food webs and food chains (sometimes also described as ecological pyramids) are often represented graphically according to various trophic levels. Such representations may depict the number of individuals, the biomass, or the relative amount of energy available within or from each trophic level. For example, one representation might depict organized plants on the bottom, herbivores above the plants, and carnivores above the herbivores. If the ecosystem sustains top carnivores, they are represented at the apex of the ecological pyramid.

As energy is transformed along a food chain through trophic interactions, substantial energy losses occur during each transfer. These energy losses are a consequence of the second law of thermodynamics, which states that whenever energy is transformed from one state to another, entropy increases. In biological energy transfer, increases in entropy generally result in the production of heat. Energy is converted from a highly ordered state in biomass to a much less-ordered condition as heat. Transfers of energy between organisms along food chains are inefficient, resulting in a pyramid-shaped representation of productivity in ecological food webs.

■ Historical Background and Scientific Foundations

Ecological food webs are based on the productivity of autotrophs, which are organisms capable of utilizing inorganic forms of energy to synthesize organic compounds. The major autotrophs in ecosystems are plants, which perform photosynthesis for growth and reproduction. On average, plant photosynthesis utilizes less than 1 percent of the solar radiation that is received at the surface of the Earth. Higher efficiencies are impossible for a number of reasons, including the second law of thermodynamics, but also because of additional constraining factors such as the availability of nutrients and moisture, appropriate temperatures for growth, and other environmental limitations. Even relatively fertile plant communities can achieve conversion efficiencies of only 10 percent or so, and only for relatively short periods of time.

The solar energy fixed by green plants in photosynthesis is the energetic basis of the productivity of heterotrophic organisms such as animals and microorganisms. The biomass of plants is consumed by herbivores, animals in the next trophic level. However, herbivores cannot convert all of the energy that they consume into biomass. The efficiency of this process is about 1 to 20 percent. The rest of the energy of the plants is either not assimilated or is converted into heat. Similarly, when carnivores eat other animals, only some of the fixed energy of the prey is converted into biomass of the predator. The rest is ultimately excreted, or is converted into heat.

Ecological Pyramids

Because of the second law of thermodynamics, the trophic structure of energy, or productivity, is always pyramid shaped. In many ecosystems this shape is reflected in the number of individuals and the biomass at different trophic levels. However, these latter variables are not pyramid-shaped for all ecosystems. In the open ocean planktonic ecosystem, the phytoplankton (or single-celled algae) typically have a biomass similar to the small animals (called zooplankton) that feed on them. However, the phytoplankton cells are relatively short-lived, and their biomass is regenerated quickly. The herbivorous zooplankton have longer life cycles, and their turnover rates are slower than the phytoplankton. Consequently, the productivity of the phytoplankton is much larger than that of the zooplankton, even though at any particular time their biomasses may be similar.

In some ecosystems, the pyramid of biomass may be inverted, that is, characterized by a larger biomass of herbivores than of plants. Inverted ecological pyramids may occur in grasslands, where the dominant plants are relatively small but quite productive. In this case, the

WORDS TO KNOW

AUTOTROPHS: Organisms that make their own food.

CHEMOSYNTHETIC AUTOTROPH: An organism that uses carbon dioxide as a carbon source but obtains energy by oxidizing inorganic substances.

CHEMOTROPHS: Animals that make energy and produce food by breaking down inorganic molecules.

DETRITUS: Dead organic matter.

HETEROTROPHS: Organisms that do not make their own food.

MONOCULTURES: Cultivation of single crops over large areas.

PHOTOSYNTHESIZING AUTOTROPHS: Animals that produce their own food by using sunlight to convert other substances to food.

TROPHIC LEVEL: The division of species in an ecosystem by their main source of nutrition.

IN CONTEXT: FOOD CHAINS AND ECOLOGICAL COMMUNITIES

All organisms, dead or alive, are potential food sources for other organisms. Consumers are ultimately also consumed by decomposers.

Organisms in an ecological community are related to each other through their dependence on other organisms for food. In a simple and hypothetical food chain, a producer is eaten by an herbivore that is in turn eaten by a carnivore. Eventually, the carnivore dies and is eaten by a decomposer. For example, in a lake, phytoplankton are eaten by zooplankton and zooplankton are eaten by small fish. The small fish are eaten by large fish. The large fish eventually die and decompose. Nothing goes to waste. Food chains are channels for the one-way flow of solar energy captured by photosynthesis through the living components of ecosystems. Food chains are also pathways for the recycling of nutrients from producers, through herbivores, carnivores, omnivores, and decomposers, finally returning to the producers.

The perfectly linear relations represented by food chains are almost never found in natural ecosystems. Although all organisms have somewhat specialized diets, most can eat a variety of different foods. Thus, each trophic level—the division of species in an ecosystem by their main source of nutrition—appears as part of several different interconnected food chains. These food chains combine into highly complex food webs.

plants will not have much biomass at any time, but the rates of energy fixation are high. Indeed, the annual productivity of the plants in grasslands is much larger than that of the herbivores. In these regions, the herbivores that feed on the plants may be relatively large, long-lived animals, and they may maintain a larger total biomass than the vegetation. Inverted biomass pyramids of this sort occur in some temperate and tropical grasslands, especially during the dry seasons when there can be large populations of long-lived herbivores such as deer, bison, antelopes, gazelles, hippopotamuses, rhinos, elephants, and other large animals.

When building ecological pyramids from numbers of individuals, inversions can also occur. For example, insects are the most important herbivores in most forests, where they can be found in great numbers. In contrast, the numbers of trees are much smaller, because each individual is large and occupies a great deal of space. However, building an ecological pyramid using energy in the forest is still governed by the second law of thermodynamics, and it is much wider at the bottom than at the top.

Transfer of Energy

As with food chains, a food web's source of energy is the sun. Solar energy is utilized by producers, such as green plants or algae. These producers are known as autotrophs or photosynthesizing autotrophs. Almost all other organisms obtain their energy, directly or indirectly, from the sun. The exceptions are the communities found around deep ocean thermal vents, which are supported by various bacteria that convert heat energy into stored chemical energy. These bacteria are known as chemotrophs or chemosynthetic autotrophs.

Autotrophs are always found at the first trophic level. In an ecosystem, this trophic level may include monerans, protists, and several different phyla of plants. They can all be placed at the first trophic level because they all have the same source of energy, and the entire food web depends on the energy harvested by them. For example, in a grazing food web, an herbivore eats living plant tissue and is eaten in turn by an array of carnivores and omnivores. Herbivores and the carnivores that prey on them are known as heterotrophs. In contrast, a detrivore (also a heterotroph) harvests energy from dead organic material and provides energy for a separate food chain.

Each step in a food web or food chain involves a transfer of matter and energy (in the form of chemical bonds stored in food) from organism to organism. Thus food webs are energy webs because the relationships represented by connections in the web represent the flow of energy from a group of organisms at one trophic level to another group of organisms at a different level. Because energy is lost (as waste heat) at each step, food chains rarely involve more than four or five steps or trophic levels.

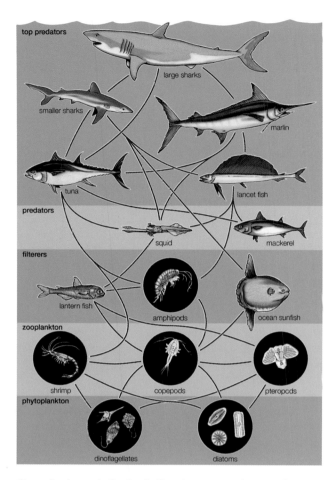

Generalized aquatic food web. Parasites, among the most diverse species in the food web, are not shown. © *Universal Images Group Limited / Alamy.*

At each level, the organisms waste much energy in the form of heat generated by normal activity. Only a fraction is stored as food or used for growth. Only about 10 percent of the food entering a link is available for the next organism in the chain. After about five links, there is insufficient energy to support a population of organisms (other than decomposers). For example, in the food chain starting with diatoms and ending with killer whales, only about 0.01 percent of the initial energy stored by the diatoms is delivered to the killer whales.

Energy flow through a food web depends greatly on the nature of the producers at the first trophic level. These are usually photosynthetic plants, phytoplankton, or algae. In forest ecosystems, trees are the largest and most abundant organism. They determine the physical structure of the ecosystem, and they can be eaten directly by small or even very large animals. However, much of the matter and energy harvested by the trees goes to build a supporting structure. These supporting structures are composed of cellulose and other wood fibers that are poor sources of energy (although they

may be good sources of valuable minerals and other nutrients).

In contrast, grasses do not invest much energy in supporting structures, so more energy is available per kilogram of plant material present to the grazers that obtain energy from plants. Consequently, all of the above-ground parts of the grass plants are eaten by herbivores.

Energy capacity spreads out through the food web, from the lowest trophic level to the highest. At the "top of the food chain," large carnivores harvest the remaining energy. However, all things eventually die, no matter where they are in the food web, and the dead organic matter accumulates in the soil, lake bottom, or forest floor. This detritus becomes the basis for a completely different ecosystem, the detritus food web.

Detritus feeders and decomposers harvest solar energy from the detritus by breaking down the organic material into simpler organic compounds and inorganic compounds. By this process, the matter is recycled and made available for reuse by plants. The detritus food web is vitally important to all ecosystems on Earth. Without it, dead organic matter would over-accumulate.

■ Impacts and Issues

Because of the serial inefficiencies of energy transfer along food chains, there are intrinsic, energetic limits to the numbers of top carnivores that ecosystems can sustain. If top predators such as lions or killer whales are to be sustained in an ecosystem, there must be a suitably large biomass of prey that these animals can exploit. Their prey must in turn be sustained by a suitably large biomass of autotrophs. Because of these energetic constraints, only very productive ecosystems can sustain top predators.

Humans are omnivores. They can operate on several trophic levels, eating plants, insects, mammals, birds, fish, mollusks, and many other organisms. Humans can also shorten the food chain when resources are scarce. In areas of the world where the population may be straining resources, people commonly increase the total food supply by eliminating one or more steps in the food chain. For example, to obtain more energy humans can switch from eating herbivores that obtain their energy from cereal grains to eating the cereal grains themselves.

Research has shown that ecological communities with complex feeding relationships have greater long-term stability and are less affected by external stresses. This suggests an evolutionary basis for the diverse and complex ecological relationships found in many communities of organisms. However, humans often violate this sound ecological principle in order to increase agricultural productivity by creating artificial ecosystems that contain only one plant, such as corn. These systems are called monocultures. While greater agricultural productivity is

IN CONTEXT: FOOD CHAIN INFILTRATION

In November 2010, researchers from the Dauphin Island Sea Lab and University of South Alabama in Mobile, Alabama, confirmed that petroleum hydrocarbons (from both Sweet Louisiana Crude (SLC) and methane gas) linked to the *Deepwater Horizon* spill were detectable in the marine ecosystem. Microbial consumption of oil proceeds faster in warm water currents such as those found in the Gulf, but microbiologists further assert that the controversial use of chemical dispersants during the spill and in subsequent clean-up operations accelerated microbial consumption of oil fractions upon which the microorganisms feed. Using molecular tracers, researchers found that oil from the spill was detectable in plankton, a cornerstone of the food web.

Only about 25 percent of the oil spilled was recovered or burned at sea; the remaining 75 percent was subject to chemical dispersants or degradation by marine microorganisms. In the months following the capping of the well in July, multiple research teams reported finding subsurface oil and a mixture of oil, chemical dispersants, and methane at depths where the water is cold, but confirmation of oil in warmer shallow waters (generally waters above 77°F [25°C]) was more fleeting.

A large amount of carbon derived from the hydrocarbons spilled was available in the food chain, both via consumption of prokaryotic microorganisms that feed on the hydrocarbons and then, via consumers of the microorganisms that are transported into the animal food chain via zooplankton. Initial movement of the carbon through the food chain is then mediated by zooplankton grazers.

possible with monoculture crops, they are very unstable ecosystems. Disease, too much rain, too little rain, or a new insect pest can destroy an entire year's harvest.

SEE ALSO *Agroecology; Calories; Cannibalism; Dietary Guidelines for Americans; Meats; Nutrition and U.S. Government Food Assistance; Nutrition's Role in Human Evolution; Seafood; Sustainable Agriculture; Veganism; Vegetarianism.*

BIBLIOGRAPHY

Books

Cardinale, B. J. *Microbial Ecology.* Sudbury, MA: Jones & Bartlett Learning, 2011.

Carson, Walter P., and Stefan A. Schnitzer. *Tropical Forest Community Ecology.* Chichester, UK: Wiley-Blackwell Pub, 2008.

Davies, Lee, et al. *Dynamic Changes in Marine Ecosystems: Fishing, Food Webs and Future Options.* Washington, DC: National Academies Press, 2006.

De Ruiter, Peter C., Volkmar Wolters, and John C Moore, eds. *Dynamic Food Webs: Multispecies Assemblages, Ecosystem Development and Environmental Change.* Burlington, MA: Academic Press, 2005.

Miller, G. Tyler, Jr., and Scott Spoolman. *Living in the Environment*, 16th ed. Pacific Grove, CA: Brooks Cole, 2008.

Morgan, Kevin, Terry Marsden, and Jonathan Murdoch. *Worlds of Food: Place, Power, and Provenance in the Food Chain.* Oxford Geographical and Environmental Studies series. Oxford, UK: Oxford University Press, 2006.

Web Sites

"Pollutants/Toxics: Toxic Substances: Persistent Bioaccumulative Toxic Pollutants (PBTs)." *United States Environmental Protection Agency (EPA).* http://oaspub.epa.gov/webimore/aboutepa.ebt4?search=9,45,345 (accessed October 27, 2010).

Foodborne Diseases

■ Introduction

Foodborne disease is a public health problem worldwide. It is caused by consumption of contaminated food or beverages. Disease-causing microbes, known as pathogens, are an important cause of foodborne disease, often also known as food poisoning. *Campylobacter*, *E. coli*, and *Salmonella* are among the leading food poisoning pathogens. However, poisonous chemicals found in foods, such as natural toxins in certain mushrooms and shellfish or contaminants such as mercury in fish, may also cause disease. The symptoms of food poisoning often include nausea, vomiting, diarrhea, and stomach pain, as the microbe or toxin enters the body via the gastrointestinal tract. Some foodborne illnesses, such as Minamata disease caused by mercury contamination, may affect the nervous system. Often an attack will clear up within a few days, leaving no lasting damage. But foodborne illness can be fatal, particularly to the elderly and infants who are in danger of dehydration from diarrhea. To keep foodborne illness under control, public health surveillance is needed so that outbreaks can be tracked promptly to their source, which can then be dealt with. The public and those who handle food can also play their part in preventing the occurrence and spread of foodborne disease by observing food hygiene rules.

■ Historical Background and Scientific Foundations

Foodborne disease has always been a public health problem but the specific illnesses of concern have changed over the course of history. In the nineteenth century typhoid fever, cholera, and tuberculosis were major problems but they have receded in significance thanks to improvements in food safety such as pasteurization of milk. Other infections have taken their place, some of which have emerged unexpectedly. For instance, a new form of Creutzfeldt-Jakob (vCJD) disease, a fatal disorder of the brain, was reported in the United Kingdom in 1996 and was attributed to eating meat from cattle with bovine spongiform encephalopathy (BSE), also known as mad cow disease. The infective agent in BSE is not a conventional microbe, but is an infectious protein called a prion. Fortunately, the predicted epidemic of variant CJD has not materialized, but each case is a tragedy for the victim and the victim's family because this is an extreme case of foodborne illness.

There are 76 million cases of foodborne illness each year in the United States, leading to 5,000 fatalities. The most common diseases are caused by *Campylobacter*, *Salmonella*, and *E.coli* O157:H7. *Campylobacter* is a bacterial pathogen that is the most commonly identified bacterial cause of foodborne illness worldwide. The bacteria live in the intestines of healthy birds and most raw poultry contains *Campylobacter*. Eating undercooked, or even raw, chicken is the most usual cause of infection, which causes fever, diarrhea, and abdominal cramps. Salmonella bacteria can live in the intestines of birds, reptiles, and mammals. The illness it causes, called salmonellosis, exhibits similar symptoms to *Campylobacter* infection. In those with weakened immunity, salmonella may invade the bloodstream and cause life threatening infection. Infection with *E. coli* O157:H7 may result in severe bloody diarrhea and painful abdominal cramps. In 3 to 5 percent of cases, a complication called hemolytic uremic syndrome may occur and possibly lead to kidney failure. Norwalk virus is another common cause of foodborne illness, causing acute illness with vomiting and diarrhea. Norwalk virus passes from one infected person to another, and infected food handlers may contaminate food during preparation.

Laboratory tests, usually on stool samples, can identify the cause of a foodborne disease. Treatment depends on the specific illness. Oral rehydration is important when diarrhea has predominated. Antibiotics should be prescribed with caution: Many foodborne illnesses are viral in origin and will not respond to antibiotics. The indiscriminate prescription of antibiotics leads to the spread of antibiotic resistance.

■ Impacts and Issues

Foodborne disease is a problem around the world. Public health authorities, food handlers, and the general public all have a part in stopping the spread of foodborne disease. A surveillance system can detect an outbreak and investigate its cause if the reporting system is robust. In the United States, salmonellosis and *E. coli* O157:H7 are both notifiable illnesses, and the data reported enables outbreaks to be contained, investigated, and lessons learned. The World Health Organization is working to establish similar systems in countries where the health infrastructure is weaker.

Foods of animal origin are the most likely to be contaminated. Particular risks include filter-feeding shellfish, which strain microbes from the sea for many months, and foods involving the combination of products of many animals, such as ground beef. A single hamburger might contain meat from hundreds of animals; a pathogen present in just one animal may contaminate the entire batch. Raw fruits and vegetables

A Chinese street market vendor sells fresh seafood. More than 40 different parasites residing in fish can be transmitted to humans, most often by consuming local-caught fish that has not been inspected, or that is served raw or undercooked. *Brenda Lerner / Lerner & Lerner / LernerMedia Global Photos.*

IN CONTEXT: TRICHINELLOSIS

A parasite is an organism that lives on or in a host organism. It is dependent upon the host for food and protection. For hundreds of thousands of years, parasites and humans have co-existed. Many parasites do no damage, particularly protozoa in low numbers, but some can cause significant harm. Parasitic infections strike millions of people annually in every region of the world. These infections are often painful, debilitating, and may be fatal. There are three main classes of parasites that can cause disease in humans: protozoa, helminths, and ectoparasites. Protozoa are microscopic, one-celled organisms. A serious infection can develop from just a single organism that then multiplies. Helminths are flatworms, thorny-headed worms, and roundworms. Ectoparasites are ticks, fleas, mites, and lice that burrow into the skin. Arthropods, including mosquitoes, serve as the vectors of many different pathogens (disease-causing organisms).

Transmission of protozoa typically occurs by a fecal-oral route through contaminated food or water or by person-to-person contact. Arthropod vectors, such as ticks, transmit protozoa that thrive in human blood or tissue. Helminths are spread by ingestion, usually through contaminated meat or water.

One parasitic disease transmitted by contaminated meat is Trichinellosis—also known as trichinosis or trichiniasis—an infection caused by a roundworm of the genus *Trichinella*, usually the species *Trichinella spiralis*. The infection is contracted by eating meat that contains live helminth (parasitic worm) cysts. Globally, eating undercooked pork is the most common path of trichinellosis infection worldwide, but in North America eating wild game is the most common path of infection.

When meat containing encysted larvae is eaten, the larvae are liberated by the digestive process. They develop into adults in the small intestine, then mate and produce offspring. These adult worms are eventually excreted. The new larvae drill through the wall of the intestine and enter the bloodstream, which conveys them to destinations throughout the body, including the muscles, eyes, lungs, and brain. The larvae encyst themselves in muscle and become dormant. Because humans with the disease are usually not eaten by other animals or people, that is usually the end of the disease cycle in human beings. If the encysted larvae are in the muscle of any animal that might be eaten by human beings or other carnivores, the life cycle can continue.

Abdominal symptoms appear a day or two after infection and may include nausea, diarrhea, vomiting, and abdominal pain. Other symptoms may appear two to four weeks after infection and include headaches, fevers and chills, muscle and joint pain, itching, diarrhea, rash, and swelling of the eyes. The later-stage symptoms are caused by the larvae encysting in the muscles and the body's immune response to their presence. Not all cases of infection, even in humans, produce noticeable symptoms. Death can occur, but is rare.

The Centers for Disease Control and Prevention (CDC) asserts that U.S. regulations and consumer awareness have reduced cases of trichinellosis to just a few dozen cases per year. New cases in the United States are more commonly associated with eating raw or undercooked wild game meats rather than pork. To prevent trichinellosis, the CDC recommends cooking pork to a temperature of 160°F (71°C) before eating, or freezing pork less than six inches thick for 20 days at 5°F (−15°C). Microwaving does not reliably kill larvae in meat.

In recent years, an increase in trichinellosis cases related to travel prompted many countries to adopt stricter bans on the importation of pork and game products by travelers to some regions. Many popular tourist destinations, such as Argentina, Croatia, Mexico, Romania, Serbia, and Laos, have endemic problems with trichinellosis. In 2005 nearly two-thirds of the reported cases of trichinellosis in the United Kingdom and France were in people who had contracted the infection while traveling abroad or who had consumed infected products imported by travelers. Many nations now include trichinellosis in traveler health warnings.

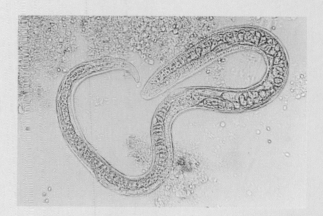

The intestinal disease trichinosis is caused by *Trichinella spiralis*, a parasitic nematode. © *Biodisc/Visuals Unlimited / Alamy.*

are another potential source of foodborne illness. This is a danger when produce is processed under unsanitary conditions, with contaminated washing water being used.

Consumers can take a few simple precautions to protect themselves from foodborne illness. Meat, poultry, and eggs always should be cooked thoroughly. Bacteria grow quickly at room temperature, so leftovers should be chilled promptly. Cross contamination should be avoided by never letting utensils that have been used on raw meat or poultry touch other foods until they have been washed. Produce should be washed thoroughly because bacteria multiply quickly on a cut surface. Hands should be washed thoroughly before preparing food so that bacteria on the hands are not transferred. Everyone coming into contact with food should be aware these are frontline precautions against foodborne disease.

SEE ALSO *Bioterrorism: Food as a Weapon; Cartagena Protocol on Biosafety (2000); Center for Food Safety and Applied Nutrition; Cholera; Consumer Food Safety Recommendations; Disasters and Food Supply;* E. Coli *Contamination; Factory Farming; Food Inspection and Standards; Food Irradiation; Food Recalls; Food Safety and Inspection Service; Hepatitis A;* Listeria; *Mad Cow Disease and vCJD; Meat Inspection Act of 1906; Norovirus Infection; Paralytic Shellfish Poisoning; Pasteurization; Produce Traceability; Pure Food and Drug Act of 1906; Raw Milk Campaign;* Salmonella; *Staphylococcal Food Poisoning; Waste and Spoilage.*

BIBLIOGRAPHY

Books

Morrone, Michele. *Poisons on Our Plates: The Real Food Safety Problem in the United States.* Westport, CT: Praeger, 2008.

Watson, Ronald R., and Victor R. Preedy. *Bioactive Foods in Promoting Health: Fruits and Vegetables.* Amsterdam: Academic Press, 2010.

Periodicals

Hoffman, Richard E. "Preventing Foodborne Illness." *Emerging Infectious Diseases* 11, no. 1 (2005): 11–16.

Kuehn, Bridget M. "Surveillance and Coordination Key to Reducing Foodborne Illness." *JAMA: The Journal of the American Medical Association* 294, no. 21 (2005): 2683–2684.

Machado, Antonio E. "Preventing Foodborne Illness in the Field." *Journal of Environmental Health* 72, no. 3 (2009): 56.

Noèel, Harold, et al. "Consumption of Fresh Fruit Juice: How a Healthy Food Practice Caused a National Outbreak of Salmonella Panama Gastroenteritis." *Foodborne Pathogens and Disease* 7, no. 4 (2010): 375–381.

"The Price of Foodborne Illness in the USA." *The Lancet* 375, no. 9718 (2010): 866.

Web Sites

"Foodborne Disease." *World Health Organization (WHO).* http://www.who.int/topics/foodborne_diseases/en/ (accessed October 2, 2010).

"Foodborne Illness." *U.S. Centers for Disease Control and Prevention (CDC).* http://www.cdc.gov/ncidod/dbmd/diseaseinfo/foodborneinfections_g.htm (accessed October 2, 2010).

Susan Aldridge

Foodways

■ Introduction

Everything about the way people eat defines them socially and culturally. What individuals eat, where their food comes from, who prepares it, and with whom they eat, even their attitudes and rituals around food, all underlie the rich fabric of vastly diverse cultures and cultural histories.

Foodways is a term that describes all of these things: the cultural, social, and economic practices relating to the procurement, production and preparation, and consumption of food. Another way of framing the term: Foodways are the connections between food-related behavior and patterns of membership in a cultural community, group, and society.

The study of foodways provides a window into the most basic beliefs about humans and the world around them. It is the term used to describe the cross-disciplinary study of why people eat what they eat and what this means culturally, historically, and socially, by anthropologists, folklorists, sociologists, historians, and food scholars.

Themes such as power, social inclusion and exclusion, and social organization are explored under the umbrella term *foodways*, both how food shapes these cultural constructs and how food is shaped by them. Typically foodways refers to a distinct group, region and/or time, local or national cultures. For example, an anthropologist might write "it is in their foodways that Northern Italians are most easily distinguished from Southern Italians and Sicilians." Examples of cultural foodways are presented in this article.

■ Historical Background and Scientific Foundations

The first usage of "foodways" is thought to come from the folklore initiative within the cultural development of 1930s America. Folklorists gathered evidence of tradition and creativity among America's living regional, ethnic, occupational, and spiritual communities such as work songs, festivals, superstitions, and foodways.

Foodways are really activities that can be observed, and sampled in the case of food itself. In many ways it is a "performed" tradition. The term itself reflects the popular anthropology of the 1950s in America when language was carefully tailored to avoid ethnocentrism and to embrace the broadest possible level of cultural comparison. The term *foodways* survived its period in folklore studies and transitioned into current use.

■ Impacts and Issues

In an increasingly interwoven global society, foodways not only reflect the vast cultural diversity around the world, but also help people connect to their culture and social roots. In this section foodways are brought to life, through two examples.

American Southern Foodways

The American Southern Foodways Alliance, a member-based organization, documents, studies, and celebrates the diverse food cultures of the changing American South. Their mission is revealing: "We set a common table where black and white, rich and poor—all who gather—may consider our history and our future in a spirit of reconciliation." In a region where the history of slavery is not so distant foodways provides a celebratory means of dealing with the past.

Southern cooks have always creatively drawn from the mix of cultures that once collided in the South: Native American, European, and African cultures. It was from the Native Americans that the first English settlers learned how to grow, prepare, and eat corn. The wheat or rye grains, for making bread that formed part of everyday meals in Britain, did not thrive in the local soil, and corn provided an alternative.

Evidence of the European settlers abound in various regions of the South: English, Scottish and Irish,

WORDS TO KNOW

ASCETICISM: The practice of voluntary, rigorous self discipline and self denial in an effort to attain enlightenment or a spiritual ideal.

ETHNOCENTRISM: The belief that one's own particular ethnic group or culture is superior to others.

FOLKLORE: Key legends, stories, beliefs, anecdotes, superstitions, and customs passed among generations in a particular culture.

Youths pelt each other with about 150 tons of tomatoes in the streets of Buñol, eastern Spain in the annual La Tomatina festival, a tradition that began in the late 1940s, anecdotally by accident, that increased in size each year until eventually it became a large annual festival. Tomatoes were introduced to Europe in the early sixteenth century after the Spanish explorer Christopher Columbus brought them from the Americas, but have become a central part of southern European cuisine. *AP Images.*

Spanish, and French. It is the French influence in Louisiana that is perhaps the most distinctive European influence on Southern cooking, because it not only sets this region apart from other regions of the South but from the rest of the country as well.

But it is African traditions that have perhaps had the most impact on the flavors and the methods of Southern cooking. Slaves did not cook only for themselves, but also for the plantation owners, and their cooking in this arena resulted in the subtle but very real transformation of the tastes of the American South.

Culinary influences include many uses of okra for gumbos (soup/stews), the use of smoked meats and fish as seasonings, and the use of nuts as thickeners. Along with dishes such as fried chicken and a host of fritters (deep fried), the African influence represented some of the best cooking the South had to offer.

Halal Foodways

Halal is an Arabic word that means "lawful, permitted, or acceptable." Observant Muslims must adhere to specific dietary laws also known as Halal foodways. Halal foodways are based on conditions set out in the *Quran.*

Halal food and drink must be lawful. This includes, for example, the way food and drink has been acquired; it cannot have been acquired through theft or cheating. Halal food must also be good both in the sense of pleasant, delicious, or sweet as well as pure and clear. The intent of the prohibitions is because the *Quran* links the physical and spiritual sides of humans. As such, errors committed in the physical realm are reflected in the spiritual. At a general level, there are two additional guidelines on diet, banning excess and self-denial or asceticism.

The details of Halal foodways describe in particular detail the way animal meat may and may not be consumed, from the type of meat (no swine) to the method of slaughter and the invocation of the name of God during slaughter.

Foodways have evolved into traditions and religious laws, and other times the stamp of the past may be completely forgotten although its evidence is in the spices, dishes, or habits of a modern community. However deeply one aims to explore foodways, the study provides a rich and appetizing window of discovery into the cultural past.

■ Primary Source Connection

Mark Twain wrote *A Tramp Abroad* in 1880. It is a description of his travels through Europe with a friend. This particular excerpt is from Chapter XLIX: Hanged with a Golden Rope. Using the humor devices of satire and exaggeration, it serves as a historical and literary standard from which to derive insights into changes and similarities in the American diet over the past 130 years.

A Tramp Abroad

It has now been many months, at the present writing, since I have had a nourishing meal, but I shall soon have one—a modest, private affair, all to myself. I have selected a few dishes, and made out a little bill of fare, which will go home in the steamer that precedes me, and be hot when I arrive—as follows:

Radishes. Baked apples, with cream

Fried oysters; stewed oysters. Frogs.

American coffee, with real cream.

American butter.

Fried chicken, Southern style.

Porter-house steak.

Saratoga potatoes.

Broiled chicken, American style.

Hot biscuits, Southern style.

Hot wheat-bread, Southern style.

Hot buckwheat cakes.

American toast. Clear maple syrup.

Virginia bacon, broiled.

Blue points, on the half shell.

Cherry-stone clams.

San Francisco mussels, steamed.

Oyster soup. Clam Soup.

Philadelphia Terapin soup.

Oysters roasted in shell-Northern style.

Soft-shell crabs. Connecticut shad.

Baltimore perch.

Brook trout, from Sierra Nevadas.

Lake trout, from Tahoe.

Sheep-head and croakers, from New Orleans.

Black bass from the Mississippi.

American roast beef.

Roast turkey, Thanksgiving style.

Cranberry sauce. Celery.

Roast wild turkey. Woodcock.

Canvas-back-duck, from Baltimore.

Prairie liens, from Illinois.

Missouri partridges, broiled.

'Possum. Coon.

Boston bacon and beans.

Bacon and greens, Southern style.

Hominy. Boiled onions. Turnips.

Pumpkin. Squash. Asparagus.

Butter beans. Sweet potatoes.

Lettuce. Succotash. String beans.

Mashed potatoes. Catsup.

Boiled potatoes, in their skins.

New potatoes, minus the skins.

Early rose potatoes, roasted in the ashes, Southern style, served hot.

Sliced tomatoes, with sugar or vinegar. Stewed tomatoes.

Green corn, cut from the ear and served with butter and pepper.

Green corn, on the ear.

Hot corn-pone, with chitlings, Southern style.

Hot hoe-cake, Southern style.

Hot egg-bread, Southern style.

Hot light-bread, Southern style.

Buttermilk. Iced sweet milk.

Apple dumplings, with real cream.

Apple pie. Apple fritters.

Apple puffs, Southern style.

Peach cobbler, Southern style.

Peach pie. American mince pie.

Pumpkin pie. Squash pie.

All sorts of American pastry.

Fresh American fruits of all sorts, including strawberries which are not to be doled out as if they were jewelry, but in a more liberal way. Ice-water—not prepared in the ineffectual goblet, but in the sincere and capable refrigerator.

Americans intending to spend a year or so in European hotels will do well to copy this bill and carry it along. They will find it an excellent thing to get up an appetite with, in the dispiriting presence of the squalid table d'hôte.

Foreigners cannot enjoy our food, I suppose, any more than we can enjoy theirs. It is not strange; for tastes are made, not born. I might glorify my bill of fare until I was tired; but after all, the Scotchman would shake his head and say, "Where's your haggis?" and the Fijian would sigh and say, "Where's your missionary?"

Mark Twain

TWAIN, MARK. *A TRAMP ABROAD*. AMERICAN PUBLISHING COMPANY, 1880.

SEE ALSO   *Family Meal Benefits; Food as Celebration; Food Fads; Gastronomy; Immigration and Cuisine; Religion and Food; Women's Role in Global Food Preparation.*

BIBLIOGRAPHY

Books

Bower, Anne. *African American Foodways: Explorations of History and Culture.* Urbana: University of Illinois Press, 2007.

Edge, John T. *Foodways.* Chapel Hill: University of North Carolina, 2007.

Nguyen, Andrea Q. *Into the Vietnamese Kitchen: Treasured Foodways, Modern Flavors.* Berkeley, CA: Ten Speed Press, 2006.

Periodicals

Cannuscio, Carolyn C., Eve E. Weiss, and David A. Asch. "The Contribution of Urban Foodways to Health Disparities." *Journal of Urban Health: Bulletin of the New York Academy of Medicine* 87, no. 3 (2010): 381–393.

Debevec, Liza, and Blanka Tivadar. "Making Connections through Foodways: Contemporary Issues in Anthropological and Sociological Studies of Food." *Anthropological Notebooks* 12, no. 1 (2006): 5–16.

Rahn, Millie. "Laying a Place at the Table: Creating Public Foodways Models from Scratch." *Journal of American Folklore* 119, no. 471 (2006): 30–46.

Web Sites

Hispanic Foodways. http://hispanicfoodways.com/ (accessed October 9, 2010).

Southern Foodways Alliance. http://www.southernfoodways.com/ (accessed October 9, 2010).

Melissa Carson

Free Trade and Agriculture

■ Introduction

Almost as long as trade has existed, governments have been taxing and otherwise restricting trade. Free trade is neither taxed nor restricted. However, because completely free trade very rarely occurs, more realistically, free trade involves situations in which taxes and other restrictions do not impose an unnecessary burden that prevents trade from taking place. Proponents of free trade have a long history of economic justifications and real economic gains that have been attributed to trade. Since World War II (1939–1945), agricultural trade has certainly been altered both in ways that free it and in ways that bind trade to a system of rules. In a rule-based trade system, free trade is the absence of trade barriers, governmental restrictions that prohibit or inhibit trade. Agricultural products of both plant and animal origin continue to face more trade barriers than non-agricultural goods for a variety of reasons including concerns about health and safety, the perceived benefits of protection of domestic agricultural and food processing industries, and concerns about food security and hunger. However, many economists argue that there are benefits to more free trade in agriculture, also known as the liberalization of agricultural trade.

■ Historical Background and Scientific Foundations

One of the first modern efforts to liberalize trade was the movement to repeal the Corn Laws in Great Britain, a tariff on grains and cereals implemented in 1815 to protect domestic producers and ensure control of the domestic price of grains. By keeping out less expensive foreign grain, landowners who grew grains benefited from a protected market. David Ricardo (1772–1823), an English economist, had argued that tariffs limited the benefits from trade that could be accrued due to comparative advantage. According to comparative advantage, two countries gain from trade even if both countries can produce a product. Because they produce the product at different levels of efficiency, countries face different opportunity costs. If one country is efficient at producing every product, it gains from specializing in products it is comparatively more efficient at producing. The country can discontinue producing products for which it lacks comparative advantage and trade with other countries for those products. This benefits both trading partners by enabling the countries to use their resources more efficiently. Comparative advantage was one reason Parliament repealed the Corn Laws in 1846.

Comparative advantage is one of three reasons countries trade, according to classical economic theory. Countries also may trade due to absolute advantage. In agricultural trade, countries that cannot grow tropical products, such as bananas and coffee, trade for them. The absolute advantage refers to the ability to produce something that another country cannot produce or the ability to produce at the very lowest cost in the world. Economies of scale also lead to international trade. Economies of scale refers to the tendency that larger markets and more production lower costs for both producers and consumers.

Trade in the nineteenth century continued to be limited, as countries with colonial empires such as France, the Netherlands, and Great Britain tended to trade primarily with their own colonies. Increasing efforts to protect domestic industries and interests using tariffs caused a collapse of world trade during the Great Depression (1929–1941). In an attempt to revive trade and its benefits following World War II (1939–1945), 13 countries negotiated the General Agreement on Trade and Tariffs (GATT) in 1947. More countries joined the agreement and subsequent rounds of negotiation were held to lower tariffs. Each round lowered tariffs and sought to reduce other restrictions on trade, often referred to as non-tariff barriers. However, in the first six rounds of negotiations, agricultural trade was largely excluded from being liberalized. At the same time, countries were

WORDS TO KNOW

COMPARATIVE ADVANTAGE: Efficiency in production of one good over another that makes trade possible even if one country lacks absolute efficiency in either good. Even if one country is more efficient at producing every product, it can gain from specializing in the products it is comparatively more efficient at producing. Then the country can move out of producing products in which it lacks comparative advantage and trade with other countries for those products. The resulting trade benefits both trading partners due to specialization that enables countries to use their resources more efficiently.

LIBERALIZATION: In trade, the reduction or removal of tariffs and other barriers to trade. In agricultural policy, liberalization refers to reduction or elimination of domestic subsidies, price and production controls, export subsidies, and other agricultural support programs.

NON-TARIFF BARRIER: Any barrier to trade other than tariffs. Usually refers to quotas and restrictions on trade or to rules and regulations that affect trade but may be set for other reasons.

SANITARY AND PHYTOSANITARY (SPS) MEASURES: Laws, rules, and regulations intended to help protect human and animal health (sanitary) or plant health (phytosanitary). Regulations regarding food safety, animal diseases, plant disease, and pests are referred to as SPS restrictions.

TARIFF: A tax on trade, usually on imports.

TRADE BARRIER: Anything that impedes or distorts the movement of goods between countries. Examples of trade barriers include tariffs, export taxes, export subsidies, quotas, country of origin rules, safety regulations, licensing requirements, and product standards.

establishing a wide variety of restrictions on trade in agricultural goods; this was designed to protect domestic agricultural producers, to control prices of agricultural products, and to promote rural economic growth. Despite these limits on trade, agricultural trade increased more than thirteen fold between 1961 and 1995.

In the Uruguay Round negotiations (1986–1993), nations began to bring agriculture into the international trading system. The result of the Uruguay Round was the establishment of the World Trade Organization (WTO) in 1995. As of July of 2008 the WTO had 153 member states. These states have agreed to a variety of rules for trade, including rules for agricultural trade. Under the Agreement on Agriculture (1995), the signatory countries agreed to reduce agricultural tariffs and subsidies for agricultural exports. Also, more controversially, the Agreement on Agriculture attempts to limit the total amount that countries can spend on domestic agricultural subsidies. In addition, the WTO attempted to deal with

some non-tariff barriers to agricultural trade. Some of these barriers are designed to prevent the spread of animal diseases, protect the health of consumers, and prevent plant diseases or pest infestations. Under the Agreement on Sanitary and Phytosanitary (SPS) Measures, known as the SPS Agreement (1995), countries may continue to impose rules that protect human, plant, and animal health. However, they must base these rules on scientific assessment of the risks posed by imports and in a way that is least trade distorting. Worldwide trade in agricultural products more than doubled in the first decade of the WTO's existence from 1995 to 2005.

At the same time that the GATT rounds were being negotiated, countries began to enter into many preferential trading agreements (PTAs). These agreements tend to be regional and may not cover all areas of trade. They attempt to lower tariffs, decrease non-tariff barriers, and possibly harmonize standards between members. PTAs may create new trade, which is one of their goals and why they were permitted under GATT and the WTO. However, some studies have suggested that trade diversion may sometimes occur instead of trade creation. In trade diversion, countries in the agreement trade with each other but decrease or divert trade with partners from outside the agreement. As of July 2010, 474 PTAs had been officially registered with the WTO. Some of these existed prior to the formation of the WTO. Among the more prominent agreements are the North American Free Trade Agreement (NAFTA), which took effect in 1994 among the United States, Canada, and Mexico. The European Economic Community was implemented in 1957 among six western European countries and had expanded to include 27 countries of the European Union by 2007.

Under the Doha Round of multi-lateral trade negotiations that began in 2001, countries sought further liberalization of agricultural trade. However, disagreements between countries led to the collapse of the Doha Round negotiations in 2008.

■ Impacts and Issues

Proponents of free trade of agricultural products point to the possibility of large benefits. In 2002 the U.S. Department of Agriculture's (USDA) Economic Research Service (ERS) estimated that the world's consumers would be able to purchase an additional $56 billion worth of goods every year under liberalization. A 2006 study conducted by the International Food Policy Research Institute (IFPRI) concluded that the developing countries alone could gain $20 billion in increased welfare, an economic measure of costs and benefits. A 2008 study by Antoine Bouët (1962–), a French economist at IFPRI, estimates the worldwide welfare gains at $100 billion. In general, the benefits would accrue to consumers around the world who would pay lower prices

Demonstrators carry an oversized replica of a corn cob to protest the removal of import tariffs on farm goods from the United States and Canada, as agreed by the North American Free Trade Agreement (NAFTA) timetable, in Mexico City, January 31, 2008. With large parts of the world clamoring for food and governments trying every play in their books to stave off food riots, many experts are saying the way out of the crisis could be by massively investing in small farmers, instead of watching them sink beneath the waters of global trade and agribusiness. *AP Images.*

on some agricultural goods, some groups of poor small farmers whose incomes increase due to rising prices of some goods, and agriculturally productive exporters that would be able to expand their exports even more.

A number of countries and citizens continue to oppose further liberalization of the rules of trade under the WTO for a variety of reasons. Some countries want to be self-sufficient in food production and not dependent on imported staple foods. Others want to protect rural lifestyles, small farms, and rural areas from the perceived risks of liberalization. Still others point to a shift in agricultural production, especially a shift away from European and rich Asian countries with high environmental and labor standards, that might degrade the environment or harm laborers. There are also those who suggest that further liberalization would actually hurt the poor due to their markets in the developing world being flooded with inexpensive agricultural products from major low cost exporters such as the United States and Brazil.

SEE ALSO *Agribusiness; Agricultural Land Reform; Agriculture and International Trade; Community Supported Agriculture (CSAs); Decollectivization; Ethical Issues in Agriculture; Fair Trade; Family Farms; Food and Agriculture Organization (FAO); Green Revolution (1943); International Fund for Agricultural Development; Produce Traceability; World Trade Organization (WTO).*

BIBLIOGRAPHY

Books

Davis, Christina L. *Food Fights over Free Trade: How International Institutions Promote Agricultural Trade Liberalization.* Princeton, NJ: Princeton University Press, 2005.

Kiple, Kenneth F. *A Movable Feast: Ten Millennia of Food Globalization.* Cambridge, UK, and New York: Cambridge University Press, 2007.

Nützenadel, Alexander, and Frank Trentmann. *Food and Globalization: Consumption, Markets and Politics in the Modern World.* Oxford, UK, and New York: Berg, 2008.

Thomas, Harmon C. *Trade Reforms and Food Security: Country Case Studies and Synthesis.* Rome: FAO, 2006.

Periodicals

Hemphill, Thomas A. "Globalization of the U.S. Food Supply: Reconciling Product Safety Regulation with Free Trade." *Business Economics: The Journal of the National Association of Business Economists* 44, no. 3 (2009): 154–168.

Trentmann, Frank. "Before Fair Trade: Empire, Free Trade, and the Moral Economies of Food in the Modern World." *Environment and Planning: D, Society & Space* 25, no. 6 (2007): 1079–1102.

Web Sites

"Agriculture: Fairer Markets for Farmers." *World Trade Organization (WTO).* http://www.wto.org/english/thewto_e/whatis_e/tif_e/agrm3_e.htm (accessed September 18, 2010).

Institute for Agriculture and Trade Policy. http://www.iatp.org/ (accessed September 18, 2010).

Blake Jackson Stabler

French Café Culture

■ Introduction

Café culture is often associated with the quintessential Parisian way of life, sitting unrushed to contemplate philosophical questions, or just sitting and watching the world go by. And Parisian cafés have been around for centuries in one form or another: The oldest café in Paris, Café Procope, has been in operation since 1686.

French cafés are meeting places, neighborhood hubs, places for relaxing or refueling. The French café is often the pulse of the social and political mood of the community. Students, political leaders, philosophers and artists, locals, and tourists enjoy more than a coffee, but also an idea that sitting unrushed is a worthy way to spend time.

But what made French café culture the symbol of this kind of approach to life? What drives this ethos and will it last in twenty-first century high-speed society? These questions are the focus of this article.

■ Historical Background and Scientific Foundations

Whereas some say coffee was consumed for spiritual reasons as early as the ninth century, the earliest reliable evidence of coffee drinking, by roasting and brewing coffee beans in a similar manner to modern day preparation, comes from mid-fifteenth century Arabia, modern day Yemen. From there, coffee drinking spread through the Middle East, Turkey, and North Africa and into Europe via Italy by the seventeenth century.

The café or coffeehouse culture appeared first in the Middle East. In Mecca, the heart of the Muslim world, coffeehouses were hubs of political gatherings. Despite a brief period of banning both coffee and coffeehouses between 1512 and 1524, the coffeehouse spread to other major cities in the Middle East from Damascus to Cairo.

The arrival of the very first café in Europe is said to have been in Venice in 1645, which was established as a result of trade with the Ottomans. Trade gave birth to cafés across the rest of Europe too. Within 30 years coffeehouses had spread across England and had started up in France, in Paris in 1672, and in America, in Boston in 1676.

The origin of the modern day French "café culture," as distinct from other parts of the world, is linked historically to the period pre-dating the French Revolution (1789–1799). This was a period of radical upheaval in French history and by extension in European history also. During the revolution, the monarchy that had ruled for centuries collapsed, and French society transformed into a liberal political system from its previous system of feudal, aristocratic, and religious privileges. During this period, known as the Enlightenment, old ideas about hierarchy and tradition were questioned and gave way to new principles of citizenship and inalienable rights and a strong belief in rationality and science. Leading intellectuals and figures in the French Revolution met regularly at Paris' Café Procope during this time, and were joined by Benjamin Franklin (1706–1790) and Thomas Jefferson (1743–1826).

Café culture around the world, not only in France, inspired similar kinds of political and philosophical exchanges, as evidenced by periods in history when coffee and cafés have been banned. In seventeenth century England, for example, coffee houses were outlawed by King Charles II (1630–1685) for their association with rebellious political activities, although he was forced to back down from the banning after loud public outcry.

The café society swelled again in Paris in the early 1900s as the world's literary and artistic avant-garde converged on Paris. Free thinkers such as Ernest Hemmingway (1899–1961), Jean-Paul Sartre (1905–1980) and Simone de Beauvoir (1908–1986) enjoyed the creative freedom that these meeting places engendered.

Late in the twentieth century a café philosophique ("café-philo") movement in Paris proved to be reinvigorating for traditional French café culture. In part founded by Marc Sautet (1947–1998) the movement repopularized café-centered philosophical debates in the

WORDS TO KNOW

ARRONDISSEMENT: In France, an administrative division or compartment. The city of Paris is currently subdivided into 20 municipal arrondissements. There are also national departmental *arrondissements* dividing France into one hundred *departments*.

EXISTENTIALIST: A philosopher who argues existential philosophical principles, typically (but with many variations) emphasizing the uniqueness of the individual and the isolation of the individual imposed by mortal existence in an indifferent natural world. The philosophy stresses freedom of individual choice and responsibility for personal actions.

debating events spread across Paris to hundreds of cafés around the world.

In the twenty-first century, many of the world's cities have their own distinct café cultures including Vienna, Budapest, Rome, and Buenos Aires.

■ Impacts and Issues

The French take their cafés seriously, and in many respects this passion is less about the character of the coffee and more about the social environment. Coffeehouses bring comforting rituals, offer time to be spent with friends, or space for reflection while watching the world go by. The French enjoy their café culture at all times of the day, with the morning paper and after meals. The key to the French café culture is the sense of not hurrying. The American model of seating two parties per table during lunch or dinner does not apply to café service; a table may be occupied by the same person for hours, who may begin with a coffee, then study, work, or meet with friends at the café, and keep the same table until time to have lunch or dinner. This sense of not rushing tends to include the pace of the waiters and service staff as well, which sometimes does not appeal as much to a foreign visitor as to the locals.

style led by French existentialist philosophers Sartre and de Beauvoir centered at the Café de Flore and other 6th *arrondissement* cafés prior to and immediately following World War II (1939–1945). The modern cafe-philo movement also placed an emphasis on the inclusion of viewpoints from people without formal education in philosophy. The modern café-philo movement and

Patrons drink coffee outdoors at the Café de Flore in Paris, France.   *© Alex Segre / Alamy.*

Some of the most recognizable Paris cafés include Café de la Paix, Les Deux Magots, and Café de Flore. And the cafés are not just coffee shops, but typically offer a full restaurant menu with meals for any time of the day, a full bar, and a wine selection. However, French café culture is struggling. For tourists, the experience is still sought after, but locals seem to be going less, and the number of cafés is shrinking. In 1960 there were about 200,000 cafés across France, whereas by the year 2010 only about 40,000 were in existence, according to industry statistics.

On a sunny day in Paris, the cafés in the more expensive neighborhoods and tourist areas continue to be full of locals and visitors alike, but less so in the working-class neighborhoods around the country. Although some blame the decline on a 2007 smoking ban and new drinking and driving legislation, others say that the traditional café culture is simply not keeping pace with the evolving needs of ordinary people, who expect good quality coffee, drinks, and food, along with services such as newspapers, an Internet signal, or a television. Additionally, lawmakers in France are considering bans on the large outdoor gas heaters that have become synonymous with cafés in the wintertime, due to their carbon emissions.

Whereas many elements of coffeehouses have their origins in the early café culture and continue to form part of the concept of the coffee culture, a new café culture has evolved, particularly in the United States. In the United States the term *coffee house* is frequently interchanged with Starbucks, the ubiquitous franchise where quality product, environment, and services are all at the fore of the service model. But some argue that the chain's Internet-service shops are perhaps counter to café culture, as they fill up with individuals and their laptops, rather than inspiring modern-day philosophers. Regardless, modern coffee culture is clearly evident in the sheer number of coffee establishments within walking distance of one another in urban centers across the world.

Just how far the visceral pleasures of café culture have woven themselves into the fabric of modern life cannot be underestimated. In the United Kingdom, for example, the government launched a "Café Culture" campaign in 2009 aimed at helping companies to improve their workers' skills by replicating a more informal, relaxed working environment to inspire positive behaviors and greater staff unity. And, anecdotally, the World Barista Championships currently attracts entrants from 54 countries.

SEE ALSO *Coffee; Food and the Internet; Foodways; Gastronomy; Social Media and Food.*

BIBLIOGRAPHY

Books

Clark, Val. *The Parisian Café: A Literary Companion.* New York: Universe, 2002.

DeJean, Joan E. *The Essence of Style: How the French Invented High Fashion, Fine Food, Chic Cafés, Style, Sophistication, and Glamour.* New York: Free Press, 2005.

Fitch, Noel R., and Rick Tulka. *Paris Café: The Sélect Crowd.* Brooklyn, NY: Soft Skull Press, 2007.

Flandrin, Jean-Louis. *Arranging the Meal: A History of Table Service in France.* Berkeley: University of California Press, 2007.

Graf, Christine *Cafe Life: Paris.* Northampton, MA: Interlink Publishing Group, 2005.

Nuffer, David. *The Walkable Feast: (Left Bank Communion with Ernest) Five Café to Café Walks to the Places of Ernest Hemingway in His Early Years in Paris.* San Diego, CA: Bookman Publishing Marketing, 2005.

Periodicals

Kleinman, Sharon S. "Cafe Culture in France and the United States: A Comparative Ethnographic Study of the Use of Mobile Information and Communication Technologies." *Atlantic Journal of Communication* 14, no. 4 (2006): 191–210.

Web Sites

Askin, Jennifer. "Starbucks Set to Rock Italy's Cafe Culture." *ABC News,* April 30, 2007. http://abcnews.go.com/Business/story?id=88256&page=1 (accessed October 17, 2010).

Le Procope. http://www.procope.com/ (accessed October 17, 2010).

Oger, Genevieve. "French Cafe Culture Struggles to Stay Alive." *Deutsche Welle,* August 14, 2009. http://www.dw-world.de/dw/article/0,,4562836,00.html (accessed October 17, 2010).

Melissa Carson

French Paradox

Introduction

Rates of obesity and coronary heart disease vary among different countries because of diet and lifestyle factors. One of the first of these differences to become apparent was the French paradox. Rates of obesity and heart disease in France have long been noted to be significantly lower than in other Western countries, including the United States. The French typically eat rich, high-fat foods, which would be expected to increase heart disease risk, and they smoke more than people in the United States, so the health benefits they enjoy seem contradictory.

Originally it was argued that consumption of red wine accounted for the French paradox, because studies show that alcohol and red wine can have some benefits for heart health. However, red wine is one factor among many accounting for the paradox. More important is the attitude towards food in France compared to the United States and elsewhere. Enjoyment of food is a priority, and the French make time to shop for, prepare, and eat their food. Importantly, portion sizes are small so even high-fat, rich foods are not consumed in excess. The French drink more water and fewer soft drinks, which may also contribute to lower obesity rates. However, the French may not enjoy their paradoxical health advantages for much longer: Rates of obesity are creeping up in France as traditional lifestyles are beginning to change.

Historical Background and Scientific Foundations

The French Paradox has been recognized for about 50 years, when coronary heart disease (CHD) statistics revealed that rates in France were much lower than elsewhere in the West. Moreover, in 2009 just 14.5 percent of the French population was obese, compared to more than 33 percent of the American population. Obesity is a strong risk factor for CHD. The paradox lies in the fact that the traditional French diet often includes cream, butter, and some very high-fat products such as foie gras. Intense physical activity is not part of the French lifestyle, and smoking is popular. Therefore, it seems that the French contravene many healthy lifestyle guidelines without paying the price in increased rates of CHD.

For many years, it was argued that the explanation for the French paradox lay in the French people's consumption of red wine. Many studies have shown that moderate alcohol consumption has various health benefits. Moderate drinkers have lower mortality rates than non-drinkers and heavy drinkers. Alcohol has a number of potentially beneficial effects: For instance, it stops blood platelets from clumping together, which may prevent the formation of the clots that cause heart attacks. Alcohol also increases levels of high-density lipoprotein cholesterol, which may inhibit the formation of plaque in the coronary arteries. Red wine, in addition, contains various antioxidants from the skin of the grapes, which could also slow the development of CHD.

More recent research has suggested that it is not just red wine consumption that accounts for the French paradox. What is probably more important is French attitudes concerning food and their behavior around it. Traditionally, the French have taken food seriously and have seen it as a major source of pleasure. They do not eat on the run, but will stop work for more than an hour to have a leisurely lunch. Eating more slowly allows the brain to process a sensation of satiety before too much food is consumed. Cooking is also more popular than in the United States, and the French tend to shop daily at small shops and markets where they invest in high-quality produce, shopping less frequently in large supermarkets that stock processed foods.

Although rich foods such as foie gras and pastry are popular in France, portion sizes are relatively small. Researchers from the French national scientific research institute and the University of Philadelphia conducted a comparison study on portion sizes in restaurants in Paris and Philadelphia. They found that the average portion size in Paris was 25 percent smaller than in Philadelphia, at 277 grams compared to 346 grams. Chinese restaurants in Philadelphia served dishes that were 72 percent larger than at Chinese restaurants in Paris. A typical candy bar in Philadelphia was 41 percent larger than in Paris. Finally, soft drinks and hot dogs were more than half again as big in Philadelphia compared to those items in Paris.

Research has also linked the rise in obesity to a corresponding increase in soda-like soft drinks, which usually contain sugar or high fructose syrup. These drinks are less popular in France than in the United States; French consumers are more likely to drink bottled water. The French drink 52 liters of soft drinks per person per year on average, compared to 216 liters per person per year in the United States. The amount of bottled water drunk in France is 147 liters per person per year compared with 47 liters per person per year in the United States. And, whereas going to the gym is not popular in France, their culture is less centered around the automobile than is the case in the United States: Walking and climbing stairs are seen as a normal part of everyday life. People, especially in the city, will take public transport rather than use their cars for short journeys and then walk from the various forms of transit to their final destinations.

■ Impacts and Issues

The French have not been immune to the pressures of globalization. The pace of life is less unhurried than it was. Lack of time means people more often are

A woman drinks coffee and eats croissants at a café in Montpelier, France. © Eastern Photography / Alamy.

buying food from fast food outlets, which are present in most French towns. Obesity rates increased at 5 percent per year from 1997, when 8.5 percent of the population was obese, to 2005, when the rate had risen to 11.3 percent. By 2009, 14.5 percent of the French population was considered obese (15.1 percent of French women and 13.9 percent of men). If this trend continues, the gap between obesity statistics in France and other countries will close. Public policy measures in France are focused upon combating child obesity, as one French child in seven was considered obese in 2005. Measures include banning the sale of snacks and soft drinks from machines at schools, promoting increased physical activity in schools, and fostering awareness about health and physical fitness. There is discussion on monitoring children's weight and banning the advertisement of certain foods.

SEE ALSO *Diet and Cancer; Diet and Diabetes; Diet and Heart Disease; Diet and Hypertension; Fast Food; Foodways; Gastronomy; Slow Food Movement; Standard American Diet and Changing American Diet; Viniculture.*

BIBLIOGRAPHY

Books

Brette, Isabelle. *The French Paradox*. Monaco City, Monaco: Alpen, 2010.

Cooper, Frank A., and Charles T. McGee. *Cholesterol and the French Paradox* . Burleigh, Queensland, Australia: Zeus Publications, 2006.

Periodicals

De Leiris, Joël, and Francois Boucher. "Does Wine Consumption Explain the French Paradox?" *Dialogues in Cardiovascular Medicine* 13, no. 3 (2008): 183–192.

El Masri, Firas, et al. "Is the So-Called French Paradox a Reality?" *Journal of Bone and Joint Surgery. British Volume* 92, no. 3 (2010): 342–348.

Mochly-Rosen, Diana, and Samir Zakhari. "Focus On: The Cardiovascular System: What Did We Learn from the French (Paradox)?" *Alcohol Research and Health* 33, nos. 1–2 (2010): 76–86.

Vidavalur, Ramesh, Hajime Otani, Pawan K.Singa, and Nilanjana Maulik. "Significance of Wine and Resveratrol in Cardiovascular Disease: French Paradox Revisited." *Experimental and Clinical Cardiology* 11, no. 3 (2006): 217–225.

Web Sites

Bays, Jan Chosen. "Mindful Eating: The French Paradox." *Psychology Today*, March 21, 2009. http://www.psychologytoday.com/blog/mindful-eating/200903/mindful-eating-the-french-paradox (accessed October 9, 2010).

Ferrières, Jean. "The French Paradox: Lessons for Other Countries." *National Institutes of Health (NIH)*. http://www.ncbi.nlm.nih.gov/pmc/articles/PMC1768013/pdf/hrt09000107.pdf (accessed October 9, 2010).

Susan Aldridge

Fruits

■ Introduction

Fruits are one of nature's ways of disseminating plant seeds to make new plants. Most taste good and have considerable nutritional value. When animals, including humans, eat fruits they ingest the seeds of the plant as well and, at least in the wild, spread them about when they excrete them. Botanists define fruit as the ovary of a plant, whereas cooks tend to define fruits as sweet, rather than savory, foods. Fruits vary widely in their shape, color, texture, flavor, and nutritional value. They provide vitamins, antioxidants, and fiber to the human diet. Fruits have been part of the human diet since pre-historic times and have been exported from their native countries for cultivation elsewhere many times during the course of history. However, of the many thousands of varieties of fruit in the world, only a few hundred are consumed often. Selective breeding by humans led to new varieties of fruits such as apples and bananas that resist disease and have better flavor characteristics. Genetic modification is beginning to take these advances a step further but remains a controversial technology.

■ Historical Background and Scientific Foundations

Fruits were probably the earliest foods to be eaten by humans, because they can be plucked from a tree or bush and eaten raw. Fruits can be classified into groups depending upon their botanical characteristics, although some, such as figs, bananas, and pineapples, do not readily fall into a particular group. Many fruits consist of the tissue of the ovary of a plant but the way this is structured can vary. Citrus fruits are native to southeast Asia, with the exception of the grapefruit, which comes from the West Indies. They are segmented fruits, in which each segment is full of juice-bearing cells and corresponds to the carpal component of the ovary. The Pome group comprises apples and pears, which have small seeds surrounded by a large amount of fibrous ovarian tissue. Apples have long had a symbolic importance. For instance, the Trojan Wars were said to be triggered by Paris giving Aphrodite a golden apple. The drupes, including apricots, cherries, plums, and peaches, have been cultivated for several thousand years and consist of a relatively large seed with a hard coat, and flesh with a characteristic texture that changes on ripening. Berries are an important group of fruits. True berries, such as blueberries, cranberries, and grapes, consist of a single fruit. There are also complex berries such as blackberries and raspberries that are botanically classed as members of the Rose family, and are known as aggregate fruits, because they are made up of many tiny fruits, each with its own seed. The strawberry is not a berry at all, but rather a false fruit in which the flesh is the base of the flower and the fruits themselves are the tiny seed-like structures on the outside. Melons, which were first described about 6,000 years ago in Egypt, are members of the squash family, and their tissue is more placental rather than ovarian.

Fruits can also be classified by how and where they grow. Sub-tropical fruits, such as oranges, avocados, and dates, are similar to the temperate-climate fruits, except that they are not hardy to extreme cold. They will tolerate mild frost and some may need a period of cold to ripen. Tropical fruits, including banana, mango, and papaya, will grow only in a frost free climate.

In cuisine, fruits are defined as sweet foods. Thus rhubarb is a fruit in the kitchen, even though in the botanical sense it is a stem. The tomato is a vegetable in the kitchen, even though it is actually a fruit. However a fruit is classified, it is formed by broadly the same biological process. Once a seed is fertilized, a fruit begins to grow. The ovary wall may become fleshy, as in berries and drupes. Nuts, which are also fruits, are formed from ovary walls that become hard. Simple fruits, such as pomes, drupes, and bananas, come from one ovary. Aggregate fruits come from many ovaries, each producing a fruitlet that joins with others to form the individual fruit. Multiple fruits, such as pineapple, are very similar

WORDS TO KNOW

OVARY: The part of a plant that produces a seed and nourishes it until it is ready to grow into another plant.

RIPENING: A series of chemical processes occurring in a fruit that make it more attractive to animals. Ripening includes increasing sweetness and decreasing starch and acid content, as well as characteristic color changes from green to red or yellow and the development of texture and aroma.

TEMPERATE CLIMATE FRUITS: Fruits that grow on trees, bushes, and vines and need a period of cold before they flower.

but come from multiple flowers, each of which produces one ovary. The ovary wall, or pericarp, has three layers that develop into the fruit skin, its center, and the seed coating. Fruits are the only parts of a plant that undergo the ripening process, through which many chemical and physical changes occur. Cells in the middle layer of the pericarp expand and fill up with sugars and minerals from the rest of the plant, while the fruit expands and develops texture as its cell walls are reinforced with pectin and cellulose. Many secondary compounds are synthesized, a number of which are bitter and astringent to help fight off predators. These complex changes are triggered by the hormone ethylene, which is produced by the ripening fruit. The produce industry uses ethylene to ripen fruit artificially because it is often harvested before it is naturally ripe to make its transport easier. Once fruit is ripe, its sugar content becomes attractive to bacteria and fungi, which bring about the less desirable changes known as rotting.

■ Impacts and Issues

Fruits are well known for their nutritional content, being high in vitamins, minerals, antioxidants, and fiber. Bananas are valued in Africa and Asia as a staple food because of their high carbohydrate content. Some fruits

Fresh fruit is displayed in a market in Barcelona, Spain. *Image copyright compuinfoto, 2010. Used under license by Shutterstock.com.*

Vendors sell dried fruit at a street market in China.   *Adrienne Lerner / Lerner & Lerner / LernerMedia Global Photos.*

have been particularly noted for their health giving properties. For instance, in 2004 the United States Department of Agriculture found that the blueberry had the highest antioxidant content of all fruits. Antioxidants are important because they can limit the damage that free radicals do within the cells of the body, which may reduce the risk of cancer and heart disease.

The nutritional qualities of fruits and the agronomic characteristics of the plants they come from have been greatly improved over the history of agriculture by plant breeding. A detailed knowledge of plant genetics and application of genetic engineering technology have led to the creation of genetically modified fruits. Crops that

have been genetically modified (GM) include papaya, apples, bananas, pineapple, plums, and tomatoes. Not all of these are yet commercially available. Possible benefits of GM plants, including those bearing fruit, are improved resistance to disease and insects, better flavor, longer shelf life, and greater nutritional value. However, there are many concerns over GM fruit, including loss of traditional species and spread of the foreign genes that are introduced by the GM plant to other crops. Genetic engineering also tends to be done by multinational companies, leading to the fear that they will come to dominate global food production at the expense of local farmers and producers.

SEE ALSO *Agricultural Demand for Water; Banana Trade Wars; Climate Change and Agriculture; Commission on Genetic Resources for Food and Agriculture; Convention on Biological Diversity (1992); Diet and Cancer; Diet and Diabetes; Diet and Heart Disease; Diet and Hypertension; Dietary Guidelines for Americans; Dietary Reference Intakes; Ethical Issues in Agriculture; Extreme Weather and Food Supply; Farm-to-Table Movement; Food as Celebration; Food Packaging; Genetically Modified Organisms (GMO); Import Restrictions; Indigenous Peoples and Their Diets; Locavore; Migrant Labor, Immigration, and Food Production; Political Food Boycotts; Preservation; USDA Food Pyramid; Veganism; Vegetarianism.*

BIBLIOGRAPHY

Books

Gollner, Adam. *The Fruit Hunters: A Story of Nature, Adventure, Commerce and Obsession.* New York: Scribner, 2008.

Koeppel, Dan. *Banana: The Fate of the Fruit That Changed the World.* New York: Hudson Street Press, 2008.

Lozano, Jorge E. *Fruit Manufacturing.* New York: Springer, 2006.

Parsons, Russ. *How to Pick a Peach: The Search for Flavor from Farm to Table.* Boston: Houghton Mifflin, 2007.

Watson, Ronald R., and Victor R. Preedy. *Bioactive Foods in Promoting Health: Fruits and Vegetables.* Amsterdam and Boston: Academic Press, 2010.

Periodicals

Gupta, Vikrant, et al. "Genome Analysis and Genetic Enhancement of Tomato." *Critical Reviews in Biotechnology* 29, no. 2 (2009): 152–181.

Solomon, Diane. "The Devil's Fruit: The Strawberries That You Get at the Supermarket Come at a Cost to Pickers." *The Progressive* 72, no. 1 (2008): 22–24.

Web Sites

Rose, Joel. "I-95 a Trap for Migrant Fruit Pickers." *National Public Radio (NPR)*, September 4, 2010. http://www.npr.org/templates/story/story.php?storyId=129580744&ft=1&f=1006 (accessed September 7, 2010).

"Safe Handling of Raw Produce and Fresh-Squeezed Fruit and Vegetable Juices." *U.S. Food and Drug Administration (FDA)*. http://www.fda.gov/Food/ResourcesForYou/Consumers/ucm114299 (accessed September 7, 2010).

Susan Aldridge

Functional Foods

■ Introduction

Health claims for specific foods have always existed. However, starting in the 1980s, a new category of nutritionally enhanced foods hit the market as functional foods. Functional foods are foods that have been somehow modified or changed to possess certain health characteristics. Functional foods include fortified foods, foods to which micronutrients have been added. Some functional foods are also known as nutraceuticals, foods that are intended to treat or prevent illness or disease. In addition to foods with added ingredients or particular nutrients, functional foods include foods modified during their production, such as feeding chickens a particular diet to produce eggs with certain nutritional qualities. The size of the functional food market is difficult to define, but it appears to be growing. Some consumer advocates and regulatory authorities worry that the health claims of functional foods have not been examined, but producers of and proponents of functional foods point both to the long history of fortified foods and of food for treating disease as proof of the potential benefits of functional foods.

■ Historical Background and Scientific Foundations

Health claims have been made about specific foods since ancient civilizations. Hippocrates (c.460–370 BC), an ancient Greek physician influential in Western medicine, said, "Let food be your medicine." However, foods were rarely marketed with specific health claims until the nineteenth century. One early proponent for diet as a treatment for and preventative measure against disease was the Reverend Alexander Graham (1794–1851), an American reformer and Presbyterian minister. Graham prescribed a vegetarian diet as a cure for alcoholism and sexual desires. He created recipes for foods to improve health including Graham bread, a whole grain wheat bread; and Graham crackers, a honey-sweetened cracker that included wheat bran and wheat germ to aid in digestion.

Fortifying food on a large-scale commercial basis began in the 1920s. In the United States and Switzerland, iodized salt started to appear as a way to prevent goiter, a disease of the thyroid gland. Other public-private partnerships (PPPs) emerged to fortify foods with specific nutrients to prevent specific diseases. For example, vitamin D was added to milk in the United States and Canada starting in the 1930s as a way to prevent rickets, a disease that softens children's bones. Also, Vitamin A was added to milk, butter, margarine, sugar, and other products in Europe, the United States, Central America, Asia, and Africa to combat multiple health problems and diseases related to a deficiency of this micronutrient. In the 1980s, partly as both a treatment and preventative measure for osteoporosis, a disease of the bones, food manufacturers in the United States began to add calcium to fruit juices, soft drinks, cereals, and other processed foods. Though originating in PPPs to prevent common diseases, fortification of food with micronutrients became a way to market foods to increasingly health-conscious consumers.

The term *functional food* first appeared in the 1980s in Japan, and Japan remains one of the only countries to have tight regulations over the health claims that can be made about functional foods. In Japan functional foods have been regulated as Foods for Specified Health Use (FOSHU) since 1991. This separate category of regulation distinguishes functional foods from general food safety regulations designed to prevent foodborne illnesses and from the regulation of medicines. FOSHU foods receive a special label that shows their health claims have been tested and the relevant governmental authority has verified those claims. Functional foods face less strict marketing requirements for their labeling in the United States. The European Union does not have a harmonized set of rules on their labeling and sale.

Functional foods lack an agreed-upon definition, so many foods may be considered functional. This would

WORDS TO KNOW

FOODS FOR SPECIFIED HEALTH USE (FOSHU): A legal term in Japan used to regulate the health claims made by functional foods. FOSHU producers can receive a seal and verification of their health claims from the Japanese government.

MICRONUTRIENTS: Vitamins and minerals necessary for growth, metabolic functions, and other biological processes in humans, other animals, and plants.

NUTRACEUTICAL: A food that may treat illness or prevent disease due to its nutritional qualities.

An upscale supermarket in Beijing, China, features a knot of ginseng, a root prized in traditional Chinese medicine. While ginseng is commonly found in affordable sizes and qualities, this cluster of roots is priced at the equivalent of $65,000 USD. Ginseng is a common ingredient in herbal teas, tonics, and natural digestive aids worldwide. *Joseph Hyder / Lerner & Lerner / LernerMedia Global Photos.*

include natural, whole foods with specific health claims such as fruits, vegetables, nuts, fish, and grains. When one or more of the preceding is used as an ingredient, packaged processed foods may make health claims related to their ingredients: For example, a fruit juice that contains pomegranate juice may claim special properties from the antioxidants found in this fruit. Functional foods that are processed foods are often fortified by the addition of micronutrients or other ingredients. During processing, vitamins, minerals, antioxidants, or other nutrients are added. With earlier fortified foods, the focus was on the addition of micronutrients—vitamins, and minerals—though now functional foods often include probiotics, fiber, and fatty acids. Danone, a French food company known for producing yogurt, has conducted a great deal of research on the health benefits of live and active cultures found in yogurt and other fermented products. These cultures, known as probiotics, have been one of the key areas of growth in functional foods as their popularity has been steadily rising since the 1990s. In addition to adding ingredients for health benefits; fortifying food; or conducting a special processing step such as fermentation to create functional foods, actual agricultural practices and livestock feeding practices are being changed to create new functional foods. For example, chickens are fed a diet high in flaxseed and other foods that contain omega-3 fatty acids so that they will produce eggs with a higher content of omega-3 fatty acids. Some studies suggest omega-3 fatty acids may lower the risk of heart disease. Also, new functional foods are marketed to persons with food allergies. For example, gluten-free foods, lactose-free dairy products, and specially formulated foods for diabetics have found growing sales and an increasing amount of shelf space in food retail outlets. Functional foods are also created by modifying the content of processed foods or even modifying the actual whole foods.

■ Impacts and Issues

As there is no agreed upon definition of functional food, measuring the sales of functional foods is difficult. For example, the *Nutritional Business Journal* posits that functional foods are a $130 billion per year industry in the United States, but the article includes all organic and natural foods in this calculation. A 2007 report in *Marketing Daily* states that functional foods were only a $24.8 billion market in the United States in 2006. In a 2009 report, the accounting firm Price Waterhouse Coopers (PWC) estimated that functional foods were a $20–30 billion dollar per year industry in the United States, comprising around five percent of total food sales. However, PWC cited growth rates between 8.5 and 20 percent annually for functional foods, significantly higher than the food markets' overall predicted rate of 1 to 4 percent annual growth. It appears that increasing population. Also, they feel that existing regulation of functional foods is sufficient, as these regulations generally already cover food safety concerns and some labeling requirements about the nutritional value of foods.

SEE ALSO *Dietary Guidelines for Americans; Dietary Reference Intakes; Nutrient Fortification of Foods; Phytochemicals (Phytonutrients).*

BIBLIOGRAPHY

Books

Bagchi, Debasis. *Nutraceutical and Functional Food Regulations in the United States and around the World.* Amsterdam: Elsevier/Academic Press, 2008.

Chen, Nancy N *Food, Medicine, and the Quest for Good Health: Nutrition, Medicine, and Culture.* New York: Columbia University Press, 2009.

Eskin, N. A. Michael, and Snait Tamir. *Dictionary of Nutraceuticals and Functional Foods.* Boca Raton, FL: Taylor & Francis Group/CRC Press, 2006.

Shetty, Kalidas. *Functional Foods and Biotechnology.* Boca Raton, FL: CRC/Taylor & Francis, 2007.

Periodicals

"The Fad for Functional Foods: Artificial Success." *Economist* 392, no. 8650 (2009): 84.

Hasler, Clare M., and Amy C. Brown. "Position of the American Dietetic Association: Functional Foods." *Journal of the American Dietetic Association* 109, no. 4 (2009): 735–746.

Henry, C. Jeya. "Functional Foods." *European Journal of Clinical Nutrition* 64, no. 7 (2010): 657–659.

Lang, Tim. "Functional Foods." *BMJ* (clinical research ed.) 334, no. 7602 (2007): 1015–1016.

Web Sites

"Antioxidants, Phytochemicals, and Functional Foods." *U.S. Department of Agriculture (USDA).* http://fnic.nal.usda.gov/nal_display/index.php?info_center=4&tax_level=3&tax_subject=358&topic_id=1610&level3_id=5947&level4_id=0&level5_id=0&placement_default=0 (accessed October 15, 2010).

Kleinerman, Rachel. "Functional Foods?" *American Council on Science and Health,* June 30, 2004. http://www.acsh.org/factsfears/newsID.396/news_detail.asp (accessed October 15, 2010).

Blake Jackson Stabler

Young woman in a health food store looking at the medicinal properties of herb teas. © *David Grossman / Alamy.*

health consciousness, especially among aging population groups, drives the demand for functional foods.

Some consumer advocates and regulatory authorities are concerned that many of the health claims made about functional foods have not been adequately tested and examined. These people may want greater testing and regulation of labeling such as is required in Japan for FOSHU. However, as of 2010 neither the United States nor the European Union has required similarly strict regulation of functional foods' health claims. Functional food producers and supporters see the risks posed by functional foods as relatively low and the added or altered nutritional content as potentially very beneficial. They point to the long history of fortified foods and see functional foods as the next step in creating more healthful processed foods and enhancing nutrition of broader

Fusion

■ Introduction

In the culinary world, fusion refers to the blending of techniques and ingredients from various cultures. Whereas throughout history cooking techniques and recipes have been shared through travel and immigration, often when one uses the word fusion in the early twenty-first century it refers to the movement of chefs creating their own fusion recipes and techniques. One of the first and still most popular blends is the combination of French and Asian cooking, often referred to as "Asian-fusion" cooking, which originated in California in the late 1960s. Since then, fusion cooking has expanded to include traditional cuisines from all over the globe, and it is a common and popular restaurant cooking style.

■ Historical Background and Scientific Foundations

Fusion cuisine first started to appear in the late 1960s and early 1970s with chefs such as Richard Wing (1921–2010), Wolfgang Puck (1949–), and Alice Waters (1944–). These pioneers of fusion cuisine often combined cooking techniques, flavors, and/or ingredients from French and Asian cooking to create their styles. An example of Asian fusion cooking is the use of Asian ingredients such as lemongrass, miso, teriyaki, and ginger as flavoring elements. Prior to the fusion trend, these ingredients were seen very rarely outside of Asian restaurants. Another example is the filling of spring rolls with ingredients more common to French or American cooking, such as sausage or vegetables with a balsamic vinegar dressing. As fusion became more popular and chefs started to explore the possibilities, Indian fusion started to become popular as well: Chefs started using the traditional Indian curry and chutney techniques with local ingredients to make completely new dishes. Later, chefs influenced by these originators of fusion combined Middle Eastern, Spanish, and many other cuisines to create

new styles of fusion cooking. In the second decade of the 2000s there is almost no limit to what cuisines may be combined in a fusion style, and one can find restaurants that pull influences from all over the world.

With the ease of communication provided by mass media and the Internet, fusion cooking could be the combination of countless different cuisines, and chefs or home cooks can order spices and ingredients to be shipped from across the world. By allowing access to ingredients that previously could only be used locally, modern technology has removed the barrier of distance that restricted certain cuisines to a particular area. This allows both for traditional cuisines to travel and for fusion cuisines to be less restricted by ingredient availability.

■ Impacts and Issues

By combining food that guests found familiar with new techniques and flavors, fusion cuisine causes disparate cooking styles from areas all over the globe to become more accessible to the average diner. For example, Japanese sushi originally was strange to the palate of the average diner of the United States because sushi is often garnished with raw fish and seaweed, neither of which appeared in traditional U.S. cuisine. However, when certain chefs started altering the garnishes to items more accessible to the U.S. palate, such as fresh fruit for a light breakfast dish or beef for an entrée, traditional Japanese sushi became much more accessible and much more popular.

Fusion can be a result of immigration and the mixing of cultures as well. Occasionally when people immigrate to a new country, instead of bringing their cuisine with them unaltered they develop a fusion of their culture's traditional cooking and the cooking culture of their new home. Sometimes this happens simply because there are different ingredients available in their new location, and they have to use what is fresh and produced locally. Though it predates the current fusion trend, Creole cuisine in Louisiana could be used as an example of

Local food sources and ingredients combine with new flavors and traditions in the growing trend of food fusion. Shown here are Asian pastries with Italian cheese and Mexican dip. © *Bon Appetit / Alamy.*

immigration-based fusion, as it developed from groups of European immigrants adapting their recipes to the ingredients that were readily available.

Fusion cooking has impacted non-fusion restaurants, making the lines between different cuisines much thinner and easier to cross, and as a result it is easier for other restaurants to broaden their menus and serve dishes that might not fall in to their normal style of cuisine. In a way, this may be one of the more profound impacts of fusion cuisine. Fusion cooking legitimized the combination of foreign ingredients or techniques in a single dish, and as such it lessened the pressure on restaurants to maintain a strict cuisine theme on their menu. Prior to fusion cooking, an Italian restaurant would have thought it impossible to feature a Spanish or Indian special on their menu. Now it is far more acceptable for restaurants to cross cuisine boundaries, so even if a restaurant does not identify as cooking in a fusion style it is still freer than before to break away from a single-cuisine mold.

Fusion cooking has caused some controversy. Traditional cuisine is deeply tied to cultural identity, and there are those who question whether or not fusion cooking detracts from traditional cuisine. Particularly in situations in which fusion was the result of immigration, there is an argument that traditional cuisine should be preserved and that fusing it with other cuisines causes a risk of the original cuisine being forgotten. The Internet has greatly advanced the globalization of cooking techniques, which can be a source of concern for traditionalists who want to see local cooking preserved and protected.

SEE ALSO *Asian Diet; Food and the Internet; Foodways; Immigration and Cuisine; Latin American Diet; Mediterranean Diet; War, Conquest, Colonialism, and Cuisine.*

BIBLIOGRAPHY

Books

Bau, Frédéric, and Jean B. Lassara. *Fusion Chocolate: Chocolate in Cuisine.* Barcelona: Montagud, 2006.

Chat, Mingkwan. *Vietnamese Fusion: Vegetarian Cuisine.* Summertown, TN: Book Publishing Co., 2007.

Civitello, Linda. *Cuisine and Culture: A History of Food and People.* Hoboken, NJ: John Wiley, 2007.

Hauck-Lawson, Annie, and Jonathan Deutsch. *Gastropolis: Food and New York City.* New York: Columbia University Press, 2009.

Kiple, Kenneth F. *A Movable Feast: Ten Millennia of Food Globalization.* Cambridge, UK: Cambridge University Press, 2007.

Millstone, Erik, and Tim Lang. *The Atlas of Food: Who Eats What, Where, and Why.* Berkeley: University of California Press, 2008.

Nimji, Noorbanu. *A Spicy Touch, Volume III: A Fusion of East African and Indian Cuisine.* Calgary: Spicy Touch Pub, 2007.

Nützenadel, Alexander, and Frank Trentmann. *Food and Globalization: Consumption, Markets and Politics in the Modern World.* Oxford, UK: Berg, 2008.

Fusion

Periodicals

Fra, Molinero B., Charles I. Nero, and Jessica B. Harris. "When Food Tastes Cosmopolitan: The Creole Fusion of Diaspora Cuisine: An Interview with Jessica B. Harris." *Callaloo* 30, no. 1 (2007): 287–303.

"From Nouvelle Cuisine through Fusion Confusion to Modern Habits." *Asian Hotel and Catering Times* (April 2006): 68–71.

"New Twists on Latin American Foods: Latin American Cuisine Is a Mix of Worlds, Old and New, Near and Far, Native and Imported." *Prepared Foods* 172, no. 7 (2003): 57–64.

Pham, Vu H. "Secret Kitchen & Trade: An Amalgam of Family, Fortune, and Fusion Food in Asian American Cuisine." *Amerasia Journal* 32, no. 2 (2006): 37–48.

"Plate of Nations: Canada's Culinary Variety and Fusion Cuisine Are Not to Be Missed." *Successful Meetings: SM* 53, supp. 5 (2004): 4–7.

Web Sites

Lothar, Corrina. "Chinese Food in America." *Washington Times*, August 31, 2008. http://www.washington-times.com/news/2008/aug/31/chinese-food-in-america/ (accessed October 21, 2010).

"New Orleans: Gumbo as History." *PBS.org.* http://www.pbs.org/wgbh/amex/neworleans/sfeature/food.html (accessed October 21, 2010).

David Brennan Tilove

Gastronomy

■ Introduction

Gastronomy refers to the study of food and its role in societies. In addition to studying the ingredients and cooking techniques used, this school of philosophy also includes food's relationship with other aspects of culture, such as art and history, as well as the physiological study of taste, aroma, digestion, and the chemical and physical effects of cooking. The people that have interest and passion for this subject go by several names: They can be referred to as gourmands, gastronomes, or gourmets. A gourmet could be a food writer who spends his or her time researching gastronomy professionally, or it could simply be someone who enjoys food and seeks out the knowledge independently.

A gastronome is different from a "foodie," which is a term that was coined to describe people who have an interest in sophisticated cuisine. Gastronomy includes the societal influences and history of the food as well. For example, of the different schools of thought, a "foodie" view of Spanish paella might include how the pan is shaped, what sort of rice should be used, and a description of the technique used to make it. Alternatively, the gastronomic view might state that *paella* has its roots in the casserole dishes made by the people of Moorish Spain, which popularized rice along the coastal regions, but when the Moors were later expelled, Spanish Catholics used the basic techniques to make a meal that was acceptable for Lent. The gastronome would also consider that the short grain rice varieties used to make classic *paella* have a high starch content that thickens the cooking liquid and causes the final dish to have a texture similar to that of Italian risotto. Gastronomy studies the world-view picture of food through the lens of culture, society, and history.

■ Historical Background and Scientific Foundations

The two classic food writers credited with founding the study of gastronomy are Alexandre Grimod (1758–1837) and Jean Anthelme Brillat-Savarin (1755–1826), both of whom lived in France in the early nineteenth century. Grimod was a famous public figure who released an annual publication reviewing restaurants and discussing fine food and wine. Brillat-Savarin wrote the seminal work *The Physiology of Taste*, which was one of the first major works to approach food and dining as though it were a science. Brillat-Savarin's book was later translated into English by American author M. F. K. Fisher (1908–1992), who was a well-known gastronomic writer in her own right.

The questions that gastronomy asks pull information from many different scientific disciplines. A culture's cuisine can be affected by religious taboos, agricultural availability, historical *aversions*, and myriad other details. For example, Japan has little room to grow crops, but as an island nation has unrestricted access to the sea. As a result, its cuisine has almost no wheat products, but countless different preparations for seafood. This includes ingredients to which Western countries have cultural aversions, such as seaweed, whale, and shark fin. Israel historically has a religious taboo against eating pork products, and its local cuisine has hardly any at all. However, just on the other side of the Mediterranean is Italy, where there is no taboo against pork, and it is commonly found in Italian food.

Gastronomy also studies physiological issues relating to food. For example, cuisines in hot climates tend to be spicier because the chemical that causes the sensation of "heat" in food, *capsaicin*, also causes most people to sweat, which helps to cool the skin in the daytime heat. Also, most cuisines that use spicy food as a cooling mechanism tend to pair the spicy food with wheat, rice, or dairy side dishes because *capsaicin* is an oil that does not dilute in water, so in order to clean the oil from one's teeth and gums and kill the heat sensation, it needs to be absorbed in bread, rice, or the dairy fat in milk or yogurt.

■ Impacts and Issues

Gastronomy has faced societal pressure since its inception in the early nineteenth century. Grimod's work was often disparaged as being too similar to the sin of gluttony,

WORDS TO KNOW

CAPSAICIN: The chemical in peppers and other plants that produces the sensation of heat in spicy food.

FOOD AVERSION: The dislike or distaste for a particular food based upon cultural and societal preferences instead of biological incompatibility.

PHYSIOLOGY: A branch of biological science that focuses on the functioning of an organism.

in the local culture and history. Using this information, creative chefs are able to combine cultural cuisines in novel ways to create new styles and trends. In addition, a greater understanding of the science of food and how the human body reacts to it can be invaluable information when creating or altering a recipe, as well as creating dishes for people with health restrictions, which most chefs are called upon to do at some point in their careers.

Gastronomic study also introduced the concept of a *food aversion*, which refers to a dislike or distaste for a specific food or ingredient based upon societal reasons as opposed to biological reasons. More simply, it refers to a food that is distasteful to a certain group of people, while not being poisonous or harmful. One practice of gastronomy is to look at one's own cultural food aversions and their foundations and compare them to those of other cultures. Often when gourmets first start to learn about gastronomy, food and culture can seem separate, and one is usually quite tied to his or her own cultural aversions and taboos. Learning where food taboos and aversions are rooted in various cultures can open one's awareness to new foods and experiences and reveal the startling complexity with which food and culture are intertwined, as well as offer perspective on the culture in which one is born.

and there was backlash against his work as being focused on decadence. In her books during the 1930s and 1940s, Fischer described meals using intense, sensual language, which was criticized at the time as being lewd and inappropriate. However, with the globalization of cooking techniques and recipes, an understanding of gastronomy is almost inextricable from a culinary career. Most culinary education programs involve some form of gastronomy or food theory education to ensure that their students understand not only how to make certain dishes, but also where those dishes come from and what they represent

Restaurant patrons dine outdoors at a restaurant while an orchestra plays on St Mark's Square in Venice, Italy. Italian food and culture are inextricably linked.   *Image copyright Paul Prescott, 2010. Used under license from Shutterstock.com.*

In addition to uncovering food and cultural history, gastronomes follow current trends as they develop. In the Midwest area of the United States, for example, where there is little to no access to coasts and seafood, the cuisine tends to focus on farm-raised products such as meat, dairy, wheat, and potatoes, and there is a traditional cultural aversion to fish and seafood. However, as parcel services become cheaper and fresh seafood can be sent from the coasts into the Midwest daily, fish is becoming more readily available and the cuisine is changing. Gastronomy follows trends such as this as technology develops and changes the world of food with it.

SEE ALSO *Celebrity Chef Phenomenon; Culinary Education; Food and the Internet; Foodways; Gourmet Hobbyists and Foodies; Molecular Gastronomy; Organics; Slow Food Movement; Social Media and Food; Tasting Food; Viniculture.*

BIBLIOGRAPHY

Books

McGee, Harold. *Modern Gastronomy A to Z: A Scientific and Gastronomic Lexicon.* Boca Raton, FL: CRC, 2010.

Savage, Brent, and Nick Hildebrandt. *Bentley: The New Gastronomy.* London: Murdoch, 2010.

Trubek, Amy B. *The Taste of Place: A Cultural Journey into Terroir.* Berkeley: University of California Press, 2008.

Periodicals

Parry, Jovian. "Gender and Slaughter in Popular Gastronomy." *Feminism and Psychology* 20, no. 3 (2010): 381–396.

Petrini, Carlo. "The New Gastronomy Agriculture, the Land and the Table Are Totally Interconnected." *Resurgence London Navern Road* 236 (2006): 17.

Wurgaft, Benjamin. "Economy, Gastronomy, and the Guilt of the Fancy Meal." *Gastronomica: The Journal of Food and Culture* 8, no. 2 (2008): 55–59.

Web Sites

La Chaîne des Rôtisseurs—International Gastronomic Association. http://www.chaine-des-rotisseurs.net/ (accessed September 25, 2010).

Slow Food International. http://www.slowfood.com/ (accessed September 25, 2010).

David Brennan Tilove

Gender Equality and Agriculture

■ Introduction

According to research by the Food and Agriculture Organization (FAO) of the United Nations, women in Sub-Saharan Africa are responsible for 90 percent of food produced in the region. In addition to time spent gathering fuel, fetching water, cooking, and cleaning, women in rural areas of the developing world also contribute the majority of agricultural labor in many areas. Women in poor countries may have full control over household gardens—valuable sources of food—but lack access to other household lands. Even in the developed world, women in 15 European countries in 2008 held only 20 percent of agricultural land. Gender inequality in agriculture such as unequal access to land or unequal market access may lead to poor nutrition, education, and health outcomes for children in poor, rural households. Recognition of gender inequality in agriculture has led to efforts to improve such disparities. Some of these attempts have led to gains in some areas by women, while others have been criticized from a variety of perspectives as being insufficient and as actually perpetuating gender inequality.

■ Historical Background and Scientific Foundations

Women have certainly provided farm labor and tended crops, gardens, and livestock since agriculture began. However, the study of gender differences in agriculture is a more recent phenomenon. These studies and programs usually focus on the developing world and on the gendered division of agricultural and household labor in poor, rural households. By the 1960s, women in development (WID) approaches became common in international aid agencies, international organizations, and charities working in rural areas of the developing world. WID offices and special WID officers attempted to draw attention to how development might affect women differently than men and to how women might participate in agriculture in ways that were not always apparent to outside observers. At the same time, academic work focused on women became more common in a variety of fields, so more information about gender and agriculture became available. By the launch of the United Nation's Decade of Women in 1975, WID was criticized as not incorporating women's concerns into development practices, and a more inclusive women and development (WAD) approach was initiated. By the 1980s, however, most international organizations began an effort that was eventually labeled *gender mainstreaming*, in which the different roles played by men and women in rural development would be incorporated into all aspects of rural development work.

The research associated with these different gender approaches to development has produced a clearer picture of how women in poor rural areas work and participate in agriculture. Gender inequality occurs at many levels and in many areas of concern for agriculture. One area of gender inequality in agriculture is in land tenure. Land tenure refers to how people gain access to land, choose to use land, and pass land on to others. Women's formal land tenure rights are not always recognized by law. Women in some countries may not be able to buy or sell land. One special area of concern is that women who are widowed, abandoned, or divorced may not be able to hold on to land if there are claims from the current or former husband's family. In other cases, women's rights to inherit and use land are recognized in law, but women are not always aware of these rights or customary practice may prevent women from exercising these rights. Land tenure concerns and access to land are especially important for women-headed households. The FAO estimates that worldwide one in five farms are headed by women.

In addition to issues surrounding land tenure and access in agriculture, women also may face other constraints that limit their agricultural productivity. Market access refers to the ability to get goods to market and sell them to willing buyers of choice. For female-headed households in some areas, women may not be allowed to go to open-air markets in another city or to even be at any market, and thus they must work through male intermediaries. Market roles are often gendered. Whereas women may sell most products in market stalls and grow most of the products sold in their gardens or on land they use, the wholesale trade and shipment of products from the countryside to the city may be controlled by men or simply conducted by men. Women may be at a disadvantage to adopt new agricultural technologies. According to a study by the FAO, women receive less than 5 percent of all agricultural extension services worldwide though they make up 40 percent of the agricultural labor force. Women may face barriers to gaining access to agricultural credit. Women in Africa and the Caribbean contribute 80 percent of basic foodstuffs from their agricultural labor. Despite these obvious agricultural skills, women may be excluded from agricultural education opportunities, agricultural marketing associations and cooperatives, and a variety of other opportunities. Varied reasons for these exclusions exist, including traditions

WORDS TO KNOW

GENDER MAINSTREAMING: The incorporation of concern and understanding about how women and men work, live, and earn money differently into organizations, development programs, and research.

LAND TENURE: A system under which land is acquired, used, and possibly bought and sold. A variety of land tenure systems exist including legal land titles, land use rights without land ownership, untitled family farms, and shifting cultivation.

MARKET ACCESS: The ability to get goods to market and sell them to willing buyers of the seller's choice.

that exclude women from meeting with unrelated men, labor requirements that tie women to household work, lack of mobility, and a lack of awareness among policy makers and government officials of the contributions women make in agriculture.

A row of women planting corn in Zimbabwe. © *Chad Ehlers / Alamy.*

■ Impacts and Issues

Although gender equality in agriculture is, in some ways, like gender equality in other occupational fields, the research on gender in agriculture reveals many benefits to increasing women's income from agriculture and increasing gender equality in agriculture. Women's equality has important long-term development consequences. In fact, increasing women's incomes within the household may be more important than increasing men's incomes. Numerous studies have demonstrated that women spend more—potentially all—of their income on household needs. This includes food for infants and children, investments in children's education, and health care expenses for the household. Because men's agricultural income, often cash crops instead of food crops, tends to be diverted to other purposes (estimated at 25 percent of male income by the FAO), income increases for men from agriculture have less immediate benefit for the children in the household, the health of the household, and the elimination of malnutrition in the household. By empowering women to profit more from their agricultural activities, better educational, nutritional, and health outcomes for the whole household may occur.

Gender mainstreaming in agricultural development activities at international aid agencies and gender-focused agricultural research have been criticized from a variety of feminist, environmental, and Marxist perspectives. These critics contend that even referring to the issue as gendered hides the fact that most of these issues are about women's inequality, not about gender per se. They suggest the studies and efforts to mainstream gender continue to marginalize women. They may critique the very structure of international organizations as being unfair to women and misogynistic. They claim that the attention of international scholars or workers from the developed world to women in the developing world only serves to make the developing world subjugated to the developed world and to world markets controlled by males in rich nations. Also, they may criticize programs to improve land tenure or women's market access as too timid. Instead, these critics argue that women's issues in agriculture and in other fields require political solutions or solutions based on women claiming new rights.

■ Primary Source Connection

The United Nations Food and Agriculture Organization (FAO) aims to reduce and eliminate world hunger. It works in four main areas: providing information, sharing knowledge and policy expertise, providing working groups for nations, and aiding organizations working in the field of agricultural development.

In 2010, the FAO announced the launch of a new database focusing on global gender equality in land relations. The Gender and Land Rights Database provides information for policymakers and researchers on national and international legal frameworks, customs, land use statistics, and other issues. The FAO maintains that gender disparity in land ownership and land access is a significant contributor to economic inequalities between men and women. Worldwide, women are more likely than men to live in poverty or experience food insecurity.

Improving Gender Equality in Access to Land

The rules of land tenure reflect the structure of power and beliefs in society. People who are landless or who have weak rights to land are usually those without power. Disparities in rights may not be immediately apparent in the rules. For example, in a common property resource system there may be the impression that all members of the community have equivalent rights, but a closer analysis may show disparities between genders.

In some societies, women cannot hold rights to land independently of their husbands or male relatives. Their rights are also often different from those of men.

Many countries do have legislation or constitutions that recognise equal rights of both men and women, including rights to land. The formal rules, however, are not always observed in practice.

Despite legislated equal rights, groups such as rural women still may be at a disadvantage in defending their rights. There may be a lack of awareness, capacity or will to implement and enforce the formal legal rules at different levels, especially for those who are financially or politically weaker than others, or when local customs conflict with the legislation.

Changes to the ways in which people gain access to land may thus change the power structure within a family, within a community, or within a nation. The promotion of gender equity may be in direct contrast with the "traditional way of doing things."

Without changes in the attitudes of much of the population, traditional practices are likely to continue regardless of the formulation of new policies or the enactment of new legislation. Advocacy of more equitable land rights is important in any effort to transform institutions and practices relating to access to land.

Susan Nichols, et al.

NICHOLS, SUSAN, ET AL. "IMPROVING GENDER EQUALITY IN ACCESS TO LAND." *LAND TENURE NOTES*. FOOD AND AGRICULTURE ORGANIZATION OF THE UNITED NATIONS (FAO), 2006.

SEE ALSO *Agriculture Brings Hierarchical Societies; Ethical Issues in Agriculture; Food and Agriculture Organization (FAO); Foodways; UN Millennium Development Goals; Women's Role in Global Food Preparation.*

BIBLIOGRAPHY

Books

De, Dipak, Basavaprabhu Jirli, and K. Kiran. *Empowerment of Women in Agriculture.* Varanasi, India: Ganga Kaveri, 2010.

Hovorka, Alice, Henk de Zeeuw, and Mary Njenga. *Women Feeding Cities: Mainstreaming Gender in Urban Agriculture and Food Security.* Warwickshire, UK: Practical Action, 2009.

Jacobs, Susie M. *Gender and Agrarian Reforms.* New York: Routledge, 2010.

Kristof, Nicholas D., and Sheryl WuDunn. *Half the Sky: Turning Oppression into Opportunity for Women Worldwide.* New York: Knopf, 2009.

Periodicals

De Brauw, Alan, Qiang Li, Chengfang Liu, Scott Rozelle, and Linxiu Zhang. "Feminization of Agriculture in China? Myths Surrounding Women's Participation in Farming." *China Quarterly London* (2008): 327–348.

Giarracca, Norma, and Miguel Teubal. "Women in Agriculture." *Latin American Perspectives* 35, no. 6 (2008): 5–10.

Gill, Jatinderjit Kaur, M. K. Dhillon, and Muninder K. Sidhu. "Women in Agriculture." *International Journal of Rural Studies* 14, no. 1 (2007): 2–6.

Motzafi-Haller, Pnina, and Paul J. Kaldjian. "Geographical Reviews—Women in Agriculture in the Middle East." *Geographical Review* 96, no. 4 (2006): 721–722.

Ngowi, Aiwerasia Vera Festo. "Women's Work in Agriculture." *African Newsletter on Occupational Health and Safety* 18, no. 3 (2008): 48–49.

Web Sites

"Agriculture and Achieving the Millennium Development Goals." *International Food Policy Research Institute.* http://www.ifpri.org/publication/agriculture-and-achieving-millennium-development-goals (accessed September 18, 2010).

Sustainable Development Department, Food and Agriculture Organization of the United Nations (FAO). "Asia's Women in Agriculture, Environment, and Rural Production: India." *SD Dimensions.* http://www.fao.org/sd/wpdirect/WPre0108.htm (accessed September 18, 2010).

Blake Jackson Stabler

Genetically Modified Organisms (GMO)

■ Introduction

Genetically modified foods are derived from genetically modified organisms (GMOs) with deliberately altered genes and genetic sequences. As of 2011, the vast majority of genetically modified foods are plants, and the majority of political struggles over GMOs relate to the planting and use of GMO crops. However, experts predict an increasing level of debate over the use of genetically modified animals.

Advocates of GMO foods, supported by the majority of scientific studies, argue that the use of GMO crops and animals is broadly safe, offers environmental benefits, lowers food costs, and helps reduce hunger worldwide. Critics of GMO foods counter that these benefits come at too high a social and economic cost, engender dependency upon technology, or are outweighed by risks attendant on altering genes and gene sequences in open environments, where transfer to wild species may occur with a variety of negative consequences.

■ Historical Background and Scientific Foundations

Humans have selected plants for desirable characteristics since the dawn of agriculture. At first, the only way to improve crop plants was to collect seeds from the best performing individuals for planting the next year. Once plant reproduction was better understood, people selectively bred plants to create offspring that were hardier, larger, more flavorful, or more disease resistant than their predecessors. In the early twenty-first century, in the age of genetically modified organisms (GMOs), the genetic code of plants is manipulated to create new varieties.

The genetic material in plants, like that of animals, is deoxyribonucleic acid (DNA). DNA carries a code containing the information required for cell metabolism and reproduction. The information consists of sequences of four bases: adenine (A), thymine (T), guanine (G), and cytosine (C). Via the processes of transcription and translation the four bases ultimately specify the sequences of amino acids to be used in the synthesis of proteins that control cell structure and function.

Genes are portions of DNA molecules that ultimately code for specific proteins that, in turn, determine specific structural and functional attributes for cells and ultimately for the observable characteristics of organisms as a whole. Differences in species and differences within species are due to differences in genes.

Transgenetics

In addition to sequence alterations, DNA sequences can be inserted in plant and animal chromosomes. Transgenic plants and animals contain DNA from species other than the plant itself. The foreign DNA can be from a related species, an unrelated plant species, or from completely different organisms such as bacteria, fungi, or even animals. In addition to the transfer of specific genes, other regions of DNA (e.g., promoter sequences, vector sequences, marker sequences, etc.) are also usually transferred.

The ability to modify the genomes of crop plants with genes from other organisms enables the creation of novel strains possessing useful traits with respect to disease or pesticide resistance, nutritional value, or for ability to synthesize drugs and other useful substances.

Although agricultural seed producers have used traditional breeding methods to create hybrid plant varieties for many decades, they became interested in developing and patenting genetically modified species in the 1970s and 1980s. This interest was triggered by changes to intellectual property laws that created a favorable environment for investing in research and development designed to produce legally protected and commercially viable products.

Beginning in the late 1980s, agricultural biotechnology companies began submitting applications for the approval of field testing of genetically engineered (GE) plants. Since then, more than 10,000 of these applications have been approved by the U.S. Department of Agriculture (USDA) Animal and Plant Inspection Service.

Herbicide-resistant, genetically modified rice grows in a field in Brazil. © *SDBEnvironment / Alamy.*

Most applications are for crop species grown in high volumes such as corn, soybean, potatoes, and cotton.

The goal of any plant genetic engineering program is to reduce or eliminate undesirable traits, to enhance desirable traits, and/or to introduce previously non-existent traits. To date, most approved genetically engineered (GE) plants have been modified for better herbicide, insect, disease, or drought resistance; in some cases the enhancement of attributes enables the plants to better withstand shipment and storage perils. Some species have enhanced traits that are perceived to increase their market value (i.e., size, color, amount of moisture, etc.).

The first genetically engineered crop to be approved by the U.S. Food and Drug Administration (FDA) and made available to consumers was the Flavr Savr tomato in 1994. In the Flavr Savr, antisense technology was used to suppress the synthesis of polygalactouronase to slow the degradation of pectin in the fruit cell walls. This kept the fruit on the vine without becoming soft, enabling growers to avoid having to pick tomatoes while still green and plan for after harvest ripening. The product was accepted by consumers but eventually failed in the marketplace because of high production and distribution costs.

The majority of transgenic plants that are commercially grown have been modified for herbicide tolerance (HT). The second most common modification is for insect resistance (IR), for example, plants transformed with a gene from the bacterium *Bacillus thuringiensis* (Bt) produce a protein that is toxic to certain insects. The majority of acreage planted in corn, soybean, and cotton in the United States is now devoted to transgenic HT and/or IR varieties. Other transgenic plants are modified for improved resistance to viral diseases (VR).

Currently GE corn, soybeans, potatoes, and cotton are in widespread cultivation. GE squash, canola, and papaya have also been introduced but without sustained success. Transgenic rapeseed and rice varieties have also been developed.

In general, farmers in the United States have adopted GMO crops (including transgenic crops) more enthusiastically than farmers in other industrialized nations. In the United States, despite a growing organics-based industry, the percentage of the total acreage devoted to HT and IR varieties continues to rise.

These GE varieties offer better yields and have less intensive management requirements than non-GE varieties. Products derived from transgenic corn and soybeans have been consumed regularly in the United States since the beginning of the twenty-first century, largely without the consumers' knowledge because there is no legal requirement for the labeling of GE foods. The FDA has ruled that GE foods, including transgenics, are substantially equivalent to non-engineered foods.

Popular GMO Crops

The two most common types of GMO crop plants are those that are genetically engineered to be resistant to the herbicide glyphosate and those that are genetically

Farmers protest against genetically modified crops outside the National Farmers' Union building in London, England.
© *David K. Hoffman / Alamy.*

engineered to produce *Bacillus thuringiensis* toxin (Bt toxin), an insecticide.

Glyphosate-resistant crop plants can withstand spraying by glyphosate-containing herbicides used to reduce undesired plant growth surrounding the desired crop (a technique also known as chemical weeding). Such crops are often termed "Roundup ready" crops (e.g., Roundup ready corn) for the chemical company Monsanto's herbicide with the trade name Roundup.

Bt-producing crops are intended to poison insects that feed on them and so may require little or no general spraying of Bt toxins or other insecticides to control those pests killed by Bt toxin. For example, one of the most common GMO crops is "Bt corn," a corn that is genetically altered to produce Bt toxin that kills the crop-destructive larvae of the European Corn Borer.

GMOs in the Wild

GMO proponents argue that the vast majority of modifications, although improving performance in selected areas, generally weaken modified organisms toward the sum of environmental or evolutionary pressures and render them less likely to do substantial environmental harm if they escape and mix with native populations. Simply introducing a new gene into a population, even if it offers superiority in selected areas, is usually not sufficient to ensure that the gene will be retained in future generations. There are pressures toward genetic equilibriums that require that, in addition to a gene offering some form of evolutionary advantage, the gene must also be introduced into a population in sufficient numbers to be retained as part of the genome. In natural populations, genome change is rarely caused by a lone mutation, instead requiring a sufficient number of independent mutations that allow new gene variants to gain traction in a population.

Genetically modified organisms have, however, escaped into the wild. Agricultural practices and transport accidents have resulted in genetically engineered canola plants growing along roadsides in North Dakota. Experts claim that the discovery of the wild-growing genetically engineered canola offers proof that genetically modified crops can become established in the wild. During a study of wild-growing canola plants along North Dakota highways, up to 80 percent of samples showed evidence of genetic engineering or of being derived from genetically engineered plants resistant to the herbicides glyphosate (commonly known by its trade name, Roundup) or glufosinate. An herbicide is a plant-killing chemical. Genetically altered canola has also been found growing in the wild in Oregon and Japan.

Transfer of genes coding for particular traits can occur from one variety or species to another. Scientists have, for example, voiced concerns that genes for pesticide resistance might transfer from glyphosate-resistant

Activists protest in Mexico City, Mexico, against a bio-security law, which activists claim will not prevent transgenic contamination of corn. *AP Images.*

GMO crops to the very weeds that glyphosate is meant to kill, producing "superweeds." Also, the production of glyphosate by some crops, and the increased application of glyphosate on resistant crops could potentially cause plants to evolve resistance to the herbicide. By 2007, according to one scientific study, five weed species exposed to glyphosate-resistant crop fields eventually showed evidence of evolving levels of glyphosate resistance.

There is research interest in whether antibiotic resistance genes introduced into other species may be transferred to bacteria in the environment, but there is no evidence that this happens, and dramatic genetic and cellular differences make this impossible or highly unlikely in many cases. Some GMO use proponents contend that it would be prudent if experimental organisms carried genes (often termed "suicide genes") that render genetically altered organisms unable to survive openly without specific support (e.g., special nutrient mixtures).

GMO Safety

Research is ongoing, but feeding studies in both humans and animals have found no significant differences in either the safety or nutritional value of most transgenic foods. With respect to Bt foods, experiments designed to see if the Bt gene is transferred from Bt soybean to bacteria that reside in the human gut have been negative. Nucleic acids (such as DNA) do not survive passage through the human digestive system intact, so there is little direct risk from consuming transgenes, although genetic fragments from transgenes have been isolated in the blood of animals that have eaten GE food.

In the 1990s a transgenic soybean was developed that contained a Brazil nut gene designed to increase the concentration of the amino acid methionine. Tests showed that people with Brazil nut allergies were also allergic to the transgenic soybeans, which led to the termination of the project. This suggests that in rare instances, some individuals may experience allergic reactions to transgenic proteins present in GE foods.

As of 2010 no scientific studies have shown conclusively that currently licensed GMO foods harm human health. However, in many cases there is continued concern that the data and studies supporting GMO use are insufficient to declare GMO use safe, especially with regard to use in the open environment and over successive generations.

■ Impacts and Issues

Concerns about GMO (especially transgenic) crops often revolve around human health, ecological safety, and issues surrounding the patenting and legal protection of naturally occurring gene sequences and GE organisms. Separate and wide ranging debates also continue in the United States and other countries about whether, and how, genetically altered species should be labeled for consumers.

Although polls show that most Americans remain personally skeptical about the safety and testing of genetically modified foods, the United States is a particularly strong advocate and large producer of GMO foods. In 2008 more than 90 percent of U.S. soybeans were raised from genetically modified seed, and 75 percent of corn was genetically modified (the United States produces 40 percent of the world's corn). For more than a decade, a vigorous debate has divided the U.S. government and biotech corporations from states in Africa and the European Union (EU) that block the importation of GMO crops. The United States has sought, through several legal actions including appeals to the World Trade Organization (WTO), to force European states to drop barriers to GMO foods. In 2006, in a major victory for U.S. GMO policy, the WTO ruled that Europe's moratorium on new licenses to grow GMO crops was a violation of global trade agreements. Despite the decisions of the WTO, some countries still openly prohibit or restrict GMO use.

Whereas some countries show broad acceptance or resistance to genetically modified foods, however, others are selective about allowing or banning them. For example, China began to allow the introduction of a lone species of genetically modified rice in 2009.

Critics of the use of GMOs argue that there are also justifiable grounds for resistance to GMO use related to local political, cultural, or economic interests. For example, in February 2010 India's environment minister Jairam Ramesh (1954–) announced a ban on the introduction of the genetically modified vegetable Bt brinjal (eggplant) as part of a pledge to overhaul India's regulatory oversight of genetically modified organisms. Farming factions in India generally have opposed the introduction of GM crops because seeds are expensive, and limitations on harvesting require farmers to purchase new seeds for each growing season. That the use of genetically modified seed ties farmers tightly to the policies of large international agriculture companies is a common and widespread concern.

Critics of GMO use often question the impact of such use on agricultural economics, expressing concern about making farmers overly dependent on GMO technology, and thus more vulnerable to proprietary interests. For example, weeds are a major pest for farmers, and the development of transgenic varieties has been a boon to production, especially for soybeans. Although the use of herbicides often poses separate environmental concerns, such herbicide-resistant varieties generally permit more flexibility with regard to acreage used and promote greater yields in crops. For example, the "Roundup ready" HT Soybean (i.e., resistant to the commercially popular "Roundup" herbicide) produced by Monsanto is popular among large commercial growers. However, farmers who use the seeds must repurchase new seeds rather than follow traditional farming practices in which seeds from each crop are saved and replanted. Monsanto and other companies have a history of aggressively pursuing remedies against farmers accused of attempting to save seeds or otherwise attempting to avoid repurchasing patented seeds.

Because a low level of transfer of HT genes to non-HT crops does occur, determining intent can be contentious and complex, often making it difficult for a farmer to grow a non-GE crop anywhere near fields where HT plants are grown. Issues regarding the long-term ecological safety of releasing HT and other genetically altered varieties into the environment and what effect it may have on endemic plants, microbes, and insects is far from settled among scientists.

The patenting of the genetic sequences of living organisms also remains controversial. Historically, the U.S. patent office has looked favorably upon such applications, although the legal status of such claims is in flux. Early in 2010, two patents on human genes important in breast cancer were ruled invalid by a district court judge. Although this situation did not involve transgenic organisms, it did strike a blow to the general principle that naturally occurring DNA sequences are patentable, and this may have implications for GMOs in the future. Corporations counter that patent protections are required to motivate research that can reasonably be expected to provide a return on investment.

Controversy over potential GMO use is frequently the subject of protests and litigation, especially regarding the evaluation and approval policies of regulatory agencies. Questions regarding the quality and sufficiency of data needed to approve the consumption of genetically modified food are also contentious among scientists. Disagreements among scientists are predicted to flare again with proposals to use genetically altered animals. Because of animal testing restrictions and the additional complexity and expense inherent in animal testing, decisions often will be made on data produced by smaller test sample populations and from studies with more limited multi-generational data.

For example, in September 2010 an FDA advisory panel debated the science and safety surrounding the proposed use of genetically engineered salmon. The panel's conclusion was that the FDA should require more testing, especially with regard to unintended potential allergic response, before endorsing what would become the first approved use of a genetically engineered animal for food in the United States.

Advocates of GMO crop use argue that the benefits of alleviating hunger around the world through increased production brought about by use of GMO organisms provides a compelling argument for the continued use of genetically modified crops.

An animal science researcher at the University of California, Davis, holds a day-old genetically altered goat kid. Ten years ago researchers found a way to transfer a human gene into goats so they produce an enzyme in their milk that fights the bacteria that causes diarrhea. The newborn kid is part of the herd of genetically altered animals. An Atlantic salmon has now been genetically engineered to grow twice as fast as a regular salmon. If U.S. regulators approve it, the fish would be the first such scientifically altered animal to reach the dinner plate. *AP Images.*

SEE ALSO *Agribusiness; Agriculture and International Trade; Agroecology; Biodiversity and Food Supply; Commission on Genetic Resources for Food and Agriculture; Convention on Biological Diversity (1992); Organics; Political Food Boycotts.*

BIBLIOGRAPHY

Books

Brand, Stewart. *Whole Earth Discipline: Why Dense Cities, Nuclear Power, Transgenic Crops, Restored Wildlands and Geoengineering Are Necessary.* New York: Penguin, 2010.

Ferry, Natalie, and Angharad M. R. Gatehouse. *Environmental Impact of Genetically Modified Crops.* Wallingford, UK: CABI, 2009.

Fiechter, Armin, and Christof Sautter. *Green Gene Technology: Research in an Area of Social Conflict.* Berlin: Springer, 2007.

Gordon, Susan, ed. *Critical Perspectives on Genetically Modified Crops and Food.* New York: Rosen Publishing Group, 2006.

Halford, Nigel. *Plant Biotechnology: Current and Future Applications of Genetically Modified Crops.* Chichester, UK: John Wiley, 2006.

Lacey, Hugh. *Values and Objectivity in Science and Current Controversy about Transgenic Crops.* Lanham, MD: Lexington Books, 2005.

Liang, George H., and Daniel Z. Skinner, eds. *Genetically Modified Crops: Their Development, Uses, and Risks.* Binghamton, NY: Food Products, 2004.

Lurquin, Paul. *High Tech Harvest: Understanding Genetically Modified Food Plants.* Boulder, CO: Westview Press, 2004.

Sunderland, John P., and Tsutomu Ichiki. *Genetically Engineered Mice Handbook.* Boca Raton, FL: CRC Press, 2004.

Thomson, Jennifer A. *Seeds for the Future: The Impact of Genetically Modified Crops on the Environment.* Ithaca, NY: Comstock Publishing Associates, 2007.

Weirich, Paul. *Labeling Genetically Modified Food: The Philosophical and Legal Debate.* Oxford, UK: Oxford University Press, 2007.

Wesseler, Justus. *Environmental Costs and Benefits of Transgenic Crops.* Dordrecht, The Netherlands: Springer, 2005.

Young, Tomme. *Genetically Modified Organisms and Biosafety: A Background Paper for Decision-Makers and Others to Assist in Consideration of GMO Issues.* Gland, Switzerland: World Conservation Union, 2004.

Periodicals

Abbott, Alison. "European Disarray on Transgenic Crops." *Nature* 457, no. 7232 (2009): 946–947.

Charles, Dan. "U.S. Courts Say Transgenic Crops Need Tighter Scrutiny." *Science* 315, no. 5815 (2007): 1069.

Moeller, Lorena, and Kan Wang. "Engineering with Precision: Tools for the New Generation of Transgenic Crops." *Bioscience* 58, no. 5 (2008): 391–401.

Web Sites

College of Agriculture and Natural Resources. "How to Make a Transgenic Plant." *University of Delaware.* http://www.ag.udel.edu/agbiotech/transgenic-tomato-cc.php (accessed November 1, 2010).

FAO Newsroom. "The Gene Revolution: Great Potential for the Poor, but No Panacea." *Food and Agriculture Organization of the United Nations (FAO),* May 17, 2004. http://www.fao.org/newsroom/en/news/2004/41714/index.html (accessed November 1, 2010).

"Food, Genetically Modified." *World Health Organization (WHO).* http://www.who.int/topics/food_genetically_modified/en (accessed November 1, 2010).

"Oxfam International's Position on Transgenic Crops." *Oxfam International.* http://www.oxfam.org/en/campaigns/agriculture/oxfam-position-transgenic-crops (accessed November 1, 2010).

Philip McIntosh

Gluten Intolerance

Introduction

Gluten intolerance, also called celiac disease, encompasses a wide array of medical complications and conditions triggered by the consumption of barley, wheat, rye, triticale, and other grains containing gluten. Symptoms experienced by persons with gluten intolerance include skin rashes, joint pain, weight loss, diarrhea, and other digestive complaints. Nutrients from food are not efficiently absorbed in persons with celiac disease, as the villi, or projections in the intestines responsible for absorbing the nutrients in food, become inflamed. Eliminating all traces of gluten from the diet typically relieves symptoms related to gluten intolerance.

Gluten intolerance has been linked to a wide range of medical conditions such as dermatitis herpetiformis, type-1 diabetes, epilepsy, asthma, and assorted autoimmune disorders. The development of the gluten-free diet in the 1950s changed the food habits of millions of persons with gluten intolerance worldwide. Currently, the gluten-free diet remains the only method for controlling the autoimmune reaction in persons with gluten intolerance.

Historical Background and Scientific Foundations

First-century Greek physician Aretaeus of Cappodocia's words, later translated by the Scottish physician Francis Adams (1796–1861) in 1856, read like the medical chart of a modern gluten-intolerant patient. Aretaeus describes fatigue, bloating, flatulence, weakness, and diarrhea. In addition, he notes "… not only does the disease cause failure of digestion, but there is failure to distribute even the partly digested product required for body growth." His advice that "drinks [be] taken before meals, for otherwise bread is very little conducive to trim vigour" both hits and misses the point for what

Aretaeus labeled "coeliac disease" or "coeliac affection," referring to a disease of the abdomen.

Later, English pediatrician Samuel Gee (1839–1911) picked up the ancient Greek physician's work in 1888, and described a specific case of "coeliac affection" in *St. Bartholomew's Hospital Reports*. Gee applied Aretaeus's observation that the condition affects body growth, noting that it especially affected children between one and five years old. Gee determined that regulating the diet could alleviate symptoms, but did not isolate gluten intolerance as the cause.

In 1924 the American pediatrician Sydney Haas (1870–1964) treated eight children with celiac disease with a diet based on bananas. In addition to requiring the patient to eat four to eight bananas each day, Haas recommended the elimination of sucrose as well as bread, crackers, potatoes, and cereal. Until the early 1950s, Haas's specific carbohydrate diet was the standard treatment for celiac disease, although the diet did not exclude all sources of gluten.

Dutch pediatrician Willem-Karel Dicke (1905–1962) developed a hypothesis that wheat was the offending culprit in gluten intolerance when he observed previously ill children who improved while bread shortages occurred during World War II (1939–1945). By the early 1950s, physicians who prescribed a gluten-free diet for patients with symptoms of celiac disease noted marked improvement. Until 1955 and the invention of the duodenal biopsy scope, however, the only method for diagnosing gluten intolerance in a patient was through observation. Duodenal biopsies gave doctors tissue evidence for diagnosis.

Advancements in genetic testing in the 1990s and the first decade of the 2000s helped to pinpoint two specific genes related to celiac disease: DQ2 and DQ8. Having one or both copies, however, does not automatically mean that a person will inevitably develop a gluten-intolerance-related condition. Environmental triggers appear to be a significant component in whether patients develop gluten intolerance and are a fertile area for ongoing research.

Whereas celiac disease remains the most severe of the disorders associated with gluten intolerance, in the latter half of the twentieth century new forms of gluten intolerance were identified. Gluten intolerance differs from a true food allergy in that the two conditions trigger different immune responses. Wheat allergies, for instance, trigger immunoglobulin-E (IgE) antibodies, while for people with gluten intolerance, blood work identifies high levels of anti-tissue transglutaminase (tTG) antibodies as a marker for diagnosis. The tTG test enables doctors to determine gluten sensitivity and to screen persons with symptoms in order to rule out gluten intolerance, or to indicate the need for further testing such as a duodenal endoscopic biopsy.

■ Impacts and Issues

In 1966 scientists connected the skin condition dermatitis herpetiformis to small-intestine abnormalities similar to those experiencing gluten intolerance, and in 1969 they confirmed the usefulness of a gluten-free diet for the condition. This launched research that continues in the early twenty-first century into exploring the gluten link to a host of autoimmune conditions, including some forms of epilepsy, diabetes mellitus, connective tissue diseases, Sjogren's syndrome, Hashimoto's thyroiditis, asthma, and cancer.

One study estimated that one in 133 people in the United States has celiac disease, and a 2006 survey puts the rate at approximately one percent of the population of Europe, South America, Australasia, and the United States affected with the disorder. The highest rate of celiac disease observed in a given population is 5.6 percent prevalence among the Saharawi, an Arab-Berber group in the Western Sahara region. Aside from this anomaly, celiac disease and gluten intolerance tend to appear at higher rates in developed nations.

The gluten-free diet includes all non-processed vegetables, fruits, meats, dairy products, potatoes, legumes, and any grain that does not contain gluten. Popular grains in a gluten-free diet include tapioca, teff, sorghum, rice, buckwheat, and corn. Processed foods often use gluten as a thickener or in preservatives. Even when processed foods are gluten-free, contamination from manufacturing processes can make a seemingly gluten-free food unsafe for those with gluten intolerance to consume.

Since 1990 the market for gluten-free foods has risen dramatically. Sales from packaged gluten-free foods increased from $600 million in 2004 to $1.56 billion in 2008. With growth rates of 14 percent to 28 percent per year, the gluten-free food industry is big business.

WORDS TO KNOW

CELIAC DISEASE: Celiac (or coeliac) disease, also known as gluten-sensitive enteropathy or gluten intolerance, involves an autoimmune reaction to gluten that leaves the intestinal villi unable to absorb nutrients from food that passes through the digestive tract.

GLUTEN: Gluten is a protein present in many grains. The proteins gliadin and glutenin join to form gluten. There are four subtypes of gliadin. Persons with gluten-intolerance or celiac disease are sensitive to the α, β, and γ subtypes while the fourth, less common subtype ω can trigger exercise-induced and asthma-induced hypersensitive reactions, and may be linked to aspirin-induced sensitivity and type-1 diabetes.

tTG TEST: tTG is the standard diagnostic blood test performed when gluten intolerance is suspected. Short for anti-tissue transglutaminase antibody, the tTG test measures the presence of antibodies to gluten in the blood. Higher results indicate a likely gluten intolerance disorder.

A chef removes a gluten-free pizza from a brick oven at Tommy's Brick Oven Pizza in Jacksonville, Florida. The restaurant's owner and head chef developed his recipe for wheat-free, gluten-free pizza dough after discovering that he had developed Celiac disease. *Adrienne Lerner / Lerner & Lerner / LernerMedia Global Photos.*

Advocacy organizations such as the Celiac Sprue Association help to spread information and lessen the social impact of celiac disease and gluten intolerance. In the United States, May is Celiac Awareness Month, and in 2009 the U.S. Congress passed a resolution designating September 13, Samuel Gee's birth date, as National Celiac Awareness Day. Public schools are not required by law to change school lunch offerings for students who must follow a gluten-free diet, but schools must permit children to bring their own gluten-free food for consumption if supported by a physician's diagnosis.

For people with gluten intolerance, navigating social events such as work and school parties, birthday celebrations, field trips, and outings can be tricky if food is involved. The increased offerings of gluten-free substitutes for birthday cakes, cookies, pizza, breads and crackers help to de-stigmatize gluten intolerance. Chain restaurants such as Burger King, Pizzeria Uno, Olive Garden, P.F. Chang's, and Starbucks have joined the trend by creating gluten-free food lines and menus, often partnering with advocacy organizations such as the Gluten Intolerance Group to create safe practices that prevent cross-contamination in products and served meals.

SEE ALSO *Food Allergen Labeling and Consumer Protection Act of 2004; Food Allergies; Grains.*

BIBLIOGRAPHY

Books

Bower, Sylvia Llewelyn, Mary Kay Sharrett, and Steve Plogsted. *Celiac Disease: A Guide to Living with Gluten Intolerance.* New York: Demos Medical Pub, 2007.

Green, Peter H. R., and Rory Jones. *Celiac Disease: A Hidden Epidemic*, 2nd ed. New York: William Morrow, 2010.

Ryberg, Roben. *The Gluten-Free Kitchen: Over 135 Delicious Recipes for People with Gluten Intolerance or Wheat Allergy.* New York: Prima Health, 2000.

Wangen, Stephen. *Healthier without Wheat: A New Understanding of Wheat Allergies, Celiac Disease, and Non-Celiac Gluten Intolerance.* Seattle, WA: Innate Health Pub, 2009.

Periodicals

Megiorni, Francesca, Barbara Mora, Monica Bonamico, et al. "HLA-DQ and Susceptibility to Celiac Disease: Evidence for Gender Differences and Parent-of-Origin Effects." *American Journal of Gastroenterology* 103 (2008): 997–1003.

Van Heel, David A., and J. West. "Recent Advances in Celiac Disease." *Gut* 55 (2006): 1037–1046.

Web Sites

Aretaeus the Cappadocian. *The Extant Works of Aretaeus the Cappadocian,* edited and translated by Francis Adams. *Google Books.* http://books.google.com/books?id=v4gIAAAAIAAJ (accessed July 20, 2010).

Celiac Sprue Association. http://www.csaceliacs.org/index.php (accessed July 20, 2010).

Gluten Intolerance Group of North America. http://www.gluten.net/ (accessed July 20, 2010).

Melanie Barton Zoltán

Gourmet Hobbyists and Foodies

■ Introduction

Gourmet hobbyists, commonly referred to as "foodies," are a large and diverse hobby group united by a common love of good food. Foodies are amateur food aficionados who enjoy preparing, eating, studying, and shopping for or growing food. They are interested in learning about both fine and ordinary food, and also about the science and industry of food. Some activities they enjoy include reading food columns, blogs, and books about this topic, and finding new restaurants that prepare food in new and innovative ways (some foodies will choose to focus on finding ideal examples of particular food favorites, such as the perfect cheese steak or the best dark chocolate gelato). Foodies often tune into television programs that glorify food and the exploits of celebrity chefs, and they gravitate toward gourmet shops and farmers' markets in search of artisan food varieties and the latest trends in kitchen tools.

Although *foodie* and *gourmet* are often used interchangeably, the two terms are not synonymous. The word *foodie* has become a populist alternative to *gourmet*, which some perceive has taken on connotations of pretentiousness or elitism. Whereas the word *gourmet* could bring to mind someone who spends time and money on only the finest and most rarified dining experiences, such as dinner at a four-star restaurant, a *foodie*, conversely, is generally considered to be an average person with an uncommon love for high-quality foods. Foodies are keenly interested in foods and food trends of all kinds, not just the sophisticated delicacies that a gourmet might seek out. Foodies can appreciate the basics, just as long as the finest ingredients are used, and they are well prepared. A foodie might enjoy scouring city diners to find the best French fries rather than searching expensive restaurants in a quest to find the most exquisite truffles.

■ Historical Background and Scientific Foundations

A number of factors have combined over the years to create the robust gourmet/foodie culture seen in the early twenty-first century. A thriving middle class and strong U.S. dollar in the 1950s helped spawn a travel boom and introduced a large segment of the American public to French and other European cuisines. Early television celebrities such as Julia Child (1912–2004) demystified sophisticated French cookery for the average American, and popular writers such as Craig Claiborne (1920–2000), food writer and restaurant critic of *The New York Times*, turned food writing into a widely accepted form of journalism. A vibrant counterculture emerging in the 1960s and 1970s rebelled against the frozen TV dinners and processed foods of their childhood and brought about a broad awareness of naturally-raised, organic, and vegetarian food alternatives.

In 1971 Alice Waters (1944–) opened Chez Panisse, a restaurant that has a legitimate claim to being one of the most influential dining establishments in the United States. The success and fame garnered by Waters's Berkeley, California, restaurant, with its emphasis on fresh, local, seasonal ingredients and its use of available organic products, has changed the way both professional and amateur cooks approach their work and the way average Americans think about food. The high profile the organic foods movement enjoys and the popularization of gourmet name brands such as Laura Chenel's Chévre and Niman Ranch meats are some of the changes credited to Alice Waters and Chez Panisse, and they are some of the culinary shifts that have helped bring about the emergence of modern foodies and a new American cuisine.

The etymology of the word *foodie* is unclear, though most people attribute the first use of the word to writer and food journalist Paul Levy (1941–), who is credited with coining the term *foodie* in a *Harper's Magazine* article in 1981, and, most famously, using it in the title of his 1984 book (co-written with Ann Barr), *The Official Foodie Handbook*. Despite this commonly-held belief, food writer Gael Greene (1935–) does hold the rights to the first published use of the word *foodie* in a

The owner and artisan cheesemaker of Sweet Grass Dairy in Georgia cuts a vat of goat cheese curds by hand. Organic, slow food, and artisan products are on the rise in the United States, including the South. *Adrienne Lerner / Lerner & Lerner / LernerMedia Global Photos.*

lesser-recognized column published in *New York Magazine*'s June 2, 1980, issue. In separate interviews, both Paul Levy and Gael Greene each claim to have been the first to coin the term *foodie.*

Further adding to the controversy, in David Kamp's 2006 book, *The United States of Arugula*, he asserts that it was in fact Joseph Baum (1920–1998), the creative force behind many of the finest restaurants in the United States—including the famous Four Seasons Restaurant in New York City—who first uttered the word *foodie*. Baum purportedly used *foodie* in conversations with friends and colleagues in referring to people who are inordinately obsessed with restaurant-going and cooking fashions. As likely as it seems, Kamp's claim is impossible to verify because there is no actual record of Joseph Baum ever using the word.

Despite conflicting accounts of the term's origin, it appears that Gael Greene's 1980 foodie, Paul Levy's 1981 foodie, and Joseph Baum's foodie, while essentially having the same meaning, are all likely to have been independent coinages. Although a significant portion of food lovers will bristle at the mere mention of the word, *foodie* appears to have become a permanent part of the language lexicon.

■ Impacts and Issues

Modern gourmet hobbyist/foodie culture exists largely as a media phenomenon. In the 1980s and 1990s, food lovers supported the Food Network and other new, specialized food programming such as *Top Chef*, *Boy Meets Grill*, and *Iron Chef*. Many of these television programs have made international celebrities out of cooks who might otherwise be working anonymously in a hot restaurant kitchen. Famous cooks such as Mario Batali (1960–), Emeril Lagasse (1959–), and Rachael Ray (1968–) enjoy a status and lifestyle that was formerly reserved for movie stars. This food television trend has in turn helped feed other businesses specializing in food such as the kitchenware and publishing industries.

Companies such as Williams Sonoma and Sur la Table that specialize in gourmet kitchen items have benefited directly from the foodie phenomenon, and their sales have increased markedly as a result of food programming sponsorship, especially when their products are demonstrated by celebrity chefs on television. When Rachael Ray uses and endorses a particular kitchen tool on her show, these stores have been known to sell out of it the next day, demonstrating how effective a sales tool such a program can be and the commercial power of its target audience.

A strong foodie culture has paved the way for many successful food books and several widely-circulated food magazines such as *Gourmet* (which ceased publication in 2009) and other respected periodicals such as *Saveur* and *Cook's Illustrated*. Books that offer frank portrayals of what goes on behind the scenes in fine restaurants such as Anthony Bourdain's (1956–) *Kitchen Confidential* and Bill Buford's (1954–) memoir of working in one of Mario Batali's (1960–) kitchens, *Heat*, were best sellers, and books focusing on the history and science of food production, such as Michael Pollan's (1955–) *The Omnivore's Dilemma* and *The Botany of Desire* have sold millions of copies worldwide.

The foodie phenomenon is also alive and well on the Internet. Any food-related Web search will bring up dozens of Web sites and amateur blogs dedicated to the appreciation of good food. Web sites that feature restaurant reviews and other food articles such as Zagats.com and Yelp.com have mushroomed in popularity, enabling diners to review instantly a restaurant they have tried—often while still seated at the table. Many foodies like to blog or read other people's blogs about food topics. Some foodies even take and post pictures on the Internet of every single meal they prepare or consume. This lively network of social media has become a main source of regenerative discourse for keeping the gourmet hobbyist movement, and foodies worldwide, alive and well fed.

SEE ALSO *Alice Waters: California and New American Cuisine; Celebrity Chef Phenomenon; Culinary Education; Food and the Internet; Food Critics and Ratings; Food Fads; Gastronomy; Michael Pollan: Linking Food and Environmental Journalism; Movies, Documentaries, and Food; Television and Food.*

Foodies attend the Great British Cheese Festival in Cardiff, Wales, United Kingdom. © *Jeff Morgan 12 / Alamy.*

BIBLIOGRAPHY

Books

Cohen, Jan. *Memoirs of a Travelling Foodie.* Hamilton, New Zealand: J. Cohen, 2007.

Kamp, David. *The United States of Arugula: How We Became a Gourmet Nation.* New York: Broadway Books, 2006.

Smith, Andrew F. *The Oxford Companion to American Food and Drink.* Oxford, UK, and New York: Oxford University Press, 2007.

Techamuanvivit, Pim, and Jenny Acheson. *The Foodie Handbook: The (Almost) Definitive Guide to Gastronomy.* San Francisco: Chronicle, 2009.

Web Sites

Blount, Hagan. "The Final Word on Foodies." *The Wandering Foodie,* November 16, 2009. http://wanderingfoodie.com/2009/the-final-word-on-foodies/# (accessed October 15, 2010).

Greene, Gael. "What's Nouvelle? La Cuisine Bourgeoise." *Insatiable Critic,* June 20, 1980. http://www.insatiable-critic.com/Article.aspx?id=1131 (accessed October 15, 2010).

Hochman, Karen, Rowann Gilman, and Ruth Katz, eds. "Letters to the Editor: FAQs about Food." *The Nibble.* http://www.thenibble.com/nav2/letters/food.asp (accessed October 15, 2010).

Reichl, Ruth. "The Ruth of the Matter." *Time Out New York,* January 24, 2008. http://newyork.timeout.com/articles/tv/25772/the-ruth-of-the-matter (accessed October 15, 2010).

Restione, Dan. "A Call for Revolution." *Food Musings,* March 17, 2009. http://www.mynorthwest.com/?nid=408&sid=146250 (accessed October 15, 2010).

Matthew Munsey

Government Food Assistance for Citizens

■ Introduction

Government food assistance for citizens is a form of food aid supplied by a government for those of its citizens who face hunger or malnutrition. Government food assistance for citizens is distinguishable from other forms of food aid, including foreign food aid and emergency food assistance. Foreign food aid generally refers to food aid supplied by one country or nongovernmental organization for the citizens of another country who are at risk of hunger or malnutrition. Emergency food aid refers to food aid supplied by a national government, nongovernmental organizations, or foreign government to victims of natural disasters or other emergencies that require immediate aid.

Historically, religious groups and other charities supplied food aid for low-income people. By the mid-twentieth century, however, most developed nations had initiated programs to provide food assistance to low-income citizens. Food assistance programs sometimes attract controversy, including allegations of wasteful spending and concern over the lack of healthy food options. Most developing nations lack food assistance programs for their citizens and often rely on foreign food aid for people at risk of hunger or malnutrition.

■ Historical Background and Scientific Foundations

Around 100 AD, Roman emperors Nerva (30–98) and Trajan (53–117) implemented one of the earliest government programs to provide food assistance to poor citizens. Trajan's program expanded the number of Roman citizens entitled to free grain distributions. Early Christian leaders and philosophers, including St. Augustine, advocated providing assistance to the poor out of spiritual devotion. In the following centuries, the Roman Catholic Church evolved a substantial network to provide alms to the poor, which were distributed through local parishes or monastic orders.

Judaism, meanwhile, continued to stress the role of individuals in providing assistance to the poor, including financial assistance and allowing the poor to harvest crops from certain parts of fields. Islamic law promotes charitable contributions of food or money for the poor. The Rashidun Caliphate, the caliphate established immediately after the death of Muhammad (c.571–632), even implemented a state-sponsored program of alms distribution to the poor, elderly, disabled, orphans, and widows.

Food and monetary assistance to the poor remained the obligation of religious orders and other charities in Europe throughout the Middle Ages and Renaissance. During the Industrial Revolution of the nineteenth century, large numbers of people relocated to urban areas in search of factory work. Under the existing system in Britain, a levy on wealthy landowners supplied parishes with money to provide workhouses—communal living houses for poor laborers and migrant workers—and outdoor aid (financial and food assistance provided to persons with their own housing). The over-reliance of the poor on these services, and fears about increased crime, led Britain to pass laws restricting access to assistance for the poor.

During the Great Depression (1929–1941), people turned to the government for assistance. Many of the programs initiated in the United States and Europe during the Great Depression focused on providing jobs for the poor rather than direct aid. Many people, therefore, continued to rely on religious orders and charities for food assistance. A few European nations, including Germany and Great Britain, however, had instituted unemployment insurance and other welfare programs that provided some financial assistance to unemployed workers during the Great Depression. By the mid-twentieth century, most developed nations had adopted comprehensive welfare programs, including government food assistance for citizens.

■ Impacts and Issues

Food assistance programs for citizens frequently draw criticism from some who view such programs as indicative of excessive government spending. Many also view food assistance programs as conferring a benefit upon people who refuse to work. Others assert that food assistance is essential government spending that helps people who, for various reasons, need assistance.

The role of government food assistance programs for citizens increased during the financial crisis and global economic recession that began in 2007. Many developed nations with food assistance programs experienced unemployment rates of higher than 10 percent. Even more people were underemployed during the recession. Underemployment refers to a person engaged in employment that does not fully utilize that person's skills and education. Underemployed people also do not realize their full earning potential. In the United States, the number of people receiving assistance from the Supplemental Nutrition Assistance Program (SNAP), colloquially referred to as food stamps, increased by 70 percent between 2007 and 2010. As of 2010, more than

WORDS TO KNOW

ALMS: Money or food given to the poor, typically by religious groups or by individuals for religious reasons.

FOOD STAMPS: A form of government assistance to low-income citizens that enables the recipient to acquire food from grocery stores, markets, or other locations.

WORLD FOOD PROGRAMME: The front-line food agency of the United Nations, World Food Programme (WFP) is the largest food aid organization in the world dedicated to hunger issues, delivering aid to more than 90 million persons in more than 70 countries per year.

42 million Americans—one out of every eight American citizens—received food stamps.

In addition to increased need for food assistance during the recession, many U.S. states relaxed food stamp eligibility to accommodate families with underemployed members. Food stamp eligibility rules vary

A single mother and full-time college student in Chicago, Illinois, prepares lunch for her three children with food purchased with government assistance. *AP Images.*

by state, but some states allow individuals or families to qualify for benefits if income is less than double the federal poverty limit. Alaska and Hawaii permit food stamp recipients to earn more than double the federal poverty limit due to the high cost of living in those states. Many health and consumer advocates, however, criticize the food stamp program for enabling the purchase of, and reliance on, highly processed foods.

The majority of developing nations, meanwhile, have limited or nonexistent food assistance programs. Often, developing nations cannot afford to provide food assistance programs for their citizens, because tax revenues are too low and demand for such programs would be too high. Many of these nations, however, receive foreign food assistance from the United Nations World Food Programme or foreign government aid. Despite having a nominally Communist government, China has limited food assistance programs for citizens. The Chinese government is hesitant to take investment capital from corporations in the form of business taxes for food assistance or other welfare programs. Chinese policy favors allowing corporations to retain capital in order to create additional jobs or raise wages.

■ Primary Source Connection

The United States Department of Agriculture (USDA) is the United States federal government agency responsible for agricultural policy and regulation. USDA identifies its missions as providing "leadership on food, agriculture, natural resources, and related issues based on sound public policy, the best available science, and efficient management." To that effort, the department publishes the *Economic Research Report* on timely topics as well as other educational materials. The accompanying article discusses the effects of government food assistance programs on household food security.

Does SNAP Decrease Food Security: Untangling the Self-Selection Effect

The Supplemental Nutrition Assistance Program (SNAP), formerly the Food Stamp Program, is the largest Federal food assistance program, serving over 28 million households monthly in 2008. This study examines households' food security (their access to adequate food for active healthy living) month by month just prior to and just after SNAP entry in order to estimate the influence of benefits on the food security of recipient households.

What Is the Issue?

SNAP benefits are intended to increase the access of eligible low-income households to food and a nutritious diet—to improve their food security. However, it has proven difficult to demonstrate this positive effect or estimate its extent using household survey data. Food insecurity has always been found to be more prevalent in households enrolled in SNAP than in other low-income households. The hypothesized reason for this seeming anomaly is that food-needy households are more likely to enroll in SNAP, and that the initial difference in food security between SNAP participants and nonparticipants is greater than the ameliorative effect of the program. Researchers have used various statistical methods to untangle these opposite forces, but have not obtained consistent or convincing results.

This report provides greater detail on the timing of food insecurity relative to a household's first receiving SNAP benefits (or beginning to receive them again after being off the program for a year or more). The extent of food insecurity in households month by month in the year prior to their enrolling indicates whether signup generally occurred after a period of deteriorating food insecurity, as the self-selection hypothesis suggests. The prevalence of food insecurity among households in the months just after versus just before enrollment may reflect the effect of SNAP benefits on food security.

What Did the Study Find?

Households' food security deteriorated substantially beginning 7 or 8 months prior to SNAP entry and improved shortly after benefits began. The prevalence of very low food security among sample households increased from around 8 percent 1 year prior to entering SNAP to nearly 20 percent in the 4–6 months prior to entry. Within a few months of entering SNAP, the prevalence of very low food security declined to around 12 percent, where it settled for the first 10 months on the program.

These patterns could not be observed either in cross-sectional or 1-year longitudinal analysis of the food security survey data. Only with finer-grained detail of the month-by-month analysis can the deterioration in food security prior to receipt of SNAP benefits and the improvement after be observed.

These results clearly demonstrate the self-selection by households into SNAP at a time when they are more severely food insecure. The results are consistent with a moderate ameliorative effect of SNAP—reducing the prevalence of very low food security among recent entrants by about one-third—although they do not conclusively demonstrate that extent of amelioration.

Mark Nord
Anne Marie Golla

NORD, MARK, AND ANNE MARIE GOLLA. *DOES SNAP DECREASE FOOD INSECURITY? UNTANGLING THE SELF-SELECTION EFFECT.* ECONOMIC RESEARCH REPORT NUMBER 85. UNITED STATES DEPARTMENT OF AGRICULTURE, OCTOBER 2009.

SEE ALSO *Dietary Guidelines for Americans; Dietary Reference Intakes; Food Security; Improving Nutrition for America's Children Act of 2010; Nutrition and U.S. Government Food Assistance; School Lunch Reform; U.S. Department of Agriculture (USDA); USDA Food Pyramid; World Food Programme.*

BIBLIOGRAPHY

Books

How to Use Your SNAP Benefits at Farmers' Markets. Oklahoma City: OK-SNAP, Supplemental Nutrition Assistance Program, Oklahoma OKDHS, 2010.

Kaushal, Neeraj, and Qin Gao. *Food Stamp Program and Consumption Choices.* Cambridge, MA: National Bureau of Economic Research, 2009.

Nord, Mark, and Anne Marie Golla. *Does SNAP Decrease Food Insecurity: Untangling the Self-Selection Effect.* Economic Research Report Number 85. Economic Research Service, U.S. Department of Agriculture, 2009.

Roush, Margaret. *U.S. National Debate Topic, 2009–2010: Social Services for the Poor.* New York: H.W. Wilson Company, 2009.

SNAP Can Make a Big Difference in Feeding Your Family. Salem, OR: DHS, Children, Adults and Families Division, Supplemental Nutrition Assistance Program, 2010.

SNAP: Supplemental Nutrition Assistance Program. Indianapolis, IN: Family and Social Services Administration, 2010.

Periodicals

Christian, Thomas "Grocery Store Access and the Food Insecurity-Obesity Paradox." *Journal of Hunger & Environmental Nutrition* 5, no. 3 (2010): 360–369.

Issar, Sukriti. "Multiple Program Participation and Exits from Food Stamps among Elders." *The Social Service Review* 84, no. 3 (2010): 437–459.

Wilde, Parke E., Lisa M. Troy, and Beatrice L. Rogers. "Food Stamps and Food Spending: An Engel Function Approach." *American Journal of Agricultural Economics* 91, no. 2 (2009): 416–430.

Web Sites

"Food Stamps and Other Nutrition Programs." *Social Security Administration.* http://www.ssa.gov/pubs/10100.html (accessed November 2, 2010).

"SNAP/Food Stamps." *Food Research and Action Center.* http://frac.org/federal-foodnutrition-programs/snapfood-stamps/ (accessed November 2, 2010).

"Supplemental Nutrition Assistance Program (SNAP)." *Food and Nutrition Service, U.S. Department of Agriculture.* http://www.fns.usda.gov/snap/ (accessed November 2, 2010).

Joseph P. Hyder

Grains

Introduction

The grains of cereal plants are a rich source of both calories and protein and have long played a major role in the human diet. Along with legumes, cereals account for two-thirds of the world's consumption of protein in the early twenty-first century. Grains are a good food source because they store well and can be processed into many familiar products such as bread and other baked goods, sauces, and breakfast cereals. However, processing and refining remove some of the most nutritious parts of the grain, which contain needed fiber, minerals, and vitamins. A healthy diet includes several servings per day of whole grains. Usually whole grain products are manufactured by putting the bran and germ back into the processed grain. The demand for grains has not only shaped human civilization since the dawn of agriculture, but has also led to huge changes in agricultural practices, with intensive large-scale farming becoming the standard in many parts of the world. Genetic engineering technology is helping push grain yields higher still by improving the traits of cereal crops, although there is resistance in many areas to adopting genetically modified food sources.

Historical Background and Scientific Foundations

Cereals and legumes were probably the first plants to be domesticated at the establishment of agriculture some 10,000 years ago. The shift from hunter-gatherer societies to a more settled way of life, with a stable and centralized food supply, had a great impact upon human culture. It is significant that some of the earliest written texts concern transactions of grains. Although there are around 5,000 species of grass, only a few cereal plants have ever been cultivated for human nutrition. The cultivation of wheat, barley, rice, and maize goes back to the beginnings of agriculture, whereas cultivation of oats and rye dates back for only around 2,000 years. Tricale, which is a hybrid of wheat and rye, was developed in the nineteenth century to produce a grain that had the culinary properties of wheat combined with the disease resistance of rye. The importance of cereal crops varies with location: Wheat, barley, oats, and rye are grown in the Middle East and Europe, whereas rice is of more significance in Asia. Maize, also known as corn, is the main grain of the New World, and sorghum and millet are grown mainly in Africa. Among the less well-known cereals is amaranth, a tiny seed, only one millimeter across, which has been grown in Central America for the last 5,000 years. Meanwhile, quinoa was one of the Inca's staple foods.

Grains differ in their nutritional and agronomic characteristics. Wheat contains gluten protein (as do barley and rye, but in smaller amounts), which is the structural basis of all leavened baked goods. Most wheat currently grown is of one species that has been cultivated for bread baking. Most barley is converted into malt, in which the grain is germinated and then fermented to make beer or whisky. Oats do not grow well in hot climates, where they are a minor grain crop. They tend to be used more for animal feed, although they contain glucan carbohydrates, which are good for lowering blood cholesterol. Rye is a hardy crop that can grow in cold climates and at high altitude. It has long been a staple food in less affluent cultures. Rye has the ability to retain moisture because it is rich in carbohydrates called arabinoxylans, which is why rye products have a long shelf life. Sorghum grows in arid and semi-arid climates and contains as much protein as wheat, but lacks gluten. Grains contain significant amounts of protein, although most of them lack the amino acid lysine. Exceptions include buckwheat, quinoa, and amaranth, which provide complete protein with all the essential amino acids. Often grains without lysine are served with legumes, such as the combination of tortillas and beans, to provide the complete range of amino acids.

All grains have the same structure in which the outer layer, or bran, is made up of several thin layers and includes the pericarp, which is the part of the ovary well that is fleshy in other fruits. The aleurone layer, which lies just under the bran, is the most nutritious part of the grain, even though it may be only one cell thick. Inside the aleurone lies the endosperm, which accounts for most of the volume of the grain and contains most of the protein and carbohydrate. The seed, at the base of the grain, consists of the embryo, or germ, which will grow into a new plant, and the scutellum, a projection that carries nutrients from the endosperm to the embryo. Barley, oats, and rice have a tough husk surrounding the grain, which has to be removed. Whole grains are not very easy to cook or chew, which is why they have long been treated to remove their tough outer layers. In primitive mills, grains were crushed between rocks and the bran picked out of the broken endosperm. Around 800 BC, the rotary grinding machine was invented, which meant that the milling process could be powered by animals or waterwheels. In a modern mill, grooved

WORDS TO KNOW

ALEURONE: The thin layer just beneath the outside of a grain that is rich in proteins, oils, vitamins, minerals, and fiber. The aleurone layer is the outer layer of the endosperm.

ENDOSPERM: The central and largest portion of a grain, filled with starch granules embedded in a protein matrix.

GRAIN: The edible part of a cereal grass plant. A grain is a whole fruit, containing a seed and a thin, dry layer of ovary tissue.

rollers are used to shear, scrape, and crush the whole grains, providing a clean separation of germ, endosperm, and bran. Refined flour is only endosperm, whereas whole grain flour has the germ and bran added back in. Whole grains are more nutritious than refined ones. Refined flour, like white sugar, was seen as a status symbol for many centuries, because it appeared to be purer than the unrefined, whole grain, version. However, in the mid-nineteenth century, a Presbyterian minister from

A woman uses her fingers to pick up every leftover grain of rice after harvest in Shovondaha, Kurigram district, Rajshahi division, Bangladesh, in 2008. Thousands of extremely poor women scavenge each grain of discarded rice in order to provide at least one meal per day. Severe unemployment, poverty, and lack of opportunities in northern Bangladesh cause millions of people to survive on less than one U.S. dollar per day. *AP Images.*

A farmer harvests wheat with a combine. During the bountiful June 2010 harvest, almost 353 million bushels of wheat were harvested nationwide in the United States. *Image copyright Orientaly, 2010. Used under license from Shutterstock.com.*

Philadelphia named Sylvester Graham (1794–1851) began to argue in favor of whole grain flour, which became known as Graham flour, on nutritional grounds. The first breakfast cereal, Granula, was developed by James Caleb Jackson (1811–1895) a follower of Graham. Then John Harvey Kellogg (1852–1943) popularized whole grain cereals at the Battle Creek Sanitarium from 1875. He and his brother went on to invent flaked cereal made from corn, and later wheat bran.

■ Impacts and Issues

Maize, rice, and wheat account for nearly 90 percent of all grains grown. They play an essential role in the human diet. In less developed countries, the diet may consist almost entirely of grains. Farmers, therefore, are always trying to increase yields to meet demand. One significant development in this respect was the Green Revolution of the 1950s and 1960s, which doubled global production of wheat. The major factors were use of higher-yielding varieties of cereals, application of modern agrochemicals such as fertilizers and pesticides, and more intensive large-scale methods

of cultivation. The Green Revolution provided more food, but at a cost: The accompanying reduction in genetic diversity leaves crops open to disease and pests. More agrochemicals have to be applied, which degrades the environment and leads to domination of large corporations that manufacture them. In more recent years, genetic engineering has been applied to cereal crops to build in resistance to insects and disease. Genetically modified crops are, however, still not accepted everywhere, although they have led to increased yields.

Grain harvests are always vulnerable to climatic factors and this can have negative effects on exports. For instance, in summer 2010 Russian Prime Minister Vladimir Putin (1952–) warned that his country's wheat harvest would be reduced to 66 million tons because of a combination of fires and drought. Russia normally exports around 110 million tons of wheat each year. Because of domestic shortages, a ban on grain exports from Russia, including rye, maize, wheat, and barley, was likely to be extended until at least September 2010. As a result, global wheat prices were up to a two year high and Russia's biggest customers, which are Egypt, Turkey, and Syria, were hit by the shortages.

SEE ALSO *Agribusiness; Baking Bread; Biodiversity and Food Supply; Biofuels and World Hunger; Commission on Genetic Resources for Food and Agriculture; Convention on Biological Diversity (1992); Ethical Issues in Agriculture; Fermentation: Alcohol; Food Price Crisis; Genetically Modified Organisms (GMO); Gluten Intolerance; Green Revolution (1943); Population and Food; Rome Declaration on World Food Security (1996); Sustainable Agriculture.*

BIBLIOGRAPHY

Books

Abdel-Aal, Elsayed, and Peter J. Wood. *Specialty Grains for Food and Feed*. St. Paul, MN: American Association of Cereal Chemists, 2005.

Bennet, Gregory S. *Food Identity Preservation and Traceability: Safer Grains*. Boca Raton, FL: CRC Press, 2010.

Cohen, Marc J., and Jennifer Clapp. *The Global Food Crisis: Governance Challenges and Opportunities*. Waterloo, Ontario: Wilfrid Laurier University, 2009.

Marquart, Len. *Whole Grains and Health*. Ames, IA: Blackwell, 2007.

The U.S. Market for Whole and Other Grains: Trends and Developments. Rockville, MD: Packaged Facts, 2009.

Periodicals

Brett, John. "The Political-Economics of Developing Markets versus Satisfying Food Needs." *Food and Foodways* 18 (2010): 1–2.

Carr, Edward. "The Millennium Village Project and African Development." *Progress in Development Studies* 8, no. 4 (2008): 333–344.

Web Sites

"Grain Market Report: 26 August 2010." *International Grains Council*. http://www.igc.int/downloads/gmrsummary/gmrsumme.pdf (accessed September 21, 2010).

Harvard School of Public Health. "Health Gains from Whole Grains." *Harvard University*. http://www.hsph.harvard.edu/nutritionsource/what-should-you-eat/health-gains-from-whole-grains/ (accessed September 21, 2010).

Susan Aldridge

Green Revolution

■ Introduction

The Green Revolution refers to a transformation in worldwide agricultural practices that began in the early 1940s and continued through the 1960s. It was not a singular movement; rather, it describes the implementation of science-based farming practices and the development of agricultural biotechnology to improve food security. The Green Revolution is credited with improving crop yields and preventing famine in developing nations.

Several basic practices formed the foundation of the Green Revolution. The development and use of hybridized, improved, or genetically modified seeds prevented crop disease and increased yields. Improved irrigation, better land clearing practices, and mechanization expanded farmlands. Crop rotation and multi-cropping made farmland more productive and promoted crop variety.

The Green Revolution garnered its name from a 1968 U.S. government report authored by the administrator of the United States Agency for International Development (USAID). When describing improvements in poverty and famine reduction in India and Pakistan, the official noted that "it look[ed] like a Green Revolution."

As a social and scientific movement, the Green Revolution shares little in common with the environment-focused green social and political movements that arose in the late 1960s and are active in the twenty-first century. The Green Revolution endeavored to prevent famine and poverty, whereas current green movements focus on the environmental impacts of human activities. The aims of the Green Revolution continue to influence biotechnology research, sustainable development initiatives, and foreign aid programs.

■ Historical Background and Scientific Foundations

The Green Revolution relied on the development of high-yield crops—plants bred to respond well to fertilizers and produce an increased amount of crop per acre planted. Thus, the Green Revolution originated in agricultural and genetics research facilities. Scientists interested in improving yields from staple crops such as wheat experimented with varieties to find valuable traits, including bountiful harvest, disease resistance, ease of planting, and suitability to multiple climate growing zones. In 1946, after assessing agricultural difficulties in postwar Japan on behalf of the United States government, agronomist S. Cecil Salmon (1885–1975) selected a short, stiff, heavily seeded variety known as Norin No. 10 for further processing. Over the following 15 years, researchers created several hybrids from the initial seed lines. Farmers in Washington state planted the seeds so that researchers could study each crop's needs and yields.

During this same period, American agronomist Norman E. Borlaug (1914–2009) was working on hybridized wheat varieties in Mexico. Borlaug crossed genetic material from the Washington state project with several varieties of Mexican wheat. The resultant seeds demonstrated strong stems that prevented breakage and crop loss, improved disease resistance, and increased tolerance of dry conditions. Borlaug's wheat varieties yielded two to three times more grain than the unhybridized varieties that were commonly planted at the time.

Borlaug combined his developed seeds with recommendations on mechanized farming and the use of herbicides, pesticides, and nitrogen fertilizers. His work enabled Mexico to move from needing to import nearly half of the total wheat consumed in the country in 1940s to being able to export surplus wheat crops in by the mid-1960s. Borlaug sought investment in the research so that improved crop and agricultural technologies could be used to fight food insecurity worldwide. In 1963, with financing from several national governments and the Rockefeller and Ford Foundations, the International Maize and Wheat Improvement Center was established.

In 1943, in India and present-day Bangladesh, crop failures, inadequate long-term food stores, distribution

A farmer walks in a field near Ciudad Obregon in 2008. After the pioneering agronomist Norman E. Borlaug introduced his green revolution of hardier seeds and chemicals in this region more than 60 years ago, he was credited with saving hundreds of millions from starvation worldwide. Today, in a global food crisis of lagging productivity and punishing prices, world leaders are calling for a second revolution but it won't be that easy this time, experts say. *AP Images.*

Green Revolution technologies also aided the highly mechanized agriculture of the world's most developed nations. The United States produced a self-sufficient wheat crop in the early 1950s, but became a wheat exporter by 1960.

In 1970 Borlaug won the Nobel Peace Prize for "providing bread for a hungry world" with his pioneering work on the development of high-yield and disease-resistant wheat crops.

■ Impacts and Issues

In 1950 the world's grain production was slightly less than 700 million tons. By 2010 world grain output approached 2 billion tons per year, with 600 million more hectares (almost 1.5 billion acres) actively farmed than in 1950. Borlaug claimed that without Green Revolution technologies, it would have required three times as much land to achieve the same global yields.

The Borlaug Hypothesis states that increasing agricultural productivity on the very best farmland can stem the large-scale ecosystem destruction and deforestation that accompanies the creation of new farmland, especially in the environmentally sensitive developing areas such as the Amazon River basin. Borlaug asserted that without the Green Revolution: "[W]e would have cut down millions of acres of forest, thereby destroying wildlife habitat, in order to increase cropland to produce enough food for an escalating population. And we would have to use more herbicides in more fields, which would damage the environment even more. Technology allows us to have less impact on soil erosion, biodiversity, wildlife, forests, and grasslands."

Criticism of the Green Revolution often focuses on its potential environmental impacts. Most of the seed varieties developed during the Green Revolution were designed to work best with applications of natural and chemical fertilizers. When seeds were introduced to regional farmers, so too were fertilizers that eventually ended up contributing to water pollution and

problems, and a food price crisis caused an acute famine that killed approximately 4 million people. India was again on the brink of large-scale famine in the early 1960s. Rapid population growth and urbanization undermined food security in the region. The International Rice Research Institute in Los Baños, Philippines, developed a new type of rice, IR8, that when combined with modern irrigation and fertilization practices, dramatically improved crop yields on existing farmlands. Over a five-year period from 1965 to 1970, IR8 enabled annual rice production in India to increase from 12 million to more than 20 million tons, helping the nation feed its booming population. IR8 became a popularly planted rice variety throughout much of Southeast Asia.

Successes with wheat in Mexico were duplicated in Asia. Throughout the 1960s, Borlaug and other researchers taught local farmers in India and Pakistan to cultivate new wheats. Pakistan raised its annual production of wheat from 1965 levels of 4.6 million tons to 8.4 million tons by 1970. In the 1980s successful wheat hybrids and yield-boosting farming practices were introduced in China, which now produces the largest volume of food in the world.

placing farm populations at risk for exposure to toxins. Similarly, farming practices of the Green Revolution also encouraged the routine use of selective herbicides to control weeds and pesticides to control insects. Irrigation projects diverted freshwater sources, which prevented devastating crop failure from drought but contributed to depletion of freshwater sources and the transfer of damaging farm chemicals into those freshwater sources.

Development-oriented criticism of the Green Revolution charges that large parts of the world have not benefited from agricultural reforms. Whereas the Green Revolution raised yields in parts of Asia and the Americas, critics note that Africa has not significantly benefited. During the peak decades of the Green Revolution, decolonization, political unrest, and corruption made working with agricultural interests difficult and exacerbated food insecurity on the continent. Critics also assert that the Green Revolution overlooked essential structural inequities that affect agricultural production, including the ability to own the land one farms, the ability to pay for farming technology, the regulation of agricultural markets, and the construction of reliable storage and transport infrastructures.

Whereas the seeds that drove the Green Revolution were developed in Mexico, the United States, the Philippines, and other nations, current biotechnology is largely developed and owned by companies based in the world's wealthiest nations. Critics claim that the Green Revolution's reliance on biotechnology makes farmers in developing nations increasingly reliant on Western corporations and transfers aid dollars back to donor nations instead of remaining in the local areas in need of aid.

Biodiversity of food crop species also worries some observers. Several thousand rice varieties were planted routinely in Asia before the Green Revolution. In 2010 twelve varieties of rice comprised more than 80 percent of all the rice production in Asia. Ecologists are concerned that a lack of biodiversity facilitates the spread of blights and crop diseases and makes each incident likely to affect a significant portion of the region's food crops. To prevent such catastrophic crop failures and prevent disease, farmers may turn to increased use of pesticides, fertilizers, and fungicides—all of which have some negative ecological impacts.

However, proponents of biotechnology in the form of genetically-modified organism (GMO) foods view GMOs as an extension of the original high-crop yield aims of the Green Revolution. In 2009, while speaking at the Borlaug International Symposium following the World Food Prize award ceremony, U.S. business leader Bill Gates (1955–) asserted that GMO foods may have "the potential to address farmers' challenges more efficiently than conventional techniques."

Critics also assert that the Green Revolution did nothing to address rapidly growing populations. High birth rates often contribute to incidence of food scarcity in places where food is endemically insecure or where there is little surplus.

Climate change raises new problems for global agriculture. Proponents of the ideals espoused by the Green Revolution assert that biotechnology offers solutions for adaptation. Crop plants likely will face new environmental stresses. Sea-level rise could inundate farmlands and salinate freshwater irrigation sources. Changing weather patterns may lengthen growing seasons in some places while shortening growing seasons in others. New outbreaks of crop diseases likely will emerge. Climate change thus threatens global food security as Earth's population continues to grow. The United Nations Intergovernmental Panel on Climate Change (IPCC) urges agricultural researchers to focus on adapting crops to use less freshwater during a warmer growing season. Agricultural adaptation to climate change is already being called the Second Green Revolution.

■ Primary Source Connection

The Honorable William S. Gaud gave this speech to the U.S. Agency for International Development (USAID) in March 1968. Gaud served as administrator of USAID before serving as executive vice president of the International Finance Corporation, a member of the World Bank Group that promotes private sector investment in developing nations. Gaud is credited with coining the term "green revolution" regarding how agricultural discoveries and improvements could better feed the world population.

The Green Revolution: Accomplishments and Apprehensions

Today's developments have been more than a few seasons in the making. Twenty-five years ago, the Rockefeller Foundation began its highly successful work to strengthen wheat production in Mexico. The Foundation concentrated next on rice, the most important crop in the world. More people eat rice than any other food. Over 90% of the billion and a half people of Asia live mostly on rice, and about 80% of them spend most of their time growing it.

In 1962 the Rockefeller and Ford Foundations established the International Rice Research Institute at Los Banos in the Philippines. Their object was to develop new varieties which would increase rice production in countries such as India, Thailand, Pakistan, the Philippines, Cambodia, and Laos—countries where rice was important but yields were low.

The Institute canvassed the world for samples of rice seed, looking for varieties to cross in order to form the hardiest, most adaptable, most nutritious strain. 10,000 varieties were collected. Para, a tall Philippine variety which originated in Indonesia, was crossed with a short variety from Taiwan, Dee-gee-woo-gan. The result was named IR-8. By 1966 it was fully developed. IR-8 has a stiff, strong, short straw. It does not fall over, or lodge, when the plant is heavily fertilized or when it is buffeted by wind and rain. It matures quickly, allowing for two—sometimes three—crops in a single year. Some call it the "miracle rice." Under favorable conditions, each planting yields four to six times as most traditional varieties.

High-yield varieties of wheat, maize, sorghum, and millet have also been developed in recent years. The best known—and most important—of these are the "Mexican wheats" developed by the Rockefeller Foundation which have quadrupled Mexican yields from 11 to 40 bushels per acre.

It is a long way, however, from breakthroughs in laboratories and test fields to the record crops now being harvested by tens of thousands of farmers in half a dozen or more countries. Transforming the new seeds into food for millions of mouths requires many things. Some of these the developing countries can supply, some they cannot.

To begin with, of course, there must be a will for improvement in the developing countries themselves. In many of them such a will exists—particularly in Asia—where the pressures of food and population are so intense. Given this will, the people of the developing nations can put the new seeds, the fertilizer, and the pesticides to work. And their governments can provide the credit, the price incentives, and the market that will begin to change their lives.

But the developing nations—their governments, their institutions, and their farmers—cannot sustain the Green Revolution without outside support. They lack the skills to do the necessary adaptive research. They lack the capital to build fertilizer plants. They lack the facilities and the technicians needed to train their people in the new ways.

If this agricultural revolution is to succeed, it can only do so as the result of a working partnership between the advanced and the developing nations.

William S. Gaud

GAUD, WILLIAM S. "THE GREEN REVOLUTION: ACCOMPLISHMENTS AND APPREHENSIONS." HTTP://WWW.AGBIOWORLD.ORG/BIOTECH-INFO/TOPICS/BORLAUG/BORLAUG-GREEN.HTML (ACCESSED NOVEMBER 15, 2010).

SEE ALSO *Agriculture and International Trade; Agroecology; Biodiversity and Food Supply; Climate Change and Agriculture; Ethical Issues in Agriculture; Ethical Issues in Food Aid; Extreme Weather and Food Supply; Famine; Famine: Political Considerations; Food and Agricultural Organization (FAO); Food Security; Genetically Modified Organisms (GMO); International Food Aid; International Fund for Agricultural Development; Population and Food; Subsistence Farming; Sustainable Agriculture; World Food Prize.*

BIBLIOGRAPHY
Books

Glaeser, Bernhard. *The Green Revolution Revisited: Critique and Alternatives.* London: Routledge, 2010.

Jain, H. K. *Green Revolution: History, Impact and Future.* Houston: Studium Press LLC, 2010.

Kidd, Jerry S., and Renee A. Kidd. *Agricultural versus Environmental Science: A Green Revolution.* New York: Chelsea House, 2006.

McInerny, Ralph. *The Green Revolution.* New York: St. Martin's Minotaur, 2008.

Reeder, Kevin, Jonathan Tisdall, and Arne Cartridge. *Catalyst for Action: Towards an African Green Revolution.* Oslo, Norway: Yara International ASA, 2007.

Shrivastava, Mohan P. *Second Green Revolution vs. Rainbow Revolution.* New Delhi: Deep & Deep Publications, 2010.

Periodicals

Archibald, John M. "Genomics: Green Evolution, Green Revolution." *Science* 324, no. 5924 (2009): 191–192.

Bagla, Pallava. "A Guru of the Green Revolution Reflects on Borlaug's Legacy." *Science* 5951 (2009): 361.

"The Next Green Revolution." *The Economist* 386, no. 8568 (2008): 67.

Rull, Valenti. "Food Security: Green Revolution Drawbacks." *Science* 328, no. 5975 (2010): 169.

Sachs, Jeffrey D. "The African Green Revolution." *Scientific American* 298, no. 5 (2008): 42.

Web Sites

Bourlaug, Norman. "Biotechnology and the Green Revolution." *Action Bioscience.* http://www.actionbioscience.org/biotech/borlaug.html (accessed October 25, 2010).

"The End of India's Green Revolution?" *BBC News,* May 29, 2006. http://news.bbc.co.uk/2/hi/south_asia/4994590.stm (accessed October 25, 2010).

Adrienne Wilmoth Lerner

Gulf of Mexico Oil Spill Food Impacts

■ Introduction

On April 22, 2010, fires from an explosion two days earlier sank the *Deepwater Horizon* oil rig located in the Gulf of Mexico off the Louisiana coast. The deadly explosion aboard the drilling rig under lease to BP (formerly British Petroleum) resulted in a massive oil spill from a deep-water well located 5,000 feet (1,500 meters) below the surface. The spill continued for 87 days, closing a significant portion of the Gulf to fishing. Oil slicks and subsurface oil fouled approximately 600 miles (966 km) of coastline and washed into marshes, wetlands, and inland waterways. The spill delivered a crippling blow to the economic base of the region, disrupting lives and livelihoods of people in the seafood industry, restaurants, and associated businesses along the central and northern Gulf Coast.

U.S. President Barack Obama (1961–) described the BP spill as the worst environmental disaster in U.S. history. In addition to killing fish, mammals, and migratory birds, the oil slick and subsurface oil, often mixed with chemical dispersants, polluted and poisoned oyster beds, crab habitats, and shrimp nurseries.

WORDS TO KNOW

BARREL (OF OIL): The traditional unit of measure by which crude oil is bought and sold on the world market. One barrel of oil is equivalent to 42 U.S. gallons (159 liters).

EMULSIFIER: A chemical used to suspend oils in water.

HYDROCARBON: A chemical containing only carbon and hydrogen.

VOLATILE: Easily vaporized at moderate temperatures and pressures.

VOLATILE ORGANIC COMPOUND: Any organic liquid that changes easily (volatilizes) to a gas.

■ Historical Background and Scientific Foundations

Estimates of the volume of oil gushing into the Gulf increased steadily throughout the spill, ultimately reaching 5 million barrels (210 million gallons) of oil. This amount surpassed the estimated 3.3 million barrels (approximately 140 million gallons) of oil released during the 1979 Ixtoc I spill in the Bay of Campeche (the southern Gulf of Mexico off Mexico's coast), making it the worst accidental marine oil spill in history. The 2010 BP spill far exceeded the 11 million gallons of oil released into Alaskan waters following the 1989 grounding of the tanker *Exxon Valdez*.

Although the composition of crude oil varies somewhat according to its source, crude oil is a naturally occurring brown or black liquid that is composed of a mixture of hydrocarbons and other organic compounds. Crude oil is toxic, flammable, and contains volatile organic compounds (VOCs) that have known adverse effects on human health, such as benzene, a carcinogen, and polycyclic aromatic hydrocarbons (PACs), which are toxic to the central nervous system. A substantial portion of the volatile components of petroleum, about 25 to 40 percent of the total volume of spilled oil, dissolved in the water column as oil rose to the surface or evaporated at the ocean surface.

After the spill, hundreds of vessels immediately began skimming and containment operations. Both ships and aircraft began applying oil dispersants to the slick. Marine wildlife experts warned against indiscriminate use of dispersants as emulsifying agents because the scale of the application was untested and some dispersants were known to be directly toxic to marine organisms. In addition, dispersed oil globules can also be highly toxic. Concentration is the key to a tricky environmental trade-off: Cleanup engineers and crews relied on the correct dilution of dispersants and dispersed oil to minimize levels of toxicity. At one point, the U.S. Environmental Protection Agency (EPA) ordered a halt to the spread of selected dispersants pending further review of toxicity. The extensive use of the oil dispersant Corexit remains controversial and under scientific investigation.

■ Impacts and Issues

Throughout the spill, public health officials expressed a range of concerns about direct health impacts from the spill. U.S. Surgeon General Regina Benjamin (1956–) said that scientific predictions ranged from little or no toxic effect (especially from short-term exposure) to levels of serious concern. However, multiple federal and state agencies stepped in to ban the harvesting and sale of potentially contaminated fish and other seafood.

The spill crippled the regional seafood industry, destroying or closing oyster beds and prime fishing grounds for shrimp and crab. In May 2010, federal and state agencies instituted temporary bans on commercial fishing from the mouth of the Mississippi river to the Florida panhandle. By the following month the fishing ban extended over 33 percent of the Gulf. Unable to fish, many skippers of shrimp boats and other fishing vessels volunteered to assist in cleanup efforts.

Thousands of businesses and people across the region lost employment and income because of the spill. Numerous restaurants and other businesses closed or were forced to seek financial compensation from BP. There were chronic and widespread complaints about the handling of claims by BP, with many businesses asserting

that claims were unfairly delayed or denied. Ultimately the compensation process was taken over by the independently administered Gulf Coast Claims Facility to independently evaluate and pay compensation claims.

With a temporary cap on the well and waters apparently clearing, in August 2010 the National Oceanic and Atmospheric Administration (NOAA) began to reopen sections of federally controlled waters to commercial fishing. Although health officials attempted to reassure consumers that Gulf seafood was safe, lingering doubts diminished consumer confidence. Restaurants that proudly boasted of Gulf seafood to show their support for Gulf Coast residents during the early days of the spill quietly removed the labels or replaced menu items with seafood selections from other regions. Many fishermen initially resisted returning to formerly closed waters.

Consumer confidence was further shaken by competing claims about the fate of the oil. Government and BP officials initially claimed the oil was consumed by microbes or otherwise dissipated within weeks of stopping the spill. In September and October 2010, however, a series of research reports documented additional areas of submerged oil mixtures and residues. Researchers also discovered oil and traces of chemical dispersants in underwater sediment samples and in blue crab larvae. Environmental experts claim it will take many years of study to fully assess the ecological and economic impacts of the BP spill.

A young man fishes within sight of booms intended to protect the eastern shoreline of Mobile Bay from the Deepwater Horizon oil spill that began in April 2010. Towns along the bay boomed off beaches, boat ramps, marinas, creeks, marshes, and estuaries hoping to protect sensitive ecosystems from surface oil. However, incident response officials and researchers discovered underwater plumes of dispersed oil in the waters where the bay meets the Gulf of Mexico. *Adrienne Lerner / Lerner & Lerner / LernerMedia Global Photos.*

IN CONTEXT: GULF OIL SPILL CREATES FOOD CHAIN UNCERTAINTY

Commercial harvests were imperiled by the massive oil spill in the Gulf of Mexico that resulted from the fiery destruction of the *Deepwater Horizon* oil rig in April 2010. The resulting oil spill continued for 87 days to become the largest unintentional marine oil spill in history. Oyster beds were poisoned by toxic hydrocarbon residues. By July 2010 oyster supplies along much of the Northern Gulf coast were either contaminated or exhausted.

Shrimp and crab populations depend on coastal marshes and estuaries, and many of those waters were exposed to some combination of surface oil and subsurface emulsified oil and oil dispersant mixture. Studies of damage to basic elements of the food chain continue, with experts predicting that it will take years to measure the full extent of the oil spill damage. Measuring the impacts on deepwater species, including royal red shrimp, redfish, mackerel, and the already threatened bluefin tuna may also require several seasons of study.

SEE ALSO *Consumer Food Safety Recommendations; Food Inspection and Standards; Food Webs and Food Chains; Seafood.*

BIBLIOGRAPHY

Books

Freudenburg, William R., and Robert Gramling. *Blowout in the Gulf: The BP Oil Spill Disaster and the Future of Energy in America.* Cambridge, MA: MIT Press, 2011.

Maczulak, Anne E. *Pollution: Treating Environmental Toxins.* New York: Facts on File, 2010.

Rees, Gareth. *Safe Management of Shellfish and Harvest Waters.* London: International Water Association, 2010.

Web Sites

U.S. Government: Unified Command's Joint Information Center (JIC). *Restore the Gulf.gov.* http://www. restorethegulf.gov/ (accessed October 31, 2010).

U.S. Government: Unified Command's Joint Information Center (JIC). "Seafood Safety." *Restore the Gulf.gov.* http://www.restorethegulf.gov/health-safety/seafood-safety (accessed October 31, 2010).

U.S. National Commission on the BP Deepwater Horizon Oil Spill and Offshore Drilling. "Media Advisories." *OilSpillCommission.gov.* http://www. oilspillcommission.gov/news#media-alerts (accessed October 31, 2010).

Wentzell's Oyster House restaurant in Point Clear, Alabama, advertises local seafood and assures tourists that the catch is clean in June 2010. The BP oil spill has disrupted the local economy. Gulf Coast towns in oil spill zone are seeing fewer tourists during the usually busy summer season. Menu's at seafood restaurants are shrinking as fresh local seafood caught by local fishermen becomes more difficult to procure. *Ellie Lerner / Lerner & Lerner / LernerMedia Global Photos.*

K. Lee Lerner

Head-to-Tail Eating

■ Introduction

Head-to-tail eating, also referred to as nose-to-tail eating, refers to a culinary movement that encourages consuming or using every part of a slaughtered animal. Whereas many cultures in developing nations have a long history of consuming every part of slaughtered animals out of economic necessity, the head-to-tail movement generally refers to a return to traditional ways of eating in developed countries that have moved away from such eating practices over the last century.

The head-to-tail movement began in earnest in the mid-1990s, when British chef Fergus Henderson (1963–) and others began advocating consuming offal and utility cuts that had fallen out of favor with restaurants and home cooks in Western countries. Offal, or the internal organs of animals, and utility cuts, including tails and trotters (feet), provide a source of nutrition that differs from traditionally consumed skeletal muscle. Head-to-tail eating encourages consumers to have an appreciation of culinary tradition and greater understanding of the meat production. The head-to-tail movement also promotes an ecologically sound use of meat by requiring the slaughter of fewer animals and consequently a reduction of production inputs required to produce meat.

■ Historical Background and Scientific Foundations

Until about two million years ago, hominids lived almost exclusively on a diet of plants. Changing climatic conditions in Africa, however, diminished the supply of edible plants and forced hominids to scavenge for meat from carcasses killed by other animals. Born of necessity, this development brought about a significant transformation in human evolution. The protein and fat contained in the concentrated flesh, fat, marrow, and organs of animals provided hominids with the energy required to enlarge brain size and evolve into more intelligent hominids, ultimately resulting in modern *Homo sapiens*. A reliance on meat also enabled hominids to migrate from the equatorial regions of Africa to Eurasia, where plants for food are not available year round.

Since the dawn of hunting about 100,000 years ago, however, humans have been inclined to use every part of animals for food or for the production of clothing or other household goods. Complete usage of the animal made the most of a rare, life-sustaining hunt. Even after humans domesticated animals about 9,000 years ago in the Middle East, communities continued to consume virtually every part of slaughtered animals out of economic necessity. Humans developed agriculture around the same time that they domesticated animals. As growing grains and vegetables makes more productive use of land than raising animals, eating meat became a rare occurrence for most people.

By the late nineteenth century, meat consumption among the general population began to increase, especially in the United States, which had expansive prairie land for grazing. The development of railroads and refrigeration also ensured that meat could be transported quickly from pasture to the slaughterhouse and from the slaughterhouse to consumers. Even though meat, the skeletal muscle of animals, has always been one of the most prized parts of slaughtered animals, many people continued to consume offal and other utility cuts, which were cheaper than meat.

By the mid-twentieth century, however, rising incomes and a growing middle class in industrialized countries meant that more people could afford meat. Consumers also began to eschew offal and flavorful utility cuts in favor of more tender, and often blander, cuts of meat. Changes in society drove this change in consumer habits to a great extent, as two-income households sought cuts of meat that could be prepared quickly after work rather than tougher cuts that require hours of braising or roasting.

WORDS TO KNOW

MEAT: Meat typically refers to the skeletal muscle of animals used as food.

OFFAL: The internal organs of animals prepared for consumption.

VARIANT CREUTZFELDT-JAKOB DISEASE (vCJD): A fatal neurological disorder that is transmitted by prions, or protein-based infectious agents, contained in the brains or spinal cords of cattle infected with bovine spongiform encephalopathy (BSE).

■ Impacts and Issues

British chef Fergus Henderson launched the modern head-to-tail movement in Western nations when he opened St. John Restaurant in London in 1994. St. John Restaurant focuses on traditional British cooking, many aspects of which use long-neglected offal and

A man eats an intact salted herring in the Netherlands. The United States remains one of a few countries where meat consumption is mostly comprised of prime cuts. The head-to-tail movement encourages using as much as possible of the whole animal as a source of food. *Lourens Smak / Alamy.*

other cuts of meat. Henderson's crusade to return to this traditional method of cooking inspired chefs and gourmands in Britain, the United States, and other nations. In the early twenty-first century, head-to tail cooking is viewed as a way to return cooking to its traditional roots in an ecologically sound and often healthy way.

Offal contains tissue and muscle that differ from the striated muscle contained in the flesh of the animal. These characteristics give offal a different nutritional quality than found in traditional cuts of meat. Non-skeletal muscles—tongue, stomach, heart, and intestines—contain smooth muscle fibers that have far more connective tissue than meat. Slow cooking of non-skeletal muscles is required to break down the high levels of collagen contained in them. Liver, which absorbs many of the nutrients consumed by the animal, contains high levels of nutrients, including up to 18 times as much iron as meat. Brains, in contrast, contain high levels of fat and cholesterol. Brains from cows over the age of 30 months are not allowed into the food supply due to concerns of bovine spongiform encephalopathy (BSE), also called mad cow disease, which causes a variant and inevitably fatal form of Creutzfeldt-Jakob disease (vCJD) in humans.

Head-to-tail eating also uses slaughtered animals in a more productive and ecologically friendly manner. Choice cuts of meat in the West generally comprise only about half of an animal body. The remaining organs, bones, and tissues often go to waste in areas where consumers do not favor them. Many of these products, however, are used in the production of animal feed or other products. The consumption of the entire animal, therefore, makes better use of the production inputs including water and grains that go into raising animals for slaughter. Instead of raising many animals for the use of only a few parts, head-to-tail eating encourages the complete use of fewer animals.

Despite the ecological benefits of head-to-tail eating over prevailing Western meat consumption patterns, even head-to-tail eating carries a more significant ecological impact than vegetarianism. Raising cattle, hogs, and chickens for slaughter requires a significant input of water and grain. A 2004 study by the International Water Management Institute (IWMI) found that one kilogram (2.2 pounds) of beef requires approximately 9,680 liters (2,557 gallons) of water input. A kilogram (2.2 pounds) of wheat, however, only requires 1,790 liters (473 gallons) of water. Animals raised for slaughter also consume significant amounts of grain. One kilogram of chicken meat (2.2 pounds) requires two kilograms (4.4 pounds) of grain input, and one kilogram (2.2 pounds) of pork requires four kilograms (8.8 pounds) of grain. The production of one kilogram of beef requires approximately eight kilograms (17.6 pounds) of grain.

SEE ALSO *Ethical Issues in Agriculture; Meats; Veganism.*

BIBLIOGRAPHY

Books

Anderson, Shauna, and Elizabeth L. Place. *Offal Great: A Memoir from the Queen of Chitlins.* Erie, PA: First Place Publishing Company, 2006.

Birnbaum, Charlotte, and Christa Näher. *A Journey Within: Cooking with Offal.* Köln, Germany: König, 2009.

Helou, Anissa. *The Fifth Quarter: An Offal Cookbook.* Bath, UK: Absolute, 2004.

Henderson, Fergus, and Anthony Bourdain. *The Whole Beast: Nose to Tail Eating.* New York: CCC, 2004.

Weis, Anthony J. *The Global Food Economy: The Battle for the Future of Farming.* London: Zed Books, 2007.

Wright, Simon, and Diane McCrea. *The Handbook of Organic and Fair Trade Food Marketing.* Oxford, UK: Blackwell, 2007.

Zimmern, Andrew. *The Bizarre Truth: How I Walked out the Door Mouth First and Came Back Shaking My Head.* New York: Broadway Books, 2009.

Periodicals

"The Good Life—Offal Good." *Newsweek* 154, no. 19 (2009): 65.

"So Good, It's Offal—Top Chefs Are Bringing New Finesse to Old Bistro Fare: Organ Meats." *Business Week* (March 28, 2005): 116.

Web Sites

Soller, Kurt. "Head to Hoof: A Butcher Helps Lead a New Carnivore Movement." *Newsweek,* January 28, 2009. http://www.newsweek.com/2009/01/27/head-to-hoof.html (accessed October 21, 2010).

Team Planet Green. "Eating Head-to-Tail? Dressing Up Less Popular Cuts of Meat." *PlanetGreen.com.* http://planetgreen.discovery.com/food-health/eating-head-tail.html (accessed October 21, 2010).

Joseph P. Hyder

Heifer International

■ Introduction

Heifer International began in 1938 as the Heifers for Relief Committee, a project of the Church of the Brethren started by Dan West (1893–1971), a missionary and World War I conscientious objector. West's vision to "give a cow, not a cup" originated from the idea that education and holistic development could build stronger families, communities, and ecological networks. By donating a heifer to a family in need and teaching animal husbandry and agricultural self-sufficiency, the organization seeks to use the multiplier effect to reach as many families in need as possible. As of 2010 Heifer International assists nearly 200,000 families per year in more than 90 countries, with three educational farm centers designed to give hands-on training to aid workers and the general public. Known for its unique fundraising catalog, in which donors "buy" various animals to give to families and villages in places of need, Heifer International has changed the way that economic development charities perform outreach, marketing, education, and operations.

■ Historical Background and Scientific Foundations

During the Spanish Civil War (1936–1939), Dan West, an American farmer and Church of the Brethren missionary, handed out rations to children in Spain. According to Church of the Brethren Network documents, West "observed that as fast as you give milk to these children they drink it and it is gone, and the cost of importing more milk was economically prohibitive for a war torn nation engrossed in a monumental recovery effort." He determined that providing cows, not milk, was the solution to helping Spain rebuild its food supply and to help with post-war development.

In 1938 West returned to the United States and convinced his church to start a Heifers for Relief Committee to make his vision a reality. West chose heifers to be raised and shipped overseas to families who would be educated on basic animal husbandry. Each heifer would produce many offspring, and each offspring would be given to a new family, creating a chain of holistic development in areas of need. In 1944 the Heifers for Relief Committee shipped 17 heifers to Puerto Rico. In the years since its inception, the organization changed its name to The Heifer Project, and subsequently to Heifer International.

Shipments expanded from the original heifers to include honeybees, pigs, ducks, chickens, goats, water buffaloes, llamas, and sheep. As with the heifers, all animals donated through Heifer International are given with the express mission of building sustainable, holistic development in areas of need, and for the offspring of existing Heifer International donations to be spread to a new family. Heifer International uses the concept of "seven Ms"—animals that provide meat, money, milk, muscle, motivation, manure, and materials—to drive this holistic developmnent. As of 2010 the organization claimed to have helped more than 62 million people in 125 countries.

■ Impacts and Issues

Heifer International's food and education programs are not without critics. At its education center in Perryville, Arkansas, middle school students experienced meat production first-hand as Heifer educators killed, gutted, and skinned a rabbit in front of the schoolchildren, then cooked it for the students' consumption. A 2007 complaint from a parent of one child from Birch Kirksey Middle School in Arkansas caused Heifer International to suspend this part of the farm lesson, and also prompted People for the Ethical Treatment of Animals (PETA) to dispatch emergency vegetarian kits to the students' school. Heifer International includes the killing as part of a curriculum designed to expose children to the cycle of life on farms, sustainable development, food chain and supply issues, and agricultural practices.

Kenyan woman with twin goats born to her Heifer Project International goat, which was received by her family as a part of the community dairy goat project. She will keep one twin and give the other to another family in her community.
© *Tina Manley / Africa / Alamy.*

2008, the highest rankings for charitable organizations, with the BBB noting that Heifer International meets all 20 criteria for charity accountability.

■ Primary Source Connection

Heifer International is an organization that makes gifts of crops and livestock and provides education in sustainable agriculture to financially-disadvantaged families around the world. For over 65 years, in 128 countries, Heifer International has attended to its mission of helping people "obtain a sustainable source of food and income."

Mukta Kamaiya—Discovering True Freedom

In many parts of Nepal, poor and uneducated families have been working the land for generations. The irony of the legacy of these peasants called "Kamaiya" is that the land they put their sweat and blood into was not and would never be theirs. Toiling from sun-up to sun-down entitled them to two measly meals a day and nothing more, these people are basically modern day slaves. Born into this form of slavery, many have served their landlords to their deaths and borne more slaves to serve them in the future. The government of Nepal abolished the Kamaiya practice in July 2000, deeming it illegal. They became freed bonded laborers, "mukta-kamaiyas"; free to live and work as they pleased. Though without education, land and capital their freedom has brought more challenges than happiness.

Sitapati Chaudhary, is 45 and a mukta-kamaiya from Banke. When she joined Heifer's project in January 2008, she was landless and in search of a stable income. Sitapati and her husband had to struggle as daily-wage laborers to support their four children. Unable to make ends meet, they resorted to taking loans at an exorbitant interest rate from money lenders. Her freedom from bonded labor did not free her from the endless cycle of poverty.

Then Sitapati joined a Heifer initiated group of women who were seeking to help each other rise from poverty.

Heifer International has made gender equity among recipients a major factor in its outreach efforts, working to empower women and girls as part of economic development. The organization actively promotes a children's book called *Beatrice's Goat* to illustrate this concept. Based on the story of an Ugandan girl named Beatrice Biira, the picture book explains how one goat given to the family led to her ability to enroll in school and come to the United States to attend college, marry, form a family, and eventually complete a master's degree.

Biira's story epitomizes founder Dan West's "Give a cow, not a cup" (of milk) philosophy, and the group focuses most of its fundraising outreach on promoting this concept, encouraging volunteers to create fundraising teams to "pass on the gift of self-reliance to a thriving world." Through fundraising events that are based in communities, schools, and home schools, Heifer International also earns high praise from such charity watchdog groups as the Better Business Bureau (BBB) and Charity Navigator. Both organizations give Heifer International, with nearly $140 million in income in

Sitapati's Santoshi Women's Group began to save money together monthly and generated additional income through creative ways like working for an hourly wage on farms. Her group received Heifer's core trainings— Cornerstones, Self Help Group Management, Improved Animal Management, Gender Justice and Reproductive Health and HIV/AIDS awareness trainings.

Through the women's group Sitapti became the recipient of two goats from Heifer that were pregnant and soon filled her pens with kids. With a stable income from her farm and animals, Sitapati is now able to send all her four children to school. Sitapati took a loan of 30,000 rupees from the women's group savings at a low interest rate, added some of her family's savings and bought 3 kattha land (1/4 acre) where she grows vegetables, keeps her goats and two pigs. With her newly acquired skills in caring for livestock and organic vegetable farming, Sitapati's small venture has flourished. She once sold 12 piglets at one time, and now makes a steady monthly income by selling vegetables. Sitapati has already paid back the loan she took from the group's savings. She has also installed a hand pump to irrigate the farm. Her group formed a pass-on group, and gave them two goats each. Sitapati exceeded her pass-on commitment by passing on a pig in addition to a goat to a deprived family. "If I had not received help, I would still be in grinding poverty. Realizing this, I wanted to help someone in need," says Sita. When asked about her plans, she says "I will buy 2 kattha land this year and expand my vegetable farm."

With a little help and skill this mukta-kamaiya and many more like her are doing what their ancestors could never do—they are discovering the true meaning of freedom.

Puja Singh

SINGH, PUJA. "MUKTA KAMAIYA—DISCOVERING TRUE FREEDOM." *CHARITABLE GIFT GIVING THAT MAKES A DIFFERENCE.* HEIFER INTERNATIONAL, HTTP://WWW. HEIFER.ORG/SITE/C.EDJRKQNIFIG/B.6151297 (ACCESSED NOVEMBER 4, 2010).

SEE ALSO *African Famine Relief; Ethical Issues in Food Aid; Food Security; Subsistence Farming; Sustainable Agriculture.*

BIBLIOGRAPHY

Books

Aaker, Jerry. *The Heifer Model: Cornerstones Values-Based Development.* Little Rock, AR: Heifer Project International, 2007.

Ginn, Janet K. *Circle of Giving: Donors' Stories of Wisdom.* Little Rock, AR: Eudora Press, 2006.

Smith, Wendy. *Give a Little: How Your Small Donations Can Transform Our World.* New York: Hyperion, 2009.

Periodicals

Bertrand, Sue. "Heifer International: Passing on the Gift." *UN Chronicle* 41, no. 2 (2004): 65.

Rublin, Lauren R. "A Special Report on Philanthropy—Animal Spirits—Through the Gift of Livestock, Heifer International Nurtures Self-Reliance." *Barron's*, December 1, 2004: 26.

Wilkins, Jennifer. "Heifer International: Ending Hunger, Caring for the Earth." *Journal of Nutrition Education and Behavior* 39, no. 6 (2007): 358.

Web Sites

Heifer International. http://www.heifer.org/site/c.edJRKQNiFiG/b.183217/ (accessed August 18, 2010).

Melanie Barton Zoltan

Hepatitis A

Introduction

Hepatitis is an inflammation of the liver that can be caused by exposure to chemicals including alcohol, or by any one of six Hepatitis viruses. Hepatitis A infection is caused by the Hepatitis A virus (HAV), and was formerly known as infectious Hepatitis. HAV was discovered in the early 1970s in the stool of a patient incubating the disease. An acute disease, Hepatitis A symptoms include nausea, malaise, diarrhea, and enlarged liver. Some infected people, particularly children, have no symptoms. Unlike other forms of Hepatitis, it does not progress to chronic disease, which damages the liver.

Hepatitis A has been on the decline in developed countries since the 1970s, although epidemics continue to occur, especially under conditions of overcrowding and poor hygiene. It remains a risk to travelers, as HAV can be spread through seafood, fruit, and vegetables that have been in contact with contaminated water. Those at risk can be protected through vaccination against HAV.

Historical Background and Scientific Foundations

Hepatitis A is a single-stranded RNA virus (that is, its genetic material is made of RNA, not DNA), unrelated to the other hepatitis viruses. During its average incubation time of 28 days, it first infects the intestines and then passes through the blood into the liver. The onset of symptoms including nausea, loss of appetite, diarrhea, and fever, is acute. The person with Hepatitis A may have a painful, enlarged liver and tenderness in the upper right abdomen. Many go on to develop jaundice, a yellowing of the skin and eyes resulting from liver inflammation. The urine may be dark and stools a pale clay color.

The vast majority of cases of Hepatitis A clear up within a week or so, although 15 percent are prolonged and relapsing over a period of months. The disease does not, however, become chronic like Hepatitis B and

Hepatitis C. Only 0.3 percent of the cases reported to the Centers for Disease Control and Prevention (CDC) prove fatal, although the mortality rate rises to nearly two percent in those over 50 years of age. Hepatitis A is transmitted through the fecal-oral route, commonly through eating seafood, raw fruit, or vegetables that have come into contact with water contaminated with infected sewage.

Adults are more likely than children to develop symptoms of Hepatitis A. Household and sexual partners of those with Hepatitis A are at elevated risk of contracting the disease, as are men who have sex with men, and both injecting and non-injecting drug users. Epidemics of Hepatitis A are fairly common in institutions such as prisons and nursing homes and among those of low socioeconomic status living in overcrowded conditions.

According to CDC data, there are about 25,000 new cases of Hepatitis A infection in the United States each year. Many infections are asymptomatic. Although epidemics may still occur where hygiene is poor, in the United States and in other developed countries new Hepatitis A infections have generally declined since the year 2000. Hepatitis A most often represents a risk to those traveling into less developed countries where sanitation, including food sanitation, is compromised.

There is no definitive treatment for Hepatitis A, and often the disease resolves with adequate nutrition and rest. Those at risk of infection can be given immune serum globulin, prepared from pooled plasma, or a vaccine against Hepatitis A, or both. There are two Hepatitis A vaccines, both made of inactivated virus. One protects against Hepatitis A only, whereas the other is a combined Hepatitis A and Hepatitis B vaccine.

Impacts and Issues

People travel more widely now than ever before, which means they may be exposed to diseases they otherwise would not be. For travelers, Hepatitis A is the most

WORDS TO KNOW

FECAL-ORAL ROUTE: The transmission of minute particles of fecal material from one organism (human or animal) to the mouth of another organism.

IMMUNE GLOBULIN: Globulins are a type of protein found in blood. The immunoglobulins (also called immune globulins) are Y-shaped globulins that act as antibodies, attaching themselves to invasive cells or materials in the body so that they can be identified and attacked by the immune system. There are five immune globulins, designated IgM, IgG, IgA, IgD, and IgE.

INACTIVATED VIRUS: Inactivated virus is incapable of causing disease but still stimulates the immune system to respond by forming antibodies.

JAUNDICE: Jaundice is a condition in which a person's skin and the whites of the eyes are discolored a shade of yellow due to an increased level of bile pigments in the blood resulting from liver disease. Jaundice is sometimes called icterus, from a Greek word for the condition.

common preventable infection. The extent of the risk depends upon the length of stay, the living conditions in the place visited, and the level of Hepatitis A in the country visited. In general, the risk of contracting Hepatitis A is low in North America (except Mexico), New Zealand, Australia, and developed European countries. However, epidemics still occur even on standard tourist itineraries. Before traveling, it is advisable to check out the latest information on proposed destinations through public health departments and the CDC.

The National Center for HIV/AIDs, Viral Hepatitis, STD and TB Prevention recommends that with regard to prevention of Viral Hepatitis A:

- Hepatitis A vaccine is the best protection.

- Short-term protection against Hepatitis A is available from immune globulin. It can be given before and within two weeks after coming in contact with HAV.

- Always wash hands with soap and water after using the bathroom, changing a diaper, and before preparing and eating food.

Street food vendor in Bangkok, Thailand. Challenges for space and hygienic facilities make street food, if contaminated, efficient spreaders of the Hepatitis A virus. People in developing countries around the world both depend on street food and have higher rates of Hepatitis A illness than those in industrialized nations. © *Bea Cooper / Alamy.*

In destinations where high standards of hygiene and sanitation may be lacking, it is recommended to stick to bottled water and avoid ice, seafood, raw fruits and vegetables, and foods sold by street vendors. Personal hygiene is also essential—thorough handwashing after using lavatories and bathrooms and before eating or preparing food will help avoid transmission of HAV.

Despite food safety measures, outbreaks of Hepatitis A sometimes occur. Health authorities and epidemiologists generally attempt to track down and contact people potentially exposed to the disease by, for example, an infected kitchen worker or server. The standard precaution is for potentially exposed individuals to undergo immune globulin injections to prevent Hepatitis A infection.

SEE ALSO *Food Safety and Inspection Service; Foodborne Diseases.*

BIBLIOGRAPHY

Web Sites

"Hepatitis A." *World Health Organization (WHO).* http://www.who.int/entity/mediacentre/fact sheets/fs328/en/index.html (accessed September 6, 2010).

"Hepatitis A Vaccination." *Centers for Disease Control and Prevention (CDC).* http://www.cdc.gov/vaccines/vpd-vac/hepa/default.htm (accessed September 6, 2010).

Herbs and Spices

Introduction

Herbs and spices have shaped human cuisine and culture for thousands of years. The essential oils in local plants add to the flavor of typical dishes and give them their character. Herbs are generally used locally, whereas spices, which can be dried and stored, can travel and have played a significant part in trade over the course of human history. The aromatic components of herbs and spices are biologically active and usually give the plant a survival value by deterring predators. For humans, this means eating a whole spice might be unpleasant but adding a pinch to a dish enhances its flavor. The biological properties of herbs and spices also mean that they can have medicinal properties, which led to the early establishment of herbal medicine and folk remedies. Modern methods of analysis are revealing the complexity of the aromatic oils synthesized by plants, and experiments show that many have antioxidant or anticancer properties that might be developed. In the diet, however, herbs and spices have little nutritional value in their own right. Their main role is to enhance the pleasure of eating.

Historical Background and Scientific Foundations

Herbs and spices have been used in human cuisine and for medicinal purposes for thousands of years. Coriander, mint, and ginger are just a few of these plants that are mentioned in ancient texts. Spices, in particular, have played an important role in trade, because they can be dried and stored. It was the spice trade that led to the development of Portugal, Italy, Spain, Holland, and England into major sea powers during the years of the Renaissance. The explorers of this era were looking for ways to import cloves, nutmeg, and pepper from the Indies, to break the monopoly on spice trading that had long been held by Venice and neighboring countries. This led to the discovery of the New World and vanilla, now the world's most popular spice, along with new vegetables such as tomatoes and potatoes.

Botanically, herbs and spices fall into four main groups, although many cannot be readily classified. The mint family includes many of the classical cuisine herbs such as mint, thyme, oregano, marjoram, sage, and rosemary. The main active ingredient in the mint oils in menthol, which is remarkable for its ability to bind to receptor proteins in the mouth and produce a cooling effect. The carrot family provides fruits that are often perceived as seeds such as caraway and dill, whereas parsley is a leaf belonging to the carrot family. The ginger family produces the rhizome that has long been known in cuisine. The main herbs from the onion family are garlic, which is a bulb, and chives. Finally, the cabbage family produces mustard and horseradish, which is a root. Then there is a miscellaneous group of herbs and spices including bay, capers, cinnamon, vanilla, and chili.

The aroma and flavor of an herb comes from many different compounds in its oils. But typically, one or two compounds will dominate. For oregano and thyme, these compounds are carvacrol and thymol. As the name suggests, thymol is more predominant in thyme. For oregano, the reverse is true. Depending on how a flavor compound affects receptors in the nose and mouth, it can be classified as having elements of sweetness, freshness, citrus, floral, and so on. Each herb or spice contributes its own spectrum of elements to the experience of flavor and aroma. When cooling with herbs and spices, it is important to know when, and in what form, to add these ingredients so they give out their maximum flavor without dominating the dish. Chopped fresh herbs are best added just before serving, whereas dried herbs and spices need time to rehydrate and develop flavor during cooking. Most of the flavor compounds in herbs and spices are soluble in oil, which is why it is best to use some olive oil or butter in cooking.

■ Impacts and Issues

Although trade in spices has a long history, local cuisine tends to retain the flavors of plants that grow nearby. Thus thyme, rosemary, and sage are characteristic of France and Northern Italy, whereas many dishes from North Africa and India will have mint as a signature ingredient. Despite the global nature of modern cuisine, there are still many herbs and spices waiting to be widely discovered. One example is screwpine leaf, also known as pandan, which is sometimes added to Southeast Asian and Indian rice dishes. The aroma of pandan is similar to that of the compounds used in basmati and jasmine rice, but it is hardly known outside Asia, which is surprising considering the popularity of the region's cuisine around the world.

Herbs and spices also have medicinal properties, which may be another reason why people are attracted to flavored dishes. Garlic, turmeric, and capsaicin, the active ingredient of chili peppers, are among the many active ingredients of herbs and spices that research has shown to have beneficial effects on human health. For instance, capsaicin has antibacterial and analgesic effects and actually consists of several different compounds. Its main impact, however, is in its immediate physiological impact. Chili pepper can produce pain, watery eyes,

and runny nose and yet has been popular in cuisine for the last several hundred years and is arguably one of the most popular of the spices. Some scientists, such as Paul

Spices for sale in an Indian market include items such as cardomom, cayenne, chili, cinnamon, clove, coriander, cumin, curry, nutmeg, paprika, pepper, and turmeric. *Image copyright kykykis, 2010. Used under license from Shutterstock.com.*

A woman at an outdoor greenmarket chooses among organic herb plants grown to be well suited for container gardens and small urban gardens. *Adrienne Lerner / Lerner & Lerner / LernerMedia Global Photos.*

Rozin (1936–), professor of Psychology at the University of Pennsylvania, say that for many people, consuming capsaicin results in a controlled thrill, like riding a rollercoaster, exposing the body to perceived danger without any real physical risk. It may be that the brain's pleasure and pain-relieving circuits are both triggered by the experience of consuming capsaicins.

Although herbs and spices do not, in themselves, contribute any significant nutrients to the diet, they add an extra dimension to eating and contain interesting and still unexplored compounds that may have some potential to improve health and protect against disease. Herbal medicines are an essential element of long-established medical traditions in China, India, and some European countries, where they are usually dispensed by medical doctors, pharmacists, traditional healers, or apothecaries. Authorities in the United States, however, classify most herbal compounds as dietary supplements rather than medicines. The National Center for Complementary and Alternative Medicine (NCCAM), the primary body for scientific research on medicinal herbs in the United States, in 2010 formed five centers designed to step up research into the potential health benefits of herbal and botanical dietary supplements. Studies conducted by NCCAM showed that 18 percent of Americans reported using at least one non-vitamin herbal or botanical supplement in 2008, and that number is expected to rise at least another 18 percent by 2015. Many of the centers' studies will focus on quantifying any potential benefits of top-selling herbs in the United States.

SEE ALSO *Asian Diet; Dietary Supplement Health and Education Act of 1994 (DSHEA); Foodways;*

Functional Foods; Latin American Diet; Spice Trade; Tasting Food.

BIBLIOGRAPHY

Books

Freedman, Paul H. *Out of the East: Spices and the Medieval Imagination.* New Haven, CT: Yale University Press, 2008.

Teuscher, Eberhard, Ulrike Bauermann, and Monika Werner. *Medicinal Spices: A Handbook of Culinary Herbs, Spices, Spice Mixtures, and Their Essential Oils.* Boca Raton, FL: CRC Press, 2006.

Wells, Donald. *The Spice Trade.* New York: Weigl Publishers, 2005.

Periodicals

Prudhomme, Paul. "Herbs and Spices Can Help Restore a City." *U.S. News & World Report* 140, no. 7 (2006): 72–73.

Web Sites

Culinary Herb Guide. http://culinaryherbguide.com/index.html (accessed September 21, 2010).

"Herbs at a Glance." *National Center for Complimentary and Alternative Medicine (NCCAM).* http://nccam.nih.gov/health/herbsataglance.htm (accessed September 21, 2010).

Susan Aldridge

History of Food and Man: From Hunter-Gatherer to Agriculture

■ Introduction

The emergence of agriculture was one of the most pivotal transformations in human history. Humans and their ancestors lived as hunters and gatherers for more than a million years, populating the world. Beginning around 12,000 years ago, some of these foragers fundamentally changed the nature of their interactions with their surrounding environments: They began modifying landscapes, cultivating plants, and feeding and herding animals, and in the process, changing the genetic makeup, behaviors, and physical attributes of these plant and animal species by domesticating them.

Understanding domestication is a key part to a broader understanding of natural selection and evolution. Domesticated plants and animals are also the linchpins of agricultural economies, and the differences in these artifacts of cultural selection and their natural environs contributed to the incredible variation in human cultures—and not just in food—but in the course of world history. It is worth noting that agriculture emerged independently in several different parts of the world, most famously in the Middle East in an area known as the Fertile Crescent, but also in China, Africa, the Andes, Mexico, and eastern North America. In all of these areas, agriculture and surplus food is linked to the emergence of increased social complexity, including settled villages and social inequality. In some areas, the intensification of agricultural economies went hand-in-hand with centralized political hierarchies, leading to ancient states and civilizations with cities, social classes, monumental architecture, laws, educational structure, and armies—all of the building blocks of modern life.

■ Historical Background and Scientific Foundations

English naturalist Charles Darwin (1809–1882) was one of the first scientists to write about the origins of domesticated animals in *On the Origin of Species* in 1859.

Books on the origins of cultivated plants, published in Paris in 1883, included descriptions of the archaeological remains of fruits and grains found in the prehistoric houses recently discovered on the edges of several Swiss lakes. Russian agronomist Nikolai Vavilov (1887–1943) was the next major figure to write about the origins of agriculture, and his articles on the "centers of diversity" and the geographic origins of the world's crops in the 1920s and 1930s influenced many scientists who went on to examine plant and animal domestication and its role in the evolution of human societies.

By the 1940s most researchers had abandoned the idea that domestication began with the "eureka" discovery that seeds could be planted and animals could be tamed, although scenarios such as this continue to be prominent in popular novels. Instead, conjectures about the causes of the Neolithic Revolution, which highlighted such factors as climate change and the nature of different environments, inspired multidisciplinary projects aimed at finding archaeological evidence for agricultural origins. Projects in Neolithic villages in the Middle East, excavations in Mexico, and analysis of the plant remains from dry rock-shelters of the eastern United States all successfully provided data on early crops and the prehistoric peoples who cultivated them. Subsequent theories emphasized the factors that these areas (and other places where early domestication occurred) had in common, rather than trying to find the "invention" of agriculture and documenting its dispersal. Population growth, risk management, feedback in hunter-gatherers' systems of resource collection, scheduling, optimization, resource diversification, and coevolutionary models were all examined and tested against a growing body of archaeological evidence. The domestication of both plants and animals came to be seen as more of a process than an event.

Technological advances and new methods of archaeological recovery in the 1960s and 1970s produced some dramatic changes in understanding the worldwide diversity and timing of domestication. Radiocarbon dating finally enabled archaeologists to securely date plant and other organic remains. Flotation recovery provided a method for separating microscopic pieces of charred seeds, rinds, stems, bone, shell, and wood from large quantities of soil, enabling researchers to discover many previously unknown aspects of food production.

Archaeobotany and zooarchaeology became important subfields of archaeology. Pollen profiles from prehistoric lake beds were analyzed to recreate ancient environments reflecting forest clearing, gardens, and new crops. Scanning electron microscopes aided in the examination of some of the morphological changes that accompanied domestication, revealing thinner seed coats, larger seeds, and less brittle seed dispersal mechanisms. Most recently, molecular biology has helped measure genetic relationships and the amount of time since species have diverged.

In this manner, the evolutionary history of many familiar plants and animals has been documented. Dogs appear to be the oldest domesticates: They diverged from Middle Eastern wolves around 100,000 years ago, perhaps living in a commensal scavenging relationship with humans, and began to reveal some morphological changes in Europe around 30,000 years ago, accompanying humans to the New World at least 12,000 years ago.

The oldest domesticated rice was found in cave deposits dating between 12,000 and 14,000 years ago in south China, and figs that could not reproduce without human aid have been found in archaeological sites in the Jordan valley that are more 11,000 years old. Other familiar crops and livestock of great antiquity include wheat, barley, chickpeas, peas, lentils, sheep, goats, and cattle in the Middle East; barley, soybeans, millet, bottle gourds, rice, pigs, and horses in Asia; taro and chickens in southeast Asia; maize, beans, squash, peppers, amaranth, and turkeys in Mexico; quinoa, peanuts, beans, potatoes, tomatoes, manioc, llamas, and guinea pigs in South America; sorghum, pearl millet, rice, yams, cowpeas, and donkeys in Africa; and sunflowers, squash, and gourds in eastern North America. Many less well-known plants and animals were locally important, and show similar signs of domestication, such as tef in northeast Africa; sumpweed, knotweed, and maygrass in eastern North America; and muscovy ducks in Mexico.

■ Impacts and Issues

Archaeologists in the twenty-first century assume that many different plant and animal species were domesticated multiple times in multiple places. This realization has led scientists away from universal explanations for the origins of agriculture towards an appreciation for the historical complexity and the variability displayed by people's interactions with plants and animals in different locations.

Current anthropological models for the origins of domesticated plants have been disengaged from

WORDS TO KNOW

ARCHAEOBOTANY: Also known as *paleoethnobotany*, this is the identification and interpretation of plant remains from archaeological sites. Zooarchaeology is the related specialization that focuses on animal remains.

COEVOLUTION: The joint evolution of two different species, interacting with and changing each other in turn. Human societies and domesticated plants and animals evolved together, with human actions altering the other species, and the domesticates in turn altering human cultures. Coevolution is generally seen as the unintentional consequence of long-term interactions.

DOMESTICATION: The process by which human behaviors alter plants and animals, resulting in varieties or species with different behaviors and morphology. Plants may become larger and hang onto their seeds longer, for example, and animals may become more docile and smaller. Domesticates rely on humans to reproduce themselves; without human aid they will go extinct or revert back to wild forms.

NEOLITHIC: The archaeological period when agriculture first appeared, no earlier than 12,000 years ago in the Middle East. The Paleolithic, or "Stone Age" and the Mesolithic or "Middle Stone Age" preceded the Neolithic, and in Europe, the Neolithic is followed by the Bronze Age. The Neolithic Revolution refers to the changes in human societies correlated with agricultural economies. As a general term, Neolithic may also refer to the characteristics of sedentary agricultural societies as opposed to hunter-gatherer societies, instead of a particular time period.

models for the origins of large-scale agriculture, which is typically associated with more complex societies. As archaeological evidence for long periods of "low-level food production" accumulated in many areas, scientists suggested that different types of cultivation, including collecting, sowing, transplanting, and burning, may have unintentionally lead to domestication. These mutually beneficial interactions confer selective advantages to both humans and domesticates, and typify coevolution. It is also likely that the behavioral changes that accompany this kind of domestication manifest themselves well before any of the structural changes that signal domestication become apparent in the archaeological record.

Research among modern and historic hunter-gatherers has demonstrated that people have drastically altered the natural landscape on every continent they have inhabited. There are no historically pristine, untouched habitats anywhere humans have lived. In some areas, such as Australia, an extreme climate and the nature of the native plants and animals made foraging with minimal cultivation more advantageous. In other areas, cultivation

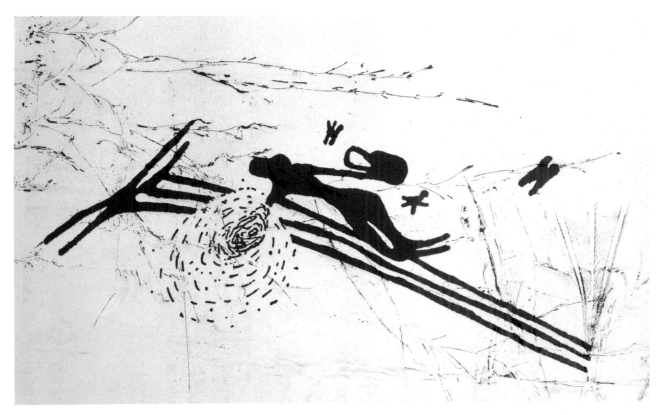

Cave painting near Valencia, Spain, drawn an estimated 10,000–12,000 years ago and enhanced by an artist in modern times, depicts an ancient honey gatherer on a tree being attacked by a swarm of bees.   *© INTERFOTO / Alamy.*

led to more sedentary communities with gardens, sometimes with domesticated animals. Under some circumstances, these societies intensified production, and agriculture was born. Although some authors argue that large-scale agriculture is an economic trap that led irrevocably to the afflictions as well as the benefits of modern civilization, it is difficult to know which of the many different types of interactions with plants and animals and the historic pathways that led to agriculture were most responsible for both.

SEE ALSO   *Ethical Issues in Agriculture; Foodways; Grains; Nutrition's Role in Human Evolution; Paleolithic Diet.*

BIBLIOGRAPHY

Books

Cohen, Mark N., and Gillian M. M. Crane-Kramer, eds. *Ancient Health: Skeletal Indicators of Agricultural and Economic Intensification.* Gainesville, FL: University of Florida Press, 2007.

Standage, Tom. *An Edible History of Humanity.* New York: Walker, 2009.

Zeder, Melinda A., Daniel G. Bradley, Eve Emshwiller, and Bruce D. Smith. *Documenting Domestication: New Genetic and Archaeological Paradigms.* Berkeley: University of California Press, 2006.

Periodicals

Kislev, Mordechai E., Anat Hartmann, and Ofer Bar-Yoself. "Early Domesticated Fig in the Jordan Valley." *Science* 312, no. 5778 (2006): 1372–1374.

Mietje, Germonpré, et al. "Fossil Dogs and Wolves from Palaeolithic Sites in Belgium, the Ukraine and Russia: Osteometry, Ancient DNA and Stable Isotopes." *Journal of Archaeological Science* 36, no. 2 (2009): 473–490.

VonHoldt, Bridgett M., et al. "Genome-Wide SNP and Haplotype Analyses Reveal a Rich History Underlying Dog Domestication." *Nature* 464 (2010): 898–902.

Weiss, Ehud, Mordechai E. Kislev, and Anat Hartmann. "Autonomous Cultivation before Domestication." *Science* 312, no. 5780 (2006): 160–161.

Web Sites

"Early Agriculture and Development." *Oregon State University.* http://oregonstate.edu/instruct/css/330/one/index.htm#EarlyAgriculture (accessed October 27, 2010).

"Go West, Early Man: Modeling the Origin and Spread of Early Agriculture." *PLoS Biology* 3, no. 12, December 2005. http://www.plosbiology.org/article/info:doi%2F10.1371%2Fjournal.pbio.0030436 (accessed October 27, 2010).

Sandra L. Dunavan

History of Home Cooking

■ Introduction

Home cooking has changed rapidly since the eighteenth century in the industrialized world. Labor saving devices such as improved oven design, refrigeration, and dishwashers have helped reduce the domestic demands for most twenty-first-century households that lack servants and in which women often work outside the home. In addition to refinements in the technology used for food preparation, ingredients in food have changed as storage and preservation techniques have improved, and more convenience and ready-to-eat and processed foods have been introduced. These foods are often viewed negatively by nutritionists and may contribute to health problems, but they are voluntarily purchased and enjoyed in many parts of the world. In rural areas of the developing world, cooking mostly remains a makeshift operation carried out by women in the family with locally acquired ingredients.

■ Historical Background and Scientific Foundations

Cooking both over fire and in fire was one technique that enabled agricultural products that are not otherwise edible, such as cereal grains, to enter the human diet in prehistoric times. Communal fires and outdoor ovens continue to predominate in many developing countries, and these ovens and similar ones would have been found everywhere as recently as the fifteenth century. Bread was probably the first ready-to-eat food, and bakeries the first marketers of a convenience food that could be purchased from a market in an urban area instead of made at home. However, technological change, increasing urbanization, and women entering the workforce have all greatly altered the home cooking environment in the developed world since the eighteenth century.

Incremental improvements in oven design began in the fifteenth century and continue to this day. Cast-iron ovens first appeared in the early eighteenth century, followed by ovens that used gas or kerosene in the early 1800s. Modern electric or gas ovens became established in cities in Europe, the Americas, Australia, and Asia in the 1920s, though their prototypes were developed in the 1880s. This long-time delay between invention of an easy-to-use, labor saving device and its movement into homes often has to do with economies of scale. Early versions of inventions are expensive to manufacture, but as more are produced, the total cost of production falls, as does the cost for each household. For example, Percy Spencer (1894–1970), an American engineer, discovered that microwaves could be used for cooking while working with radar. He worked with the company Raytheon to produce his patented invention, the microwave oven, starting in 1947. The microwave oven utilizes microwaves to heat the food itself, instead of heating the air around the food, distinguishing it from other ovens. However, due to the high cost of the Raytheon model, which gradually fell as more companies started to produce microwave ovens, the product was not common in American kitchens until the 1970s and was not ubiquitous until the 1980s.

Ovens were only one of the technological areas that changed how people cook and saved time from cooking to be devoted to other tasks including widespread employment of women outside the home. These devices also had long delays between their inventions and their widespread use. Mechanical refrigeration machines were invented in the early 1800s, and the first refrigerator patent was received by Jacob Perkins (1766–1849), an American inventor, in 1834. Josephine Cochrane (1839–1913), an American woman who enjoyed throwing lavish dinner parties, but hated when her servants chipped dishes while washing them, invented the first workable dishwashing machine in 1886. The company she founded eventually became KitchenAid, a large multinational brand of kitchen appliances. Following electrical ovens and refrigerators, a wide variety of electrical devices have entered contemporary kitchens, including electric tea kettles, rice cookers, blenders, food processors, steamers, bread makers, and other tools for specific dishes.

Ingredients have changed in addition to tools and appliances. In the 1790s canning techniques began to make it possible to can a wider variety of foods. Nicholas Appert (1750–1841), a French industrialist, opened the first commercial cannery in 1804. Clarence Birdseye (1886–1956), an American inventor, began to market his frozen foods in 1925. In 1953 C.A. Swanson and

Sons, an American processed foods brand, introduced the TV Brand Frozen Dinner. An entire meal for a family could be purchased frozen and then prepared simply by placing the aluminum tray in the oven. This process became significantly faster when adapted to the widespread use of microwave ovens in the 1970s.

■ Impacts and Issues

Convenience foods, processed foods, and ready-to-eat foods that require little or no actual home cooking have been criticized for their fat and sodium content, along with an inadequate inclusion of fruits, vegetables, and whole grains. A variety of health ailments including high blood pressure and obesity are partially blamed on their proliferation. However, convenience foods depend both on supply and demand to be successful in the market. The technology to create, store, and market these foods influences their supply and their cost. As more women in the developed world entered into the workforce beginning in the 1970s, the time allotted to cooking has decreased. For this reason, demand for convenience foods has been high. This demand continues to grow in rapidly developing and middle income countries as women move into cities and start to work outside the home.

As demand for healthier, fresher foods has also increased over time, food processors have responded. Aseptic packaging, in which food is more minimally processed and less salt and sugar are added, has become more common and is likely to enable healthier foods to become convenience foods. Philip E. Nelson (1934–), an American food scientist, won the World Food Prize in 2007 for his work in aseptic packaging and storage techniques for food. Nelson's techniques for aseptic bulk food packaging and storage have been used in responding to widespread disasters including the 2004 Indian Ocean Tsunami.

Among the poor in the developing world, home cooking is most often managed over a single rudimentary heat source, usually consisting of an open fire or open stove that burns wood, charcoal, dung, or other organic material. According to the Global Alliance for Clean Cookstoves (GACC), more than 1.9 million premature deaths occur annually from pollution relating to open cookstoves in the developing world. Most of these deaths are of women or children in India, South Asia, or Sub-Saharan Africa. The United States contributed $50 million to the GACC in 2010 towards their goal of providing cleaner cookstoves and fuels to 500 million households worldwide.

■ Primary Source Connection

The Art of Cookery Made Plain and Easy is an early cookbook intended to aid the home preparation of meals. Published in 1784, it was the staple reference for most cooks in the English speaking world.

Colored woodcut from "Kuechenmeisterei" (Fine cooking), 1516, Germany, depicting a household kitchen with an open hearth and its kitchenware. © *INTERFOTO / Alamy.*

Hannah Glasse, the author of this pinnacle cookbook, was born in or near London in 1708. She was a member of the household staff of the 4th Earl of Donnegall in Broomfield Essex from 1728 to 1732. She wrote *The Art of Cookery* after those years. The cookbook was published with the author simply listed as "By a Lady." Glasse was not revealed as the cookbook's author until she sold its copyright in 1754.

To Make a Grand Dish of Eggs

You must break as many eggs as the yolks will fill a pint bason, the whites by themselves, tie the yolks by themselves in a bladder round, boil them hard: then have a wooden bowl that will hold a quart, made like two butter dishes, but in the shape of an egg, with a hole through one at the top. You are to observe, when you boil the yolks, to run a packthread through, and leave a quarter of a yard hanging out. When the yolk is boiled hard, put it into the bowl-dish; but be careful to hang it so as to be in the middle. The string being drawn through the hole; then stop the hole, then clap the two bowls together, and tie them tight, and with a funnel pour in the whites through the hole; then stop the hole close and boil it hard. It will take an hour. When it is boiled enough, carefully open it, and cut the string close. In the mean time take twenty eggs, beat them well, the yolks by themselves, and the whites by themselves; divide the whites into two, and boil them in bladders the shape of an egg. When they are boiled hard, cut one in two long-ways, and one cross-ways, and with a fine sharp knife cut out some of the whites in the middle; lay the great egg in the middle, the two long halves on each side with the hollow part uppermost and the two round flat between. Take an ounce of truffles and morels, cut them very small, boil them in half a pint of water till they are tender, then take a pint of fresh mushrooms clean picked, washed, and chopped small, and put into the truffles and the morels. Let them boil, and add a little salt, a little beaten nutmeg, a little beaten mace, a gill of pickled mushrooms chopped fine. Boil sixteen of the yolks hard in a bladder, then chop them and mix them with the other ingredients; thicken it with a lump of butter rolled in flour, shaking your sauce-pan round till hot and thick, then fill the round with this, turn them down again, and fill the two long ones; what remains, save to put into the sauce-pan. Take a pint of cream, a quarter of a pound of butter, the other four yolks beat fine, a gill of white wine, a gill of pickled mushrooms, a little beaten mace, and a little nutmeg; put it over all, and garnish with notched lemon.

This is a grand dish as a second course. Or you may mix it up with red wine and butter, and it will do for a first course.

GLASSE, HANNAH. "TO MAKE A GRAND DISH OF EGGS." *THE ART OF COOKERY MADE PLAIN AND EASY,*

During the 1950s, electric appliances held the promise for less labor and time spent in the kitchen for the American homemaker. © *ClassicStock / Alamy.*

REPRINT OF ORIGINAL FOLIO EDITION. FARMINGTON HILLS: GALE ECCO, 2010.

SEE ALSO *Building Better Ovens; Family Meal Benefits; Farm-to-Table Movement; Food as Celebration; Food Preparation Methods; Foodways; Gourmet Hobbyists and Foodies; Slow Food Movement.*

BIBLIOGRAPHY

Books

Aratow, Paul, and E. Saint-Ange. *La Bonne Cuisine de Madame E. Saint-Ange: The Original Companion for French Home Cooking.* Berkeley: Ten Speed Press, 2005.

Davis-Gibson, Katonya. *Plantation Sweetness: The True History of African-American Home Cooking.* Baltimore: PublishAmerica, 2008.

Hughes, Kathryn. *The Short Life and Long Times of Mrs. Beeton.* New York: Knopf, 2006.

Jamison, Cheryl A., and Bill Jamison. *American Home Cooking: Over 300 Spirited Recipes Celebrating Our Rich Tradition of Home Cooking.* New York: William Morrow, 2005.

McNamee, Gregory. *Moveable Feasts: The History, Science, and Lore of Food.* Westport, CT: Praeger, 2007.

Shapiro, Laura. *Perfection Salad: Women and Cooking at the Turn of the Century.* Berkeley: University of California Press, 2009.

———. *Something from the Oven: Reinventing Dinner in 1950's America.* New York: Viking, 2004.

Periodicals

Clark, Maggie L., et al. "Indoor Air Pollution, Cookstove Quality, and Housing Characteristics in Two Honduran Communities." *Environmental Research* 110, no. 1 (2010): 12–18.

Petrick, Gabriella M. "Manly Meals and Mom's Home Cooking: Cookbooks and Gender in Modern America." *Journal of Social History* 38, no. 2 (2004): 515–517.

Tolley-Stokes, Rebecca. "Appalachian Home Cooking: History, Culture, & Recipes." *Gastronomica: The Journal of Food and Culture* 7, no. 1 (2007): 118–119.

Web Sites

"Cooking in the 1940s." *Retro Housewife*. http://www.retro-housewife.com/1940-cooking-and-recipes.html (accessed October 27, 2010).

Global Alliance for Clean Cookstoves. http://cleancookstoves.org/ (accessed October 27, 2010).

"Of Hearth and Home: Cooking In the Late 18th Century." *Minisink Valley Historical Society*. http://www.minisink.org/hearthhome.html (accessed October 27, 2010).

Blake Jackson Stabler

Human Gastrointestinal System

■ Introduction

The human gastrointestinal system, also called the gastrointestinal tract or alimentary canal, is a group of organs and glands responsible for converting food into substances that the body can absorb. These substances are then used to provide energy for cellular growth and repair.

The human digestive system consists of the mouth, esophagus, stomach, small intestine, and large intestine, along with several glands such as the salivary glands, liver, gall bladder, and pancreas. These glands secrete digestive juices containing enzymes that chemically metabolize food into smaller molecules that are more readily absorbed by the body. In addition to providing the body with the nutrients and energy it needs to function, the digestive system also separates and disposes of a variety of waste products associated with food.

■ Historical Background and Scientific Foundations

Food Movement

Food moves through the alimentary canal, propelled by a wavelike muscular motion called peristalsis. Peristalsis consists of alternate contractions and relaxations of the smooth muscles lining the tract. In this way, the body passes food through the gut in much the same way that a person squeezes toothpaste from a tube. Other organs in the gastrointestinal tract perform a variety of other mechanical processes. For example, churning is another type of movement that takes place in the stomach and small intestine; these movements mix food with liquids so that the digestive enzymes can break down the food molecules.

Digestive Mechanics, Physiology, and Regulation

In human beings, the digestible components of food include carbohydrates, proteins, fats, vitamins, and minerals; the remainder of most foods is made up of fiber

and water. The majority of vitamins and minerals pass through to the bloodstream without the need for further digestive changes, but the other nutrient molecules must be broken down into simpler substances before they can be absorbed and used in the body. The various steps of this breakdown process occur at several points in the digestive system. Once taken into the mouth, food is prepared for digestion in a two-step process known as mastication. In the first stage, the teeth tear food and break it down into smaller pieces. In the second stage, the tongue and other muscles form the chewed food into balls known as boluses.

A number of senses play a key role in the eating process. Sensory receptors on the tongue (taste buds) detect taste sensations of sweet, salt, bitter, and sour; sense data from these receptors can cause people to eat more or cause them to reject bad-tasting food. The olfactory nerves contribute to the sensation of taste by picking up the aroma of the food and providing the brain with information about its smell. The sight of food also stimulates the salivary glands, located in the mouth. Working together, taste, smell, and sight cause the salivary glands to release saliva into the mouth, which helps to soften and mix the food. A variety of enzymes in the saliva, called amylase, initiate the breakdown of carbohydrates (starch) into simple sugars such as maltose. Ptyalin is one of the main amylase enzymes found in the mouth; ptyalin is also secreted by the pancreas.

The bolus of food—now crushed, moistened, and partially digested—is swallowed, moving to the throat at the back of the mouth (pharynx). In the throat, rings of muscles force the food into the esophagus. The esophagus extends from the bottom part of the throat to the upper part of the stomach.

The esophagus does not perform any enzymatic functions. Its role in digestion is strictly mechanical, functioning as a pathway by which boluses of food travel to the stomach. There is a powerful muscle at the junction of the esophagus and stomach, called the

WORDS TO KNOW

BILE: A bitter, greenish fluid secreted by the liver and stored in the gall bladder that aids in the digestion of fats and oils in the body.

DIGESTION: The physiological process by which food is broken down, mechanically and chemically, into particles small enough to pass through the walls of the intestinal tract and into the blood.

ENTERIC: Involving the intestinal tract or relating to the intestines.

FLORA: In microbiology, flora refers to the collective microorganisms that normally inhabit an organism or system. Human intestines, for example, contain bacteria that aid in digestion and are considered normal flora.

INTESTINAL MOTILITY: Intestinal motility refers to the movement of smooth muscles in the small and large intestine that aids in mixing, digestion, absorption, and movement of foodstuffs. The smooth muscle controlling intestinal motility is called the muscularis. This layer of muscle tissue consists of two types of muscle: circular and longitudinal smooth muscle. Within the muscularis is nervous tissue called the myenteric plexus that controls these muscles. Additionally, some hormones such as gastrin can affect intestinal motility. Finally, intestinal distention (e.g. when attempting to pass a bolus of food) is a contributing factor that initiates motility in the intestines.

esophageal sphincter. This muscle acts as a valve, keeping food, stomach acids, and bile from flowing back into the esophagus and mouth.

Much of the chemical digestion process takes place in the stomach. This organ is a large, hollow, pouch of muscle shaped roughly like a lima bean. When empty, the stomach becomes elongated; when filled, it balloons out. In the stomach, food is broken down by the action of gastric secretions that contain hydrochloric acid and a protein-digesting enzyme called pepsin. The lining of the stomach secretes these substances, as well as mucus that helps protect the stomach lining from the action of the acid in the secretions. Three layers of powerful stomach muscles work to churn the food into a fine, semi-liquid paste called chyme. At intervals, the chyme is passed through an opening called the pyloric sphincter, which controls the movement of chyme between the stomach and the beginning of the small intestine.

Several mechanisms regulate the release of gastric secretions in the stomach. The stomach begins producing these secretions while food is still in the mouth. Nerves from the cheeks and tongue are stimulated by food and the actions of chewing, and these nerves send information to the brain. In turn, the brain sends messages to nerves in the stomach wall, stimulating the secretion of a variety of gastric substances in anticipation of the food's arrival. The second signal for gastric secretion production occurs when the food arrives in the stomach and touches the lining. This mechanism only moderately increases the amount of gastric secretions; most of them are released when food is in the mouth.

Additional gastric secretions are sometimes required, primarily as a supply of pepsin to help digest protein. If, for example, someone eats a hamburger on a bun, there is no need for extra gastric secretions to break down the carbohydrates in the bun. However, the protein in the hamburger will require a much greater supply. The gastric secretions already present will begin to break the hamburger's large protein molecules down into smaller molecules called polypeptides and peptides. These smaller molecules in turn stimulate the cells of the stomach lining, causing it to release a hormone called gastrin into the bloodstream.

Gastrin then circulates throughout the body, eventually reaching the stomach, where it stimulates cells in the stomach lining to produce more gastric secretions. The proportion of protein in the stomach controls the amount of gastrin that is produced, and hence the overall production of gastric secretions. This process represents the third mechanism that regulates gastric secretions.

The small intestine, or small bowel, is a narrow tube approximately 20 feet (6 m) long, which runs from the stomach to the large intestine. The small intestine occupies the area of the abdomen between the diaphragm and hips, and is greatly coiled and twisted. The small intestine is lined with muscles that move the chyme toward the large intestine. Digestion continues to some extent in the small intestine, but this organ is also a major site for the process of absorption, in which digested food passes into the bloodstream and is transported to the rest of the body. The mucosa, which lines the entire small intestine, contains millions of glands that aid in digestive and absorptive processes.

Anatomists subdivide the small intestine into three sections: the duodenum, the jejunum, and the ileum. The duodenum is about 1 foot (0.3 m) long; this part of the small intestine connects with the lower portion of the stomach. When chyme reaches the duodenum, it undergoes further enzymatic digestion and is subjected to pancreatic secretions, intestinal secretions, and bile.

The pancreas is a large gland located below the stomach; it secretes pancreatic juice into the duodenum via the pancreatic duct. There are three enzymes in pancreatic secretions that digest carbohydrates, lipids, and proteins. Amylase breaks starch down into simple sugars, such as maltose. The enzyme maltase, contained in intestinal secretions, completes the breakdown of maltose into glucose.

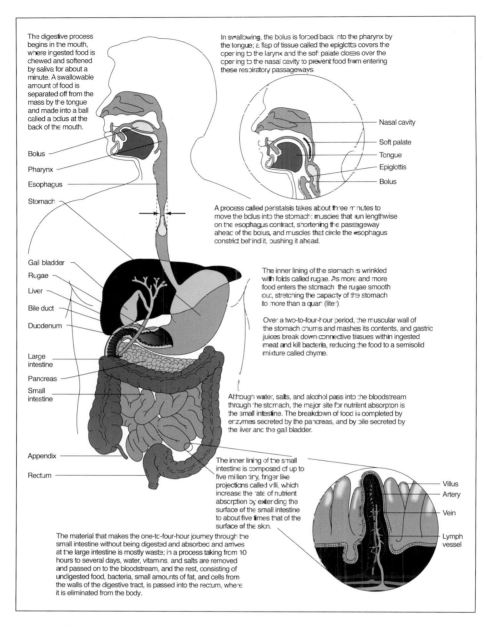

The digestive process begins in the mouth, where ingested food is chewed and softened by saliva for about a minute. A swallowable amount of food is separated off from the mass by the tongue and made into a ball called a bolus at the back of the mouth.

In swallowing, the bolus is forced back into the pharynx by the tongue; a flap of tissue called the epiglottis covers the opening to the larynx and the soft palate closes over the opening to the nasal cavity to prevent food from entering these respiratory passageways.

Nasal cavity
Soft palate
Tongue
Epiglottis
Bolus

Bolus
Pharynx
Esophagus
Stomach

A process called peristalsis takes about three minutes to move the bolus into the stomach: muscles that run lengthwise on the esophagus contract, shortening the passageway ahead of the bolus, and muscles that circle the esophagus constrict behind it, pushing it ahead.

Gall bladder
Rugae
Liver
Bile duct
Duodenum

The inner lining of the stomach is wrinkled with folds called rugae. As more and more food enters the stomach the rugae smooth out, stretching the capacity of the stomach to more than a quart (liter).

Over a two-to-four-hour period, the muscular wall of the stomach churns and mashes its contents, and gastric juices break down connective tissues within ingested meat and kill bacteria, reducing the food to a semisolid mixture called chyme.

Large intestine
Pancreas
Small intestine

Although water, salts, and alcohol pass into the bloodstream through the stomach, the major site for nutrient absorption is the small intestine. The breakdown of food is completed by enzymes secreted by the pancreas, and by bile secreted by the liver and the gall bladder.

Appendix
Rectum

The inner lining of the small intestine is composed of up to five million tiny, finger like projections called villi, which increase the rate of nutrient absorption by extending the surface of the small intestine to about five times that of the surface of the skin.

Villus
Artery
Vein
Lymph vessel

The material that makes the one-to-four-hour journey through the small intestine without being digested and absorbed and arrives at the large intestine is mostly waste; in a process taking from 10 hours to several days, water, vitamins, and salts are removed and passed on to the bloodstream, and the rest, consisting of undigested food, bacteria, small amounts of fat, and cells from the walls of the digestive tract, is passed into the rectum, where it is eliminated from the body.

Diagram of the human digestive system. *Diagram by Hans & Cassidy. Cengage Learning.*

Lipases in pancreatic secretions break fats down into fatty acids and glycerol, while proteinases continue the breakdown of proteins into amino acids. The gall bladder, located next to the liver, secretes bile into the duodenum. Bile does not contain enzymes, but it contains bile salts and other substances that help to emulsify (dissolve) fats, which are otherwise insoluble in water. Breaking the fat down into small globules also provides lipase enzymes with a greater surface area for their action.

Passing from the duodenum, chyme next reaches the jejunum of the small intestine, which is about 3 feet (0.91 m) long. Most of the digested breakdown products of carbohydrates, fats, and proteins are absorbed here, as well as many vitamins and some minerals. The inner lining of the small intestine is covered with up to five million tiny, fingerlike projections called villi. The villi vastly increase the rate at which nutrients can be absorbed into the bloodstream by extending the small intestine's surface area to about five times that of the skin.

Two transport systems pick up nutrients from the small intestine. Simple sugars, amino acids, and glycerol, as well as some vitamins and salts, are conveyed to the liver in the bloodstream. Fatty acids and vitamins are absorbed and then transported through the lymphatic system, a network of vessels that carries lymph and white blood cells throughout the body.

IN CONTEXT: THE HEIMLICH MANEUVER

Every year thousands of people die because they accidentally inhale rather than swallow food. The food blocks their windpipe (trachea), making breathing impossible. Death follows rapidly unless the food or other foreign material can be displaced from the airway. In children under the age of one year, choking is the leading cause of unintentional injury-related death, and children under the age of five years are especially vulnerable to choking. Accordingly, many people in food service industries receive basic training to deal with choking emergencies. The Heimlich maneuver is a common emergency procedure for removing food or a foreign object lodged in the airway that is causing airway obstruction. American physician and inventor Dr. Henry Heimlich (1920–), a specialist in digestive disorders, developed the Heimlich maneuver in the mid–1970s as a means of saving the lives of choking victims. Since then his maneuver has garnered wide acceptance by most medical professionals in helping victims of choking accidents.

The Heimlich maneuver is a series of abdominal thrusts that is simple enough that it can be performed immediately by almost anyone trained in the maneuver. By compressing the abdomen, air is forced out of the lungs, dislodging the obstruction and bringing the foreign material up into the mouth. The maneuver is used mainly when solid material, often a bolus of food, blocks the tracheal airway. The Heimlich maneuver can be performed on all people, but modifications are necessary if the choking victim is obese, pregnant, a child, or an infant.

Indications that a person's airway is blocked include:

- The person can not speak or cry out;
- The face turns blue from lack of oxygen;
- The person desperately grabs at his or her throat;
- The person has a weak cough, and labored breathing produces a high-pitched noise; and
- The person does all of the above, then becomes unconscious.

About 95 percent of deaths from choking could be prevented by using the simple technique of the Heimlich maneuver. Information on how to sign up for classes that teach the proper way to administer the Heimlich maneuver and other emergency techniques can be obtained at many local clinics and hospitals. Additional information is also available at the Heimlich Institute Web sites located at <http://www.heimlichinstitute.org/page.php?id=34>.

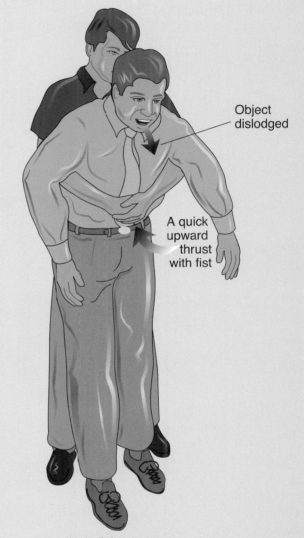

Object dislodged

A quick upward thrust with fist

The Heimlich maneuver

SOURCE: *Electronic Illustrators Group/Cengage Learning.*

The last section of the small intestine is the ileum. It is smaller and thinner-walled than the jejunum, and it is the preferred site for vitamin B12 absorption as well as bile acids derived from bile.

The large intestine is the last part of the gastrointestinal tract. It is wider and heavier then the small intestine, but much shorter—only about 4 feet (1.2 m) long. It has three basic parts: the caecum, the colon, and the rectum. The caecum is a pouch connected to the ileum; the appendix is part of this pouch. The colon rises up on one side of the body (the ascending colon), crosses over to the other side (the transverse colon), descends (the descending colon), and then forms an S-shape (the sigmoid colon of sigmoid flexure). The colon then reaches the rectum and anus, from which the waste products of digestion (feces or stool) are passed, along with gas. The muscular rectum, about 5 inches (13 cm) long, expels the feces through the anus, which consists of sphincters that control the passage of waste matter.

The large intestine is where water and many minerals are absorbed into the body. This organ extracts water from the waste products of digestion and returns some of it to the bloodstream, along with some salts. Fecal matter contains undigested food, bacteria, and a variety of cells from the walls of the digestive tract. Certain types of bacteria in the large intestine, called the intestinal flora, play important roles in the digestive process. They help to break down food that might otherwise be indigestible, and they can synthesize certain vitamins needed in the body. These vitamins then find their way to the bloodstream along with the water absorbed from the colon.

■ Impacts and Issues

A deeper understanding of digestive development and process has enabled medical and public health workers to refine dietary recommendations. Conversely, misinformation about the way the digestive system processes food and vitamins is often the basis for pseudoscientific claims about the nutritional or medicinal values of certain foods. For this reason, basic anatomy and physiology of the digestive system is often part of the curriculum in food science related programs.

The gastrointestinal system is also the target for one of the latest weight loss methods for the severely obese. Surgical resection, restriction, and attenuation of the digestive system, known as bariatric surgery (usually gastric banding or gastric resection) have become common methods for treating severe obesity. One area of concern, however, is the increasing youth of candidate patients. Clinicians and public health officials continue to debate the criteria and parameters used to recommend these procedures.

SEE ALSO *Culinary Education; Eating Disorders; Nutrition's Role in Human Evolution; Obesity; Tasting Food.*

BIBLIOGRAPHY

Books

Carlson, Bruce M. *Human Embryology and Developmental Biology*, 4th ed. Philadelphia: Mosby/Elsevier, 2009.

Drake, Richard L., ed. *Gray's Anatomy for Students*, 2nd ed. Philadelphia: Elsevier/Churchill Livingstone, 2010.

Kohlstadt, Ingrid, ed. *Scientific Evidence for Musculoskeletal, Bariatric, and Sports Nutrition*. Boca Raton, FL: CRC/Taylor & Francis, 2006.

Lipski, Elizabeth. *Digestive Wellness*. New York: McGraw-Hill, 2005.

Moore, N. Anthony, and William A. Roy. *Gross and Developmental Anatomy*, 2nd ed. Rapid review series. Philadelphia: Mosby Elsevier, 2007.

National Institutes of Health. *Your Digestive System and How it Works*. Bethesda, MD: National Institute of Diabetes and Digestive and Kidney Diseases, 2004.

Netter, Frank H. *Atlas of Human Anatomy*, 4th ed. Philadelphia: Saunders Elsevier, 2006.

Schoenwolf, Gary C., and William J. Larsen. *Larsen's Human Embryology*, 4th ed. Philadelphia: Churchill Livingstone/Elsevier, 2009.

Web Sites

"Digestive System." *National Geographic Society.* http://science.nationalgeographic.com/science/health-and-human-body/human-body/digestive-system-article.html (accessed September 29, 2010).

IN CONTEXT: ROUNDWORM (ASCARIASIS) INFECTION

Ascariasis (as-kuh-RYE-uh-sis), or roundworm infection, is an infection caused by the parasitic helminth, or roundworm *Ascaris lumbricoides*. The largest parasite to infect humans, commonly called the giant intestinal roundworm, it can grow up to a length of 6–12 in (15–30 cm) by a diameter of 0.12–0.32 in (0.3–0.8 cm) in males and 8–14 in (20–35 cm) by 0.2 in (0.5 cm) in females.

Humans become infected by direct contact of the worms with skin and through the ingestion of soil and vegetation that contain fecal matter contaminated with eggs. Transmission can also occur when wastewater is recycled onto crop fields as fertilizer—a practice that is common in developing countries.

When ingested, the larvae hatch and burrow into the moist lining (mucosa) of the intestines. They then travel to the lungs, where they further mature—usually for 10 to 14 days. They eventually travel through the respiratory tract and up into the throat where they are swallowed and sent to the small intestines. They mature as worms while attached to the walls of the small intestines.

Roundworm infection is found throughout the world, but especially in tropical regions and among the poorest areas that have inadequate sanitation and the worst of hygiene conditions. It is pronounced along the rural areas of the Gulf Coast within the United States; in Africa, especially Nigeria; and in Southeast Asia, especially Indonesia. It is believed that up to one-fourth of the world's population is infected with the roundworm *A. lumbricoides*. The National Institutes of Health (NIH) estimates that more than one billion people are infected worldwide, with children being affected more seriously and more frequently than adults. About 2 percent of people in the United States are estimated to be infected with roundworms.

Children are highly vulnerable, especially those aged three to eight years. The disease can create or exacerbate iron-deficiency, anemia, and malnutrition, and result in impairment of growth and intelligence.

Humane Animal Farming

■ Introduction

Humane animal farming is a method of raising animals for food or clothing while best providing for their welfare. Animal welfare itself is the viewpoint that animals, especially those under human care, should be treated in such a way that they are provided with everything they need in order to live comfortably and not be subjected to any unnecessary suffering. This position usually focuses on the morality of human action (or inaction), as opposed to making deeper political or philosophical claims about the status of animals, as is the case for the viewpoint of the animal rights movement.

Concern for farm animals primarily has focused on factory farming, a system of large-scale farming that seeks to maximize profits by increasing stocking density, often resulting in severely confined living conditions for the animals. Techniques that include limiting space, restricting movement, and eliminating natural animal behaviors with the use of battery cages for hens, gestation crates for sows, and veal pens for calves, as well as other more invasive methods such as the debeaking of hens, are some of the main issues of concern for those interested in animal welfare. Humane animal farming focuses on ways of creating the best possible conditions for farm animals from the moment of birth to the time they are to be slaughtered.

At least one organization provides certification for farmers and ranchers that produce animal products under humane conditions. These products carry a "Certified Humane Raised & Handled" label on the package. Standards created by Humane Farm Animal Care, an independent third-party certification and inspection organization, require that farms provide animals with ample space, shelter, and gentle handling to limit stress and additionally require that:

- The use of growth hormones and antibiotics is prohibited.
- Animals must be free to move and not be confined—cages, crates and tie stalls are prohibited.

This means that chickens are able to flap their wings and dust bathe, and pigs have the space to move around and root.

- Livestock have access to sufficient, clean, and nutritious feed and water.
- Animals must have sufficient protection from weather elements and an environment that promotes well being.
- Managers and caretakers must be thoroughly trained, skilled and competent in animal husbandry and welfare, and have good working knowledge of their system and the livestock in their care.
- Farmers and ranchers must comply with food safety and environmental regulations.

■ Historic Background and Scientific Foundations

At one time, animals were considered without sensations of feeling that humans possess, and thus the concept of animal welfare was meaningless. Among those who were of this opinion was the French philosopher and physician René Descartes (1596–1650), who assumed that animals acted without consciousness, much like a machine. In his *Discourse on the Method*, published in 1637, Descartes wrote that without the ability to use language, animals merely react out of instinctual response to external stimuli by making noises.

Throughout the next two centuries, public opinion regarding the humane treatment of animals shifted dramatically, thanks in part to influential Christian thinkers and secular thinkers in Europe. Though they did not always agree on the reasons, many believed animals should not be mistreated by humans. Jean-Jacques Rousseau (1712–1778) argued that animals had sentience, which obligated man to treat them kindly. John Wesley (1703–1791), the founder of Methodism, preached that both humans and animals are the offspring of one God and should therefore be treated with a degree of reverence and kindness. The utilitarian philosopher Jeremy Bentham (1748–1832), asked a question regarding animal welfare that was revolutionary for its time: "The question is not, Can they reason? Nor Can they talk? But Can they suffer? Why should the law refuse its protection to any sensitive being?"

The first meaningful animal welfare legislation was enacted in 1822, when British Member of Parliament Richard Martin (1754–1834) championed a bill protecting cattle, horses, and sheep from cruelty (earning himself the nickname Humanity Dick). Martin also helped to found the Society for the Prevention of Cruelty to Animals, or SPCA, the world's first organization interested in animal welfare and protection, in 1824. Soon afterwards, Queen Victoria (1819–1901) of England lent her support to the organization, and it became known as the Royal SPCA. Inspectors employed by the organization contacted authorities when they identified evidence of animal abuse or neglect.

It was more than 100 years before major animal welfare legislation was again addressed by the British government, spurred in part by reaction to the publication of Ruth Harrison's (1920–2000) 1964 book *Animal Machines*, which documented the welfare of intensively farmed animals like veal calves, chickens, and pigs, exposing the overcrowded conditions, inhumane treatment, and use of antibiotics and growth hormones. The well-publicized book included a foreword written by scientist Rachel Carson (1907–1964), the author of *Silent Spring*, and shocked the public and Parliament members into action. In 1965 an investigation into intensive farming techniques led by Professor Roger Brambell was commissioned by the government. The Report of the Technical Committee to Enquire into the Welfare of Animals kept under Intensive Livestock Husbandry Systems (also called The Brambell Report) served as the impetus for the creation of the Farm Animal Welfare Advisory Committee in 1967, which became the Farm Animal Welfare Council in 1979. The committee's first guidelines recommended that animals "have the freedoms to stand up, lie down, turn around, groom themselves and stretch their limbs." The guidelines have since been elaborated to become known as the Five Freedoms:

- Freedom from thirst and hunger—by ready access to fresh water and a diet to maintain full health and vigour;

- Freedom from discomfort—by providing an appropriate environment including shelter and a comfortable resting area;

- Freedom from pain, injury, and disease—by prevention or rapid diagnosis and treatment;

- Freedom to express normal behavior—by providing sufficient space, proper facilities and company of the animal's own kind;

WORDS TO KNOW

ANIMAL RIGHTS MOVEMENT: Individuals and groups concerned with protecting animals from perceived abuse or misuse. Supporters are specifically concerned with the use of animals for medical and cosmetics testing, the killing of animals for furs, hunting for pleasure, and the raising of livestock in restrictive or inhumane quarters. Many animal rights activists argue that animals have inherent rights just as humans do, and that they should not be exploited for food, clothing, scientific research, or entertainment and should not be abused in any way. Concern for inhumane treatment of animals has led many supporters of the animal rights movement to advocate vegetarianism.

BATTERY CAGES: An industrial agricultural confinement system used primarily for egg-laying hens. The battery cage has generated conflict among advocates for animal welfare and animal rights and industrial egg producers due to the restrictions on movement these high-density cages impose on the hens.

DEBEAKING: Also called beak trimming, this is the partial removal of the beak of poultry, especially chickens and turkeys. Most commonly, the beak is shortened permanently, although regrowth can occur. The term debeaking implies that the entire beak is removed during the trimming process, though in reality only half or less of the beak is removed. Debeaking is done in order to reduce instances of cannibalistic pecking among birds in dense populations, where such behavior is more common.

GESTATION CRATE: A metal pen typically two feet wide and seven feet long in which a pregnant sow is kept during its four-month gestation period. The use of these enclosures is controversial because they often do not include any kind of bedding material, and the cramped conditions within the pen do not allow the animal to turn around or even to lie down comfortably. Most sows in factory farms are kept in a lifelong state of impregnation and birth and will therefore spend most of their lives in a gestation crate. Also called a sow pen.

THIRD-PARTY CERTIFICATION: A system in which an organization independent of all the companies in a supply chain certifies that a good reaches particular standards or has particular attributes. Most international organic standards, fair trade standards, humane animal treatment standards, and claims of being not genetically modified, as well as a variety of environmental claims, are certified using third-party certification.

- Freedom from fear and distress—by ensuring conditions and treatment which avoid mental suffering

These guidelines, and others like them, became the model for current laws and regulations concerning the treatment of farm animals.

IN CONTEXT: FOIE GRAS, CULTURAL HERITAGE OR CRUELTY?

In the European Union, *foie gras* is both a delicacy on the plate and a problem on the political agenda. The demand for *foie gras* (meaning fat liver) is so great that although France is the largest producer of *foie gras* in the world, it is unable to make enough to satisfy the demands of its own population. Other countries, especially Hungary, have tried to fill the gap in producing the goose-liver specialty food.

Geese are force fed via gavage, a tube placed in the esophagus, in order to quickly fatten their liver for *foie gras*, a process that animal rights activists contend is inhumane. The EU has suggested, but not mandated that *foie gras* producers convert to alternative feeding methods and eliminate gavage feedings by 2020. More humane *foie gras* production methods include increasing the time period for intensive feeding, allowing the geese to roam freely between feedings, and hand feeding using a pliable funnel instead of gavage. Some EU countries, including Poland, Denmark, Germany, and Italy, along with other countries such as Norway, Israel, Argentina, and Turkey, have banned the production of *foie gras* using all force-feeding techniques. In the United States, *foie gras* produced by gavage feeding was briefly banned in 2006 by the city of Chicago (the ban was lifted in 2008) and will be illegal in the state of California beginning in 2012.

Food purists contend that gavage feeding is necessary to produce the highly fattened *foie gras* liver, which becomes six or more times its natural size, and to meet the legal definition established in France to qualify as *foie gras*. Official policy in France states that "*Foie gras* belongs to the protected cultural and gastronomical heritage of France."

■ Impacts and Issues

Interest in humane animal farming techniques continues to grow, with increasing attention being paid to it by the media and governmental and nongovernmental organizations. Recent polling and voting results in the United States show that a majority of consumers place a high value on the welfare of farm animals. Seventy-three percent of those who participated in a 2008 Humane Research Council poll indicated that they would support a law requiring farm animals to have enough space to move around and behave naturally. Both free-range poultry and meat from pastured, grass-fed animals (as opposed to animals confined to cages and feed lots) has gained popularity despite its higher cost, and is now available in most markets in the United States.

A number of laws have been passed in the United States that protect the welfare of farm animals, including the federal Humane Slaughter Act, or the Humane Methods of Livestock Slaughter Act (the earliest version of which became law in 1958), which was written to prevent the unnecessary suffering of livestock when they are killed. This law requires that all livestock, including cattle, horses, sheep, and pigs, are rendered senseless before they are slaughtered.

More recently, several voter-passed state laws protecting farm animals have been enacted. In 2002 Amendment 10, an amendment to the Florida Constitution, banned the confinement of pregnant pigs in gestation crates. In 2006 Arizona voters passed Proposition 204, which prohibits the confinement of calves in veal crates and breeding sows in gestation crates. This was followed by California's Proposition 2 in 2008, which prohibited similar crates, as well as battery cages for egg-laying hens. In other states, such as Colorado, Maine, Michigan, and Oregon, veal crates and/or gestation crates have been outlawed by state legislators, and ballot initiatives and legislation dealing with anti-confinement laws are pending in several more states, including New York and Massachusetts. Due to such pressure, the American Veal Association has recommended the phasing out of veal crates by 2017.

Europe has been ahead of the United States in this trend. Veal crates were banned in Great Britain in 1990 and in the entire European Union in 2007. Several European countries, including Germany, Switzerland, Sweden, and Austria, currently have bans on battery cages for egg-laying hens. The entire European Union will be phasing out gestation crates by 2013 and battery cages by 2012. The battery cages are to be replaced with so-called "enriched cages"—a new type of battery cage in which hens are kept, where the bird's living conditions have been improved by an increase in the size of the cage and the inclusion of perches, nests, and litter so that the bird can peck and scratch.

These animal welfare measures designed to make farming more humane are not without their critics. Many animal rights groups feel that merely bettering conditions for animals without abolishing the use of and slaughter of animals is illogical and serves only to make people feel better about killing animals. These groups tend to view farms as death camps, weigh stations for animals' inevitable slaughter. There are, however, some animal rights groups, such as People for the Ethical Treatment of Animals (PETA), that support animal welfare measures in the short term to alleviate animal suffering until all animal use is ended.

Regardless of where people stand on the issue of animal farming, an alliance between humans and animals has existed for more than 10,000 years. In this symbiotic relationship, animals have been given food, care, and protection, in exchange for which these animals have provided humans with milk, eggs, meat, and clothing fiber.

Cows graze in an area of a certified humane animal farm in Virginia. Standards require that animals have necessary shelter, sufficient space to engage in natural behavior during their lives, and that the animals have to be stunned or otherwise rendered insensible before they are killed. *AP Images.*

SEE ALSO *Agribusiness; Agroecology; Ethical Issues in Agriculture; Factory Farming; Organics; Sustainable Agriculture.*

BIBLIOGRAPHY

Books

Pollan, Michael. *The Omnivore's Dilemma: A Natural History of Four Meals.* New York: Penguin, 2006.

Web Sites

"Animal Tracker—Wave 1, an HRC-Managed Research Study. *Humane Research Council,* June 2008. http://www.humanespot.org (accessed October 17, 2010).

"Facts about Farm Animal Welfare Standards." *Farm Sanctuary.* http://www.upc-online.org/welfare/standards_booklet_FINAL.pdf (accessed October 17, 2010).

"Five Freedoms." *Farm Animal Welfare Council.* http://www.fawc.org.uk/freedoms.htm (accessed October 17, 2010).

"Frequently Asked Questions." *Humane Farm Animal Care.* http://www.certifiedhumane.org/index.php?page=frequently-asked-questions" (accessed October 17, 2010).

People for the Ethical Treatment of Animals. http://www.peta.org/ (accessed October 17, 2010).

Matthew Munsey

Hunger

Introduction

The United Nations Food and Agriculture Organization (FAO) reports that hunger has increased during the first decade of the present century, and that an estimated 925 million people will go hungry each day in 2010. Among the world's hungry, women account for more than 60%, and close to two-thirds live in the Asia and Pacific region. In developing countries, children are the most vulnerable, and undernutrition contributes to 53% of the 9.7 million deaths of children under the age of five. An individual is defined as suffering from hunger when he or she does not consume at least 2,100 kilocalories per day. Hunger is categorized as either acute/temporal or chronic, and within these categories the severity of hunger can vary. Acute hunger is a temporary state that is usually more visible, whereas chronic hunger is less visible and takes place over a long period of time. Those who experience chronic hunger usually suffer from undernutrition or malnutrition, have a weakened immune system, and possibly experience irreversible damage to their physical and cognitive development. Hunger is caused by a variety of factors that affect food security at the household, village, community, and national level: Unemployment, homelessness, increasing food prices, and natural disasters are just a few events that contribute to hunger. Food insecurity, poor conditions of health and sanitation, and inappropriate care and feeding practices are the major causes of poor nutritional status. Food insecurity can be a chronic, seasonal, or transitory situation.

Historical Background and Scientific Foundations

Thomas Robert Malthus (1766–1834) introduced the notion that hunger is caused by population growth in his "Essay on the Principle of Population," in which he describes population growth as naturally overtaxing the production of food on earth. According to

Michael O'Flynn's article "Food Crises and the Ghost of Malthus," Malthus's theory predicted "terrible disasters" based on the fact that: 1) All living creatures need subsistence to survive, and 2) the capacity to subtract the means of subsistence from nature is finite. Biologist Paul Ehrlich (1932–) agreed with Malthus' basic principles that a growing population would lead to food shortages in his 1968 book *The Population Bomb*. Events such as the Irish Famine (1845–1849) and the Great Leap Forward Famine in China (1959–1961) resulted in the deaths of millions of people due to starvation. Economist Amartya Sen (1933–) challenged the common notion that famine was caused solely by the shortage of food in 1981 in *Poverty and Famines* by stating that starvation is the characteristic of some people experiencing the "loss of entitlements to food," through failed crops, death of livestock, or loss of means to access food. Sen proposed famine is not caused by a slump in the overall availability of food, but the ability to acquire food. Sen reasoned that when addressing the problem of hunger there must be less emphasis on food quantities and more emphasis on studying the relationship of people at the household level to the commodity of food.

Enough food is produced globally to ensure that everyone has 2,720 kilocalories (kcal) per day. When a person eats less than the standard 2,100 kilocalories per day the body reacts by slowing down the metabolism in order to conserve energy, thus impacting physical and mental development. This minimum caloric intake of 2,100 is an average and varies among people depending on factors such as their age, sex, body size, occupation, and their climate. In general, for a healthy diet the recommended intake for men ranges from 2,500–3,000 kilocalories per day, whereas for a woman the daily range is 1,900–2,500 kilocalories. When calories are consumed by the body through the food that is ingested, the body breaks down the food into the basic compounds of amino acids, fatty acids, carbohydrates, vitamins, minerals, and water. This process releases the energy that humans need to carry out daily physical activities.

An undernourished and hungry girl from Senossa, Mali, exhibits abdominal distension. *Image copyright Attila Jandi, 2010. Used under license from Shutterstock.com.*

According to the 2009 FAO report on the State of Food Insecurity in the World, food and economic shocks typically initiate shorter-term acute hunger; longer-term chronic hunger is symptomatic of extreme poverty.

■ Impacts and Issues

Debates surrounding dependency on food aid and sustainable solutions for fighting hunger emerged during the FAO International Freedom from Hunger Campaign in 1960 and set the stage for the issues that were to be addressed for the decades to come. By 1962 the United Nations World Food Program (WFP) was established in an effort to ensure food access for every man, woman, and child. As some countries began to experience rapid population growth, more governments began to voice concerns about the state of national food security at the UN World Food Conference in Rome by 1974. Ultimately they reacted by increasing investments in agriculture, but did not recognize the importance of achieving food security at the individual and household

FAMINE: Unusually high mortality rate caused by a severe threat to food intake of some segment of a population.

FOOD AID: Emergency food aid is distributed to victims of natural or human-made disasters. It is freely distributed to targeted beneficiary groups and usually provided on a grant basis. Food aid is channeled multilaterally, through nongovernmental organizations (NGOs), or sometimes bilaterally, given by one country directly to another.

FOOD INSECURITY: A situation that exists when people lack secure access to sufficient amounts of safe and nutritious food for normal growth and development and an active and healthy life. It may be caused by the unavailability of food, insufficient purchasing power, inappropriate distribution, or inadequate use of food at the household level.

FOOD SECURITY: When all people at all times have both physical and economic access to sufficient food to meet their dietary needs in order to lead a healthy and productive life.

HUNGER: No internationally recognized legal definition of hunger exists. However, it is widely accepted that it goes beyond a minimum calorific package sufficient to prevent death by starvation. The term "starvation" refers to the most extreme form of hunger; death by starvation is the end result of a chronic, long-lasting, and severe period of hunger.

MALNUTRITION: A condition in which a person is not consuming or absorbing adequate and balanced nutrients in order to sustain a healthy, active life. Diets with caloric deficits, deficits of protein or fat, or deficits of key vitamins and minerals cause malnutrition. Obesity is also sometimes considered a form of malnutrition if it contributes to a state of decreased health or disease.

UNDERNUTRITION: Describes the status of people whose food intake does not include enough calories (energy) to meet minimum physiological needs. The term is a measure of a country's ability to gain access to food and is normally derived from Food Balance Sheets prepared by the United Nations Food and Agriculture Organization (FAO).

UNITED NATIONS FOOD AND AGRICULTURE ORGANIZATION (FAO): Organization that leads international efforts to defeat hunger. Serving both developed and developing countries, FAO acts as a neutral forum where all nations meet as equals to negotiate agreements and debate policy. FAO is also a source of knowledge and information and assists developing countries and countries in transition to modernize and improve agriculture, forestry, and fisheries practices and ensure good nutrition for all.

level before being able to reach it at the national level until the 1990s. It was also during this time that international development institutions and agencies began to shift away from the technical definition of hunger, as defined as surviving on less than 2,100 calories per day, and began to accept hunger as an indicator of food consumed in the household, and therefore the result of food insecurity. The concept that every human deserves the "right to adequate food" was the focus of the FAO World Food Summit in 1996, and since then several governments have adopted this rights-based approach to food security.

Regardless of the attention that was given to improving global food security, progress made in the 1980s and early 1990s ended when the number of undernourished around the world increased during the time periods from 1995 to 1997 and 2004 to 2006. The adoption of the 2000 UN Millennium Development Goal to halve poverty and hunger between 1990 and 2015 repositioned hunger or food security as a priority, but many were not prepared for the food crisis of 2007–2008. During this period, the prices of major commodities such as rice and wheat increased to levels that were unaffordable for populations across several nations that were living on less than one U.S. dollar per day. As a result of the growing linkages between energy and agriculture markets the food price surge produced food riots in several countries including Mexico, Pakistan, India, and Burkina Faso. The events of the 2007–2008 food crisis and resulting increase in the number of hungry people around the world signaled the need to shift away from emergency food aid approaches to food insecurity and to a focus on sustainable agricultural development in developing countries.

SEE ALSO *African Famine Relief; Biodiversity and Food Supply; Biofuels and World Hunger; Desertification and Agriculture; Disasters and Food Supply; Ethical Issues in Agriculture; Ethical Issues in Food Aid; Extreme Weather and Food Supply; Famine; Famine: Political Considerations; Food and Agriculture Organization (FAO); Food Security; Food Sovereignty; Gender Equality and Agriculture; International Food Aid; International Fund for Agricultural Development; Land Availability and Degradation; Malnutrition; Nutrition; Population and Food; Subsistence Farming; Sustainable Agriculture; UN Millennium Development Goals; Undernutrition; U.S. Agency for International Development (USAID); Water Scarcity; World Food Day; World Food Programme.*

BIBLIOGRAPHY

Books

Bread for the World Institute. *A Just and Sustainable Recovery: Hunger 2010: 20th Annual Report on the State of World Hunger.* Washington, DC: Bread for the World Institute, 2009.

Food and Agriculture Organization of the United Nations (FAO). *The State of Food Insecurity in the World 2009: Eradicating World Hunger.* Rome: FAO, 2009.

Stanford, Claire. *World Hunger.* Bronx, NY: H. W. Wilson, 2007.

Periodicals

Day, Michael. "Deadline to End World Hunger by 2025 Is Being Allowed to 'Quietly Wither Away.'" *BMJ: British Medical Journal* 339 (2009): b4977.

Kaufman, Frederick. "World Hunger: A Reasonable Proposal." *BMJ: British Medical Journal* 339 (2009): b5209.

O'Flynn, Michael. "Food Crisis and the Ghost of Malthus." *Journal of Marxism and Interdisciplinary Inquiry* 3, no. 1 (2009): 33–41.

Sanchez, Pedro A., and Monkombu S. Swaminathan. "Cutting World Hunger in Half." *Science* 5708 (2005): 357–360.

"The World: Hunger Levels in the U.S. Rise to an All-Time High." *Time* (November 30, 2009): 16–17.

Web Sites

"Get Involved: United against Hunger: World Food Day." *Food and Agriculture Organization of the United Nations (FAO).* http://www.fao.org/getinvolved/worldfoodday/en/ (accessed September 23, 2010).

"Hunger." *World Food Programme.* http://www.wfp.org/hunger (accessed September 23, 2010).

Tiffany Imes

Hydrogenated Fats and Trans Fats

■ Introduction

Fats and oils play an important part in cuisine, nutrition, and health. Oils from plant sources, such as corn, olive, and soy, are liquid at room temperature and have a lower degree of saturation. Fats, such as butter and lard, tend to come from animal sources, are solid at room temperature, and generally have a higher degree of saturation. The margarines, which include products such as low-fat spread, are synthetic butter substitutes that are made by hardening oils through a hydrogenation process. Margarines have a higher degree of saturation than oils because hydrogen breaks up the double carbon bonds in the unsaturated fats, changing the double carbon bonds into hydrogen-carbon bonds and creating either completely or partially saturated fats. If the hydrogenation process is incomplete, the partially hydrogenated oils created can also produce fatty acids not known in nature called trans fatty acids. The higher the partially hydrogenated fat content of a margarine and the higher its trans fatty acid content, the more detrimental it is to heart health. Both saturated fats and trans fatty acids increase cholesterol and lead to fatty plaque deposit on the walls of the arteries. Healthier margarine spreads without trans fatty acids are becoming increasingly available. Some are also fortified with vitamins and other substances that promote health.

■ Historical Background and Scientific Foundations

Margarine is a butter substitute that was invented in 1869 by the French chemist Hippolyte Mège-Mouriés (1817–1880). At the time, Europe was running short on oils and fats because of growing demand for lubricants and soap, so Napoleon III (1808–1873) issued a challenge to researchers to find a synthetic edible fat. Mège-Mouriés managed to make suet palatable through his process but it was not until 1905 that French and German chemists invented the catalytic hydrogenation of fats and oils that is the basis of margarine manufacture in the early twenty-first century. Margarine was popular among consumers from the start, but less so with the dairy industry and government, which levied a high tax on it. It was not until the butter rationing of World War II (1939–1945) that margarine became a popular commodity item.

Most margarine is made from soy or corn oil, which is hydrogenated and then fortified with vitamins A and D and sometimes other ingredients such as omega-3 fatty acids and plant stanol esters. It is colored with either synthetic carotene or annatto, a pigment from a tropical seed. Then the water or skimmed milk phase is added along with emulsifiers such as lecithin to disperse the water throughout the oil. There is a wide range of margarines available. Harder margarines are more highly hydrogenated than the softer tub margarines.

WORDS TO KNOW

FATTY ACIDS: A group of organic chemicals consisting of a carbon backbone linked to a carboxylic acid group. The length of the carbon backbone varies. The simplest fatty acid is acetic acid, the main ingredient in vinegar, which has a backbone consisting of just one carbon atom, bonded to three hydrogen atoms. Naturally occurring fatty acids have carbon backbones containing up to 35 carbon atoms.

HYDROGENATED FAT: The fatty acids in fats and oils may contain carbon-carbon double bonds that are capable of reacting with hydrogen. The hydrogenation of a fat, as in the manufacture of margarine, increases the degree of saturation of a fat.

TRANS FAT: A fat containing trans fatty acids, which are produced from the hydrogenation of vegetable oils to make margarine. The term trans refers to the geometrical arrangement of hydrogen atoms in a carbon-carbon double bond.

Artificial trans fats, short for trans fatty acids, are partially hydrogenated vegetable oils commonly used for deep frying. *Image copyright Lana Langlois, 2010. Used under license from Shutterstock.com.*

IN CONTEXT: TRANS FATS

Research published in the *New England Journal of Medicine* in 2006 indicates that an overall 2 percent increase in calorie intake from trans fats can raise an adult's risk of heart disease by more than 23 percent. Industrial trans fats have been shown to increase health risks more than naturally occurring trans fats.

Because trans fats have little nutritional value and increase health risks in consumers, several health organizations and governments have taken steps to reduce trans fat, and especially industrial trans fat, consumption. In addition to educating consumers about reducing the amount of fast foods, packaged snack foods, fried foods, and shelf-stable baked goods that are consumed, regulations often require specific labeling of foods containing trans fats. Several nations have also revised dietary guidelines to discourage consumption of industrial trans fats. Public awareness campaigns, restrictions on the percentage of trans fats permitted in certain products, programs encouraging manufacturers to replace trans fats with other fats in processed foods, taxing products with trans fats, and banning oils and margarines with industrial trans fats in restaurants are examples of measures that some governments are using to respond to the public health risks associated with trans fats and also general obesity. Although pressures on restaurants and fast-food chains by health advocates in the United States have resulted in some voluntary restrictions on the use of trans fats, an increasing number of cities and states are resorting to legal restrictions on the use of trans fats, or at minimum greater public disclosure of the use of trans fats.

Fats are triglycerides, also known as triacylglycerols. A triglyceride consists of a glycerol backbone bonded to three fatty acids, which may be the same or different. A given fat will be a complex mixture of different triglycerides. Each carbon atom in a fatty acid molecule backbone can make four bonds. Two are taken up with bonding to the neighboring carbon in the chain. There are then two possibilities: The remaining two bonds can be two hydrogen atoms, in which case that carbon atom is said to be saturated; or one bond is with hydrogen and the other forms a double bond with the neighboring carbon atom in the chain, in which case the carbon atom is unsaturated. Hydrogenation breaks up double bonds into single bonds and adds extra hydrogen atoms to the carbon atoms, turning unsaturated double carbon bonds into saturated carbon-hydrogen bonds. In short, hydrogenation of fats and oils increases their degree of saturation. If the hydrogenation process is incomplete, another consequence is the production of trans fatty acids in which the geometry of the molecule differs from that found in nature.

■ Impacts and Issues

Margarines are products in the fat and oil category and have similar health impacts. Hard margarines contain a higher proportion of saturated fats because of their higher degree of hydrogenation. Conventional hard margarines with partially hydrogenated oils also contain trans fatty acids. Both saturated fat and trans fatty acids have similar adverse effects upon health, according to clinical studies. Higher consumption increases the risk of fatty plaque being deposited on the inner linings of the arteries. This buildup, called atherosclerosis, can lead to a heart attack or stroke by narrowing the arteries so they are more likely to be blocked by a blood clot. Fats that are solid at room temperature are more likely to have this effect.

In response to research showing that trans fatty acids are a health hazard, manufacturers have adjusted their processes so that partial hydrogenation does not occur, thus eliminating the presence of trans fat in margarine. Trans fatty acids play no useful role in the human diet, and eliminating them will benefit health. Trans fatty acids had been distributed widely in baked and processed goods, because traditional margarines are a key ingredient in these products. However, products increasingly are being labeled as free of trans fatty acids, and these are recommended for heart health. As of 2007, the U.S. Food and Drug Administration required all products containing trans fats to have this information presented and quantified on the food label. Additionally, the American Heart Association claims that consuming even small amounts of trans fatty acids is unhealthy and encourages the consumption of unsaturated vegetable oils such as canola, peanut oil, olive oil, flax seed oil, corn oil, or safflower oil for heart health.

Margarine, being a totally synthetic product, can also be developed as a healthy food. There are margarine-like spreads, which are fortified with vitamins A and D, to help meet daily intake needs, and with omega-3 fatty acids, which reduce inflammation and blood clotting and so promote heart health. There are also spreads that have added plant stanol esters, which can help lower cholesterol levels with just one or two servings per day.

SEE ALSO *Cooking Fats; Diet and Heart Disease; Diet and Hypertension; Dietary Guidelines for Americans; Mediterranean Diet; Monounsaturated and Polyunsaturated Oils.*

BIBLIOGRAPHY

Books

Ettlinger, Steve. *Twinkie, Deconstructed: My Journey to Discover How the Ingredients Found in Processed Foods Are Grown, Mined (yes, Mined), and Manipulated into What America Eats.* New York: Hudson Street, 2007.

Stanfield, Maggie. *Trans Fats: The Time Bomb in Your Food.* London: Souvenir, 2008.

Periodicals

Foster, Rebecca, Claire S. Williamson, and Joanne Lunn. "Briefing Paper: Culinary Oils and Their Health Effects." *Nutrition Bulletin* 34, no. 1 (2009): 4–47.

Kummerow, Fred A. "The Negative Effects of Hydrogenated Trans Fats and What to Do about Them." *Atherosclerosis* 205, no. 2 (2009): 458–465.

A sign on a restaurant counter informs patrons that the restaurant uses frying oil that has zero trans fat per serving, contains Omega 3 fatty acids, and is low in saturated fat. Public campaigns have raised awareness of the dangers of saturated and trans fat consumption. © Ilene MacDonald / Alamy.

Sanders, Tom A. 3. "The Role of Fat in the Diet—Quantity, Quality, and Sustainability." *Nutrition Bulletin* 35, no. 2 (2010): 138–146.

Web Sites

"Meet the Fats." *American Heart Association.* http://www.heart.org/HEARTORG/GettingHealthy/FatsAndOils/MeettheFats/Meet-the-Fats_UCM_304495_Article.jsp (accessed October 2, 2010).

My Pyramid.gov. "Inside the Pyramid: How Are Oils Different from Solid Fats?" *United States Department of Agriculture (USDA).* http://www.mypyramid.gov/pyramid/oils_how.html (accessed October 2, 2010).

"Trans Fats." *American Heart Association.* http://www.heart.org/HEARTORG/GettingHealthy/FatsAndOils/Fats101/Trans-Fats_UCM_301120_Article.jsp (accessed October 2, 2010).

Susan Aldridge

Hydroponics

■ Introduction

The term *hydroponics* describes all methods used to grow plants without soil using nutrients supplied in a water solution. The term literally means "water work" or "working water" and is derived from the Greek roots *hydro* (meaning water) and *ponos* (labor).

Although the details vary considerably, hydroponics involves placing plants in an inert medium such as rock wool, gravel, vermiculite, perlite, sand, expanded clay, or other root supporting material, and providing nutrients to the roots in an aqueous solution. The solution is provided either continuously or intermittently to supply the required minerals while allowing for adequate aeration of the root zone.

Much of what is known about plant mineral nutrition has been learned through research on plants grown hydroponically. This is because of the extreme control of the makeup of the nutrient solution afforded in a hydroponic system.

Commercial and hobby hydroponics are an earthbound pursuit at the current time, but there is no doubt that if humans venture further into space for extended periods, hydroponics will figure prominently in providing food for astronauts and extraterrestrial colonists.

■ Historical Background and Scientific Foundations

It is impossible to know when the first use of hydroponics took place, but there are a few possibilities. The hanging gardens of Babylon may have used a form of hydroponics. The floating gardens constructed by the Aztecs and Chinese can rightly be considered early hydroponic systems.

During the seventeenth century, British scientist Sir Francis Bacon (1561–1626) undertook a series of experiments on soil-free gardening that generated the first wave of interest in what would eventually be called

hydroponics. After Bacon, John Woodward (1665–1728) grew plants in water from various sources that had been mixed with soil and then filtered to some extent. He showed that water exposed to soil was more effective than pure water for growing spearmint.

During the 1800s advances were made by a number of scientists, including French chemist Jean Baptiste Boussingault (1802–1887), who grew plants in a soilless medium using only water and chemical mineral nutrients. German botanist Julius von Sachs (1832–1897) is credited with publishing a recipe for the first nutrient solution in 1860. From that time on, soil-free culture was used to investigate the mineral element requirements of plants, and methods continued to be improved in the laboratory.

The modern era of hydroponics was ushered in during the 1920s by William Gericke at the University of California at Berkeley. He produced enormous, highly productive tomato plants using soilless culture techniques. He was a strong proponent of the commercial potential of his methods. Gericke originally called his technique "aquaculture," but finding that term already in use, he came up with the name still in use in the early twenty-first century—"hydroponics." His work was followed up by two other researchers at Berkeley, Dennis Hoagland (1884–1949) and Daniel Arnon (1910–1994). Their work culminated in the publication of the important work *The Water Culture Method for Growing Plants without Soil* in 1938.

The simplest hydroponic installations use a system called ebb and flow (or fill and drain). A basic ebb and flow system can be constructed by placing seedlings in a tray of gravel or other medium and raising and lowering a bucket of nutrient solution connected to the tray with tubing, to alternately fill and drain the root region. Commercial ebb and flow systems use a combination of pumps and valves to accomplish the filling and draining. Drip systems are commonly used on tomato and cucumber crops to provide an intermittent supply of nutrients to a root container, with the runoff collected and sent back to a central reservoir for reuse. Plants can be placed in floatation devices with their roots submerged in an aerated nutrient solution. In the Nutrient Film Technique (NFT) system, developed in England during the 1970s, a thin layer of nutrient solution is continually passed over the roots and returned to a reservoir by gravity. This method provides excellent oxygenation of the root zone and is the method of choice for growing lettuce and other leafy greens.

Aeroponics is a technique for growing plants that requires no root support substrate at all. Plants are grown individually or in small batch containers with their root systems totally enclosed. A steady or intermittent fine mist of nutrient solution is directed onto the roots to provide required mineral elements while allowing a high degree of aeration. Due to the difficulty of maintaining the pumping and misting components, this method is usually restricted to small-scale hobby or research operations.

Aquaponics is a relatively new development that combines fish farming (aquaculture) with hydroponics. The enhanced nutrient content of water in which fish are grown is used to support the growth of plants. In turn, the plant roots act as a filtering and purifying system for the water to keep it healthy for the fish. Once an aquaponic system is established it forms a complex ecosystem of plants, animals, and microbes designed to operate in a harmonious balance addressing the needs of both aquaculture and hydroponics.

■ Impacts and Issues

Hydroponics is used to produce a small but growing fraction of the world's food and ornamental crops. Hydroponic culture is not optimal for all plant species: With the exception of potatoes, plants grown primarily for their roots are not well suited to the method. Leaf, fruit and flower crops, however, are grown hydroponically in many parts of the world.

The cut flower industries in Holland, Mexico, and the United States make extensive use of hydroponics. Hydroponic production of roses, tulips, chrysanthemums, and carnations is well established.

The range of food crops grown hydroponically is diverse. Lettuce and other leafy green salad vegetables are the easiest crops to produce and can be grown to market-ready size in as little as six to eight weeks. Herbs such as basil, oregano, cilantro, chives, thyme, rosemary, dill, parsley, and mint also do well. Included in this class are the *microgreens*, which include any seedlings harvested for their inclusion in salads (e.g. all kinds of lettuce, spinach, watercress, radish, mustard, and many sprouts). The most common commercially grown hydroponic fruits are tomatoes, cucumbers, peppers, and strawberries. Many other crops are grown on a small scale or for research purposes, including green beans, corn, okra, melons, and tropical fruits.

Terry Fujimoto, plant sciences professor at California State Polytechnic University, Pomona, is at the forefront of an effort to use hydroponics—a method of growing plants in water instead of soil— to bring farming into the urban areas where consumers are concentrated. *AP Images.*

Although hydroponics can be implemented outdoors, greenhouse hydroponics offers significant advantages over traditional outdoor farming. Advantages include optimum control of light, temperature, airflow and humidity; precise control of conditions in the root zone; efficient use and recycling of water and nutrients; reduced space requirements; year-round crop production; avoidance of soil pests; ability to grow species outside of their natural range or where suitable soil conditions do not exist; adaptability of production systems to urban settings; and, if applied correctly, higher yields.

There are disadvantages to hydroponics to be considered as well. The main barrier to wider adoption of hydroponics is the initial high cost of system installation. The greater the degree of environmental monitoring and control desired, the higher the cost and greater complexity of the required system. Hydroponics requires specialized skill in both agricultural practice and the required technology, and there is a learning curve to be negotiated before an operation achieves success. Other disadvantages include the requirement of daily expert monitoring of plants and system operation (although this can usually be done by a single person); rapid plant death in the event of a major system failure; and potentially rapid spread of disease because many plants are connected to the same nutrient supply system.

Population growth and industrial expansion are putting increased demands on the world's resources including the water supply. These factors, in combination with increasing global temperatures, will make traditional soil-based agriculture that relies on natural rainfall or irrigation less viable. Fewer regions will be able to support food production at their current levels. For these reasons, the greater water efficiency of hydroponics will make it an increasingly attractive option in the future.

SEE ALSO *Agribusiness; Agricultural Demand for Water; Biodiversity and Food Supply; Organics; Population and Food.*

BIBLIOGRAPHY

Books

Jones, J. Benton. *Hydroponics: A Practical Guide for the Soilless Grower*, 2nd ed. Boca Raton, FL: CRC Press, 2005.

Kessler, J. Raymond. *Hydroponics for Home Gardeners*. Auburn, AL: Alabama Cooperative Extension System, 2006.

Mason, John. *Commercial Hydroponics*, 2nd ed. Pymble, New South Wales: Kangaroo Press, 2005.

Raviv, Michael, and Johann Heinrich Lieth. *Soilless Culture: Theory and Practice*. Amsterdam; Boston: Elsevier Science, 2008.

Singh, Dharm, and Devender Pratap Singh. *Hydroponics: Soilless Culture of Plants*. Jodhpur: Agrobios, 2009.

Periodicals

Anslow, Mark. "News Focus—Can We Really Grow Good Food without Soil? Mark Anslow Looks into Hydroponics." *The Ecologist* 38, no. 4 (2008): 12–13.

Despommier, Dickson. "The Rise of Vertical Farms." *Scientific American* 301, no. 5 (2009): 80–87.

Web Sites

"Welcome to the Controlled Environment Agriculture Center." *University of Arizona*. http://www.ag.arizona.edu/ceac/ (accessed July 20, 2010).

Philip McIntosh

Immigration and Cuisine

Introduction

Most immigrants migrate for increased opportunity, and many have come to the United States with this hope. In addition to the many other perceived benefits immigrants to the United States expect, the United States has a global reputation as a place where food is relatively plentiful and affordable. In all countries receiving large groups of immigrants, the newcomers bring their foodways with them, but they are also shaped by their adopted communities. The cuisine of the United States offers a good example of the integration of diverse foods and culinary practices brought by immigrants from around the world. In just the span of the 100 years from 1820 to 1920, about 30 million Europeans came to the United States. In the twentieth century, thousands of Central Americans, Caribbeans, and South Americans joined Mexicans in the immigration surge. With the passage of the 1965 Immigration Act, Asians began to immigrate in significant numbers. Africans have been in North America since 1619, a few years after the English arrived. All of these immigrant groups have different cultural constructions around food, and many of these cultures have dietary taboos. The only constant is that food intensifies group identity. With food so tightly woven around childhood and family, it serves as an agent of memory. Migrants, regardless of how long they plan to stay in their new homes, often attempt to recreate familiar foods. Stores, bakeries, and restaurants all bear witness to the desire of the newcomers to capture the foodways of places left behind.

Historical Background and Scientific Foundations

As a nation of immigrants, the United States has a national cuisine that is a mix of other national cuisines. As the first European immigrants, the English tried to replicate their traditional diet, which remains the foundation of the American diet. They consumed wheat and barley as well as the corn that they obtained from Native Americans. Given a choice, however, the English replaced cornmeal with their traditional wheat flour. The few Dutch living in the New York area introduced the waffle to American cuisine. African influences on southern cuisine were monumental and generally not acknowledged until the late twentieth century. Whereas slaves were provided with European food by their owners, most were able to supplement these rations with foods grown around their living quarters. The most important of these crops included peas, peanuts, okra, watermelon, and rice, with sorghum also possibly farmed.

After the English, the Germans were the largest ethnic group in the United States in the nineteenth century. The higher consumption of pork in the Midwest is one of the most obvious reflections of the Germanic stamp on settlement, as is the generally heavier Midwestern diet. The hot dog may be all-American, but its ingredients and the technology to make it reflect German influence. German settlers also brought a potato-consuming tradition, as did the Irish and others. From the Germans, the American diet has gained potato salad, egg noodles, holed doughnuts, and, probably, coleslaw. Lager beer is also a German contribution.

After the Civil War, many European grain farmers headed to the United States. The Scandinavians brought smörgasbord as well as lutefisk. Smörgasbord traditionally consists of a number of small appetizers rather than American version of all-you-can-eat. Typical of many imported food traditions, it has been modified for American tastes. Eastern and central Europeans had a greater influence on American cuisine than the Scandinavians, partly because of their greater numbers. They ate ducks, geese, sausages, stuffed cabbage, and stews as well as potato-filled ravioli. Jews brought bagels, cream cheese, and cheesecake. Italians added pasta and pizza to the mix. Mexican immigrants brought tacos, salsas, and burritos but few other Latin American groups have yet had much of an impact

WORDS TO KNOW

DIETARY TABOO: A prohibition of a food or a type of food preparation.

FOODWAYS: Customs and traditions that accompany the production, selection, and preparation of food.

FUSION: Fusion cuisine blends the ingredients and traditions of food preparation from different cultures into hybrid dishes.

on American foodways. Chinese food has made few inroads into the traditional American kitchen except for the widespread adoption of stir-fry cooking, which does not always employ traditional Chinese ingredients.

■ Impacts and Issues

The arrival of millions of immigrants on American shores during the past four centuries obviously has shaped the American national cuisine. Less obvious is the impact of the settlement patterns of the newly arriving immigrants. German, Scandinavian, and African ethnic groups did not randomly settle in the new land: They tended to concentrate in a few places. As a result, their impact on

the American diet has tended to be more highly concentrated in some areas than others.

Regional cuisine is affected by history as well as the availability of foods. The cuisine of New England has been shaped predominantly by Native American preparation techniques combined with British cooking. Roasting, boiling, and stewing are preferred whereas strong seasonings are avoided. The Mid Atlantic region shows a strong German influence in a greater use of pork, dairy products, and baked goods as well as stronger seasonings. Dutch influence is evident in the use of cinnamon, pickled fruits, coffee cakes, and rye breads. The Midwest cuisine reflects internal migration from the Northeast and New England as well as strong German and Central European traditions such as the consumption of pork and horseradish. The foods most associated with the South reflect both the bounty of the plantations and the scarcity of the slave diet. Corn dishes, rice, all parts of the hog, and greens are characteristic components. Large numbers of ethnic groups reside in the West, making this a very eclectic cuisine that shows the influences of Native Americans, Asians, Latinos, and Europeans. Fish and game are as popular as tacos, sushi, and egg rolls.

The immigrant has been a part of the evolution of American cuisine from the arrival of the first English settlers on Jamestown. As time passes, it is likely that American cuisine will become an even greater mixture of

Polish immigrant Julia Balik, left, has been making pierogies for more than 70 years. She and daughter Helen Mannerino work at their drive-thru Perfect Pierogie shop in McKees Rocks, Pennsylvania, in 2002. Also helping fashion the traditional eastern European comfort food are Elizabeth Andrzewski, of Poland, and Olga Shakraba, rear, of the Ukraine. *AP Images.*

A worker prepares an Indian dish called "pav bhaji," a mixture of vegetables and potatoes, that will later be packaged and frozen at a warehouse in New York. Ethnic grocers and food companies are enjoying explosive growth in sales of frozen meals to immigrant and second-generation customers with less time, inclination or ability to cook the foods of their homeland. *AP Images.*

global cuisine to reflect the increasingly diverse heritage of Americans. Restaurants and food carts on the coasts in the early twenty-first century have popularized new forms of fusion food, including Korean-Mexican blends such as kimchi tacos (fermented vegetables in a taco shell). Such trends have historically moved inland. It is possible that American cuisine will eventually emerge as blend of Asian, European, African, and Latin American influences instead of the mostly European flavor of American cuisine over the past few centuries.

SEE ALSO *Asian Diet; Foodways; Fusion; Indigenous Peoples and Their Diets; Latin American Diet; Mediterranean Diet; Wage Slavery in Food Production; War, Conquest, Colonialism, and Cuisine.*

BIBLIOGRAPHY

Books

Anderson, Lynn Christie. *Breaking Bread: Recipes and Stories from Immigrant Kitchens.* Berkeley: University of California Press, 2010.

Civitello, Linda. *Cuisine and Culture: A History of Food and People.* Hoboken, NJ: John Wiley, 2007.

Kiple, Kenneth F. *A Movable Feast: Ten Millennia of Food Globalization.* Cambridge, UK: Cambridge University Press, 2007.

Smith, Andrew F. *Eating History: Thirty Turning Points in the Making of American Cuisine.* New York: Columbia University Press, 2009.

Periodicals

"New Twists on Latin American Foods: Latin American Cuisine Is a Mix of Worlds, Old and New, Near and Far, Native and Imported." *Prepared Foods* 172, no. 7 (2003): 57–64.

Web Sites

Evans, Dale. "Documentaries: New Film Links Food to Immigration." *Rochester City Newspaper,* May 29, 2007. http://ns.rochestercitynewspaper.com/entertainment/movies/DOCUMENTARIES-New-film-links-food-to-immigration/ (accessed October 21, 2010).

Lothar, Corrina. "Chinese Food in America." *Washington Times,* August 31, 2008. http://www.washingtontimes.com/news/2008/aug/31/chinese-food-in-america/ (accessed October 21, 2010).

"New Orleans: Gumbo as History." *PBS.org.* http://www.pbs.org/wgbh/amex/neworleans/sfeature/food.html (accessed October 21, 2010).

Caryn E. Neumann

Import Restrictions

Introduction

Import restrictions are measures imposed by governments to restrict the free trade of goods between nations. Nations typically impose import restrictions to protect domestic jobs, stabilize prices, or otherwise prevent foreign incursions into domestic markets. Commonly employed import restrictions include tariffs, import quotas, and subsidies. A tariff is a government tax, or duty, levied on a good upon importation to make domestically-produced goods more competitive with that good. Import quotas limit the quantity of a particular class of goods that may be imported into a nation within a certain period. Import quotas decrease the supply of foreign goods, thereby driving up their cost. Subsidies are a form of financial assistance paid by a government to domestic producers to stabilize commodity prices or make that particular industry competitive in global markets. Governments frequently employ subsidies to assist agricultural producers.

Prevailing capitalist sentiments disfavor import restrictions and other protectionist trade policies, including currency manipulation. Nevertheless, nations continue to impose import restrictions for several reasons, including promoting domestic industries, protecting infant industries, and to compensate for high taxes on domestic businesses. The use of import restrictions remains a controversial subject. Many policymakers and economists argue that import restrictions punish workers in developing nations and prevent market conditions from determining supply, demand, price, and investment.

Historical Background and Scientific Foundations

Beginning in the late fifteenth century, mercantilism, an economic theory that advocated increasing capital through a beneficial balance of trade with other nations, promoted the imposition of import restrictions. Nations asserted that protectionist policies, including tariffs and import quotas, were necessary to increase that nation's share of capital, which economic philosophers of the period argued to be static. Mercantilism encouraged European maritime powers to promote imperialism as a way to obtain cheap raw goods from their colonies to turn into more valuable finished goods for export. Mercantilism prevailed as the dominate economic model until the late eighteenth century.

The works of Adam Smith (1723–1790), David Hume (1711–1776), and other late eighteenth- and early nineteenth-century economic philosophers resulted in the abandonment of mercantilism and the adoption of capitalism as the dominant economic theory. Capitalism is an economic system that calls for private ownership of the means of production. The control of supply, demand, prices, and investment through market forces rather than central government planning are central tenets of capitalism. Capitalism, therefore, eschews import restrictions as a means of manipulating prices, supply, demand, or investment.

At the beginning of the Great Depression (1929–1941), however, many capitalist nations imposed import restrictions as a means of protecting domestic industries and agriculture. To protect American jobs, the United States passed the Smoot-Hawley Tariff Act of 1930, which called for steep increases in tariffs on foreign goods. The act pushed the tariffs on some goods to 50 percent and resulted in many nations imposing retaliatory tariffs on American goods. American exports fell by two-thirds due to foreign tariffs. The price of goods in America, particularly agricultural goods, plummeted and forced many American farmers to default on loans. Most economists assume that the retaliatory tariffs and other import restrictions of the 1930s exacerbated and prolonged the Great Depression.

Realizing the disastrous consequences that import restrictions had during the Great Depression, the international community rededicated itself to free trade following World War II (1939–1945). The United Nations Conference on Trade and Employment produced the General Agreement on Trades and Tariffs (GATT). GATT was the major international agreement governing international trade from 1949 until 1993. GATT reduced import tariffs by hundreds of billions of dollars on tens of thousands of goods over nearly five decades. The World Trade Organization (WTO), which replaced GATT in 1993, has continued GATT's preference for liberal trade policies.

■ Impacts and Issues

Most economists oppose import restrictions in favor of the free trade of goods across international borders. Under the principle of comparative advantage, each nation benefits from free trade because each nation is allowed to specialize and engage in those economic activities in which that nation has a competitive advantage. Competitive advantages that nations may possess include the availability of natural resources, labor costs, an educated workforce, or any other factor that makes their economic activities productive and profitable.

Unemployment decreases if each nation participates in those economic activities in which it has a comparative advantage. Protectionism, on the other hand, results

The U.S. government finally allowed the import of Spain's succulent and exceedingly expensive jamon Iberico, the cured ham long sought by American gourmets, in 2007, and the even more rare jamon Iberico de bellota (fed only on acorns) in 2008, after a quagmire of regulations and trade wars. *AP Images*

IN CONTEXT: SELECTIVE RESTRICTIONS

In a move that surprised many international experts, Egypt announced a ban on importing or exporting genetically modified foods in 2009. The move surprised the international community because GMO crops comprised a substantial portion of Egypt's current food imports. Starting late in 2009, food imported into Egypt required a certificate from the country of origin attesting that the product was not genetically modified. Egyptian exports will carry similar certification.

Within months, China and India also took stands on GMO use. In December 2009, China announced it would allow the introduction of some strains of genetically modified rice. In an opposing stand, in February 2010 India's environment minister, Jairam Ramesh (1954–), announced a ban on introduction of the genetically modified vegetable, Bt brinjal (eggplant or aubergine), as part of a pledge to overhaul India's regulatory oversight of GMOs. Farming factions in India have generally opposed the introduction of genetically modified crops because seeds are expensive, and there are limitations on seed harvesting that require farmers to purchase new seeds for each growing season.

Chinese shoppers buy pork at a supermarket in Nantong, Haian county, Jiangsu province in 2009. China began demanding testing and health certificates on pork imported from the European Union in 2009, citing the need to prevent the spread of A/H1N1 flu, a move seen as protectionist by suppliers. China is a major consumer of imported meat products. *AP Images.*

in economic inefficiency, known as "deadweight loss" in the field of economics. Furthermore, economists argue that free trade lifts wages and standards of living in developing nations by increasing competition among producers. Economists, including Nobel Prize laureate Paul Krugman (1953–), note that rapidly developing nations, including China and Indonesia, have succeeded economically in large part because free trade allowed their low-cost labor to compete and succeed on the international stage.

Whereas most economists support free trade, a few economists and politicians continue to favor protectionism for a variety of reasons. Proponents of protectionism argue that import restrictions may help a nation foster a particular industry during that industry' infancy. Startup industries have to bear the financial burden of shifting production. Import restrictions enable the infant industry remain competitive, at least domestically, until the industry becomes profitable.

Protectionism proponents also assert that trade restrictions actually level the playing field for producers and make markets more competitive. Protectionists argue that countries with higher taxes are at a competitive disadvantage, because producers in high-tax countries must raise the cost of their goods to account for certain taxes, including payroll, national healthcare, and social security taxes. Most developing nations do not impose these taxes on employers, or they tax at a lower rate. Most developing nations, therefore, may charge less for exports. A developed nation that collects both the additional taxes that it imposes on its producers and tariffs imposed on imports benefits financially from both sources of revenue.

The payment of subsidies to agricultural producers in developed nations enables that nation's products to be competitive against a developing nation with lower taxes. Subsidies are a form of commodity price control in which the government may make payments to agricultural producers in order to stabilize prices. Often subsidies guarantee a producer a certain price for goods. If the producer cannot receive that price on the open market, then the government pays the producer the difference between the commodity price and the price guaranteed by the government subsidy program. Under the Common Agricultural Policy, agricultural subsidies are the single largest expenditure of the European Union (EU) and account for one-third of all EU expenditures. Agricultural subsidies in the United States account for between one-quarter and one-third of all agricultural revenue.

Many policymakers, economists, and non-governmental organizations, however, assert that subsidies, which they view as a protectionist measure, punish agricultural producers in developing nations. Most developing nations and the WTO argue that the payment of subsidies by Brazil, the EU, the United States, and other large agricultural nations protect agricultural jobs in those countries and manipulate world commodity markets. Large subsidies drive down the global price of agricultural commodities. Farmers in nations that cannot afford to pay subsidies must sell their goods for less because they do not receive subsidies from their governments. In some instances, however, the payment of subsidies in major agricultural exporting nations supplies developing nations with cheap food subsidized by the taxpayers of developed nations. Many economists and policy analysts also cite high subsidies as a major contributing factor in the food price crisis of 2007 and 2008.

SEE ALSO   *Banana Trade Wars; Center for Food Safety and Applied Nutrition; Embargoes; Ethical Issues in Agriculture; Fair Trade; Free Trade and Agriculture; Subsidies; World Trade Organization (WTO).*

BIBLIOGRAPHY

Books

Peterson, E. Weseley F. *A Billion Dollars a Day: The Economics and Politics of Agricultural Subsidies.* Malden, MA: Wiley-Blackwell, 2009.

Schmitz, Andrew. *International Agricultural Trade Disputes: Case Studies in North America.* Calgary, Alberta, Canada: University of Calgary Press, 2005.

Periodicals

Devadoss, Stephen. "Optimal Tariff Analysis of India's Apple Import Restrictions." *Journal of Food Products Marketing* 13, no. 1 (2006): 45–59.

"Mexico Mulls Dairy Import Restrictions." *Food Chemical News* 50, no. 50 (2009): 18.

"Mexico's Shrimp Sector Questions U.S. Import Restrictions." *Food Chemical News* 52, no. 1 (2010): 25.

Web Sites

"Import Alerts." *U.S. Customs and Border Protection (CBP).* http://www.cbp.gov/xp/cgov/trade/trade_programs/agriculture/import_alert/ (accessed October 23, 2010).

"Understanding the WTO: The Agreements: Antidumping, Subsidies, Safeguards." *World Trade Organization (WTO).* http://www.wto.org/english/thewto_e/whatis_e/tif_e/agrm8_e.htm#subsidies (accessed October 23, 2010).

Joseph P. Hyder

Improving Nutrition for America's Children Act of 2010

■ Introduction

Introduced in the Senate in March 2010 by U.S. Senate Committee on Agriculture, Nutrition, and Forestry chairperson Blanche Lincoln (D-AR), the Healthy, Hunger-Free Kids Act of 2010 provides an increase in funding for school-provided lunches for the first time in nearly 30 years and an overall increase of $4.5 billion in child nutrition funding over the 10 subsequent years. The House of Representatives' version of the bill, the Improving Nutrition for America's Children Act of 2010, goes further, adding $8 billion in funding

for child nutrition programs. With provisions for adding organic fare to food options in schools, increasing out-of-school nutrition funding, streamlining eligibility and enrollment procedures for free and reduced school meal programs, integrating local farms and produce into school meals, and improving food safety in school cafeterias, the more comprehensive Improving Nutrition for America's Children Act of 2010 aims to reform federal government food programs that date back to the mid-1940s.

■ Historical Background and Scientific Foundations

Dating back to 1966, the first Child Nutrition Act was passed during the Lyndon Johnson administration as part of the relatively new War on Poverty. The Child Nutrition Act expanded the National School Lunch Program, a 1946 law that provided free and reduced-cost lunches to income-eligible students while simultaneously providing farmers with an outlet for crop surpluses. The 1966 legislation added the National School Breakfast Program and increased the reach of national child nutrition programs, making service institutions such as child care centers, recreation centers, settlement houses and certain non-profit institutions eligible for funding to provide qualified meals to children enrolled in these programs.

In addition to the National School Lunch Program and National School Breakfast Program, federal child nutrition programs include the Special Milk Program, in operation since 1954, and the Fresh Fruit and Vegetable Program, established in 2002. The annual cost of these programs exceeds $16.3 billion. In 2010 U.S. president Barack Obama called for additional funding of more than $10 billion over the next 10 years, a sum that Congress did not meet in either the Senate or the House version of the revised child nutrition acts proposed in 2010.

WORDS TO KNOW

FARM TO SCHOOL PROGRAMS: Local partnerships that public school districts, or individual schools, can form with area farmers to deliver agricultural and nutrition curricula to students while serving local produce and crops. These programs often include field trips to farms, cooking classes that incorporate local crops, and unit studies on nutritional composition and growing conditions for local foods.

FREE AND REDUCED LUNCH: Students from families with incomes below 130 percent of the federal poverty line generally qualify for free school lunches through the National School Lunch Program, with the fee for lunch reduced for children from families earning between 131 percent and 185 percent of the federal poverty line, per United States Department of Agriculture Guidelines.

WIC: The Special Supplemental Nutrition Program for Women, Infants, and Children (WIC) provides nutrition assistance to more than 45 percent of all infants in the United States. WIC supplies specific foods via a voucher system to pregnant women, postpartum women, breastfeeding mothers, infants, and children through age five for families with incomes below 185 percent of the federal poverty line.

The Improving Nutrition for America's Children Act of 2010 increases the rate of reimbursement to schools by 6 cents per meal, which is the first increase, aside from inflation adjustments, since 1973. More than 31 million students receive meals from the National School Breakfast and National School Lunch programs, with additional food provided for snacks in approved after-school programs and summer nutrition offerings.

■ Impacts and Issues

As the Senate and the House worked to align the two acts to create legislation that President Obama would sign, retaining as much of the Improving Nutrition for America's Children Act of 2010 as possible was the goal of Representative George Miller (D-CA), the bill's sponsor and chairman of the House Education and Labor Committee. In addition to increasing direct reimbursement rates for meals, the bill would provide funding of one half cent per meal for nutrition education; food standards for all food offered in schools, including vending

machine items; grants for equipment and new food programs; green grants for school cafeterias that follow specific environmental standards; special diet considerations; expansion of farm-to-school programs to increase local and organic produce offerings in cafeterias; and extension and expansion of WIC with an increased emphasis on supporting breastfeeding mothers.

A student makes a selection in a school lunch line. Though some American schools are making efforts to offer more healthful choices in school lunches, the most popular foods are items like chicken strips, pizza, french fries, and desserts. Concern about childhood obesity has made food served in school settings a priority, especially in schools in which many low income children receive free lunches as part of the Title 1 federal school food program. © *Marc F. Henning / Alamy.*

The Improving Nutrition for America's Children Act of 2010, unlike the Senate's Child Nutrition Act, automatically enrolls any child in Medicaid health insurance programs in the National School Lunch Program, reducing gaps for children who may qualify for food assistance but are not enrolled due to paperwork mistakes, parents or guardians who do not complete paperwork, or other outside factors. In addition, all foster children automatically receive free school lunch as part of the act. This streamlining integrates various child nutrition and low-income assistance programs, making the act the most comprehensive piece of legislation aimed at child nutrition and health since the 1966 Child Nutrition Act.

SEE ALSO *Edible Schoolyard Movement; Farm-to-Table Movement; Nutrition and U.S. Government Food Assistance; Obesity; School Lunch Reform.*

Web Sites

"Improving Nutrition for America's Children Act." *American Dietetic Association.* http://www.eatright.org/Media/content.aspx?id=6442452566 (accessed July 20, 2010).

"National School Lunch Program." *Food and Nutrition Service, U.S. Department of Agriculture (USDA).* http://www.fns.usda.gov/cnd/lunch/ (accessed July 20, 2010).

Melanie Barton Zoltan

Indigenous Peoples and Their Diets

■ Introduction

Given the number of indigenous peoples living in landscapes with remarkably varied climates, with their distinctive histories of migration, trade, and colonization, it is not surprising that their traditional diets were—and sometimes still are—incredibly diverse. In some Arctic regions, all but a minor part of the diet of several ethnic groups was animal-based. In other parts of the world, native peoples had almost entirely vegetarian diets. Some groups gathered an incredible assortment of wild tubers, fruits, seeds, nuts, fish, shellfish, and insects, and hunted virtually every animal that could be eaten in their region. Others cultivated familiar crops (though in a bewildering number of varieties), raised domesticated animals, and tended bees, orchards, or herds. Many traditional peoples combined agriculture with hunting and gathering.

One thing that all of these traditional foodways or ethnic cuisines shared was their local nature and lack of industrial-era processing. Traditional foods were harvested in season, or preserved in a variety of old-fashioned ways: dried, smoked, fermented, pickled, or frozen in the winter in temperate and Arctic regions. Highly refined flours, sugars, and fats were absent. Trade may have been important, but most food came from the land that indigenous people lived on, regularly traveled, and knew intimately. In many indigenous groups, a large percentage of the population was engaged in food production, and they consumed an amazing diversity of species, especially in times of scarcity. Despite all of the products found on the supermarket shelves in industrialized nations, most modern diets are not nearly as varied as those of indigenous peoples. More than half the food in industrialized nations is based on rice, corn, and wheat. The remaining portion is made up of an assortment of meats, fruits, vegetables, and nuts that is tiny in comparison to the number of plants and animals used by most indigenous societies.

■ Historical Background and Scientific Foundations

European and American scholars began paying closer attention to the plants used by various indigenous peoples in the late 1700s and early 1800s, especially in the New World. This "aboriginal botany" focused largely on finding new medicines that could be useful to colonial doctors and businessmen. In 1895 American botanist John W. Harshberger (1869–1929) coined the term *ethnobotany*, and during the following century the study of plants utilized by native peoples expanded to include more detailed examinations of diet, agriculture, "primitive" technology, animal husbandry, and hunting. Eventually, cultural perceptions and classifications of plants and animals, and the interactions between people and other species—their interrelationships—became important topics.

Anthropologists, economic botanists, and biologists were particularly interested in this new field, now called *ethnobiology*, especially as many indigenous groups were rapidly decreasing in size, losing traditional lands, and becoming acculturated or assimilated into more dominant ethnic groups. In the twenty-first century, according to American ethnobotanist Gary Paul Nahban, "most truly authentic ethnic cuisines are in peril, even though they have displayed resiliency and continuity over hundreds if not thousands of years."

The interest in the traditional foods eaten by indigenous peoples is not limited to academia, however, and several popular works by anthropologists, medical practitioners, and culinary thrill-seekers were published in the twentieth century, promoting foodways markedly different from those in the mainstream in industrial nations. In 1935 and 1936, Canadian-American ethnologist Vilhjalmur Stefansson (1879–1962) published a series of articles in *Harper's Magazine*, documenting his life among the Invialuit people who lived above the Arctic Circle in the Northwest Territories of

WORDS TO KNOW

ASSIMILATION: The process by which one ethnic group is absorbed by another, losing or altering unique cultural traits, customs, and attitudes, including those about food. Less pervasive changes associated with colonialism and migration are more accurately described as acculturation, with cultural groups remaining distinct but altering each other's cultures.

ETHNOBIOLOGY: The study of the interrelations between people and the plants and animals in their environment, including cultural classifications and perceptions of other species, as well as traditional ecological knowledge and the utilization of plants and animals. Researchers may specialize in ethnobotany or ethnozoology.

FOODWAYS: Another term for culinary practices, including social as well as nutritional aspects of ethnic cuisines or traditional cultures of food.

INDIGENOUS: Native to a certain area. The definition of indigenous peoples varies across the world, but usually refers to those whose ancestors were born in a particular area and who retain traditional knowledge of their environment and culture (including food). Indigenous peoples also may be described as ethnic groups, and aboriginal, tribal, or First Peoples. Some groups include the Ainu of Japan; the Baffin Inuit of Canada, along with many other Canadian First Nations; the Igbo of Nigeria; the Tononi O'Odham (Papago), various Native American nations of the United States and Mexico; the Chukchi of Russia; Maori of New Zealand; and hundreds of other groups.

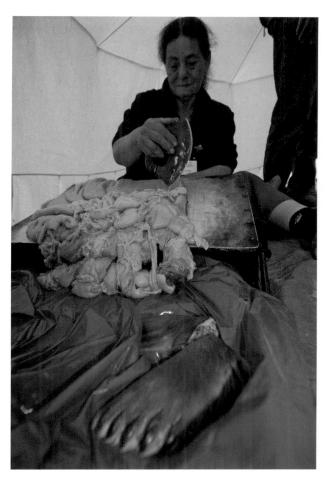

Local Inuit woman in the Canadian Arctic fishing community of Kimmirut cuts and peels a seal using the traditional knife for women (ulu). *AP Images.*

Canada. His "Adventures in Diet" advocated an all-meat and fat diet, and many current Paleo Diet enthusiasts continue to refer to Stefansson's "Eskimo Diet" articles and books.

In the 1930s Canadian-born American dentist Weston A. Price (1870–1948) traveled the world comparing the nutrition and health of "isolated and modernized" peoples, publishing a book entitled *Nutrition and Physical Degeneration* in 1939. Price argued that cavities and many of the other illnesses associated with modern civilization (which researchers agree include metabolic syndrome, diabetes, some cancers, and arteriosclerosis) were caused by modern diets. Price promoted an alternative diet that includes large quantities of raw milk, eggs, meat, fats, and nuts, augmented with fermented vegetables and cooked grains. Like Stefansson's work, Price's book gained renewed popularity during the first decade of the twenty-first century, and the Weston A. Price Foundation currently promotes "traditional foods" and "nourishing traditions" based largely on Price's interpretations of several indigenous diets.

In the 1980s, American physicians S. Boyd Eaton and Melvin Konner, along with anthropologist Marjorie Shostak (1945–1996) wrote *The Paleolithic Prescription*, partially inspired by the hunter-gatherer diet that Konner and Shostak observed during their fieldwork amongst the !Kung San who live in the Kalahari Desert in Botswana and South Africa. The authors endorsed a diet based on whole grains, fruits, vegetables, and lean meats, which they argued was most like that eaten by ancestral humans. They did not recommend mongongo nuts, baobob pods, or any of the other hundred or more plant species consumed by the indigenous peoples of southern Africa, or the insects, caterpillars, reptiles, or the other foods of this type that rounded out traditional !Kung San diets.

■ Impacts and Issues

In 2004 Gary Paul Nabhan (1952–) summarized how ethnic food traditions do not "simply consist of random ingredients brought together through some

Tiriós indigenous child holds hummingbird with fingers, in Tracuateua. Pará, northern Brazil. People of this tribe use the bird as food. *AP Images.*

serendipitous experimentation by a master chef," but actually reflect "the evolutionary history of a particular human population as it responded to the availability of edible plants and animals." Nabhan went on to explain how natural selection for particular human genes in a local population can even be mediated through food choices. Some researchers call this avenue of research evolutionary gastronomy. Researchers have explored how ethnic cuisines are the product of local evolution, examining how food combinations, preparation techniques, and even the rituals of eating affect human health in areas called epidemiological "cold spots"—places with the lowest incidences of the "diseases of civilization" such as diabetes.

Many indigenous peoples are especially vulnerable to "civilized" diseases, particularly diabetes, when they adopt a modern diets with remarkably high quantities of refined carbohydrates and sugars. Nabhan and others hypothesize that the very genes that were most adaptive in local environments with traditional cuisines are the ones that make native peoples more susceptible to these "diseases of civilization." Many different indigenous diets contain plants that are high in fiber, phytochemicals, and omega-3 fatty acids, and much leaner meats, including wild game and fish—except in the Arctic, where few carbohydrates or sugars were eaten at all. Many of the plants found in native diets help stabilize blood sugar, slow digestion, and improve diabetic control or the incidence of the disease. Plants such as garlic, onion, chicory roots, Jerusalem artichokes (historically cultivated by native peoples across eastern North America), agave, and jicama are all high in a polysaccharide called inulin, which has several health benefits, including being high in fiber and having little effect on glucose levels. In processed foods, inulin has become valuable as a sweetener that can replace sugar without increasing blood sugar levels and as a low-fat replacement for fats. It has also become an important source of fiber for many processed foods.

Although few people in industrialized nations have the means or the desire to adopt many traditional peoples' diets—with the exception of a Mediterranean peasant diet—the promotion of native foodways has had a significant impact. More people are trying to eat locally produced, less highly processed "real food" like their great-grandparents did, as Slow Food advocates recommend. Some formerly obscure indigenous crops, such as amaranth, quinoa, and fava beans, have become more widely appreciated. And perhaps most importantly for people with indigenous ancestry worldwide, more communities are sharing traditional knowledge, food processing techniques, and recipes. Native and aboriginal food groups such as the Indigenous Food Systems Network of North America (Working Group on Indigenous Food Sovereignty 2010) are active on the Internet, and the FAO (Food and Agriculture Organization) of the United Nations and other nonprofit groups are also helping preserve traditional foodways.

SEE ALSO *Biodiversity and Food Supply; Climate Change and Agriculture; Food Sovereignty; Foodways; Paleolithic Diet; Whaling.*

BIBLIOGRAPHY

Books

Kuhnlein, Harriet V., Bill Erasmus, and Dina Spigelski, eds. *Indigenous Peoples' Food Systems: The Many Dimensions of Culture, Diversity and Environment for Nutrition and Health.* Rome: Food and Agriculture Organization of the United Nations, Centre for Indigenous Peoples' Nutrition and Environment, 2009.

Miller, Daphne, with Allison Sarubin-Fragakis. *The Jungle Effect: The Healthiest Diets from around the World—Why They Work and How to Make Them Work for You.* New York: Harper, 2009.

Nabhan, Gary Paul. *Why Some Like It Hot: Food, Genes, and Cultural Diversity.* Washington, DC: Island Press/Shearwater, 2004.

Periodicals

Gombay, Nicole. "Shifting Identities in a Shifting World: Food, Place, Community, and the Politics of Scale in an Inuit Settlement." *Environment and Planning D: Society and Space* 23, no. 3 (2005): 415–433.

"Indigenous Peoples' Food Systems for Health: Finding Interventions That Work." *Public Health Nutrition* 9, no. 8 (2006): 1013–1019.

Web Sites

"Safeguarding Traditional Foodways." *Bioversity International.* http://www.bioversityinternational.org/announcements/safeguarding_traditional_foodways.html (accessed October 27, 2010).

Working Group on Indigenous Food Sovereignty. *Indigenous Food Systems Network.* http://www.indigenousfoodsystems.org/#content (accessed October 27, 2010).

Sandra L. Dunavan

Infant Formula and Baby Food

■ Introduction

Infant formula, also known as artificial baby milk or artificial breast milk, is a product made with a combination of dried cow's milk or soy powder, thickeners, sugars, vitamins, and amino acids; it is designed to replace a mother's breast milk. Breast milk or infant formula is the sole form of nutrition for most babies worldwide through the first three to four months of life, although the World Health Organization (WHO), American Academy of Pediatrics (AAP), and other health groups recommend that mothers breastfeed exclusively through the first six months of life or, if breastfeeding is not possible, that formula be provided exclusively through the first six months. The AAP maintains the position that "breastfeeding ensures the best possible health as well as the best developmental and psychosocial outcomes for the infant," but also recognizes that there are personal, economic, cultural, and political pressures that may make using infant formula necessary.

The infant formula market, and international food giant Nestlé in particular, have been the subject of controversy for many years. Criticized heavily by nongovernmental organizations, public health authorities, and child nutrition advocates for its aggressive campaigns to encourage artificial baby milk use in countries with poor water supplies, Nestlé has been the target of an ongoing boycott since 1977.

In many societies solids are introduced around the age of three to four months, although in others babies do not receive any nutrition aside from breast milk or infant formula through the first year. Worldwide sales of formula exceeded $20 billion in 2009, whereas the baby food market reached $21 billion in 2005.

■ Historical Background and Scientific Foundations

Until the invention of artificial baby milk by the German confectioner Henri Nestlé (1814–1890) and German chemist Justis von Liebig (1803–1873) in 1867, the only substitute for a mother's breast milk was cow's milk, goat's milk or to hire another lactating woman to breastfeed the infant and act as a wet nurse. Most wet nurses stepped in when a mother died or provided wet nurse services to the children of royalty, aristocrats, and the upper classes. Goat's milk and cow's milk were recognized as nutritionally inferior to breast milk for a human infant even before researchers discovered that some animal proteins can challenge an infant's kidneys, but at times these substitutes were fed to infants when breast milk was not available.

Breast milk substitutes, called "dry nursing" in the 1800s, increased after the invention of the artificial rubber nipple in the 1840s. A common dry nursing concoction was called "pap," a mixture of boiled milk, wheat flour, and an egg yolk. As bottle feeding of these non-breast milk preparations increased in the United States and Europe, infant illness and mortality increased as well, pushing researchers such as Nestlé and von Liebig to create a commercial substitute that would include protein, fat, and carbohydrates in a formula that was closer to that of breast milk. Later, vitamins and minerals were added to aid in providing proper nutrition for development.

The introduction of infant formula in the 1860s did not cause an immediate change in breastfeeding patterns in most countries, but as the quality of formula and baby bottle technology improved, more parents adopted infant formula as a feeding solution. The Progressive Era of the 1890s to the 1920s and its attending "scientific management" movement espoused the theory that anything made via science was inherently better than anything human made. Many doctors began to recommend infant formula over breastfeeding, and in the United States and England breastfeeding often became a class issue—a social signal that the parents could not afford formula.

Production of evaporated milk in cans, and pasteurization of cow's milk throughout the 1920s–1940s made homemade breast milk substitutes far safer than they had

WORDS TO KNOW

CODEX ALIMENTARIUS COMMISSION: Formed as a joint effort between the Food and Agriculture Organization of the United Nations and the World Health Organization in 1963, the Codex Alimentarius Commission works to supervise international cooperation for safe food practices across borders.

DRY NURSING: The term for 1800s and 1900s feeding of infants, via spoon, finger or bottle, any mixture of animal milk and other foods as a substitute for breast milk.

RECALL: In a recall in the United States, the Center for Food Safety and Applied Nutrition (CFSAN) asks the public to return products from a specific batch produced by a manufacturer, for reasons such as contamination or foodborne illness. Most CFSAN-originated recalls involve voluntary recalls, in which the manufacturer works proactively with CFSAN to remove a product from shelves and to educate consumers to return or destroy defective products.

been in previous years, and physicians began to prescribe either commercial formulas or hybrid concoctions that included evaporated milk and vitamin supplements to maintain infant development in non-breastfed babies. Upper class women abandoned breastfeeding throughout the twentieth century and other women soon followed; by 1972, 78 percent of all babies in the United States were formula-fed.

Gerber introduced jarred baby food in 1928. Until this point, babies were fed what the rest of the family ate, though mashed, strained, or pureed for easier feeding. Strained peas, prunes, carrots and spinach were the first processed baby foods available in the Gerber line, and sales quickly skyrocketed. Until the Gerber line of baby food, the only prepared baby food available was sold by pharmacists, and the Gerber jars were priced at nearly 60 percent less than baby food sold in pharmacies. Gerber dominated the prepared baby food market until the 1980s.

■ Impacts and Issues

The 1970s and 1980s saw enormous changes in the public's view of artificial breast milk and prepared baby food. In 1977 some consumers instigated a boycott against Nestlé that extends into the present day, fueled by child nutrition activists who claim that the company's advertising and marketing practices compromise infant health in developing and developed countries. Possibly the most important complaint is articulated by the WHO: "[I]nfant formula does not contain the antibodies found in breast milk" which protect against "diarrhoea and pneumonia, the two primary causes of child mortality worldwide."

Other complaints, voiced by groups such as War on Want and Infant Formula Action Coalition, include the fact that formula must be prepared with safe water, which is often in short supply in developing countries. Mothers living in poverty often water down formula powder to stretch supplies, leading to infant malnutrition. Additionally, formula feeding substitutes for breastfeeding, which normally promotes healthy bonding and delays fertility.

These groups initiated a boycott against Nestlé after the company offered free formula samples worldwide, especially in developing countries. Mothers shifted to formula feeding with the free powder, and by the time the powder was depleted the mothers' breast milk would dry up, leaving the poorest mothers with no money to buy adequate additional formula, and no way to breastfeed even if they desired.

The WHO promotes breastfeeding for the reasons above, however there is recognition by the WHO that infant formula is necessary and useful in some cases, so it considers infant formula that is prepared according to Codex Alimentarius procedure to be safe for infant consumption. The WHO created the International Code of Marketing of Breast-milk Substitutes in 1981. A voluntary code, it covers all forms of baby feeding, including infant formula, baby food, and devices such as bottles and nipples. Companies are not permitted to promote their products in hospitals or freestanding birth centers, nor to give free samples to mothers or heathcare workers, and all documentation and product literature must avoid aggressive language and use clear terminology that explains the health risks of using formula over breast milk. Some infant food companies, including Nestlé, do not follow the WHO code in full, prompting the continuation of the Nestlé boycott; however, compliance with the WHO code is on the rise worldwide.

The infant formula and baby food industry has experienced a series of recalls for contaminated products or faulty formulation. In 1984 and 1986, shards of glass were found in some lines of Gerber jarred baby food, prompting a large-scale recall of products and a 4 percent decline in Gerber sales. In 2003 German manufacturer Humana Milchinion produced infant formula sold in Israel that contained less than 10 percent of the required amount of vitamin B1, leading to three infant deaths and reports of more than 20 infants with medical problems resulting from the error. In 2008 another contaminated infant formula story led to public furor when infant formula manufactured and sold in China (and also sold in the United States), was found to contain melamine, a plastic used to increase the protein content and cut manufacturing costs. Melamine consumption can cause kidney complications, and the product sickened more than 50,000 infants in China and killed four.

Additional contamination issues related to baby food and infant formula include 2009 research studies confirming the presence of bisphenol A (BPA) in

Attorneys representing infant formula companies sit beside products inside the Supreme Court in Manila in 2007. The issue that all new moms face on breastfeeding has moved into the courtroom, where Philippine health officials claim aggressive advertising has many women believing that formula is better than their own milk. *AP Images.*

baby food lids. BPA can act as an endocrine disruptor, and the chemical purportedly leached from the lids into the food. In addition, baby bottles containing BPA have been banned in Canada, and in January 2010 the FDA announced it was taking reasonable steps to reduce human exposure to BPA in the food supply, including the support of industry actions to eliminate BPA-containing baby bottles and infant feeding cups in the United States. A 2010 recall of Similac, an infant formula brand that captured $5.3 billion in sales in 2009, garnered new headlines, as the source of contamination was reported to be ground beetles.

These recalls and contamination have triggered advocacy in the United States and Canada for increased breastfeeding and a return to homemade baby food. The AAP, WHO, and groups such as La Leche League promote breastfeeding as the most healthful means of feeding infants, and some pediatricians recommend that parents make their own baby food and avoid packaged foods. Proliferation of products designed to support these efforts, from electric breast pumps to specially designed food processors, has created a niche market in the United States.

SEE ALSO *Advertising Food; Breastfeeding; Ethical Issues in Food Aid; Food Recalls; Women's Role in Global Food Preparation.*

BIBLIOGRAPHY

Books

Chen, Viola. *The Evolution of the Baby Food Industry 2000–2008.* Washington, DC: Bureau of Economics, 2009.

Palmer, Gabrielle. *The Politics of Breastfeeding: When Breasts Are Bad for Business,* 3rd ed. London: Pinter & Martin, 2009.

Periodicals

"Growth Spurt Continues for Organic Baby Food and Infant Formula Sales." *Nutrition Business Journal* 13, no. 3/4 (2008): 26–28.

Herbold, Nancie H., and Elizabeth Scott. "A Pilot Study Describing Infant Formula Preparation and Feeding Practices." *International Journal of Environmental Health Research* 18, no. 6 (2008): 451–459.

Lee, Mendoza R. "Breast Milk versus Formula." *Infant, Child, & Adolescent Nutrition* 2, no. 1 (2010): 7–15.

Morin, Karen H. "Organic Baby Food: What Do You Tell Parents?" *American Journal of Maternal Child Nursing* 34, no. 2 (2009): 129.

Olstad, Dana, and Linda McCargar. "Prevention of Overweight and Obesity in Children under the Age of 6 Years." *Applied Physiology, Nutrition, and Metabolism* 34 (August 2009): 551–570.

Thulier, Diane. "Breastfeeding in America: A History of Influencing Factors." *Journal of Human Lactation* 25, no. 1 (2009): 85–94.

Web Sites

"Infant Feeding & Nutrition." *International Formula Council.* http://www.infantformula.org/ (accessed October 4, 2010).

"Infant Formula." *Food and Drug Administration (FDA).* http://www.fda.gov/Food/FoodSafety/Product-SpecificInformation/InfantFormula/default.htm (accessed October 4, 2010).

Melanie Barton Zoltan

International Federation of Organic Agriculture Movements

■ Introduction

The International Federation of Organic Agriculture Movements (IFOAM) was formed in 1972 to promote organic agriculture and unite organizations involved in organic agriculture from many countries. Organic agriculture attempts to reduce the impact of agriculture on the environment by prohibiting the use of artificial inputs. IFOAM has created its own organic standard, which has been influential on standards adopted by national and international authorities. IFOAM's organic standard relies on third-party certification as do most world organic standards. In addition to standard setting, IFOAM organizes information and research about organic agriculture; promotes and helps protect the interests of organic agriculture in the developing world; and functions as an umbrella organization made up of many commercial and nonprofit organizations involved in organic agriculture in both developed and developing countries.

■ Historical Background and Scientific Foundations

The International Federation of Organic Agriculture Movements (IFOAM) was formed in November 1972 at a conference on organic agriculture held in Versailles, France. *Nature et Progrès*, a French farmers' association, organized the conference as a way to exchange information among organic movements in various countries. Representatives of organizations in the United States, the United Kingdom, Sweden, South Africa, and France formed the International Federation of Organic Agriculture Movements (IFOAM). The organization was intended to promote organic agriculture and make available more information about organic agriculture. From five initial members, IFOAM grew to include 750 member organizations from 116 countries by 2010. Initially based in Cannes, France, IFOAM moved to Tholey-Theley, Germany, in 1987. The organization's head office subsequently relocated to Bonn, Germany, where it remains as of 2010.

By the late 1970s, IFOAM began work to establish what would be called the IFOAM Basic Standard. Early organic producers sold products directly to consumers or were taken at their word to be using actual organic production techniques. However, as the market for organic foods widened, standards became necessary. Standards are a way to distinguish between certified organic production, which can be labeled as such, and uncertified producers who may employ organic methods but lack auditable records, organic plans, and outside observers of the producer. Standards assure consumers that they are, in fact, purchasing organically produced goods, because consumers cannot distinguish how a product is produced solely with their senses. The IFOAM Basic Standard outlines the basic boundaries that are widely regarded as constituting organic agriculture. IFOAM's standards were influential in writing national or regional organic standards adopted by the European Union, India, China, and other areas. For example, IFOAM began to lobby the European Community as early as 1986 to help coordinate the eventual single organic standard that was adopted across the customs union. In other cases, those adopting standards examined IFOAM's existing Basic Standard and modified or added to it to meet local conditions. The most recent IFOAM standard was adopted in 2005.

Also in 1986 IFOAM began an accreditation process that would accredit certification bodies to certify to its standards. Organic agriculture relies primarily on third-party certification in which a certification organization is accredited to certify producers in a particular standard. A regulator for a national government standard or an international organization such as IFOAM accredits the organizations that actually certify farms, production, and goods as organic. IFOAM does not itself certify farmers or producers to its standards.

WORDS TO KNOW

ORGANIC AGRICULTURE: Agriculture and livestock production that uses no chemical, mineral, or otherwise artificial inputs. Organic agriculture is thought to be more natural and to have less impact on the environment than the conventional methods associated with the input-dependent technologies of the twentieth century. Certain human-made fertilizers, soil amendments, herbicides, and pesticides are prohibited by organic standards that define organic agriculture.

THIRD-PARTY CERTIFICATION: A system in which an organization independent of all the companies in a supply chain certifies that a good reaches particular standards or has particular attributes. Most international organic standards, fair trade standards, claims of being not genetically modified, and a variety of environmental claims are certified using third-party certification.

UMBRELLA ORGANIZATION: A federation or other grouping of organizations for a single purpose. An umbrella organization unites many organizations, often from various countries, to represent a cause or movement on a broader level or internationally.

Impacts and Issues

In addition to standard setting, IFOAM represents the organic movement and organic trade to many international bodies including having official observer status at the Food and Agriculture Organization (FAO) of the United Nations and the United Nations Economic and Social Council (ECOSOC). IFOAM has a long history of encouraging the development of organic agriculture in the developing world. IFOAM also invites leaders of organic organizations in the developing world to its conferences and meetings both as a way to educate developing world leaders and as a way to ensure broad participation in the organization. Partly out of concern for small-scale organic producers in the developing world, IFOAM has been a proponent of group certification in which a group of small farmers receives a single certification so that they can take advantage of reduced certification cost, but still access the market for certified organic production.

In 1992 there was a controversy within IFOAM over allowing for-profit traders and processors of certified organic foods to participate. By including for-profit entities, IFOAM has successfully managed to link processors, traders, and farmers' associations from all along the value chain in a single umbrella organization. Individuals are not members of the organization, but instead organizations join IFOAM. These organizations include research centers, certification bodies, farmers' associations, and trade organizations. In addition to being an umbrella organization for those involved in organic agriculture, IFOAM itself is a member of another umbrella organization, the International Union for Conservation of Nature (IUCN). Umbrella organizations bring together groups of similar organizations to provide a more prominent platform for action. The transnational structure of many umbrella organizations enables them to disseminate information across national lines.

Primary Source Connection

Consumer demand fuels today's worldwide market for foods that are both sustainably produced and organically grown, and food producers are responding by incorporating these philosophies into their production methods. Earlier motives for ramping up organic and sustainable production are discussed in the accompanying article published by the International Federation of Organic Agriculture Movements (IFOAM). The mission of IFOAM is "leading, uniting, and assisting the organic movement in its full diversity." Founded in 1972, its goal is a worldwide adoption and expansion of organic agriculture. Part of the international "green movement" and active in environmental issues, this organization spans 116 countries.

Building Sustainable Organic Sectors

When we speak about the early stage of organic agriculture we most often refer to the period when awareness arose about the negative effects of the so called conventional agriculture in the USA and Europe during the 1960s and 1970s. The reactions were at first centered around pesticides and chemical fertilizers, but later included a more holistic view criticizing the whole modern/conventional production system. The organic farming ideas and methods that sprung from this criticism of course were not new. There already existed health food movements in the early part of the century that saw the connections between production methods and human health, and the early developments of Demeter go back to 1924, when Rudolf Steiner gave his 'Agriculture Course' in Koberwitz. Long before that, there are numerous examples of exquisite, sustainable production systems building on careful use of natural resources and satisfying basic human needs. Green manure was systematically used in China to fertilize rice paddies over 3,000 years ago. Efficient water use, essential to survival, was technically and socially organized in the water canals of Ladakh in the Northern Himalayas, in the rice terraces of Ifugao in the Philippines, and in the Mayan 'cenotes' (underground fresh water holes) in Yucatán hundreds of years before the peak of the Roman Empire.

The market for organic products such as this organic corn grown in southwestern France has increased worldwide during the past two decades. The International Federation of Organic Agriculture Movements sets standards that help nations to define and regulate organic farming. *AP Images.*

Traditional agricultural methods from around the world have to a great extent inspired today's modern organic agriculture. For example, Sir Albert Howard, one of the founders of the organic movement in the UK, was inspired by the composting methods used by traditional farmers in India. Still, in this study we have chosen to limit ourselves to examples of experiences from the movement that started to grow during the latter half of the 20th century, what could be defined as the 'modern' organic era.

Motives Behind the Early Initiatives

Some of the earliest initiatives of the 'modern' organic era took place in the 1940s through the 1960s in Europe and the USA, and many of the pioneers were people who were not farmers from the beginning but came from the city looking for an alternative life-style. The first initiatives sprung from a concern about the impacts of food production methods on human health. But because of the intensive use of pesticides and synthetic fertilizers in western countries, environmental awareness grew, and already in the 1960s environmental aspects

became one of the strongest motives for organic agriculture. The book *Silent Spring*, written by Rachel Carson, started an environmental movement worldwide, highlighting the harmful effects of pesticides on the environment we depend on. Pesticide use and environmental aspects are still fundamental concerns in the organic agriculture concept.

Developing countries have in many cases entered organic agriculture with the main goal of supporting small-scale farmers to adopt sustainable farming practices in order to improve their livelihoods and agro-ecological conditions in rural areas (e.g. the Philippines and Southeast Brazil in the early 1980s). Organic agriculture has sprung from a reaction against modern, industrialized agriculture, the so-called Green Revolution, which was considered to have devastating effects on rural populations, causing poverty and dependence alongside with soil erosion, decreased biodiversity, water pollution, and health problems. These problems called for a redesign of agriculture methods with a broad approach, including a strong social and economic focus besides development of appropriate technologies.

In countries where organic agriculture developed comparatively late (e.g. China, Serbia Turkey, and Uganda), the economic potential of the increasing global trade in organic products has often been the first and main driving force for organic. Awareness of environment, health, and rural development developed later. In these cases the initiative often came from buyers or exporters who convinced farmers to go for organic conversion. There is a parallel in countries with an older organic sector (e.g. Sweden) where farmers nowadays convert their farms for economic reasons, but broaden their conception and attitudes about organic once they start practicing organic. In other cases (e.g. Thailand), the economic incentives of export markets are working in parallel with rural development perspectives.

Inger Källander
Gunnar Rundgren

KÄLLANDER, INGER, AND GUNNAR RUNDGREN. *BUILDING SUSTAINABLE ORGANIC SECTORS.* THOLEY-THELEY, GERMANY: IFOAM, 2008.

SEE ALSO *Agriculture and International Trade; Organic Foods Production Act of 1990; Organics; Sustainable Agriculture.*

BIBLIOGRAPHY

Books

The World of Organic Agriculture, 11th ed. Bonn: International Federation of Organic Agriculture Movements, 2011.

Web Sites

farmingsolutions: Success Stories for the Future of Agriculture. http://www.farmingsolutions.org/ (accessed October 9, 2010).

International Federation of Organic Agriculture Movements. http://www.ifoam.org/ (accessed October 9, 2010).

Blake Jackson Stabler

International Food Aid

■ Introduction

International food aid refers to transfers of food or resources for the purchase of food to developing countries. Food aid began in the 1950s and the 1960s as a way for developed countries whose agricultural policies led to the government purchasing surplus food commodities, usually grain, to dispose of these commodities outside of the domestic market. International food aid takes the form of program food aid sold at a concessional rate to developing countries, project food aid used for specific project objectives or to produce funds for projects, and emergency or humanitarian food aid used to feed vulnerable populations in an emergency. Over time, food aid has improved targeting of food distributions, introduced purchases of food for food aid at the local and regional level in developing countries, and developed special foods for use in emergencies. International food aid tends to be evaluated on whether it actually provides additional food resources to those in need. Some critics of food aid complain that donors drive food aid and that it serves the interests of donor countries instead of recipient countries.

■ Historical Background and Scientific Foundations

In 1954 the Agricultural Trade Development and Assistance Act, U.S. Public Law 480, often called PL480, became law in the United States. Because at the time, U.S. agricultural support programs, also called subsidies, supported prices, the government of the United States would buy commodities that could not find commercial buyers at the stipulated prices. To dispose of these surplus commodities, usually grains, PL480 allowed the U.S. government to donate these commodities or sell them at discounted prices to developing countries. By removing these commodities from the U.S. market, the domestic supply of a commodity was reduced, thus helping support a higher domestic market price. In 1965 international food aid made up 22 percent of aid flows to the developing countries. From 1954 until 2004, the PL480 programs of the United States supplied more than 340 million metric tons of food aid. This excludes food aid from other countries and from the other food aid programs of the United States.

International food aid comes in three general forms. Program assistance offers governments free, discounted, or otherwise specially priced commodities, usually grain. A government facing a shortage of foreign currency to purchase food can substitute this program food aid to cover food imports. The government then sells the program food aid on the domestic market. In the 1950s and 1960s, the United States and Canada provided more than 90 percent of all food aid, and the majority of it came in the form of program food aid through government-to-government concessional sales. Project food aid, the second form, is used in or to fund projects, often to increase agricultural productivity or improve maternal and child health (MCHT). Some project food aid is monetized and sold in the recipient country to provide project funds. While founded in 1963 as a specialized agency of the United Nations (UN), the World Food Programme (WFP) became a major player in food aid in the 1970s as the European countries donated more and the United States began to work more through this multilateral mechanism. The third form of food aid, emergency or humanitarian food aid, is when food is actually given to a food-insecure population such as during a civil war, after a natural disaster, or in a refugee or internally displaced persons (IDPs) camp. Emergency or humanitarian food aid became the dominant form in the 1990s.

Changes in how food aid is delivered reflect not merely the shift from program to project and to humanitarian or emergency food aid over time. One innovation is the growth in the use of local and regional procurement (LRP) since the early 1980s. During the 1960s all food aid was shipped from the developed country to a developing country. However, as developed countries changed their agricultural policies so as not to have government surpluses or warehouses full of food belonging to the government, they began merely to purchase food from their own producers to ship as food aid. Concerns about food aid grew

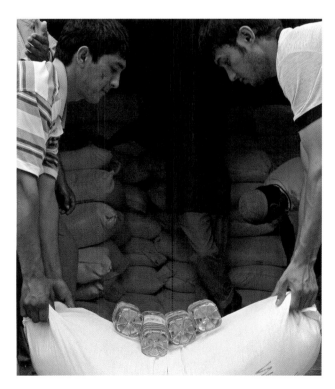

Local residents collect humanitarian aid at the distribution point of the World Food Programme in the southern Kyrgyz city of Osh, Kyrgyzstan, in June 2010. *AP Images.*

though, as sometimes food aid may have led to farmers in the recipient country or in neighboring countries losing markets by being displaced by the imported food aid. By purchasing food for food aid either within the recipient country or in a neighboring country, the costs of transportation are reduced, the time it takes food to reach the intended beneficiaries is reduced, and farmers in the developing countries do not lose a market. By 2010 the World Food Programme, for example, acquired three fourths of the food it purchased through local and regional procurement LRP. Also, by targeting food distributions to populations that would not otherwise buy food in the market due to low incomes or lack of functioning markets, food aid began experiencing less leakage over time. Leakage refers to recipients selling food aid, bartering donated food for other goods or services, or giving away the food aid to non-recipients.

Lastly, new foods first adapted from military and maritime uses and then made especially for emergency or humanitarian distribution appeared in the 1980s. These included high energy biscuits (HEB), a single, ready-to-eat serving that covers most nutritional needs of an adult; and later nutrient-dense peanut-based foods for supplemental feeding of malnourished infants.

■ Impacts and Issues

Concerns about leakage, where food is purchased, and discussions of who is targeted tend to depend on the concept of additionality. If food aid is additional, meaning it would not otherwise be purchased or would not be able to enter these households through purely commercial means, food aid does not displace food imports or food produced by local farmers. Concerns about additionality have led to the use of cash or vouchers in many emergency programs instead of direct food aid. Cash and voucher programs allow markets to provide food instead of being displaced with imported food aid or having the food aid program make all market decisions as with an LRP program. The concern with vouchers and cash is that they may be used for non-food needs and may not adequately address the nutritional needs of women and children. However, in situations where markets do not exist, where purchasing power is too weak to attract food imports even with additional cash, or when markets and trade have been completely destroyed by war or natural disaster, then direct, imported food aid may continue to be a more appropriate response.

The primary criticism of food aid remains that it is driven by the donors and serves the agricultural interests of the donor countries. In the negotiations at the World Trade Organization (WTO), the European Union (EU) contends that U.S. food aid is an export subsidy that should be eliminated. The EU and Canada, while continuing to be major food aid donors,

IN CONTEXT: FAMINE AND INTERNATIONAL AID FOR NORTH KOREA

Since the mid-1990s, frequent flooding, inefficient food production, and economic mismanagement have led to frequent famine in North Korea, or the Democratic People's Republic of Korea (DPRK). During this period North Korea has relied on international humanitarian aid from the World Food Programme (WFP), China, South Korea, Japan, the United States, and other nations. However, North Korea's relationship with many of its largest donors has been strained by North Korea's closed, Stalinist (authoritarian and based on communist principles) government and its nuclear weapons program.

Because it is a closed society, information related to North Korea is either classified or difficult to verify. Journalists and other experts have publicly estimated that even with the contribution of millions of tons of humanitarian food aid, at least one million North Koreans died in the 1990s from starvation and famine-related diseases. Other media sources placed the death toll as high as two million.

North Korea is a totalitarian regime, in which the state controls every aspect of economic production and distribution. Throughout most of its history following the partition of Korea in the Korean War (1950–1953), North Korea has relied on subsidized food, oil, fertilizer, and machinery from its allies the Soviet Union and China. These subsidies declined dramatically following the breakup of the Soviet Union in the early–1990s. North Korean food production, which relied on outdated methods of production, decreased significantly. Without subsidized food imports, the price of food in North Korea also increased. North Korean food production could not meet demand.

Under North Korea's Son'gun, or military first policy, the government began to divert scarce food supplies to military and other government applications. Consequently, in 1995 the North Korean government cut the annual state-allowed food allotment for a rural family from 368 pounds (167 kilograms) of grain per person to 236 pounds (107 kilograms) per person.

Flooding of farm land in 1995 and 1996, followed by extreme drought in 1997, produced further declines in North Korean food production. The international community responded: China and the United States in particular sent millions of dollars in humanitarian aid. Between 1995 and 1998, the worst years of the famine of the 1990s, North Korea received almost 3.5 million metric tons of food. During the late 1990s, the United States donated more aid to North Korea than any other nation. In 1999 the United States Agency for International Development (USAID) donated almost 700,000 metric tons of food to North Korea.

Despite international efforts, millions of North Koreans died. "The Politics of Famine in North Korea," a report issued by the United States Institute of Peace in August 1999, lists several reasons for famine-related deaths despite foreign aid. First, the aid did not always coincide with the time of year when food aid was needed most, typically in late winter and spring when the previous year's harvest had rotted or spoiled. Second, North Korean officials often diverted the food aid for sale in urban markets, which prevented the aid from reaching people in rural areas.

Some countries ultimately refused to provide aid. Japan and South Korea scrapped a plan to send almost 500,000 tons of food to North Korea due to political pressure at home.

International politics continue to affect international aid to North Korea. North Korea's efforts to develop nuclear weapons caused some nations to condition food aid on North Korean concessions during nuclear negotiations. Food aid from the United States dropped from 350,000 tons in 2001 to 50,000 tons in 2004 following a dispute between the United States and North Korea over North Korea's nuclear program.

In 2005 North Korea formally informed the United Nations and the World Food Programme that it would no longer accept international food aid. The UN and WFP estimated that more than six million North Koreans could face starvation or death from famine-related diseases without international aid. However, following flooding in 2007 that decreased harvest yields, North Korea indicated that it would accept international aid again. The changes are part of a pattern and practice of rapid shifts in North Korean internal and foreign policies.

In October 2010, South Korea reversed its previous policy and sent shipments of rice and other food supplies to North Korea, the first food aid from South to North Korea since the election of South Korean President Lee Myung-bak in 2008. The International Red Cross arranged logistics for the shipment, which was destined to travel by sea from South Korea to Dandong, China, where Chinese officials arranged truck transport into North Korea.

Aid shipments to North Korea were complicated by an exchange of artillery shells between North and South Korean forces on November 24, 2010. South Korea suspended delivery of government-financed aid. Previously shipped food aid (including noodles and rice) and some building supplies (mainly cement) were already in North Korean ports (shipped via China) but nearly 7,000 tons of cement and medical supplies were stopped in transit. South Korea announced a limited ban on private organization humanitarian aid, including food aid, to North Korea.

have largely limited the amount of direct food donated from their own domestic stocks. However, although the United States no longer has agricultural policies that lead to the government owning surplus grains that must be distributed abroad, the United States continues to purchase the majority of its PL480 food aid domestically. The United States remains by far the largest player in food aid, providing more than $1 billion of the World Food Programme's $3 billion budget in 2010. When all forms of food aid are considered, the United States has, with the exception of a few years in the 1990s, provided more than half of the world's food aid funding and food according to the U.S. Department of Agriculture's Economic Research Service (USDA/ERS).

Being driven by the donor countries means that more food aid tends to be available in good budget years for the donor countries, which tend to be when the economies of the developing countries are less likely to want or need food aid. With more food aid being budget based, instead of based on supply of surplus commodities, rising food prices also decrease the amount of food aid available. The erratic supply appears not to respond to actual emergency and humanitarian needs and instead to reflect the conditions of supply. Other criticisms of food aid include that it forces developing countries to accept donations of genetically modified foods and that it forms dependence in recipient countries on food aid and food imports.

SEE ALSO *African Famine Relief; Disasters and Food Supply; Famine; Famine: Political Considerations; Food Security; Hunger; International Fund for Agricultural Development; Malnutrition; Rome Declaration on World Food Security (1996); UN Millennium Development Goals; Undernutrition; U.S. Agency for International Development (USAID); World Food Day; World Food Programme.*

BIBLIOGRAPHY

Books

Barrett, Christopher B., and Daniel G. Maxwell. *Food Aid after Fifty Years: Recasting Its Role.* London: Routledge, 2005.

Jensen, Heather. *Reevaluating U.S. Food Aid to Africa: Food Aid for Food Security.* Cambridge, MA: John F. Kennedy School of Government, 2007.

Reilly, Katherine V. *Food Aid Policy and Challenges.* New York: Nova Science Publishers, 2009.

Stanford, Claire. *World Hunger.* Bronx, NY: H.W. Wilson Co, 2007.

Periodicals

"Do Handouts Harm?: Rethinking Food Aid." *Time New York, American Edition* 169, no. 26 (2007): 64–66.

"Famine, Prices, and Aid—Food for Thought." *The Economist* 386, no. 8573 (2008): 63.

"Food Aid for Africa: The Politics of Hunger." *The Economist* 394, no. 8674 (2010): 58.

"Food Aid Needs Reform." *Lancet* 369, no. 9580 (2007): 2134.

"Sudan—Over Six Million People Need Food Aid." *UN Chronicle* 43, no. 1 (2006): 57.

Web Sites

Schalch, Kathleen. "All Things Considered: U.S. Food Aid Critics Call on Congress for Overhaul." *National Public Radio (NPR)*, November 6, 2007. http://www.npr.org/templates/story/story.php?storyId=16053196 (accessed October 17, 2010).

"World Food Programme: Fighting Hunger Worldwide." *World Food Programme.* http://www.wfp.org/ (accessed October 17, 2010).

Blake Jackson Stabler

International Fund for Agricultural Development

■ Introduction

The International Fund for Agricultural Development (IFAD) is a specialized agency of the United Nations (UN) dedicated to eradicating rural poverty and increasing food security in developing nations. IFAD focuses on achieving these goals by addressing structural problems related to poverty, rather than by improving food production or increasing international food aid. IFAD works with governments, non-governmental organizations (NGOs), local partners, and the rural poor to develop rural poverty reduction solutions tailored to a particular country or region.

An international finance institution, IFAD achieves its objectives by issuing low-interest loans and grants for rural development and agriculture projects. Since 1978, IFAD loans and grants have funded more than 800 programs and projects that have assisted more than 350 million rural poor people. IFAD projects provide rural poor people with financing and technical assistance required to better utilize natural resources through resource management and conservation, improve agricultural technologies and production, open competitive agricultural markets, provide funding for enterprise development, provide access to a wide range of financial services, and shape local and national agricultural policies and programs to assist rural poor people.

■ Historical Background and Scientific Foundations

In 1974 the United Nations (UN), in cooperation with the Food and Agriculture Organization (FAO) of the United Nations, hosted the World Food Conference in Rome, Italy. Motivated by a number of world food crises in the early 1970s, delegates to the World Food Conference addressed food security, hunger, and malnutrition issues. The Conference resolution states that "every man, woman and child has the inalienable right to be free from hunger and malnutrition." Delegates to the

World Food Conference set the ambitious goal of eliminating world hunger within ten years. The establishment of the World Food Council, which suspended operations in 1993, and the adoption of Resolution XIII, which would establish IFAD, were two concrete actions taken by delegates to the World Food Conference.

Between 1975 and 1977, UN member nations held a series of meetings that laid the groundwork for the establishment of IFAD, including drafting a charter for the new organization. The charter states that the objective of IFAD shall be to "mobilize additional resources to be made available on concessional terms for agricultural development in developing Member States." In order to achieve this objective, IFAD is charged with providing "financing primarily for projects and programmes specifically designed to introduce, expand or improve food production systems and to strengthen related policies and institutions within the framework of national priorities and strategies." Nations that participated in establishing IFAD also drafted IFAD's Lending Policies and Criteria, which contains the rules and terms under which IFAD lends money.

On December 13, 1977, the first Governing Council of IFAD convened with representatives from 120 nations joining IFAD. The Governing Council is IFAD's highest decision-making authority and meets annually. Each IFAD member nation has one seat on the Governing Council. IFAD's Executive Board oversees general operations and approves IFAD loans and grants. The Executive Board consists of 18 members and 18 alternate members. The Governing Council elects IFAD's president to manage the organizations ongoing affairs.

■ Impacts and Issues

IFAD's *Rural Poverty Report* states that the world's poorest people—about 1.4 billion people who live on less than one dollar per day—rely heavily on local agriculture and related activities for their livelihoods. IFAD focuses on assisting the rural poor in developing

WORDS TO KNOW

FOOD SECURITY: Access to sufficient, safe, and nutritious food to meet dietary needs and food preferences for an active and healthy life.

NON-GOVERNMENTAL ORGANIZATION: A private organization, usually a nonprofit entity, that typically pursues human rights, poverty, environmental, or developmental issues through direct action, lobbying, or other means.

RURAL DEVELOPMENT: Rural development refers to actions, programs, or projects designed to increase the living standards of people living in rural areas, typically through agricultural improvement or poverty reduction.

nations, because IFAD estimates that 70 percent of the world's poorest people live in rural areas in developing nations. Despite the difficulties faced by rural poor people in developing nations, the World Bank estimates that only 4 percent of official development assistance goes to agricultural projects in developing nations.

IFAD has been successful in mobilizing contributions and funding for rural development projects from governments, NGOs, and other donors. From 1978 until 2010, IFAD supplied more than \$11.5 billion in funding for rural development programs and projects. During the same period, IFAD mobilized more than \$10 billion in additional funding from governments and over \$8 billion in funding from other donors.

IFAD's implemented and funded projects face numerous challenges raised by working in some of the poorest and most isolated rural areas of the world. Lack of both infrastructure and effective local governments in some areas complicate IFAD programs and projects. IFAD maintains local-level operations in more than 115 nations and territories to assist in the formulation and implementation of programs and projects. The knowledge that IFAD's local contacts supply to the organization enable IFAD to design projects around the needs and constraints presented by a particular location.

IFAD also responds to global agricultural crises by making funds available to poor farmers in developing nations. In April 2008 IFAD participated in the UN's High Level Task Force on the Global Food Security Crisis, a group designed to address skyrocketing food costs during the food price crisis of 2007 and 2008. IFAD made \$200 million in existing funds available to provide a boost to agricultural production in the developing world. The funds were dispensed so that farmers

The International Fund for Agricultural Development is dedicated to reducing poverty in developing countries, mainly through low-interest loans and grants that fund agricultural projects like this rice paddy field. *Image copyright Zastol'skiy Victor Leonidovich, 2010. Used under license from Shutterstock.com.*

in the developing world would use them to purchase seeds, fertilizers, and other agricultural inputs to increase agricultural production quickly.

SEE ALSO *African Famine Relief; Agriculture and International Trade; Agroecology; Biofuels and World Hunger; Ethical Issues in Agriculture; Fair Trade; Food and Agriculture Organization (FAO); Food Security; U.S. Agency for International Development (USAID).*

BIBLIOGRAPHY

Books

Calaguas, Belinda. *Failing the Rural Poor: Aid, Agriculture, and the Millennium Development Goals.* Johannesburg: ActionAid International, 2008.

Planet Aid, USDA. *5 Years of Rural Empowerment: Planet Aid in Partnership with USDA.* Columbia, MD: Planet Aid, 2009.

Reeder, Richard, and Faqir Bagi. *Geographic Targeting Issues in the Delivery of Rural Development Assistance.* Washington, DC: U.S. Department of Agriculture, Economic Research Service, 2010.

Periodicals

Brett, John. "The Political-Economics of Developing Markets versus Satisfying Food Needs." *Food and Foodways* 18, nos. 1–2 (2010): 28–42.

Marchione, Thomas, and Ellen Messer. "Food Aid and the World Hunger Solution: Why the U.S. Should Use a Human Rights Approach." *Food and Foodways* 18, nos. 1–2 (2010): 10–27.

Web Sites

"Agriculture." *U.S. Agency for International Development (USAID).* http://www.usaid.gov/our_work/agriculture/ (accessed October 6, 2010).

International Fund for Agricultural Development. http://www.ifad.org/ (accessed October 6, 2010).

"Rural Poverty Report 2011." *International Fund for Agricultural Development.* http://www.ifad.org/rpr2011/index.htm (accessed October 22, 2010).

Joseph P. Hyder